BLIC OF CHINA

1945)

R

HEILUNGCHIANG
Tsitsihar

KIRIN
Kirin

LIAONING

CHAHAR

JOHEL
Chengteh
Shenyang

SUIYUAN
Kueisui   Changyuan Kupeikow
Yellow
Paotou   Peiping
Tientsin

KOREA

SEA OF JAPAN

Taiyuan   HOPEI

HANtingchuan

Tsinan Tsingtao
SHANSI
SHANTUNG   YELLOW
River   SEA
Lanchow

SHENSI   kaifeng
Sian   Loyang   Hsuchow
HONAN   KIANGSU

Hofei Nanking
Sui   ANHWEI   Shanghai

EAST
su ZECHUAN   HUPEI Hankow   Anking Hanschow
Chungking River Wuchang   CHINA
Yangtze   CHEKIANG
Changteh   Nanchang   Chu   SEA
Changsha
HUNAN   KIANGSI

KWEICHOW   Hengyang   FUKIEN
Kweiyang
Tuhshan   Kweilin   Foochow
Liuchow Chuchiang Amoy kinmen Taipei
KWANGSI Si   Taiwan
Nanning River KWANGTUNG
Canton

Haikang   SOUTH

Hainan   CHINA

SEA

HISTORY OF
THE SINO-JAPANESE WAR
(1937-1945)

History of
The Sino-Japanese War
(1937-1945)

Compiled by
Hsu Long-hsuen and Chang Ming-kai

Translated by
Wen Ha-hsiung

Revised by
Kao Ching-chen, Hu Pu-yu, Liu Han-mou,
Liu Ih-po, and Lu Pao-ching

Chung Wu Publishing Co.
Taipei, Taiwan
Republic of China

Printed by

CHINA PRINTING, LTD.

Republic of China

Excerpts from
"Soviet Russia in China"
written by
President Chiang Kai-shek

"*Our decision for this campaign was in conformity with Clausewitz' principle that national policy should determine military strategy. In economic resources, industry, science, and technology as well as in the striking power of her armed forces and weapons, China was weak as compared with Japan. After the Mukden Incident of 1931, therefore, we had to be patient and to negotiate with Japan; and for six years thereafter we did not lightly talk of armed resistance.*

"*Once hostilities were forced on us in 1937, however, we did not hesitate to adopt the scorched-earth policy, to 'fall back into the interior,' or to pit the new spirit of the age, motivated by the Three People's Principles and the new methods of warfare developed in the course of our National Revolution, against the Japanese militarists in an 'absolute war.' We held fast to this strategic principle throughout the eight years of war and, despite the intrigues of Soviet Russia and the insurrection of the Chinese Communists, we achieved victory in concert with the Allies in August 1945.*"

Preface

China's War of Resistance against Japan which began with the Manchurian Incident of Sept. 18, 1931 and ended with Japan's surrender on Sept. 3, 1945 took fourteen years. During this time the period which began on July 7, 1937 when Japan launched full-scale war against China with the Marco Polo Bridge Incident was the bloodiest and most difficult. Under Generalissimo Chiang's call of "fighting to the end," Chinese people courageously plunged themselves into the rage of the War of Resistance. Altogether they took part in 23 campaigns, 1,117 major battles, 38,931 engagements, spent Fapi $1,464.3 billion, lost 3,237,916 officers and men in casualties and 5,787,352 civilians in casualties before achieving final victory.

China's bloody War of Resistance not only crushed the Japanese Militarists' aggression scheme since the Meiji reform, defended our territory of 11,000,000 sq. km., protected China's history and culture of more than 5,000 years and removed her humiliation at being a sub-colony for one hundred years, but also tied down 2.3 million Japanese troops in the China Theater and covered the mighty counter-offensive of the Allied forces to win a total victory. This was a sad but heroic epic of the Chinese people as well as an unparallelled glory of our National Revolutionary Forces.

The Military History Bureau of the Ministry of National Defense, Republic of China, compiled and published the 100 volume "History of the Sino-Japanese War (1937-1945)" in order to provide a detailed account of what is also known as the War of Resistance. In the interest of convenience, the decision was made to condense it into "A Concise History of the Sino-Japanese War (1937-1945)" which proved most popular abroad since its publication. It has been used as an important reference by many people in the study of China's modern history. In order that our foreign friends may have an accurate understanding of the truth of China's War of Resistance and thereby promote the interflow of Chinese and Western military thinkings, this book has translated into English for publication. Suggestions and comments of our readers are solicited so that we may make the necessary corrections in the next printing.

Hsu Long-hsuen
Chang Ming-kai

Contents

CHARTS

MAPS

History of
The Sino-Japanese War
(1937-1945)

After the outbreak of the Marco Polo Bridge Incident, President Chiang issued a statement at Lu Shan in which he considered that the critical moment had arrived, and decided to fight against Japan. (July 19, 1937)

Lukouchiao (Marco Polo Bridge) unveiling full-scale War of Resistance. (July 7, 1937)

President Chiang reading reports of victories in the Eastern Theater of War.

Leng-kou Command Post in the Northern Theater of War.

800 gallant warriors defending the isolated 4-Bank Warehouse after withdrawal of our forces from Shanghai. (Nov. 1937)

Mme. Chiang led women to sew clothes for the soldiers.

President Chiang reiterating his determination on fight to the end. (Jan. 18, 1938)

President Chiang leaving conference room after a joint briefing of Allied Forces. (Dec. 1941)

President Chiang, Supreme Allied Commander, China Theater, posing with Mme. Chiang. (Jan. 1942)

Chinese National Forces rescued British troops in Burma. (April 1942)

President Chiang inspecting Chinese Expeditionary Forces in India. (1942)

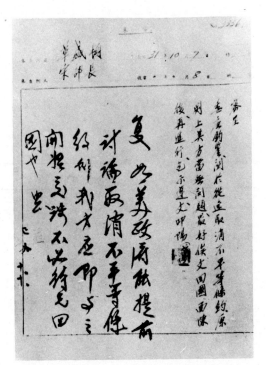

Message sent by Foreign Minister T. V. Soong giving an account of negotiations with U.S. on the abolition of unequal treaties and President Chiang's instruction. (Oct. 1942)

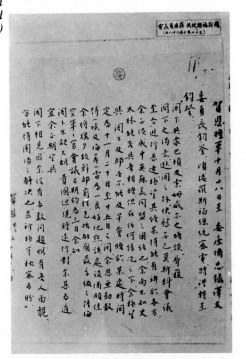

Chinese Text of President Roosevelt's cable inviting President Chiang to Cairo as forwarded by Gen. Thomas G. Hearn. (Oct. 1943)

I deeply appreciate your kind message informing me of the date and place of our conference. I look forward with the greatest pleasure to meeting you and President Roosevelt and of having a full exchange of views concerning our joint offensive against our common enemies and the means of assuring effective and whole-hearted co-operation of our countries in the post-war world. The already close relations between Great Britain and China, will, I am sure, become still closer through our personal contact.

I wish to express my sincere thanks for your kindness in taking the trouble to make arrangements for my stay during the conference.

蔣委員長勛鑒頃奉相電

尊電告如吾人會議之日期與地點

深為感幸綏余將以極愉快之心情與閣

下及羅斯福總統相會略覺而充分交

換將合作戰之意見並冀進同盟團結開

戰後有效與堅誠之合作余信吾人晤

敘後中英兩國之關係必將更光密切

會議期間蒙閣下對余之居留預為

安排謹致謝忱

Text of Prime Minister Churchill's cable inviting President Chiang to Cairo and President Chiang's replying cable. (Nov. 1943)

President Roosevelt has already told you of our hope that you may be able to join our conference in Cairo by November 22nd. May I say what importance I attach to your participation and how much I look forward to this opportunity of making your acquaintance and of seeking together and finding the way to complete victory at the earliest possible moment over our common enemies and assuring the future cooperation of our countries in all spheres for their better security and greater prosperity.

As the President has told you I think we can make arrangements for your stay in Cairo that will be satisfactory to you and we shall count it an honour to play the host on this occasion.

邱吉爾首相致　蔣委員長電

羅斯福總統已告如閣下吾人希望閣下能

參加十一月二十二日在開羅舉行之會議余

深覺余得附驥閣下共同出席此一會議關係

之重要蓋吾人藉此良機不僅得以相認識

並得以共同商討如何早日先服共同之敵人

獲得完全之勝利以及相互保證同盟團結將

來各方面之合作以促進其安全與繁榮也

吾幸對於閣下在居留開羅期間當妥備招

待以盡同盟之誼

President and Mme. Chiang conferred with U.S. President Franklin D. Roosevelt and British Prime Minister Winston Churchill in Cairo. (Nov. 22, 1943)

In November, 1943, Generalissimo Chiang Kai-shek, President Roosevelt and Prime Minister Churchill, together with their respective military and diplomatic advisers, met and conferred at Cairo. The following general statement was issued:

"The several military missions have agreed upon future military operations against Japan. They covet no gain for themselves and have no thought of territorial expansion. It is their purpose that Japan shall be stripped of all the islands in the Pacific which she has seized or occupied since the beginning of the First World War in 1914, and that all the territories Japan has stolen from the Chinese, such as Manchuria, Formosa, and the Pescadores, shall be restored to the Republic of China. Japan will also be expelled from all other territories which she has taken by violence and greed. The aforesaid three great powers, mindful of the enslavement of the people of Korea, are determined that in due course Korea shall become free and independent.

"With these objects in view the three Allies, in harmony with those of the United Nations at war with Japan, will continue to persevere in the serious and prolonged operations necessary to procure the unconditional surrender of Japan."

President Chiang inspecting units of the Youth Corps. (Oct. 1944)

On behalf of President Chiang, Gen. Ho Ying-chin, C-in-C Chinese Army, accepted the surrender text from Gen. Neiji Okamura, C-in-C Japanese forces in China, at the Central Military Academy in Nanking. (Sept. 9, 1945)

*President Chiang receiving the Japanese sur-
render text forwarded by Lt. Gen. Leng Hsin.
(Sept. 10, 1945)*

*President Chiang's photograph autographed
by himself for sending to the Allied Forces
during the time of V-J Day. (Sept. 1945)*

Japanese prisoners of wars being repatriated safely to Japan. (Nov. 1945)

Following the return of the National Government to Nanking after the glorious victory, President Chiang led a group of government officials to pay respects to Dr. Sun Yat-sen's Mausoleum. (May 5, 1946)

President and Mme. Chiang visited Taiwan and received a hearty welcome from the people of Taiwan. (Oct. 21, 1946)

CHAPTER ONE

Introduction

Ever since Japan dispatched military forces to Tsinan in 1928 to obstruct our Northward Expedition[1] and then withdrew the forces in 1929, Russian forces invaded the Chinese Eastern Railway and instigated their fifth columnists, the Chinese Communists, into staging city uprisings. In 1930, they succeeded in taking Changsha. In 1931, Japanese forces staged the Manchurian Incident by seizing the northeastern provinces.[2] Meanwhile, Chinese Communists raised havoc in the border areas of the seven provinces in South China.[3] Thus, the anti-Japanese and anti-Communist war was gradually unveiled. At this time, the democratic camp was troubled by economic panic and the rise of fascism. The United States adopted the isolation policy, while Britain and France were too preoccupied to look to the East. Shouldering the responsibilities in the name of democracy and freedom, China alone carried out the struggle.

Far-sighted and observant, Generalissimo Chiang had always regarded Russia and the Chinese Communists as the most dangerous public enemy to mankind. The Chinese Communists told lies to deceive the farmers under the disguise of land reform, in particular, shook the nation's foundation and posed a serious threat. Accordingly, Generalissimo Chiang concentrated strong forces to fight them by first eliminating the nation's traitors. In resisting the aggression of the Japanese militarists, he sought peaceful solutions through diplomatic channels in the beginning and then offered only limited resistance. He made concessions time and again in the hope that they would awaken. Nevertheless he persisted in

---

[1] To obstruct China's unification which would affect their intrigue of aggression in China, the Japanese militarists conspired with the northern warlords by dispatching military forces to interrupt the launching of the Northward Expedition by the National Revolutionary Forces. Initially, three Japanese companies occupied the Chiaochow-Tsinan Railway. On May 1, the Japanese dispatched the 6th Division to occupy Tsingtao, Tsinan, Lungkou and Yentai. On May 3, they took provocative actions by firing on the Northward Expeditionary Forces. At night, under the pretext of searching our Negotiation Office, the Japanese troops kidnapped Commissioner Tsai Kung-shih and more than ten members of his staff, cut off their ears and noses and finally killed them, resulting in the tragic "May 3 Incident." This was followed by bombing and shelling of Tsinan to continue the massacre. The Japanese did not relent until the Northward Expeditionary Forces crossed the Yellow River and recaptured Peiping and Tientsin. 11,062 Chinese soldiers and civilians were killed and other heavy losses were incurred.

[2] See Section 1, Chapter Six of this book for details.

[3] Meaning the provinces of Hunan, Kiangsi, Chekiang, Fukien, Hupei, Anhwei and Kwangtung.

pursuing his objectives, sought China's freedom and equality and called upon the nations in the world's democratic camp to march onto the road of collective security.

Hard pressed by the sieges of the Government forces, the Chinese Communists in their hideouts in the Honan-Hupei-Anhwei border area, the Hung-hu area in northern Hupei and southern Kiangsi were successively disorganized. In the summer of 1935, they fled through Szechuan and Yunnan to northern Shensi. Having suffered prohibitive losses and having found themselves at the end of their wits, the Chinese Communists were directed by Communist International to advance the slogan of "Anti-Japanese National United Front."[4] They launched a peace offensive to relax our efforts in combating communism and instigated the Japanese aggression of China.

Greatly intoxicated by the trend at the time and the war doctrines, Japanese militarists were unaware that armed colonial policy was no longer applicable in the face of high national spirit. When a nation became an organic body, limited war could not be waged. In addition, they lacked a thorough understanding of the Russian-Chinese Communist intrigue of turning a war into indirect aggression, and the power of matching guerilla tactics with attrition strategy. They did not distinguish friend or foe, nor did they assess their national power. As they initiated the July 7 Incident by attacking Peiping and Tientsin, they attempted to achieve the specialization of the five provinces in North China. Under such circumstances, China was unable to make further concessions. The painful sacrifices in the 8-year War of Resistance made it possible for the Chinese Communists to rise from ashes and the Russians to achieve victory without fighting. At the time of the Cairo Conference and the Japanese capitulation, Generalissimo Chiang's magnanimity of returning love for hatred was indeed the manifestation of Christian spirit, and the concrete display of vision in the world's anti-Communist strategy.

Now that the Chinese Communists have seized the China mainland, the sufferings they have heaped on our people far surpass those of the Japanese militarists. As we recall the tremendous hardships during the War of Resistance, we should all the more remain firm in our will to stage counteroffensive and achieve national recovery. Indeed, the proverb that "those who are kind have no peer; those who are virtuous receive much help" is quite right. The vicious Japanese ate their bitter fruits and the brutal Russian and Chinese Communists will not last long. We who carry out the will of our Leader and believe the Three People's Principles will achieve final victory.

---

4 In July, 1935, the Soviet Communist International called the 7th Conference. The decision was made to abandon temporarily the armed seizure of political power and adopt "united front." It then directed the Chinese Communists to act in accordance with the "Outline of United Front."

CHAPTER TWO
Causes of the War

With the Shoguns' Revolution of 1868, the abolition of feudalism in 1871, the activation of national army in 1873 and the convocation of the parliament in 1889, the political system of Japan gradually became westernized. However, the military hierarchy which was the reincarnation of the feudal chiefs retained special political and social privileges. In the chain of command, the Japanese army and navy were directly subordinated to the Emperor, yet the Emperor, by tradition, was not permitted to interfere with politics. In spite of the fact that the military hierarchy was under the cabinet in the administrative channel, the cabinet frequently accommodated itself to the military. Like an unbridled horse, the military hierarchy was able to get what it wanted in both personnel and military expenses. The Japanese army, in particular, was patterned after Germany and intoxicated in fascism and in the sweet dreams of 18th-19th century colonialism. As the Japanese military was opposed to the Oriental culture of moderation and was misled in the trend of modern revolution, it paid no heed to the consciousness of China's nationalism and the Russian and Chinese Communists' intrigue of transforming the war into something else. The fact that Japan did not identify friend or foe and did not assess accurately her national strength was the primary cause which led to her blind, impulsive and blatant aggression of China. Meanwhile, local cheap labor and European and American economic aid enabled the Japanese industries to leap from an agricultural society into a capitalistic and industrialized nation. As a result, production surplus and food shortage ensued. These accounted for the main reasons why the Japanese financiers supported the militarists in seeking foreign markets and colonies.

Taking full advantage of World War I, the Russian Communists overthrew the Czar and seized political power to play a key role in bringing chaos to the world. They aimed to communize the world by means of manufacturing wars and sabotage. The agents and party organizations of the Communist International were scattered everywhere. They infiltrated every level in the society fanning chaos with such trickeries as intelligence, propaganda, discord and incitement. Since the failure of Russia's invasion of Poland in 1920 when her westward advance was stopped, Lenin left the will that the shortest route from Moscow to Paris was via Peiping and Calcutta. Hence the arrow of Russia's invasion was directed toward East Asia with China bearing the brunt. While Russia did all she could to help the Chinese Communists grow and to sabotage the Chinese

Government, she made full use of the international Communist agents to engineer the Japanese invasion of China.

When the Northward Expedition was successfully accomplished in 1928, the National Government sought international equality in foreign affairs and reconstruction, reorganization of the armed forces, and mopping-up of the Chinese Communists in domestic affairs. As China's international prestige grew higher and higher, the designs of the Japanese militarists and the Russian Communists on China were stepped up. In 1928, when the northeastern provinces swore allegiance to the Central Government,[1] the aggressors' intrigues to divide China fell through. The expansion of railroads in the northeast and the port construction at Hulutao led the Japanese militarists into the belief that their gained interests were at stake. In the same year, Russian forces invaded the Chinese Eastern Railway and urged the Chinese Communists to harass Hunan and Kiangsi so as to tie down and wear out Chinese forces and to encourage the swift advance of the Japanese forces. In 1931, Shumei Ogawa, head of the Daikokai (a rightist organization) mobilized 10,000 people of the rightist and leftist organizations to stage the March Coup which ended in failure. Thus, the rightist elements of the Japanese forces decided to take provocative actions by a blind promotion of the continental policy. At a time when the world was in an economic panic (which began in 1929 and lasted for ten years) and the United States and Britain were too busy to look to the East (United States was insisting on an isolation policy and was advocating disarmament), Japanese economy was also tottering In order to monopolize China's northeastern markets, Japanese financiers were in favor of the militarists' staging of the Manchurian Incident which broke out on September 18, 1931. The intrigues of the Russian and Chinese Communists helped turn it into a full-scale war.

---

1 When the Northward Expeditionary Forces captured Peiping and Tientsin, warlord Chang Tso-lin escaped to Huang-ku-tun beyond Shan-hai-kuan and was killed when his train was blown up by a mine planted by the Japanese. His son, Chang Hsueh-liang led his remnant forces back to Feng-tien (Manchuria). Knowing he could no longer depend on his armed forces, feeling that the Three People's Principles could save China and pained by his father's death because of Japanese intrigue, Chang Hsueh-liang finally cabled to pledge his allegiance to the National Government and changed to the national flag of blue sky, white sun with crimson background in 1928.

CHAPTER THREE
Political Warfare

Section 1. Wartime Political Organizations

Revision of Organic Law of the National Government

On 12 May, 1931 the National Convention passed the provisional constitution of the period of political tutelage. The main contents were divided into eight chapters covering people's rights and obligations, outline of political tutelage, people's livelihood, national education, delineation of responsibilities between the central and local governments, and organization of government. On 1 June of the same year, the provisional constitution was promulgated by the National Government for implementation. Several months later, the Manchurian Incident broke out with the Japanese invasion of the northeast. Thus, China entered into a period of national emergency. In December, 1931, in an effort to meet the existing situation so as to achieve political flexibility, the Central Government revised the organic law of the National Government and reorganized the National Government. The highlights of the revised organic law are as follows:

1. The chairman of the National Government is the chief of state of the Republic of China. He represents the state internally and externally; however, he is not charged with practical political responsibilities nor with other concurrent duties. His term of office is two years, and may be re-appointed. However, at the promulgation of the Constitution, he should, by law, be re-elected.

2. The National Government Committee has 24-36 members. The heads of the yuans and ministries cannot serve concurrently as members of the Committee.

3. Before the promulgation of the Constitution, the five yuans perform their duties independently with each yuan responsible individually to the KMT Central Executive Committee.

4. The president of the Executive Yuan shoulders actual, administrative responsibilities.

5. A ministry is organized to be responsible for judicial affairs under the Executive Yuan.

6. The chairman and the members of the National Government and the presidents and the vice-presidents of the five yuans are elected by the KMT Central Executive Committee.

The organic law of the National Government has undergone no revision since then.

Meanwhile, the Central Political Conference was organized to provide direction and supervision to the National Government on major issues and to dispose of political affairs. In December, 1935, the Central Political Conference was reorganized into the Central Political Committee. The committee had 19-25 members filled by those who were not heads of the yuans or ministries. The standing members were abolished, while a chairman and a vice-chairman were created. The functions of the committee included the passage of resolutions on legislative principles, administrative policies, military and financial policies as well as the selection of officials by special appointment for the execution of the National Government.

Readjustment of Central Political Organizations

When the War of Resistance broke out on 7 July, 1937, the Supreme National Defense Council was established by the Central Government to meet the requirements in combining political strategy and military strategy. The functions of the council are as follows:

1. In time of war, the chairman of the Supreme National Defense Council may dispense with peacetime procedure in the discharge of party, political and military affairs by issuing orders as expedients.

2. When the council deems it necessary to act immediately on those cases which should be turned over to the Legislative Yuan, it may take expedient measures first and then refer to the Legislative Yuan in accordance with legislative procedure.

3. Cases submitted to the Legislative Yuan which are related to the war should be first reviewed by the Supreme National Defense Council.

The above functions were the same as those of the Central Political Committee. When the Central Political Committee was not in session, necessary actions were taken by the Supreme National Defense Council.

In November of the same year, the Central Government promulgated "The Readjustment Measures of Central Party-Political-Military Organizations in National Emergency." The National Military Council became the supreme command in the War of Resistance. Hence, the organization of the National Military Council was expanded. A secretariat was established. In addition, six ministries respectively responsible for military operations, military administration, economy, political strategy, public information and organization and training were established.

On 1 January 1938, the Central Government promulgated an order readjusting central administrative organizations. Key points of the order are as follows:

1. The Ministry of the Navy is deactivated for the time being. Its activities will be consolidated under the GHQ Navy.

2. The Ministry of Industries is redesignated the Ministry of Economic Affairs. The water conservancy activities of the Commission on Reconstruction

and of the National Economic Commission and the activities of the Third and Fourth Ministries of the National Military Council are consolidated under the Ministry of Economic Affairs.

3. The highway operations of the Ministry of Railways and the National Economic Commission are consolidated under the Ministry of Communications. The Ministry of Railways is hereby deactivated. The Joint Transportation Office established by the three readjustment commissions on agriculture, industries and trades are redesignated under the Ministry of Communications.

4. The health activities of the National Economic Commission are integrated into the Directorate of Health under the Ministry of Interior.

Later, the Executive Yuan consolidated the Accounting Division and the Refugee Relief Association into the Relief Commission. Additionally, the relief activities formerly handled by the Ministry of Interior were turned to the Relief Commission.

On 14 January, the National Government promulgated the revised organic law of the Executive Yuan stipulating that, apart from directing other special organizations, the Executive Yuan exercised rule over the Ministries of Interior, Foreign Affairs, War, Finance, Economic Affairs, Education and Communications as well as the Commissions on Mongolian and Tibetan Affairs, Overseas Affairs, and Relief. On 17 January, after revision the National Military Council was designated the wartime supreme command in the military chain of command. The National Military Council was directly subordinated to the National Government with a chairman at the head and 7-9 members. These officials were selected by the Central Political Committee and were specially appointed by the National Government. Furthermore, the chief of the general staff, the vice chief of the general staff, the ministers of the Ministry of War, the Ministry of Military Operations, the Ministry of Military Training and the Ministry of Political Affairs and the president of the Board of Military Councillors were members of the council by virtue of their positions. The National Military Council was reorganized to include the Ministry of Military Operations, the Ministry of War, the Ministry of Military Training and the Ministry of Political Affairs under its direction. The Judge Advocate General, the Commission on Aeronautical Affairs, the Rear Area Services Ministry and the Administrative Office of the Council remained unchanged.

In January, 1939, the Central Government established the Supreme National Defense Commission to meet the requirements of total war in the War of Resistance in the light of the need "to organize a unified party-political-military command agency so that party-political efforts could be geared to military efforts to develop the full effectiveness of joint actions." This commission assumed the authorities of the Central Political Committee with the deactivation of the Supreme National Defense Council.

The KMT director-general was also the chairman of the Supreme National Defense Commission. The commission had 11 standing members who were the presidents of the five yuans, the minister of foreign affairs, the chief of the general staff, the vice chief of the general staff and three recommended standing members of KMT Central Standing Committee. The standing members of the Central Executive Committee and the Central Supervisory Committee, the secretary-general of the Central Executive Committee and the secretary-general of the Executive Yuan were observers at the standing conferences of the Supreme National Defense Commission. As the commission was more flexible in the combined employment of political strategy and military strategy, it contributed immensely to leading the nation in the War of Resistance and in national reconstruction. The commission was finally deactivated in 1947.

In the same year, the National Military Council added the Battle-field Party-Political Commission, the Executive Yuan added the Ministry of Agriculture and Forestry. The Ministry of Social Affairs which had been subordinated to the KMT Central Party Headquarters was placed under the Executive Yuan.

In July, 1940, the Central Government redesignated the Ministry of Economic Affairs into the Ministry of Industries and Commerce to be responsible for industries, commerce, and mining. In addition, the Ministry of Economic Warfare and Wartime Economic Conference were added. In order to implement the administrative interlocking system of planning, execution and evaluation so as to perfect government and increase efficiency, the decision was made to create a Central Planning Bureau under the Supreme National Defense Commission. In September, the organization outline of the bureau was passed by the Central Standing Committee. Subsequently, the bureau was established in February, 1941. Before the start of each fiscal year, the Central Planning Bureau formulated the administrative guide lines. When passed by the Supreme National Defense Commission, they were distributed to the government at various echelons which, in accordance with the directed guide lines, passed on to the responsible agencies the preparation of the administrative programs and the budget estimates required to execute these programs. The programs were submitted and screened at each level to be reviewed and consolidated by the Central Planning Bureau. The bureau would then prepare a nationwide administrative program. The program was then submitted to the Supreme National Defense Commission for execution and to the Party-Political Work Review Committee as a basis for future evaluation.

The chairman of the Supreme National Defense Commission was concurrently the director-general of the Central Planning Bureau. There were 7-9 reviewers and a number of planners who either selected or invited by the director-general to render their services. The director-general presided over the meetings of the review board. The items being reviewed are as follows:

(1) Political and economic reconstruction plans and budgets.
(2) Readjustment of party-political organizations and important regulations.
(3) Recommendations on important policies.

The secretary-general was the convener of the planners' conference. In addition, there was the Budget Committee to review the budgets.

Section 2. Wartime Political Measures

On 18 September, 1931, when the Manchurian Incident erupted, the National Government called on the nation to unite and resist aggression. Similarly, the Kuomintang urged solidarity and sincerity to meet the national crisis. Yet, the Chinese Communist Party issued a manifesto on 30 September denouncing the call for a "united front to resist foreign aggression" as an outrageous and deceitful lies. It further declared that "the Chinese Communist Party is still arch enemy to the imperialists and the Kuomintang." The Executive Committee of the Communist International in Moscow passed a resolution saying that the Chinese Communist Party must devote itself to the overthrow of the Kuomintang.

On 28 January, 1932, when the Shanghai Incident broke out, the Chinese forces fought valiantly in Shanghai.[1] The Chinese Communist Party, therefore, moved the Red Army to occupy Kanchow, Nanhsiung, and Changchow and made plans to attack Nanchang and Wuhan. It openly called for strikes in Shanghai and incited the masses to oppose the Government. Meanwhile, Government authorities decided on the general policy of "Internal pacification before resisting foreign aggression" by proceeding with national defense reconstruction on the one hand and laying siege of the Communist-occupied areas on the other.[2] Accordingly, in the winter of 1932, the Honan-Hupei-Anhwei border areas were mopped up. In 1934, the Communists in Kiangsi-Hunan were destroyed. The Communists fled west to Yunnan, Kweichow, Szechuan and Sikang. In 1935, Communist remnants fled to northern Shensi. During this period, currency system was revamped, armed forces were reorganized, Lushan Officers' Training Corps and Omei Training Corps were organized, the New Life Movement was initiated,[3] the National Economic Reconstruction Movement was promoted,[4] na-

---

[1] See Section, Chapter 6 of this book for detail.

[2] To save the country from the crisis of having to fight Japan and the Chinese Communists at the same time, Gereralissimo Chiang proclaimed after the Shanghai Incident of Jan. 28, 1932 the policy of "internal pacification and unification before resisting foreign aggression" and proceeded with operations against the Chinese Communists.

[3] In order to streamline living habits, complete psychological reconstruction, develop national spirit and eliminate Communist ills, Generalissimo Chiang launched the "New Life Movement" at Nanchang on Feb. 19, 1934. The promotion of this movement enabled us to eliminate bad practices in the society, achieve success in operations against the Chinese Communists and win victory in the War of Resistance.

[4] To urge the people to improve national economy and cooperate fully with the government and the armed forces, Generalissimo Chiang launched the "National Economic Reconstruction Movement" in Kweiyang on Apr. 1, 1935. Ever since then, improvement in people's living conditions was evidenced and gradual prosperity took place, balance of receipts and payment was achieved. Thus, the operations against the Chinese Communists were concluded satisfactorily marking the realization of the first step of the Principle of People's Livelihood.

tional defense was strengthened, traffic communication was realigned and the air force was built up. In August, 1931, the area administrative supervisory commissioner system was installed and the Pao Chia system (a system of mutual assistance and security, dating back nine centuries) was implemented.[5] In 1933, the conscription law was promulgated. By the time the law went into effect in 1936, conscription began on a trial basis. In July, 1934, the system of having all the agencies of the provincial government work in the same compound was instituted. In 1936, the draft constitution was prepared ahead of schedule.

When the War of Resistance broke out in July 1937, various parties and cliques all recognized the Three People's Principles as the main theme in the war for national reconstruction. On Sept. 22, the Chinese Communist Party announced the abolition of the Soviet government and the reorganization of the Red Army into the National Revolutionary Army to struggle for the realization of the revolutionary Three People's Principles. In April, 1938, the National Socialist Party and the Young China Party separately wrote to KMT Director-General Chiang reiterating their desire to fight the war under the leadership of the Kuomintang. The representatives of the various parties and cliques participated in the People's Political Council. Later, the Han, Manchurian, Mongolian, Moslem, and Tibetan peoples as well as the Miao and Yao tribes announced their support of the Government and actively made preparations for the war.

At this time, the Chinese people, regardless of parties, races or localities were solidly united under the leadership of the Central Government to meet the national crisis. For the first time since the establishment of the republic, national political and military unity was achieved. Such an achievement was the result of the employment of political strategy.

On 29 March, 1938, the KMT Provisional National Congress was convened. Lasting ten days, it passed the following four important resolutions:

1. It formulated the Program of Resistance and National Reconstruction as the guiding principle for the nation.

2. It elected Generalissimo Chiang as the KMT director-general. It clearly stipulated that Generalissimo Chiang was the leader of the party so that our revolutionary camp could have a stabilizing force.

3. It decided to terminate the National Defense Advisory Council and establish the People's Political Council as the highest wartime people's organ.

4. It decided to establish the Three People's Principles Youth Corps. As

---

[5] To seek perfection in civil organization and coordination with the military so as to eliminate disturbances created by the Chinese Communists, Generalissimo Chiang decided to implement the "pao chia" system (a system of mutual assistance and security, dating back nine centuries). Each household was regarded as a unit. Ten households were organized into a "Chia," and ten "chia's" were organized into a "pao." Two or more "pao's" formed a "lien pao." This system was instrumental in laying the foundation of people's self-defense and in enabling the operations against the Chinese Communists to be concluded smoothly.

the ruling party, the KMT should train the youths of the nation, so that everyone would believe in the Three People's Principles. The establishment of the Youth Corps eliminated the preparatory membership.

As the Program of Resistance and National Reconstruction was the wartime administrative guideline and the basis for the unified employment of political strategy and military strategy, it was fully supported by the People's Political Council. The original text of the Program of Resistance and National Reconstruction is as follows:

Program of Armed Resistance and National Reconstruction (Adopted by the Extraordinary Kuomintang National Congress on April 1, 1938):

The Kuomintang is leading the entire nation in carrying on armed resistance and national reconstruction. Success in both tasks will require not only the efforts of members of this Party but also the acceptance of responsibility by the people as a whole in a united endeavor. Consequently, this Party has deemed it necessary to call on the people to abandon their prejudices and sink their differences in favor of oneness of purpose and unity in action. For this particular reason, at its Extraordinary National Congress, this Party has formulated and adopted various principles governing diplomacy, military affairs, politics, economic affairs, mass movement and education, and caused their promulgation for general observance so that the nation's strength may be collected and general mobilization may be attained. These principles are as follows:

1. General Provisions:

a. The Three People's Principles and other teachings bequeathed by Tsungli (Dr. Sun Yat-sen) are hereby declared as the highest authority regulating all war activities and the work of national reconstruction.

b. The nation's war strength shall be centralized under the leadership of this Party and of Generalissimo Chiang Kai-shek in order to make possible the fullest progress.

2. Diplomacy:

a. In accordance with the spirit of independence and sovereignty, China is prepared to ally herself with all states and peoples that sympathize with her cause, and to wage a common struggle for peace and justice.

b. China is prepared to exert her utmost to uphold and increase the authority of any international peace structure as well as all treaties and conventions that aim at safeguarding world peace.

c. China is prepared to ally herself with all forces that are opposed to Japanese imperialism in order to check Japanese aggression and to establish and maintain a lasting peace in East Asia.

d. China is prepared to improve still further the existing friendly relations with various nations in order to win greater sympathy for her cause.

e. All bogus political organizations which Japan has set up in Chinese territory now under her military occupation, and all their actions, both internal and external, are declared null and void.

3. Military Affairs:

a. Political training in the army shall be intensified in order to familiarize all officers and men with the meaning of armed resistance and national reconstruction and to make them, one and all, ready to lay down their lives for the nation.

b. All able-bodied citizens shall be trained; the people's military ability for self-defense shall be strengthened; military units engaged in war shall be reinforced; and overseas Chinese who have returned to offer their services at the front shall be given special training in the light of their skills and abilities to fit them for participation in the defense of their fatherland.

c. People in various localities who have their own arms shall receive direction and support from the Government; under the command of the various war area commanders, they shall cooperate with the regular troops in military operations for the defense of their homeland against external foes, and also for the purpose of starting widespread guerilla warfare in the enemy's rear in order to destroy and harass enemy forces.

d. In order to heighten military morale and boost the people's enthusiasm for national mobilization, both the wounded and dependents of the killed shall be looked after, the disabled shall be rehabilitated, the families of soldiers shall be given preferential consideration.

4. Politics:

a. An organ shall be set up for the people to participate in affairs of state thereby unifying the national strength and collecting the best minds and views for facilitating the formulation and execution of national policies.

b. The hsien (county) shall be taken as the basic unit in which self-defense organizations shall be strengthened through training the people and increasing their power, and in which conditions for local self-government shall be fulfilled as soon as possible in order to provide a strong political and social foundation during wartime and to pave the way for constitutionalism.

c. There shall be a thorough reform in the machinery of all levels of government, simplifying it and making it systematic, and administrative efficiency shall be heightened in order to meet the needs of war.

d. The conduct of officials of all ranks shall conform to rules; they shall be dutiful, ready to sacrifice themselves for the country, observe discipline and obey orders so that they may serve as models for the people; those disloyal to their duty and obstructing the prosecution of the war shall be court-martialed.

e. Corrupt officials shall be severely punished and their property shall be confiscated.

5. Economic Affairs:

a. Economic reconstruction shall concern itself mainly with matters of military importance and, in addition, with matters that contribute to the improvement of the people's livelihood. With these objects in view a planned economy shall be put into operation, investments by people both at home and abroad shall be encouraged, and large-scale wartime production shall be undertaken.

b. The greatest measure of energy shall be devoted to the development of rural economy, the encouragement of cooperative enterprises, the regulation of foodstuffs with regard to their demand and supply, reclamation, and the improvement of irrigation installations.

c. Mining shall be undertaken, the foundations for heavy industries shall be laid, light industries shall be encouraged, and handicraft industries in the various provinces shall be developed.

d. Wartime taxes shall be levied and the financial administration shall be thoroughly reformed.

e. The banking business shall be controlled so that industrial and commercial activities may be properly adjusted.

f. The position of fapi (legal tender) shall be fortified, foreign exchange shall be controlled, and imports and exports shall be regulated, all for the sake of financial stability.

g. The communication systems shall be reorganized, connecting transportation by waterways, overland routes and airways shall be instituted, more railways and highways shall be built and more airlines shall be opened.

h. No hoarding, speculation and manipulation shall be allowed, and a system of price stabilization shall be enforced.

6. Mass Movement:

a. The people throughout the country shall be aroused and organized by occupational groups such as unions of farmers, laborers, merchants, and students. The rich shall be asked to contribute in money and the able-bodied shall contribute in labor service. All classes of people shall be mobilized for the war.

b. The freedom of speech, the freedom of the press, and the freedom of assembly shall be fully protected by law, in the course of the war, provided they do not contravene the Three People's Principles which are the nation's highest principles, and provided they are within the scope of laws and ordinances.

c. Refugees from the war areas and unemployed people shall receive relief and shall be organized and trained so that their services may be available for the war.

d. The people's national consciousness shall be promoted so that they may assist the Government in eradicating reactionaries. Traitors shall be severely punished and their property shall be confiscated in accordance with law.

7. Education:

a. Both the educational system and teaching material shall be revised. A program of wartime education shall be instituted with emphasis on the cultivation of the peoples' morale, and the enhancement of scientific research, and the expansion of necessary facilities shall be effected.

b. Technical personnel of all kinds shall be trained and given proper assignment in order to meet the needs of war.

c.   Youths shall be given training to enable them to work in the war areas or rural districts.

d.   Women shall be given training so that they may be of service to social enterprises and thereby of help to the nation's war strength.

On April 12, 1938, the People's Political Council promulgated its organizational regulations listing its members at 150.   The membership was distributed as follows:

1.   88 members were chosen from among those who had served in government organs, public bodies, various private institutions in the provinces and municipalities (directly subordinate to the Executive Yuan) for more than three years.

2.   6 members (4 from Mongolia and 2 from Tibet) were chosen from those who had served in government organs, public bodies, various private institution in Mongolia and Tibet or were familiar with the local political and social conditions.

3.   6 members were chosen from those who had served with distinction in overseas Chinese communities or were familiar with their living conditions.

4.   50 members where chosen from those who had served for more than three years in key cultural and economic bodies or had been long devoted to political activities.

The first plenary session met in Hankow and its tenure ended in 1940.   In September of the same year, the Central Standing Committee resolved at its 158th meeting to continue the convocation "and to improve the selection of councillors, increase the number of councillors and expand the authorities of the Council taking into consideration the experiences in the past two years and the desire of the social leaders.   In addition, the speaker system was changed into the presidium system so as to insure smooth discharge of the Council's responsibilities and collective efforts."   Briefly, the stipulations governing the organization, functions, length of session and presidium are as follows:

1.   Organization:

The Council had a membership of 200 delegates.   Chinese citizens, male or female, who reached the age of 30, were not incumbent government officials were eligible to become delegates so long as they met the necessary qualifications.   The distribution and the selection of delegates are as follows:

a.   90 delegates were elected by provincial or municipal councils with unsigned ballots.   In provinces or municipalities which had no council, the candidates were nominated by the provincial or municipal government concerned in consultation with the local Kuomintang offices.   Twice as many candidates were nominated to be selected by the Central Executive Committee.

b.   4 delegates from Mongolia and 2 delegates from Tibet.

c.   6 delegates from overseas Chinese.

Delegates to the first and second People's Political Council were selected by the Central Executive Committee. Twice as many candidates were separately nominated by the Mongolian and Tibetan Affairs Commission and the Overseas Chinese Affairs Commission.

d. Twice as many candidates for the 180 delegates representing various major cultural and economic bodies and political parties were nominated by the Supreme National Defense Council and were selected by the Central Executive Committee. The tenure of office of the delegates was one year and might be lengthened by the government.

2. Authority:

a. Power to make resolutions: During the War of Resistance, major domestic and foreign policies of the government were submitted to the People's Political council for discussion and resolution before implementation. These resolutions, when passed by the Supreme National Defense Council were turned over to the responsible agencies in accordance with the nature of the resolutions. The agencies concerned would make laws or promulgate orders. In the event of an emergency, the Supreme National Defense Council could take improvised measures by issuing orders.

b. Power to make proposals: The People's Political Council could make proposals to the government.

c. Power to make interpellations: The People's Political Council had the power to receive the government's administrative reports and to interpellate the government.

d. Power to make investigations: The People's Political Council organized an investigation committee to investigate matters entrusted by the government. The results of the investigations could be presented by the Council to the government for action.

3. Length of Session:

The People's Political Council was convened for a period of ten days every six months. The government might prolong a session or call a provisional session. When each plenary session adjourned, the Council formed a resident committee. The 25 members of this committee were elected by the presidium and the delegates. Its functions were as follows:

a. To receive the government reports.

b. To insure the implementation of resolutions and to check on the progress from time to time.

c. To exercise the Council's power to make proposals and investigations within the scope of the Council's jurisdictions.

4. The Presidium:

During the first People's Political Council, apart from the delegates, there were a speaker and a deputy speaker who were selected by the Central Executive Committee. At the second People's Political Council, a five-man presidium was elected by the Council. Candidates for the presidium were not confined to delegates only. When the People's Political Council and the resident committee met, the presidium elected one of its members as the chairman.

From the formation of the People's Political Council to its termination with the implementation of a constitutional government in May, 1947, the number of delegates was increased to 360. From the first through the fourth People's Political Council, a total of 13 plenary sessions was held contributing greatly to the basic national policy in the War of Resistance and national reconstruction. Members of the Chinese Youth Party, the National Socialist Party, the Communist Party as well as those prominent personages having no party affiliations were participants. During the War of Resistance, the People's Political Council, representing the people, made many proposals to support the Program of Armed Resistance and National Reconstruction, continue the War of Resistance, make laws to establish a democratic system, denounce traitor Wang Ching-wei, discuss and prepare the Draft Constitution, impeach officials, and organize such bodies as the "Szechuan-Sikang Inspection Team, Committee for the Promotion of Constitutional Government, Committee for the Promotion of Economic Reconstruction in Szechuan and Sikang" which were most practical organizations. Under the major premise of resisting Japan, all the other political parties, with the exception of the Communist Party which harbored its own designs, were united in realizing the common objective. These organizations regarded the Program of Armed Resistance and National Reconstruction as their guide post and the repulse of the Japanese their duty. Despite Wang Ching-wei's betrayal and his subsequent surrender to the enemy and Japanese manufacture of the puppet regime in Nanking, the various political parties were united in forming the anti-Japanese front, they remained unwavered and fought on until final victory was achieved.

Meanwhile, the various provisional provincial and municipal councils were successively organized. A number of provinces had even organized hsien (county) councils. The guerilla areas behind enemy lines in North China held popular election of magistrates, district chiefs and village chiefs.

Subsequent to the Government's removal to Chungking, greater emphasis was placed on border problems. In January, 1939, Sikang officially became a province. Thus, the Sikang-Tibet dispute which had been stalemated for seven years was satisfactorily solved. In February, 1940, the 14th Dalai Lama was installed. The installation ceremony was officiated by Chairman Wu Chung-hsin of the Mongolian and Tibetan Affairs Commission who was dispatched by the Central Government.

On July 30, 1940, the Executive Yuan decided to establish the National Food Administration in order to handle the production, marketing, storage and transportation of the nation's foodstuff and to regulate the supply and demand of it. In mid-July, the Stage Transportation Conference was held in Chungking.

The conference decided to prepare an organizational outline and budget estimates for submission and approval of the Central Government. Subsequently, the Ministry of Communications organized the National Stage Transportation Administration with branches in the various provinces.

On September 6, 1940, the National Government promulgated an order which reads as follows:

"Szechuan, known as heavenly palace in ancient times, is gifted with majestic landscape and abundant resources. Strategically located along the Yangtze River in the southwest, Chunking has been selected as the temporary seat of government at which the nation began to reestablish itself in the War of Resistance. Three years have elapsed in our preparations for what may take place in the future. With a common hostility of the enemy, the people of Szechuan have given generously and have been resolute in their determination to lay a solid foundation in the War of Resistance and to undertake the task of national reconstruction. At present, the position of the nation's wartime capital is more consolidated than ever, as it has become the pivot in military, political and economic affairs. After the termination of the war, it will become the center of reconstruction in the southwest. The people are unanimously agreed that efforts will be directed to rebuild the nation. Accordingly, Chunking is hereby designated as the nation's wartime capital. The Executive Yuan is directed to supervise the responsible agencies and take into consideration the organizational system of Hsiking so as to realize the long-range plans, fulfill the wish of the people, and prepare for great celebrations."

With the official designation of Chungking as the nation's wartime capital, people throughout China rejoiced in the celebrations. Since his assumption of duties as Chairman of the National Government in 1932, Chairman Lin Sen had long been admired by the people and the servicemen. During his 12-year tenure, he had been kind, modest and dedicated. During the War of Resistance, he led the civilian and military officials of the National Government in their removal to the nation's wartime capital. While sharing hardships under most difficult circumstances, he had enabled the nation to engage simultaneously in the War of Resistance and national reconstruction. His advanced age and his devotion to duty led to the illness from which he never recovered. On August 1, 1943, he passed away in Chungking. In mourning his death, the government ordered that all flags be flown at half mast.

On September, 1943, Generalissimo Chiang was unanimously elected Chairman of the National Government and concurrently Supreme Commander of the Army, Navy and Air Force. On October 10 of the same year, Generalissimo Chiang took office as the Chairman.

In addition to the above mentioned, there was employment of many wartime political strategies. Outstanding among them were domestic and foreign affairs which are stated as follows:

Internal Affairs

The relationship between the Central Government and the local authorities has been a basic political problem in China for several thousand years. Historically, when a nation was able to achieve unification and power, the central government and local government were able to maintain political equilibrium. Thus, the nation was able to remain consolidated internally and externally. Maladjustment of this relationship led to the collapse of previous dynasties. By the same token, it also led to foreign aggression. In a country in which power was centralized, more emphasis was placed on domestic affairs, and less emphasis was given to foreign affairs ending invariably in collapse and destruction. When power was decentralized to the local governments, the disadvantage was the opposite resulting in inflexible encumberance. In view of China's past historical lessons, our National Father advocated the system of power equalization which was a happy medium between centralization and decentralization of power. It did not overlook real local autonomy because it supported the Central Government. This system was derived from the historical thinking of power equalization and was tested by the trend of thinking at the time. Thus, it emerged and became a brand new political system in the period of national reconstruction. Inheriting Dr. Sun Yat-sen's mantle, Generalissimo Chiang devoted his efforts in the planning. In 1932, he formulated the district administrative commissioner system and in 1934 the joint provincial office system. Subsequently, he drafted "The Proposal on the Delineation of Authority and Responsibility between the Central Government and the Local Government." This proposal was intended to achieve better coordination between the Central Government and the various provinces. Thus, the Central Government had adequate authority, while the local government still had driving force. Equal emphasis was given to both. In 1939, the "Organic Outline of Various Levels under Hsien," i. e. the new hsien system, was promulgated. This marked a major revamping in local administration, and the ground work in the implementation of constitutional government. The purpose in implementing the new hsien system was to achieve parallel improvement in administering, teaching, supporting and protecting the people. Similarly, no effort was spared to expedite the completion of training for the people to exercise administrative power, promote conscription, mobilize economy, implement the land policy and intensify primary education. Additionally, the establishment of wartime hsien and provincial councils developed considerable effectiveness. As the hsien council represented the people to supervise the organizations below the hsien and to assist in the promotion of local self-government, it marked a basic move to realize the Principle of Democracy. As the War of Resistance and national reconstruction supplemented each other, the Government sought soundness and effectiveness at the various basic level administrative organizations. On the one hand, it tried to meet the requirements of wartime political system. On the other hand, it sought to carry out the spirit of democracy. Some of the major actions taken in domestic affairs are stated as follows:

1. Delineation of Authority and Responsibility between the Central and the Local Government:

In the light of Dr. Sun Yat-sen's teaching on the system of power equalization, the National Government cabled the nation in 1934 delineating the authority and responsibility between the Central Government and the local government. Originally, Generalissimo Chiang made the proposal at the Fifth Plenary Session of the KMT Fourth Central Executive Committee. On December 12 of the same year, the proposal was passed for implementation. This proposal aimed to lay the foundation of mutual confidence and common confidence in the hope of guiding political affairs onto the right track, and was the only route which would lead to peace and unification. The original text of the proposal is stated as follows:

"If we remain firm in our faith that peace and unification will be achieved and work individually for the joint effort, we shall be victorious in saving the nation from disaster and in national renaissance. The fact that we have not been able to achieve effective results in our individual and collective effort is largely due to the lack of clear cut delineation of authority and responsibility between the Central Government and the local government. The most apparent weaknesses are the unclear responsibility of the local government and inflexible employment of the Central Government which have lowered administrative efficiency and have obstructed the development of various reconstruction projects. Therefore, it is most urgent that the authority and responsibility between the Central Government and the local government be newly delineated and political measures be adequate. To achieve this aim, the Central Government must rid the local government of the fear that the former is in its way and must remove its suspicion. Meanwhile, the local government must be sincere in the belief that its fate and that of the Central Government are interrelated. It must adhere to the nation's policy bearing in mind the gravity of the nation's difficulties. To be law-abiding, it must make every effort to eliminate the past practices of 'divide and rule" and counteracting. Thus, the feudal practices of the Middle Age will be transformed and a new nation practising Three People's Principles will be created. If responsible officials in the Central Government and the local government are united in carrying out the above, they will not only save the party and the nation, but also themselves.'

"What Dr. Sun Yat-sen instructed in the Fundamentals of National Reconstruction is the highest principle in delineating the authority and the responsibility between the Central Government and the local government. However, during the transition period, discretion must be exercised in order to cope with contingencies and to guide the various activities onto the right track. In the light of the above, an outline is prepared delineating the authority and the responsibility between the Central Government and the local government as follows:

"a. On the recommendation and appointment of government officials:

"In view of the multitudinous activities of the nation, talent is urgently needed Although personnel power is in the hands of the Central Government, the authority to make recommendations can be vested in the local government. In fact, most of the present regulations governing the appointment of officials at various levels carry this spirit. However, in selecting the worthy and the competent, it is imperative that the responsible officials making the selection be able to turn down the ill-considered recommendation before they can insure flexible direction and specific responsibilities. Hence, it is advisable to reiterate the above giving the responsible officials freedom to choose the qualified civilian and military candidates and recommend them for appoinment to the Central Government. Every effort should be made to meet the practical need and to select the most qualified. Thus, in unifying the command and authority of the Central Government, the authority and the responsibility of the local responsible officials will be further developed. Henceforth, regulations governing the recommendation and appointment of officials throughout the nation must be revised and implemented accordingly.

"b. On the tenure and protection of government officials:

"In administering affairs of the state improvement will depend on pinning specific responsibilities. If one acts without foresight, carelesness and perfunctoriness will result. Terms of offices for civilian and military officials in the various localities must be specifically prescribed. The teaching of the ancient sages to rate a person for three years advises us that the term of office should, in principle, be set at 3 years. The regulations should provide them with protection and should be carried out. No officials should be dismissed without justification. Those who have served with distinction may be reappointed by the Central Government upon completion of their terms of office so that they may remain in their posts for a longer period of time. Given additional time and coupled with efficiency ratings, the competent officials, conscious of the heavy responsibilities that the nation has placed on their shoulders, will be able to fulfill their tasks and and will better serve the nation. Hence, it is imperative that regulations governing the terms of office and the protection of government officials be separately and further edited.

"c. On local administration and economy:

"To seek development of local enterprises, we must place greater responsibilities on the local responsible officials. To avoid mutual conflicts and irregular development, the Central Government must assume direction and supervision so as to insure smooth progress of various activities under the nation's overall policy. Therefore, the local administrative guideline and economic reconstruction should be considered by the local government with discretion. Plans should be made and budget prepared for the approval of the Central Government. Upon approval, the agencies concerned will be rated in accordance with the schedule and without interference or frequent changes. Other major activities which are local in nature may also be handled in accordance with this principle to achieve greater results.   This explains why local enterprises must be permitted free development by the local government.

"d.   On the financial problems between the Central Government and the local government:

"The finances between the Central Government and the local government must be clearly delineated in accordance with the current measures.   National finance should be handled by the Central Government.   Custom duties, in particular, must be handled by the Central Government.   Local government must not interfere.   Other revenues must also be handled in accordance with the regulations and taxation provisions promulgated by the Central Government.   However, during the transition period, assistance may be rendered by the Central Government to local government which does not have sufficient funds so that proper adjustment can be made.   This is something which is in urgent need of solution between the Central Government and the local government.

"e.   On the national defense force and the local militia and police forces:

"The national defense force is designed to safeguard the nation.   Therefore, the nation's regular forces should be placed under the unified command of the Central Government.   However, during the present transition period, the highest local officer may make recommendation on the appointment and relief of their subordinates for approval of the Central Government.   As to local militia and police forces such as the peace preservation forces, defense units and police forces, they may be trained and transferred by local administrative officers.   Be it national defense forces or local militia and police forces, the Central Government will consolidate the procurement of weapons so as to avoid different makes of similar models and not to hinder effectiveness.   Therefore, the authority and the responsibility between the Central Government and the local government on military matters must be clearly delineated.

"f.   On the formulation of legal system:

"Due to the vastness of the country, disparity of customs in various places, lack of uniformity in the people's educational levels, and differences in economic conditions and geographical locations, care must be exercised in administrative measures in accordance with urgency of the matters.   Educational differences make it necessary to take into consideration the time, the place and the people. Promulgation of a set of unified and complicated legal system for the compliance of all is comparable to trimming the toes to fit the shoes and is highly unworkable.   In order to insure the nationalwide smooth promotion of to-day's legal systems, it is necessary that the Central Government approve the principles and the outlines permitting flexibility.   The provinces and municipalities should, based on the principles and outlines, prepare draft regulations with regard to the implementing measures and details.   These measures, being practical, will be submitted to the Central Government for perusal.   Hence, all the nation's legal regulations must meet the actual need."

2.   Institution of Joint Provincial Office System:

In 1934, when Generalissimo Chiang took personal charge of the Generalissimo's Headquarters in Nanchang, he observed that the various offices of the provincial government ran parallel to each other and formed their own cliques. They fought for power and put the blame on others.   In many respects, they were concerned only with their own interests and lacked the spirit to place group interest over their own.   Hence, he initiated the joint provincial office system for immediate implementation by the five provinces of Kiangsi, Hupei, Honan, Anhwei and Fukien in which campaigns were undertaken against the Communists. By May, 1936, the Executive Yuan called the Local Senior Administrative Officers' Conference at which a resolution was passed for the nationalwide adoption of this system.   Thus, it became an established system.

Provisions of the joint provincial office system: The provincial secretariat, the department of civil affairs, the department of education, the department of reconstruction, and the peace preservation department should have their offices jointly located within the provincial government.   All agencies that are directly subordinated to the provincial government should be abolished, amalgated, reduced or resubordinated under the interested departments.   Upon amalgation of the department offices, all the documents will be dispatched in the name of the provincial government.   The receipt and dispatch of documents will be handled by the provincial secretariat.   Meanwhile, the departments and their subordinate agencies should institute drastic reforms.   Their funds and procurement would be centralized.   As the secretariat was burdened with such activities as clerical work, accounting and housekeeping affairs, it was permitted to add offices of technical affairs, legal affairs and statistics.   The surplus funds accrued as a result of the amalgation would be allocated to the various hsiens as additional administrative funds.

3.   Special administrative inspector system:

In view of the two-level (provincial and hsien) system in local administration and the vastness of a province, it was extremely difficult for the provincial government to exercise adequate supervision over scores of hsiens and even more than one hundred hsien's and resulting in misunderstandings and corruptions. The Nanchang Headquarters of the National Military Council decided to form the Party-Political Committee in the Nanchang Headquarters.   The commander-in-chief was concurrently chairman of the committee.   Kiangsi Province was divided into a number of districts with a sub-committee in each district.   In compliance with the chairman's order, each sub-committee exercised rule over the various hsiens in the district.   The chairman of the sub-committee acted concurrently as the magistrate of the hsien in which he was stationed.   Thus, the party, political and military authority was centralized giving one person full responsibility of the party affairs, administration and security in the various hsiens of a district. The introduction of this new system met with considerable success. Later, other provinces also adopted the district system; however their designations varied somewhat.

In 1932, the Honan-Hupei-Anhwei Communist Suppression General Headquarters formulated the organizational regulations governing the office of the administrative inspector for implementation in the three above-mentioned provinces. Meanwhile, to standardize the system in the various provinces, the Ministry of Interior also drafted the provisional regulations governing the administrative inspectors for implementation in the various provinces. The regulations stipulated that, in principle, the administrative inspector acted concurrently as the magistrate of the hsien in which he was stationed. Later, as the War of Resistance broke out, the administrative inspector also served as the peace preservation commander. It was not possible for him to take charge of the hsien administration. Therefore, the Executive Yuan issued an order relieving all administrative inspectors of the responsibilities as the magistrates of the hsiens in which they were stationed.

The inspector districts bore only numerical designations in accordance with the sequence of their formations. The selection of candidates for the administrative inspector was made by a screening committee organized by the Executive Yuan. The functions of the administrative inspectors were to review the administrative programs, the central work, budget estimates and regulations of the hsiens and municipalities under their jurisdictions; inspect and guide them in local administration and self-government; evaluate the performance of the administrative personnel; settle the disputes between the hsiens and the municipalities; and call the district-wide administrative conference. Although the administrative inspector's office, by law, had considerable authority, it resembled a mid-level organization in the three-level system. In reality, it was a "supplementary agency of the provincial government" but not an agency between the provincial government and the hsien government. Its relationship to the provincial and hsien government was comparable to that of the district office to the hsien and hsiang (or chen) office. Hence, the levels of local administrative organization remained at the 2-level provincial-hsien system. Should the provincial area be reduced in the future, there, of course, would be no need to retain the administrative inspector system.

4. Promotion of experimental hsien:

Dr. Sun Yat-sen's teachings long ago had provided that local self government should be considered the most important major theme during the period of political tutelage. In 1933, the government authorities and the people felt there were a number of problems pertaining to hsien administration which needed to be resolved. They were uncertain as to the best ways to solve problems. Thus, an experimental movement in hsien administration was initiated to employ concrete measures so as to exploit the practical effectiveness of various reform programs. At that time there were a number of people who were engaged in work seeking improvement in reconstruction of village and hsien administration. Different localities were selected for the experiment. Most well-known at the time were Tsou-ping and Ho-tse in Shantung Province and Ting Hsien in Hopei Province. There were many other social organizations which were engaged in village reconstruction. This explained how the experimental hsien was developed.

With regard to the formation of the experimental hsien, the Ministry of Interior stipulated the following conditions:

a. The conditions of the area were representative of the province.

b. Convenient communications and suitable locations.

c. Marked progress was achieved in previous local self-government.

d. There were local leaders who had the leadership ability and were able to help.

e. Adequate facilities in the experimental sites.

Further, those who undertook reconstruction were mostly specialists. Supported with special funds, they had greater authorities. Hence, the experimental hsiens fared better than the average hsiens in general conditions.

Of the experimental hsiens, Kiangning in Kiansu Province and Lanhsi in Chekiang Province were most outstanding. Generalissimo Chiang felt that training of political personnel should place equal emphasis on academic subjects and experiment. During the formation of the Kiangning Experimental Hsien, he stated. "As Kiangning is the key locality in the capital area, self government marks the basis of constitutional government. As the magistrate assumes his duties in administering the hsien, the eyes of many people are fixed upon him. I strongly urge that he stand on solid ground, establish good practices, and take exemplary actions." Subsequent to the redesignation of Kiangning and Lanhsi as experimental hsiens, graduates of the Central Cheng Chih College were assigned there, and work proceeded smoothly and efficiently. In organizational system, the two hsiens underwent thorough reorganization turning bureaus into branches, reducing the number of administrative and self-governing levels, abolishing chu (district) offices and lu and lin, and establishing the two-level system of hsiang (or chen) and tsun (or li). These had an impact on subsequent reforms. Considerable progress was noted in various activities. Most significant was the progress achieved in land administration (land reporting of Kiangning and land inspection of Lanhsi).

5. Initiation of new hsien system:

The implementation of new hsien system aimed to expedite local self government. Ever since the Ching Dynasty, China had advocated self-government, but without noticeable effect. When the National Government was established in Nanking in 1927, efforts were made to promote local self-government in accordance with Dr. Sun Yat-sen's teaching. Successively, the hsien and municipal organic law, and the chu (district), hsiang and chen self-government laws were promulgated contributing immensely to improvements in local self-government; however, much remained to be done.

In the winter of 1935, in an effort to promote local self-government so as to complete the preparation for political tutelage, the KMT Central Party Headquarters established the "Local Self-Government Planning Committee," redrafted the "Principles of Local Self-Government Regulations," and simplified hsien-level organizations. As a result, the "pao-chia" (a system of mutual defense and security) system was integrated into the self-government organization. It was prescribed in the organizational system of the local self-government that the hsiang (or chen) be the unit below the hsien. In the hsiang (or chen) there were pao and chia. Originally, the "pao chia" system was an improvised measure introduced during the Communist suppression campaign in 1932 with emphasis on self defense. After revision of the self-government regulations, the "pao chia" system was incorporated. Ever since then, the "pao chia" officially became the basic organization in self-government.

On April 8, 1938 when the Fourth Plenary Meeting of the KMT Fifth Congress was held, Director-General Chiang spoke on "Improving Party Operation and Adjusting Party-Political Relationships" with "Draft Chart Showing Relationships between Party and Political Organizations below the Hsien" and legends as annexes. Later, the Central Training Corps organized the Party-Political Personnel Training Course. In June, 1939, Director-General Chiang spoke on "The Question of Determining Various Levels organizations under Hsien" and further revised and supplemented the original draft and chart. Three essential points of the address are listed as follows:

a. With regard to the party, the party district headquarters and the hsiang (or chen) organization should be synchronized. A cell is set up under the chia so as to mesh with the appropriate administrative levels.

b. As the hsien is the unit of local self-government, there were three to six classes of hsien, depending on their area, population, economic conditions, cultural status and communication facilities. Each hsien administers all affairs of the hsien self-government under the supervision of the provincial government. It also executes, under the direction of the provincial government, all orders of the Central Government and the provincial government. As to the basic level organization, there are hsiang (in rural areas) or chen (in urban areas) which are the basic units below the hsien level. The pao (or village or street) is the cell organization of hsiang (or chen). Between the hsien and hsiang (or chen) the provisions are more flexible. Depending on the localities, district offices can be set up when necessary, to act as the liaison agencies. If there is no such need, the hsiang (or chen) can be directly subordinated to the hsien government. Similarly, between the hsiang (or chen) and pao, there are also more flexible provisions in accordance with the geographical locations. In densely populated places such a village or a street which forms a natural and indivisible unit, two or three pao may jointly establish a cell organization with a senior pao chief in charge of the affairs so as to avoid arbitrary division.   In order to solve the problems of funds and talent, all the clerks in hsiang (or chen) and pao (or village and street) should be filled by school teachers.   All the principals of the pao primary schools and the commanders of the pao able-bodied men's corps might be the same persons, but in economically developed areas, the principal of the primary school should be, in principle, a full-time worker so as to centralize his responsibilities and functions and relieve him of added difficulties.   Additionally, the people were organized so that they could shoulder various activities and meet practical needs.

c.   The people's representative organizations, in turn, organized the pao general council, the hsiang (or chen) council, and the hsien council and were delegated considerable authority so as to stimulate the people's interest and ability to take part in political activities and to fully develop the people's strength in establishing a nation by the people.

After careful study and discussion of the above address, experts formulated "The Organic Outline of Various Level Organizations under Hsien" which was promulgated by the National Gevernment on September 19, 1939.   This new hsien system included the regulations from which the promotion of local self-government was derived.

In the Organic Outline of Organizational Levels in the Hsien, there was the "pao chia" system in the organization of hsiang (or chen).   Each chia, in principle, comprised ten households, but the number of households must not be fewer than six or more than fifteen.   Each pao, in principle, ten chia, but the number of chia must not be fewer than six or more than fifteen.   The division of the hsiang (or chen) called for ten pao in principle, but the number of constituent pao should not be fewer than six or more than fifteen.   If a hsien is unusually large or has special conditions, it may be divided into a number of chu (district).   The division of the chu, in principle, should be from fifteen to thirty hsiang (or chen).   Both the hsien and the hsiang (or chen) are legal persons.   All citizens of the Republic of China over twenty years of age, irrespective of sex, having lived within a hsien for over six months or having had a domicile there for over one year, are citizens of the hsien concerned, and may, in accordance with law, exercise the rights of election, recall, initiative and referendum.

After the above outline was promulgated, the Executive Yuan prepared three implementing principles and directed the provinces to formulate implementing plans for approval.   In compliance with the orders of the Supreme National Defense Council and the Executive Yuan, the Ministry of Interior drafted local self-government implementing programs and various supplementary regulations of the Organic Outline of Various Graded Units in the Hsien as the basis for implementation which was to begin in 1940.

As to the various people's representative organizations in the hsien, they were regarded as the foundation in establishing local self-government.   In hsien's which had implemented the new hsien system for more than two years, and when the provincial government concerned considered that hsien council and hsiang (or chen) council could be convened, it could request the Executive Yuan for approval to form these councils. Similarly, the regulations governing the establishment of the Youth Council were also promulgated so as to link with the hsien council. The main point was for each hsien to produce one provincial assemblyman who was elected by the hsien council. In addition, legally organized professional groups might also send delegates to the hsien council, but their number should not exceed three-tenths of the total.

6. Improvement in personnel administration:

Personnel administration included such problems as the appointment, rating, promotion, protection, discipline and payment of public functionaries. Reasonable resolutions of these problems had much to do with administrative, examination and inspector systems. The appointment, relief and rating of local officials were the functions of the Ministry of Interior. Hence, the Ministry of Interior constantly paid close attention to the performance of officials. In accordance with the "Measures Governing the Appointment of Hsien Magistrates," "Measures Governing the Criteria in the Rating Percentage of Hsien Magistrates," "Regulations Governing the Appointment of Public Functionaries," "Regulations Governing the Appointment of Hsien Administrative Personnel," "Outline Measure for the Training of Local Administrative Personnel," "Provisional Regulations on the Ratings of Various Graded Units in Provinces and Hsiens," "Measures Governing the Criteria in the Rating Perecentage of Hsien Magistrates," "Regulations Governing the Award for Battlefield Defense," "Measures Governing the Punishment of Civilian Officials," and "Provisional Regulations Governing Corruption Punishment," efforts were made to insure the implementation of these measures and regulations by the provinces and municipalities concerned. Furthermore, "Outline Plan for the Improvement of Local Personnel Administration" prepared in 1940 and submitted to the Executive Yuan for approval and implementation provided concrete measures on the appointment, protection, training, award and punishment, and gratuity of the various graded administrative personnel.

7. Maintenance of local security:

A nation has two major undertakings—one is internal pacification and the other is resistance to foreign aggression. The responsibility for resisting foreign aggression lies with the armed forces, while the responsibility for internal pacification rests with the police. In peacetime, the police maintains local order and promotes local peace. Therefore, the police plays an important role in internal administration. In wartime, the police leads the people and assists the armed forces to increase self-defense capability and maintain local security. In war or in peace, the police is closely related to the nation. It was the police which enabled the people in various places to live in peace after the War of Resistance broke out. In these years, the Ministry of Interior revamped police administration, intensified police officer training, promoted police training, improved the quality of policemen, bettered the living conditions of policemen, improved police techniques and increased the size of the police force.   All these aimed to produce a sound police system.   Generalissimo Chiang had always paid the closest attention to police administration.   When he was concurrently superintendent of the Central Police Academy, he frequently visited the academy to address the students.   On May 9, 1937 at the opening ceremony of the Central Police Training Class, he stated the following.

"The responsibility of the police rests in protecting and training the people so as to win their support.   Only by knowing how the people feel and winning them over, can you accomplish your mission.   As to how you can achieve it, it is necessary that every policeman be close to the people, understand their frame of mind and get rid of their difficulties.   Like fathers and elder brothers to their sons and younger brothers, like tutors to their children, the policemen should teach them, guide them and protect them so that people, irrespective of sex or age, learn to maintain order and do their work.   The policemen must do everything possible to wipe out theft, robbery and vices in the areas within their jurisdiction so that people improve in knowledge, virtues physical fitness, and social, economic and cultural reconstructions continue to develop.   Only then shall we consider ourselves as having fulfilled our obligations as policemen."

In compliance with Generalissimo Chiang's instructions, police cadres marched forward to accomplish their missions of leading the people and defending the nation.   Due to the vastness of China, country police was not organized.   Hence, the Ministry of Interior prepared "Measures Governing the Liaison of the Police, Pao Chia and National Guards," "Measures Governing the Intensification of Police Defense Force to Maintain Security," and "Measures Governing the Intensification of Maintenance of Security by the Magistrates."   It was hoped that efforts could be concentrated to achieve coordination in the destruction and prevention of the bandits.

8.   Implementation of land policy:

One of the major policies in Dr. Sun's Principle of Livelihood was the equalization of land ownership, it was necessary to check the actual area of land and to implement the return of the increase of the land price to the national treasury.   This would equalize the burden of the people and increase national income.   In accordance with the "Second Wartime Administrative Program," the Ministry of Interior conducted survey of land in the provinces in rear areas beginning with the provincial capital and key hsien's and municipalities.   In 1941, the KMT 8th National Congress resolved that the Ministry of Interior establish the "Central Division of Land Price Reporting" responsible for the nationwide reporting of land price.

Foreign Affairs

Our original purpose in fighting the full-scale War of Resistance against Japan was to resist Japanese aggression, maintain the survival of the Chinese people, protect international justice, and seek to establish permanent world peace. Accordingly, during the war, our diplomatic efforts were oriented in this direction. Our foreign affairs at this time were multitudinous complicated. They can be generally divided into four major headings: our diplomatic efforts in the preliminary phase of the War of Resistance, seeking Allied support to check the enemy, diplomatic accomplishments after combined operations with Allies, and diplomatic activities on the eve of V-J Day. Briefly, these efforts are stated as follows:

1.   Diplomatic efforts in the preliminary phase of the War of Resistance:

When the Manchurian Incident broke out on September 18, 1931, our government lodged three protests with the Japanese Government and urged it to withdraw its forces from Manchuria. Meanwhile, the Chinese Government appealed to the League of Nations and the signatories to the Pact of Paris to uphold justice. Although the League of Nations repeatedly passed resolutions urging Japan to withdraw her forces and the United States time and again sent notes to Japan by referring to the Nine Power Treaty and reminding Japan of her obligations to international treaties, Japan, on the one hand, stated that her forces had been gradually withdrawn, and on the other hand stated informally that international treaties were no longer applicable and that she refused the arbitration and judgement of the League of Nations. Japan poured all her efforts into the realization of her pre-determined plans. After her occupation of Manchuria, Japan created the Shanghai Incident on January 28, 1932. Meanwhile, she manipulated the deposed Ching Emperor Henry Pu Yi into organizing a puppet government. On March 9, 1932, the puppet government of Manchukuo was formally established. Through the hands of the puppet regime, Japan seized all the revenues, telephone and telegraph rights and roads in Manchuria. Thus, the aftermath of the Manchurian Incident became more complicated than ever. As to the Shanghai Incident, efforts of Britain, the United States and France led to the signing of ceasefire in Shanghai on May 5, 1932 and the Japanese withdrawal agreement.

To find ways to end the Manchurian Incident, the League of Nations sent an investigation team to Manchuria in the spring of 1932 headed by Viscount Lytton of Britain with members representing Britain, the United States, Germany, France and Italy. The team arrived in Tokyo on February 29 and was joined by Japanese delegates. It called on the Japanese emperor and held discussions with Prime Minister Takeshi Inukai and the ministers of foreign affairs, army and navy. On March 14, when the team arrived in Shanghai, it was joined by Chinese delegates. Upon arrival in Nanking on March 20, it was entertained at dinner by Generalissimo Chiang who sincerely explained that China would support

international laws and pacts and world humanitarianism and justice and that
she would fight to the end.

From April to June, 1932, the investigation team spent approximately six weeks
in Manchuria making an on-the-spot inspection and invited many specialists
to assist it in its work.   On July 20, it drafted a report which was signed on
September 4.   The report was later translated by the Chinese Ministry of Foreign
Affairs and was named "Report of the League of Nations Investigation Team."
The report was divided into ten chapters and contained 180,000 words.   The
main points of the various chapters are as follows:

"(1)   A description of the present situation in China regarding that excellent
progress had been achieved vastly surpassing the situation at the time of the
Washington Conference.

"(2)   The report recognized the relationship between Manchuria and China
not only as one of sovereignty but also that Manchuria belonged to China as her
territory.

"(3)   Determined that Japan's military actions on the night of September
18, 1931 could not be regarded as proper.

"(4)   The creation of Manchukuo was the result of the activities of the Japanese forces and the Japanese civilian and military officials.   'Therefore, the present Manchurian regime cannot be regarded as one which appeared as a result
of purely self-acting independence movement.'

"(5)   With regard to the Japanese actions in Manchuria since September
18, 'although there was no official declaration of war, without doubt vast areas
in China have been captured by Japan.   It is a fact that the result of such actions
has separated these areas from other parts of China.'

"(6)   The continuation of Manchukuo violated the basic principles of international obligations and was an obstacle to peace in the Far East.   It not
only ran contrary to China's interest but also was complete disregard of the wish'
of the Manchurian people.   Furthermore, it was against the interests of the Japanese people."

Based on the above six points, the investigation team brought out ten principles and conditions for solution.   It made recommendations to the League
Council; however, it accommodated itself to realities.   As a result, there were
contradictions.   When the investigation team visited Manchuria, Dr. Wellington
V. K. Koo who was a member of the team made public many exchanges of notes
giving a detailed account of negotiations pertaining to land, emigration, trade and
investment.   Later, it was compiled into a book known as "Exchanges of Notes
by the Chinese Delegation to the League of Nations Joint Investigation Committee"
and became an important document.

The attitude of the Japanese Government had been militant.   Foreign Minister Yasunari Uchida even said, "Even though our country were turned into
scorched earth, Japan's lifeline, Manchuria, must be held."   The Japanese press

responded to the government and treated the investigation team coolly. Upon his return to Britain via Bombay, Viscount Lytton said, "The situation in Manchuria is extremely serious. Placing 30 million Chinese under the rule of 200,000 Japanese is a monumental task. Japan may be able to occupy Manchuria, but the world will be plagued with problems." On Feb. 24, 1933, Viscount Lytton submitted to the League of Nations his report which was passed by a vote of 42 to 1. Feeling helpless and enraged, the Japanese delegate withdrew from the League of Nations. On Feb. 27, Japan formally served notice to the Assembly that it would withdraw from the League of Nations. Then, the negotiations of the League of Nations to the Sino-Japanese disputes came to an end.

When the War of Resistance broke out on July 7, 1937, China took the dispute to the League of Nations in the hope that the major powers would realize that the Japanese invasion of China constituted a direct threat to peace and collective security of the entire world and would learn to cope with it by applying economic sanction or other measures against Japan. On July 30, China sent her first statement to the League of Nations. On Sept. 12, the Chinese Government addressed two supplementary statements invoking Articles X, XI and XVII of the Covenant and appealed to the League of Nations to take appropriate actions. The League Council turned the statements to the Far Eastern Advisory Committee for review. After review, the committee submitted the first and second reports both of which were passed and adopted by the League Assembly on Oct. 6. The conclusion of the first report stated that the military operations carried on by Japan against China were in contravention of Japan's treaty obligations under the Nine-Power Treaty of 1922 and under the Pact of Paris. The second report recommended ways to settle the Sino-Japanese dispute. Its main points are as follows:

"(1) The present situation in China involves not only the two parties to the dispute but also concerns all the other nations somewhat.

"(2) The present dispute in the Far East involves Japan's violation of her treaty obligations. Hence, it is considered that the dispute cannot be settled directly by the two nations concerned.

"(3) The first step that should be taken now appears to be the invitation of the members of the League of Nations which are concurrently signatories of the Nine-Power Pact for discussion in the nearest future.

"(4) It appeals to the Assembly to express its moral support for China and recommends that members of the League should refrain from taking any action which might have the effect of weakening China's resistance and thus of increasing her difficulties in the present conflict and should also consider how far they can individually extend aid to China."

In September, 1938, when the League Council met, Japan declined the invitation. The League Council passed a resolution adopting the report of October 6 and stated that in view of Japan's refusal of the invitation extended to her, the provisions of Article XVII, paragraph 3, applicable in present conditions and the members of the League are entitled not only to act as before on the basis of the said finding, but also to adopt individually the measures provided for in Article XVI. The fact nonetheless remains that China, in her heroic struggle against the invader, has a right to the sympathy and aid of the other members of the League. The grave international tension that has developed in another part of the world cannot make them forget either the sufferings of the Chinese people, or their duty of doing nothing that might weaken China's power of resistance, or their undertaking to consider how far they can individually extend aid to China.

On January 17, 1939, when the League Council met, China renewed the following appeal:

(1) It requested the member nations to invoke the economic sanction measures stipulated in Article XVI of the Covenant as passed in the last council.

(2) It requested the member nations to seek practical and effective measures in their aid to China.

(3) It requested the League of Nations to insure the facilitation in transporting munitions to China.

(4) It requested the League of Nations to institute a committee of coordination in order that concrete measures might be worked out to step up aid to China.

Unfortunately, the League of Nations failed to produce practical measures with regard to the above appeal and was merely engaged in empty talk.

As to the Nine-Power Pact conference, Japan's refusal to attend ended the conference.

Apart from the above-mentioned official diplomacy, people of nations rose to give their moral support to China, banned the sale of Japanese goods and staged the International Anti-Aggression Campaign. The campaign yielded great influence.

The International Anti-Aggression Association was the driving force in the International Anti-Aggression Movement and the pioneer in the campaign to provide aid to China. It had 35 member nations with a chapter in every nation. Since the outbreak of the War of Resistance, it had held four well-known conferences. One was "World Conference to Save China and Peace" held in February, 1938 in London. Another was the "Anti-Bombing Conference" held in July of the same year in Paris. The former divided its activities into 8 sections, namely labor union, cooperative, consumption, propaganda, technology, congress, religion and ethical aid to China. Its central themes were to ban Japanese goods, collect funds to help the wounded soldiers and refugees in China, and appeal to the Red Cross of various nations to help China. The Anti-Bombing Conference passed the following resolutions:

"(1) With regard to all the resolutions passed by the Nine-Power Pact, the League of Nations Covenant, Pact of Paris and League Assembly on aid to China, this conference is determined to mobilize world opinion to support all the legitimate requests of China to the League Assembly.

"(2)   This Conference is opposed to all arrangements which impair China's independence and territorial integrity.

"(3)   This Conference requests that direct loans to the Chinese Government in order to assist it and that the aid to China campaign be intensified to demonstrate concretely our concern over and deep sympathy with China.

"(4)   This Conference reaffirms the resolutions passed at the rally which it had called in February, 1938.

"(5)   It reiterates the former proposal which is in progress, i.e. it requests all the peace-loving nations not to supply Japan with military items."

Although many of the above-mentioned were not implemented, the righteousness of mankind remained.   Furthermore, the world came to better appreciate China's War of Resistance and expressed sincere sympathy.   Hence, the aid to China campaigns in various nations mushroomed.   These diplomatic achievements all contributed to the prosecution of the War of Resistance against Japan.

2.   Seeking Allied assistance to check the enemy:

In addition to maintaining national survival, our War of Resistance was fought to uphold international treaties and faith.   Although diplomatic progress was affected by the international situation, the nation depended on the application of foreign policy.   Based on the "Program of Armed Resistance and National Reconstruction" and pertinent diplomatic articles, China proceeded to promote collective and individual international actions in order to realize her aim of enlisting international aid to check the enemy.   All these were basic principles of strategy in the diplomatic warfare.   The so-called collective international actions united the other nations with China for common actions such as the League of Nations and the Nine-Power Pact Conference as stated earlier.   The so-called individual international actions were actions taken separately by the individual nations.   Our diplomatic relations with Britain, the United States, Soviet Russia and France are separately described as follows:

a.   Foreign relations with Britain: When the War of Resistance broke out, British Prime Minister Neville Chamberlain adopted an appeasement policy toward Japan in order to maintain British interest in the Far East.   Chamberlain's realism led to the fruitless results of the League of Nations and the Nine-Power Pact.   However, the Chinese Government, conscious of the spirit of the traditional Sino-British frendship, continued diplomatic negotiations with Britain in the correct manner.   Continuing changes in international relations eventually turned Britain's assistance to China from passive to active. Similarly, Britain's attitude toward Japan turned from perfunctory to firm.   By the time the war in the Pacific broke out on December 7, 1941, all peace-loving nations in the world rose in unison to strike a heavy blow against aggression.   Thus, China and Britain marched forward hand in hand as allies.   A few major events illustrating the transformation in Sino-British foreign relations are stated as follows:

On May 3, 1938, Britain and Japan reached an understanding in Tokyo on the custom revenues in China and payment of foreign debts and interests. The main point of this understanding stated that all the custom revenues in the areas under control of the Japanese forces should be deposited in the Yokohama Shokin Bank. Such an arbitrary agreement in disposing China's custom revenues not only hindered China's custom administration, but also impaired her sovereignty. Our Ministry of Foreign Affairs immediately sent a note to Britain stating that China would not be subjected to the binding of the agreement and would reserve all the rights for customs and freedom of action.

In June, 1937, when the Japanese failed to extradite the four suspects in the Cheng Hsi-keng's case, they sealed off the British Concession in Tientsin and used it as an excuse to increase their demands on Britain. At first, the British Government indicated its desire to settle the case on the spot, but later gave in to Japan. Thus, a "preliminary agreement" was reached on July 25. Our Ministry of Foreign Affairs issued a stern statement hoping that Britain would resort to actions to indicate her determination not to change the established policy with regard to the situation created by the Japanese aggression in China. In August, Britain decided to turn over the four suspects in the Cheng case to the puppet regime in Tientsin. Such a move by Britain violated international law and entailed the suspicion that Britain might recognize the puppet regime. Our Ministry of Foreign Affairs and Chinese Embassy in Britain separately lodged strong protests with the British Embassy in China and the British Foreign Office.

In mid-June, 1940, as the war in Europe took a turn for the worse, France surrendered after her defeat. Britain's position became increasingly difficult. Taking advantage of this opportunity, Japan applied pressure on Britain. Eventually, Japan and Britain reached an agreement on the blockade of the Yunnan-Burma Road. On July 16, China's Ministry of Foreign Affairs issued a statement pointing out that the British acceptance of the unreasonable Japanese demand was not only illegal but also greatly facilitated the aggressor. In the meantime, Generalissimo Chiang issued a statement saying that China's efforts in the War of Resistance could not be nullified by the extortion of any third nation.

The above-mentioned was unfavorable to China. However, the following facts proved that because of our continued efforts, the British Government came to have an accurate understanding.

On November 3 and 22, 1938, the Japanese prime minister issued two absurd statements. On January 17, 1939, the British Government, in a note to the Japanese Government sternly repudiated these statements and formally stated that "it is not prepared to accept or recognize the activities of the nature indicated which are brought about by force. It intends to adhere to the principles of the Nine-Power Treaty."

By the end of March, 1940, the puppet organization headed by Wang Ching-wei was created. Britain indicated that there was no change in her attitude toward the legitimate government of China. By the time Japan signed a treaty with Wang's puppet regime, Britain again expressed her recognition of the National Government in Chungking as China's legitimate government.

On October 8, 1940, Prime Minister Churchill announced in the Lower House that "Beginning October 17, the Yunnan-Burma Road will be reopened." Such an attitude provided great moral and material assistance to China. The main reasons which prompted Britain to take such an action were that after the blockade of the Yunnan-Burma Road, Japan arrested British nationals in many places in China, invaded Vietnam, and signed military agreement with Germany and Italy causing the British pacification policy to achieve no satisfactory results. Additionally, Britain's position in the war in Europe was more stable than before.

On August 26, 1941, British Prime Minister Winston Churchill and U.S. President Franklin D. Roosevelt issued a joint declaration in which they mentioned eight principles. In his address, Churchill stated that the United States was beginning important negotiations with Japan with regard to the settlement of the Far Eastern problems. Should these negotiations fail, Britain would undoubtedly place herself on the side of the United States.

The three British credit loans totalling £23 million and the stabilization fund, assistance to Burma to build the Burma Railroad, the exchanges of ambassadors between China and Canada and between China and Australia and the equal treaty between China and Britain are ample indications that Sino-British foreign relations became better coordinated and the Sino-British friendship closer.

b. Foreign relations with the United States: Sino-U.S. relations have always been most cordial. When the Manchurian Incident broke out, the United States called for justice. Secretary Stimson's non-recognition policy was adopted by the League Assembly and became one of the obligations of many nations toward China. By the time all-out war against Japan began in 1937, U.S. Secretary of State Cordell Hull delivered an address on July 14 advocating international justice and international peace, avoidance of the use of force as an instrument in promoting national policy, adherence to peaceful means in settling disputes between nations, honoring the dignity of treaties, disarmament and abolition of trade barriers as the basis of establishing excellent understanding between nations. On October 5, U.S. President Roosevelt delivered his famous address in Chicago on quarantining and isolating the aggressors. In February, 1938, Japanese Prime Minister Konoye issued his ridiculous statement of the so-called "Establishing East Asia New Order." On the 31st of the same month, the United States sent a memorandum to Japan refusing to admit that she had undermined the Nine-Power Pact and opposing the East Asia New Order. Her wording was

strong. In July, 1939, when Britain and Japan reached the so-called preliminary agreement in Tokyo, the United States announced the abolition of U.S.-
Japanese Trade Pact. In June, 1940, the U.S. Senate and House of Representatives passed the National Defense Act authorizing the president to exercise import
and export control. China made every effort to urge its implementation. On
July 2, the U.S. President announced that 46 items were subject to export control.
Subsequently, on July 25 and 31, September 26 and December 1, announcements
were made on materials subject to export control. Of these items most were
military. All these reflected the attitude of the U.S. Government on aggressive
actions and world peace. They struck a blow on Japan and provided us with
moral support.

As to economic assistance, the United States had furnished China with
financial support long before the Pearl Harbor Incident. On July 14, 1937,
the United States and China signed the Currency Stabilization Agreement. On
April 1, 1941, a second agreement was signed and the Stabilization Board was
organized with the purpose of assisting China to stabilize the rise of commodity
prices and to maintain the normal exchange rates between U.S. dollars and fapi
(legal tender). Furthermore, through the Import and Export Bank, four credit
loans in the amount of US$25 million was made after the Battle of Wuhan in
December, 1938. The second US$20 million credit loan was made in March,
1940 after the establishment of Wang Ching-wei's puppet regime. The third credit
loan of US$25 million was made in September, 1940 after the signing of the
Japanese-German-Italian Axis alliance. The fourth credit loan of US$50 mil-
lion loan was made in December, 1940 after Japan had signed a treaty with
Wang's puppet regime. By the time the war in the Pacific broke out in December, 1941, U.S. President Roosevelt, upon request of China, asked the Congress for
additional financial assistance. The request was submitted to Congress on January 31, 1942 asking for a US$500 million loan to China, and was quickly passed.
In his cable message to Generalissimo Chiang, President Roosevelt stated: "This
bill was unprecedentedly, swiftly and unanimously passed in the Senate and the
House of Representatives..." On June 2, 1942, Foreign Minister T. V. Soong
represented the Chinese Government to sign the Sino-American Mutual Agreement on Resistance against Aggression.

c. Foreign relations with U.S.S.R.: Subsequent to the all-out War of
Resistance in 1937, Soviet Russia pretended to sign the Non-Aggression Treaty
with China. The treaty stipulated that two High Contracting Parties solemnly
reaffirm they undertake to refrain from any aggression. In the event that either
of the High Contracting Parties should be subjected to aggression on the part
of one or more third Powers, the other High Contracting Party obligates itself
not to render assistance of any kind to the aggressor nation. Briefly speaking,
during the Sino-Japanese War, Soviet Russia must not render assistance to the
enemy. In fact, Soviet Russia was incapable of rendering any assistance to

the enemy.

In June, 1939, China and Soviet Russia signed the Equal Reciprocal Commercial Treaty. Materially speaking, the Pact provided China with certain amount of assistance; however, most of it was given on a barter basis.

On April 13, 1941, Soviet Russia signed a neutrality pact with Japan and jointly issued a declaration announcing the mutual recognition of the puppet Manchukuo and the puppet People's Republic of Mongolia which violated the territorial and administrative integrity of China.

Accordingly, the Chinese Ministry of Foreign Affairs issued the following statement on April 14: "It is an indisputable fact that the four Northeastern Provinces and Outer Mongolia are an integral part of the Republic of China and always remain as Chinese territory." "The Chinese Government and people cannot recognize any engagements entered into between third parties which are derogatory to China's territorial and administrative integrity, and wish to state that the Soviet-Japanese declaration just announced has no binding force whatsoever on China." Article 2 of the Soviet-Japanese Treaty stated, "In the event that either of the High Contracting Parties should be subjected to military actions on the part of one or more third powers, the other High Contracting Party obligates itself to maintain neutrality during the period of the conflict." Since then, Soviet Russia's insincere friendship toward China was fully unmasked.

d. Foreign relations with France: France's Far Eastern foreign policy. had always followed the lead of Britain. In the beginning, France expressed her sympathy with China and consistently took the same actions with Britain and the United States in denouncing the Japanese aggression and in providing material assistance to China. By the time France was defeated and surrendered in the war in Europe, she was incapable of maintaining her former position in the Far East. The Japanese, therefore, took advantage of this situation to apply pressure and to extort the helpless Vichy Government which could do nothing but to comply with the Japanese demands. Some of her major concessions included the stopping of our transportation via Vietnam in 1940, granting Japanese forces permission to attack China via Vietnam in September, 1941, permitting the Japanese to take over Chinese courts in the French Concession in Shanghai in November, 1941, the signing of the Joint Defense of Vietnam Pact with Japan in July, 1942, permitting the Japanese forces to occupy Kwangchou-wan in 1943, and the transfer of the embassy grounds in Peiping, the administrative authority of the International Settlements in Shanghai and Amoy, and the French Concessions in Tientsin, Hankow and Canton to the puppet regime in Nanking. All these were indicative of the extent of submission on the part of the Vichy Government to the enemy. Nevertheless, our Government asked nothing of France. However, each time our Government refuted the French actions which violated her treaty obligations and our country's sovereignty, and made known our position. Our Ministry of Foreign Affairs, therefore, lodged strong protest with the Vichy Government in stating that "through the Vichy Government's own illegal acts, the provisions of the treaties and agreements granting to France special rights and concessions, have become null and void and are no longer binding on China." Accordingly, the Chinese Government severed diplomatic relations with the Vichy Government. In the same year, due to military necessity, the Chinese authorities took over the Chinese section of the Yunnan-Indo-China Railway.

In the fall of 1943, as China fought side by side with the Allies and continued the traditional friendship with the French people, China after consultation with the United States, Britain and Soviet Russia, issued a declaration on August 27 announcing official recognition of the French Committee of National Liberation in North Africa. In the fall of 1944, France was liberated and the new government was established by September 11. On October 25, China, the United States, Britain and Russia extended recognition. Thus, a new page began in the annals of Sino-French foreign relations.

3. Diplomatic accomplishments after combined operations with Allies:

Subsequent to the outbreak of war in the Pacific and China's simultaneous declaration of war on Japan, Germany and Italy, the Inter-Allied Military Council was created in Chungking on December 23, 1941. The United States was represented at the council by Lt. Gen. George H. Brett and Britain by General Sir Archibad Wavell, Commander-in-Chief, India. The council coordinated on military cooperation of the nations concerned against aggression. It was an achievement unprecedented in the annals of China's diplomacy. In parting, Generalissimo Chiang said to the British delegate: "Between Britain and China, neither must fail. If China should fail, then India of the British Commonwealth will be at stake." To the American delegate, he said: "The war in the Far East depended on the coordinated efforts of China's army and the British and American air forces. It is hoped that the United States will have Sino-U.S. combined operation plans, particularly concrete plans on the employment and availability of U.S. air forces in the Far East and in China." Meanwhile, the materials under the U.S. Lend Lease Act, having arrived in Rangoon, were detained by the British Government. The Chinese Government was not informed in advance. The lack of faith and the insult on China were intolerable. On December 29, Generalissimo Chiang became concurrently the acting minister of foreign affairs (Foreign Minister T. V. Soong was then in the United States on official business).

The United States, Britain, China and U.S.S.R. and 22 other Allied nations signed a joint declaration in Washington on January 1, 1942 pledging to use their full resources against the Axis and not to make separate armistice or peace with the enemy. As this joint declaration centered around China, the United States, Britain and U.S.S.R., China became one of the world's four major powers. On January 3, 1942, the White House announced that Generalissimo Chiang Kai-shek has accepted the supreme command of all land and air forces of the 26 nations which are now or may, in the future, be operating in the Chinese Theater including such portions of Indo-China and Thailand. A strategic executive agency of the Allies in East Asia was formally established. British and American opinions spoke highly of Generalissimo Chiang regarding him as a most outstanding leader in the history of China—determined, courageous and magnanimous.

Since China participated in combined operations with the Allies, there had been many diplomatic activities. Some of the highlights are enumerated as follows:

(1) Generalissimo Chiang's visit to India: Since the war in the Pacific broke out, in January 1942, Generalissimo Chiang asked President Roosevelt to convey to Prime Minister Churchill his hope that British would grant autonomy to India and that India would join the anti-aggression front so as to contribute her manpower and resources to the war effort. The British Government responded favorably by inviting Generalissimo and Madame Chiang to visit India. It hoped that Generalissimo Chiang would issue a statement before his departure from India urging the Indian people to achieve full cooperation.

On February 4, 1942, Generalissimo and Madame Chiang, accompanied by a group including Wang Chung-hui and Chang Tao-fan, took off from Chungking. They reached Calcutta on February 5 and the Indian capital of New Delhi on February 9. In issuing the official communique, the Indian Government stated: "The purpose of Generalissimo Chiang's visit is to confer with the Indian Government, particularly the British commander in India on problems which concern China and Britain, and to avail himself of this opportunity to meet the leaders of the various circles." While sharing their welcome with the Indian people, British political leaders considered that "the gravity of the war situation in the Far East and Generalissimo Chiang's visit to India which so many people watch intently form a contrast unprecedented in history. They shed a speck of light in gloom-ridden London."

At 3:30 P.M., February 9, Generalissimo Chiang called on British Viceroy in India Marquess of Linlithgow. On the 10th, Marquess and Marchioness of Linlithgow returned the call. In the afternoon, Generalissimo Chiang and Marquess of Linlithgow discussed political problems. Generalissimo Chiang advised the British that they should take the initiative to declare India as an autonomous state and that the Indian should abandon, for the time being, the demand for complete independence. Later, Generalissimo Chiang received Jawaharlal Nehru, former chairman of the National Congress, with whom he talked for an hour.

In the morning of February 11, Generalissimo Chiang went to the square in front of the Viceroy's Office where he inspected the troops. In the afternoon, he met with the Indian maharajahs, Nehru, and Abdul Kalam Azad, incumbent chairman of the National Congress. On the 12th, Nehru called on Generalissimo Chiang for the third time and later delivered a public address in which he said: "On behalf of the nation's people, I extend a warm welcome to Generalissimo Chiang of China. India is determined not to accept any rule, be it Japanese or

German. India can only accept the rule of the Indian masses...."

At midnight, February 14, upon receipt of a cable and a letter from Mohandas Karamchand Gandhi, Generalissimo Chiang was so distressed that he could not sleep. He felt more than ever the pain of the loss of freedom of a person without a country. In the morning of February 15, he sent for British Ambassador of China Sir Archibald Clark Kerr and conveyed to him the need for him (Generalissimo Chiang) to meet with Gandhi. Subsequently, Calcutta was chosen as the meeting place.

On February 18, Gandhi arrived in Calcutta. Generalissimo and Madame Chiang called on him but were disappointed in his attitude.

On February 20, Generalissimo Chiang conferred with Nehru for three hours and told him the need for the two great peoples of China and India to struggle together. However, Nehru did not pay too much regard to foreign affairs. Nehru made a statement in which he said: "Generalissimo Chiang's visit to India has a historical significance. This visit marks the beginning of a new era in Indian-Chinese relations. China's War of Resistance is a part of the great war in the entire world to seek freedom. Portions of the world or the entire world have always achieved victory in the war to seek freedom; other portions will also achieve victory in the future."

On February 21, upon conclusion of his visit in India, Generalissimo Chiang issued a statement to the Indian people hoping that the two great nations of China and India would strive for the freedom of mankind and sincerely expecting that Britain would soon delegate political power to India. This statement is an important document in Indian-Chinese relations. The full text of Generalissimo Chiang's message to the Indian people is as follows:

"During my two weeks' stay in India I had the opportunity of discussing very frankly with the highest civil and military authorities as well as with my Indian friends questions concerning joint plans against aggression and the objective of our common efforts. I was happy to find that there was full sympathy and general understanding between us. My mission is now drawing to a close. On the eve of my departure I wish to bid farewell to all my friends in India and to thank you for the many kindnesses showered upon Madame Chiang and myself. The briefness of my stay has not permitted me to tell the Indian people all that I wished to say. I avail myself of this opportunity to address to them this farewell message. It is an expression of my high and warm regard and of long cherished hopes for India. It comes from the depth of my heart.

"Since my arrival in this country I found to my great satisfaction that there exists among the people of India a unanimous determination to oppose aggression.

"China and India comprise one half of the world's population. Their common frontier extends three thousand kilometers. In the two thousand years' history of their intercourse, which has been of a purely cultural and commercial character, there has never been any armed conflict. Indeed nowhere else can one find so long a period of uninterrupted peace between two neighboring countries. This is irrefutable proof that our two peoples are peace-loving by nature. Today they have not only identical interests but also the same destiny. For this reason they are duty bound to side with anti-aggression countries and to fight shoulder to shoulder in order to secure real peace for the whole world.

"Moreover our two peoples have an outstanding virtue in common, namely the noble spirit of self-sacrifice for the sake of justice and righteousness. It is this traditional spirit which should move them towards self-negation for the salvation of mankind. It is also this spirit which prompted China to be the first to take up arms against aggression in the present war to ally herself unhesitatingly with other anti-aggression countries, not merely for the purpose of securing her own freedom, but also for the purpose of securing justice and freedom for all.

"I venture to suggest to my brethren people of India at this most critical moment in the history of civilization that our two peoples should exert themselves to the utmost in the cause of freedom for all mankind, for only in a free world could the Chinese and Indian peoples obtain their freedom. Furthermore, should freedom be denied to either China or India, there could be no real international peace.

"The present international situation divides the world into two camps, the aggression camp and the anti-aggression camp. All those who opposed aggression by striving for the freedom of their country and of other countries should join the anti-aggression camp. There is no middle course and there is no time to wait for developments. Now is the crucial moment for the whole future of mankind. The issue before us does not concern the dispute of any one man or country, nor does it concern any specific questions now pending between one people and another. Any people therefore which joins the anti-aggression front may be said to be cooperating, not with any particular country, but with the entire front. This leads us to believe that the Pacific War is the turning point in the history of nationalism. The method, however, by which the peoples of the world could achieve their freedom might be different from what it used to be. The anti-aggression nations now expect that in this new era the people of India will voluntarily bear their full share of responsibility in the present struggle for the survival of a free world, in which India must play her part. The vast majority of world opinion is in full sympathy with India's aspirations for freedom. This sympathy is so valuable and so difficult to obtain that it cannot be appraised in terms of money or material and should therefore by all means be retained.

"The present struggle is one between freedom and slavery, between light and darkness, between good and evil, between resistance and aggression. Should the anti-aggression front lose the war, world civilization would suffer a setback for at least one hundred years and there would be no end of human suffering.

"So far as Asia is concerned, the cruelties committed by the Japanese militarists are beyond description. The suffering and oppression, which have been the fate of Formosans and Koreans since their subjugation by Japan, should serve as a warning. As regards barbarities committed by the Japanese army since our war of resistance, the fall of Nanking in December 1937 is a case in point. Over 200,000 civilians were massacred within one week. For the last five years the civilian population of Free China has been subjected almost daily to bombings from the air and bombardments by heavy artillery. In every place invaded by Japanese troops, men, women and children were either assaulted or killed. The young men and the educated people received their special attention with the result that men of intelligence and ideas have been tortured. Nor is this all. Institutions of culture, objects of historical interest and value and even articles necessary for livelihood, such as cooking utensils, ploughs, tools, and domestic animals, have been either forcibly taken away or destroyed. In places under Japanese military occupation, rape, rapine, incendiarism, murder are frequent occurrences. Moreover they have with official connivance everywhere opened opium dens, gambling houses and houses of ill-fame in order to sap the vitality of the people and destroy their spirit. Such is the disgraceful conduct of the Japanese, the like of which is not found in countries invaded by other aggressor nations. What I have just said is but an inadequate description of the true state of affairs as reported by Chinese and foreign eyewitnesses.

"In these horrible times of savagery and brute force, the people of China and their brethren people of India should for the sake of civilization and human freedom give their united support to the principles embodied in the Atlantic Charter and in the joint declaration of twenty-six nations, and ally themselves with the anti-aggression front. I hope they will whole-heartedly join the allies, namely China, Great Britain, America and the Soviet Union, and participate in the struggle for the survival of a free world until complate victory is achieved and the duties incident upon them in these troubled times have been fully discharged.

"Lastly, I sincerely hope and I confidently believe that our ally Great Britain, without waiting for any demands on the part of the people of India, will as speedily as possible give them real political power so that they may be in a position further to develop their spiritual and material strength and thus realize that their participation in the war is not merely aid to the anti-aggression nations for securing victory but also the turning point in their struggle for India's freedom. From the objective point of view, I am of the opinion this would be the wisest policy which will redound to the credit of the British Empire."

When the message was made public, Indian newspapers expressed welcome and respect. Similarly, various Indian political parties expressed unprecedented warm welcome. They considered that Generalissimo Chiang had the privilege and obligation to advance his erudite views in settling the Indian political issues. On February 26, Foreign Minister T.V. Soong cabled from Washington transmitting President Roosevelt's subscription to Generalissimo Chiang's observations in India. Unfortunately, the British authorities were reluctant in making decisions at an early date.

(2) Sino-U.S. and Sino-British exchanges of visits: Prior to the outbreak of the war in the Pacific when China was fighting alone against Japan, the world lacked an understanding of the aggressor's actions. In the winter of 1942, Madame Chiang visited the United States. American political leaders attached great importance to her visit believing that her integrity would strengthen Sino-American cooperation and the war efforts of the Allies. On February 17, 1943 Madame Chiang visited the White House in Washington, D. C., where she was cordially entertained by President Roosevelt. Upon invitation of the U.S. Congress, she visited the U.S. Senate on February 18, followed by a visit to the U.S. House of Representatives. The entire nation was waiting to hear her address in the U.S. Congress which was broadcast by four major networks. Such an arrangement had been made in the past only when something of great significance took place.

In her address in the U.S. Senate, she advanced two major points which are stated as follows: (a) Despite the differences in languages, the Chinese people and the American people shared the same ideal and fought for the same objective. (b) Our ideal could not be realized by empty talk but by practical actions. Later in her address in the U.S. House of Representatives, she began by saying "In my address in your Congress, I speak, in fact, to the American people. On behalf of the American people, the 77th Congress declared war on the aggressors and fulfilled the obligations and responsibilities entrusted by the people. Your immediate tasks are to assist in winning victory and to create and maintain a permanent peace so that all the sacrifices and pains suffered in the hands of the aggressors may be meaningful." Next she described the struggles of the American soldiers in various parts of the world. Later she said, "Defeating Japan is not secondary in importance. Indeed, the Japanese are a stubborn people. The natural resources in the Japanese-occupied areas at present far exceed those in the hands of Germany. The longer it is, the greater will be the strength of Japanese. As a result many more Chinese and American lives will be sacrificed. It is necessary to destroy thoroughly the armed power of the Japanese in order to remove the threat to civilization."

Madame Chiang was the first Chinese who ever addressed the U.S. Congress. It was also unprecedented that the U.S. Congress invited a foreign visitor to the United States who was there in a private capacity. American public opinion regarded Madame Chiang's visit in the United States representing a people who were liked and respected by the United States. Such respect was based on the Chinese people's heroic resistance against Japan during the past five years.

Madame Chiang's 7-month visit in the United States covered New York, Wellesley University, Chicago, San Francisco and Los Angeles. Finally upon invitation of the Canadian Government, she visited Canada's capital of Ottawa contributing immensely to China's prestige and diplomatic situation. One of her major accomplishments in the United States was the U.S. abolition of the Chinese Exclusion Act (an act which restricted Chinese immigration into the United States).

In order to promote Sino-U.S. friendship, President Roosevelt invited Republican leader Wendell Wilkie and Vice President Henry A. Wallace to visit China. Additionally, he sent Patrick Hurley and Donald Nelson to China to discuss important political matters. The visits of these important people were most significant and indicative of the firm friendship of the United States toward China. The visits of Wilkie and Wallace are briefly stated as follows:

On October 2, 1942, U.S. Presidential Representative Wendell Wilkie arrived in Chungking and was warmly welcomed by tens of thousands of people. On the 4th, Generalissimo Chiang conferred with Mr. Wilkie. Their conversation centered on the following three main points: (a) Whether or not the former U.S. isolation policy and its traditional concept could be thoroughly changed. (b) The misunderstandings and the attitudes of the U.S. civilian and military officials in China would lead to unfortunate consequences in the relations between the two nations. (c) If there were no special cooperation or alliance between China and the United States, the Pacific Ocean would lose its safeguard for permanent peace. This was the joint responsibility of the Chinese and American statesmen.

On the 6th, they continued their talk on the situation in the Pacific saying that the four provinces in the Northeast (including Port Arthur and Dairen) and Taiwan must be returned to China. However, the naval port of Port Arthur could be jointly used by China and the United States with the former shouldering the responsibility in the actual defense. If this was the case, the Sino-U.S. joint defense concept might have been realized.

On May 21, 1943, President Roosevelt announced the dispatch of Vice President Henry A. Wallace as his representative to visit China and stated that East Asia would play a key role in future world history. On June 21, Vice President Wallace arrived in Chungking and was entertained at dinner by Generalissimo Chiang. Between June 21-24, Generalissimo Chiang and Vice President Wallace held five talks for more than ten hours. Highlights of their talks are as follows:

a. Soviet Russia would like the United States to help settle the disputes and improve the relations between China and Soviet Russia; however, she did not wish to see the United States as the arbitrator.

b. The United States Government indicated to Soviet Russia that Sino-U.S. friendship was the cornerstone of her Far Eastern policy. The United States Government would support firmly the only government led by Generalissimo Chiang.

c.   Soviet Russia stated the following to the American ambassador to Russia:

(a)   Dissatisfaction with the National Government of China.

(b)   Telling Chinese Communists that non-theoretical positions were not real Communists and had nothing to do with Soviet Russia.

(c)   Russia hoped that China would be united internally for the War of Resistance meaning that our government should integrate Communist strength for the war effort.

d.   Wallace advised our government to solve speedily the Chinese Communist problem.

e.   Wallace relayed President Roosevelt's views as follows:

(a)   The United States would not be prejudiced in favor of the Chinese Communist Party.

(b)   If China permitted him to arbitrate, he would make an attempt and would be impartial favoring neither side.

f.   Generalissimo Chiang's general replies are as follows:

(a)   The thinking of Chinese people was such that they regarded the Chinese Communist Party as internationalized fifth columnists but not truly Chinese people and soldiers.

(b)   The Chinese Communists were no trustworthy and would deceive people to realize their aims. Generalissimo Chiang made a detailed analysis of the advantages and disadvantages in President Roosevelt's arbitration.

(c)   Our government would accommodate itself to set a policy aiming to reach political settlement with Chinese Communists.

(d)   China hoped that the United States would not be intoxicated by the Chinese Communist propaganda which took advantage of U.S. public opinion and government power to press the Chinese Government into accommodating or submitting to the intrigues of the Chinese Communists.

(e)   Our government welcomed U.S. mediation in improving Sino-Soviet relations. It also hoped that a Sino-Soviet or a Soviet-U.S. conference could be arranged.

In October, 1942, Britain organized the British Parliamentary Mission to visit China. The mission arrived in Chungking on November 10 to promote Sino-British friendship and to increase mutual understanding. Its contributions were many and outstanding. In November, 1943, upon formal invitation of Britain, the Chinese Government sent a goodwill mission, headed by Wang Shih-chieh, to reciprocate their visit. Among its members was Wang Yun-wu. When the Chinese Goodwill Mission arrived in London on December 3, it was warmly welcomed. The visit of the Chinese Goodwill Mission strengthened the contact between China and Britain in combined operations.

(3)   Signing of new equal treaties: When the eastern and western theaters were combined, the greatest Chinese diplomatic achievements were the aboli-

tion of unequal treaties and the signing of new equal treaties.   On July 16, 1937, the United States Government issued a statement indicating its regard for world order by law, international equal treatment, international trade freedom and principle of large-scale cultural exchange.   On August 23, U.S. Secretary of State Cordell Hull again issued a statement describing U.S. Far Eastern foreign policy. Apart from abiding by the principles in the usual foreign policy, it included the spirit of the Nine-Power Pact and the Pact of Paris. On May 31, 1941, Secretary Hull announced that as soon as peace was restored in China, the United States Government wished to confer with the Chinese Government on the abolition of U.S. extraterritorial rights in China.   On July 4, British Ambassador to China Sir Archibald Clark Kerr sent a note to the Ministry of Foreign Affairs indicating the British desire to confer on the abolition of consular jurisdiction in China, the return of the International Settlement and the revision of unequal treaties when war came to an end in the Far East. Through our continued efforts, the British and U.S. Governments announced the abolition of the extraterritorial rights in China on October 10, 1942 and were prepared to discuss and sign new treaties with us.   Subsequently, the drafts of the new treaties were separately brought forth prescribing the abolition of consular rights and concessions and the Peking Agreement of 1901. After careful study of the British and the American drafts, the Ministry of Foreign Affairs felt that they have not included all the special rights in China. The Ministry of Foreign Affairs, therefore, worked out a counter measure by adding an exchange of note to the treaties abolishing such special rights as the commercial port system, special courts in the International Settlement, employment of foreign navigational pilots, random entrance and exit of foreign warships in Chinese territorial waters, foreign operation of inland navigation and coastal trade. After many negotiations, agreement was finally reached with Britain and the United States. The new Sino-British and Sino-U.S. treaties were separately signed in Washington, D.C., and Chungking. On May 20 of the same year, China exchanged instruments of ratification with Britain and the United States rendering the treaties effective on that day.

Subsequently, China signed the Treaty of Friendship with Cuba, the Sino-Brazilian Treaty of Amity and a new treaty with Belgium. Later the Netherlands, Norway, Venezuela, Mexico, Peru, Colombia. British Dominion of Canada, Australia and Union of South Africa successively gave up their special rights in China. The Ministry of Foreign Affairs engaged in separate negotiations with them and signed new treaties.

(4) The Four-Power General Security Declaration: On October 30, 1943, after Moscow conference, the Governments of the United States of America, the United Kingdom, the Soviet Union and China, united in their determination in accordance with the declaration by the United Nations of January 1, 1942, and subsequent declarations, to continue hostilities against the Axis powers with which they respectively were at war until such powers have laid down their arms

on the basis of unconditional surrender. Conscious of their responsibility to secure the liberation of themselves and peoples allied with them from the menace of aggression, recognizing the necessity of insuring a rapid and orderly transition from war to peace and of establishing and maintaining international peace and security with the least diversion of the world's humanity and economic resources for armaments, these governments jointly declared:

a. That their united action will be pledged for the prosecution of the war against their respective enemies and will be continued for the organization and maintenance of peace and security.

b. That those of them at war with a common enemy will act together in all matters relating to the surrender and disarmament of that enemy.

c. That they will take all measures deemed by them to be necessary to provide against any violation of the terms imposed upon the enemy.

d. That they recognize the necessity of establishing at the earliest practicable date a general international organization, based on the principle of the sovereign equality of all peace-loving nations, and open to membership by all such states, large and small, for the maintenance of international peace and security.

e. That for the purpose of maintaining international peace and security pending the reestablishing of law and order and the inauguration of a system of general security they will consult with one another and as occasion requires with other members of the United Nations for joint action on behalf of the community of nations.

f. That after the termination of hostilities they will not employ their military forces within the territories of other states accept to complement the purpose envisaged in this declaration and after joint consultation.

g. That they will confer and cooperate with one another and with other members of the United Nations to bring about a practicable general agreement with respect to the regulation of armament in the postwar period.

V.M. Molotov of U.S.S.R., Cordell Hull of the United States, Anthony Eden of Britain and Chinese Ambassador to Soviet Russia Fu Ping-chang represented the respective nations in signing the declaration.

After the declaration was made public, all peace-loving nations in the world were deeply gratified.

(5) Cairo Conference: Cairo Conference marked the first time that a Chinese leader was invited to attend an international big power conference which listened to his views which had decisive effects on the major issues in the Far East and on the problems pertaining to China. In July, 1943, U.S. President Roosevelt expressed the desire to meet with President Chiang before his conference with Stalin of Soviet Russia. Generalissimo Chiang was in favor of having the meeting in the fall followed by the announcement of a declaration. He was of the opinion that the declaration should include the following seven points:

a.   The Atlantic Charter was applicable to the peoples of other nations in the world.

b.   Unconditional victory must be achieved.

c.   Manchuria and Taiwan must be returned to China.

d.   Korean independence and the position of Indo-China Peninsula.

e.   Establishment of an effective postwar international peace organizations.

f.   Establishment of Combined Staff Headquarters in Chungking and Washington, D.C., for the prosecution of war against Japan in the Pacific.

g.   Mutual assistance in Sino-U.S. wartime finances and cooperation in postwar economic reconstruction.

In October, President Roosevelt sent three cable messages inviting Generalissimo Chiang to the conference. The wordings of the messages were most sincere. On November 12, President Roosevelt sent Patrick Hurley as his personal representative to Chungking. His purpose was for the United States to act as the third party in the mediation after listening to the policies of the Chinese and the British leaders. Generalissimo Chiang accepted his invitation. On November 18, Generalissimo and Madame Chiang, accompanied by a party headed by Wang Chung-hui, departed from Chungking. On November 21, they arrived in Cairo via India and met with Prime Minister Churchill. The following day, President Roosevelt arrived and conferred with Generalissimo Chiang. Having learned that the original agenda was prepared by the British and American staffs without taking into consideration China's position and proposal, Generalissimo Chiang brought the matter to the attention of President Roosevelt who changed the meeting to a Sino-British-U.S. conference. This was the first success scored by Generalissimo Chiang before the conference was convened.

The conference began on November 23 and ended on November 26, Generalissimo Chiang was deeply impressed by President Roosevelt's enthusiasm toward China, his vision and fortitude, and by Prime Minister Churchill's farsightedness, experiences and steadfastness. In his first broadcast to the nation after his return, President Roosevelt spoke on his impression of Generalissimo Chiang. He said: "I met in the Generalissimo a man of great vision, great courage and remarkably keen understanding of the problems of today and tomorrow."

The agreements reached at the conference were contained in the three leaders' declaration which was officially made public on Dectmber 3, 1943. The full text of the declaration is as follows:

In November, 1943, Generalissimo Chiang Kai-shek, President Roosevelt and Prime Minister Churchill, together with their respective military and diplomatic advisers, met and conferred at Cairo. The following general statement was issued:

"The several military missions have agreed upon future military operations against Japan. They covert no gain for themselves and have no thought of territorial expansion. It is their purpose that Japan shall be stripped of all the islands in the Pacific which she has seized or occupied since the beginning of the First World War in 1914, and that all the territories Japan has stolen from the Chinese, such as Manchuria, Formosa, and the Pescadores, shall be restored to the Republic of China. Japan will also be expelled from all other territories which she has taken by violence and greed. The aforesaid three great powers, mindful of the enslavement of the people of Korea, are determined that in due course Korea shall become free and independent.

"With these objects in view the three Allies, in harmony with those of the United Nations at war with Japan, will continue to persevere in the serious and prolonged operations necessary to procure the unconditional surrender of Japan."

In the Cairo Conference Declaration, most of the main points brought up by Generalissimo Chiang had been adequately settled. President Roosevelt spoke highly of Generalissimo Chiang. He solicited the latter's views on such matters as the form of government Japan should adopt. The latter replied: "It is my opinion that all the Japanese militarists must be wiped out and the political system must be purged of every vestige of aggressive elements. As to what form of government Japan should adopt, that question can be left to the awakened and repentent Japanese people to decide for themselves. In this war, we must not create permanent mistakes between peoples." The declaration which was drafted by the United States was forwarded to Generalissimo Chiang for comments before being transmitted to Churchill. Originally, the declaration included the abolition of the Japanese emperor system. As Generalissimo Chiang did not think it was necessary to bring it up, it was deleted by President Roosevelt. All these indicate President Roosevelt's high regard for Generalissimo Chiang.

4. Diplomatic activities on the eve of V-J Day

a. Initiation of the United Nations: After the war in the Pacific broke out in December, 1941, China's international prestige was elevated. This was evidenced in the initiation and organization of the United Nations. Earlier on August 14, 1941, Roosevelt and Churchill issued a joint declaration which mentioned not only Europe but also included the world. Although it mentioned only eight principles and did not include major issues in the Far East, in intangibly regarded Japan in the same light as it did Germany and greatly influenced the situation in the Far East. This indicated that Britain and the United States had abandoned the compromise policy and adopted an active policy. As the declaration is a historical document, its full text is stated as follows:

"President Roosevelt and Prime Minister Churchill, meeting on 9-12 August 1941 in a series of conferences aboard ship, at an undisclosed point off the Newfoundland coast, agreed on the statement of principles which was publicly announced on 14 August as the Atlantic Charter. The charter was intended to set forth certain principles relative to the national policies of both the United States and Great Britain, and on which the two nations based their vision of a better future for the world. Its eight points were as follows:

"First, their countries seek no aggrandizement, territorial or other;

"Second, they desire to see no territorial changes that do not accord with the freely expressed wishes of the people concerned;

"Third, they respect the right of all peoples to choose the form of government under which they will live; and they wish to see sovereign rights and self government restored to those who have been forcibly deprived of them;

"Fourth, they will endeavor, with due respect for their existing obligations, to further the enjoyment by all states, great or small, victor or vanquished, of access, on equal terms, to the trade and to the raw materials of the world which are needed for their economic prosperity;

"Fifth, they desire to bring about the fullest collaboration between all nations in the economic field with the object of securing, for all, improved labor standards, economic adjustment and social security;

"Sixth, after the final destruction of the Nazi tyranny, they hope to see established a peace which will afford to all nations the means of dwelling in safety within their own boundaries, and which will afford assurance that all men in all land may live out their lives in freedom from fear and want;

"Seventh, such a peace should enable all men to traverse the seas and oceans without hindrance;

"Eighth, they believe that all nations of the world, for realistic as well as spiritual reasons, must come to the abandonment of the use of force. Since no future peace can be maintained if land, sea or air armaments continue to be employed by nations which threaten, or may threaten, aggression outside of their frontiers. They believe, pending the establishment of a wider and permanent system of general security, that the disarmament of such nations is essential. They will likewise aid and encourage all other practicable measures which will lighten for peace-loving peoples the crushing burden of armaments."

This declaration was the world famous Atlantic Charter which was the principles of the United Nations organization. At that time, President Roosevelt suggested that each nation be considered as a unit in establishing the new international peace organization known as the United Nations. On January 1, 1942, headed by China, the United States, Britain and Soviet Russia, 26 nations which fought against the Axis issued a declaration proclaiming the establishment of the United Nations as one of their objectives. The declaration was known as the United Nations Declaration. China became one of the initiators of the United Nations.

Since then, China has played an important role in the many activities of the United Nations. These activities included the Food Conference held in May-June, 1943, the United Nations Rehabilitation and Relief Administration (UNRRA) Agreement in November of the same year, the U.N. Monetary and Financial Conference held at Bretton Woods, N.H. in July 1944. All these which were convened by the United States, were attended by China. From August 1 to

October 7, 1944, the United States invited China, Britain and Soviet Russia to meet at Dumbarton Oaks to discuss the United Nations Charter. On March 5, 1945, as initiators of the United Nations, China, the United States, Britain and Soviet Russia jointly invited those nations which indicated the desire to join the United Nations organization (totalling 46) to meet at a conference in San Francisco on April 25 of the same year. The conference ended on June 26 after 62 days. The conference passed the United Nations Charter. In the organization of the United Nations, the Security Council which was the most important was composed of five permanent members and six non-permanent members. The five permanent members had the veto power, although the veto power, after indiscriminate use by Soviet Russia was synonymous with dishonor. However, at that time the provision for the permanent members and their veto power was regarded as an international status symbol. Since China was an initiator of the United Nations as well as a permanent member with veto power, her international prestige could well be imagined.

b. Potsdam Conference: In May, 1945, after the collapse of Nazi Germany and Fascist Italy, the Allied forces in the Western European theater brought the war to an end in the midst of victories. Accordingly, the leaders of the United States, Britain and Soviet Russia met at Potsdam in the vicinity of Berlin on July 17, discussing the German issues and problems of the Axis powers and their satellites. China, the United States and Britain conferred on operations against Japan and the provisions for the unconditional surrender of Japan. On July 26, the three leaders of China, the United States and Britain issued a communique in which they pointed out the need for the complete destruction of the Japanese militarists and warned that Japan must surrender unconditionally. This communique was known as the Potsdam Declaration (see Section 1, Chapter Nine) which was divided into 13 articles; however, the articles which concerned the unconditional surrender were 7.

c. Foreign relations with Soviet Russia: After the outbreak of the war between Germany and Soviet Russia on June 22, 1941, Soviet Russia suffered a series of reverses. As she was too occupied to pay attention to the east, Sheng Shih-tsai, governor of Sinkiang Province, showed his inclination toward the Central Government in June, 1942 and reported on the treaties he had signed with Soviet Russia. The contents of these treaties were so vicious that they surpassed the Twenty-One Demands which Japan forced Yuan Shih-kai to sign. As Russian forces were compelled to withdraw, Soviet Russia severed relations with Sinkiang. In May, 1943, Soviet Russia instigated a Kazak by the name of Othman to stage a rebellion at Mt. Altai under the support of Mongolia. Under the cover of Russian planes, the Mongolian forces entered into Sinkiang. This became known as the Altai Incident. Although Othman later realized that he was manipulated and defected to the Central Government, the Altai Incident was out of hands. Soviet Russia engineered the Eli Incident by smuggling a Russian Tartar by the name of Fahati to incite the mobs in Eli. In time, Eli fell. All in all, Soviet Russia did not relax in her aggression of China. Subsequent to the defeat of Germany, her aggressive actions were stepped up.

The basic principle of China had always been one of toleration and consideration of the overall situation. On June 27, 1945, Premier and Foreign Minister T. V. Soong visited Moscow to engage in negotiations. After many talks lasting for days, he and the Russian delegates had exchanged views on all the issues concerned. On July 15, he returned to China for instructions. On August 5, Premier T. V. Soong and the newly appointed Foreign Minister Wang Shih-chieh flew to Moscow once again to re-open negotiations. On August 14, the Sino-Soviet Treaty of Friendship and Alliance was signed. On August 27, it was made public.

The treaty included six documents which are as follows:
(1)   Basic text of the Treaty of Alliance.
(2)   Agreement on the joint operation of the Chinese Changchun Railway.
(3), (4)   Agreement on the joint use of Port Arthur and Dairen.
(5)   Agreement on the relationships between the Soviet forces and the Chinese administrative authorities after the former's entrance into the Three Eastern Provinces (Manchuria).
(6)   Two communications pertaining to the exchanges of notes on the recognition of Mongolian, independence and non-interference of Sinkiang problems.

In addition, there was a record which contained Stalin's guarantee that Soviet forces would withdraw from the Three Eastern Provinces three months after V-J Day.

Diplomatic Warfare and Psychological Warfare Against the Enemy

When the Manchurian Incident broke out on September 18, 1931, our diplomatic authorities repeatedly lodged protests with the Japanese and appealed to the League of Nations for arbitration. Yet the Japanese Government pretended that the actions were taken by the Japanese forces themselves who acted on their own will but not on that of the Japanese Government. Apart from directing the Kwantung Army to prevent the incident from spreading, the Japanese Government notified the League that most of the forces had been withdrawn to the areas bordering the railroad and that the Japanese Government was determined to complete the withdrawal. Nevertheless, the Japanese forces proceeded in accordance with pre-determined plans. In less than three months, the entire Northeast was occupied by Japan.

When the Shanghai Incident took place on January 28, 1932, China continued negotiations with Japan through diplomatic channels on the one hand, and appealed to the League of Nations for effective actions on the other. In the beginning Japan thought that victory was in sight and would not accept negotiations. Later, her attitude softened as a result of repeated, overwhelming defeats. By March 4, the League of Nations resolved that "China and Japan, through the assistance of the naval and army representatives of the interested nations, execute ceasefire and consult on the withdrawal measures of the Japanese forces." Later, Britain, the United States and France made efforts to mediate. On May 5, the agreements governing the ceasefire of Shanghai and the withdrawal of Japanese forces were signed.

In the spring of 1933, Japan created the Manchukuo on the one hand and began to have designs on Jehol and the land within the Great Wall under the pretext that Jehol was a part of the puppet regime. In February, the League of Nations failed in its mediation. In March, after Japan had established the puppet Manchukuo and had withdrawn from the League of Nations, she acted more and more without restraint. She attacked toward Jehol and the Great Wall. Soon Luantung was overrun and Peiping and Tientsin were in danger. The efforts of the British minister in mediation finally led to the signing of the Tangoo Agreement on May 31. On June 7, the League of Nations passed the resolution on the non-recognition of the puppet Manchukuo. By then, although China scored a diplomatic victory, the enemy had already seen through the impotence of the League of Nations.

Since then, Japan's pressure on China became increasingly serious. To relieve the pressure and the threat, China was compelled to pretend playing around with Japan. Thus, Japan employed diplomatic strategy to protect her military gains.

On April 17, 1934, Amane issued an abused statement, the main theme of which included "the clarification of special position and special responsibilities" and "the objection of China using the influence of other nations to attempt resisting Japan with any actions." The so-called special position indicated political leadership and economic monopoly. The so-called special responsibilities meant the use of force to compel China into submitting herself to Japan's will and direction so as to maintain Japan's aim of the so-called East Asia peace and order. In order to realize her objective, Japan had to take "natural and necessary actions" with regard to China. Japan regarded that China's ability to make use of the influence of other nations, techniques or financial assistance, particularly the provision of military supplies and the dispatch of military training officers and loans was intended to undermine the East Asia New Order and was, therefore, strongly opposed by Japan.

On April 25, the Chinese Ministry of Foreign Affairs issued a stern statement which indicated that "China's sovereignty and independent integrity must not be impaired by any nation under any pretext. China's relationships with other nations and the League of Nations which were legal were based on China's own development and security and must not be interfered by any nation under any pretext." Meanwhile, the British London Times, on April 19 and 25, refuted the Japanese statement in its editorials. Conscious of the unfavorable international situation, Japan then changed her position saying that the statement was merely the opinion of a number of people in her Foreign Ministry and did not represent the views of the Ministry. Later, the Japanese Foreign Ministry stated that "the statement no longer existed." Thus, the incident came to an end.

In January, 1935, after Hirota announced the so-called peaceful foreign policy toward China, the Northern Chahar Incident, the Hopei Incident and the Northern Kalgan Incident took place one after another. On June 8, the Japanese vice-consul Einai Kuramoto in Nanking suddenly disappeared. Believing that he had been killed by men of influence in China, Japan sent many gunboats to Hsiakwan in Nanking. She shifted all her marines and police from Shanghai to Nanking in anticipation of the occupation of Hsiakwan before conducting negotiations. Several days later, Einai Kuramoto appeared in Hsiaolingwei. It was said that he had attempted suicide. For days he hid himself in the mountain. He did not succeed in killing himself. As he was too hungry, he came down from the mountain to find food. He was discovered by the local people and was taken to the Ministry of Foreign Affairs which notified the Japanese authorities to take him back. By September, Hirota brought out the so-called three principles to Chinese Ambassador to Japan Chiang Tso-pin. These principles are as follows:

(1) China must recognize Manchukuo.

(2) China must end anti-Japanese movement.

(3) China must sign an anti-Communist agreement with Japan.

Later, Japan sent Ambassador Ariyashi to China to negotiate with the Chinese Ministry of Foreign Affairs. Knowing Japan's intentions, the Ministry proposed five countermeasures which are stated as follows:

(1) Abolition of the Shanghai and Tangoo Agreements.

(2) Abolition of the puppet Eastern Hopei organization.

(3) Actions to check smuggling in North China.

(4) Prohibition of Japanese planes to fly at will in China.

(5) Non-interference of the Japanese forces with the Communist suppression activities in Suiyuan.

As Ariyashi returned voluntarily to Japan, the conferences ended without results.

Upon Ariyashi's return to Japan, he was succeeded by Kawakae as the Japanese ambassador to China. Kawakae held three meetings with the Chinese Ministry of Foreign Affairs discussing the Chengtu Incident. The meetings were fruitless, as the enemy's conditions were too severe. On October 8, he called on Generalissimo Chiang hoping to conduct direct negotiations with the latter on Sino-Japanese foreign relations. Apart from explaining China's main attitude toward Japan which was based on mutual and reciprocal principles and the safeguarding of territorial sovereignty and integrity, Generalissimo Chiang instructed Foreign Minister Chang Chun to continue discussions with Kawakae. On October 19, the fourth negotiation was held. The scope of the discussion included the following seven main points:

    (1)   Japanese demand for autonomy of North China.

    (2)   Signing of Sino-Japanese anti-Communist agreement.

    (3)   Ending of anti-Japanese movement.

    (4)   Reduction of customs duties in favor of Japan.

    (5)   Opening of flying route between Fukuoka and Shanghai.

    (6)   Suppressing the Korean Independence Party.

    (7)   China must recognize Manchukuo.

Achieving no fruitful results, the negotiations came to a stop. The talks of Japanese settlement of the China problem by force prevailed. The situation was so critical that all-out war was imminent.

In June, 1937, Prince Konove became Japan's prime minister. On July 7, the Lukouchiao (Marco Polo Bridge) Incident took place. Despite Konoye's policy of not expanding the war, he was unable to control the Ministry of War. The Japanese Army took provocative actions in North China. Similarly, the Japanese Navy opened the war in Shanghai on August 13. Finding the situation intolerable, China rose in all-out resistance and made known to the world her determination to fight to the end. Nevertheless, the Japanese imperialists were as stubborn as ever not abandoning their predetermined intrigues. Again Konoye reiterated the so-called "policy of not expanding the war." Taking advantage of the situation when our capital was besieged, Japan asked Germany to mediate in the hope of bringing the war to a quick peace and to a quick end.

In the end of December, 1937, German Ambassador to China Oskar Trautmann claimed that he had his government's instructions to act as messenger in negotiating for peace between China and Japan and gave a resume of the talks between the Japanese authorities and the German ambassador in Tokyo. Its four basic conditions for peace are as follows:

    (1)   Abandonment of the Chinese Government's policy against Japan and Manchukuo, and the need for China's joint effort with Japan against communism.

    (2)   Necessary areas should be set aside and designated as areas where no troops would be stationed, and special organizations should be established.

    (3)   Economic cooperation between China and Japan and between China and Manchukuo.

    (4)   Considerable indemnities.

In addition, there were the following two annexes:

    (1)   No ceasefire during negotiations.

    (2)   Need for China to dispatch personnel to the designated area for direct negotiations.

As these conditions were too harsh and inclusive, China refused to consider them. Embarrassed and enraged, Japan made the "not to deal with the Chinese National Government" statement on January 16, 1938. In general, the statement mentioned the following: "Even after the capture of Nanking, the Japanese Government has until now continued to be patient with a view to affording a final opportunity to the Chinese National Government for a reconsideration of their attitude. However, the Chinese Government, without appreciating the true intentions of Japan, blindly persists in their opposition against Japan, with no consideration either internally for the people in their miserable plight or externally for the peace and tranquillity of all East Asia. Accordingly, the Japanese Government will cease from henceforward to deal with that Government, and they look forward to the establishment and growth of a new Chinese regime, harmonious coordination with which can really be counted upon. With such a regime she will fully co-operate for the adjustment of Sino-Japanese relations and for the building of a rejuvenated China." At this time, Japan recalled her ambassador to China. Similarly, China recalled Ambassador Hsu Shih-ying from Japan. On January 18, China issued a declaration to the world. The complete text of the declaration is quoted as follows:

"After the occurrence of the Lukouchiao Incident in July, 1937, the Chinese Government repeatedly made known its readiness to seek an equitable settlement through any peaceful channel recognized by international law.

"Japan, however, spurning all peaceful efforts, mobilized her army, navy and air forces, launched an attack on Chinese territory and slaughtered Chinese people.

"China was then compelled to adopt defensive measures and check the outrages. Several months have elapsed since the beginning of hostilities, but not a single Chinese soldier has intruded into Japanese territory. On the other hand, many Chinese cities and towns are still under the unlawful occupation of the Japanese forces.

"Chinese lives and properties have been subjected to wanton destruction; disarmed Chinese warriors and non-combatants and even the old and feeble, women and children were murdered in cold blood. Material destruction and cultural losses caused by the Japanese are beyond description.

"That the Japanese action has constituted a flagrant violation of international law, the Kellogg Pact and the Nine Power Treaty, has been recognized by nearly all nations in the world. It is therefore, Japan, not China, who should be held responsible for the breach of international tranquillity.

"Japan still finds it convenient to announce that she respects China's territorial integrity and administrative rights and that she respects the interests of third powers. But what is meant by Japan's reiteration of her respect of China's territorial integrity and administrative rights is nothing else but the setting up by military force of various kinds of unlawful organizations on Chinese territory for the purpose of bringing about China's disintegration and seizing China's rights through these bogus organizations. What is meant by her respect of the interests of third nations simply an attempt to establish her monopolistic rights in China by means of her superior position acquired by military force.

"The object of China's present War of Resistance is to preserve her own existence and to uphold the sanctity of international treaties. China has not altered her policy of peace, but since territorial rights and administrative integrity constitute the prerequisites of an independent nation formally recognized in sacred treaties which she entered into with all nations concerned, she naturally cannot countenance their being infringed upon by any foreign country.

"No matter under what circumstances, China will exert her utmost to maintain her territorial rights and administrative integrity. Any plan for the restoration of peace, if not based on the principles of independence and equality, will never be recognized by her.

"In the same vein, any unlawful organization, which is being set up in areas under occupation of Japanese troops and which usurps political powers, will be regarded by China as null and void, both internally and externally."

On December 22 of the same year, Japanese Prime Minister Konoye issued the so-called statement on "rejuvenating China" and readjusting the relations between China and Japan. On December 26, Generalissimo Chiang readily refuted the statement calling it "a confession of the enemy's intrigue to conquer China and dominate East Asia and even the whole world and a complete exposure of the enemy's plans to destroy China and the Chinese people."

On March 30, 1940 traitor Wang Ching-wei established the puppet organization in Nanking. 77 leaders of the puppet regime were placed on the wanted list of our Government in order to let the world know where we stood. Our Ministry of Foreign Affairs sent notes to the diplomatic representatives of various nations in China so as to clarify our position. On November 30, Japan formally extended recognition to Wang's puppet regime and signed a secret agreement with it. The agreement carved China into the Northeast, Mongolia, North China and Central China for administrative purposes. Accordingly, our Ministry of Foreign Affairs issued a statement. The last paragraph of the statement is as follows:

"The National Government of the Republic of China has repeatedly declared, and desires to reiterate most emphatically, that Wang Ching-wei is the archtraitor of the Republic and that the puppet regime at Nanking is an illegal organization whose acts of whatever character are null and void in respect of all Chinese citizens and all foreign countries. The so-called treaty just signed at Nanking is totally devoid of legality and has no binding force what so ever.

"Should any foreign country choose to accord recognition to the puppet organization, the Government and people of China would consider it a most unfriendly act and would be constrained to discontinue their normal relations with such a country.

"Whatever Japan may attempt or conspire to do in China or in the Pacific, China is determined to fight on till victory is won, and she is confident of victory because to freedom and right and justice victory inevitably belongs."

On July 1, 1941, Germany and Italy recognized Wang's puppet regime so as to please Japan. The following day, China resolutely announced her severance of diplomatic relations with Germany and Italy. Subsequently, Rumania and Denmark followed the footsteps of Germany and Italy by recognizing Wang's puppet regime in Nanking and Manchukuo. Similarly, China severed diplomatic relations with these two nations.

On December 7, 1941, Japan launched a sneak attack on Pearl Harbor. The attack led to the war in the Pacific. To uphold justice and maintain civilization of mankind the National Government announced simultaneous declaration of war on Japan, Germany and Italy. The full texts are as follows:

1. Declaration of War on Japan

China formally declared war on Japan on December 9, 1941. The declaration reads:

"Japan's national policy has always aimed at the domination of Asia and the mastery of the Pacific. For more than four years China has resolutely resisted Japan's aggression, regardless of suffering and sacrifice, in order not only to maintain her national independence and freedom but also to uphold international law and justice and to promote world peace and human happiness.

"China is a peace-loving nation. In taking up arms in self-defense, China entertained the hope that Japan might yet realize the futility of her plan of conquest. Throughout the struggle all the other Powers have shown the utmost forbearance, likewise in the hope that Japan might one day repent and mend her ways in the interest of peace in the entire Pacific region.

"Unfortunately, Japan's aggressive propensities have proved to be incorrigible. After her long and fruitless attempt to conquer China, Japan, far from showing any sign of penitence, has treacherously launched an attack on China's friends, the United States of America and Great Britain, thus extending the theater of her aggressive activities and making herself the arch-enemy of justice and world peace. This latest act of aggression on the part of Japan lays bare her insatiable ambition and has created a situation which no nation that believes in international good faith and human decency can tolerate.

"The Chinese Government hereby formally declares war on Japan. The Chinese Government further declares that all treaties, conventions, agreements and contracts concerning the relations between China and Japan are and remain null and void."

2. Declaration of War on Germany and Italy

On July 2, 1941, China had severed her diplomatic relations with Germany and Italy upon German and Italian governments' recognition of the puppet regime at Nanking. On December 9, 1941, China formally declared war on Germany and Italy. The declaration reads:

"Since the conclusion of the Tripartite Pact September, 1940, Germany, Italy and Japan have unmistakably banded themselves into a bloc of aggressor States working closely together to carry out their common program of world conquest and domination. To demonstrate their solidarity, Germany and Italy successively accorded recognition to Japan's puppet regimes in Northeast China and at Nanking. As a consequence, China severed her diplomatic relations with Germany and Italy last July.

"Now, the Axis Powers have extended the theater of their aggressive activities and thrown the whole Pacific region into turmoil, making themselves the enemies of international justice and world civilization. This state of affairs can no longer be tolerated by the Chinese Government and people.

"The Chinese Government hereby declares that as from midnight, December 9, 1941, a state of war exists between China and Germany and between China and Italy. The Chinese Government further declares that all treaties, conventions, agreements and contracts concerning the relations between China and Germany and between China and Italy are and remain null and void."

Since Germany and Italy were enemy nations, the Ministry of Foreign Affairs, in conjunction with organizations concerned, drafted Regulations Governing the Disposal of Enemy Nationals, and Regulations Governing the Disposal of Enemy Properties which were promulgated on January 1, 1942. Later, Measures Governing Inspection, Registration, and Change of Address of Enemy Nationals, Regulations Governing the Refugee Detention Houses, Measures Governing the Assembly, Protection and Supervision of Enemy Missionaries, Measures Governing the Registration, Handling and Clearance of Enemy Properties and Organic Regulations of the Commission on Enemy Properties were promulgated for implementation by the Executive Yuan on January 11, 1942.

CHAPTER FOUR
Economic Warfare

Section 1. Wartime Economic System

Formulation of National Economic Reconstruction Program

Due to her vast territories and abundant resources, China was well-equipped for economic reconstruction. Unfortunately, China was weakened by a succession of wars from within and the aggression of foreign powers from without. It was not until May, 1931 when the National Convention passed the provisional constitution during the period of political tutelage and promulgated the same that the National Government decided to proceed with economic reconstruction on June 1 in accordance with the fourteen articles of Chapter Four, People's Livelihood, of the Constitution. Since the Manchurian Incident, China was determined to march toward modernization. On September 25, the National Economic Commission was established. At this time, such basic industries as steel, iron, copper, coal, petroleum and machinery manufacturing were not firmly established, China had to seek the development of people's economy in order to improve the people's living conditions and to have the nation stand on solid ground. On November 17, the Six Guide Lines on the Reconstruction of People's Livelihood was formulated as follows:

1. Economic relations in the modern world are closely interwoven. All the organizations engaged in economic production have passed the age of purely national economy and have entered into the age of world economy. The meaning of national economy both politically and economically becomes more important in the organization of world economy. As a nation which lags behind in production, China has to make use of her domestic and overseas Chinese capitals in order to develop rapidly her national economy and the reconstruction of all production industries. In particular, she has to take full advantage of foreign capital and technology. Our National Father's Plans of National Reconstruction and the guide lines in implementing the fundamentals are the unchangeable principles in China's economic policy. Of course, the most important basic prerequisite lies in unimpaired sovereignty, legal jurisdiction and economic administrative power. We survive if we have these in our hands; we perish if we do not.

2. Water conservancy has always been China's greatest problem. The present flood disaster spread all over the great rivers. The danger in the future

will be more unpredictable. Since the establishment of the nation's capital in Nanking, special agencies have been established for the control of the Yellow River and the Huai River. Unfortunately, military operations continued, and the measures taken were ineffective. It is felt that the Government should organize special agencies to engage in water conservancy construction with forestation as a supplementary driving force in water conservancy engineering.

3. Permanent reconstruction plans: Our National Father's Plans for National Reconstruction had already mapped out the details. What should be decided now are the guidelines for the next several years but not the general plans. Dr. Sun's Plans for National Reconstruction considered that the completion of a national railway net was the basis of all economic activities. Taking into consideration the present situation, we feel that our future railway policy should be as follows:

Firstly, we should realign the present railways.

Secondly, we should expedite the completion of the half-finished Canton-Hankow Railway and the Lunghai Railway.

Thirdly, immediate actions should be taken to proceed with the construction of railways from Kwangtung to Yunnan to Szechuan to Shensi in order to link up with the Lunghai Railway. The construction of these railways is most urgent. As to the other railways, they can be planned by the National Government taking into account the actual situation.

4. As China is an agricultural country, efforts should be made to undertake the construction of basic industries. However, emphasis should be placed on the development of agriculture, the promotion of cooperative enterprises and the implementation of the Kuomintang land policy. All the reconstruction guidelines on water and land communications, transportation and financial activities should aim at facilitating the development of agriculture and the livelihood of the farmers.

5. Exploitation and tilling of border land should be regarded as important guidelines in developing national economy. Plans must be made, actions taken and financial and other assistance rendered. Planning for the livelihood of the local people in the border areas is of utmost importance. In exploiting the border land, the livelihood of the local people must be taken into consideration.

6. All the national economic enterprises should be protected by law and under the principle of controlling capital in the Principle of Livelihood of the Three People's Principles. At present there is much to be desired in the taxation laws and industrial regulations. In addition, the maintenance of security is most pressing.

In March, 1932, Generalissimo Chiang who was concurrently Chief of the General Staff invited specialists to establish the National Defense Planning Board with emphasis on the relations between national defense economy and economy. This was the predecessor of the Commission of Resources.

On January 23, 1934. "Basic Guide Lines on the Establishment of Future

Material Reconstruction" was formulated. Its main purpose was to match the National Defense Center with the Economic Center. The original text is as follows:

1. Establishment of a center for national economy in the interior provinces which are rich in natural resources and are not subjected to the influence of foreign commercial and financial firms. The following steps should be taken.

a. Unification under the Central Government.

b. Major national and private industries should avoid concentrating on seaports in the future.

c. Various cooperatives should plan on agricultural finances. The Government should help market their agricultural products.

d. Revision of taxation system to protect the growth of industries and business.

e. Opening of roads and sea routes. In establishing communication hubs, efforts should be made to complete westward trunk lines first, so that apart from seaports, we have exits and entrances which are not subject to enemy blockade.

2. Establishment of a national defense military center which is in the vicinity of economic center but is not threatened by foreign military forces.

3. All constructions of major plants, railways and wire lines in the nation should be based on National Defense Military Plans and National Economic Plans. Their sites and facilities will be reviewed by the Government.

Since the promotion of national economic reconstruction, development was noticed in many fields. In order to expedite and consolidate the basic conditions in our national defense economy and to meet the wartime requirements, Generalissimo Chiang felt it necessary to increase encouragement and to expand the influences. On October 10, 1935, he initiated the "National Economic Reconstruction Movement." In his talk, he solemnly stated: "This National Economic Reconstruction Movement is designed to stimulate agriculture, improve agricultural products, protect mines, assist industries and businesses, regulate the relations between management and labor, open roads, develop communications, adjust finances, and insure flow of capital to promote industrialization." On December 4, "Implementing Outline Program for the Establishment of National Economic Reconstruction" was formulated. The principles of the implementing program included 28 articles which are stated as follows:

1. The essentials in production are "manpower," "land power," "material power" and "organizational power." To seek continuation of the production enterprises in being and the development of future production actions, manpower, land power, material power and organizational power must be oriented and employed enabling them to become systematic, organized and meaningful activities. Of course, reasonable orientation of production essentials cannot be achieved readily, neither can the planned development of national economy be carried out overnight. Therefore, in making the approach, the only way is to realign and integrate the

existing economic organizations and production units so that they become an organic organized entity. Thus, meaningful and planned control and promotion can be achieved.

2. Various economic activities are complex and interwoven making it extremely difficult to draw sharp lines of distinction. Hence, in national economic reconstruction, if these activities are arbitrarily and partially divided, no satisfactory results will be achieved. For instance, the management of commodities should run parallel to price control and foreign trade control before the anticipated results can be achieved.

3. The objective of the national economic reconstruction should be the entire people. Under the present international situation, careful consideration should be given to the situation of communication geography of the various places. The establishment of basic industries and the construction of important engineering works should be located in the security zone to the rear of key areas in national defense.

4. In order to adapt to the present international situation, hsien should be taken as the basic, local unit. The agencies which perform such economic acts as production, exchange, consumption and transportation within a hsien must be flexible and integral so as to facilitate mobilization in national defense economy. At the same time, efforts must be made to adapt to individual survival in the event of traffic stoppage or invasion by force so that social and economic life may continue without immediate collapse.

5. Local self-defense organizations and educational organizations should be coordinated with economic reconstruction so that they help each other grow under the overall objective.

6. "Manpower" is a key factor in production. In the reconstruction of national economy, all the "manpower" in the society should be given planned mobilization. All able-bodied males and females (presumably between the ages of 18-45) have the obligations to render labor services. Depending on the actual needs of various places, provisions will be made for the length of their service.

7. A thorough survey should be made of the number of able-bodied males and females in a hsien, the nature of their ability such as the types of work that best suit them—farming, military service, medicine, nursing or teaching—and record them so that these people can be mobilized at all times.

8. To facilitate "manpower" mobilization and control, the recorded "manpower" should be carefully organized and properly trained. Apart from cultivating their production skills and the spirit of collective work, they should be taught the ability to defend themselves (i. e. proper military training). Thus, where possible they can safeguard the security of the economic reconstruction enterprises by means of their ability to undertake self-defense.

9. Land is the necessary tool in production. The various hsiens should survey or investigate the areas and types of land within their jurisdictions, control

their utilization and readjust their relationships.

10. Actively undertake such water conservancy work as irrigation, dredging and filling so as to increase the tillable area.

11. Farmers with no land should be given land where possible so as to make full use of "manpower" and increase the "value of the land."

12. Various places should use discretion in setting up model farms, adopt proper methods and machinery to increase production.

13. Demonstrate the superior productivity of the model farms to encourage the farmers so that they voluntarily adopt the new farming techniques or organize cooperative farms to improve agricultural economy and production. The Government should offer special privileges to the cooperative farms (such as the use of public machinery, technical guidance, transportation facilities, economic assistance and culture safeguarding enterprises) so as to stimulate the people into undertaking collective production.

14. Side lines contribute to the proper use of the farmers' excess labor and have an effect on the farmers' incomes. In accordance with the distribution of the side lines, the Government should provide the farmers with guidance, improve their products and increase their productivity.

15. Sound farm credit organizations should be established to regulate farm finances, assist the newly established cooperative farms and the general development of farming with funds.

16. All large-scale and basic industries should be operated or supervised by the Government. Appropriate terms and measures for "rental" should be worked out in order to attract the investments by capitalists at home and abroad.

17. Various handicraft industries which have special effects should be encouraged and improved by the Government in accordance with their business volume so as to remedy the inadequacy of our present machinery production.

18. In accordance with the financial power and needs of the Government, gradually distribute "power nets" in various places so as to provide the power such as light, heat and electricity for housing, manufacturing and transportation.

19. The construction of plants for light industries should meet the following principles:

a. In the vicinity of the source of the raw materials, concentrate the plants manufacturing similar products as much as possible so that production costs may be cut and production standards unified.

b. Where possible, widely establish small-scale factories in the agricultural centers so that farmers may participate in manufacturing. If such is the case, the farms will not suffer from depression due to decrease in population. Similarly, cities will not suffer from having too many factories. Crowded population and air pollution are damaging to sanitation, for they create undesirable environment and render the distribution of population unbalanced. As the rich resources of the various places are widely exploited, despite possible destruction by force, it will only be partial but not total.

20.   Under the principle of protecting investment security and of safeguarding the welfare of labor, efforts should be made to adjust management-labor relations so that they contribute to the development of national economy.

21.   Barter trade should be adequately controlled so as to balance supply and demand and facilitate transportation and marketing.

22.   The method is to have the local associations jointly organize an import and export center. All imports and exports must be handled by the center. Any member of the center acting independently will be severely dealt with.

23.   The types, amount and sources of consumers' goods in the various places and those of the local products and their marketing places should be carefully investigated and be made available statistically so that barter trade may become reasonable. All non-essential consumers' goods which are not produced domestically will be placed under control as much as possible.

24.   The prices of goods should be reasonably controlled in order to insure adequate profits for the producers and to balance the profits or losses of the sellers.

25.   The financial organizations in the various places should be concentrated under the overall economic reconstruction program so as to fully develop their effectiveness.

26.   Reconstruction of communications and transportation should meet the requirements in economic reconstruction and the national defense conditions and should be planned by the Central Government and the provinces and hsiens concerned.

27.   To undertake economic reconstruction, we need the participation of large numbers of specialists or adequately educated people. In the beginning, personnel in the party and administrative organizations at national and local levels may be drafted. They will be classified and assigned work which best suits them.

28.   As to the guide lines of school education at the various levels, they must be geared to the requirements in economic reconstruction. Meanwhile, the various cultural organizations should pool their efforts in widely publicizing and encouraging economic reconstruction.

In March, 1936, Generalissimo Chiang advanced the "Program of China's Economic Reconstruction" hoping to complete all the necessary reconstruction within the next five years so as to lay solid foundation for the people's livelihood and the nation's future. The five-year program was then decided upon and implemented. The original text of the program was divided into five parts. Excerpts of the program are as follows:

1.   Objective: China's economic reconstruction aims to meet the requirements in national defense and to improve the people's living conditions. The former are designed to carry out the Principle of Nationalism, the latter the Principle of Livelihood.

2.   Policy: The policy of China's economic reconstruction should emphasize planned economy. Based on actual situation and requirements, the Government

should prepare detailed plans embracing the entire nation's economy such as production, trade, distribution and consumption as the guide lines in undertaking all economic reconstruction. Under this policy, the nation's manpower and resources, irrespective of boundaries, are to be adequately distributed in order to develop maximum effectiveness. The result of the production will be jointly used and fairly distributed to improve the welfare of the masses.

3. Contents: The Central Government, the local governments and the people should combine their efforts in economic reconstruction so that work can proceed under the overall system and the overall plans. At present, the following six items require immediate action:

    a. Establishment of a financial system.

    b. Formulation of a budget policy.

    c. Preparation for land reform.

    d. Development of communication enterprises.

    e. Construction of national water conservancy works.

    f. Promotion of industrial reconstruction.

4. Funds: Funds for economic reconstruction are divided into two parts:

    a. Regular funds: All administrative funds (including interests and various incentive pay and allowances' and technical funds (including funds for the permanent agencies engaged in experiments, research, promotion, investigation and planning) are grouped under regular funds. These funds are of indirect production nature. The regular funds from the Central Government should be made available by it from its regular budget, while the regular funds from the local government should be made available by it from its regular budget. Technical funds can be used as cash awards to public and private organizations at home and abroad and as individual allowances.

    b. Enterprise foundations: All those which are of investment and profit-making nature are direct production capital and known as enterprise foundations. These foundations can be classified into five categories:

    (1) Central enterprise funds should be made available from sources outside of the central regular budget and should be placed in the safekeeping of the Central Reconstruction Capital Committee.

    (2) Local enterprise funds should be made available from sources outside of the local regular budget and should be placed in the safekeeping of the Local Reconstruction Capital Committee.

    (3) People's capital should, of course, be fully utilized by the Government People should be encouraged to make investments in all the civilian-operated industries, major and minor local light industries, various agricultural processing enterprises and such profit-seeking enterprises in farming, fishing and animal husbandry.

    (4) Floating enterprise capital is used as investment in long-term or short-term loans and credit loans basis and should be made available by the central

financial organizations in conjunction with commercial banks and local financial organizations.

(5) Funds from international credit loans should be made available where possible to privately or government-operated enterprises. The payment can be made by installments through the years in order to increase the effect in the utilization of funds. When international credit is increased and foreign capital can be borrowed, various methods will be used to facilitate the imput of foreign capital.

Methods used in making funds available are as follows: Beginning 1937 for a period of five years, a capital of two billion dollars was needed for China's communication, water conservancy and industrial reconstruction of which 600 million dollars was to be made available by the Central Government, 100 million dollars by the local governments and the remaining 1.3 billion dollars from the financial markets at home and abroad. Of the 600 million dollars, 200 million dollars for railway construction and 50 million dollars for highway construction were to be defrayed by the national treasury. The balance could be paid by the Central Government for industrial and water conservancy construction by issuing 100 million dollars worth of reconstruction bonds each year for a period of five years.

5. Organization: The undertaking of central economic reconstruction such as heavy industries, basic chemical industries, railway communication and large-scale water conservancy construction should be separately carried out by the responsible agencies in the Central Government. The major and minor light industries in the various economic zones could be jointly promoted by the Central Government, the local government and the people by organizing companies. As to the conduct of local economic reconstruction such as the public communication enterprises, agricultural and industrial reconstruction and local cooperative enterprises, they would be taken up by the local governments or by joint local government-civilian efforts. However, to assume overall supervision in obtaining reconstruction funds, centralized planning and review, a top economic reconstruction agency should be established at the Central Government level to formulate and promulgate policies and plans which concerned national economic reconstruction. This agency would be held responsible for the supervision and evaluation of the progress and results of the various reconstruction projects undertaken by the Central Government. Local economic reconstruction was subject to the technical guidance of the Central Government, but the ratings would be made by the local governments and timely submitted to the Central Government. In establishing the top economic reconstruction agency by the Central Government, the functions of the present responsible economic agency in the Central Government should be properly readjusted so as to avoid duplication and increase working efficiency.

Throughout the nation at the time this policy was strictly adhered to, the nation was marching toward reconstruction objective with remarkable achievements. Such rapid progress won much international praise and also expedited the aggression of the Japanese imperialists who then created the Lukouchiao (Marco

Polo Bridge) Incident on July 7, 1937. As a result, China's national defense economy and national economic reconstruction were affected.

Formulation of Wartime Economic Program

When the War of Resistance broke out in 1937, China moved the materials of her ports inland. By the end of the year, Nanking and Shanghai fell. In March, 1938, China decided on her national policy of fighting a protracted war, with emphasis on measures in wartime economy. Hence, the "Economic Program in the National Emergency" was drafted. Excerpts of the program are indicated as follows:

"Economic policy should meet the requirements of our time. Therefore, in the national emergency, all the economic measures should contribute to our war efforts, and should aim at the seeking of final victory. Anything which contributes to the war efforts should be given first priority and pursued vigorously. Thus, our material power and financial power may be combined to achieve early success.

"At present our production enterprises should consider supplying materials to the frontline operations their primary task. ... for materials needed in operations which can be produced domestically, effort must be made to achieve self-sufficiency. Materials for which our manufacturing facilities are inadequate and need to be procured from abroad, efforts should be made to export goods in exchange of these materials. Production should be increased to furnish the materials needed by the frontline areas.

"In the War of Resistance, the needs of the frontline soldiers should, of course, be met, but the daily necessities of the people in the rear areas must also be made available.

"In order to increase production, finance must be stable and flexible before farming, industries and mining can nurture and prosper. Additionally, communication agencies should be developed to facilitate the flow of materials. Furthermore, foreign trade will be improved to increase the export of domestic products and to reduce the import of luxury and non-essential products. Thus, our income and expenditure will be balanced and the equipment necessary for the increase of production and for the war can be brought in. Therefore, finance, communication and foreign trade which are essential in economic planning should be given due emphasis.

"In order to meet the requirements in the War of Resistance, land and materials should be utilized to the maximum and a constant inter-flow of goods should ge maintained so that all the enterprises may fully develop their effectiveness.

"Based on the above-mentioned objective, a decision has been made on the guide lines and outline measures to be taken. They are described in details and will be turned over to the responsible agencies which will draft detailed measures for implementation.

"1. Promotion of agriculture to increase production:

"a.   Settled life for farmers: As farmers are the direct producers, they should be able to live a settled life before they can increase production. Order must be maintained in the villages. In order to prevent the villages from being troubled, every effort should be made not to disturb the farmers while conducting conscription and labor commandeering. The point is to have frontline operations and rear area production complement but not interfere with each other. No efforts should be spared in implementing the pao-chia system, mopping up bandits, avoiding disturbances and indoctrinating the people with wartime common sense.

"b.   Increase of production of useful crops: Presently, there are the following methods in increasing agricultural production:

"(1)   Banning the planting of harmful crops and restricting the excessive production of not urgently needed crops in order to increase the production of useful crops. For example, a deadline has been set on banning the planting of opium in the various provinces. Efforts should be doubled to put an end to this harmful drug.

"(2)   Urging the farmers to promote the planting of rice, wheat and cereals as well as the planting of cotton in provinces which need cotton badly so that food and clothing of the people are taken care of.

"(3)   For special products such as tung oil, tea, and silk, efforts should be expended to increase the production. Government agencies concerned should provide guidance in planting methods such as improved seeds, better fertilization, water irrigation and animal plague prevention. Personnel should be dispatched to the various places to render assistance and engage in promotion.

"c.   Storage and regulating of large quantities of agricultural products: Frequently, weather and local conditions make it difficult to match agricultural productions with the needs of various areas. Therefore, in places where there is a production surplus, warehouses should be made available to store the surplus crops. Regulating the production is necessary so that the surplus of one place can be used to fill the shortage of another. For instance, Kwangtung Province always has a shortage of rice. Therefore, the Government should see to it that the surplus rice from Hunan and Kiangsi is shipped south in order to reduce the import of rice from abroad and stop the flow of foreign exchange. Similarly, the new textile mills need the Government to purchase the cotton from Shensi to meet the present demand. Furthermore, the scale should be increased. All domestic agricultural products such as foodstuff, cotton, tung oil, tea, silk and wool should be marketed to meet the demand at home and exported to Europe and America.

"d.   Active rural economy: Frequently, farmers lack capital making it difficult to achieve development. As a result, production effectiveness suffered. The Government has always attached great importance to the needs of rural finance. The relief measures should aim at perfecting the organizations of farm cooperatives in order to facilitate the mortgage and guarantee in producing agricultural products. More cooperative banks should be established in the agricultural centers to provide loans for agricultural production. Responsible agencies should be directed by the Government to utilize funds which can be made available by the Government for these purposes. The warehouses in various places can be mortgaged for agricultural production so that rural economy may become active.

"e. Gradual improvement of land allocation: The basic solution to the problem of rural land should be sought in accordance with our National Father's policy of equalization of land rights so that the tiller may own his land and the worker may have his food. In the present War of Resistance, work should be carried out gradually, actively and steadily.

"In addition, the Government should work out measures governing the revamping of water conservancy, exploiting of desolate land, filling of swamps, repressing of tomb land, promoting forestation and increasing by-products for implementation.

"2. Developing industries and mines to meet demand:

"a. Existing industrial and mining facilities should be maintained to increase the productivity of the inland areas. Hitherto, most of China's industries and mines were located along the coast. When the War of Resistance broke out, they were subject to destruction by the enemy. Efforts should be made to protect them so as to continue the production and to meet the demand. The Government has allocated funds to assist the removal of 140 plants, 20,000 tons of machinery and materials to the interior. Special emphasis was given to such plants engaged in steelmaking, shipbuilding, chemical works, electrical engineering, rubber and machinery which had been separately moved to Szechuan, Hunan, Yunnan and western Hupei. All these plants contributed to national defense. A number of the coal mining facilities have been moved from Hopei, Shantung, and Anhwei for use in new mines in Hunan and Szechuan. Textile mills which have much to do with the people have been partly moved to Szechuan Province totalling 90,000 spindles. Active plans are being made in other places.

"b. Active preparation for the establishment of plants urgently needed in national defense: Apart from protecting the existing productivity, the government should create new productivity. Since the start of the War of Resistance, the operations of China's heavy industries and basic mining industries have not stopped. Programmed development should be more active than in the past. For instance, steel, tungsten, electrical appliance plants, copper plants presently under construction in Szechuan, Yunnan, Hunan, Honan and southern Kiangsi should be completed on schedule. As to the light industries needed as daily necessities such as paper making, match, cement, alcohol and pharmaceuticals, also needed militarily, should be established on appropriate sites in the southwest and northwest.

"c. Availability of fuel and power: Based on the criteria of raw materials supply and convenience in transportation, the Government should select industrial centers in the interior provinces so that factories may be established, and the electricity and coal, as power sources needed by the factories, can be made available. Power plants should be established and coals mined to provide power energy. For example, the power plant at Tseliuching, Szechuan Province was established to assist the chemical industries and the Hsiangtan Coal Mines mined to provide coal for Hunan and Hupei Provinces.

"d. Promotion of rural handicraft industries: Production in the interior provinces should make full use of the labor of most people. Because of the need for power and transportation, new industries have to be concentrated in certain localities. To facilitate management, workers must have regular working hours. Rural handicraft industries can make use of the leisure time of the farmers and can be scattered. The Government can provide the necessary guidance in their methods in order to effect improvement. For instance, in places where modern spinning is not available, hand spinning can be encouraged and tools modified to increase efficiency.

"e. Reward and guidance for civilian-operated industries: Reconstruction enterprises cannot be achieved single handedly by the Government. In addition to taking the lead in industries which are closely related to national defense, the Government should encourage the people to act on their own or to utilize funds of friendly nations in promoting other enterprises. The Government should render maximum assistance to those people who wish to engage in economic enterprises so that their plans may lead to success and that their interests may be safeguarded. Overseas Chinese making investments in China will be rewarded. The reward measures include the following:

"(1) Interest guarantee and allowance.

"(2) Mortgage loans to provide the materials.

"(3) Inclusion of Government shares.

"(4) Assisting in transportation.

"In its dealing with the Government-owned and privately owned enterprises, the Government should be impartial and should promote the enterprises. For those Government-owned or privately own enterprises which contribute to the promotion of national economy, the Government should make overall plans and work toward their development.

"f. Equal emphasis on the interests of management and labor: As China's industries are in their infancy, there are difficulties in planning and operation. In order to achieve success, efficiency must be increased and production costs must not be too high. On the other hand, as labor is the basis in production, due emphasis should be given to treatment and protection. The Government should look after the interests of both management and labor and make provisions so that they cooperate fully to achieve prosperity.

"3. Land reclamation to settle the refugees:

"All people in the war zone who have moved to the rear areas since the outbreak of the War of Resistance should be given comfort and assistance by the

Government. They should be given places to live and to engage in production so that they may contribute to the war effort. In production work, there is much that they can do. For instance, land reclamation is the most important. There is much desolate land which is tillable in the rear area provinces. For instance, in Huanglung Shan (Yellow Dragon Mountain), Shensi Province alone, there is a tract of land extending more than 200 li's from east to west and more than 300 li's from north to south giving an area of 4-5 million mou's in which 200,000 people can be settled. It is understood that the Government has made plans, prepared outline measures governing refugee reclamation, designated responsible agencies and supervised the various provincial governments in their implementation. In the near future, surveys will be made on the desolate land in the various provinces, refugees in land reclamation registered and various reclamation measures drafted for gradual implementation. Meanwhile, handicraft, transportation, trade and education in these areas should also be promoted. Specially qualified refugees should be given assistance in their removal so that greater effect will be achieved.

"Additionally, the Government should encourage mining, road building and factory establishment. As skilled workers and hardworking people find work to do and become self-sufficient, production and local security will be enhanced. The Government should make available the funds required in this endeavor so as to insure the realization of the plans.

"4. Developing communication and facilitating transportation:

"a. Rapid increase of domestic communication routes:

"(1) Construction of the Hunan-Kwangsi Railway should be expedited and completed within 18 months. Plans should be made for the construction of the Szechuan-Yunnan Railway. The construction of the Chengtu-Chungking Railway should be continued in order to complete the communication net in the southwest at an early date. In the provinces of the northwest, a railway should be built from Hsienyang to the west via Kansu Province.

"(2) Similarly, highway construction should be stepped up. In the northwest, the construction of the highway from Lanchow via Tienshui and Nancheng to Laohoko and improvement of the connections between the highways in Shensi, Kansu, Sinkiang, Ninghsia, and Chinghai and the various trunk lines is necessary. In the southwest, the improvement of the Szechuan-Hunan Highway, the construction of the Szechuan-Yunnan Highway, improvement of the routes in the southwest and make shipping connections, and the addition of cars to increase transportability, should proceed actively

"(3) In water transportation, original channels should be improved and more inland lines should be opened in order to link up with railways and highways. Furthermore, land-water joint transportation should be promoted to facilitate traffic. Shipbuilding should be encouraged so that adequate means of transportation may become available.

"b. Establishing and expanding international communication lines:

"(1)   Railway: Upon completion of the Hunan-Kwangsi Railway, the traffic from the Canton-Hankow Railway will lead to Indo-China via Chennankwan. Upon completion of the Szechuan-Yunnan Railway, goods produced in Szechuan may be exported to Indo-China via Kunming. It will be beneficial if railways in the northwest can reach Central Asia via Sinkiang.

"(2)   Highways: In the northwest, the Kansu-Sinkiang Highway should be improved. In the southwest, the highway from Kunming to Burma should be constructed and opened in two months. Transportation facilities for international highways should be expended.

"(3)   Telecommunications: Powerful radio stations should be established in Chungking, Chengtu and Kunming so as to maintain close communication contact with the world.

"(4)   Aviation: Air routes should be established in the northwest from Lanchow via Tihwa to the border in order to link up with Soviet Russia's Eurasian lines. In the southwest, Kunming-Rangoon line should be established in order to link up with Britain's Eurasian lines.

"5. Dividing into areas to regulate finance:

"Since her adoption of 'fapi' (legal tender), China's finance became stable. As a result, her production has been increased and her international trade has been gradually balanced. Unfortunately, foreign aggression plunged China into war. Since she has already implemented measures to stabilize finance and foreign exchange, assist industries and business and regulate rural areas, she should continue her efforts in accordance with the established policies. Lately, the enemy directed the puppet organization in Peiping to establish the so-called Joint Reserve Bank issuing banknotes without guarantee, and robbed people so as to provide for his aggression. Therefore, preventive measures must be taken and the Government must work out countermeasures for the compliance of our financial organizations. Future measures must be guided by various provisions for implementation in the different areas, so that excellent effects may result. (The four areas are: (1) enemy-occupied area, (2) enemy-near area, (3) enemy-remote area, and (4) recovery base area, details omitted).

"6. Trade management to increase foreign exchange:

"Balance in international trade is of paramount importance. To achieve this, the Government should restrict import and increase export. On the restriction of import, the use of import application and the reduction of consumption can reduce or stop the importation of non-essential and luxury items. With regard to ways in increasing export, the following should be noted:

"a. Directing water and land transportation agencies to facilitate the exportation of goods.

"b. Operating war insurance to provide protection.

"c. Directing responsible trade organizations to improve the quality and to increase the quantity of the goods to be exported and urging reasonable prices for buying at home and selling abroad.

"d.   Assisting domestic and foreign exporting firms so that they may develop their maximum effectiveness.

"e.   The Government should make available funds for purchase of large quantities of goods to be marketed abroad.

"At present, the goods which can be purchased in the rear areas for export include tung oil, hog bristle, raw silk, tea, calf hide, wool, sheep skin, guts, tungsten, antimony, tin, sesame, gall nuts and hemp, totalling 200 million dollars (equivalent to 12 million British pound sterlings) per year, or 1 million British pound sterlings each month.   However, had the transportation agencies not be affected by the military activities, and Wuchang and Changsha Stations on the Canton-Hankow Railway moved 1,000 tons of export goods daily; further, water transportation from Canton and Wuchow to Hong Kong maintained, and the highway transportation from Chungking to Kunming expanded, then, the above-mentioned goods would have been steadily exported.   In areas temporarily under enemy occupation, efforts should be made to procure goods for export to Europe and the United States in order to earn more foreign exchange and to achieve the aim of balance with international loans.   In important export points such as Hankow, Changsha, Chungking, Kunming, Canton, Wuchow, Haiphong and Hong Kong, personnel should be assigned to take charge of freight transportation so that foreign exchange may be concentrated and wartime finances consolidated. Goods will then move freely in the country, and production enterprises will prosper.

"7.   Practising austerity to economize material power:

"In the present emergency, the Government takes the lead in urging the people to economize.   In public finances, all unnecessary expenditures and reconstruction expenses in government agencies which do not have immediate results should be carefully screened and reduced.   Private economy should have material power and financial power so that all efforts contribute to the nation and the War of Resistance.   Presently, there is much waste and extravagance.   In the interest of material power and financial power, a careful review of the individual's living habits should be made so as to eliminate harmful practices.   The Committee on National Economic Reconstruction Movement and the Committee on New Life Movement should publicize and awaken the people so that they pay heed to and practice austerity."

In March, 1941, as the enemy suffered military reverses, he tightened economic blockade of China.   In an effort to break the economic shackle and to realize the aim of victory in economic warfare, ten following principles on the Basic Outline of Wartime Economic System was prepared:

a.   We should recognize that the present economic struggle against the enemy is the key to victory.   All untimely economic concepts should be abandoned and replaced by the basic concept of "military first" and national defense economy so as to establish the policy in wartime economic system.

b. We should fully understand the importance of modern national defense economic policy and should guide the people, despite any hardships and cost, to implement this system in achieving final victory in the War of Resistance.

c. Decide on a unified procedure, set minimum time period, improve and adjust various economic organizations and emphasize basic organizations. Such organizations in charge of finance, revenues, cooperatives, transportation, salt and storage, should be built into sound economic entities, so that they may serve as strong points in exercising total economic control.

d. Mobilize the nation's experts, and assign them to the economic organizations at various levels, to be responsible for management and techniques. Their authorities and responsibilities are clearly defined and their positions guaranteed, making them the cadres in the economic aspect of the War of Resistance.

e. Mobilize the nation's outstanding youths and provide them with short-term training and assign them as combatants in the economic War of Resistance. Consider them equally important as our soldiers fighting on the frontlines and give them the same preferential treatment and reward as the frontline soldiers.

f. Mobilize the nation's workers, farmers and women. Organize and train them to play active roles in production enterprises.

g. Like military establishments, economic organizations should be given scientific management, unified command, decentralization of responsibilities and simplification of procedures so as to achieve military rapidity and adequacy. Determine efficiency ratings, enforce periodic evaluations, adjust the pay scale of personnel at different echelons rendering it reasonable. When necessary, payment will be made in kind.

h. With regard to the economic activities of the people, systematic plans should be made from production to consumption. These plans should be gradually improved in order to effect overall control in conjunction with military employment.

i. With regard to key industries in finance, trade, transportation and production, effort should be made to expand Government ownership, achieve joint Government civilian ownership and strengthen liaison so that they may be turned into an entity in the economic War of Resistance. By means of public ownership and financial approaches, seek fair distribution. Excess and unjustified profits will be turned over to the Government. Meanwhile, steps will be taken to enforce austerity among the people and make the people accustomed to collective living.

j. Undertake economic struggle against the enemy. Patriotic merchants are encouraged to bring military materials and materials urgently needed in the rear through the enemy lines of blockade and sell them to the public-owned agencies. Non-essential luxury items or enemy goods will be banned by anti-smuggling agencies.

In December of the same year, as the war in the Pacific broke out, the international situation changed drastically. In order to fight shoulder to shoulder with her Allies in a sacred war against aggression, fully develop China's potentials, insure the independence and survival of our nation so that every citizen may fulfill his share in combat and every article may develop its usefulness, the government drafted "Determining the Present Wartime Basic Economic Policy." The original text is as follows:

"Since the outbreak of the Pacific War, our nation's economic posture has undergone drastic changes. Her trade policy and financial policy need to be re-examined, emphasis shifted, strategy of self-sufficiency established and the foundation of postwar economic recovery laid. The following outline is hereby presented:

"a. An overall plan with regard to the activities in national economy should be prepared to tighten control and achieve balance between production departments and between production and consumption so as to eliminate the abnormal phenomena in wartime economy.

"b. Step up economic warfare against the enemy, prevent smuggling and rush the procurement and transportation of materials from the areas which had fallen to the Japanese. To achieve the above, superfluous organization should be deactivated or integrated, authority centralized, manpower and financial power synchronized so as to eliminate duplications and hindrances of the past.

"c. Strictly implement measures governing the control of banks making it absolutely impossible for banks to engage in speculation and preventing commodity prices from rising. Commercial banks, in particular, should be controlled.

"d. Thoroughly control investments and concentrate them on necessary and effective production enterprises. The Government should encourage production enterprises which are closely related to national defense and people's livelihood.

"e. Industrial reconstruction which is non-essential in wartime for which no action has been taken will be suspended. Industrial reconstruction for which action has been taken will be deprived of its capital and facilities which will then be turned into production in national defense and daily necessities.

"f. Small industries will be given assistance. The Government should be urged to comply with previous resolutions.

"g. Due to difficulties in international shipping, foreign trade operations should be adjusted. The products which cannot be exported should be marketed at home.

"h. Responsible agencies will be designated to solicit technicians and skilled workers from areas fallen to the Japanese and other ports to engage in rear area production work."

In June, 1943, the Second National Production Conference was convened (the first conference was held in 1939), in order to match production with pressing military and civilian needs and to lay the prototype in the postwar combination of economy and national defense. The following five major resolutions were passed:

a. Wartime and postwar equal emphasis:

(1) Supplementing each other, agriculture, industry and mining should be interdependent.

(2) Assisting present production enterprises with equipment, techniques and raw materials, centralize them for control and store for allocation.

(3) Encouraging and controlling newly emerging and newly established enterprises.

(4) Planning postwar demobilization of production enterprises.

b. Rationalization and scientific management of production enterprises.

(1) Extending scientific management to all departments.

(2) Properly coordinating all production organizations.

(3) Advocating efficiency ratings and encouraging work contests.

(4) Advocating unity in manufacture and standardization of products.

(5) Strengthening trade guild organizations.

c. Readjusting mining industries and consolidating shipping and marketing.

d. Increasing food and cotton production and farmland water conservancy.

(1) Increasing food production with emphasis on areas which lack food.

(2) Parallel control and promotion of cotton production. Equal emphasis on loans and transportation. Designate Szechuan, Shensi, Hunan, Honan and Hupei as the provinces in which production will be increased.

(3) Farmland water conservancy will be carried out in accordance with the regulations governing the enforced construction of dams and wells.

e. Manpower mobilization and manpower economy.

In September of the same year, to protect the wartime economic foundation and the direction of postwar economic reconstruction, the government prepared "Postwar Policy of Economic Reconstruction" as the guiding principle in planning gradual implementation of postwar economic program.

Following is an excerpt of the resolution adopted by the Supreme National Defense Council in Chungking on December 28, 1944, outlining important principles for the first stage of economic development in China.

a. The industrial development of China should be carried out along two lines: (1) by private enterprises and (2) by state enterprises.

b. In order to facilitate the division of labor under the general plan for economic reconstruction the following provisions concerning economic enterprises are to be observed.

(1) The kinds of state monopolies should not be too numerous. Such monopolies include (a) postal service and telecommunications, (b) arsenals, (c) mints, (d) principal railroads, and (e) large-scale hydraulic power plants.

(2) Private capital may engage in any enterprise other than state monopolies.

(3) The Government may, on its own account or in cooperation with Chinese or foreign capital, engage in enterprises which private capital is not fully capable of developing or which the Government regards as being of special importance, such as large-scale petroleum fields, steel plants, air and water transportation, etc.

(4) All enterprises which are operated by the Government in cooperation with Chinese or foreign capital should be organized in the form of business corporations. The Government, apart from exercising such administrative supervision as is provided by law, is entitled to participate in the management of all matters relating to the business, finance and personnel of such corporations solely in its capacity as a shareholder.

(5) With the exception of state monopolies, all enterprises operated by the Government, whether with or without the cooperation of Chinese or foreign capital, insofar as they are of a commercial character, should, as regards their rights and obligations, be treated in the same manner as private enterprises of a like character.

c. The establishment of any important private enterprise should, according to law, be submitted to the examination and approval of the Government on the basis of the general plan for economic reconstruction. (Important matters to be considered include: location of the projected plant, production capacity, kind and quality of output, issuance of shares and bonds, etc.)

To all private enterprises that conform to the general plan for economic reconstruction the Government should give special encouragement including financial aid and technical and transportation assistance so that they may achieve their scheduled programs.

d. No restrictions shall be placed on the percentage of foreign shares of capital in any Sino-foreign enterprise. In the organization of such a corporation it shall not be made a fixed rule that the general manager be a Chinese, although the chairman of the board of the directors must be a Chinese.

e. State enterprises may contract foreign loans or seek foreign investments through competent Government organs provided that they first be approved by the Government on the basis of the general plan for economic reconstruction. Private enterprises may also directly undertake such negotiations, provided that similar approval of the competent Government organs is obtained.

f. All enterprises in China which are directly financed and operated by foreign nationals on their own account should observe Chinese laws and regulations. In the case of certain special enterprises which would require special authorization for their establishment and operation, special characters or franchises may be granted upon application to and approval by the Chinese Government.

g. Persons in the Government service are forbidden to participate in the operation and management of any enterprise that falls within the scope of their supervisory functions.

It seems inevitable that the existing laws and regulations concerned will in some cases be found to be in conflict with the above-stated principles. Such cases should be referred to the Legislative Yuan for revision with a view to harmonizing all existing legislation on the subject.

This program emphasized the four following principles:

(1)   The harmonizing and joint employment of planned economy and free economy.

(2)   Concrete decisions on Government enterprise and civilian enterprise.

(3)   Welcome to foreign investment.

(4)   Revision or annulment of provisions restricting foreign investment.

Section 2.   Wartime Productions and Resources

Agricultural Production Increase

According to the statistics prepared by the Institute of Social Sciences, Academia Sinica, China's population in 1933 stood at 430 million, her area at 11,000,000 sq. km. and her population density at 100 persons per square mile. However, China's tillable land stood at 1.3 billion mou's which was less than 8% of the country's area. The nation's farmers represented 75% of her population giving an average of 4 mou's of land per farmer. Her agricultural products are mostly foodstuffs with rice, wheat, kaoliang (sorghum), millet and corn as the staple food. Of the economic crops, cotton is most important, while soy bean in between.

The statistics of the productions of various foodstuffs (average between 1932 to 1934) are as follows: rice—1.2 billion piculs, wheat—520 million piculs, kaoliang—370 million piculs, millet—250 million piculs and corn—170 million piculs. Due to her large number of farmers, foodstuffs stood first in her imports. In 1935, she imported rice, wheat, flour and other crops totalling 136 million dollars which was two fifths of her import (340 million dollars) of that year.

Her cotton production which was 13 million piculs each year (average between 1933 and 1935) for domestic consumption was quite often inadequate. This represented approximately 15% of her import.

Silk, tea and soy bean were China's main exports. The export of the soy bean from Manchuria quite often compensated most of import surplus in foodstuffs. In 1935, the annual production of raw silk was 95,000 piculs. Export and domestic consumption roughly divided the total. Production of tea stood at 5 million piculs of which 1 million piculs worth 30 million dollars were exported each year.

In 1934, the export of tung oil totalled 40 million dollars taking the lead in all exports. Apart from making dress materials, silk was also used in the manufacture of aircraft wing. The annual production of silk was 30,000 piculs worth 20 million dollars. The provinces in the northwest annually produced 600,000 piculs of wool and 100,000 piculs of camel hair. The 1935 statistics indicated an export of 40 million dollars of wool, camel hair, fur and rugs.

Since China's industries were not highly developed and her agriculture also lagged behind, the Government spared no efforts in agricultural improvement. Parallel efforts were made in increasing acreage, seed improvement and promotion, reduction of insect disease, improved fertilization, better water conservancy and regulated transportation. As a result, steady increases were evidenced in rice, wheat, corn and sweet potato. Noticeable improvement were registered in increasing the production of cotton, raw silk, hemp, peanuts, soy bean, rape-seed, peas, tung oil and hog bristle. In 1937, the export of agricultural products represented 75.6% of the total. An analysis of the major export items revealed that tung oil stood first at $89,845,000, silk second at $53,171,000, egg products third at $52,812,000, tungsten ore fourth at $40,758,000, tin ingots fifth at $39,719,000, cotton sixth at $31,300,000, tea seventh at $27,921,000, hog bristle eighth at $27,921,000, drawn work and non-silk embroidery ninth at $20,654,000, wool tenth at $17,427,000. From the above, one can see that apart from tungsten ore, tin ingots, drawn work and non-silk embroidery, all the other exports were agricultural products. These were major foreign exchange earners contributing greatly to the war efforts.

With the outbreak of World War II, the Allies needed China's hog bristle to make guns and mechanical brushes. In 1940, the export of hog bristle which stood at 35,567 kuan piculs was worth $94,184,000. In 1941, the export of 16,921 kuan piculs totalled $68,968,312. Formerly, the silk used in the manufacture of parachutes was obtained from Italy and also to a lesser extent from China. Take the statistics of Szechuan silk for example, the export in 1937 was only 20 kuan piculs. It rose to 1,200 kuan piculs in 1943. The export of tung oil and gasoline substitute also established new records. Apart from the economic values in paying off debts, barter and earning foreign exchange, agricultural products played a key role in the war against aggression. Due to necessity and the removal of specialists to the interior, farming techniques in the interior were also improved. Progress in seed improvement, insect prevention and care of domestic animals was most outstanding.

Development of Resources

In addition to emphasizing increase in agricultural products, efforts were also made in developing war resources. They are stated as follows:

1. Coal—According to the estimate of the Geological Survey Institute, China's coal reserves stood at 246 billion tons and was the third largest in the world. In 1933, China's coal production was 28 million tons and was the eighth in the world. By the time war broke out in 1937, Hopei and Shantung were still

the major coal-producing provinces, while Szechuan and Hunan were the major coal-producing provinces in the rear areas with a total annual output of 6 million tons. Among them, Szechuan produced 2.7 million tons, Hunan 1.4 million tons, and Honan and Shensi 400,000 and 500,000 tons each.

2. Petroleum—China's pre-war petroleum reserves were estimated at 3.6 billion barrels (42 gallons in each barrel) of which Fushun contained oil shale numbering 1.9 billion barrels and representing 53% of the nation's general reserves. During the war, apart from operating coal mines, and refining petroleum, Japan explored oil fields in Taiwan and established a large refinery to refine petroleum. In the rear areas, Szechuan had natural gas, and the oil fields in Kansu became the main sources which provided liquid fuel in the northwest. The annual production stood at 6 million gallons. Due to lack of transportation, only 4 million gallons were actually produced. Although the quantity was not large, it contributed materially to the prosecution of the war.

3. Steel—China lacked iron ore. According to pre-war estimates, the nation's general reserves stood at 1.13 billion tons. Liaoning Province alone had 77% of the nation's total iron ore reserves, and Chahar Province had 9%. During the war, Japan undertook large-scale expansion greatly increasing the production of pig iron and steel. In addition to establishing the Tatukou Steel Mill in the rear areas and exploring Chichiang Iron Mines, the area in the vicinity of Chungking became the metallurgil center. Yimen and Anning in Yunnan Province were explored, yielding 84,000 tons of pig iron and 15,000 tons of steel annually. This could not compare with the production in Manchuria; however, in the southwest where the resources were poor and facilities were inadequate, the little production to meet the war demands was precious.

4. Copper—China was not rich in copper reserves and she did little mining. However, copper, as material in electrical appliances, was closely related to military requirements. The center of wartime production of copper in the rear area was Tungchuan. Scattered production was found in Szechuan and Sikang. There were copper plants in Chungking and Kunming, and copper coins were bought and melted. The annual production was as high as 1,500 metric tons. However, due to limited raw materials, the average production remained at 700-800 metric tons.

5. Tungsten—Of the world's total tungsten production of 14,000 tons, China's output represented over two fifths. During the war, antimony, tungsten, tin and mercury were the materials which were used to repay the loans and barter with the United States and Soviet Russia. As a result of the Government's efforts to step up production, the annual yield reached 12,500 metric tons. Southern Kiangsi topped the list, followed by Hunan, Kwangtung, and Yunnan. Despite the blockade of seaports and isolation from Burma and Indo-China, China's mining products were flown to India and were moved on land to Soviet Russia. Thus, the Government's credit was maintained resulting in fine international

reputation. The quality of China's tungsten was excellent, as it contained over 70% of tungstic acid greatly surpassing international standards.

6. Antimony—Hunan Province was rich in antimony. Of the world's pre-war production of 16,000 tons, China produced three quarters. During the war, pure antimony was primarily produced in Hunan. The production in Kwangsi, Kweichow and Yunnan was negligible. In 1937, the maximum output was 14,600 metric tons. Although antimony was also used to pay debts and for barter, the world's demand for antimony was not nearly so pressing as for tungsten and tin. As the unit price for antimony was low, it was uneconomical to export when there were difficulties in transportation. Therefore, production was greatly reduced. By 1944, even though production was reduced to 200 tons, there was much in stock. As to the quality of antimony, the percentage which was increased from 99.3 to 99.8 after Government management, met British and U.S. standards.

7. Tin—The nation's production of tin which stood at 9,000 tons came mostly from Kochiu, Yunnan. During the war, tin was second only to tungsten in repaying debt and in barter. At its peak, the production totalled 15,000 tons. Apart from Fuhochung in Kwangsi, Kwangtung, Kiangsi, and Hunan each producing several hundred tons, Kochiu was the main producer. The quality of fine tin was as high as 99.95%, surpassing Britain and paralleling the United States. Unfortunately, before new mining methods were introduced, lack of materials and labor made it difficult for the old mining methods to continue. Thus, no longer profitable, tin mining deteriorated.

Section 3.   Wartime Economic Reconstruction

Westward Removal of Mines and Factories

Prior to the outbreak of the war on July 7, 1937, according to reliable estimates, the total number of Chinese factories (excluding Manchuria) was over 10,000, the total power over 2 million H. P., capital of 2 billion dollars, workers over 1.6 million, production costs over 4.7 billion dollars. By the time the war broke out, the Government, in preparation for protracted war, moved most of the factories in Shanghai area first to Hunan and Hupei Provinces, and later to Szechuan, Yunnan and Kweichow. More factories moved to Szechuan. Some factories in Hupei, Hunan and Honan also moved to the interior. The Government paid for the expense in the removal. Upon arrival in the interior, these factories were given loans, capital, technicians and assistance to recruit workers. The Government paid the per diem, family settlement and provided other conveniences to workers who were enlisted from the areas which had fallen to the enemy. On the other hand, the Government exercised supervision over the production of the factories and mines so that they kept pace with the wartime requirements. According to the statistics furnished by the Statistics Division, Ministry of Economic Affairs, 410 factories had moved to the interior by the end of 1939.

A breakdown of these factories is as follows:

Description	No. of Factories	No. of Worker	Materials and Machineries Moved (tons)
Steel	1	360	1,152
Machinery	168	5,588	13,255
Electrical	28	684	5,300
Chemical	54	1,376	8,093
Textile	92	1,603	30,822
Food	22	549	3,213
Cultural	31	606	1,374
Others	14	270	560
Total	410	11,036	63,769

The above chart indicates that the number of factories which had moved to the interior represented 17% of the nation's factories which met the requirements in factory regulations. Of these factories, the major ones included Yangtze Steel Works and Hanyang Steel Works, Chen Huan Textile Mill and Shen Hsin Textile Mill, Lung Chang Paper Mill, Hua Sheng Machinery Works, Hua Hsing Machinery Works and China Industrial Works. After 1940, factories in Hunan and Kiangsi continued to move west. Over 10,000 mechanics moved to the interior representing 22% of the nation's mechanics. The mechanics who were enlisted directly by the individual factories from the Japanese-occupied areas were several times more. Over 60,000 tons of factory equipment were moved to the interior. These factories established the basis of China's industries in the War of Resistance.

Wartime Industries

In 1933, there were only 33 factories in Szechuan. By 1937, 144 factories had moved to Szechuan. By the end of 1942, there were more than 3,000 newly established factories and 1,596 small handicraft factories in the rear areas. Although most of these factories were sub-standard, they contributed to the supply of daily necessities and important military items. By the time the war ended, there were 6,000 factories in the rear areas with a capital of 8.5 billion dollars. A statistical chart showing the number of wartime rear area factories and their capitals are indicated below (statistics furnished by the Statistics Division, Ministry of Economic Affairs):

Year	No. of Factories	Authorized Capital (in 1,000 dollars)	Currency Capital (in 1,000 dollars)
Before 1936	300	117,950	117,950
1937	63	22,388	22,166
1938	209	117,740	86,583
1939	419	286,569	120,914
1940	571	378,973	59,031
1941	866	709,979	45,718
1942	1,138	447,612	9,896
1943	1,049	1,486,887	14,486
1944	549	1,119,502	3,419
Unknown year	102	113,635	7,319
1945	732	3,684,681	
Total	5,998	8,485,926	487,480

The above chart reflected the wartime rear area industrial prosperity. The changes undergone in the industries are as follows:

1. Heavy industries: Subsequent to the Manchurian Incident, China's industrial development was inclined toward light industries. By the time full-scale war broke out, the Government emphasized the establishment of heavy industries. On the one hand, factories producing power driven machineries, electrical appliances, communication equipment, chemical and medical products which were related to munitions and national defense were moved or established. On the other hand, the National Resources Commission aimed to develop heavy industries. Rapid development ensued. The following chart shows the peak of rear area industrial development in 1942.

Description	No. of Plants (%)	Capital (%)
Chemical	22.0	28.83
Textile	21.0	14.98
Machinery	18.1	17.42
Food	9.6	4.30
Cultural	6.0	1.10
Metal	4.3	1.18
Metallurgical	4.1	15.59
Dress	3.9	0.57
Utilities	3.3	7.39
Earthen Ware	3.2	3.32
Electrical	2.6	4.80
Timber & Construction	1.3	0.29
Miscellaneous	0.6	0.19

In that year the number of rear area factories totalled 3,758 with a gross capital of $1,939,026,000. Heavy industry factories represented 35% of the factories and 50% of the capital.

2. Establishment of industrial complex: Prior to 1936, most of the factories were concentrated in Shanghai and some along the coast and the Yangtze River. The southwest and the northwest had no modern industry to speak of. After the war broke out, the removal and construction of plants, and the abundance of raw materials and communication convenience in Szechuan turned it into an industrial center, supplemented by Kwangsi, Hunan, Kweichow, Yunnan and Shensi Provinces. The following chart shows the distribution of the 3,758 factories in 1942:

Province	No. of Factories %	Capital (%)	Power (%)
Szechuan	44.01	58.28	43.22
Kweichow	2.98	2.39	1.13
Yunnan	2.82	10.80	10.32
Kwangsi	7.77	7.90	7.92
Kwangtung	1.85	0.48	0.95
Fukien	2.34	0.58	8.34
Hunan	13.34	3.92	10.51
Kiangsi	2.71	1.72	3.23
Chekiang	1.89	4.71	2.46
Shensi	10.24	3.43	9.63
Kansu	3.69	3.19	1.14

3. Public enterprises: Prior to 1936, the nation suffered from many changes. Apart from such industries as munitions and communications, the Government operated few enterprises. By the time the full-scale war broke out, the National Resources Commission began to establish Government-owned heavy industries. Ten years of efforts resulted in considerable achievements. Meanwhile, various provincial governments operated small-scale enterprises. This was especially true of Kweichow, Kwangsi, Fukien and Kiangsi. Gradually, national banks made investments in industries. For example, the Central Bank invested in Szechuan and Sikang and the Bank of China in Shensi and Kansu. Additionally, the Economic Commission in the various war areas also scored achievements. All in all, the efforts in various fields yielded fruitful results. In 1942, the capital of the public-owned enterprises represented 69%+ of all the capitals in the rear area industries. In terms of provinces, of the 69%, Szechuan represented 36.68%, Yunnan 10.12%, Kwangsi 6.83%, Chekiang 4.58%, Kansu 2.77%, Shensi 2.25%, Kweichow 2.03% and Hunan 1.4%. Except Hunan and Shensi, the capitals of the Government-owned enterprises exceeded that of the private-owned enterprises. In terms of trade, of the 69%, chemical industry represented 21.66%

(of which oil refinery, alkali acid and alcohol were well developed. At that time the chemical industry operated by the National Resources Commission did not play an important role), metallurgical industry 14.18%, mechanical industry 12.17%, textile industry 7.35%, water and electricity 6.58%, electric appliances 4.21%, earthen-ware 1.64%. The above indicates that most of the capitals of the Govednment-operated enterprises were concentrated in the basic industries.

4. Scale of the Government-operated and private-operated industries: Of the 3,758 factories in 1942, only 656 were Government-operated, while 3,102 were private-operated. In numbers, the private-operated factories had the absolute majority, however, they had less capital. Approximately 40% of the Government-operated factories had capitals which were less than $100,000, while 70% of the private-operated factories had capitals less than $100,000. Further, the average capital of a public operated factory was $2,000,000 and the average capital of a private-operated factory less than $200,000. An average Government-operated factory had more than 100 workers, while an average private-owned factory had 50+ workers. An average Government-operated factory had 100 H.P., while an average private-operated factory had 30 H.P. If only the Government-operated factories of the public-operated factories were considered, excluding the small provincial industries, the disparity with the private-operated factories would be much greater.

Communication Situation

In order to implement our National Father's Industrial Program[1] and to undertake communications reconstruction, the Government formulated the "Procedure in Industrial Reconstruction" and actively promoted communications enterprise. The efforts of the Government are as follows:

1. Railways: According to the 1934 statistics, the total length of the completed railways in China was only 18,000 km, of which the length of the national railways was 12,000 km. representing two thirds of all the nation's railways. The length of the private-owned was approximately 2,400 km., while that of the foreign-owned railways was 3,300 km. representing 30% of the total length of the nation's railways. By V-J Day in 1945, the newly constructed railways during the war totalled 5,200 km. These new railways are listed below:

a. Chekiang-Kiangsi Railway: The road covered 929 km. for Hangchow via Yushan and Nanchang of Kiangsi Province to Chuchow, Hunan Province. It was completed in 1937. This road spanned across the area between the Yangtze River and the East Sea and was the main trunk line in the southeast railway net.

---

[1] Shortly after the termination of the First World War, Dr. Sun Yat-sen wrote the "Industrial Plan" which was divided into six programs of thirty-three sections. The plan was designed to better people's livelihood and lay the foundation in defense and economic planning.

b. Canton-Hankow Railway: This road crossed Kwangtung, Hunan and Hupei Provinces and linked with the Peiping-Hankow Railway becoming the main trunk line traversing Peiping, Wuhan and Canton. However, construction of the Chuchow-Chuchiang (Shaokwan) section of 456 km. was held up for a number of years. Construction began in July, 1933, and rails were laid by April, 1936. In July, 1936, the entire Canton-Hankow Railway was open to traffic. This section of the Canton-Hankow Railway contributed considerably to the moving of troops, refugees and materials. Construction of the Whampoa branch line began in 1936 and was completed in 1937, it was linked with the Canton-Kowloon Railway.

c. Lunghai Railway: This road extended west to Shensi and Kansu, and east to Haikow, traversing four provinces. Due to civil war, the entire line extended east to Tapu near Haichow and west to Lingpao in Honan Province with a length of 818 km. Construction of the other sections was stalled, and did not begin until December, 1931 when traffic reached to Tungkuan. In 1934, it was extended to Sian. In the same year, the branch line from Taierchuang to Chaotun was linked with Lin-Tsao branch line of the Tientsin Pukow Railway. The Sian-Paokis section was open to traffic in 1937. The eastern section from Tapu to Lienyunkang was completed in 1935. In order to meet the wartime requirements, the westward construction must be speeded up. The construction of the 154 km. Paoki-Tienshui (in Kansu) section passed through corrugated mountains and difficult terrain, as the road bed moved along the north bank of the Wei River. There were 125 tunnels totalling 22 km. and 520 culverts of varying sizes. The engineering was the most difficult ever encountered. Work began in May, 1939 and was not completed until the end of 1945. The construction of its 135 km. Hsienyang-Tungkuan branch line began in May, 1939 and was completed by the end of 1940.

d. New Lungsui Railway: The plan was to go from Paotou via Ninghsia and Langchow to Hami. Survey was conducted, but construction never began.

e. Soochow-Kahsing Railway (branch line of the Nanking-Shanghai Railway): In order to strengthen national defense transportation, China built the 74 km. Soochow-Kahsing Railroad. Construction began in 1935 and was completed the following year. Transportation from Nanking to Hangchow no longer had to go by way of Shanghai. The rails were dismantled by the Japanese during the war.

f. Kiangnan Railway: Construction began from Nanking in 1933, reached Sunchiafu in Anhwei Province (175 km.) in 1935. In 1936, a branch line was built from the Chunghuamen Main Station in Nanking to Yaohuamen (16 km.) linking with the Nanking-Shanghai Railway. Originally, it was planned to extend it to Wuhu and Chapu. Later, the road was changed to become a section of the Nanking-Canton Railway (the section from Wuhu to Wanchih was the old road bed of the Ninghsiang Railway).

g.   Nanking-Kiangsi Railway: The first section was the Kiangnan line and then extended to Hsuancheng and Kweihsi, Kiangsi Province to link with the Chekiang-Kiangsi Railway.   In November, 1937, the rails for the section from Sunchiafu to Hsi Hsien (155 km.) and Kweihsi to Chingtehchen (approximately 50 km.) would have been laid, had it not been for the war which interrupted the work.

h.   Tungpu Railway: The line extended north to Tatung and south to the ferry point of Fenglingtu crossing the entire Shansi Province.   It was built by the Shansi Provincial Government with troop labor.   This narrow-guage light railroad had a width of 1 m.   In December, 1933, construction began in Taiyuan heading north and south.   The southern section from Taiyuan to Fenglingtu was 514 km. long, while the northern section from Taiyuan to Tatung was over 300 km.   In 1937, the southern section was completed, and later in the same year, the northern section was mostly completed.   Unfortunately, war prevented the entire line from being opened to traffic.

i.   Extension line of Taotsing Railway (branch line of the Peiping-Hankow Railway):   Construction of the 66 km.   Taokou to Tsuwang (Neihuang Hsien) section began in 1936, and traffic was open in April of the following year.

j.   Shanghai-Hangchow-Ningpo Railway: The section from Hangchow to the north bank of the Tsaowo River (80 km.) was completed in 1937.

k.   Huainan Railway: The line began north at Tienchia-an on the south bank of the Huai River and ended south at Yuhsiko on the north bank of the Yangtze River.   Work on the 215 km. line began in March, 1934, and traffic on the entire line was open in June, 1935.

l.   Hunan-Kwangsi Railway: The road extended from Hengyang through Kweilin, Liuchow, Nanning to Chennankwan to link with Indo-China.   The total length from Hengyang to Chennankwan was 1,030 km.   Construction began in September, 1937 to meet the demand in transporting military supplies and materials and proceeded rapidly.   The 360 km.   Hengyang-Kweilin section was open to traffice in October, 1938.   Construction of the Kweilin-Liuchow section, the Liuchow-Nanning section and the Nanning-Chennankwan section started simultaneously.   The Kweilin-Liuchow section was open to traffic by the end of 1939. Work on the Liuchow-Nanning section reached Litang when the Japanese landed at Peihai.   Construction was, therefore, interrupted and was not resumed until our forces staged counteroffensive and the enemy withdrew in defeat.   By September, 1941, traffic reached Laipin (Liuchow to Laipin-72 km. Later, the 20 km. Tawan branch line was built in 1942) to link with water transportation.   The Nanning-Chennankwan section was a Sino-French joint venture.   Construction had to stop when the Japanese invaded Kweilin and Nanning.

m.   Kweichow-Kwangsi Railway: In 1939, the construction moved westward from Liuchow.   In October, 1940, traffic reached Yishan, in February to Chinchengchiang, and in May, 1943 to Tushan, Kweichow Province, and in the winter of 1944 to Tuyun.   Only Tuyun-Kweiyang section of the entire line was not completed.

n.   Hunan-Kweichow Railway: The Chekiang-Kiangsi Railway was the eastern section of the east-west major artery south of the Yangtze River, while the Hunan-Kweichow Railway marked the western section of the artery.   The construction of the latter from Chuchow to Kweiyang extending 1,000 km.   By 1939, the Chuchow-Hsiangtan section (28 km.) was opened.   Work continued and rails were laid from Hsiangtan to Lantien (175 km.).   Later, war interrupted the work. Rails were dismantled and used on the Kweichow-Kwangsi Railway.

o.   Szechuan-Yunnan Railway: It was an important line of communications of the upper stream of the Yangtze River and the southwestern border. The road began at Hsufu (Yiping), Szechuan Province and passed through Weining, Yisheng, Chanyi, Chuching to terminate at Kunming and to link with Indo-China and Burma.   The road which was 744 km. long used 1 m. gauge.   In 1938, work began simultaneously with the construction of the Yunnan-Burma Road. However, the materials which were ordered did not arrive on account of the war. Hence, the progress was slow.   Later, when the Japanese invaded Indo-China, the rails dismantled from the Yunnan-Indo-China Railway were used in the construction of the Szechuan-Yunnan Railway.   Traffic reached Chuching in February, 1943 and Chanyi (175 km.) in June, 1944.

p.   Yunnan-Burma Railway: In December, 1938 construction began simultaneously at Hsiangyun in both easterly and westerly directions.   In the fall of 1939, the railway administration was moved to Lufeng.   When the line from Kunming to the Yunnan-Burma border was divided into 20 engineering sectons, work progressed rapidly.   However, in the summer of 1940, the Yunnan-Burma Highway was closed.   As a result of the lack of construction materials, work was suspended.   In March, 1941, work was resumed.   Four engineering divisions were established to rush the work day and night.   It was estimated that the western section would take 15 months and the eastern section 2 years to complete. However, in April, 1942, the war situation on the Burma border changed drastically.   As the Yunnan-Burma Railway had lost its significance, construction was stopped.

q.   Chichiang Railway: The main purpose of the Chichiang Railway was to move the iron ore of the Chichiang Iron Mine.   Work began in April, 1942, and traffic reached Wucha by August, 1945.   By August, 1947, the entire line was completed.

2.   Highways: In 1928, the Ministry of Communications prepared a national highway plan using Lanchow as the center of the highway system and dividing the nation's roads into national highways, provincial highways and hsien highways.   It was estimated that it would take 10 years to complete 41,550 km. of highways.   By the time Manchurian Incident broke out in 1931, the National Economic Commission organized the Highway Administration to be responsible

for supervising the construction of highways in the various provinces. Financially and technically, it assisted the various provinces to regulate the routes and to set engineering standards.

First, the Economic Commission supervised the construction of the Kiangsu-Chekiang-Anhwei connecting highway. The Nanking-Hangchow, Shanghai-Hangchow, Nanking-Wuhu, Soochow-Kashing, Yihsing-Changchow and Hangchow-Huichow Highways were designated as connecting highways. Later, they were expanded to include Kiangsi, Hupei, Hunan and Honan Provinces. Within a period of two years, all the highways in the seven provinces including the highways constructed by the provinces concerned totalled 13,676 km.

Again in 1934, the Economic Commission directly constructed the Northwest Highway including the Si-Lan and Si-Han lines. The scope of its supervision extended to Kansu, Shansi, Sinkiang, Suiyuan, Szechuan and Yunnan. Its efforts resulted in the completion of the Suiyuan-Sinkiang Highway, Suiyuan-Shansi Highway, Kansu-Sinkiang Highway and Szechuan-Yunnan Highway totalling over 20,-000 km.

In addition, Kwangtung, Kwangsi, Fukien, Shantung and Hopei Provinces also undertook the construction of highways. However, some of them failed to meet the specified engineering standards resulting in stoppage when it rained. On the eve of the full-scale War of Resistance, there were 43,521 km. of surfaced road and 65,979 km. of dirt roads totalling 109,500 km.

In August, 1937, the emergency routes built to meet military requirements were found in 11 provinces, namely Kiangsu, Chekiang, Anhwei, Kiangsi, Hupei, Fukien, Honan, Shansi and Shensi totalling over 3,600 km. Most urgent among these were the emergencey repair of the Shih-Teh, Shih-Tsang, Shih-Pao and Shih-Liu military roads in the northern theater which were directly handled by the engineering division established by the National Military Council. In 20 days, the roads were open to traffic. In the southern theater, quite frequently after the enemy bombing, the highway bridges in Kiangsu and Chekiang Provinces were soon repaired.

In the summer of 1938, efforts were made to improve the Pien-Lo Highway, Canton-Shaokwan Highway, Wuchang-Changsha Highway and Hankow-Ichang Highway, to rush the repairs of the branch lines from the northeastern and southeastern parts of Hupei Province to Kiangsi and Anhwei as well as the communications net with Wuhan as the center. Most outstanding was the completion of emergency repair work on the Wuchang-Changsha Highway and the Hankow-Ichang Highway enabling the materials in Wuhan to be withdrawn five days before Wuhan was abandoned.

After the withdrawal of Canton and Hankow, highway transportation assumed an increasingly important position. The following is a brief account of the domestic international highways:

a. Domestic highways:

(1) Kunming-Kweiyang-Chungking Line: With Kweiyang as the center, the road led north to Chungking, west to Kunming, east to Chihchiang and Juanling, and south to Liuchow and Kweilin. Other than the Southwest Import Transport Supervisory Commission, the China Transportation Company was the largest firm responsible for transportation in this area.

(2) Szechuan-Yunnan East Highway: It was supplementary line of the Kunming-Kweiyang-Chungking Line. Upon arrival at Luchow from Yunnan, the materials were shipped by boat to Chungking. Much ordnance equipment and petroleum products were moved on this line.

(3) Szechuan-Yunnan West Highway: It extended from Lohshan, Szechuan Province to Hsichang via Huili, Tayao and Hsiangyun to link with the Yunnan-Burma Road totalling 1,113 km. After withdrawal from the Yunnan-Burma Road, the section south of the Gold Sand River was destroyed.

(4) Chinghai-Tibet Line: The 797 km. line began at Hsining, Chinghai Province and terminated at Yushu. The construction began in 1943 and was completed the following year.

(5) Sikang-Chinghai Highway: This 792 km. highway extended from Kangting in Sikang Province to Hsiehwu in Chinghai Province, to link with the Chinghai-Tibet Highway. Work began in 1942 and ended in 1944.

(6) Nan-Kiang Highway: The 73 km. road began at Tunhuang, Kansu Province and ended at Nuochiang, Sinkiang. Construction began in 1945 and terminated in 1946.

b. International Highways:

(1) Yunnan-Burma Highway: This road began at Kunming and ended at Wanting. It measured 960 km. The 547 km. section from Hsiakwan (near Tali) to Wanting (on the Yunnan-Burma border) traversed along deep and precipitous canyon. The entire highway was built under conditions whereby manpower and materials were lacking. The fact that 150,000 laborers were mobilized to complete the construction in 7 months amazed the world.

(2) China-India Highway: Also known as the Ledo Road, it began at Ledo in India and traversed through northern Burma to link with the Yunnan-Burma Highway. With a total length of 386 km. the road moved along breathtaking cliffs, jungles and uninhabited mountains. Traffic was opened in the end of 1944, after much hazardous work surpassing that of any highway.

(3) Pipelines: The construction of the China-India pipeline began at the same time as that of the China-India Highway. It began at Calcutta, India and passed through Tinsukia, Ledo, Myitkyina, to Kunming extending for more than 3,000 km. The pipeline from Kunming to Wanting totalled 690 km. In April, 1945, to facilitate the movement of petroleum to the airfields east of Kunming, the pipeline was extended to Chuching, Chanyi, Luliang and Chengkung totalling 280 km. The pipeline moved 54,000 tons of petroleum products each month.

3. Aviation: In August, 1930, the Ministry of Communications and the

China Airways Federal Inc., U.S.A. jointly established the C.N.A.C. (China National Aviation Corporation) to fly the major domestic routes. In February, 1931, the Ministry of Communications and the German Lufthansa Company jointly established the Eurasia Aviation Corporation to fly the major routes between Europe and Asia. Meanwhile, to actively develop this new enterprise and to assist local, and private-owned aviation, the Government established the Southwest Aviation Corporation to fly the routes in Kwangtung and Kwangsi.

In 1931, China's airline total kilometerage was 3,931 km. but in 1936, it rose to 11,841 km.

When the War of Resistance broke out in 1937, C.N.A.C. and Eurasia Aviation Corporation were moved to Hankow and Sian respectively in accordance with pre-determined plans. By the time the nation's capital fell, the Eurasia's Hankow-Changsha-Canton-Hongkong route and the C.N.A.C.'s Chungking-Kweilin-Canton-Hongkong route were subjected to the attacks of the Japanese air force. When Wuhan was threatened, the two corporations pooled all their planes to fly the Chungking-Hankow route and the Kweilin-Hankow route in order to evacuate Government personnel. As the Japanese entered Wuhan, the last plane was still taking off. The spirit of the members of these two corporations had long been remembered.

After the fall of Wuhan and Cantou, the center in the War of Resistance was moved to Chungking. Plans were under way to establish an air net. At this time, as China's relations with Soviet Russia were quite close, the Ministry of Communications signed a contract with the Soviet Central Civil Aviation Administration to jointly organize the Sino-Soviet Aviation Corporation at Tihua to be responsible for the air operations from Hami through Tihua and Ili in Sinkiang to Alma Ata in Russia. The flights were formally inaugurated in December, 1939, However, after China's severance of ties with Germany, the Eurasia Aviation Corporation was taken over by the Ministry of Communications and became Government-operated.

After the fall of Wuhan and Canton, the center in the War of Resistance was flown to the interior from Hong Kong. By the time the Japanese invaded Vietnam, the Yunnan-Vietnam Railway could no longer be used. At one time, Britain closed the Yunnan-Burma Highway (the Burma Road), and foreign materials had to be flown in. In order to meet this emergency, the Ministry of Communications directed the C.N.A.C. and the Eurasia Aviation Corporation to operate short flights between Nanhsiung, Kwangtung Province and Hong Kong for moving materials into and out of the interior. The results were quite effective.

After the outbreak of the Pacific War, C.N.A.C. and Eurasia Aviation Corporation suspended their flights to Hong Kong. Meanwhile, Rangoon Airfield was raided, and C.N.A.C. had to suspend its Chungking-Rangoon flights. When the Japanese air force raided Hong Kong, large aircraft of the two companies' parked in the airfield were totally destroyed. The Eurasia Aviation Corporation suffered heavy losses.   In March, 1943, the Ministry of Communications and the Commission on Aeronautical Affairs jointly reorganized the Eurasia into the Central Air Transport Corporation (C.A.T.C.).   A number of military aircraft were allocated to C.A.T.C. for use.

The Sino-India airlift was undertaken by C.N.A.C. under authorization of the Government.   The three routes of Kunming-Tinsukia, Yipin-Tinsukia and Luhsien-Tinsukia were established to move the Government materials.   The performance of the planes made available from the U.S. Lend Lease was excellent. In the initial stage, the number of planes was small, but it rose to 50 by 1945. These planes were barely adequate to meet the demand of materials from abroad needed by the Government, and contributed materially to the war effort.   Similarly, C.N.A.C. undertook the task of bringing in large quantities of military supplies from India, and flying tungsten ore, hog bristle and raw silk from Kunming to foreign countries.   During its peak, the monthly tonnage of imports reached 2,400 tons substituting the load carried by the Burma Road and the words "Over the Hump" became legendary in international aviation.

4.   Telecommunications: Telecommunications included telephone, telegraph and radio photo.   Radio photo included teletype, television and radar.   In 1944, teletype service was inaugurated between China and the United States; however, few messages were transmitted.   Plans for television and radar were under way. The following is a summary of telegraph and wireless telegraph.

a.   Telegraph: There were wire and wireless telegraph.   In 1927, the telegraphic lines in the nation totalled 90,000 km; however, most of them needed repair.   After 1928, steps were taken to repair the existing facilities and add new equipment. By June, 1937, the lines were increased to 105,000 km. and the number of telegraph offices to 1,270.   As the War of Resistance broke out, difficulties were encountered in maintenance, repair and replacement of parts.   Hence, in 1943, efforts were made to make telephone lines for telegraph when the telephone lines were not occupied.   On the other hand, typewriter transmitters were tried out to provide telegraphic service in an improvised manner, and the results were quite satisfactory.   As to radio (wireless) telegraph the Ministry of Communications made preparations for the establishment of shortwave communication in 1927.   A shortwave station was established in 1928.   Later, shortwave stations were established in Chungking, Ichang, Chungming, Anking and Tientsin. In the same year, the Reconstruction Commission established a national shortwave radio net which was turned over to the Ministry of Communications in 1929. Many radio stations were established in Szechuan, Sikang, Ninghsia and Suiyuan, on river banks and along the coast.   In 1935, radio stations were established in Shanghai, Hankow and Canton.

b.   Telephones: There were local telephone and long-distance telephone service.   In 1927, the Ministry of Communications operated 20 municipal telephone administrations totalling over 40,000 telephones.   Provincial-operated and private-operated telephones totalled nearly 10,000 telephones. By 1937, the number of local telephone administrations operated by the Ministry of Communications was increased to more than 50, and the obsolete equipment was replaced. As the telephone systems in Nanking, Shanghai, Wuhan and Tsingtao became automatic, the number of telephones rose to 76,000. Similarly, the provincial-operated and private-operated telephone systems in Hangchow, Swatow, Kweilin, Foochow and Changshu also became automatic, and the number of telephone was increased to more than 3,000. With regard to long-distance telephone, in 1927 the Ministry of Communications had only 4,000 km. two-way long-distance lines. The long-distance telephone lines operated by the various provinces were limited and had one-way lines resulting in poor transmission. When the National Government named Nanking the nation's capital, the Ministry of Communications first established the Nanking-Shanghai line which was extended later to Hangchow. In 1929, the Chekiang Provincial Government established the provincial long-distance net. Later, similar nets were established by Kiangsu, Shantung, Anhwei, Hunan and Hopei Provinces. Having decided to establish a nationwide communications net, the Ministry of Communications organized the 9-Province Long-Distance Telephone Engineering Division in 1934. The nine provinces were Kiangsu, Anhwei, Hupei, Hunan, Kwangtung, Shantung, Shansi, Hopei and Honan. By June, 1937, the long-distance two-way copper lines were installed totalling 52,200 paired km. The technical standards and building specifications met the latest requirements. The 160 km. underground cable built by the Kwangtung Provincial Government and the Hong Kong Government by sections were the earliest in China covering 700 places. After the War of Resistance broke out, long-distance telephone center system was instituted in order to meet the wartime requirements. Beginning 1943, Chungking, Hengyang and Sian were used as the centers from which direct telephone lines were laid, carrier telephones completed, carrier telephone equipment in the country gradually readjusted and increased to form communication lines in the form of a spoke. The entire construction was completed in early 1944 and marked the first time of a long-distance central system.

All in all, in terms of the progress in operations, a total of 200,092,708 words were transmitted in domestic telegraph in 1936. By 1943, the wordage was increased to 359,745,902. In 1936, 2,780,713 calls were made in domestic long-distance telephone. The number was increased to 5,466,376 by 1944.

c. International telephone and telegraph: In 1928, the International Radio-Telegraph Station was established in Shanghai to handle international telegraph. Communications were established with Manila and Hong Kong in 1929, with the United States (San Francisco) and Batavia in 1930, with Germany, France and Saigon in 1931, with Japan and England in 1934, with Rome in 1935 and with Soviet Russia (Khabarovsk) in 1937. Meanwhile, Tientsin, Amoy, Kunming and Canton could communicate with a number of places abroad to relieve the load on the Shanghai area. By the time the War of Resistance broke out, the International Telegraph Station was first established in Chengtu in the rear area and was later moved to Chungking. Since then, Chungking communicated with foreign conntries. In 1936, radio-telephone service was established with Japan and in 1937 with the United States.

5. Establishment of Army postal service: When the full-scale war broke out in 1937, the Army postal service was established, under the General Postal Administration. Personnel were transferred from post offices and were given special training. The expenses and facilities were provided by the post offices. Military post offices were established in major units, and military mail collecting offices in important military communications junctions. A number of military general inspection sections were established near the frontline areas augmented with personnel having received postal training to increase the efficiency of the original post offices with due consideration of the division and requirements of the various postal areas and the war areas. Under the direction of the directors of the postal administrations concerned, each general section was divided into a number of sub-sections for supervision. The military and ordinary post offices should give priority to military mails (official and personal). In addition, military stamps, reduced postage mails, and free remittances were some of the preferential treatments. Later, work was developed. At divisions or higher units, military post offices or sub-offices were organized. At regimental level or below army postal service liaison stations were attached as far as India, Burma and Indo-China. According to the statistics compiled by the end of August, 1945, there were altogether 13 general inspection sections, 12 military mail collecting offices, 292 army post offices, 173 army sub-post offices, 2,035 part-time army post offices, 223 army postal service liaison stations and 2,679 military post office employees.

Section 4. Wartime Finance and Currency

Wartime Financial Measures

For a long time, China's currency had been confusing. Although there had been talks of currency reform since the end of the Ching Dynasty, it was never implemented. In the few years since the Manchurian Incident in 1931, the world's wave of depressions hit China. Poor business transactions, declining industry and commerce, rise of the price of silver in the international market, and the exodus of silver (from July to mid-October, 1934, 200 million dollars' worth of silver drifted out of China), the currency situation was alarming. On October 15, 1934, the Ministry of Finance implemented silver export tax and also equalization charge on the export of silver. For a while these measures were effective, but they treated the symptoms instead of the disease. In order to thoroughly check the outflow of silver, consolidate currency system, stabilize currency and regulate capital, the decision was made to reform resolutely the currency system.

On November 4, 1935, a consolidated issuance measure governing the non-circulation of silver was promulgated. Beginning November 4, 1935, the banknotes issued by the Central Bank, the Bank of China and the Bank of Communications would be known as fapi (legal tender). All payment of taxes, official and private transactions would be made in fapi. No silver was allowed to be circulated. The silver of the offenders would be confiscated in order to stop the outflow of silver. Those who purposely hid their silver or intended to smuggle silver out of the country would be dealt with in accordance with the laws governing the punishment if acts which endangered the Republic. The Issuance and Preparation Commission was established to take charge of the safekeeping, issuance and exchange of fapi so as to establish confidence and credit. In order to stabilize the exchange rates between the fapi and the foreign currency, the Central Bank, the Bank of China and the Bank of Communications would buy and sell unlimited amount of foreign exchange. Since the promulgation of the new measures, the nation adhered to its observance and established the fapi's credit. In 1936 and 1937, as the nation had bumper crops and increased revenues, the fapi became even better established.

As the War of Resistance broke out in 1937, military expenses multiplied. In accordance with its established policy, the Government gave equal emphasis to national reconstruction and to the war. All economic reconstructions, such as the construction of railroads, highways, telecommunications, water conservancy, mining and industries as well as the funds needed in regulating materials were successively increased. Like previous examples in wartime finance, equal emphasis was placed on increase of revenues and floating of bonds in order to fill the gaps. However, customs duty, salt tax and consolidated tax formed the major portions of China's revenue from taxation. With the war continuing, most of China's ports along the coast and the rivers and major cities fell into enemy hands. As a result, all three of the taxes were lost. Based on the aboved-stated principle of equal emphasis on increase of revenues and floating of bonds, the financial authorities consolidated revenues by creating taxes and instituting monopolies to compensate the losses of old taxes and by consolidating bonds and funds on the one hand and by readjusting old debts to remedy the losses in the expenditures and incomes of the national treasury on the other hand. Meanwhile, efforts were made to step up collections and contributions. Some of the major measures are stated as follows:

1. Revamping revenues from taxation and promotion of Government monopoly:

In 1936, the Ministry of Finance began the levy of income tax and in 1937, excess profit and inheritance tax. Although short in history, the new system of direct taxation was established and revenues greatly increased. In 1942, the Ministry of Finance further improved the income and expenditure system, took over the business tax from the various provinces for consolidated taxation and abolished the animal tax in the northwestern provinces.   The adoption of the ad valorem rates replaced the commodity tax and raised the tax on luxuries and reduced the tax on daily necessities (the tax on such daily necessities as flour and cotton yarn was reduced).   Twice in a year, the rates of taxable items were carefully itemized as the basis for taxation.   The new measure went into effect in September, 1941 and was revised on March 1 and July 1, 1942.   Apart from taxation of tea products in the consolidated tax, leather, furs, bamboo, timber, earthenware and foil paper were also included.   Beginning March, 1943, taxation of the above products took effect in the production areas throughout the nation.   In 1943, in an effort to better control materials and prices of commodities, cotton yarn and flour were taxed in kind.   Beginning October 1, the Supreme National Defense Council resolved to levy salt surtax.   Subsequent to the abolition of salt monopoly, the salt tax was readjusted.   In 1945, a total of $1,323,289,019 was received showing rapid increase in tax revenue receipt.

The first thing in wartime economy is materials.   In 1941, the Ministry of Finance temporarily placed all the land taxes of the various provinces under the Central Government and began preparations for taxation in kind.   Meanwhile, in August of the year, land tax organizations at various levels were established.   In September, the taxation began.   Other than the seven provinces of Liaoning, Kirin, Heilungkiang, Jehol, Hopei, Chahar and Sinkiang for which the taxation in kind was deferred, 21 provinces totalling 1, 200 hsiens were taxed in kind. By early November, 1942, the actual collection from taxation in kind and in fapi exceeded the original estimates by 7% which, was totally different from 70-80% collection of previous years.   In 1942, the collection of land tax in kind and the purchase of grains were handled by the Ministry of Finance and the Ministry of Food for approval of the President and later for actions by the land tax organizations at the various levels.   Additionally, taxation of food in kind for Government workers and teachers was also handled by the same organizations in order to simplify the procedures.   The total receipts from taxation in kind and from purchase of grain far exceeded that of 1941.

Since the outbreak of the war and in an effort to regulate the supply of materials, the various provinces levied interport duty on goods being transported resulting in overlapping levy of tax and the forming of economic barriers between provinces.   Thus, the movement of goods was delayed and prices affected.   A review by the provincial representatives to the third National Financial Conference decided to abolish the former goods sales tax, special tax, salary administrative fees and all taxes in the nature of interport duty.   The wartime consumption tax was instituted by the Ministry of Finance as a substitute for the interport duty. The drafted regulations for this tax were promulgated on April 1, 1942 and were enforced on April 15.   19 kinds of goods including cotton, raw silk, and Chinese linen were to be taxed.   In 1943, the kinds of goods to be taxed were increased, and the regulations went into effect on May 11.

While paying attention to the collection of taxes and regulating supply and demand, the Ministry of Finance took steps to stop hoarding and made plans for the institution of monopoly to increase revenues and to control commodity prices. Initially, rolled tobacco, sugar, matches, wine, tea and salt were placed under monopoly on a trial basis to establish a wartime economic policy and to lay the foundation for sound postwar finance stated in the Principle of Livelihood. Accordingly, the National Monopoly Enterprises Planning Committee was established. Later, the wartime monopoly policy, as formulated at the Eighth Plenary Session of the Central Executive Committee of the Kuomintang, placed under Government monopoly sugar, salt, tobacco and matches and made provisions to check the commodity prices. The profits yielded from the monopoly contributed materially to the wartime finance. Between 1944 and 1945, the revenue system gradually returned to normal. By February, 1945, all the monopoly organizations were abolished.

2.   Arranging domestic and foreign loans and revamping provincial bonds:

In wartime, arranging loans from a third nation to exchange materials for meeting operational requirement could relieve the burden on the people on the one hand and reduce the expenditures of National Treasury on the other. Since the outbreak of the War of Resistance, China's barter loan, credit loan and currency loan with the United States, Britain and Russia all met her wartime requirements. As tension mounted in the Pacific, the United States provided materials needed in operations from the Lend Lease Act and contributed greatly to China's war effort. When war broke out between the United States and Japan, an alliance was formed between the United States, China and Britain. The United States loaned US$500,000,000 to China, and Britain loaned £50,000,000. The U.S. loan which required no interest, no guarantee and no repayment date was unprecedented in China's history of foreign debt. Apart from US$200,000,000 which was used as funds for Allied Victory Loan and American Gold Loan, the remainder was used as reserves in the issuance of fapi. In June, 1942, the Lend Lease Agreement was signed with the United States to purchase the badly needed materials. Later, gold was made available in the U.S. loan as a measure to stabilize the fapi. On the eve of the V-J Day, currency values and commodity prices were under effective control.

Since the outbreak of the war, China issued short-term treasury notes amounting to $500,000,000. Subsequently, in September, 1937, National Liberty Bonds totalling $500,000,000 and Gold Loans of $550,000,000 were floated. In July, 1938, the Relief Loan of $30,000,000 was issued. In August, 1939, the Reconstruction Loan of $600,000,000 was floated. In October, 1939, the Military Supplies Loan of $600,000,000 was issued. In May and November, 1940, another loan of £10,000,000 and US$50,000,000, called the Reconstruction Loan, was floated. March and September, 1941 saw the floating of the new Military Supplies Loan of $1,200,000,000. In 1941, additional Reconstruction Loan and

Military Supplies Loan were issued. In 1942, when a loan was obtained from the United States, the Allied Victory Gold Loan of $100,000,000 and U.S. Gold Dollar Savings Certificates of $100,000,000 and the Allied Victory Loan of $1,-000,000,000 were floated. Meanwhile, the Wartime National Bond Subscription Commission was reorganized by the Ministry of Finance into the National Bonds Subscription Commission to promote the sale and subscription of bonds among the people. The purchase of bonds by the people was, in principle, voluntary in rural districts; however, subscription by assignment had been resorted to in urban sections. To rich merchants, land owners, professionals and house property owners, the Government assigned certain amounts of war bonds in proportion to their incomes.

In accordance with the resolution on improving the system of financial receipts and expenditures at the 8th Plenary Session of the Kuomintang 5th National Congress and the proposal to take over the provincial loans at the third National Financial Conference, the Ministry of Finance prepared measures for taking over the provincial loans for approval and implementation. The implementing procedures were divided into two phases. On the one hand, further issuance of provincial would be stopped beginning 1942, including those provincial bonds which had been approved but not yet floated. Separate actions governed those bonds which had been approved and had to be floated due to special needs. Among the bonds which had been stopped were the second payment of the 1941 Reconstruction Loan of Kiangsi Province in the amount of $15,000,000, the second payment of the Reconstruction Loan of Szechuan Province in the amount of $40,000,000 and the second payment of the 1941 Reconstruction Loan of Kansu Province in the amount of $4,000,000. By the end of 1941, all the bonds which had not yet been floated were turned over to the National Treasury for safekeeping and clearance. On the other hand, old bonds were taken over and put in order. Beginning in 1942, all the bonds should be redeemed by the National Treasury to make good the Government's credit. At the same time, personnel were dispatched to the various provinces to check and take over old bonds. The provinces from which the Ministry of Finance took over the bonds included Szechuan, Hunan, Kwangsi, Kwangtung, Chekiang, Kiangsi, Shensi, Kansu, Shansi, Honan, Hupei, Anhwei, Kiangsu, Sikang and Fukien.

3. Revising receipt and expenditure system:

At the third National Financial Conference, it was resolved to divide the system of financial receipts and expenditures into two categories; namely, the national system (inclusive of Central Government and the provinces) and the local autonomy system (with hsien as the unit). Beginning in 1942, the provincial budgets were incorporated into the national budgets. Land taxes, the main source of revenue of the provinces, were taken over by the Central Government. This revamping in financial system greatly strengthened the power of the Central Government. As the provincial finance is handled by the National Treasury, the

Central Government had the consolidated strength to tide the nation over its wartime financial difficulties.   Between the provincial government and the hsien government, the promotion of the new hsien system (clearly delineating pertinent areas between hsien and hsiang or chen) finances and the revamping of the system of financial receipts and expenditures greatly enhanced the position of the hsien.

Wartime Currency Measures

The problems in currency are indeed multitudinous.   In terms of policy, China's currency measures had always adhered to the following policy.   It is to control currency with the help of finance before guiding it onto the right track; assist economy and promote its development by means of sound currency; make use of the strength of economic development to improve finance and consolidate financial foundation.   Finance, currency and economy must be closely synchronized before they could complement each other.   Before the outbreak of the war, China instituted currency reform in 1935.   As war ensued, the Government directed the Central Bank, the Bank of China, the Bank of Communications and the Farmers' Bank of China to establish a joint board and a number of sub-boards to strengthen the nation's finances.   In September, 1939, the Outline Measures for Improving Central Financial Organizations was promulgated.   A trustee office was set up at the Joint Board with a chairman appointed by the Government who took charge of the various activities.   An account of the wartime financial measures is stated as follows:

1.   Regulating currency measures:

Shortly after the outbreak of the War of Resistance, the Government promulgated the "Measures for the Stabilization of Currency."   Immediately, the Joint Discount and Loan Boards of the Four Banks were established in twelve cities throughout the nation.   The "Measures for Discount and Loan in Interior" was promulgated to govern discharge and loans in response to the needs of industries and businesses.   Further, to enable the loans to reach the rural areas and to develop production, the "Outline Measures for Improving Local Financial Organizations" was promulgated.   In accordance with the above measures, the local financial[1] organizations might draw one-dollar notes or notes less than one dollar in denomination from the four banks paying only 20% in fapi as reserves and the remainder in notes and certificates of production enterprises.   To help the average people in maintaining their livelihood, the Farmer's Bank of China was directed to grant loans to the pawnbrokers and in conjunction with the Agricultural Bureau and the various provincial cooperative banks handled cooperative loans to the farmers.

The Ministry of Finance promoted savings by using the financial organizations.   The promotion of saving deposits in various forms on a nationwide scale has been undertaken vigorously by all Government and private banking institutions.   Donations were encouraged in order to develop people's patriotic spirit and to assist the financial organizations in absorbing cash.

2. Control of foreign exchange and stabilization of the foundation of fapi:

Shortly after China adopted fapi as the legal tender, the War of Resistance broke out. On the domestic side, capitals ran away. On the external side, the Japanese and the puppet regime attempted to absord the Chinese foreign exchange. The foreign exchange situation was abnormal. The control of foreign exchange, due to various changes, could be divided into the following four phases:

a. Phase One: Beginning in March, 1938, the enemy was making preparations for the establishment of the puppet United Reserve Bank in Peiping and Tientsin attempting to absorb our foreign exchange with the puppet banknotes. To shatter the enemy's insidious scheme, the Government promulgated six regulations governing the application and approval in the purchase of foreign exchange. The regulations placed control on the purchase of foreign exchange. The head office of the Central Bank was directed to organize a Foreign Exchange Screening Division responsible for handling the application and approval of the purchase of foreign exchange. The applications were approved or disapproved according to the merits of the individual cases. In April, 1938, the Foreign Trade Commission was directed to handle the foreign exchange for export goods in addition to promotion of foreign trade and increase of foreign exchange receipts. In accordance with the measures governing the foreign exchange for merchants to export goods, all foreign exchange from export goods must be sold to the Bank of China or the Bank of Communications according to the official rates in exchange of fapi. The Government decreed that 24 kinds of goods, later revised to 13, were required to apply for foreign exchange. However, farmers and peddlers who carried small quantities of daily necessities to Hong Kong and Macao and drawn work and embroideries to these places were permitted to dispense with application for foreign exchange. The bulk of the applications for foreign exchange was tung oil, tea, raw silk and hog bristle. Since then, the control of foreign exchange was placed on both imports and exports.

b. Phase Two: Since March, 1939, the enemy began to step up his activities against fapi by banning the circulation of fapi in northeast China. The enemy established the Hua Hsing Bank in Shanghai attempting to issue puppet banknotes (without deposits and capitals) for circulation with the fapi in the Yangtze River area so as to realize his scheme of disturbing our finances and undermining our currency. Accordingly, the Government arranged loans with Britain to control currency stabilization in the hope that international assistance would strengthen our foreign exchange reserves and foreign exchange organizations. The emergence of the Board of Foreign Exchange Stabilization Fund with the Hong Kong and Shanghai Bank and the Mercantile Bank each underwriting £5,000,000, and the Bank of China and the Bank of Communications jointly underwriting £5,000,000, as the stabilization fund contributed materially to the stabilization of China's foreign exchange and the credit of her currency.

c. Phase Three: Beginning in early June, 1939, the financial situation in Shanghai underwent drastic changes. On the one hand, as the Foreign Exchange Stabilization Board insisted on the free buying and selling of foreign exchange as a means of balancing the foreign exchange market, there were large quantities of import goods. Yet the export goods in the Japanese occupied areas were tightly controlled by the Japanese and the puppet regime, and could not meet the demand for foreign exchange. Further, as the enemy made every effort to absorb our foreign exchange, the stabilization fund was endangered. On the other hand, Shanghai had become the enemy's base in carrying out aggression. In order to meet the emergency, the Board had to revise its policy. Accordingly, the foreign exchange rates were changed on June 7 and 21. The Government put into force the following countermeasures.

(1) Changed the foreign exchange application and selling measures for exports. Upon completion of the formalities in foreign exchange application and selling, the export merchants were paid the difference between the official rates and the rates posted by the Bank of China and the Bank of Communications so as to encourage exports.

(2) Similarly import goods were required to pay the same difference plus stabilization fee so as to provide fair treatment.

(3) Luxury goods and non-essential goods were banned in order to save the expenditure of foreign exchange.

(4) In the past, applications for foreign exchange needed by the various Government organizations were reviewed directly by the Ministry of Finance and those needed by business men and civilians were reviewed by the head office of the Central Bank. In order to strengthen the reviewing procedure, all the reviewing was handled by the Foreign Exchange Review Commission of the Ministry of Finance for accurate handling and simplified procedure.

(5) The location for showing the foreign exchange rates was moved from Hong Kong to Chungking, the wartime seat of Government.

d. Phase Four: Beginning in January, 1941, the enemy was about to move to the south. Knowing that Shanghai was the financial center of China and that should the Pacific War break out, Shanghai would be endangered, the Government moved the financial market in the interior in anticipation of a worsening situation. Some of the Government's countermeasures are stated as follows:

(1) The Central Bank began selling foreign exchange periodically in Chungking in order to establish separate foreign exchange markets in the interior, provide adequate supply of proper import goods into the interior, and lessen the dependability on the Shanghai market.

(2) Arranged currency loans of US$50,000,000 from the United States, £5,000,000 from Great Britain and US$20,000,000 from Government banks to strengthen the currency stabilization fund. In addition, the former Foreign Exchange Stabilization Board was reorganized into the Stabilization Board. The

operation of the Board was improved with the development of the nation's overall economy as the major premise.

(3)   Requested the British and U.S. Governments to announce the freezing of Chinese citizens capitals abroad, so that they might be placed under the control of the Government and might not be used by the enemy.

(4)   In order to strengthen the control of foreign exchange, the existing foreign exchange organizations were readjusted, their personnel better staffed, and their authorities increased.   The Foreign Exchange and Assets Control Commission was subordinated to the Executive Yuan in order to improve the control organizations and carry out thoroughly the control policy.

From July, 1942 to 1945 the official foreign exchange rates underwent no changes, but the rise and fall of foreign exchange and gold in the market retained a certain ratio.   After V-J Day in 1945 and on August 20, U.S. dollars dropped 51% in comparison with the pre-V-J Day rates.   Later U.S. dollars went up as commodity prices were increased.

3.   Unification of banknote issuance and specialization of the Four Banks:

Unification of banknote issuance is an important part of the financial policy in modern nations.   In order that the Central Bank might accomplish its mission, it must be given the right of banknote issuance before it could control currency. In 1935, it was stipulated that the right of fapi issuance be given to the Central Bank, the Bank of China, the Bank of Communications and the Farmers' Bank of China.   In 1942, with the vesting of the right of note issuance in it, the Central Bank was enabled to concentrate the issuance of fapi.   In addition, the bank notes issued by the provincial and local banks were turned over to the Central Bank, together with their bank reserves.   The Bank of China was designated as the bank which assisted in the development of international trade; the Bank of Communications in the development of industries, communications and production enterprises; the Farmers' Bank of China in the development of agricultural production, agricultural finance, land finance and cooperative finance.   Since this revamping, the financial system was clearly delineated with each bank moving forward in its own missions.

4.   Management of banks and tightening of credits.

As the war in the Pacific broke out, international communication was stopped and the enemy tightened his blockade.   Control of currency was more important than ever, as there was a shortage of goods and commodity prices rose sharply. Accordingly, the Temporary Measures Governing the Management of Banks in the Extraordinary Period was revised and amended.   In addition to closer provisions on the drawing and payment of Bank deposit reserves, utilization of deposits, restrictions on loans, banning of banks engaging in trade, and inspection of books and accounts, regulations governing the inspection of banks were prescribed and inspectors assigned to be responsible for bank inspection.

5. Promotion of saving and enforcement of acceptance and discount measures:

Savings is a policy which should be adopted in time of war. Through the years, the Ministry of Finance had made use of financial organization to encourage savings, such as the opening of savings deposits and the sales of savings certificates. In 1942, the Government issued U.S. Gold Dollar Savings Certificates amounting to US$100,000,000 backed by a portion of the U.S. loan. In order to enforce the promotion of savings, plans were made to pay a portion of the payment in the purchase of materials as savings. It was arranged that in the purchase of foodstuffs for 1942, $500,000,000 would be paid as savings and in the purchase of salt, $100,000,000 would be paid as savings. Accordingly, the savings deposits of six banks greatly increased. In October, the total was $1,-027,000,000 and in October, 1943, it rose to $2,150,000,000. Within a period of one year, other than the savings certificates which were sold together with the payment in the purchase of materials, the total deposits were doubled, resulting in considerable effect in the absorption of uncommitted cash and in thrift. The purpose of finance is to absorb the uncommitted cash in the society and invest in productive reconstruction so as stimulate economic development. Since the outbreak of the war, the Ministry of Finance directed Szechuan Province to take charge of discount measures and loans in order to meet the requirements of agricultural, mining, industrial and business enterprises. During the period when credits were tightened, the banks were still encouraged to invest in productive reconstruction on the one hand and to continue discount measures and loans on the other in order to ensure that the capitals in the society could be channeled into production. These measures benefitted materially social and economic development.

Adjustment of Material Supply

As the outcome of modern warfare depends on the availability of materials, the adjustment of wartime materials depends on the maximum efforts of the Government. The situation both before and after the Pacific War is stated as follows:

1. Since the outbreak of the Shanghai Incident on August 13, 1937, communications were blocked, flow of goods was stopped, supply of materials was out of steps and businessmen adopted a wait-and-see attitude. While doing its best to stabilize the currency, the Government also handled discount measures and loans. Meanwhile, $60,000,000 was allocated for the establishment of three adjustment commissions for agricultural production, mining and trade as operating capital to make necessary adjustments in materials, stimulate production, and increase export. Later, due to adjustment of administrative organizations, the two commissions on agricultural production and mining became subordinated to the Ministry of Economic Affairs; however, the Trade Commission was still

under the Ministry of Finance. In order to reduce the cost of local products and promote export and increase the earning of foreign exchange, Measures Governing the Maintenance of Production and the Promotion of Export was promulgated. In adjusting the silk in stock, the freight was supplemented and the payment was made in advance. Special allowance was made for shipping silk to Hong Kong for sale. Silk merchants were given guidance in improving the quality of the local silk, production cooperative organizations were set up and loans were made to purchase new silk-making equipment. The quality of silk was improved and the organizations took over the selling of silk on a cooperative basis. With regard to the promotion of tea production, Measures Governing the Nation's Tea Production and Sales Plans and the Nation's Tea Export was formulated organizing all the tea administrative agencies of the various provinces and achieving close cooperation with the tea-producing provinces. Large-scale and well-planned production and making of tea and increased control were effected to meet barter trade and export and to stabilize the international market.

In tung oil, assistance was given to the farmers growing tung trees and to tung oil merchants establishing tung oil refineries and storage facilities. Later, the Trade Commission and the Szechuan Provincial Government worked together in the management on tung oil. All the tung oil merchants in the province organized cooperative ogranizations, set up public warehouses, published the buying prices at various places, conducted open buying and selling in order to stabilize the tung oil market and protect both the tung tree growers and tung oil merchants. In improving the production and sale of furs and wool, assistance was given to the various northwestern provinces to establish wool washing factories. Similarly, the Western China University was assisted in the manufacture and sale of wool. As to trade, the barter loan with Soviet Russia, the tung oil loan, tin loan, wolfram loan and metal loan with the United States and the export guarantee and credit loan with the United States were effected, and the prices were increased. Where possible, the local agricultural and mining products were purchased and exported in exchange for machineries and equipment necessary in our defense communications and economic reconstruction. For materials in or near the war areas, their prices were increased and their purchase stepped up to prevent them from aiding the enemy. As to the means of transportation necessary in adjusting materials, efforts were made to increase the transportation fleet.

For instance, loans were made for the purchase of cars on the Chengtu-Kunming Road, cars were allocated to the Shanghai-Kunming Highway, and transportation divisions were organized to handle large quantities of exports, balance international receipts and expenditures; and strengthen the fapi reserves. In the fall of 1940, the Trade Commission underwent a reorganization which separated its administration and operations. On the administrative side, the Trade Commission consolidated the management and integrated the Material Division of the Ministry of Finance into the Commission. Thus, the Commission was greatly strengthened in carrying out the policies and pertinent laws and regulations. As to operations, the Fu Hsing (tung oil), China Tea (tea) and Fu Hua (other materials) Companies separately handled the production, manufacture and shipping of export goods. In 1942, the Fu Hsing and Fu Hua Companies were amalgated. All export goods which were controlled were purchased and sold by the Government only, while non-controlled goods could be exported freely by province-owned and private-owned companies. However, the foreign exchange they earned must be turned over to the Government. In addition, the banning of the import of non-essential goods, control of import trade, improvement of export foreign exchange measures and payment to the merchants for the differences between the official rates and the prevailing market rates all served to stimulate interest and encourage export. If there were justifications for bringing in goods which were banned, special permits could be issued for purchase. However, efforts should be made to discourage such practice.

2. Since the outbreak of the war in the Pacific, the Government shifted to the economic strategy of seeking materials in view of the circumstances. In compliance with this policy, the Ministry of Finance prepared the following:

a. Import: All the essential goods needed in the War of Resistance and national reconstruction could be moved via routes which were open. The quantity should be increased and efforts should be made to move the goods to the interior. In one year, the military items under the Lend Lease Act and the loans from Russia which were moved overland through the northwest and the Sino-Indian air routes and the procurement from British and American loans amounted to over US$30,000,000 of which 35% was industrial equipment, 20% communications equipment, 18% aircraft equipment, 12% military equipment and 15% miscellaneous equipment giving a total tonnage of 80,000 tons. The supplies arrived successively. Additionally, arrangements were made with the United States and Britain to increase the number of aircraft and transportability to meet the demand.

b. Export: In the past, export of local products was pushed to the limit in order to earn foreign exchange. Later, in compliance with the Government's newly established policy, the needs of the military and civilians were met where possible. However, those goods which were needed by the Allies and for which there was a surplus should be moved on land or by air. Efforts should be made to purchase needed goods from the Japanese occupied areas in order to meet the demand. In 1943, the Agricultural Bureau was redesignated the Cotton Yarn Cloth Control Bureau under the Ministry of Finance to effect better distribution and control on cotton, cotton yarn and piece goods.

Economic Struggle Against the Enemy

Modern warfare is not restricted to striking the enemy militarily. In the economic field, efforts should be made to thwart the enemy attempt. A brief summary of our economic struggle against the enemy is stated as follows:

1. Embargo:

According to the statistics provided by the League of Nations, of the 73 raw materials and foodstuffs, the enemy was only self-sufficient in 20. His lack of resources could well be imagined. The enemy advanced the slogan of "fighting a war by means of war"[2] in order to obtain the necessary resources in China. In October, 1938, the Government published the "Regulations Governing the Embargo of Goods Which Would Aid the Enemy." All goods in the country which could be used to strengthen the enemy were not allowed to be moved to the enemy country, enemy colonies or places under enemy trusteeship or under enemy control. The most important items were wolfram, antimony, tin and mercury. Other items which could be exchanged for foreign exchange included tung oil, hog bristle, tea and wool.

2. Destruction of the enemy and puppet economic facilities:

Shattering the enemy's design of fighting a war by means of war required additional efforts in embargo and destruction of the enemy's economic reconstruction in the Japanese-occupied areas so that the enemy could not reap any fruitful results. Iron ore is one of major ingredients in the making of steel and iron. In 1935, the enemy's domestic production of iron ore did not exceed 500,000 tons, and he had to import 3.4 million tons from abroad of which 1.3 million tons was imported from China. Before the Government's evacuation, the iron ore mines in Ta-yeh, Hupei Province and in Tang-tu and Fan-chang, Anhwei Province were extensively destroyed in order not to aid the enemy. Originally, there were plans to operate the mines in the vicinity of Phoenix Mountain in Nanking. This mine was also destroyed before the Government's evacuation. The major light industry in Japan was cotton textile and the raw materials were imported. After the outbreak of the war, the enemy was short of foreign exchange. Consequently, it was difficult for him to buy cotton. The enemy then resorted to collecting all the cotton in North China and increased the yield to 10 million metric piculs. It no longer depended on the United States and Britain for the supply of cotton. To undermine its plans, the Government made efforts to reduce the planting of cotton and to plant crops which enemy did not need badly, such as corn and kaoliang (sorghum). Then, the Government shipped all the surplus local cotton to the rear areas where possible.

3. Checking and banning enemy goods:

In October, 1938, the Government published the "Regulations Governing the Checking and Banning of Enemy Goods." All the goods produced in factories used by the enemy or having enemy capital under the enemy control in the enemy

---

[2] After the Battle of Wuhan, the Japanese forces realized that it was difficult to subjugate China. Since several peace offensives launched by Prime Minister Fumimaro Konoye fell through and the strategy of "quick ending of the military operations" and "a swift peace to end the war" was also empty talk, the Japanese then switched to the ruse of "fighting the war to support themselves" to sustain their long-term aggression.

country and its colonies were to be checked and banned. The objectives were to prevent the enemy from obtaining fapi with the goods it sold and in exchange for the goods it needed, and to weaken the enemy's markets so that his domestic industries would develop difficulties. Since August, 1940, the enemy banned our imports. In his economic warfare against us, he intended to reduce the sources of our materials and to create difficulties among the people. In order to cope with this new situation, the Government permitted the import of such goods as foodstuffs, cotton, cotton yarn, linen, steel and iron which were badly needed in the rear areas regardless of their places of origin.

4. Thwarting enemy and puppet regime's aggression:

Since the outbreak of the war in the Pacific and subsequent to the enemy's control of Hong Kong and Shanghai the enemy did everything possible to undermine the fapi, lower the exchange rates between fapi and the puppet notes. Thus, the fapi in the Japanese-occupied areas found its way into the Government-controlled areas and the materials in the rear areas were moved out. In view of this, the Ministry of Finance worked out countermeasures. On the one hand, the restriction on taking fapi out of the Government-controlled areas was rescinded in order to effect the flow of fapi for the purchase of needed materials. On the other hand, efforts were made to increase the uses of fapi in the frontline areas in order to stabilize people's confidence in fapi. Giving special emphasis to materials in the rear area in time of war, the Ministry of Finance directed the provincial banks adjacent to the war areas to purchase materials from the Japanese-occupied areas. Plans for these materials were made in advance by the provincial banks and were submitted to the Ministry of Economic Affairs for approval. These materials were mostly daily necessities and military items. Daily necessity articles were sold as they became available. All in all, what could be done financially was adequately planned and carefully implemented in order to shatter the enemy's insidious designs and to provide ample supply of needed items in the rear areas.

CHAPTER FIVE
Cultural Warfare

Section 1. Wartime Education

Formulation of Educational Policy

China's educational policy had long been established prior to the War of Resistance against Japan. Subsequent to the establishment of the seat of government in Nanking in 1927, steps were taken to proceed with educational reconstruction so as to lay the foundation for national defense. In May of the following year, the first National Educational Conference was held at which the resolution for the realization of the Three People's Principles as the educational objective was passed. In March, 1929, the Educational Objective and Implementing Policy of the Republic of China was established. In April, it was promulgated by the National Government. The full text is as follows:

1. Educational Objective:

Based on the Three People's Principles, the education of the Republic of China is designed to improve people's living conditions, help the growth of the society, develop the people's livelihood and propagate the Chinese people. Every effort should be made to achieve national independence, civil rights and development of people's livelihood in order to promote universal harmony.

2. Implementing Policy:

In implementing the above-mentioned educational objective, the following should be observed:

a. The instruction on the Three People's Principles in schools at various levels should be interrelated with the entire curriculum and extracurricular activities. History and geography instructional materials should be used to explain the essence of nationalism; group living training should be employed to develop the principle of democracy; and practice of production labor should be employed to lay the foundation for the Principle of People's Livelihood. All in all, knowledge and virtues should be combined under the Three People's Principles in order to achieve faithfulness and pragmatism.

b. Ordinary education: It should be designed in accordance with Dr. Sun Yat-sen's teaching to indoctrinate children and youths with the national virtues of loyalty, filial piety, kindness, love, faith, righteousness, harmony and peace, train the people to acquire necessary skills and increase the people's productivity.

c. Social education must enable the people to be aware of the international situation, understand national consciousness, possess knowledge on urban and rural life, skills to improve home economy, necessary prequisites for self-rule, habits to protect public enterprises and forests, and good virtues of looking after the old, helping the poor, preventing natural disasters and rendering mutual assistance.

d.   College and special education must emphasize applied science, strengthen curriculum, cultivate special knowledge and skills, and aim at character building in order that the individuals concerned may serve the society and the nation.

e.   Normal education, as the source of mass education in practising the Three People's Principles, must consider proper science education and strict physical and mental training as its primary missions so that teachers may become morally and academically prepared for their tasks.   Where possible, efforts will be made to set up these educational institutions independently and develop rural normal education.

f.   Equal opportunity in education for men and women. Women's education should emphasize character building so that they may become good mothers and live excellent family life and social life.

g.   School education and social education should stress the development of physical education.   Students in secondary schools and colleges should be given military training.   The objective of developing physical education is to improve physical stamina of the people, with emphasis on physical exercise, and to cultivate regulated habits.

h.   Agricultural promotion should be undertaken by the responsible agency. Improvement in agricultural production methods, increase in the farmers' skills, improvement in rural organization and in the farmers' living conditions, promotion of rural scientific knowledge and the establishment of farm cooperatives should be pushed to the limit.   Additionally, contact should be maintained with the production circles in order to insure practical application.

Upon establishment of the above-mentioned objective and policy, the administrative outline took shape in conjunction with the promulgation of the Provisional Constitution in the period of Political Tutelage.   This Provisional Constitution was formulated by the National Congress in May, 1931 and was published by the National Government on 1 June.   Of the eight chapters in the Constitution, Chapter Five—National Education (a total of twelve articles from Article 47 to Article 58)—became the outline in educational administration for fifteen years (from June, 1931 to Jan. 1, 1947 when the Constitution was promulgated).   The full text of this chapter is as follows:

a.   The Three People's Principles is the basic principle of education in the Republic of China.

b.   Every citizen, regardless of sex, should have an equal opportunity to receive education.

c.   All public and private educational institutions in the country shall be subject to State supervision and amenable to the duty of carrying out the educational policies formulated by the State.

d. All children eligible for schooling shall receive elementary education. Details will be covered by law to be established.

e. All persons over school age who have not received elementary education shall receive supplementary education. Details will be covered by law to be established.

f. The Central Government and the local governments should make available the funds necessary for education. Such funds, while independent in nature, should be protected by law.

g. The State shall encourage or subsidize those private educational enterprises with a high record of achievement.

h. The State shall encourage or subsidize overseas Chinese education.

i. The State shall encourage or subsidize those who have served in educational institutions with good records and long service.

j. All public and private educational institutions should make available full or partial scholarships for students who have achieved high scholastic attainments and shown good conduct but are unable to receive further education.

k. The State shall encourage or subsidize those who have made inventions and discoveries in academic or technical knowledge.

1. The State shall protect objects of historic, cultural or artistic value.

In addition, on 15 June of the same year, the Executive Yuan promulgated the following proposal on the Trend of Educational Institutions passed by the National Congress:

a. The training and education of schools at various levels must be based on Dr. Sun Yat-sen's teaching advocating the restoration of the national spirit. The implementation of this teaching must be expedited with emphasis on cultivating the habit to withstand hardships and achieve industry and on fostering rigid and regulated life.

b. Secondary and elementary school education should take into consideration the local social conditions aiming at cultivation of the skills for independent living and the capability for increased production. Every effort should be made to help those students unable to receive further education so that they may have the ability to live independently.

c. Social education should aim at increased production. The present educational level and actual living conditions of the people should be taken into account while assisting them in production knowledge and skills.

d. Establish as many vocational schools and supplementary vocational schools as possible. The systems and curriculum in vocational education should be highly flexible and economically realistic. The State shall encourage individuals planning to establish vocational schools.

e. Establish as many as possible technical colleges having much to do with productions and people's livelihood.

    f. College education should, in principle, emphasize natural science and applied science.

    On November 23, 1935, conscious of the hardships under which the people were living and of Dr. Sun Yat-sen's advocacy of revolution to save the country, the Central Government presented ten items with regard to national reconstruction and saving the nation from disaster. Of the ten items, the following two had to do with education:

    1. Undertaking realistic studies to lay the foundation of the nation: In the midst of keen competition between nations and in order to catch up with those which are ahead, efforts should be concentrated on the areas of paramount importance. They are as follows:

    a. All the research conducted by the Academia Sinica and academic research institutions should be closely related to the nation and society so that the nation and the society may benefit from it.

    b. Establish system to encourage study, and carry out of it so that those who are talented and studious may profit from it.

    c. Promote the independence and development of science in China, giving equal emphasis to natural science and humanities, so that manpower and material power may proceed on parallel lines. Thus, the nation will remain strong and civilization permanent.

    d. Emphasize proficiency in techniques and promote the provision of technical training in order to rectify the one-sided emphasis on theories, reap the benefit of division of work and meet the pressing demand in the nation's material reconstruction.

    2. Promote education to build the nation's strength: Viewing the conditions in the nation and realizing that civilian education and military education are from the same source, they are given equal emphasis in order to meet the demand of modern nations. Some of the essentials in this regard are stated as follows:

    a. Institute the uniformed revision of text books, abolish unnecessary courses and strengthen the contents of the required courses.

    b. Compulsory education should be pushed aggressively and secondary and elementary education system revamped. Elementary schools should aim at those poor students who are financially unable to receive further education. Secondary schools bear in mind the interests of both those students who are able and unable to receive further education. All in all, students from poor families should be given opportunities to receive education and profit from the practical knowledge they acquire.

    c. Strengthen the system of normal education, promote normal education and emphasize character building and patriotic concept so as to produce well-rounded teachers.

    d. Develop women's education and cultivate kindness, fraternity, physical stamina and knowledge in the future mothers in order to save our people from destruction and lay solid foundation of the society and the nation.

e. Increase funds for education, encourage the establishment of educational foundations and exercise good care to eliminate wastes in schools at various levels.

f. Promote citizen training and emphasize military teachings and military virtues so as to cultivate the habit of group living, perfect the people's physical and mental training, train cadres in social organizations and help the nation to gain independence and freedom.

g. Promote social education and adult supplementary education. By carrying out the three in one method of educating, supporting and protecting the people, and harmonizing the political-educational relationships, the people acquire the capability to help themselves and, in turn, help the nation.

In the fall of 1937 when the full-scale war against Japan broke out, our educational policy, under the two major themes of "based on nationalism" and "centered on people's livelihood" moved ahead speedily. In order to meet the promotion of wartime educational policy, the Government drafted the Program of Resistance and Reconstruction in which the portion which concerned education is as follows:

1. Both the educational system and teaching material shall be revised. A program of wartime education shall be instituted with emphasis on the cultivation of the people's morals, and the enhancement of scientific research, and the expansion of necessary facilities shall be effected.

2. Technical personnel of all kinds shall be trained and given proper assignment in order to meet the needs of war.

3. Youths shall be given training to enable them to work in the war areas or rural districts.

4. Women shall be given training so that they may be of service to social enterprises and thereby of help to the nation's war strength.

School Education

School education was divided into elementary education, secondary education and higher education. It is briefly described as follows:

1. Elementary Education: To promote compulsory education, the Ministry of Education prepared the Implementing Measures for Short-Term Compulsory Education and the Provisional Regulations Governing the Enforcement of Compulsory Education. Due to ineffective promotion, the results were not as expected. Later in May, 1935, the Ministry of Education revised the said regulations, stipulating the division of the implementing procedure into three phases. Beginning in August of the same year, the number of children entering school steadily increased each year. By the fall of 1937 when the full-scale War of Resistance began, the education at various levels in the war-torn areas suffered greatly. This was particularly true of elementary education. Apart from directing the various provinces and municipalities to continue the promotion of compulsory

education and supervising the nation's elementary schools in complying with the disposition measures of schools in the war zones, the Ministry of Education promulgated such measures as the War Zone Children's Corps and Compulsory Supplementary Children's Classes in the elementary schools. In addition, it directed the provinces in the war zones to prepare measures for the promotion of compulsory education in the guerilla areas. Despite great hardships, the nation continued to promote compulsory education. Of the elementary schools in the nation, there were 320,080 in 1936, 229,911 in 1937, 217,394 in 1938, 218,758 in 1939, 220,213 in 1940, 224,707 in 1941, 258,283 in 1942, 273,443 in 1943, 254,377 in 1944 and 269,937 in 1945. Of the school age children, there were 18,364,956 in 1936, 12,847,924 in 1937, 12,281,837 in 1938, 12,669,976 in 1939, 13,545,837 in 1940, 15,058,051 in 1941, 17,721,103 in 1942, 18,602,239 in 1943, 17,221,814 in 1944 and 21,831,898 in 1945.

In September, 1939, subsequent to the promulgation of the Organic Outline of Various Graded Units in the Hsien, the Ministry of Education sought to synchronize compulsory education-supplementary education for those who had missed schooling and the new hsien system, close political-educational relationships, and promotion of local autonomy. During the period from March to April, 1940, the Ministry successively promulgated Implementing Outline Governing Education, Regulations Governing Pao Public Schools, and Regulations Governing Facilities in Hsiang (Chen) Central School and stipulated that beginning in August, 1940, people's education would be implemented. It was hoped that in five years each pao would have a public school and each hsiang (chen) would have a central school so as to achieve universal public education. The national treasury would assist and the local governments would shoulder the responsibilities in making the required funds available. Furthermore, the fund-raising measures and award measures for the establishment of one public school in each pao and one central school in each hsiang (chen) were promulgated. The above measures were implemented. By 1943, central public school were established in Szechuan, Yunnan, Kweichow, Kwangsi, Kwangtung, Hunan, Fukien, Chekiang, Kiangsi, Shensi, Kansu, Honan, Hupei, Chungking, Anhwei, Ninghsia, Chinghai, Sikang and Sinkiang. There were 256,926 public schools and other elementary schools. As there were altogether 303,793 pao's in the various provinces and municipalities, the average was two schools in every three pao's. In five provinces, there was one school in each pao, and in seven provinces and municipalities, there was more than one school in every two pao's, and in four provinces there was one school in every two pao's. Though in very small number of provinces and municipalities in which the new system was instituted at a late date, there was one school in every three pao's. Therefore, in terms of the number of schools, the actual progress far exceeded what was scheduled in the original plan. Again, in terms of the number of children in school in 19 provinces and municipalities, 70% of all the children reaching school age were in school, and illiterates took 34%† of the total population. In 1944, promotion of education resulted in 73%− of all the school age children in school and 32%+illiterates in the entire population. In 1945, there were 66%+ of all the school age children in school and 30%+ illiterates in the population.

2. Secondary Education: Secondary education plays a most important role in the entire educational system. On the one hand, it continues the basic training in elementary training, develops the body and the mind of youths and cultivates well-rounded citizens. On the other hand, taking into consideration the interest and ability of youths, secondary education provides what they need, prepares them for study and research in higher learning and trains middle level cadres for the society. In 1932, the National Government promulgated the middle school law, the normal school law and the vocational school law. It was not until the Ministry of Education promulgated the middle school curricula, the normal school curricula and the vocational school curricula in 1935, did China have a sound foundation in her secondary education system. By the fall of 1937 when the full-scale War of Resistance broke out, efforts were made to push secondary education in order to meet the wartime situation and to align with defense and economic requirements. Major measures with regard to secondary education are stated as follows:

a. Promotion of Policy to Establish Middle Schools in Different Zones: In order to achieve balanced development in the establishment of different types of secondary schools and to coordinate with local requirements, the Ministry of Education promulgated measures governing the delineation of zones for secondary schools of various types. In accordance with transportation, population, economy and cultural conditions of the respective provinces, an overall plan was prepared dividing secondary schools into three categories, and prepared plans for implementation. By 1942, the Ministry of Education set the ratio for classes in the senior middle schools, normal schools and senior vocational schools, and the number of classes in the junior middle schools for the observance of the schools concerned. Thus, the foundation in planned education was established and the training of personnel met the actual requirements.

b. Improvement in the Curricula of Secondary Schools: In order to meet the requirements of national reconstruction in the War of Resistance, the curricula of the secondary schools of various categories were consolidated and revamped. In February, 1940, the curricula and total number of class hours for senior and junior middle schools were revised and promulgated. Subsequently in 1941, the revision of all secondary school curricula was completed.

c. Improvement in Instruction and Character Guidance: As text books are the direct tools used in instruction, they have an important bearing on educational effects. Among them, civics, Chinese, history and geography have a great impact on the thinking of youths. Beginning in 1940, the Ministry of Education organized a Text Books Editing Committee to do the editing. As compilation and review of the above-mentioned text books were completed, they were put to print.

Subsequently, other text books were edited. As to character guidance, students in senior middle schools were given military training, while students in junior middle schools were given scout training. Positions for teachers responsible for character guidance were filled by qualified personnel. Based on the nation's educational objective and the spirit of the Three People's Principles, student bodies practised self rule in schools. In 1936, the Ministry of Education promulgated Measures Governing Military Discipline for Senior Middle and Higher Schools and in 1938, the Outline Governing Tutor System in Secondary and Higher Schools (In 1944, it was revised and was known as Implementing Measures for Tutor System in Secondary Schools). Since then, all middle schools adopted tutor system in their character guidance and emphasized the students' ideological training. In the same year, the Outline governing Youth Training was promulgated. The Outline Governing Character Guidance which was promulgated in 1939 described in details the significance, objectives and implementing methods in character guidance. In March of the same year, the Ministry of Education held the Third National Education Conference in Chungking. In accepting KMT Director-General Chiang's recommendation, the conference resolved to use the characters "Propriety, righteousness, integrity and self-respect" as the motto for all schools. In May, all schools were directed to comply with the resolution. In November, 1941, to revamp the practices of schools, the Implementing Measures Governing the Cultivation of Practices in Secondary Schools was promulgated for the observance of schools concerned. In 1942, the 12-article Youth Dicta was designated as the objective for character guidance in secondary schools. As the objective for character guidance was clearly defined, its implementation was greatly facilitated.

d. Establishment of National Secondary Schools and Receiving of Youths in War Areas Having Missed Schooling: According to the delineation of authority in the nation's educational administrative system, secondary schools fall within the realm of the department of education or education bureau in the provinces and municipalities, while the Central Government had always refrained from operating national middle schools. However, as the War of Resistance broke out in 1937, secondary schools in the war areas were closed resulting in large number of students having no school to attend and evacuating to the rear areas. In order to augment the nation's strength and to meet practical requirements, the government directed the Ministry of Education to establish national secondary schools in the provinces in rear areas by the end of 1937 to receive and educate these displaced students. From the spring of 1938 to 1942, a total of 30 national middle schools, 11 national normal schools and 7 national vocational schools (excluding secondary schools affiliated with the various technical colleges and universities and secondary schools established in border provinces) were established receiving more than 50,000 students. In 1938, the Ministry of Education promulgated the Outline Curricula for National Secondary Schools which was divided into spiritual training, physical training, academic training, production labor training, special teaching and wartime rear area service training. 80% of the students were provided free boarding by the Government. Needy students were given uniforms, text books and pocket money. Beginning in 1941, in order not to have the students in the war areas travel long distances to the rear areas, the Government directed the provincial departments of education in the war areas to establish provisional middle schools or increase the number of classes in the existing schools so as to take in the youths evacuated from the war areas. All the funds required and boarding were provided by the Ministry of Education. A total of ten schools in 168 classes accommodating 8,600 students were established in Kiangsu, Honan, Anhwei, Kiangsi, Chekiang, Fukien, Hunan, Shensi and Kansu.

As V-J Day came, the nation had 5,073 secondary schools and 1,566,392 students. For the number of secondary schools and students from 1936 school year to 1945 school year, see Chart 1.

CHART 1

Statistics Showing the Number of Students in Secondary Schools
from 1936 to 1945

Year	No. of Schools	No. of Students
1936	3,264	627,246
1937	1,896	389,948
1938	1,814	477,585
1939	2,278	622,803
1940	2,606	768,533
1941	2,812	846,562
1942	3,187	1,001,734
1943	3,455	1,101,187
1944	5,745	1,163,113
1945	5,073	1,566,393

3. Higher Education: Higher education includes universities, independent colleges, technical colleges and post-graduate schools. In April, 1929, the National Government promulgated the Educational Objective and Implementing Policy of the Republic of China stipulating that college and specialized training must emphasize applied science, improve academic subjects, cultivate technical knowledge and skill and build sound character in students to serve the society and the nation. Students in universities and technical colleges should be given military training. In July of the same year, the National Government promulgated the organic laws of universities and technical colleges. By 1931, the nation had 36 national universities, 37 private universities, 20 national technical colleges and 10 private technical colleges. Most of the universities and technical colleges were concentrated in three major cities along the coast resulting in lopsided development. Subsequent to the Manchurian Incident in 1931 when Manchuria was

lost to the Japanese, the universities and colleges in Peiping and Tientsin were oppressed by the Japanese imperialists. As the full-scale War of Resistance broke out on July 6, 1937, the universities in Peiping and Tientsin were the first ones to suffer from wanton Japanese bombing. Later, the war areas expanded and the students, unwilling to live in shame in the war areas, gradually moved to the designated provinces in the rear areas. The provinces in the southwest and north-west in which higher education had not been well-developed now had a number of universities and technical colleges. In the past, there was a lack of system in the establishment of schools and departments in the educational institutions higher than technical colleges. There were instances in which redundant departments and colleges were found in the same locality. Some colleges were poorly equipped, lacked a central objective or did not meet the needs of the society. Beginning in 1938, the Ministry of Education carefully reviewed the existing situation and consolidated these departments and schools. Those which were poorly equipped were eliminated. In addition, newly established departments were required to have the necessary faculty and facilities and to emphasize balanced development. Through the years, as close supervision was exercised, the establishment of various departmental became adequate. Additionally, the National Treasury appropriated large sums of money to increase the number of classes each year. In the spring of 1939, 2-year courses in mechanics, mining, telecommunications, laboratory tests, automotive engineering, animal husbandry, veterinary, agriculture, economics, sanitation, engineering, silkworm farming, accounting and statistics were established. Since the autumn of 1940, 25 classes were set up to train per-sonnel in mechanical engineering and electrical engineering. As to the institution of the new technical school system the Ministry of Education gave the matter careful consideration. Formerly, the regulations prescribed that technical schools would admit senior middle school graduates or students with equivalent academic standing for a period of 2-3 years. Such regulations were adhered to for a number of years. However, the technical schools felt that the duration was too short making it difficult to train students to become proficient in special skills. At the Third National Education Conference in 1939, a resolution was passed advocating the institution of a 5-year course in arts and music by admitting junior middle school graduates. As to whether or not the same should be applied to the other courses, it was felt that the decision be made after the Ministry of Education had invited specialists and held discussions with them. Subsequently, the decision was reached to begin the 5-year courses in music, arts, veterinary medicine and agricul-ture in 1939. Later, the duration of medical college course which had been 5 years and had had difficulties in finding students was changed to a 6-year course in 1941 by admitting junior middle school graduates. Beginning in 1941, the Kiangsi Provincial Medical College instituted the 6-year course.

In order to meet the wartime special requirements, the Ministry of Educa-tion instituted a number of temporary measures. For example, it promulgated the

Regulations Governing Normal Colleges in order to turn out well-rounded teachers for secondary schools. In January, 1939, the Outline Measures Governing Various Technical Courses was promulgated in order to produce technical personnel. In September, 1939, the Outline Measures Governing College Preparatory Classes was promulgated. It stipulated that the Ministry of Education should provide preparatory college training to those who failed the consolidated college entrance examination but whose grades were close to passing. In July, 1939, the Ministry promulgated the Measures Governing the Establishment of Temporary Political Colleges in the Guerilla Areas and in the Provinces near the Frontlines which gave permission for the establishment to meet the local requirements. These colleges were designed to propagate the Three People's Principles by taking in youths in the guerrilla areas and in areas near the frontlines. These youths were given adequate training so as to prepare them for work in the War of Resistance and in national reconstruction as cadres. In December, 1940, the Ministry of Education prepared the Supplementary Measures Governing the Establishment of Temporary Political Colleges specifying the locations, students to be admitted, service and payment.

The development of higher education included the establishment of academic screening institutions, reviewing of educational qualifications, publication of college curriculum, conduct of consolidated and joint college entrance examination, formulation of loan and government-financed schooling systems and the institution of scholarships. However, in terms of the number of technical and higher colleges there were 103 in 1932, 108 in 1936, 91 in 1937. Beginning in 1938, the number was increased each year. In 1941, there were 129. By V-J Day in 1945, the number rose to 141. In terms of the number of students, there were 31,188 in 1937 and 83,498 in 1945. The increase is evidence of the development of higher education during the war. For the number of students, graduates and schools of higher education, see Chart 2.

CHART 2

Statistics Showing the Number of Students and Graduates in Schools of Higher Education from 1936 to 1945

Year	No. of Schools	No. of Students	No. of Graduates
1936	108	41,922	9,154
1937	91	31,188	5,137
1938	97	36,110	5,085
1939	101	44,422	5,622
1940	113	52,376	7,710
1941	129	59,457	8,035
1942	131	64,097	9,056
1943	133	73,669	10,514
1944	145	78,909	12,078
1945	141	83,498	14,463

Social Education

In 1929, the Ministry of Education made it known that the nation's educational objective was the Three People's Principles and that its implementing policy was social education which "must enable the people to possess knowledge on urban and rural life, skills to improve home economy, necessary pre-requisites for self-rule, habits to protect public enterprises and forests, and good virtues of looking after the old, helping the poor, preventing natural disasters and rendering mutual assistance." At the Second National Education Conference in 1930, resolutions were passed to eliminate illiteracy, cultivate productivity, emphasize civic training and foster national independence as the guidelines in social education. By May, 1931, the National Convention discussed and passed the proposal on the Trend of Educational Facilities. "Increase production" was taken as the central objective in social education. Provisions were made to improve the production skills of the people taking into consideration the people's present educational levels and their actual living conditions. In September of the same year, the Central Government prepared the Implementing Principles in the Education on the Three People's Principles. On social education, the five following objectives were set:

1. Increase the people's knowledge so that they may possess knowledge on urban and rural life.

2. Increase the people's vocational skills so that they may improve home economy, and increase productivity.

3. Train the people to familiarize themselves with the four powers so that they may practice autonomy and be imbued with such virtues as loyalty, filial piety, kindness, love, faith, righteousness, harmony and peace and practice the Three People's Principles.

4. Emphasize physical education and public recreation so that the people may improve in body and mind.

5. Cultivate cadres in social education in order to develop social education enterprises.

Based on the five objectives above, three implementing outlines were made in the following activities: (1) Public schools, (2) Parks, movie and theaters, (3) Libraries, museums, newspaper reading services. In 1933, the Mass Education Specialists' Conference was convened and passed resolutions on the five proposals pertaining to mass education during national crisis. It was felt that mass education should emphasize the following eight points.

1. Culture the spirit of hatred against the enemy.

2. Work up the courage of independence and self-reliance.

3. Understand the responsibility in joint efforts to meet national crisis.

4. Cultivate the habit for fortitude and ability to withstand hardships.

5. Help the organizations in the ability for self-defense.

6. Acquire the physical stamina to withstand hardships.

7. Cultivate the habit to buy native products.

8. Indoctrinate the people with knowledge in national defense.

These eight points were simultaneously important items in the implementation of other social education. In the same year, the Generalissimo's Headquarters in Nanchang directed the responsible officers in the frontline areas to operate Chung Shan People's Schools. In 1934, Generalissimo Chiang initiated the New Life Movement by applying the four cardinal virtues of propriety, righteousness, integrity and self-respect in the fields of clothing, eating, housing and moving in daily life. He personally edited the Outline of New Life Movement as the guideline for the movement. As the entire nation rose in response to the movement, it became the main work in social education at the time. In 1938, the Ministry of Education prepared the "Program Governing the Implementation of Wartime Education at Various Levels." In 1939, the Third National Education Conference passed the proposal on "Greater Emphasis on Education to Meet Wartime Requirements during the Period of War of Resistance and National Reconstruction" which clearly described the missions of wartime social education. Its main contents stressed the following objectives:

(1) Awakening of nation consciousness.

(2) Stimulating sentiments in carrying on the War of Resistance.

(3) Indoctrinating knowledge on the War of Resistance.

In general social education, the emphasis was the elimination of illiterates, the promotion of word-recognition education, adult education or supplementary education. Similarly, selection of Mandarin as the national dialect in the interest of standardization was made. In June, 1928, the National Government passed a resolution on people's training listing the "rigid promotion of word-recognition movement" as one of the seven major endeavors. In 1929, the Ministry of Education published the Outline Measures for People's Schools and the Outline Plan for Propaganda to Promote Word-Recognition Movement." According to the statistics of the Ministry of Education, there were 6,708 people's schools in the nation in 1928 and 38,565 people's schools in 1934, while there were 257 supplementary schools in 1928 and 2,184 supplementary schools in 1936. As regards to consolidated organizations in social education, the Central Government and the various provinces and municipalities set up 185 people's education agencies in 1928 and 1,600 in 1936. In 1928, there were 14 museums and in 1936 there were more than 80 museums. There were 896 libraries in 1928 and 1,632 in 1936. The number of art galleries was 53 in 1936. The number of theaters rose from 40 in 1928 to 1,083 in 1933. In radio broadcasting, upon completion of installation of hi-power equipment in 1932, the Central Broadcasting Station began broadcasting education and achieved great results.

As the War of Resistance broke out in 1937, the Chinese people found themselves facing a challenge which could mean life or death. Hence, raising the educational level of the people, cultivating strength in production reconstruction and developing national spirit and virtues were primary conditions in overcoming the enemy to achieve victory.

In March, 1938 and May, 1945, important decisions were made by the Central Government with regard to social education. Top on the list was the elimination of illiterates. Earlier in 1936, the Ministry of Education made a 6-year plan to wipe out illiteracy and prepared the Program Governing the Implementation of Supplementary Education to Adults Who Had Missed Schooling. It was estimated that there were 320 million illiterates in the nation. The number of people below the age of 45 who had missed schooling stood at 200 million. According to the above program, illiteracy would be wiped out by 1942. Later, as the War of Resistance broke out and subsequently the coastal provinces fell into enemy hands, the program was only effective in the interior provinces. In March, 1940, the Ministry of Education published the Implementing Outline of People's Education stipulating that each hsiang (chen) should establish a central public school and that each pao should establish a public school. It also specified that each school should be divided into a department for children's education and a department for adult supplementary education. The latter was further divided into adult class and women's class combining compulsory education and supplementary education. Thus, children, youths, women and adults found themselves in the same schools but in different classes. Later, Measures Governing the Institution of Adult Supplementary Education by the Various Schools for Those Who Had Missed Schooling, Measures Governing the Establishment of People's Schools by Various Organizations, and the Word-Recognition Education for Adults Who Had Missed Schooling were successively published. In 1942, the Ministry of Education designated 18 national educational institutions in the vicinity of the nation's wartime capital to operate affiliated supplementary schools in the summer. In 1943, it directed all the schools at various levels and people's education agencies to consider the operation of supplementary schools as their main task. Subsequently, Regulations Governing Supplementary Schools was promulgated dividing supplementary schools into ordinary and vocational types with each subdivided into elementary, intermediate and advanced sections. The number of such schools rose from 408 in 1938 to 2,840 in 1942, In 1945, despite financial difficulties, there were still 916 supplementary schools. During the period from 1937 to 1945, a total of 69,887,323 illiterates were wiped out.

Other activities in social education are stated as follows:

1. Art Education: As drama, music and arts inspire people the most, they are the most effective tools in promoting social education.

a. Drama Education: Apart from the drama education in the armed forces which was handled by the Board of Political Training of the National Military Council, civilian drama education was taken up by the Department of Social Education in the Ministry of Education. The National School of Drama was renamed the College of Drama. In addition, the National College of Musical

Drama and the Department of Drama of National College of Social Education were established. In 1938, a play editing section was organized to review, edit and collect new and old scripts. On the one hand. the 1st, 2nd and 3rd Circuit Drama Educational Teams were successively organized. The 4th Circuit Drama Educational Team was organized in 1939, and the Experimental Drama Educational Team in 1941. These teams were actively touring Kiangsu, Chekiang, Fukien, Kiangsi, Hunan, Kwangsi, Kwangtung, Hupei, Yunnan, Kweichow, Szechuan, Sikang, Shensi, Ninghsia, Chinghai and Kansu Provinces. In 1943, efforts were made to consolidate the 1st and 2nd Circuit Drama Educational Teams into the Ministry of Education Circuit Drama Educational Team operating along the highways in the southeastern part of the country. The 3rd Circuit Drama Educational Team was integrated into the Social Educational Team operating along the Szechuan-Sikang Highway. The 4th Circuit, Drama Educational Team was integrated into the Social Educational Team operating along the northwest highways. Apart from the above, there were the Experimental Drama Troupe of the Ministry of Propaganda, the Central Youth Drama Club of the Three People's Principles Youth Corps and ten troupes of the Board of Political Training which toured many important cities giving performance for a total of over 10 million people. Their efforts greatly helped the propaganda work in the War of Resistance.

b. Musical Education: The Ministry of Education organized the Musical Education Committee to be responsible for the promotion of musical education. Among the music schools, three were national and one was provincial. 21 music departments and 4 orientation or training classes were established by the various universities and schools. Additionally, there were four orchestras and choruses including the China Symphony Orchestra and the Experimental Circuit Chorus. There were also hundreds of magazines, musical compositions, music writings published. Group singing and performances by accomplished musicians aroused the interest of many people in the society.

c. Art Education: In 1940, the Ministry of Education organized the Committee on Education in Fine Arts. In the autumn of the year, the Art Objects Inspection Team was organized and went to the northwest via Sian, Lanchow, Hsining, Changyi, Tunhuang and Laprang to study ancient art objects and famous relics. The trip which lasted several years and covered thousands of miles was most fruitful. In 1942, the Tunhuang art treasures were transported to Chungking for display. Over 20,000 people saw the exhibition. In December, 1942, the Third National Arts Exhibition was held in Chungking. Of the 1,668 pieces of art objects submitted, only 663 pieces were displayed after screening. In 1943, preparations were under way for the establishment of the National Central Museum of Fine Arts. In the next year, the Tunhuang Arts Institute was established. In September of the same year, as the Regulations Governing Provincial Art Gallery was promulgated, various provinces were directed to proceed with the establishment of art galleries.

All in all, the promotion of art education did much to uplift the morale of the people and the armed forces.

2. Audio-visual Education: In July, 1936, the Ministry of Education organized the Motion Picture Education Committee and the Broadcasting Education Committee which marked the inception of administrative organizations for audio-visual education in China for which the Ministry of Education spared no effort in its promotion. In August, the Ministry published "Measures Governing Implementation of Motion Picture Education in the Various Provinces and Municipalities" indicating that the provinces should delineate educational motion picture circuit showing districts. A total of 81 districts were organized throughout the nation. In October, 1938 the organization was renamed Motion Picture Education Circuit Instruction District. By November, 1940, the two committees were combined to be known as the Audio-visual Education Committee. Another branch, known as the Third Branch, was established in the Department of Social Education to be responsible for such activities. The provinces were directed to expand the original Broadcasting Education Service Departments which were redesignated Audio-visual Education Service Department. By 1943, it was renamed Audio-visual Education Assistance Department. Apart from the war zones and border provinces, such departments were organized in 18 provinces outside of the war zones. In 1944, the previous measures governing motion picture and broadcasting education were combined to be known as the Implementing Essentials in Audio-visual Education. According to the provisions of the Essentials, the implementation of audio-visual education was divided into school audio-visual education and social audio-visual education. As to the implementation, the provinces should designate "provincial audio-visual education districts" in line with the administrative supervision districts. Each provincial or municipal audio-visual education district should organize an "Audio-visual Education Circuit Team" to provide motion picture and slide showing and broadcasting in the designated district. Statistics showed that the nation had 52 such teams by the end of 1943 and 39 by April, 1945.

The instructional materials in audio-visual education can be divided into films, slides and broadcasting. These educational films were either produced locally, purchased from abroad, jointly produced or edited. Prior to 1942, the Ministry of Education produced 4 films including "Our Capital." Since 1942 with the establishment of the China Educational Motion Pictures Production Corp., over 40 short-length educational films were produced. As to educational slides, 8 stories totalling 14 reels and including the story of "Wen Tien-hsiang" were completed. Later, the China Educational Motion Pictures Production Corp. completed 8 slide stories including "Sinkiang". Beginning on Double Ten, 1935, the Ministry of Education asked experts to write articles for broadcasting by the Central Broadcasting Station. Prior to 1937, such broadcasts were directed toward the general public and middle school students. During the first phase of the War of Resistance, the broadcasts were divided into three categories with each aiming at a different group, i.e., college students and intellectuals, youths who had missed schooling, and general public. Beginning in 1940, they were changed to youth forum, educational news and civic education. Again in 1942, they were revised into 20 topics such as Mandarin education, musical education, children's education, youth education, war area education, and border education. In 1944, they were all grouped under "Education Talk." In 1945, the entire project was turned over to the Central People's Education Agency.

As to the training of personnel in audio-visual education, a total of 5 audio-visual education personnel training classes were operated from 1936 to V-J Day. In 1943, one class in training personnel in motion picture art, and six classes of technical courses in audio-visual education were jointly operated with the Nanking University. In 1941, the National College of Social Education was directed to add special courses in audio-visual education. Later in September, 1944, the National Audio-visual Education Technical College was established.

3. Science Education: As China's science education had always lagged behind the Ministry of Education initiated the science movement and held a national defense science exhibition in an effort to make science more popular and to expedite national defense reconstruction. Beginning in 1941, it directed the various provinces and municipalities to plan for the establishment of science halls. In February of the same year, the Regulations Governing Provincial and Municipal Science Halls was promulgated. In August, the Work Outline Governing Provincial and Municipal Science Halls was promulgated. By the end of 1942, nine such science halls had been established by the various provinces. In 1944, the Kansu Science Education Hall became subordinated to the Ministry of Education.

Border Area Education

In February, 1930, the Ministry of Education organized the Department of Mongolian-Tibetan Education to be responsible for the educational administration of Mongolia-Tibet and other border areas. During its inception, there was much to be desired in manpower and financial resources. Apart from translating and compiling a number of grade school Mandarin text books and short-term grade school and public school text books which combined Mandarin and one of the three languages—Mongolian, Tibetan and Moslem, it was difficult to proceed with the work in this field. In view of the significance of Mongolian-Tibetan education, the Ministry of Education decided to allocate a portion of the funds originally set aside by the Central Government to subsidize the financially stringent border provinces for assistance in initiating border education. The money was jointly allocated by the department and the Department of Elementary Education. The border provinces were directed to prepare plans for the promotion of border education. This marked the beginning of border education. In October of the same year, the Ministry of Education felt that there was need to make on-the-spot inspections in order to understand the actual requirements as references for future promotion and improvement. Meanwhile, a number of local princes and tribal chiefs felt differently and needed persuasion. Responsible officials of the Department of Mongolian-Tibetan Education were dispatched to Chahar, Suiyuan and Ninghsia for an inspection. Upon their return to the Ministry in the following year, they proceeded to make plans for the promotion of Mongolian Banner education in Chahar, Suiyuan and Ninghsia as well as the plans for the establishment of National Suiyuan Mongolian Banner Normal School, which were promulgated for implementation.

In 1935, based on the plans prepared by the various border provinces, the Ministry of Education continued to subsidize these provinces. Apart from the special fund of $500,000, another $200,000 was made available from the Sino-British, Sino-U.S., and Sino-Belgian indemnities for compulsory education. 15 provinces including Chahar, Suiyuan, Ninghsia, Kansu, Chinghai, Sinkiang, Shensi, Szechuan, Sikang, Tibet, Hunan, Kweichow, Yunnan, Kwangsi and Kwangtung were subsidized. With the exception of Kwangtung and Shensi which did not establish border schools, the border educational institutions established by the various provinces are as follows:

1. Schools:

Kansu-One Mongolian-Tibetan-Moslem Teachers' Training Class affiliated with the Langchow Rural Normal School and 55 Mongolian-Tibetan-Moslem primary schools.

Chinghai-1 Hsining Mongolian-Tibetan Normal School, 2 middle schools, and 143 Mongolian-Tibetan-Moslem primary schools.

Ninghsia-2 Mongolian Banner normal classes operated by the Provincial Normal School and 14 Mongolian-Moslem primary schools.

Suiyuan-1 Mongolian Banner middle school and 29 Mongolian Banner primary schools.

Chahar-1 Mongolian Banner normal class affiliated to the Provincial Normal School and 13 Mongolian Banner primary schools.

Sinkiang-5 Mongolian-Moslem normal classes affiliated with the Provincial Tihua Normal School, 1 A-ke-su Normal School, 1,412 Mongolian-Moslem primary schools.

Szechuan-Provincial Pingshan and Mao Hsien Normal Schools and 15 border primary schools.

Sikang-Provincial Kangting Normal School and 5 provincial primary schools.

Yunnan-3 provincial border normal schools, and 35 border primary schools.

Kweichow-Provincial Kweiyang Rural Normal School and 12 border primary schools.

Hunan-Provincial Western Hunan Special District Teachers' Training Class and 100 short term primary schools.

Kwangsi-Provincial Special Teachers' Training School and 541 border primary schools.

Tibet-Lhasa Municipal First Primary School.

There were totally 11 normal schools and 9 classes, 3 middle schools, 3,374 primary schools.

2. Social Education:

Ninghsia Provincial Mongolian Banner Education Circuit Team.

Laprang Tibetan Cultural Promotion Association Circuit Instruction Team.

Mongolian Cultural Hall.

Chahar Provincial Second Circuit Social Education Hall.

Chahar 12-Banner Associated Mongolian Translation and Compilation Office.

Of the above mentioned border educational institutions, apart from a small number which were operated by the various provinces, most were subsidized by the Central Government. Based on the reports of the various provinces and taking into consideration the actual requirements of the border areas, the Ministry of Education published the "Promotion of Mongolian-Tibetan-Moslem-Miao Educational Program" in the spring of 1935. In the following year, the National Suiyuan Mongolian Banner Normal School was established. Steps were taken to compile and print Chinese-Mongolian, Chinese-Tibetan, and Chinese-Moslem primary school text books as instructional materials for the bordar primary schools.

As the War of Resistance broke out, the need to develop the border areas and to consolidate national defense preparations was most pressing. As the Government moved to the west, a number of border schools which were affected by war had to be closed. In May, 1939, the Ministry of Education promulgated "Temporary Measures Governing the Implementation of Mongolian Banner Education" to meet the existing situation. Mongolian Banner education was divided into the following:

a. In Japanese-occupied areas, pay attention to the removal and disposition of various schools, registration of faculty members and students, and relief.

b. In war areas and in places which were near the war areas, make every effort to maintain the school and conduct people's education to assist the war effort.

c. Establishment of schools in the rear areas, promotion of social education and training of teachers.

Supplementary measures were incapable of coping with the turbulent situation. In an effort to concentrate manpower and financial resources for massive development of border education, the Ministry of Education decided to take direct charge of the border schools in the interest of promotion and demonstration. In view of the significance of improving border culture and assisting the war effort. the Central Ministry of Organization, Central Political Institute, and Sino-British

Board of Trustee of the British Boxer Indemnity successively set up schools in the border areas. Gradually, educational institutions in the border areas took shape. During the War of Resistance, the following organizations were directly under the supervision of the Central Government:

3 technical colleges (National Border College, National Sea Frontier College and Oriental Language College).

12 normal schools (National Southwestern, Kweichow, Hsining, Kangting, Northwestern, Tali, Suchow, Suining, Lichiang, Pa-an, Chengta, and Lungtung Normal Schools).

3 middle schools (National Yimong, Huangchuan and Ho-hsi Middle Schools).

7 vocational schools (National Ninghsia, Chinghai, Laprang, Sungpan, Sikang, Chinchiang and Chinghsi Vocational Schools).

23 primary schools (Lhasa, Triangle City, Kweita, Tingyuanying, Anlung, Yuehsui, Tunhuang, Tehkeh, Tsaidam, Jasag Banner, Octo Banner, Dalat Banner, Kolo, Yushu, Jashlump, Jauggin Hoshu Banner, Ordos J.G.E. Banner, Ketsinah Banner, Ordos J.G.D. Banner, Muli, Hsikung Banner, Ushen Banner and Liang-shan).

Promotion of border education: The National Government successively promulgated the Implementing Regulations on Education in Three People's Principles (Chapter 6 Mongolian-Tibetan Education) in 1931. Program Governing the Promotion of Border Education passed by the Third National Educational Conference in 1939 and the Implementing Outline in Education and Personnel Administration in 1941. Although the three programs differed, they aimed to increase and popularize the education and culture of the people living in border areas, meet the environment of the localities in which various people resided, honor their freedom of belief, retain the original good customs, habits, languages, and written languages, cultivate national consciousness in order to achieve harmony and unification in the nation's culture. The objectives and the procedures in the promotion can be summarized as follows:

a. In compliance with the border education policy, formulate implementation program as the yardstick in promoting border education.

b. Improve the administrative organization of border education and complete the administrative triumvirate system to expedite border education.

(1) Establishment of planning organization.

(2) Research.

(3) Execution of evaluation work.

c. Emphasize investigating research in order to thoroughly understand the border situation and the requirement as a basis in the promotion of border education.

(1) Investigations.

(a) Southwestern Border Education Investigating Team.

(b) College Students Summer Border Service Corps.

(2) Research.

(a) Subsidizing private research.

(b) Subsidizing group research.

(c) Subsidizing various colleges to set up courses, lectures and departments on border reconstruction.

(d) Establishing research organizations.

d. Making available funds to seek the development of border education.

(1) Subsidy to border provinces.

(2) Border education funds.

(3) Funds for border area schools operated by the Ministry of Education.

(4) Specially allocated funds and other subsidies.

e. Train teachers and increase their salaries in order to meet the requirements in border area education.

f. Emphasize production training to improve the living condition of the people.

(1) Production training of the various border schools.

(2) Vocational education.

g. Edit and print instructional materials and reading materials to increase teaching efficiency and to strengthen cultural interflow.

h. Coordinate with sanitation work to improve the health of people living in border areas.

i. Extend privileges to border area students and encourage border area youths to pursue advanced studies.

j. Respect freedom of belief and the traditional culture of the border area people in order to achieve harmony in feelings.

No effort was spared by the Ministry of Education in conducting border education which also strengthened national defense during the entire period of the War of Resistance.

Boy Scout Training and Military Training

1. Scout Training:

Scout training was originated in England and flourished in Europe and the United States. In 1912, the first scout detachment came into being at the Wen Hua College in Wuchang. Subsequently, other scout detachments were organized and made good showing.

On March 5, 1926, cognizant of the importance of scout training, the Central Government organized the China Scout Committee which became the first national scout organization to take charge of scout activities.

Upon completion of the Northward Expedition in 1928 and the unification of the country, the Central Government underwent reorganization. The KMT Scout Headquarters was established under the Ministry of Training to be responsible for training the nation's scouts. The following year, the official name of scouts was "Chinese Scouts." General Ho Ying-chin, Deputy Minister of the Ministry of Training served concurrently as commander of the Chinese scouts. On April 18, 1930, the first general inspection and jamboree of the Chinese scouts were held in Nanking. Some 3,600 boy and girl scouts representing various provinces and municipalities came to the nation's capital for the occasion which marked the first national assembly of the Chinese scouts.

In 1931, Tai Chi-tao and Ho Ying-chin made a proposal on the "Organization of the Chinese Scout Organization." The proposal was passed by the Central Executive Committee in Loyang in April, 1932. President Chiang was elected chairman, and Tai Chi-tao and Ho Ying-chin vice-chairmen. Both the chairman and the vice-chairmen were honorary titles. In addition, there was the Chinese Scout National Supervisory Committee headed by a director-general who, as concurrently minister of education, was responsible for the administration of the nation's scouts.

On November 1, 1934, the China Scout Association was established. Under the leadership of the nation's leader, its educational outline was worked out. Scout activities spread from the interior to the border areas and from inside the country to overseas.

In 1935, a scout detachment was sent to the United States for a visit. On October 10, 1936 the Second National Scout Review and Jamboree were held in Nanking. Over 11,000 scouts participated, and Generalissimo Chiang addressed the scouts who distinguished themselves in many activities. In August, 1937, two scout detachments were sent to Holland to participate in the 5th World Scouts Jamboree and the Youth Jamboree in Italy. Delegates were sent to the International Scout Conference to seek China's admission as a member of the international scouts. In 1943, Chinese scouts came under the direction of the Three People's Principles Youth Corps.

Since its inception, Chinese scouts have striven to serve the community and have contributed greatly to the nation. For instance, in 1931 when 16 provinces suffered from serious floods, many people were homeless and starved. The nation's charity-minded scouts took an active part in the famine relief and solicited donations. When the Shanghai Incident broke out on January 28, 1932, the Shanghai Scout War Area Service Corps rendered its service both in the frontline and rear areas by evacuating refugees, rescuing wounded soldiers and undertaking communications, transportation and troop-comforting activities. Four scouts, Lo Yun-hsiang, Pao Cheng-wu, Mao Cheng-hsiang and Ying Wen-ta, went deep into the battlefield to evacuate refugees and gave their lives to the country. Despite personal danger, other scouts continued to serve in the frontline areas. Their bravery and fortitude wrote a most glorious page in the history of the Chinese scouts. In 1933, the scouts of Shanghai donated and solicited money to purchase a plane, the "Shanghai Scout," for presentation to the Government. The Nanking

Scouts collected more than 17,000 pieces of clothes for distribution to refugees thereby fully demonstrating the scout's spirit of pragmatism. As the War of Resistance broke out in 1937, over 300,000 boy and girl scouts rendered their service by undertaking various types of work and achieving remarkable deeds. For example, a girl scout swam across a river in the midst of heavy enemy fire to deliver a national flag to an isolated force defending the Four-Bank Warehouse in Shanghai; boy scouts rescuing refugees in Taichang were killed by the enemy; and scouts in Szechuan collected over 110,000 pieces of clothing for the soldiers. Instances like these were countless. All these indicate that Chinese youths, boys and girls, who received scout training proved themselves capable of practising such good virtues as loyalty, filial piety, kindness, faith, righteousness, harmony and peacefulness, helping mankind in general and serving the public. Where righteousness stood, they unhesitatingly gave all they had. As a result of the nation's efforts in promoting scout education, excellent achievements were scored.

2. Military Training:

China's ancient education was built on the six arts of propriety, music, archery, charioteering, writing, and mathematics which were blended with wisdom, virtues, physical fitness and beauty. Such an education was designed to produce individuals who were well-balanced culturally and militarily, in wisdom and in virtues, and in body and in mind, to enhance the stability and progress of the society. In later generations, drastic changes placed more emphasis on culture rather than on military science. Thus, the people became stagnant in morale and weak in physical stamina.

In 1927, the National Government established the nation's capital in Nanking and in the following year the May 3 Incident in Tsinan took place at a time when the Ta Hsueh Yuan (loosely translated as the Ministry of Education and Research) called the First National Education Conference in Nanking. With the sentiments of the people greatly agitated, the conference passed a resolution directing all the national and provincial educational administrative organizations to include no less than three hours each week in military science subjects for a period of two years in all schools higher than technical colleges. Similarly, emphasis was placed on physical education in all the schools below secondary schools by providing physical education subjects for three hours each week until graduation. Based on the resolution of the conference, the National Military Council prepared military education programs for schools higher than senior middle schools. The programs together with essential items in academic instruction, the schedule of military education and similar proposals made by the conferees were submitted to the conference for discussion, revision and resolution. Boys in schools higher than senior middle schools were required to take military subjects, while girls were required to study nursing. The Ta Hsueh Yuan requested the National Military Council to assign graduates of the Military Academy as instructors. In addition, students undergoing military training were required to receive more than three consecutive weeks of rigid military training in summer each year. This marked the implementation of military training in schools.

In 1929, the Ta Hsueh Yuan was renamed the Ministry of Education. Subsequently, the Ministry of Military Training was established. It was stipulated that military subjects be given three credits in each school year. A total of six credits would be given in two school years. The entire military education program was submitted through the National Militay Council to the National Government for promulgation and subsequent compliance by all secondary and higher schools throughout the nation. Since then, military training began to play an important role in the curriculum of all the secondary schools.

During the inception of military training in schools, there was a lack of experience and preparations resulting in unsatisfactory performance. By May, 1934, the Ministry of Education and the Ministry of Military Training jointly invited specialists to supplement and revise the original program dividing it into five chapters and twenty-six articles. The main contents included peacetime training, assembled training, instructional subjects, instructional hours, field exercise, medical nursing, assignment of instructors, uniforms and equipment. In August of the same year, the revised program was submitted to the National Government for promulgation and implementation. In September, these two ministries issued a Regulations of Reward and Punishment of Military Education in Senior Middle and Higher Schools. There were five chapters of fourteen articles. Again, to reinforce discipline, the Ministry of Education and the Ministry of Military Training jointly prepared the Measures Governing Military Training in Senior and Higher Schools which was promulgated for implementation. In December, 1936. The text included general, organization, uniforms, leaves, passes, classroom regulations, mess hall regulations, drill ground regulations, field regulations, duty regulations, discipline guards, dispensary regulations and annexes giving a total of 14 chapters and 98 articles. Thus, military training in schools was placed on the right track.

In the fall of 1937 when the War of Resistance broke out, the Ministry of Military Training was deactivated. Military training for students was subordinated to the Board of Political Training. In 1938, it was again subordinated to the Board of Military Training. In May, 1946, when the Ministry of National Defense was organized, military training for students was placed under it. Since the conduct of school military training in 1928 to V-J Day in 1945, responsible organizations for school military training were changed four times, pertinent regulations and laws numbered over 30 and important regulations and laws totalled 7 which were jointly prepared by the Ministry of Education and the Ministry of Military Training. Of these three were most important. In August, 1944, as the Central Government had separate programs for military training in schools higher than technical colleges, college military training was suspended. As to military training in middle schools, stepped-up demobilization after V-J Day in 1945 rendered it to a standstill.

For the number of students in schools higher than technical colleges receiving training from the time military training was officially inaugurated in 1929 to V-J Day in 1945, see Charts 3 and 4.

Youth Movement

President Chiang had said: "The nation needs revolutionary youths; youths need revolutionary education." Hence, revolution and education in youth movement are interrelated and interlocked.

Shortly after the Manchurian Incident which broke out on September 18, 1931, our three provinces in Manchuria were lost. At the time, youths throughout the nation were so aroused that they proceeded to undertake anti-Japanese activities in order to save the nation from destruction. Student organizations in various places organized student volunteer corps. Patriotic youths and intellectuals in Manchuria rallied behind the banner of the Anti-Japanese Volunteer Corps. In an effort to assist and promote this movement, the Central Government formulated "The Educational Outline of Student Volunteer Corps," and directives issued by the National Government for implementation throughout the nation. Article 1 of the outline stipulated: All students in senior middle and higher schools organize Youth Volunteer Corps and junior middle schools organize Scout Volunteer Corps to receive military training. They will take oaths to indicate their belief in the Three People's Principles, restore the Chinese people to their proper places and pledge allegiance to remove the nation's disgrace and to save the nation. They should vouch to observe the following discipline:

1. Sacrifice themselves, guard the nation and serve the country as loyal and courageous citizens.

2. Obey orders and discipline.

3. Cultivate the custom of self-rule and live group life.

4. Help other people at all times and render public service.

The Student Volunteer Corps in various provinces grew rapidly. The Student Volunteer Corps in Shanghai rendered battlefield service during the Shanghai Incident in 1932. The Student Volunteer Corps of the Chiang Huai Middle School in Anhwei Province marched long distance to support the defenders of Heilungchiang.

During this period, several anti-Japanese student organizations in the main cities made remarkable progress. Employing the provincial or municipal student associations as the basic units, they continued to consolidate and develop. According to incomplete statistics, by 1934, student associations in the nation totalled 658. As a number of them were manipulated by the Chinese Communist Youth Corps, a series of tumultuous unrest, numerous killings and deceiving traps cast an ominous shadow on the history of youth movement. Indeed, as President Chiang said: "At that time Communist leaders included Chen Tu-hsiu...Toward

CHART 3

Statistics Showing the Number of Students in Schools of Higher Education Receiving Military Training

School Year	No. of Students Receiving Military Training
1929	4,164
1930	4,583
1931	7,034
1932	7,311
1933	8,665
1934	9,622
1935	8,673
1936	9,154
1937	5,137
1938	585
1939	5,622
1940	7,710
1941	8,035
1942	9,056
1943	10,514
1944	12,078
1945	14,463
TOTAL	132,406

CHART 4

Statistics Showing the Number of Students in Secondary Schools Receiving Military Training

School Year	No. of Trainees			Total
	Senior Middle School	Normal School	Senior Vocational School	
1931	10,761	22,711	—	33,472
1932	12,240	22,450	2,988	37,678
1933	9,591	5,729	3,272	38,592
1934	13,161	9,104	4,779	27,044
1935	—	—	—	—
1936	13,270	24,162	4,447	41,879
1937	9,701	9,396	3,494	22,591
1938	10,188	10,600	3,111	23,899
1939	11,762	12,487	8,411	32,652
1940	15,279	18,964	3,438	37,681
1941	22,833	23,065	5,014	50,962
1942	31,318	22,931	8,043	62,292
1943	37,157	24,528	6,393	68,078
1944	41,667	26,808	6,612	75,087
1945	53,125	28,163	8,705	89,993
TOTAL				641,500

the youths, they regarded those receiving schooling and study as counterrevolutionary elements....Between 1931 and 1936, chaos reigned in southern Kiangsi, eastern Hunan, western Anhwei, western Honan, Szechuan and Shensi."

By 1937 when the War of Resistance broke out, China's youths entered into the second phase of the second great union. The Three People's Principles (San Min Chu I) Youth Corps was responsible for this phase. Mr. Chiang, leader of our people's revolutionary war, said: "Subsequent to the outbreak of the War of Resistance, I organized the Three People's Principles Youth Corps to meet the pressing needs of the nation's youths and to create new life in China and the sources of new momentum in the Chinese people." On Youth Day, March 29, 1938, the Central Government made the following resolution: "... Our efforts in the War of Resistances rest with our people. Among them, our youth are most valuable. The Youth Corps is organized with excellent youths of the nation who are given training to become faithful disciples of the Three People's Principles." On July 9 of the same year, the Three People's Principles Youth Corps was established in Wuhan with Generalissimo Chiang as its director. On August 1, Director Chiang was sworn in.

Under its objective of "uniting and training revolutionary youths, realizing the Three People's Principles, guarding the country and reviving the nation," Director Chiang made the following remarks on the special missions for youths in his first message to the nation's youths:

1. In accordance with the national general mobilization plan, rally the nation's youths to actively participate in wartime mobilization.

2. Conduct strict military training in order to cultivate the skills of youths in guarding the country.

3. Actively conduct political training so as to equip the people with necessary political ingredients for a modern constitutional government.

4. Make every effort to promote cultural reconstruction in order to raise the cultural level of the people.

5. Promote labor service to develop the spirit that "the objective in human life is to serve."

6. Actively cultivate production skill, emphasize scientific knowledge in order to expedite the completion of national reconstruction.

On September 31, 1939, the Central Secretariat of the Three People's Principles Youth Corps issued "Guidelines in the Work of the Sub-Corps at Various Levels" which reads as follows:

1. This Corps should enable all its members and the nation's youths to understand that it unites and trains the youths so that they may practice the Three People's Principles, guard the country, and revive the nation. It is the only youth revolutionary organization which injects new blood and new life into our youths. It is by no means a political party as the average people think.

2. In leading the nation's youths, the attitude of the Corps is one of ab-

solute justice and sincerity in order to develop the traditional spirit and virtues of our country as the guideline for the thinking and conduct of youths. Every efforts should be made to achieve self-help and to help others. Additionally, obstacles in natural environment, discriminatory thinking and childish actions should be overcome.

3.   Cadres at various level should bear in mind their responsibility which is to serve the nation's youths and people so that they may accomplish the mission of guarding the nation and striving for national recovery.

4.   As to the recruiting of Corps members, outstanding and competent young comrades should, of course, be selected; however, emphasis should be placed on the performance of the Corps in order to inspire the youths. Magnanimity should be blended with strictness.   While attempt to achieve solidarity, every effort should be made not to edge out others but to inspire them into joining the Corps voluntarily so as to achieve the Corps' ultimate objective of uniting the nation's youths.

5.   The main work of the Corps in various schools must be coordinated with the education of the schools and must have the guidance and support of the principals and teachers in order to develop the political consciousness of the youths, their physical stamina, and academic research, and to cultivate their capacity for organization and gregariousness.

6.   The theme of the Corps lies in developing the youths in schools as well as youths in the communities with emphasis on those who have production skills and vocations.   All these youths will be united in the spirit of mutual assistance and mutual requirement to form a strong force capable of accomplishing the mission of revolutionary national reconstruction.

7.   The Corps will furnish guidance on the actual situation in national reconstruction, the trend in international situation, and the intrigues of the enemy and traitors during the entire period of the War of Resistance so that youths may differentiate right from wrong and advantages from disadvantages. The Corps will assign youths to engage in work which is related to the war or national reconstruction, so as to strengthen their faith and to seek the nation's independence and freedom.

8.   The work of the Corps must be reflected in the daily life of youths.   The Corps must furnish guidance and assistance to youths in such pressing problems as employment and schooling.   In these respects, the Corps must make every effort to solve the problems.   Thus, the youths will consider the Corps their home, and the Corps will not degenerate into an ordinary office.

In November, 1940, the Corps promulgated is 35-article "Working Outline" of which the 9-article General Outline on which the spirit and the main contents hinged are given below:

1.   Develop the organization of the Corps, its organizational power by

means of training, and employ propaganda service to develop organizational effectiveness.

2.   Promote physical education, sports, military training and the New Life Movement in order to develop the bodies and the minds of youths.

3.   Promote national defense movement and science movement; organize and train technical personnel needed by the various agencies in national defense reconstruction.

4.   Promote labor service and collective production reconstruction.

5.   Develop the spirit to serve by starting with youths. Promote the welfare of youths, lead the youths and serve the people so as to increase their welfare.

6.   Strengthen youth political leadership, concentrate efforts to actively participate in national reconstruction in the War of Resistance and eliminate all the obstacles in the national revolution.

7.   Intensify the training of cadres at various levels and cultivate youth leaders.

8.   The Corps should make full use of various youth organizations in its activities.

9.   Establish supervisory systems and go to various places to promote the work of the Corps.

Under the inspiration and leadership of Director Chiang, the Three People's Principles Youth Corps established correct goals and guide lines in its struggles and concretely planned its central themes and working outlines. Its repeated efforts resulted in its valuable contributions. During the preliminary phase of the War of Resistance, its political and social influences were at a peak cultiminating in the enlistment of the educated youths into the armed forces in the final phase of the war. President Chiang had said: "I attribute our victory in the War of Resistance to the second great union of China's youths and the opening of the drive to save the nation." Indeed, he was quite right.

The organizations of the Three People's Principles Youth Corps rapidly developed in war areas, border areas, schools and overseas areas (In countries or places which had overseas Chinese youths such as Malaya, the Philippines, Dutch East Indies, Burma, Thailand, Vietnam, Canada, Cuba, Mexico, Australia, Honolulu, New Zealand, Batavia, Singapore, Penang, Malacca, Johore, Bahru, Negri Sembilan, Selangor, Perak...). As the organizations were established, various activities were stepped up. By June, 1946, the nation had 4 sub-corps, 7 direct subordinate corps and 197 branch corps. There were 84 branch corps in schools higher then technical colleges and 250 detachments in secondary schools giving a total of 1,338,507 members.

On March 29, 1943, the Corps held its First National Congress in Chungking, attended by 320 delegates and 82 central secretaries, secretary candidates, supervisor and supervisor candidates. The Congress lasted from March 29 to April 12. After candid review and critique on the report rendered by the Central

Secretariat, the Congress considered that "during the past five years which was a great period in national reconstruction and the War of Resistance, the missions of the Corps have been heavy and the environment most arduous. From its establishment to the present development, the Corps has remained firm in seeking progress. Its responsibilities in unifying youth movement and cultivating the lives of the people are heavy...The Corps organizations spread far and wide. Despite the Japanese and puppet suppressions, Corps activities continued in the occupied areas. Indeed, the foundation of the Corps has been firmly laid." The 573 proposals received by the Congress were consolidated in 24 proposals after review. The major proposals included "General Outline of the Ten Year Plan in Developing Corps Activities," "Outline Plan in Unifying the Organization and Training of the Nation's Youths," "Calling upon Youths to Reconstruct New China," "Establishment of Agency to Take Charge of Youth Activities," and "Promotion of Youth Welfare." The General Resolution of the First Plenary Meeting of the Corps' First Central Secretariat giving a resume on the above-mentioned proposals is given below:

1. Proposal—"Unifying the Organization and Training of the Nation's Youths:" This is a general policy which delegates the Corps the authority to organize and train the nation's youths in the hope that the nation's youths and adults will be organized and trained by the Corps to strengthen the organizations of the people and society and expedite the realization of our principles.

2. Proposal—"General Outline of the Ten Year Plan in Developing Corps Activities:" This proposal outlines the key areas in the Corps' work in the fields of organization, training, publicity, and social service. Objectives are established toward which all the Corps' efforts will be directed in order to accomplish the great missions.

3. Proposal—"Calling upon Youths to Reconstruct New China:" This is the general direction toward which all our efforts in leading the nation's youths will be pooled. In compliance with our National Father's "Plans for National Reconstruction" and Director Chiang's "China's Destiny," the nation's youths will be called upon to reconstruct a new China combining national defense, economy and culture into one entity.

4. Proposal—"Establishment of Agency to Take Charge of Youth Activities:" This is the central theme in the Corps' direction of its members and the nation's youths. Efforts to help youths find schooling and employment should coincide with plans for national reconstruction, and the policy of the Corps in organization and training, develop the revolutionary practices of youths, and rectify the corruptive practices in the society.

5. Proposal—"Promotion of Youth Welfare." This proposal insures that the nation's youths are developed mentally and physically in the midst of the nation's difficulties. It is designed to encourage youths in their studies, improve their physical fitness, and boost their morale so that they may help themselves

and help others and serve as the driving force in building a new China.

The above-mentioned resume reflected the ideals and aspirations of the San Min Chu I Youth Corps which gave new life to our revolutionary history. Director Chiang also stated: "The convocation of the National Congress by the Youth Corps has an important bearing on the rise or fall of our party and our nation and our people, and on the success or failure in the War of Resistance."

Subsequent to the inspiring and educational National Congress the younger generation in China fully displayed the vitality of youth and made still greater contributions to national reconstruction and war efforts.

In the winter of 1943, China entered into a most difficult period in the War of Resistance. Students of over 300 universities and middle schools including the Northern University in Santai, Szechuan Province, the National 18th Middle School, the hsien middle schools volunteered for military service. College and middle school students in areas from Chengtu to northwest Szechuan and from Chungking to southeastern Szechuan rushed to enlist in the expeditionary forces. Government workers, even monks in the World's Buddhist School, Han and Tibetan Religious School and Shihchu Monk Training Class, enlisted en masse. By Dec. 20, the various hsiens in Szechuan recorded a total of 14,000 volunteers. Chengtu alone had 8,000 volunteers and the number of volunteers in various hsiens and municipalities kept increasing. Similarly, youths in Shensi, Kansu, Hunan, Kiangsi, Kwangtung, Kwangsi and Yunnan followed suit. The drive caught on like bushfire.

On January 10, 1944, Director Chiang addressed the youths who volunteered for military service. He said: "The fact that the educated youths in the nation's schools at various levels have volunteered for military service to wipe out the past practice of physical weakness among students and have fulfilled their duties as citizens in guarding the nation is most gratifying since the War of Resistance broke out." Meanwhile, Director Chiang issued the call for "An inch of ground an inch of blood. Ten thousand youths, a force of ten thousand." This call which was both courageous and heartwarming epitomized youth movement. Students from such colleges as the Yenching University, Western China University, Fu Tan University, Nan Kai University, Central University, Szechuan University, Kwangsi University, Chung Cheng University, Social Education College, Ming Hsien College, Central Engineering College, Northwestern Technical College, National Medical College, College for the Dumb and Blind and Academy of Fine Arts enthusiastically responded. By the spring of 1945, 120,000 youths had signed up. Due to transportation difficulties, 86,000 reported in by the end of April. Later, a number of student were assigned to the expeditionary forces in India and other units. The remaining 76,000 students were organized into 9 divisions. According to the original plans, training would be completed in August, and they would take part in the counteroffensive in September to seek final victory in the War of Resistance and add luster to the glory of youths. Little did the enlisted youths realize that Japan surrendered unconditionally on August 14. Hence, the forces organized by youths did not receive the baptism of fire.

The Northward Expedition and the War of Resistance formed the second mission in the history of our national revolution. Defeat of the warlords and defeat of imperialism formed the two phases in the second union of the nation's youths. The missions in the two phases were successively accomplished in a manner befitting our history and times. The statement made by some people that "the Three People's Principles did not go to college and the San Min Chu I Youth Corps did not open its gates" indicated the high expectations people had of the Youth Corps. In reviewing the work of the Corps, it is felt that there were much to be done in youth movement.

Youth Vocational Guidance

In the past, the Ministry of Education had no agency exclusively responsible for youth schooling and vocational guidance. By the time the War of Resistance broke out in 1937, China was not adequately prepared for war. In quick succession, the war moved from Peiping-Tientsin to Shanghai, Central China and southeastern provinces including Wuhan. Educational and cultural facilities in the occupied areas were extensively damaged rendering many patriotic youths without schools to attend. The dispatch of personnel to Kaifeng, Chengchow, Chinghua and Tunhsi to hold examinations, register, take in and provide schooling and employment for youths marked the beginning of youth vocational assistance.

As time went on, the war areas increased in size, and puppet regimes were set up in the various occupied areas. In order to prevent youths from being used by the enemy, measures taken moved from passive rescue of youths to active organization and training of youths. Education in the occupied areas continued in order to keep on the struggle against the enemy and the puppet regime. Later, permission was obtained from the Executive Yuan to formulate the Implementing Program for Education in the War Areas. In 1938, 50 war area education supervising districts were delineated in Kiangsu, Chekiang, Anhwei, Honan, Hopei, Shangtung, Shansi, Chahar, Suiyuan, Peiping, Tientsin, Shanghai and Hankow. Supervising commissioners, supervisors and assistants were installed to handle youth guidance and promote war area education. Later, supervising personnel were sent to Peiping, Tientsin, Kiangsu, Shantung and Anhwei to effect close cooperation with local party, political and military organizations as well as civil organizations. They entered into the occupied areas to draw the college and middle school students who were still in school. Supplementary schools were established to admit and provide normal education for those students who had missed schooling. In addition, private and free informal schools were set up in the village strong points to substitute primary school education. By this time, educational measures in the war areas and youth guidance were on the right track progressing steadily.

In May, 1939, the Ministry of Education, in an effort to step up its activities, received the approval to formally establish the Ministry of Education War Area Education Supervising Committee. In 1940, due to war requirements, the occupied areas were again divided into 70 supervising districts. Shanghai, Peiping-Tientsin-Hopei-Chahar, Shansi-Suiyuan-Jehol and Kiangsu-Chekiang-Anhwei border districts were named War Zone Education Supervising Commissioner Districts headed by a chief supervisor and a number of supervisors. Additional funds were appropriated to step up the activities. It was only then that war area education had complete administrative organizations and mobile units to make overall planning in accordance with the changes in the war situation. The division of the above-mentioned supervising districts was made in line with the natural environment and the pre-war administrative districts. However, military changes and different environments in the war areas led to frequent adjustments. In 1941, due to military reasons and the existing situation, the four, Kiangsu-Shantung, Honan-Anhwei, Hunan-Hupei, and Fukien-Kwangtung, Supervising Commissioner Districts were added. In 1942, the number of districts was increased to 90, and in 1943, to 102. As work continued, progress was achieved.

In 1939, at the risk of their lives, youths in war areas flocked to the rear areas. With the increase in size of the war areas, the number of people was increased. Suffering from geographical difficulties, displacement, loss of schooling, unemployment and homelessness, youths found it difficult to maintain minimum living. It was found necessary to set up organizations, conduct training, comfort the displaced and look after the youths. In December of the same year, the National Military Council established in Chungking the Training Board for the Unschooled and Unemployed Youths in the War Areas, National Military Council, National Government. The Board was formally established in March of the next year. Initially, General Hsiung Pin, director of the Administrative Office, National Military Council, was concurrently chairman. Representatives of the Ministry of Education, Ministry of Interior, Ministry of War, Board of Political Training, War Area Party Political Committee, and Central Training Committee served as members of the Board. Later, as the people to be recruited were youths, it was taken over by the Central Headquarters, San Min Chu I Youth Corps.

In May, 1941, in view of the fact that most of the youths trained were students who come from the Japanese-occupied areas and that training and schooling fell within the realm of the Ministry of Education, the Central Government decided to turn over the related activities to the Ministry of Education. In September the same year, the Training Board for the Unschooled and Unemployed Youths in the War Areas was composed of a chairman, 2 vice chairmen, 5 standing members and 10 members. Education Minister Chen Li-fu served concurrently as chairman. The vice chairmen and the remaining members were filled by personnel assigned by the Ministry of Education, Central Ministry of Overseas Affairs, Central Training Committee, San Min Chu I Youth Corps, Battlefield

Party-Political Committee, Board of Military Training, and Board of Political Training. The routine work was handled by the War Area Education Steering Committee which was divided into the admission section and the management-training section, plus secretaries and clerks, filled by personnel from the War Area Education Steering Division of the Committee. In March, 1943, the Battle-field Party-Political Committee was deactivated. Responsible officials from the Ministry of War, Ministry of Economic Affairs, Ministry of Social Affairs, and Ministry of Education were invited to serve as standing members and take charge of various activities.

In compliance with the organizational regulations approved by the Executive Yuan, the Ministry of Education made the Committee an independent organization in July, 1944. The Committee consisted of admission, training and general affairs sections. The War Area Student Steering Division of the Ministry of Education War Area Education Steering Committee was integrated into the Committee. With the new organization to take charge of the nationwide training, the various activities such as the admission, management and training, schooling, employment, relief, communications and guidance of battlefield youths were consolidated.

In December of the same year, as Chu Chia-hua became the education minister, he served concurrently as chairman of the Committee. Kan Chia-hsing became the vice chairman. As the war area increased in size, it was necessary to meet the actual requirements, make new plans and step up the activities. Recruiting and training subcommittees were established in key localities throughout the nation. Altogether there were 87 reception stations, registration stations, training and guidance posts and preparatory middle schools. To facilitate supervision and management, recruiting commissioner's offices and battlefield working teams were established in Kwangsi-Kwangtung border area, southern Kiangsi, Honan and Anhwei in 1945. In spring of the same year, war in southwestern Honan broke out. As many youths in Honan-Shensi border area needed relief, personnel were dispatched to the frontline areas to evacuate and move them to the west. A total of 132,700 students were admitted, trained and given relief in that year. This number far exceeded the total number of students recruited and trained in the past years.

In August, 1945 when V-J Day came and the Japanese surrendered, it was hoped that problems of schooling and employment for youths could be solved together with the nation's demobilization and the termination of training. Unfortunately, the Government was busy with the Japanese surrender and demobilization by staging rebellious activities. They began by refusing to obey Government orders and went from the seizure of points to fullscale rebellion. As the civil war was escalated and communications were disrupted, not only the youths who had gone to the interior were unable to return to their homes to resume schooling, youths in the recovered areas and Communist-controlled areas also were unschooled and unemployed needing relief. Solutions to various problems pertaining to the resumption of schooling, employment and relief at this time were even most pressing than the time when the War of Resistance was in progress. In order to meet the actual requirements, the Ministry of Education requested and received permission from the Executive Yuan to reorganize the War Area Unschooled and Unemployed Youths Training Committee and the Ministry of Education War Area Education Steering Committee into the Youth Resumption of Schooling and Vocational Assistance Commission which was an independent organization under the Ministry of Education. This Commission handled the relief for the nation's displaced, unschooled and unemployed youths by helping them to resume schooling, find employment, and prepare for later turnover of these activities to the local authorities. Subsequently, vocational assistance divisions were established in various provinces and municipalities to assist the local authorities in education and demobilization. Preparatory classes for entrance to middle schools, vocational training classes, teachers' training classes, middle schools and normal schools were established in key localities to provide necessary training.

All in all, between 1940 and 1945, 372,271 youths were admitted and trained making valuable contributions to the war effort.

Section 2. Wartime Culture

Cultural Movement

After the Manchurian Incident in 1931, China's culture began to flourish. By the time the War of Resistance broke out in 1937, much progress was evidenced. National Resistance Associations were organized by the literary, art, drama and music circles under the supervision of the Cultural Movement Committee and other related organizations. Their activities which were fully aligned with the national policy, took the members to the frontlines, frontiers and rear areas to develop the supplementary education and to keep the public informed. They not only stepped up the people's patriotism and enthusiasm, they also stimulated the youths and service men to develop a high morale against the enemy and added luster to China's culture.

1. Drama: In order to meet wartime requirements, promotion of drama developed rapidly. The following achievements were noted:

a. Going deep into the villages—Taking drama into villages was a pre-war slogan which had seldom been implemented. However, during the War of Resistance, this slogan was actively pushed. In frontline areas, this was particularly evident.

b. Professionalism and pragmatism—Before the War of Resistance, professionalism, though budding, had not flourished as it did during the war. Professional actors and actresses appeared in government-operated troupes, special troupes organized by various organizations as well as well-established professional troupes such as the China Drama Society, New China Drama Society and China Arts and Drama Society. The troupes were highly professional. What was more, the average people believed that professionalized plays were more excellent.

c. Technical improvement—During the War of Resistance, despite material difficulties, technical improvements compensated material deficiencies in such areas as lighting and scenery. This progress was evidenced in the private operated and Government operated professional troupes in the rear areas as well as the mobile troupes in the frontline areas and the troupes scattered in the various schools.

d. Increase in drama education and number of theaters—Prior to the war, the nation had only one school of drama to turn out actors and actresses. As drama contributed greatly to the nation during the war the Government and far-sighted people realized its significance. Hence, the National School of Drama was redesignated as a technical college. On the other hand, another school of drama was established in Szechuan, the Academy of Arts in Kwangtung set up a course in drama; the Nan Hung Academy of Arts in Chengtu established a department of drama; the National College of Social Education added a drama section; the Military Culture Class of the Board of Political Training organized a department of drama; the Youth Corps Cadre Training Class set up a drama section. In addition, there were the Kuang Hua Drama Club and the private Hsia Sheng Peiping Opera School and other short-term courses. All these reflected the fact that drama education flourished.

As to theatres, there were not enough and many were inadequate. However, the Resistance and Reconstruction Hall and the Youth Hall in Chungking and the well-equipped Arts Hall in Kweilin, Kwangsi Province helped the presentation tremendously.

Concurrent with the progress in drama, motion pictures achieved balanced development. The newsreels and featured films of the Central Motion Pictures under the Ministry of Information, China Motion Pictures of the National Military Council and the Northwest Company showed steady progress.

2. Folk Arts: Being relatively simple, folk arts were rapidly promoted and improvements noted. Chess teams were sent to the South Sea areas in the interest of overseas Chinese. Magic shows for troop-cheering and lectures were given. Yuan Chen-nan, a magician, displayed much enthusiasm entertaining the troops and led the Ministry of National Defense Magic Troupe after the war. The lyrics of ta-ku (singing accompanied by drum beating) were stimulating after revision. In the performances in rear areas, propaganda effect was achieved. Other local dramas such as the pang-tzu of Honan and chin-chiang were also improved.

3. Music: New contributions were noted in composition, chorus, foreign broadcasting and alignment of Chinese music. Important music organizations included the following:

a. China Symphony Orchestra—Established in 1940, it was the only symphony orchestra in the rear areas during the war. With more than 30 members, it was located in Chungking and was moved to Nanking after the war.

b. New Music Club—The club was established in 1938. It was the most aggressive music organization in the promotion of new music in China during the war. Its 5,000 members were scattered in many parts of the nation. It also published such periodicals as "New Music" and "Musical Art." In post-war Shanghai, it operated the "Sunday Music Hall."

In addition, there was the National Academy of Music under the Ministry of Education which contributed immensely in musical education and turned out musically talented people.

4. Fine Arts: Sketching and cartoon moved ahead rapidly. Many artists took their easels with them to various places. They travelled as far north as Mongolia and as far south as Yunnan and Burma painting the gallantry of our soldiers, the fierce fighting and the sufferings of our people. In 1941, these productions were exhibited in Chungking achieving excellent propaganda effect in the War of Resistance and national reconstruction. Similarly, there were new creations in cartoon.

5. Woodcut: Subsequent to the outbreak of the War of Resistance, woodcut artists organized the "China Woodcut Association" to contribute to the prosecution of the war. The "China Woodcut Society" which was organized in 1942 held woodcut exhibitions in 30 areas.

Academic Research

Following the designation of Nanking as the nation's capital, the National Government devoted great efforts in the promotion of academic research. Accordingly, academic research organizations and academic and cultural agencies scored many achievements. Between 1928-1929, the Academia Sinica, the National Peiping Academy and independent consolidated research organizations were successively established. Private research organizations included the Ching Sheng Institute of Biology supported and organized by the Board of Trustees of the China Educational and Cultural Foundation in 1928 and the Institute of Tropical Diseases established in Hangchow in the same year. Academic or research organizations affiliated with the various ministries of the Central Government included the National Institute of Compilation and Translation, Central Industrial Laboratory and Central Hydro-Work Laboratory were successively established. In 1931, the Provisional Constitution during the period of Political Tutelage was promulgated. In it, two articles in the chapter on education had to do with academic research. Article 57 reads, "The State should encourage and protect academic and technical research and inventions." Article 18 reads, "The State should protect and keep historical, cultural and art relics and objects." These two articles reflect the emphasis of Government on academics and culture. However, academic awards at the time were handled by academic organizations and agencies. These awards included scholarships in memory of Yi Yen, Yang Chuan and Ting Wen-chiang awarded by the Academia Sinica. Beginning in 1972, the Board of Trustees of the China Educational and Cultural Foundation made available scientific research scholarship; however, the Government did not make available any national academic scholarships. Though China was subjected to foreign aggression, the society was relatively stable, and academic research was on the right track. Progress in natural science, applied science, social science and humanities was noted. Thesis written by Chinese scholars appeared in international conferences and periodicals at home and abroad and won the attention of the world's academic circles. Meanwhile, various societies such as China Mathematics Society, China Physics Society, China Zoology Society, China Mechanical Engineering Society, China Political Science Society, China Economics Society, China Sociology Society, China Statistics Society and China Education Society were established. Gradually, various publications reached international academic levels.

Despite heavy losses suffered by the academic institutions in the coastal cities, the Government adhered to the highest principle of "peace time consciousness of wartime requirements" by moving to the interior. Thus, academic research was not disrupted. In April, 1838, the Ministry of Education promulgated the "Outline Plan for the Wartime Implementation of Education at Various Levels," which stipulated 9 policy guidelines and 17 key points. The following includes 3 of the 9 policy guidelines which had to do with academic research:

1. Apply scientific methods to consolidate and develop the literature, history, philosophy and arts on which the traditional Chinese culture rests in order to establish self-confidence of the Chinese people.

2. Based on actual needs, make improvements in natural science to meet defense and production requirements.

3. On social science, study the merits of other peoples to compensate our weaknesses. Rearrange the principles and create systems in order to meet the requirements necessary in our country.

The above guidelines were quite accurate and could be adhered to at the present time. Of the 17 key points, one pertained to academic research. It reads, "The nation's highest academic reviewing institution should be established to elevate academic standards."

In 1940, the Ministry of Education established the Academic Reviewing Board. Its main activities were as follows:

1. Beginning in 1941, awards were given to outstanding writings, inventions and art works. During the first year, 29 recipients were selected, the second year 48, and the third year 54. More awards were given in the fields of social science and applied science. By 1947, 301 scholars had been given awards (14 won first prizes, the remainder were given second and third prizes or cash prizes).

2. Screening the qualifications of faculty members in technical and higher colleges. From September, 1940 to April, 1948, 8,685 faculty members were

screened and passed. They included 2,658 professors, 1,260 associate professors, 2,068 instructors and 2,699 teaching assistants.

3. Reviewing the theses of candidates for master degrees. From May, 1943 to April, 1948, 232 theses were reviewed including 43 in liberal arts, 40 in science, 22 in law, 26 in normal education, 64 in agronomy, 17 in engineering and 6 in medicine.

4. Reviewing the qualifications of professors contracted by the Ministry of Education and selecting professors to receive sabbatical leaves and planning the award of doctor's degrees.

At this time, key academic research institutions had been moved to the rear areas. And the China Institute of Geography, the China Institute of Sericulture, the China Institute of Medicine and the Provincial Institute of Fukien were newly reestablished. In addition, the Central Bureau of Meteorology, the Central Hygienic Experimental Station, the Central Experimental Station on Forestry and the Central Experimental Station on Animal Husbandry were established. Private institutions included the Fu Hsing Institute, National Culture Institute and the China Institute of Land Administration. According to the statistics of 1945, there were 45 institutes in universities and independent colleges, of which 10 were in liberal arts, 9 in science, 5 in law, 1 in commerce, 5 in agronomy, 6 in engineering, 6 in medicine, 3 in normal education far surpassing the pre-war number of 23. However, they were inadequate as they could not provide the advanced studies to be pursued by college graduates. At that time, the capacity was only for 300 post-graduate students.

Despite tumultuous conditions during the war, academic research was not interrupted. This was especially true of regional scientific research which uncovered much mystery in the universe. The research and invention of wartime substitutes contributed greatly to the protracted war effort.

Originally, the establishment of academic and cultural organizations required the authorization of the Ministry of Education. By the time the Ministry of Social Affairs was organized in November, 1940, it replaced the Ministry of Education as the responsible agency. However, according to Article 2 of the Organic Laws Governing People's Organizations during the Emergency Period, the activities of these organizations came under the direction and supervision of the responsible Government agencies. Academic and cultural organizations were under the direction and supervision of the Ministry of Education. Although these organizations suffered somewhat during the war, they achieved much more progress than they did before. Hence, some of them also made valuable contributions to the country. The outstanding organizations contributing to the war effort are listed as follows:

1. General academics and culture—China People's Society, China People's Customs Society and Life Philosophy Institute.

2. Education—China Education Society, China Social Education Society, China Children's Education Society, China Society of Tests, and China Society of

Scout Education.

3. Science and technology—China Science Society, China Chemistry Society, China Physics Society, China Geography Society, China Textile Society, and China Zoology Society.

4. Medicine—China Medical Society and China Nursing Society.

5. Agronomy and forestry—China Agronomical Society and China Horticultural Society.

6. Sociology, politics and economics—China Sociological Society, China Social Administration Society, China Political Science Society, China Local Autonomy Society, China Administration Society, China Examination Society, China Personnel Administration Society and Economic Research Society.

7. Literature and history—China Society of Philosophy and China Society of History.

8. Engineering—China Engineering Society, China Mechanical Engineering Society, China Hydraulic Engineering Society, China Civil Engineering Society, China Mining Engineering Society, China Chemical Engineering Society and China Shipbuilding Engineering Society.

9. International culture—China League of Nations Association and Sino-Korea Cultural Association.

10. Physical education—China Physical Education Association.

After V-J Day, academic institutions and cultural organizations either returned to their pre-war locations, moved to the nation's capital with the Government, or selected permanent sites in other cities. Similar organizations operated by the puppet regimes were turned over to designated agencies.

International cultural cooperation: International cultural cooperation promotes cultural exchange between countries and academic and ideological progress which are conducive to friendly relationships between nations and to world peace. Upon termination of the First World War, people with foresight who attended the peace conference believed that the avoidance of catastrophic war depended on mutual understanding. Hence, international cultural and educational cooperation was one of the most important tasks of the then League of Nations. During the Second World War, the governments of those democratic nations in exile in London maintained constant contact with each other as early as the period from 1942 to 1944. Other allies also considered the restoration of cultural and educational activities in the war-stricken countries as well as the post-war international cultural and educational cooperation. This premise led to the establishment of UNESCO (United Nations Education, Science and Culture Organization). China also sent delegates to UNESCO in order to further mutual cooperation in education, science and culture among peoples.

As early as 1930, China participated in the international cultural cooperation enterprises sponsored by the League of Nations. In 1933, the China Chapter of the World Cultural Cooperation was organized to establish contact with international cooperaion organizations. China successively attended many important international academic conferences. During the War of Resistance, British and American scholars such as Professors Johnson, Brown and Eden lectured in China. Six Chinese college professors were invited to do research or lecture in the United States. In addition, a cultural and educational mission was sent to India to repay a similar visit by an Indian mission. Three Indian scholars were also invited to lecture in China. Ten graduate students were exchanged between India and China. There was also talk that Britain might send one professor and 39 students to do research in China. The United States Government also gave permission for a number of books to be reproduced by universities in China.

As early as 1925, China participated in the International Publications Exchange Pact to exchange books with other countries and in the international cultural and educational activities such as expositions and exhibitions. Through the years, many books were exchanged with other countries.

For years, China had sent students to study abroad. By June, 1932, the Ministry of Education promulgated Regulations Governing Studies Abroad which specified the necessary qualifications and management of students. Since then, the qualities of students studying abroad at their own expenses improved a little and management also showed improvement.

By 1937, the Sino-British Board of Trustees, British Boxer Indemnity, held six examinations for students to study abroad with expenses paid. Later, the qualified candidates who had passed the last examination were sent to Canada instead of Britain as the war in Europe had broken out. National Tsing Hua University held five examinations for students to study in the United States with the last examination in 1938.

In April, 1938, the Central Government formulated the Outline of the Implementing Program of Wartime Education at Various Levels. Article 13 of the program is stated as follows:

"Revision of the system, so that students to be sent abroad hereafter will become a part of the nation's overall educational program. Students studying abroad at their own expenses will also be regulated so as to elminate the past weaknesses." In accordance with this provision, the Executive Yuan promulgated Temporary Measures Governing Students Studying Abroad. The new measures provided that students going abroad be limited to those who studied military science, engineering, science and medicine. Although some liberal arts students and law students pursued advanced studies in foreign countries due to special requirements, their number was quite small. Students to study abroad were restricted to those who had graduated from public or private universities and had pursued advanced studies or had served with distinction for more than two years. Due to severe restrictions, difficulties in obtaining foreign exchange and in transportation, the number of students going abroad was drastically reduced.

In January, 1942 when China signed a new treaty with the United States, the international situation changed rapidly, "China's Destiny," written by President Chiang, stated the urgent need for competent personnel in post-war reconstruction. In order to meet the requirement and to cultivate personnel in national reconstruction, the Ministry of Education rescinded the above restrictions. Favorable considerations and assistance were given to students who wished to study abroad regardless of the subjects. In view of the wartime material difficulties and the post-war urgent need for competent personnel, the Government considered it necessary to elevate the academic standards of the students. Hence, students were required to pass examinations before they could receive certificates to study abroad. In October, 1943, the Ministry of Education promulgated "Measures Governing the Dispatch of Students to Study Abroad at Their Own Expresses." In December of the same year, a total of 327 students passed the first examination and marked the inception of such an examination. Thus, the control of students to study abroad took a step forward.

Journalism and Publication

After the full-scale War of Resistance broke out on July, 7, 1937 and as the war situation deteriorated rapidly, most of the newspaper enterprises along the coast did not evacuate to the interior with the Government. The newspapers which moved to the nation's wartime capital included Central Daily News, Ta Kung News, Sao Tang News, Shih Shih News, Hsin Min News and Freedom News (English). Later, Yi Shih News and World Daily News resumed publication in Chungking. Additionally, there were the Kuo Min Daily News, Commercial Daily News, Hsin Chu News and Southwest Daily News which had originally been published in Chungking. Later, the Chinese Communist Party published the Hsin Hua Daily News to engage in subversive comments. In the wartime rear areas, newspapers were thriving in Chungking.

Despite extreme material shortages and incessant enemy bombings day and night during the War of Resistance, Chinese newspapers displayed indomitable spirit. During the peak, there were 478 newspapers and 154 news service in the country all using coarse papers, crude carbon black and flat presses for printing. In order to avoid being bombed wantonly by enemy planes, the editors and printing presses of the newspapers were moved into caves. At times, electricity was out because of heavy bombing. However, under dim candlelight, newspapermen continued to turn out newspapers by manually operating the presses.

Apart from the above-mentioned newspapers, there were military newspapers headed by Sao Tang News. Each war area published medium-size battlefield daily newspapers, while frontline areas published small-size Sao Tang Tabloids. By 1943, there were 200 such military newspapers. In addition, there were 140 summary news squads engaged in wartime public information activities.

The Central International Broadcasting Station which was subordinated to the Ministry of Information continued to broadcast news in China to foreign countries via short wave.

During the war against Japan, the heroic struggles of newspapermen behind enemy lines were most admirable. In November, 1937 when the Chinese forces evacuated from Shanghai, the International Settlement became isolated. Nevertheless, patriotic newspapermen continued to publish newspapers under foreign registration, engaged in propaganda against Japan and exposed the treacheries of traitors. In 1939, as the Japanese and the puppets failed in their attempts to bribe our patriotic newspapermen, they resorted to terror and assassination. From August, 1939 to December, 1941, 26 newspapermen were assassinated or kidnapped. Despite these terrorist activities, none of our loyal newspapermen betrayed the country and they continued to carry on the struggle.

With regard to publishing companies, prior to 1937, they were concentrated mainly in Shanghai, Nanking, Tientsin and Canton. Shanghai, in particular, was the center of publishing activities. Other major book companies included the Commercial Press, the Chung Hua Book Company, and the World Book Company all of which were located in Shanghai. The publications of these three major companies took 61% of all the publications in the nation in 1934, 62% in 1935 and 71% in 1936. Shortly after the outbreak of the War of Resistance, most of the publishing companies in Shanghai, Nanking, Peiping, Tientsin and Canton were destroyed by Japanese planes. As only a small number of them were moved to the interior, publishing enterprise was crippled.

In October, 1938, Wuhan and Canton fell into enemy hands in succession and the war entered into a second phase. By 1939, as the war situation gradually improved, publishing enterprise showed sign of revival. In 1941, bookstores, publishing services and printing shops mushroomed everywhere, particularly Chungking, Chengtu, Kunming and Kweilin.

During this period, publishing enterprise had two major characteristics:

1. Since 1941, printing organizations or distributing agencies increased in number. Bookstores alone numbered 754 and were increased to 1,286 in 1942. Printing shops numbered 430 in 1941 and 1,311 in 1942. After 1943, the number continued to rise in Chungking, Kweilin and various provinces and cities.

2. Publishing enterprise: Publishing companies were concentrated in Chungking, Kweilin, Chengtu, Kunming and Chuchiang with Chungking and Kweilin as the centers, as Shanghai and Nanking were in the days before the war.

From July, 1937 to the end of 1939, the nation's publications totalled 10,014. During the first phase of the war, publishing enterprise suffered heavily. In 1941, publication of books solely totalled 1,891, in 1942 3,877 and in 1943 4,408. The number of books published in one year greatly exceeded that of 10 years ago and was comparable to 1935 and 1936. Since then, the publishing companies continued the heroic struggles under adverse conditions. Their fighting spirit was most commendable.

An analysis of the above-mentioned publications revealed that literary books stood first, followed by books on education, political science, economics, history and geography. Fewer books on philosophy, military science and Three People's Principles were published.

The publication of magazines showed steady increase each year. In 1941, 1979 magazines were published (the actual number is large). The magazines which were published in Chungking exceeded those in other areas and took nearly 1/3 of all the magazines published in the country. The number of magazines published continued to increase. Apart from Chungking, other cities such as Chengtu, Kweilin and Kunming published more magazines. This indicates that the centers of magazine publication were the above-mentioned cities.

In terms of contents, most of the magazines were literary, political, educational and economic, followed by science, military science, dramas and philosophy. Their contents, of course, differed from those of books; however, literary magazines and literary books still took the first places in numbers. This was an obvious phenomenon which was worthy of note in the various publications.

CHAPTER SIX
Military Operation

Section 1. Preliminary Operations

Manchurian Incident ·

In April, 1931, the Japanese Kwantung Army (under the command of General Shiguru Honjo who directed the main force of the Second Division and the Southern Manchurian Railway Garrison Force) killed many Chinese peasants in an incident which involved the forced renting of farmland at Wanpaoshan.[1] In June, when Capt. Nakamura,[2] a Japanese spy, was missing in our reclaimed land in Hsing-an-ling, the Japanese began to send in reinforcements along the Southern Manchurian Railway and moved a portion of the artillery units from Port Arthur Fortress to the Japanese barracks in Mukden. On September 18, the Japanese used their own bombing of the Liu-tiao-kou Railway as an excuse and made an unprovoked night attack on our forces at Pei-ta-ying in Mukden resulting in heavy losses sustained by the 7th Brigade under General Wang Yi-che.

General Chang Hsueh-liang who was then commander of the Northeast Frontier Command and concurrently chairman of the Northeast Political Committee was in Peiping at the time. At first, he thought that the hostilities were

---

1 Japan encouraged the Japanese people to emigrate to Manchuria. Due to cold climate there, few went. Japan then sent the Japanese people to Chosen (now Korea) and forced the Koreans to emigrate to Manchuria. Thus, frequent conflicts broke out between the Korean in Kirin Province and the local Chinese farmers. Beginning on Apr. 16, 1931, Korean immigrants dug ditches in the vicinity of Wan-pao-shan and ruined over 400 acres of farmland belonging to Chinese farmers. Later, they led in river water and built dikes inundating 50,000 acres of farmland on both banks of the river. The farmers petitioned to the Changchun Municipal Government which negotiated with the Japanese consul without avail. On July 2, the farmers decided to fill the ditches, but were fired upon by Japanese policemen. More than ten unarmed Chinese farmers were arrested and tortured. The Japanese even instigated the Koreans to antagonize the Chinese. As a result, thousands of overseas Chinese in Seoul, Inchon, Pyongyang and Pusan were massacred, deported or jumped into the ocean.

2 In the first part of June 1931, Capt. Nakamura Rietaro of the Japanese general staff, disguised himself as an agriculturist and went to Northeast China to engage in intelligence activities. When he arrived at Chao-nan in Hsing-an District on June 9, he was missing. The Japanese Foreign Office banned the publication of the news until Aug. 17 when the Japanese Consul General Moreshima in Mukden lodged a protest with the Chinese authorities in Liaoning Province. As the provincial authorities were investigating the case, the Japanese flew planes to drop leaflets to the Japanese people to stir up the feelings of the Japanese people and sent reinforcements to the south of the Northeast attempting to provoke an incident.

accidental and accommodated himself by seeking a peaceful settlement. Having received orders not to offer resistance, our forces were completely on the defensive withdrawing in succession. Thus, Japanese forces occupied Mukden and took over our military and political establishments. Futhermore, they imprisoned Tsang Shih-yi, governor of Liaoning Province, and forced him to sign a confession accepting the responsibility for the incident.

When hostilities broke out, elements of the Japanese Kwangtung Army and the Chosen Army (commander-Gen. Sentaro Hayashi) took simultaneous actions along the Southern Manchurian Railway from Changchun to Port Arthur. On September 19, they took Anshan, Haicheng, Kaiyuan, Tiehling, Fushun, Szepingchieh, Changchun, Kuanchengtzu, Yingko, Antung and Penhsihu. From September 20-25, the Japanese forces took Hsiungyueh, Changtu, Liaoyuan, Tungliao, Tiaonan, Kirin, Chiaoho, Huangkutun and Hsin-min. The entire Liaoning and Kirin Provinces fell into Japanese hands.

Judging from the above, one could see that large-scale Japanese aggressive actions were obviously pre-planned and could not possibly be covered up by their own fabrications.

While our National Government negotiated with the Japanese Government on the one hand, urging it to withdraw the Japanese forces, our Governments appealed to the League of National and the signatories of the Nine Power Pact, urging them to uphold justice on the other. The League of Nations repeatedly passed resolutions urging the withdrawal of Japanese forces and notified both the Chinese and the Japanese Governments to take actions which would prevent the hostilities from spreading. The United States in a note to Japan referred to the Nine Power Pact calling her attention to the obligations in international treaties. Subsequently, the Japanese Government issued a statement in which it stated that Japan had no territorial ambition on the northeast and that it would not aggravate the situation. It further stated that the Japanese forces were gradually being withdrawn. However, the Japanese army authorities informally stated that international laws* were no longer applicable and that they would not accept the arbitrations of the League of Nations nor the restrictions of the Japanese Government. Meanwhile, Japanese Army proceeded with its pre-determined invasion plans. On November 19, after breaking the heroic resistance of the forces led by Gov. Ma Chan-shan of Heilungchiang Province, the Japanese took Tsitsihar. On January 3, 1932, the Japanese seized Chinchow. On January 28, the Japanese attacked Chinese garrison troops in Shanghai. On March 9, Japan set up puppet Manchukuo making the Manchurian Incident all the more complicated. In an attempt to find a solution, the League of Nations dispatched the Lytton Investigation Team to the northeast in the spring of 1932. The team issued a report in October declaring that Japan was an aggressor nation and that the puppet Manchukuo was created by the Japanese military power. It also recommended solutions, means and procedures. In 1933, after the League of Nations passed the recommendation with a vote of 42 to 1, Japan withdrew from the League.

Shanghai Incident

As the Japanese Army took Manchuria without much bloodshed, it swiftly swung north. To achieve parallel development, the Japanese Navy actively made plans to move south. As the Chinese Communists took advantage of the emotionally upset people and merchants of Shanghai, to add fuel to fire, thus giving the Japanese an excuse for provocative actions.

On January 20, 1932, Japan sent spies disguised as monks to set fire to the main plant of the San Yu Industries at Yangshupu and killed several Chinese policemen who arrived at the scene to maintain order. In the afternoon of the same day, Japanese nationals roamed on North Szechuan Road and Hungchiang Road in Chapei to stage parades and demonstrations. Scores of Chinese shops were smashed and two Japanese were hurt. The Japanese consul-general in Shanghai made the following strong protest to the Shanghai Municipal Government:

(1) That the mayor of Shanghai make an official apology.

(2) That the culprits who killed the Japanese monks be arrested at once.

(3) That gratuities and medical expenses be paid to the victims.

(4) That appropriate actions be taken against the anti-Japanese movement.

(5) That anti-Japanese organizations and organizations hostile to Japan be disbanded immediately.

The brutalities of the Japanese spies touched off the incident, and Japan should be held responsible for the disturbance and destruction, yet, Japan made unreasonable demands. To keep the incident from spreading, the Chinese Government accommodated itself to seek peace and made concessions to the unreasonable demands of Japan. Unexpectedly, when the negotiations were still in progress, the Japanese poured reinforcements into Shanghai to prepare for war.

On January 27, the Japanese consul-general notified the mayor of Shanghai saying that if no satisfactory reply was received by 1800 hours, January 28 with regard to the Japanese demands, Japan would take actions to effect their realization. At 0700 hours the next day, the Japanese naval commander informed the International Settlement and the French Concession in Shanghai in the same tone. The situation was such that the outbreak of war was imminent. In compliance with the instructions of the Central Government, the Shanghai Municipal Government accepted the Japanese demands in total the afternoon. Thus, the Japanese indicated their satisfaction.

Having adopted the above-mentioned tolerant and compromising attitude, the Chinese Government had hoped that war could be averted. Yet at 1900 hours on the same day, the Japanese marines attempted to realize their predetermined invasion plans under the pretext of protecting their nationals and demanded the withdrawal of our garrison forces in Chapei and the turnover of the garrison to the Japanese forces.   Without waiting for our reply, the Japanese forces suddenly attacked our garrison forces on the 28th.   Finding this outrage intolerable, our Government and garrison forces rose in defense.   Thus, the Battle of Shanghai erupted.

In the beginning, the Japanese militarists thought that their superior equipment would enable them to take Shanghai in one stroke and threaten Nanking, thus forcing us to sue for a humiliating peace.   However, our 19th Route Corps and the 5th Corps resisted gallantly for more than 30 days repeatedly repelling the stubborn enemy.   In succession, the Japanese marine Kurume brigade, the 9th, 11th, 14th and 16th Divisions poured in as reinforcements.   Despite replacement of their commanders on 4 occasions, the Japanese did not succeed.   As the Japanese suffered heavy losses in the Battles of Chapei, Wentsaoping, Tsaochiachiao, Miaohsing and Wusung, their aggressiveness was frustrated.   Once again, they poured in additional reinforcements. On February 29, on the Wusung-Shanghai front, the 9th, 14th and 16th Divisions and the Kurume Brigade staged an air-naval-ground joint general offensive.   Meanwhile, the Japanese 11th Division made a forced landing at Liuho.   Being attacked both in the front and rear, our forces were forced to fall back to the second line of resistance in the vicinity of Nanhsiang on March 1 to continue resistance.

When the Battle of Wusung-Shanghai broke out, our Government, through diplomatic channels, appealed to the League of Nations to check the Japanese atrocities in their aggression.   Thinking that victory was certain, the Japanese would not come to terms in the beginning.   Later, their repeated reverses softened them.   It was not until March 4 when the League of Nations passed a resolution, was the Sino-Japanese ceasefire realized.   On the 24th, the ceasefire conference was held in Shanghai with the arbitration of the League of Nations and the diplomats of friendly nations.   The high morale of our forces was responsible for repelling the Japanese attacks on our second line positions.   On April 29, Admiral Shiragawa of Japan was assassinated by Korean patriot Yun Bong-gil.   It was not until May 5, that the Wusung-Shanghai Ceasefire Agreement[3] and the Agree-

---

3 The Wusung-Shanghai Cease-fire Agreement contained   five articles.   The salient points of the five articles are as follows:

   a. Cease-fire by both sides.

   b. Chinese forces will remain in their positions for the time being as the Cease-fire agreement is signed.

   c. The Japanese forces will withdraw from the International Settlement and the roads beyond the boundary in Hung-kou and revert to the positions prior to Jan. 28. However, a number of units can be stationed in the bordering areas of the above-mentioned.

   d. A joint committee to be composed of the British American, French and Italian representatives will announce the withdrawals of both sides.

   e. The agreement will become effective after signing.

ment of the Withdrawal of Japanese Forces[4] were signed. Thus, the Battle of Shanghai came to an end.

This battle exposed the military, political and diplomatic weaknesses of the enemy and reflected the high morale of the Chinese people and military forces. It also strengthened our conviction of victory in the War of Resistance. The Russian and Chinese Communist intrigues of diversions in war were noteworthy, but unfortunately the Japanese militarists failed to recognize them thoroughly and were awakened only too late.

Fall of Yukuan and Jehol and the Battle of the Great Wall

With the Wusung-Shanghai ceasefire singed on March 4, 1932, the puppet Manchukuo was established under the tutelage of the Japanese Kwantung Army on March 9. On July 12, the League of Nations Investigation Team stated that the independence of Manchuria which was tantamount to the splitting of China's territory violated the Nine Power Pact. On September 5, the Japanese Government openly recognized the puppet Manchukuo and appointed General Nobuyoshi Muto, commander of the Kwantung Army, the concurrent commander of the Manchukuo Defense Forces. On the same day, our Government lodged a strong protest with the Japanese Government. At this time, Soviet Russia proposed the signing of Russo-Japanese Non-Aggression Pact which made possible active Japanese aggression of China.

Since April, 1932, Japanese forces began to pour reinforcements into Yukuan and Suichung and repeatedly provoked our military and police forces in Yukuan. On May 15, Prime Minister Takeshi Inukai of Japan was assassinated by Ketsumeidan. Thus, the atrocities of the Japanese militarists in aggression upon China were no longer restrained. In July, Gen. Chang Hsueh-liang, director of the Peiping Pacification Headquarters appointed Gen. Ho Chu-kuo garrison commander of Linyu and Yungping. Commanding the 9th Infantry Brigade and the 3rd Cavalry Brigade, Gen. Ho was responsible for the garrison between Yukuan and Tangshan. In early December, the Japanese forces shelled Yukuan. On January 1, 1933, elements of the Japanese 8th Division began the attack on Yukuan. As Ho's forces did not fight well, they abandoned the city on January 3 and Chiumenkou on January 13. Thus, the Japanese forces took possession of the vital area between Hopei and Liaoning greatly threatening eastern Hopei and consolidated their pivoting point to the left in the subsequent attack on Jehol.

On January 21, the Japanese prime minister announced that the boundary between Manchukuo-Mongolia and China was the Great Wall and that Jehol Province was a part of the Manchukuo. Furthermore, in the name of Manchukuo

---

4 In accordance with the annex of the Wusung-Shanghai Cease-fire Agreement, the withdrawal covered the areas of Lo-tien—Liu-ho—Nan-hsiang, south of Cha-pei Railway, Ta-chang, Kiang-wan-Peng-pu, Chen-ju, north of the Cha-pei Railway, Wusung, Pao-shan, east of the Wusung-Shanghai Railway and west of Sha-ching-kang.

he issued a statement announcing the employment of military forces against Jehol. On February 12, Acting Premier T. V. Soong stated that should the Japanese forces attack Jehol, it would be tantamount to an attack on the nation's capital and that the Chinese people would mass all their forces against such an attack. On February 19, the ranking officers in North China jointly dispatched a cable vouching their determination to fight against Japan. On February 23, the Japanese Foreign Office again presented a memorandum demanding the designation of the area inside and outside of the Great Wall as the neutral zone. Our Ministry of Foreign Affairs sternly repudiated such a demand. In the evening of the 23rd, the Japanese Embassy presented a note to the Ministry of Foreign Affairs demanding the withdrawal of our forces from Jehol. In the same evening a reply was sent to the Japanese in which our Government lodged a protest.

Meanwhile, the Japanese 8th Division, 14th Composite Brigade, 6th Division, 4th Calvary Brigade and the puppet forces under Li Chi-chun and Chang Hai-peng had assembled in Suichung, Chin Hsien and Tungliao. On February 23, these forces began the attack on Jehol. Unfortunately, the military and political activities in Jehol were not properly aligned. Despite the fact that Tang Yu-lin's forces had been in Jehol for 7 years, they refused the entry of Government forces into Jehol in the beginning and later abandoned such important localities as Kailu, Pinchuan and Chengteh without fighting. However, Gen. Sun Kuei-yuan's forces fought bitterly in the vicinity of Chihfeng and were forced to fall back to the mountainous border areas in Jehol and Chahar. Having fought against the enemy south of Lingyuan, Gen. Fu-lin's army withdrew to the vicinity of Lengkou inside the Great Wall. The remainder of Gen. Chang Tse-hsiang's army withdrew to Hsifengko, as Gen. Wang Yi-che's army operated in Kupeikou. On March 4, the Japanese took Chengteh and advanced toward the various passes of the Great Wall. Indeed, the situation was most critical. As a result of Generalissimo Chiang's personal survey of the situation in the vicinity of Peiping Gen. Ho Ying-chin, Minister of War, was assigned to Peiping replacing Gen. Chang Hsueh-liang as acting Chairman, Peiping Military Council. Gen. Yu Hsueh-chung's army was ordered to take up the garrison of Tientsin and Taku, Gen. Wan Fu-lin's army in Luanho, and the forces under Gen. Shang Chen, Gen. Sung Che-yuan, Gen. Hsiao Chih-chu and Gen. Hsu Ting-yao were ordered respectively to Leng-kou, Hsifengkou, Malankukou and Kupeikou to occupy positions in depth and conduct sustained resistance. Additionally, Gen. Fu Tso-yi's forces occupied alternate positions to Huaijou and Shunyi. For two months, these forces fought bitterly against the enemy and achieved excellent combat results. Gen. Sung Che-yuan's 29th Corps operating in Kupeikou fought gallantly. Unfortunately, we were unable to send reinforcements to the north and to turn the defensive into an offensive, as our forces were tied down in Kiangsi fighting the decisive Fourth Siege against the Chinese Communists. Consequently, the Japanese 6th Division broke through the area linking Gen. Wan Fu-lin's forces and Gen. Sung Che-yuan's forces. Moving rapidly along the Ping-Yu Highway. In early May, our forces withdrew to the line along Pai Ho (White River) in preparation for further operations. In time, the Japanese forces reached Fengjun, Yutien and Huaijou along the Chiyun River line to threaten Peiping and Tientsin. As the theater of war greatly expanded in size, the Japanese felt their inadequate strength. Since they had realized their objective of seizing Jehol, they proposed a truce. The tying-down of our force by the Chinese Communists, the depletion of our forces, our adherence to the policy of internal pacification as a pre-requisite to resisting foreign aggression and the mediation of British Ambassador Miles W. Lampson made it necessary for the Government to negotiate with the Japanese. Eventually, an agreement was reached making the line east and north of Yenching-Changping-Shunyi-Tungchow-Hsiangho-Paoti-Lutai to the Great Wall as the demilitarized zone. China would station no military forces there and the police would be responsible for the maintenance of peace and security. On May 31, the Tangku Ceasefire Agreement was signed making the geographically important Jehol in North China a part of the puppet Manchukuo.

Fall of Eastern Hopei and Specialization of Hopei and Chahar

In 1934, Chinese Government forces wiped out the Chinese Communist home base in southern Kiangsi with the Chinese Communists fleeting to the north. Mao's remnants of less than 10,000 men fled to northern Shensi in the following year finding themselves at the end of their wits. In March, Soviet Russia sold the Eastern Manchurian Railway to the puppet Manchukuo. In July, the Communist International advanced the slogan calling for a united front. While they encouraged the Japanese in the aggression of China, they tried to subvert our Government in order to turn out suppression of the Chinese Communists into a war against Japan. In the autumn of 1934, Generalissimo Chiang, in an article entitled "Friend or Foe?" warned the people in and out of the Japanese Government hoping they would awaken. Unfortunately, the Japanese militarists were determined. On May 29, 1935, the Japanese Garrison Command along Pei-Ning Railway (Gen. Mijiro Umezu was the commander of the composite brigade stationed in Tientsin), under the pretext that a pro-Japanese head of a news service had been killed, made 6 unreasonable demands on Gen. Ho Ying-chin, Acting Chairman of the Peiping National Military Council. These 6 demands are as follows:

(1) That Gen. Yu Hsueh-chung retire and the Hopei Provincial Government move to Paoting.
(2) That the Government forces pull out of Hopei.
(3) That Mayor Chang Ting-ngo of Tientsin and Li Chun-hsiang, Chief of Police be replaced and that Chiang Hsiao-hsien, Commander of the 3rd MP Regiment and Tseng Kuang-ching, Director of the Political Training Department be relieved.

(4) That the Hopei provincial and municipal KMT party headquarters and the Political Department of the Peiping National Military Council cease their activities and that anti-Japanese organizations be disbanded.

(5) That the assassins of the head of the pro-Japanese news service be apprehended and dealt with and that the losses suffered by the victim be compensated.

(6) That publications hostile to Japan be repressed.

Through diplomatic channels, our Government instructed the Chinese ambassador in Japan to negotiate with the Japanese Government; however, the Japanese Government was unable to restrain the actions of the military authorities, although Foreign Minister Hirota agreed to forward our views to the latter. Despite repeated negotiations with the representative of the Japanese garrison forces, Gen. Ho Ying-chin was unable to overcome the Japanese fanaticism. Again under the pretext of troop rotation, the Japanese poured in reinforcements and claimed that if their demands were not totally accepted, they would resort to drastic actions. Not wanting to create hostilities, our Government suffered humility by accepting the Japanese demands.

After the signing of the Ho-Umezu Agreement on June 10, Gen. Ho left Peiping. Subsequently, the Hopei-Chahar Political Committee was established headed by Gen. Sung Che-yuan. There was talk of specialization. Gen. Doehara, Japanese intelligence chief, instigated traitor Yin Ju-keng to form the so-called Eastern Hopei Anti-Communist Autonomous Committee thereby exposing their insidious scheme to divide eastern Hopei and encroach on North China.

Fighting in Chahar and Suiyuan

On February 26, 1936, a coup was staged in Tokyo when the Japanese military authorities seized central political power. This led to increase in military budget, army-navy parallel development, preparations for advance to the north and south, and more fanaticism.

In spring of the same year, the Kwantung Army invaded 6 hsiens in northern Chahar and instigated Prince Teh of the Hsi Banner to organize the "Mongolian Autonomous Military Government." Manipulation of military and political activities led to the integration of bandits into the puppet forces on the one hand, and the establishment of intelligence agencies in Kueisui, Paotou, Ninghsia, Tingyuanying, Taiyuan and Tatung to reconnoiter and harass our rear areas in support of the puppet regime on the other. In early November, Japanese planes reconnoitered Suiyuan, followed by an attack on the 16th. Puppet forces under Wang Ying and Li Shou-hsin were the spearheads in the 4-pronged attack. One moved from Hsingho to Fengchen, another headed toward Chining, the third advanced from Shangtu to Taolin and the fourth proceeded from Pailingmiao to Wuchuan to press Kueisui. The puppet forces failed in the attack as they met strong resistance from our garrison forces in Suiyuan. Our counterattack led to the recapture of Pailingmiao, their home base, and the surrender of the puppet forces en masse. As remnants of the puppet forces fell back to the 6 hsiens in northern Chahar, the Japanese invasion plans on Suiyuan fell through.

Meanwhile, Japan's Hirota cabinet made unreasonable demands to our Government on joint defense against communism and specialization of the provinces (Hopei, Chahar, Suiyuan, Shansi, and Shantung) in North China. Furthermore, it announced the German-Japanese Anti-Communist Agreement on November 25. Chinese Communists and their front organizations passed the resolution on the so-called "Anti-Japanese National Salvation Grand Alliance" asking our Government to stop suppression of the Chinese Communists and to join forces against Japan. At the same time, a movement was under way to align with Soviet Russia. Generalissimo Chiang was fully aware that the real objective of Japan and Soviet Russia was not one of sincerity and alignment but one of forcing us to pull away from the West and fall into isolation ready to be cut into pieces. Our Government, therefore, established its foreign policy urging the democratic nations to promote mutual cooperation in the League of Nations. While rejecting Japan's unreasonable demands, it continued to improve Sino-Soviet relationships under the above-mentioned policy. Disappointed in the failure of their schemes and conscious of the gradual pacification of the Chinese Communists, national unification and progress in national defense, Japanese forces attacked our garrison forces at Lukouchiao (Marco Polo Bridge) on July 7, 1937 at night. Subsequently, they took Peiping and Tientsin to open fullscale war.

Section 2.   Our War Directions and Preparations

War Directions

Japan pressed China harder and harder in her aggression. Ever since the Manchurian Incident, China realized that war against Japan was unavoidable and actively made preparations. The following is an outline of our war direction in the various phases:

1. Guiding principle:

Our objective is to maintain the nation's sovereignty and territorial integrity, seek our people's survival and freedom, and establish a strong and prosperous New China. On the one hand, we urge peace and collective security. On the other hand, we should strengthen our national defense by stepping up our military preparations. When peace is hopeless, the entire nation rallies to conduct sustained war of attrition.

2. Guiding essentials in the preliminary phase (from the Manchurian Incident on September 18, 1931 to the War of Resistance which broke out on July 7, 1937)

a. In order to be adequately prepared for war against Japan, we should make every effort to tolerate Japan's challenges regardless of how humiliating they may be. We should bear in mind our basic national policy announced by Generalissimo Chiang that unless peace is hopeless, never give up peace, and that unless the critical moment for sacrifice has arrived, we do not speak lightly of sacrifice, in order to avoid the premature outbreak of war.

b. Actively increase the nation's strength, improve military preparations, reorganize the armed forces, construct defense works, realign signal communications, develop the nation's resources, develop munition industries, implement conscription system, conduct universal military training and formulate the first five year program regarding 1938 as the target date.

c. Revamp military education and conduct Lushan training to improve the quality and the military skills of the armed forces, promote spiritual solidarity and strengthen the combat effectiveness of the armed forces.

d. Before the completion of our war preparations, make every effort to localize any provocative enemy attack in order to preclude premature total war.

e. Internally, establish the national policy of "internal pacification as a pre-requisite to resisting foreign aggression, wipe out internal unrest, and pacify local and border areas, so as to achieve solidarity, and concentrate our strength to wage the War of Resistance against foreign aggression.

f. In order to stabilize wartime currency for the prosecution of war, announce the implementation of the fapi policy. Meanwhile, make every effort to seek self-sufficiency in the financial and material resources needed in war, particularly food, daily necessities and munitions.

g. In foreign affairs, seek the support of nations which are on our side, expose the design of the Japanese militarists that "In order to conquer the world, it is necessary to conquer China first," enhance the alertness of Britain and the United States and trust the arbitrations of the League of Nations with regard to the Manchurian Incident. Thus, peoples in the entire world will realize the Japanese aggressive actions in complete disregard of collective security, and international sympathy and assistance could be obtained.

h. Initiate the New Life Movement and National Economic Reconstruction Movement to condition ourselves, foster our people's fighting spirit, elevate our people's traditional morals, and develop national economic reconstruction so as to lay the foundation for protracted operations.

3. Guiding essentials during the warring phase (after July 7, 1937)

a. Military:

(1) Strategy: Take advantage of our superior man power and vast territory to conduct sustained war of attrition. While wearing out the enemy on the one hand, we should improve our combat effectiveness on the other, awaiting the opportune time to shift to the offensive, defeat the enemy and seek final victory. In accordance with the shifts in situation, this phase is divided into 3 stages:

(a) First stage operations (defensive): (From July 7, 1937 to the Battle of Wuhan)

Hold key localities, wear out and exhaust the enemy and crush the enemy attempt of a quick ending. Elements of the Chinese armed forces would be concentrated in North China to be deployed in the key points along the Peiping-Suiyuan Railway, Peiping-Hankow Railway, and Tientsin-Pukow Railway for overlapping disposition, multiple-line defense and piecemeal resistance, with emphasis on insuring the natural barriers in Shansi. The main strength of the Chinese Armed Forces was concentrated in eastern China to attack the enemy in Shanghai, protect the key localities of Wusung-Shanghai[5] and cover the nation's capital. By the end of the Battle of Nanking in late 1937, elements of the Chinese forces were shifted to the Hsuchow front to lure the enemy main force to the areas along the Tientsin-Pukow Railway, scatter the enemy and gain time so that the main strength of the Chinese Armed Forces might make active preparations to restore their combat effectiveness on the outskirts of Wuhan, take advantage of the natural barriers of Po-yang Lake and Ta-pieh Shan and the swamps on either side of the Yangtze River to conduct sustained defense, destroy the remaining strength of the enemy offensive and lay the foundation for protracted operations:

(b) Second stage operations (sustained operation): (From the Battle of Wuhan to the recovery of Kwangsi)

After staging a series of limited offensives and counterattacks, the Chinese forces continued to wear out the enemy, respond to guerilla operations behind the enemy, tighten the control of the occupied areas, turn the enemy rear areas into front areas, force the enemy to hold points and lines, prevent him from overall rule and seizure of materials, and break the enemy attempt of "checking Chinese with Chinese" and "fighting a war to support another war." Meanwhile, units were drawn for rotational reorganization and training, and combat effectiveness was strengthened in preparation for the counteroffensive. At the end of 1941, as the Pacific War broke out, Chinese forces and Allied forces fought side by side. Apart from conducting local attacks to tie down the main strength of the Japanese Army (1.2 million men) so that he could not draw units to the south and thereby reduce the pressure on the Allied forces in the Pacific, our Government dispatched Chinese forces into Burma to assist the Allied forces in their operations, clear the China-India Road,[6] obtain the necessary new equipment, build up new force and increase combat effectiveness. By the early summer of 1945 (most of the U.S.-equipped forces had completed their reorganization). Chinese forces recovered Kweilin and Liuchow, and mopped up the enemy in Kwangsi to assist the Allied forces in the Pacific and stage attacks on the sea. They were prepared to seize Leichow Peninsula, operate in Canton and open harbours in Kwangtung Province to lay the foundation for the third stage operations.

---

5 Wusung was a fortress area. Shanghai was an economic center.

6 1,044 miles from Kunming, Yunnan Province, China to Ledo on the Indian border.

(c) Third stage operations (counteroffensive): (From the recovery of Kwangsi to the surrender of the Japanese forces)

Efforts were made to synchronize with the actions of the Allied forces, launch offensives, destroy the enemy, recover lost territories and achieve final victory. When our forces were poised for the attack on Canton after mopping up the enemy forces in Kwangsi, the Japanese lacked the strength to continue the war and announced the surrender on August 10, 1945. Thus, our third stage operations were substituted by the overall Japanese surrender.

(2) Military administration: In order to maintain and increase the combat effectiveness of our armed forces, efforts were made to seek foreign military assistance, improve the organization and equipment of the armed forces, realign conscription administration and food administration. give preferential treatment to recruits, encourage the enlistment of recruits, initiate the enlistment of educated youths and improve the quality of officers and men so as to increase the combat effectiveness of our armed forces.

b. Internal affairs:

Based on the determination of continuing the War of Resistance on the one hand and the lofty ideal of creating a New China practising the Three People's Principles on the other efforts were made to increase political efficiency and thoroughly implement total spiritual mobilization in order to meet wartime requirements. With regard to the implementation of important rear area administrative measures, efforts were made to reconstruct the southwestern provinces into rear area bases for the protracted War of Resistance. Meanwhile, promotion of work during the period of political tutelage should be expedited to lay the foundation of post-war constitutional rule.

c. Economy:

All the industrial materials in the government and private enterprises along the coast in the southeast should be evacuated to the rear in order to protect the strength of our national industries. Materials which could not be evacuated were destroyed so that they might not be used by the enemy. Establishment of factories in the rear areas was expedited. Additionally, resources were developed and production was increased to meet civilian and military needs. Military materials were procured from abroad to remedy the insufficiency in domestic production and to meet the requirements in sustaining the War of Resistance. In consumption, thrift was emphasized and control was enforced to support the prosecution of war.

d. Finance:

In order to defray the tremendous wartime military expenditures, efforts were made to open new sources for taxation and to reduce expenses so as to prevent depreciation of currency and inflation. People were encouraged to make donations and purchase bonds. When necessary, foreign debts could be incurred so as to enable the National Treasury to achieve balance and financial stability.

e. Foreign affairs:

Japanese designs and brutalities in aggression were exposed and the spiritual and moral support of friendly nations were sought in order to achieve military assistance. In consonance with the international situation, we sought military cooperation with friendly states to expedite the early collapse of the Japanese forces.

f. Education:

(1) Military education—Improved facilities and implemented highlighted education so as to increase the command ability and combat skills of the commanders at the various levels. Efforts should be made to stimulate morale and develop the spirit of loyalty and courage.

(2) People's education—Developed the people's common hostility against the enemy, provided them with strong body and military knowledge and served the nation with enthusiasm.

(3) Talent education—Emphasized science and technology and gave the people necessary military training. Cultivated the spirit of hard struggle and industry and made them thoroughly realize their responsibilities in the War of Resistance and national reconstruction.

g. Propaganda, public opinion and overseas Chinese affairs:

Urged the people and servicemen at home and abroad and overseas Chinese to contribute money or efforts, under the leadership of Generalissimo Chiang, realize the significance of the War of Resistance, observe people's agreement, carry out the national spiritual general mobilization so as to stimulate their strong sense of patriotism, strength their confidence in our victory in the War of Resistance and our success in national reconstruction.

h. Transportation and communications:

In transportation, to meet military requirements, increase logistic capability, water-land-air transportation was given tight war-time control. Priorities were established in accordance with the actual urgency of military and civilian requirements so that transportability could be effectively employed. In signal communications, to guard military security, censor was effected and domestic wave lengths were controlled. People were forbidden to listen to enemy broadcast so that they might not be deceived by false enemy propaganda.

i. Sanitation:

Preventive measures were stressed to maintain the health of people and servicemen and to prevent the occurrence of plagues. Medicine and equipment were procured and stored. Factories were established to remedy shortage. Public health was emphasized and sanitation inspections were made. Medical facilities needed by the armed forces must meet operational requirements.

War Preparations

As the Manchurian Incident and the Shanghai Incident came one·after another, our Government, in self defense, formulated the preliminary 5-year plan to be carried out in 1938 with emphasis on national defense. Unfortunately, the nation was confronted with many problems and suffered from financial stringencies, and the plan was not fully completed. The war preparations at the time are as follows:

1. Readiness of the armed forces—It was found necessary to unify organizations, improve equipment, implement the principle of an elite force, reduce higher units and strengthen lower units. It was anticipated that beginning in 1936, 20 divisions would be reorganized each year with 60 reorganized divisions as the cadres in our national defense forces. In addition, the establishment of separate non-infantry units and mechanized units was to be completed by the end of 1938. The objective is as follows:

   a. Light artillery—30 regiments.
   b. Heavy artillery—5 regiments.
   c. Calvary—10 divisions.
   d. Tank—2 regiments. Armored cars—2 regiments.
   e. Anti-aircraft artillery—7 regiments.
   f. Chemical troops—5 regiments.
   g. Engineers—3 regiments.
   h. Signal—5 regiments.
   i. Transportation—4 regiments.
   j. Railway troops—1 regiment.
   k. Armored railway troops—5 groups.

2. Construction of defense work—The nation's 8 key strategic areas were divided into Kiangsu-Chekiang, Shantung, Hopei-Chahar, Shansi-Suiyuan, Honan, Kwangtung, Fukien and Kwangsi districts. Permanent fortifications were constructed in all the strategic localities as the basis for sustained operations. The Kiangsui-Chekiang District had the nation's capital as its center and extended gradually toward the national boundary constituting defense fortifications in depth. By the time war broke out, the Kiangsu-Chekiang, Shansi-Suiyuan, and Honan Districts had completed most of their first phase fortifications.

3. Strengthening of water frontier defense fortresses—Beginning with Nanking, Chenchiang and Chiangyin Fortresses in the lower reaches of the Yangtze River, old guns were renovated, new guns and observation equipment were added, Nantung Fortress was constructed and Chenghai Fortress was repaired, Foochow Fortress, Amoy Fortress, Swatow Fortress and Hu-men Fortress were reconditioned, the Naval Torpedo School was established, fortress construction was strengthened, fortress garrison units were consolidated, and preparations were made to blockade the Yangtze River.

4. Implementation of conscription system—In order to meet the demand of modern warfare, our Government promulgated the Conscription Law in June, 1933. Based on the Conscription Law, the Ministry of War prepared the 20 pertinent regulations and formulated conscription implementation plans and pro-

gram governing the delineation of conscription control area temporarily dividing the nation into 60 division control areas. It was estimated that the plans would be promoted throughout the country in 5 years and approval was given for the Conscription Law to go into effect on March 1, 1936. In the same year, 12 division control areas were activated in Kiangsu, Shantung, Chekiang, Anhwei, Honan and Hupei with 4 regimental control areas in each division control area. By the end of December, the first batch of 50,000 recruits reported in and received training in the respective control areas. In the spring of 1937, 8 additional division control areas were activated in Kiangsu, Honan, Kiangsi, Hupei, Hunan and Fukien to take charge of conscription. It was estimated that between 1936 and 1940, 60 division control areas would be activated. Each division control area would be assigned 1 adjusted division supplemented with 1 realigned division.

5. Implementation of military training:

a. Able-bodied male training—As China just started conscription, there were no reservists. As casualties resulted in actual combat, replacements were not readily available to restore the strength of units. Beginning in 1936, universal able-bodied male training was conducted to facilitate wartime personnel replacement.

b. School military training—This training was designed to produce reserve NCO's and officer candidates. Since its implementation in 1934, a total of 17,498 senior middle school students or equivalents were qualified as reserve NCO's and 880 college students were qualified as officer candidates.

6. Build-up of munition industries—The facilities of munition factories were improved. Prior to the outbreak of full-scale war, our arsenals were able to produce all rifles, heavy machine guns, mortars, shells in caliber up to 150 mm., bombs up to 1000 kg, various types of fuses, chemicals and gas masks in large quantities. On the one hand, obsolete weapons in troop units were replaced; on the other hand, weapons were stored for future needs.

7. Development of economic resources—The National Resources Commission was established. Its main activities are as follows:

a. Construction of heavy industries:

With regard to metallurgy, there were the iron smelting plants in Hsiangtan, Hunan Province and the lower reaches of the Yangtze River; the steel plants in Tayeh and Yanghsin, Hupei Province and Peng Hsien, Szechuan Province; and the aluminum and zinc plants in Hunan and Kwangsi. As to fuels, there were the coal mines in Kaokeng and Tienho in Kiangsi, Yu Hsien in Honan and Tanchia Shan in Hunan, and petroleum fields in Yungping and Yenchang in northern Shensi, Pa Hsien and Ta Hsien in Szechuan. As to chemical industries, nitrogen plants and waterless alcohol plants were built. In machine industries, the aircraft engine factory, power plant, tool factory and textile plant in Hsiangtan, Hunan, were established. In electrical industries, the electrical appliance plant in Hsiangtan, Hunan and the hydroelectric plant in Changshou, Szechuan were successively established.

b.   Control of special mines:

The Antimony Control Administration and the Tungsten Control Administration were organized and the Chi An Tungsten Plant was established, responsible for the control over the marketing of antimony and tungsten.

c.   Preparations for economic mobilization:

Conducted surveys of materials for industries, mining, agriculture, communications and economy and formulate wartime development program in preparation for economic mobilization.

8.   Revamping transportation and communication—National defense transportation and communication nets in the southeastern, southwestern and northwestern provinces were established. The Chekiang-Kiangsi Railway[7] and the Canton-Hankow Railway were linked; the Lunghai Railway[8] and the Pingsui Railway[9] were extended; and the Hunan-Kweichow Railway[10] and the Hunan-Kwangsi Railway[11] were beginning to be built. In addition, the following preparations were made in water and land transportation:

Water transportation:

a.   Investigation and statistics on river and oceangoing ships.

b.   Organizing and holding exercises for river craft.

c.   Organizing and linking civilian junks.

d.   Construction and repair of water Pao-chia piers and drydocks.

e.   Improving old waterborne means of transportation.

Land transportation:

a.   Registering and organizing public and private-owned trucks.

b.   Preparations for the production of automobiles.

c.   Award and research on gasoline substitutes.

d.   Readying various types of fuel.

e.   Improving and utilizing old trains and hand carts.

9.   Air defense measures:

a.   Organizing air defense units—The Air Defense School was established, personnel trained and pooled, and anti-aircraft weapons and searchlight and observation equipment procured. By the time total war broke out, all the nation's ground air defense forces were organized into 6 large-caliber batteries, 23 small-caliber AW batteries and 2 search light detachments. The total number of weapons included 32 75mm. anti-aircraft guns, 26 37mm. anti-aircraft guns, 40 22mm. anti-aircraft guns, 48 13.2mm. AW and 66 7.9mm. AW.

b.   Dividing air defense zones and organizing nationwide air defense warning net—The nation was divided into 9 air defense zones: The 1st Zone included

---

7 Hangchow to Chu-chow.
8 Lien-yun to Pao-chi.
9 Peiping to Kwei-sui.
10 Hsiang-tan to Kwei-yang.
11 Heng-yang to Kwei-lin.

Kiangsu, Chekiang and Anhwei. The 2nd Zone included Honan and Shansi. The 3rd Zone included Kiangsi and Fukien. The 4th Zone included Shansi and Sui-yuan. The 5th Zone included Hopei and Chahar. The 6th Zone included Hunan and Hupei. The 7th Zone included Kwangtung and Kwangsi. The 8th Zone included Shensi and Kansu. The 9th Zone included Szechuan, Yunnan and Kweichow, by the spring of 1937, the intelligence in the various zones was linked up. Long distance telephone lines between key provinces and municipalities were established. In addition, 205 observation teams, 1,445 observation posts and 104 independent observation posts were established.

c. Various air defense and protective corps were organized and given active training so that in time of war they could undertake such duties as firefighting, gas defense, first aid, air raid alarm, engineering, traffic control, blackout control, shelter control, garrison and supply. By the spring of 1937, Kiangsu, Chekiang, Kiangsi, Anhwei, Hupei, Shansi, Shensi, Hunan, Suiyuan, Nanking, Shanghai, Chungking and Tsing-tao completed their organizations. Meanwhile, such air defense measures as underground shelters, air-raid shelters, air-raid dugouts, and sirens were taken and air defense exercises were held in order to increase the air defense techniques of the armed forced and indoctrinate the people with knowledge of air defense.

Section 3. Our Strength vs. Enemy Strength

When the war first broke out, the Japanese army, navy and air force were both quantitatively and qualitatively superior. They had many well-trained reservists. Their well-developed ordnance industry produced excellent equipment. In the personnel field, they had implemented the conscription system for decades. All males between the age of 17 and 40 had the obligation to do military service. Japan's total population stood at 105 million (including Japan proper, Korea, Taiwan and other territories). In time of war she could mobilize 27.8 million men. In time of peace, she had only 380,000 regulars, 738,000 ready reserves, 790,000 reservists, 1,579,000 first line replacements and 905,000 second line replacement, totaling 4,481,000 men. A well-developed industry enabled the equipment of the Japanese army to become modernized. As the war broke out, Japan had 17 regular divisions (another 4 divisions appeared to have been secretly activated). The strength of a division included 22,000 men, 5,800 horses, 9,500 rifles and carbines, 600+ light and heavy machine guns, 108 guns, 24 tanks and attached non-infantry units when needed to meet operational requirements. Japan's navy was second only to the United States and Britain, as she took the third place in all the navies in the world (additionally the battleships Yamato and Musashi were secretly under construction) giving a total tonnage of 1.9 million tons. Her army and navy had 2,700 planes.

As China was industrially backward, her production was limited. Further, as her conscription system was newly initiated, her military preparedness was greatly inferior. When the war first broke out, the total strength of the Chinese Armed Forces stood over 2 million with 182 infantry divisions, 46 separate brigades, 9 cavalry divisions, 4 artillery brigades and 20 artillery regiments. However, China's vast territories required considerable forces to maintain security. During the preliminary phase of operations it was estimated that the forces which could be used on the first lines included 80 infantry divisions, 9 separate infantry brigades, 9 cavalry divisions, 2 artillery brigades and 16 separate artillery regiments. By 1936, as equipment of the Chinese Armed Forces consisted mainly of small arms, they were only able to develop the effectiveness of defensive operations. By 1937, each reorganized infantry division had 10,923 officers and men, 3,800 rifles and carbines, 328 light and heavy machine guns, 46 various types of guns and mortars and 243 grenade launchers. The inferiority can well be imagined. In particular, the lack of heavy weapons and artillery ammunition and inadequate logistic support capability made it impossible to increase the firepower of the strategic units. The Chinese Navy had 66 newly constructed and

CHART 5

Our Strength vs. Enemy Strength Immediately before Outbreak of War

Classification Item	Enemy forces	Our forces	Remarks
ARMY	17 regular divisions (complete with noninfantry units).	191 infantry and cavalry divisions and 52 brigades.	In the initial phase, our forces could employ only 80 infantry divisions and 9 separate brigades, 9 cavalry divisions, 2 artillery brigades and 16 artillery regiments.
NAVY	1,900,000 tons	59,034 tons	
AIRCRAFT	2,700 planes	600 planes	Our air force had only 305 fighters.
Notes	1. Enen. regulars numbered 380,000 and reservists 738,000. During the initial phase, 700,000 troops were used. The total strength, including ready reserves and reservists stood at 4,480,000. 2. Our regulars numbered 2,000,000. 40%+ could be used during the initial phase. 500,000 able-bodied males were trained. 3. The enemy secretly restored the 4 divisions which he had deactivated. The fact that the enemy 13th, 15th and 17th Divisions appeared in the Shanghai theater shortly after the outbreak of war was ample proof. Hence, the enemy army's total strength was 21 divisions. Additionally, there were the puppet Manchurian forces, the puppet Mongolian forces, and the garrison forces of Na-man Railway and Pei-ning Railway.		

old ships with the largest ship at 3,000 tons and the smallest at 300 tons, and 12 high-speed torpedo boats giving a total displacement of 59,034 tons. Although the Chinese Air Force had 600 aircraft of various types, only 305 were combat types. The remainder consisted of trainers and transports. As to personnel replacements, China had always recruited her troops. By the time the Conscription Law was promulgated in 1933, she began to establish a formal conscription system. However, the recruiting system had been implemented for a long time. To meet the actual requirements, both the recruiting system and the conscription system were implemented on a parallel basis. Officially, conscription was pro-

CHART 6

Chart Showing Comparison of Enemy and Our Conscription Systems and Manpower Mobilization Status

Item	Classification	Enemy forces	Our forces	Remarks
Population		105,000,000	450,000,000	
Conscription	System	Conscription system	Conscription-recruiting system	
	Active duty	380,000	2,000,000	
	Ready reserves	738,000	500,000	
	Reservists	879,000	none	
	1st replacement	1,579,000	none	
	2nd replacement	905,000	none	
Mobilization	Manpower	27,830,000		
	Personnel	8,860,000	14,049,024	12,267,780 were replaced
Notes	1. Enemy mobilized manpower was based on the estimate of our G-2. 2. Our mobilized manpower was based on the statistics of the Conscription Bureau.			

CHART 7

*Chart Showing Comparison of Organization and Equipment of Enemy
and Our Divisions Immediately before Outbreak of War*

Comparison of Organization

Branch	Enemy force	Our force	Remarks
Infantry	2 brigades (4 regt.)	2 brigades (4 regt.)	
Artillery	1 regiment	1 battalion	
Cavalry	1 regiment		
Engineer	1 regiment	1 battalion	
Quartermaster	1 regiment	1 battalion	
Tank	1 company		
Others	A number of non-infantry units	A number of non-infantry units	

Comparison of Equipment

Description	Enemy force	Our force	Remarks
Personnel	21,945	10,923	
Horses	5,849		
Rifle, carbine, pistol	9,476	3,821	
Grenade launcher	576	243	
LMG	541	274	
HMG	104	54	
Howitzer; pack howitzer	64	16	
Regimental and battalion gun	44	30	
Tank	24		
Vehicle	262		Belonging to enemy artillery regiment.
Truck	266		Equipment of a QM regiment.
Horse-drawn cart	555		—ditto—

Notes	
	1. The equipment listed in the organization of our forces was from the more than 10 divisions reorganized in 1937. The strength of other divisions was 50% of the above. However, there were exceptional cases. For example, each division in the 29th Corps had 4 brigades with a total of more than 700 LMG.
	2. Our artillery units lacked ammunition, observation and signal equipment. Our transportability was especially weak.

mulgated to become effective on March 1, 1936. Shortly afterwards, war broke out. At this time, China's conscription system and her mobilization of manpower and material power were incapable of meeting the war requirements. Throughout the hard struggle, China fought the war on the one hand and devoted herself to improving the conscription system on the other, culminating in the successful accomplishment of her missions in the War of Resistance.

A comparison of the enemy strength and our strength before the war is shown in Chart 5; conscription system and the status of manpower mobilization is shown in Chart 6; and a comparison of the organization and equipment of an enemy division and our division is shown in Chart 7.

Section 4. First Phase Operations

(July 7, 1937 - Late November, 1937—See Map 1)

When the war first broke out on July 7, 1937, the Japanese forces used the pretext of not wishing to aggravate the situation as the reinforced brigade which was stationed in Pingyu sector of the Pei-ning Railway suffered defeat in its night attack on Lu-kou-chiao (Marco Polo Bridge).[12] The Japanese swiftly mobilized one division and two brigades to reinforce Peiping-Tientsin. When the reinforcements arrived on July 28, they began the attack. Subsequently, they mobilized three divisions and moved them to Peiping-Tientsin.

As the units of the 29th Corps under Gen. Sung Che-yuan had hoped to reach a peaceful solution to the problems through diplomatic negotiations, their dispositions were passive. The situation in the preliminary period was highly unfavorable to the 29th Corps, the main force of which was stationed in Nanyuan and suffered heavy losses when it engaged the enemy. On July 30, the 29th Corps gave up Tientsin and on August 4, withdrew from Peiping.

On August 7, our National Defense Council decided to fight the general war and adopt the sustained strategy of attrition. On August 20, it delineated "Hopei-Northern Honan," "Shansi-Chahar-Suiyuan," "Southern Kiangsu-Chekiang," "Fukien-Kwangtung," and "Shantung-Northern Huai" as the 1st through the 5th War Areas. The following operational guiding principle was established:

"Portions of the Chinese Armed Forces would be concentrated in North China for sustained resistance, with emphasis on guarding the natural barrier of Shansi. The bulk of the armed forces would be concentrated in East China to attack the enemy in Shanghai, protect the key localities of Wusung-Shanghai, and defend the nation's capital. Minimum forces would be employed to undertake the garrison of the ports in South China."

---

12 Belonging to Wan-ping Hsien, Hopei Province. Erected across the Yung-ting River, it is 211 meters long and has nine arches. The trains of the Peiping-Hankow Railway travelled over it. It is considered as the sacred spot in China's War of Resistance as the July 7 Incident of 1937 broke out here.

On August 15, the enemy declared general mobilization. Two corps were dispatched to Peiping-Tientsin and two divisions were moved to Shanghai in an attempt to destroy our forces in Hopei in one stroke, take Shanghai and threaten the nation's capital thereby forcing us into submission.

Two of our corps under Gen. Tang En-po operated in the mountainous areas in southern Chahar to tie down the enemy. In middle and late August, they struck the enemy in Chuyung Kuan and Nankou. In September, the First Army and the Second Army in the 1st War Zone made use of the rivers in Hopei to offer piecemeal resistance so as to delay the advance of the enemy's 1st and 2nd Corps. In early October, our elite forces were pulled out to be employed in Shansi and subordinated to the 2nd War Area. The natural barrier of North China was insured. As the enemy force entering into Southern Hopei failed to catch our main force, it was forced to turn its front from facing south to facing west. The uphill attack led to a stalemated situation. Resolutely, our main force was committed in Wusung-Shanghai under the 3rd War Area. The attack began in mid-August without waiting for the completion of assembly. The attack progressed smoothly and forced the enemy to draw reinforcements from Japan and North China. For three months, our forces fought gallantly inflicting over 60,000 casualties on the enemy, enabled the materiel in our factories in the lower reaches of the Yangtze River and along the coast to move to the west, and boosted morale, contributing immensely to the prosecution of war.

In early November, enemy 10th Corps landed in the vicinity of Chinshanwei to attack the rear of our right flank. Thus, our forces were forced to abandon Shanghai and fall back to Nanking. On December 13, our forces continued the withdrawal into Chekiang and Anhwei. After taking Nanking, the enemy massacred more than 100,000 civilians and soldiers unmasking their ruthless brutality. Later, through the office of German Ambassador Oskar Trautmann, Japan proposed peace negotiations.

Generalissimo Chiang's vision and determination can be seen in his message to the nation upon the withdrawal of our forces from Nanking on December 17, in which he strongly indicated our determination to fight to the end. At the Wuchang Conference in the spring of 1938, he pointed out that the Japanese forces, poorly disciplined and brutal, would be defeated in the end. Subsequently, the supreme headquarters was reorganized, order of battle adjusted and future operational principles formulated. The principles were to insure the security of Hsuchow, and lure the enemy main force to the Tientsin-Pukow Railway so as to disperse the enemy strength, gain time, strengthen our combat effectiveness and cover our military and communication center—Wuhan. Later, taking advantage of the lack of coordination between the enemy forces in Central China and North China, our elite forces in northern Honan and southern Shansi were shifted to southern Shantung and subordinated to the 5th War Area. In late March, Generalissimo Chiang arrived in Hsuchow to give his instructions. He emphasized the importance of fighting the enemy on interior lines and defeated the enemy 2nd Corps at Taierhchuang. Thus, the enemy was forced to send in reinforcements from North China and south of the Yangtze River to the northern and southern ends of the Tientsin-Pukow Railway in an enveloping attack on Hsuchow. The enemy's 14th Division moved in from northern Honan to take Lanfeng and cut off the Lunghai Railway. In mid-May Generalissimo Chiang arrived in Chengchow to direct our army in eastern Honan which defeated the enemy's 14th Division, recaptured Lanfeng and Lowang, cleared the Lunghai Railway between Kuei-te and Kai-feng, and lured the employment of the enemy main force to the front so that our forces in Hsuchow could break out. Later, the enemy was stopped by the flood of the Yellow River and changed his axis of operations. In June, the enemy moved up the Yangtze River to attack Wuhan. Taking advantage of the natural barriers of Poyang Lake, Chiukung Shan and Tapieh Shan, our forces resisted strongly and counterattacked. Fierce fighting lasted for 5 months. When our forces abandoned Wuhan, the enemy had suffered heavy losses. As the theater of operations expanded greatly and the enemy forces were widely scattered, they had reached the ultimate in the offensive. Accordingly, the enemy forces stopped along Hsinyang-Yuehyang-Hsiuchiang and dispatched forces to capture Amoy and Canton, blockaded our ports, and adopted counter-attrition warfare. Thus, the first phase operations came to an end.

Earlier in the Battle of Taiyuan in the winter of 1937, enemy forces in North China were dealt a heavy blow by our forces at Pinghsingkuan, Hsinkou and Ladies' Pass. Later, enemy forces operated along Paotou-Fenglingtu-Hsinhsiang and took all the narrow corridors along the Peiping-Suiyuan Railway, Tungpu Railway, northern section of the Peiping Hankow Railway and the Tientsin-Pukow Railway. Our forces operated in the vast areas outside the railways and launched guerrilla operations which bogged down the enemy. Thus, our forces were able to make use of the time to regroup the units and restore combat effectiveness preparatory to subsequent operations.

During the above period, our air force destroyed the enemy Shikay and Kisarazu Squadrons, shooting down 227 planes, damaging 44 planes, destroying 140 planes, sinking 98 ships, damaging 60 ships and 1 aircraft carrier. Our navy blockaded Chiangyin and Matang, damaged the Japanese battleship Izumo and 20 ships and craft resulting in glorious achievements.

An account of army, navy and air force operations and logistic support is stated as follows:

An Account of Army Operations

1. Peiping-Tientsin operations (Early July-Early August, 1937. See Map 2 and Charts 8 and 9)

On July 7, 1937, under the pretext of conducting an exercise, elements of the Japanese garrison forces along the Ping-yu sector of the Peining Railway

CHART 8

Chart Showing Japanese Chain of Command in Peiping-Tientsin Operations
(Early July-Early August, 1937)

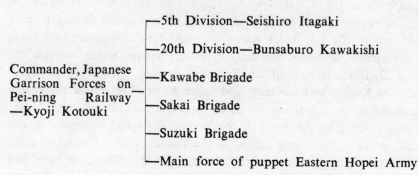

Commander, Japanese
Garrison Forces on
Pei-ning   Railway
—Kyoji Kotouki

—5th Division—Seishiro Itagaki

—20th Division—Bunsaburo Kawakishi

—Kawabe Brigade

—Sakai Brigade

—Suzuki Brigade

—Main force of puppet Eastern Hopei Army

Totalling 100,000 men, 200 aircraft and 100 tanks

Remarks: 1. Sakai and Suzuki Brigades, formerly organic to the Kwantung Army, were temporarily attached.

2. During the outbreak of hostilities on July 7, 1937, Koichiro
Tashiro was the commander. Later, when he died, Kyoji
Kotouki became the acting commander.

3. Japanese Navy took part in the Battle of Ta-ku-kou

CHART 9

Chart Showing Chinese Chain of Command during Peiping-Tientsin Operations
(Early July, 1937)

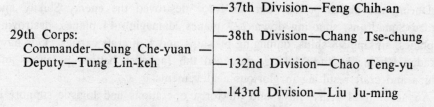

29th Corps:
   Commander—Sung Che-yuan
   Deputy—Tung Lin-keh

—37th Division—Feng Chih-an

—38th Division—Chang Tse-chung

—132nd Division—Chao Teng-yu

—143rd Division—Liu Ju-ming

Remarks: 1. Each division had 3 infantry brigades and was attached
with 1 separate brigade.

2. The 143rd Division which was stationed in Chahar did not
participate in this operation.

3: Hopei Peace Preservation forces were stationed in Pei-wan.

4. One brigade of the 53rd Corps took part in the attack on
Feng-tai.

(under Gen. Koichiro Tashiro whose command included the Tanabe Composite Brigade which was composed of 3 infantry regiments, 1 tank company and 1 field artillery regiment stationed its main strength in Tientsin and portions in Peiping and along the Peining Railway), staged a night attack on Lukouchiao (Marco Polo Bridge). One of our regiments under Col. Chi Hsing-wen, a unit of the 29th Corps (Gen. Sung Che-yuan who was concurrently the corps commander commanded 4 divisions, 4 separate brigades, 2 cavalry division, 1 cavalry brigade and Hopei peace preservation units, deployed his main force in Peiping and portions on the outskirts of Tientsin and key localities in Hopei and Chahar) fought valiantly. On July 8, the enemy sent reinforcements from Tientsin. Gen. Sung Che-yuan, director of the Hopei-Chahar Pacification Headquarters, ordered his forces to hold their positions, and accommodated himself to the situation hoping to avert war through diplomatic negotiations. After repeated negotiations, both sides agreed to stop shooting and return to their stations. However the Japanese forces did not honor their promise. In the afternoon of July 10, when the reinforcements arrived, they renewed the attack. Once again, they were repelled. On July 12, the enemy mobilized one division, two brigades and an air force regiment. Subsequently, in the latter part of July, three more divisions were mobilized and sent to Peiping-Tientsin area.

During the outbreak of the incident, Generalissimo Chiang was aware of the seriousness of the situation. On July 9, Generalissimo Chiang cabled the following message to Gen. Sung: "Peace negotiations without neglecting combat readiness." He ordered the 26th Route Army (later reorganized into the 1st Army) under Gen. Sun Lien-chung to move two divisions by rail to Paoting and Shihchiachuang to be placed under the command of Gen. Sung.

When the attack of the Japanese garrison forces was frustrated, Gen. Koichiro Tashiro suddenly died and was replaced by Gen. Kyoji Kotouki. As their reinforcements had not fully assembled, the Japanese claimed that they would not aggravate the situation and agreed to an investigation by both sides hoping to resolve it as a local incident. By July 25 when enemy reinforcements poured in, they made provocative attacks on our 38th Division in Langfang. On July 26, enemy planes bombed Langfang. Enemy units attempted to enter Kuang An Gate in Peiping but were stopped. The enemy then issued an ultimatum to Gen. Sung demanding the withdrawal of Chinese forces on the outskirts of Peiping to the west of Yungting River. Gen. Sung flatly refused the ultimatum, ordered his units to prepare for action and requested the Central Government to dispatch large reinforcements.

On July 27, the enemy laid siege to our forces stationed in Tung Hsien. One battalion of our garrison forces broke out and fell back to Nanyuan. On the same day, enemy planes bombed our forces on the outskirt of Peiping and reconnoitered Kaifeng, Chengchow and Loyang. On July 28, the enemy employed one division and three brigades in a general offensive against our forces in Peiping. His main attack was directed against Nanyuan with a secondary attack against Peiyuan. Scores of enemy planes rotated in the bombing. Our forces rose in resistance, and the fighting was most bitter. Gen. Tung Lin-ko, Deputy Commander of the 29th Corps and Gen. Chao Teng-yu, Commander of the 132nd Division, gave their lives to the nation. The Hopei peace preservation units also suffered heavy losses. However, the brigade under Gen. Liu Chen-san of the 38th Division mopped up the enemy in the vicinity of Langfang. A brigade of the 53rd Corps and another unit jointly recaptured the Fengtai RR Station. In the same night, realizing that fighting the enemy hastily was unfavorable, Gen. Sung Che-yuan led the main force of the 29th Corps to withdraw to the right bank of the Yungting River. Mayor Chang Tze-chung of Tientsin was left in Peiping to take charge of political affairs in Hopei and Chahar in an acting capacity. Gen. Liu Ju-chen's New Separate 29th Brigade was left in Peiping.

On July 29, the puppet eastern Hopei peace preservation units in Tung Hsien defected by annihilating the enemy and puppets there. At dawn on July 29, enemy 5th Division and naval forces separately attacked Tientsin and Taku-kou. Units of the 38th Division under the command of its acting commander Gen. Li Wen-tien, and the municipal peace preservation units defended Tientsin, Gen. Huang Wei-kang's brigade defended Taku. fighting gallantly, and killing many enemy troops. It also attacked the enemy airfield at Tungchutzu destroying many enemy planes. At night, Gen. Chang Tze-chung was ordered to withdraw toward Machang and Yangliuching. On July 30, when the enemy captured Tientsin and Taku, looting and burning followed resulting in heavy destruction.

On August 1, Generalissimo Chiang appointed Gov. Fu Tso-yi of Suiyuan as the commander-in-chief of the 7th Army Group, (composed of 1 division, 3 brigades, and units of the 19th Corps, 35th Corps and 61st Corps), Gen. Tang En-po as the frontline overall commander (commanding the 13th Corps and 17th Corps) reinforcing Chahar by rail from Suiyuan and Shansi, and Gov. Liu Ju-ming of Chahar as the deputy commander-in-chief (commanding the 143rd Division and 2 peace preservation brigades) responsible for the garrison of Chahar.

As the enemy forces moved into Peiping-Tientsin, their arrogance and over-bearing made it impossible for Gen. Chang Tzu-chung to carry out his duties. On August 4, he left Peiping and Gen. Liu Ju-chen's forces withdrew into Chahar. With the fall of Peiping, the puppet organization came into being.

2. Operations along the Peiping-Suiyuan Railway (Early August-late August, 1937. See Map 3 and Charts 10 and 11)

After the fall of Peiping-Tientsin, enemy forces took the key localities on the outskirts of Peiping-Tientsin to cover the massing of the their follow-up armies. In early August, the enemy's 10th Division operated in Tuliu Chen, while his 20th Division advanced toward the line from Chaili to Lianghsiang. Subsequent-ly his 11th Separate Brigade and 5th Division attacked Nankou. Additionally,

CHART 10

*Chart showing Japanese Chain of Command in Operations along the
Peiping-Suiyuan Railway (Early August, 1937)*

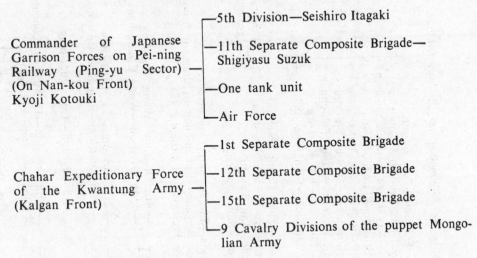

Commander of Japanese
Garrison Forces on Pei-ning
Railway (Ping-yu Sector)
(On Nan-kou Front)
Kyoji Kotouki

—5th Division—Seishiro Itagaki

—11th Separate Composite Brigade—
Shigiyasu Suzuk

—One tank unit

—Air Force

Chahar Expeditionary Force
of the Kwantung Army
(Kalgan Front)

—1st Separate Composite Brigade

—12th Separate Composite Brigade

—15th Separate Composite Brigade

—9 Cavalry Divisions of the puppet Mongolian Army

Remarks: 1. The Kwantung Army and the Pei-ning Railway Garrison
Force were under the remote control of Japan's Central
Supreme Command. There was no unified command on
the battlefield.

2. The 11th Separate Composite Brigade was subordinated to
the Kwantung Army. At the end of July, it was attached
to the Garrison Force. In early September, it was reverted
to the Chahar Expeditionary Force of the Kwantung Army.

the Kwangtung Army dispatched more than 3 brigades (the 1st, 12th and 15th
Brigades plus 7 infantry companies) from northern Chahar to Kalgan in response
to the above attack. Furthermore, 9 puppet Mongolian divisions operated in the
vicinity of Shangiyi, Shangtu, and Huateh to block the eastward advance of our
1st Cavalry Corps.

In early August, Gen. Tang En-po's 13th Corps (commanding 4th Division
and 89th Division) at Chuyung Pass and Nankou and the 17th Corps (commanding 21st Division and 84th Division) at Chihcheng, Yenching and Huailai
occupied positions in depth to stop the enemy. The 1st Cavalry Corps and Gen.
Liu Ju-ming's forces (the 143rd Division and 2 peace preservation brigades) attacked the enemy in northern Chahar.

On August 8, the enemy forces began the attack on Nankou. Taking full
advantage of natural barriers, our 13th Corps offered strong resistance employing
firepower and counterattacks in repeated fightings. Despite heavy casualties on
both sides, our forces were successful in thwarting enemy attacks.

CHART 11

Chart Showing Chinese Chain of Command during Operations along the Peiping-Suiyuan Railway (August, 1937)

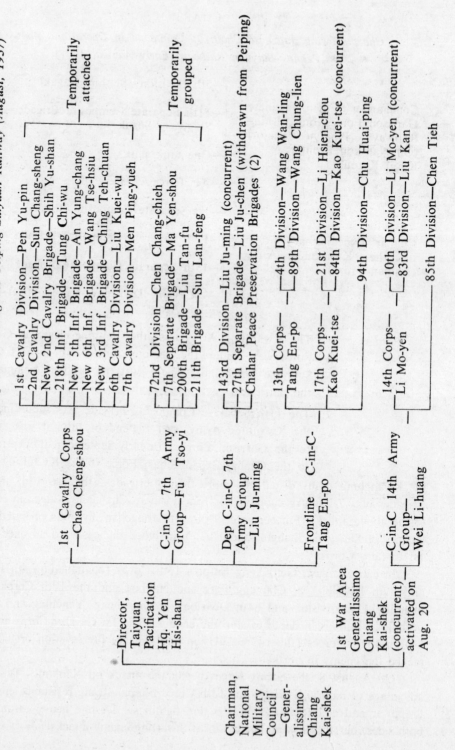

On August 11, Generalissimo Chiang ordered Gen. Wei Li-huang's forces (10th Division, 83rd Division and 85th Division) to activate the 14th Army Group. Elements of this army group were moved from the vicinity of Yingchia-chuang by rail to Yi Hsien in 10 days through the mountain plains west of Peiping for a turning movement toward Nankou in direct support of Gen. Tang En-po's forces. In addition, Gen. Sun Lien-chung's 1st Army made piecemeal attacks on the enemy forces in Lianghsiang and Chaili. Elements of the 1st Army operated in Heilung Pass to cover the advance of Gen. Wei Li-huang's forces.

After August 11, when the attack launched by the enemy's 11th Separate Brigade against our left flank failed, the enemy employed planes and tanks jointly in a frontal attack, took Nankou RR Station and continued the attack on Chuyung Pass. Our 13th Corps counterattacked and drove off the enemy. Subsequently, the enemy employed his main force, the 5th Division, in an enveloping attack on our right flank at Huanglaoyuan. Our forces shifted Gen. Shih Chueh's brigade and Gen. Li Hsien-chou's division as well as the reinforcements which were composed of the divisions under Gen. Chu Huai-ping and Gen. Chen Chang-chieh to meet the enemy resulting in violent fighting.

In northern Chahar, our 1st Cavalry Corps captured Shangtu, Nanhaochan, Shangyi and Huateh. Elements of the 143rd Division took Chungli, while, the main force reached the wall of Changpei. Meanwhile, the enemy massed the bulk of 2 composite brigades and 1 mechanized brigade for a counterattack from Changpei to Kalgan.

On August 17, Gen. Yen Hsi-shan, director of the Taiyuan Pacification Headquarters, directed Gen. Fu Tso-yi to move 1 division and 3 brigades by rail from Tatung to Huailai to reinforce Gen. Tang En-po's forces.

On August 18 and 19, enemy forces which counterattacked from Changpei took Shenweitaiko in outer Great Wall and Hanno Dam. The situation in Kalgan was critical, as our forces, scattered and ill-equipped, were unable to stop the enemy. Meanwhile, Gen. Fu Tso-yi led 2 brigades and arrived in Tumupao and Hsiahuayuan by rail. On August 20, these forces turned back to reinforce Kalgan. Gen. Chen Chang-chieh's division which had reached Huailai reinforced Chenpien City, and Gen. Ma Yen-shou's brigade defended Huailai.

On August 21, enemy forces broke through Hengling City and Chenpien City. Gen. Tang En-po's forces, having suffered over 50% casualties, defended such strong points as Chuyung Pass, Huailai and Yenching awaiting reinforcements to launch counterattacks. In northern Chahar, Gen. Liu Ju-ming's 143rd Division fell back to defend Kalgan.

On August 23, the enemy's 5th Division pushed toward Huailai via Chenpien City. The advance elements of Gen. Wei Li-huang's forces reached Chingpaikou, drove off a small number of enemy troops and contacted the enemy forces in Chenpien City. However, they were delayed in crossing the Yungting River and were unable to open the attack in time and check the enemy. As communications were poor, they were unable to establish contact with Gen. Tang En-po's forces.

On August 26, Gen. Tang En-po's forces were ordered to break out toward the right bank of Sangchien River. Later, the 13th Corps was ordered to move to Anyang. On the same day, Gen. Liu Ju-ming's forces were ordered to withdraw to the right bank of Hsiang-yang River, and later to southern Hopei. Gen. Fu Tso-yi's forces, having failed in the counterattack to recapture Kalgan, fell back to defend Chaikoupao.

On August 29, enemy Oui's column moved south from Tushihkou. On August 30, it attacked Yenching via Chihcheng. After repelling the enemy, our 17th Corps withdrew to the right bank of Sangchien River. The operations of this phase came to an end.

Later, according to reliable information, during these operations, our wounded who had not been evacuated and stragglers. other than a small number whom the enemy regarded worthy of interrogating, were all summarily executed.

3. Operation along Northern Sector of Peiping-Hankow Railway (Early August-early December, 1937. See Map 4 and Charts 12 and 13-1 13-2)

CHART 12

Chart Showing Japanese Chain of Command in Operations along the Northern Sector of Peiping-Hankow Railway (Mid-August, 1937)

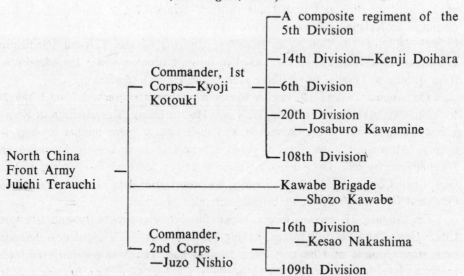

Remarks: The main force of the 5th Division was in Shansi. Originally on the Tientsin-Pukow Railway, the main force of the 2nd Corps moved from Hsiaofan Chen in early October to Ningchin to take part in the operations along the Peiping-Hankow Railway. The 10th Division was left for operations along the Tientsin-Pukow Railway.

CHART 13-1

Showing Chinese Chain of Command in Operations along the Northern Sector of the Peiping-Hankow Railway (August-September, 1937)

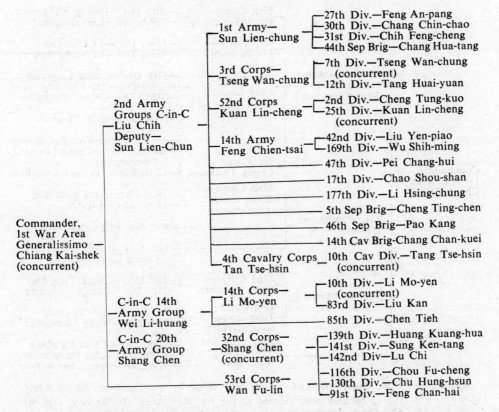

Remarks: 1. After massing in Shih-chia-chuang, Liu Mao-en's 13th Army was shifted to Ping-hsing-kuan in Shansi leaving its engineer battalion to construct defense works along the Peiping-Hankow Railway under the command of Hsu Yung-chang, director of the Generalissimo's Headquarters in Shih-chia-chuang.

2. Formerly under the command of higher headquarters along the Tientsin-Pukow Railway, the 53rd Corps became subordinated to the 1st War Area in September.

3. Between August and September, Wei Li-huang's forces participated in the operations at Nan-kou along the Peiping-Suiyuan Railway. Forces under Feng Chien-tsai, Li Hsing-chung, Cheng Ting-shen, Pao Kang, Chang Chan-kuei and Shang Chen massed in the vicinity of Shihchiachuang but did dot participate in the operations.

4. Between August and September, Director Hsu Yung-chang of the Generalissimo's Headquarters in Shihchiachuang supervised and maintained contact with the operations in Hopei. In the latter part of September, the Headquarters was deactivated.

CHART 13-2

Chart Showing Chinese Chain of Command in Operations along the Northern Sector of Peiping-Hankow Railway (October, 1937-January, 1938)

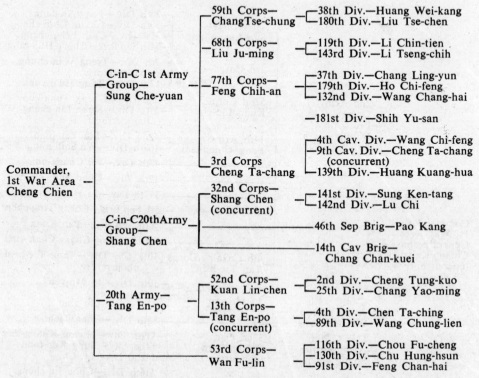

Remarks: 1. Upon deactivation of the 6th War Area in mid-October, the 1st Army Group became subordinated to the 1st War Area. In January, 1938, its 59th Corps was integrated into the order of battle of the 5th War Area, In mid-October, the 68th Corps became subordinated to the 1st War Area. In the latter part of October, it was integrated into the order of battle of the 3rd War Area.

2. The 4th Cavalry Corps was transferred to Kai-feng in mid-October. Later, the corps headquarters was deactivated.

3. After the Battle of Cheng-ting in early October, the 46th Separate Brigade was deactivated.

4. On October 2, the 14th Army Group attached with 47th and 54th Divisions and 5th Separate Brigade was integrated into the order of battle of the 2nd War Area.

5. On September 30, Liu Chih, C-in-C, 2nd Army Group, was relieved and succeeded by Sun Lien-chung. The 1st Army was reorganized into a general headquarters. In early October, this general headquarters led the former 1st Army, 14th Corps, 3rd Corps, 17th Division, and 177th Division to be integrated into the order of battle of the 2nd War Area.

6. Forces under Hopei militia C-in-C Chang Yin-wu, Hopei guerilla commander Sun Kuei-yuan, and 1st Separate Guerilla Column commander Lu Cheng-tsao conducted guerilla operations behind enemy lines. At the end of October, Tang En-po of the 20th Army led the 13th Corps to come under the command of the 2nd War Area.

In August, 1937, the National Military Council established the Paoting Headquarters with Gen. Hsu Yung-chang as its director and Gen. Lin Wei as the chief of staff to supervise the military operations in Hopei. Gen. Sung Che-yuan and Gen. Liu Chih were named respectively Commanders-in-Chief of the 1st and 2nd Army Groups responsible for the operations along the Tientsin-Pukow Railway and the northern sector of the Peiping-Hankow Railway.

In early August, the main strength of the 29th Corps was shifted to the Tientsin-Pukow Railway. The first-line forces faced the enemy north of Chinghai. Our 3rd Cavalry Corps and 53rd Corps faced the enemy across the Yungting River along Yungching, Pa Hsien and Ku-an. The 1st Army faced the enemy's 20th Division in the vicinity of Toutien and Fangshan. The 67th Corps, 3rd Army, 49th Corps and 23rd Division massed in Tacheng, Tsang Hsien and Tehchow. The 10th Cavalry Division, 3rd Corps and 52nd Corps massed in the vicinity of Paoting. The 14th Corps, 85th Division, 13th Army, 14th Army, 32nd Corps, 47th Division, 17th Division, 177th Division, 5th Separate Brigade and 46th Separate Brigade massed in the vicinity of Shihchiachuang.

On August 11, Gen. Wei Li-huang's 14th Corps and 85th Division were ordered to be reorganized into the 14th Army Group which was moved from Shihchiachuang to Yi Hsien by rail via mountain plain west of Peiping in direct support of the operations in Nankou. A force of the 1st Army occupied the high ground northwest of Fangshan to cover the advance of the 14th Army Group.

On August 15, the enemy issued the general mobilization order directing the North China Front Army (under Gen. Juichi Terauchi commanding the 1st and 2nd Corps) to mass in Peiping-Tientsin.

On August 20, our Government divided the war theater into 5 war areas. The 1st War Area included Hopei Province and northern Honan with Generalissimo Chiang as the concurrent commander exercising unified command of the operations along the Tientsin-Pukow Railway and the northern sector of the Peiping-Hankow Railway. Soon afterwards, operational plans were issued. A summary of the operational plans is as follows:

a. Objective: The 1st War Area will stop the southward advance of the enemy along the Tientsin-Pukow Railway and the Peiping-Hankow Railway, and attack the flank of the enemy storming Nankou.

b. Guiding essentials: Using the Tientsin-Pukow Railway and the Peiping-Hankow Railway as the axis, our forces will occupy deep and dispersed strongpoint type positions, control mobile forces on the flanks, be prepared to assist the defense forces and attack the flanks of the enemy. The first-line units will organize guerrilla forces, cross the Yungting River, organize the people, sabotage the lines of communications and tie down the enemy.

Additionally, a powerful mobile force will advance in the area southwest of Huailai, directly or indirectly render assistance to Nankou and insure the operations of our forces.

c.   General disposition:

(1)   1st Army Group (Tientsin-Pukow Railway): Omitted.

(2)   2nd Army Group (Peiping-Hankow Railway):

1st Army, attached with the 10th Cavalry Division will occupy positions in depth along the line from Matou Chen, Liuliho, Fangshan to Heilung Pass. It will establish contact with the 53rd Corps in Ku-an on the right to stop the enemy.

Later, the 47th Division will advance to Chochow to support the operations of the First Army.

The 3rd Corps will prepare alternate positions in the vicinity of Kaopeitien, Laishui and Yi Hsien. Afterward, it will also advance toward Chochow.

The 52nd Corps and 17th Division will prepare alternate positions in the vicinity of Hsinan Chen, Tsaoho, Mancheng and Paoting.

The boundary between the 1st Army Group and the 2nd Army Group will be Hochien-Hsiung Hsien-Kuan-Shunyi. All points along the boundary will be inclusive to the 1st Army Group.

(3)   1st General Mobile Force:

With Chaitang and Talungmen as the bases, the 14th Army Group will attack the enemy's flank to respond to the operations of Nankou and Huailai.

(4)   General Reserves:

The 32nd Corps will prepare positions in the vicinity of Anping, Shentze and Chin Hsien.

The 13th Army will prepare positions in the vicinity of Chengting and Shih-chiachuang.

Since mid-August, to respond to the operations in Nankou and facilitate the operations of the 14th Army Group, our 1st Army attacked the enemy at Liang-hsiang and Chaili. Although the enemy repeatedly counterattacked, the scale was limited and neither side made any appreciable progress. On August 26, our forces abandoned Huailai and Kalgan with the 13th Corps heading for Anyang, the 14th Army Group for Shihchiachuang and the 143rd Division for Taming. On August 27, the 1st Army fell back to prepared positions in Liuliho and Fangshan to engage the enemy.

On September 14, the enemy 1st Corps began the general offensive with the 20th Division making a frontal attack on Liuliho and the 6th Division and 14th Division making a forced crossing of the Yungting River at Kuan and Yungching for a turning attack against Chochow. From positions in depth, our 53rd Corps, 3rd Corps, 47th Division and 1st Army offered strong resistance which resulted in bitter fighting. By September 18, when our positions on the right were out-flanked by the enemy, and the situation was most unfavorable. Our forces began the withdrawal. The 53rd Corps was shifted to Hsiung Hsien, Paikouho and Jenchiu; the 3rd Corps attached with 47th Division was moved to the vicinity of Paoting; and the 14th Army Group was ordered to the vicinity of Shihchiachuang.

Meanwhile, the enemy's 1st Corps moved south along both sides of the

Peiping-Hankow Railway. On September 21, it began the attack on Tsao-ho and Mancheng. From prepared positions, our 52nd Corps, 3rd Corps, 17th Division and 47th Division resisted strongly. On September 22, Mancheng fell and portions of the enemy forces made a turning movement toward Fangshunchiao and Yuchia-chuang. On September 24, our forces abandoned Paoting, withdrawing toward the right bank of Huto River. As the 53rd Corps was in the east of Paiyangting, it did not participate in this operation, and later withdrew to the south.

In late September, our forces designated the northern sector of the Tientsin-Pukow Railway as the 6th War Area and the northern sector of the Peiping-Hankow Railway the 1st War Area with Gen. Cheng Chien as the acting commander of the 1st War Area in order to facilitate direction. The Shihchiachuang Headquarters was deactivated, and dispositions were adjusted designating the 32nd Corps (less 139th Division), 17th Division, 47th Division, and 10th Cavalry Division under the command of Gen. Shang Chen, commander of the 20th Army Group, to occupy the positions in Chin Hsien, Kaocheng, Lohcheng, East and West Tatzu Shan and the right bank of Huto River. The 3rd Corps, 14th Corps, 14th Army, 27th Division, 85th Division, 94th Division, 177th Division, 5th Separate Brigade, and 46th Separate Brigade were placed under the command of Gen. Wei Li-huang, Commander-in-Chief of the 14th Army Group for the defense of the positions in Chengting, Shihchiachuang and the right bank of Huto River. The 1st Army (less 27th Division), 139th Division, and 54th Division massed south of Pingshan as reserves preparatory to go into offensive from the left flank for a decisive battle against the enemy.

Later, as the enemy penetrated Ku-yueh-kou and took Yenmen Pass in northern Shansi, the situation in Taiyuan was critical. Generalissimo Chiang directed Gen. Wei Li-huang to reinforce Yikou on October 2 by rail with the 14th Corps, 85th Division, 47th Division, 54th Division and 5th Separate Brigade in order to guard the key localities in Shansi.

On September 29, elements of the enemy's 1st Corps took Hsinlo. In early October, its main force continued its advance from Paoting. On October 6, it attacked our advance positions in Changshou. Our 46th Separate Brigade fought bitterly for one day and sustained prohibitive losses. Later, the enemy attacked our primary positions at Chengting and Huto River. Meanwhile, the main force of the enemy's 2nd Corps moved west along the Tzu-ya River. On October 6, its advance elements passed through Hsiaofan Chen. The 67th Corps in the 6th War Area fell back successively, as it could not withstand the attack. Delayed by the flooding of the Chulung River and the Huto River, the 53rd Corps remained in the area north of the Huto River unable to establish contact. Thus, the right flank of the 1st War Area was greatly threatened. Generalissimo Chiang resolutely ordered the 1st Army, 14th Army, 3rd Corps and 17th Division to move into the prepared positions in advance in order to consolidate the gate to eastern Shansi. The 32nd Corps was left in the front of the Peiping-Hankow Railway for sustained resistance. On October 8, the enemy took Chengting and Lingshou and made a forced crossing of the Huto River. On October 10, Shih-chiachuang fell, making it possible for elements of the enemy's 20th Division to advance westward along the Chengtai Railway, and the main force of the enemy's 1st and 2nd Corps to drive southward along both sides of the Peiping-Hankow Railway. After offering piecemeal resistance at Chengting, Shihchiachuang and Yakoying, our 32nd Corps withdrew toward the southern bank of the Chang River. On October 15, the 53rd Corps withdrew to Wu-an via Jen Hsien and Shaho, leaving Col. Lu Cheng-tsao's regiment to conduct guerrilla operations in central Hopei. The 67th Corps withdrew via Lin-lo-kuan and Hsien Hsien. After offering piecemeal resistance, the 10th Cavalry Division withdrew via Shentze and Chaohsien, toward Anyang. By October 17, all the units reached the southern bank of the Chang River.

Meanwhile, the enemy's 10th Division along the Tientsin-Pukow Railway had arrived at the bank of the Old Yellow River. As our 6th War Area was deactivated, Gen. Sung Che-yuan's forces became subordinated to the 1st War Area for garrison duties in Ta-ming and Nei-huang and the 10th Cavalry Division was transferred to Kaifeng for replenishment.

After replenishment, the main force of our 1st War Area massed in Tang-yin, Lin Hsien and Hui Hsien. Gen. Tang En-po was promoted to become commander of the 20th Army commanding the 13th Corps and the 52nd Corps in defense of the positions along the Chang River.

Subsequently, the main strength of the enemy's 1st and 2nd Corps were pulled to the north. His 20th Division and 109th Division were employed to reinforce Shansi. The enemy's 6th Division and 16th Division were redeployed to Shanghai. On October 19, the enemy's 19th Division made a forced crossing of the Chang River and fought bitterly against our 52nd Corps for two days and two nights resulting in heavy casualties on both sides. Eventually, the situation became a stalemate between Anyang and Feng-loh Chen.

On October 22, our 1st War Area rearranged its disposition. The 13th Corps of the 20th Army defended Anyang, while the 52nd Corps defended the area in the vicinity of Shui-yeh Chen. Each corps kept a powerful force for mobile guerrilla operations. The 20th Army Group defended the prepared positions in Chi Hsien and Hsinhsiang, and the 67th Corps defended the prepared positions south of Hsinhsiang. The 29th Corps and the Hopei peace preservation units were reorganized into the 59th Corps, 68th Corps, 77th Corps and 88th Division for the defense of Neihuang and Taokou. With Ta-ming as its base, the 3rd Cavalry Corps advanced toward Linchang and Tzu Hsien to conduct guerrilla operations.

On October 25, Generalissimo Chiang ordered the 67th Corps to Shanghai. The 1st Army Group, with Ta-ming as its base, dispatched units to operate in the area between the Tientsin-Pukow Railway and the Peiping-Hankow Railway to tie down the enemy. Its main force was employed in conjunction with friendly forces to destroy the enemy moving south along the Peiping-Hankow Railway and to operate in Shihchiachuang in order to facilitate our operations in eastern Shansi. The 1st War Area was further ordered to advance toward Ladies Pass.

In compliance with the above instructions, the 1st War Area employed a portion of its forces to attack Hantan and Tzu Hsien and its main force in an attack on Shihchiachuang. The 20th Army Group moved from Anyang to attack the enemy at Fenglo Chen. The 20th Army crossed the Chang River at Peng-cheng to attack Hantan and Tzu Hsien. The 53rd Corps pushed to Kucheng to respond to the operations there. Later, as Gen. Tang En-po, commander of the 20th Army, led the 13th Corps via Lin Hsien to save Taiyuan, the original plans were not fully implemented. Regretfully, our strength in the attack on Tzu Hsien was insufficient.

On November 4, our 20th Army Group launched the attack. The enemy massed his forces against the 20th Army Group in a counterattack and took Anyang. The 20th Army Group fell back to defend Paolien Temple. A portion of the 52nd Corps advanced to the vicinity of Hantan, destroyed the enemy airfield and continued the attack toward Hantan and Tzu Hsien. On November 6, the 1st Army Group launched the attack, recaptured Sha-ho and Jen Hsien and disrupted the Peiping-Hankow Railway. Massing its forces from Hantan and Tzu Hsien for a counterattack against Ta-ming, the enemy took Ta-ming on November 11. By this time, all the forces of the 1st Army Group had withdrawn to the southern bank of the Wei River.

On November 22, the 1st War Area readjusted its disposition, dispatching a portion of its forces to defend the Paolien Temple advance positions and pulling its main force back to defend the Chi River. On December 1, Gen. Tang En-po led the 13th Corps to return to the order of battle of the 1st War Area. The 53rd Corps was ordered to take over the defense of the Paolien Temple advance position, and designate areas to step up guerrilla operations. Col. Lu Cheng-tsao's regiment of the 53rd Corps was designated the 1st Separate Guerrilla Column. The National Military Council appointed Gen. Chang Yin-wu commander-in-chief of the Hopei militia. At this time, people in central Hopei rose against the enemy. As the enemy did not have sufficient strength, it was only about to control the area along the railways and a small number of key localities. With the enemy lacking the strength to continue, this operation was terminated.

4. Operations along Northern Sector of Tientsin-Pukow Railway (Early August-mid-November, 1937. See Map 5 and Charts 14 and 15)

CHART 14

Chart Showing Japanese Chain of Command in Operations along the Northern Sector of the Tientsin-Pukow Railway (Early September, 1937)

```
                          ┌─── 10th Division-Rinsuke Isoya
2nd Corps — Juzo Terauchi──┼─── 16th Division—Kesao Nakashima
                          └─── 109th Division
```

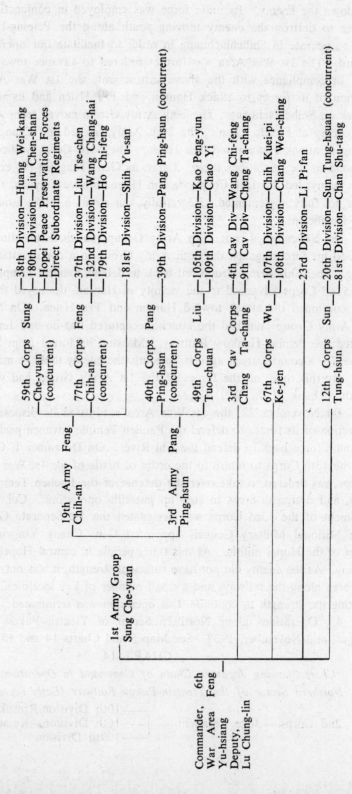

CHART 15

Chart Showing Chinese Chain of Command in Operations along the Northern Sector of
the Tientsin-Pukow Railway (Early September, 1937)

In early August, 1937, the 29th Corps (less the 143rd Division) withdrew to Ching-hai and Ma-chang from Peiping-Tientsin in a stalemate with the enemy forces on the southern outskirts of Tientsin, while the 3rd Cavalry Corps and the 53rd Corps faced the enemy across the Yungting River. The Hopei peace preservation units (2 brigades) massed toward Hochien and Jenchiu, the 67th Corps toward Wenan and Tacheng, the 39th Division of the 40th Corps toward Tsang Hsien, and the 49th Corps and the 23rd Division toward Teh Hsien. These units constructed alternate positions in the above-mentioned places.

In mid-August, our Government designated Hopei and northern Honan as the 1st War Area, Gen. Sung Che-yuan was appointed commander-in-chief of the 1st Army Group exercising command over the forces along the northern sector of the Tientsin-Pukow Railway. With this railway as an axis, the forces occupied dispersed positions in depth to stop the enemy from moving south along the Tientsin-Pukow Railway. Mobile forces were kept on the flanks ready to attack the enemy and assist the operations of the defense forces. Its operational boundary with the 2nd Army Group was Hochien-Hsiung Hsien-Ku-an-Shun-yi. All points along the boundary were inclusive to the 1st Army Group.

In early September, the enemy's 10th Division of the 2nd Corps (composed of the 10th, 16th and 109th Divisions with Gen. Juozo Nishio as the commander) successively captured our positions at Ching-hai, Tang-kuan-tun and Ma-chang with its main force massing toward the north of Tzu-ya Chen on both banks of the Tzu-ya River.

On September 6, the 29th Corps and the peace preservation units of Hopei and Chahar Provinces received orders to be reorganized into the 59th, 68th and 77th Corps and the 181st Division. After the fall of Machang on September 10, our forces withdrew to prepared positions north of Tsang Hsien. The 38th Division of the 59th Corps, 39th Division of the 40th Corps, the 49th Corps (less 109th Division), the 132nd Division of the 77th Corps occupied the line along Li-tien-mu, Ma-loh-po, Yao-kuan-tun, Hsi-hua-yuan, Hsiao-tzu-mu, and Liu-ko-chuang. The 109th Division which was the reserve was located south of Tsang Hsien. All these units were placed under the command of Gen. Pang Pin-hsun. Other units of the former 29th Corps underwent reorganization.

Since taking over the positions at Tzu-ya Chen, Yao-ma-tu, Wen-an and Ta-chen from the 132nd Division on September 4, the 67th Corps engaged the enemy's 16th Division. On September 15, it counterattacked the enemy's flank at Yao-ma-tu and North Chao-fu repelling the enemy on the left bank of the Tzu-ya River, forcing him to withdraw to the right bank and capturing 3 pack howitzers and large quantities of weapons and ammunition.

Since September 14, the 3rd Cavalry Corps and the 53rd Corps fought bitterly against the main force of the enemy's 1st Corps which had crossed the Yung-ting River at Yung-ching and Ku-an.

Since August, the heavy rains in North China resulted in flooding of the rivers in central Hopei and difficulties in communications on the Tientsin-Pukow Railway and the Peiping-Hankow Railway. In late September, our Government redesignated the northern sector of the Tientsin-Pukow Railway as the 6th War Area with Gen. Feng Yu-hsiang as the commander. The 1st War Area was directed to conduct sustained defense in the area between Tsang Hsien and Teh Hsien and then shift to the offensive upon arrival of reinforcements from the 5th War Area. Its boundary with the 1st War Area was the line along Hengshui-Hochien-Lukungpao-Wenan. All points along this line were inclusive to the 6th War Area. The 53rd Corps was subordinated to the 1st War Area.

On September 20, the enemy's 16th Division moved toward Ta-cheng. On September 21, the enemy's 10th Division attacked Yao-kuan-tun. Taking advantage of the prepared positions and the flooding, our forces resisted strongly killing many enemy troops. However, enemy air superiority, ballon observation and intense artillery fire led to heavy casualties on our forces. Successively, Ta-cheng and Tsang Hsien fell. On September 25, our defenders withdrew to Sha-ho-chiao and Nan-pi.

Between September 26 and 29, the main strength of our 6th War Area offered piecemeal resistance along the Tientsin-Pukow Railway at Feng-chia-kou, Po-tou Chen and Tung-kuang. On September 29, Gen. Lu Chung-lin, deputy commander of the 6th War Area went to Nan-pi to direct the turning attack against the enemy's left flank by employing the 59th and 49th Corps and 23rd Division. Before noon on September 30, Feng-chia-kou, Pei-hsia-kou and Tai-chuang were recovered resulting in large quantities of captured materiel. Finally, poor communications, lack of coordination among frontal units along the railway, lack of information on the enemy situation, compelled our forces to withdraw to the areas east of Teh Hsien and the railway.

In early October, the main force of the enemy's 2nd Corps moved southwestward along the Tzu-ya River, breaking the resistance of our 67th Corps. On October 6, it passed Hsien Hsien and advanced toward Ning-chin along the Fu-yang River threatening the right flank of our 1st War Area. The enemy's 10th Division advanced along the Tientsin-Pukow Railway. On October 3, it began the attack on Teh Hsien. Originally, our 3rd Army Group had been ordered to send two divisions as reinforcements, however, it acted slowly. Meanwhile, Gen. Yun-Chi-chang, a brigade commander of the 81st Division, defended the city with the 485th Regiment. Heavy fighting lasted until October 5th when most of the defenders gave their lives and Teh Hsien fell.

On October 12, elements of the enemy's 10th Division crossed the Old Yellow River. They took Ping-yuan on October 13th and Chang-chuang on the 15th. Gen. Han Fu-chu, commander-in-chief of the 3rd Army Group, ordered the 74th Division, 81st Division and a portion of the 20th Division to fall back to the southern flank of the Tu-hai River, while the 1st Army Group moved toward Lin-ching and Ta-ming, west of the Tientsin-Pukow Railway. Accordingly, our Government deactivated the 6th War Area. The 1st Group, the 67th Corps and the 3rd Cavalry Division became subordinated to the 1st War Area. The northern sector of the Tientsin-Pukow Railway which was under the command of Gen. Han Fu-chu, became subordinated to the 5th War Area. The boundary of the 5th War Area was the line running from Yun-cheng, Liao-cheng, Lin-ching to Fu-cheng. All points on the boundary were inclusive to the 5th War Area.

In late October, the enemy pulled two divisions from the 1st and 2nd Corps for an attack on Ladies' Pass and another two divisions for operations in Shanghai. As the situation in Shansi was critical, and the enemy forces along Tientsin-Pukow Railway and the Peiping-Hankow Railway were thin, Generalissimo Chiang ordered the 5th War Area to launch a counterattack with the main force of the 3rd Army Group to recapture Teh Hsien, operate in Tsang Hsien and tie down the enemy. Meanwhile, the 1st War Area was directed to employ the 1st Army Group in a counterattack to retake Shih-chia-chuang; however Gen. Han Fu-chu hesitated. Thus, the enemy in the northern sector of the Tientsin-Pukow Railway wrested the initiative and once again launched a counteroffensive. As the enemy took Hui-min on November 11, and Chi-yang on November 13, Gen. Han Fu-chu's forces gradually withdrew to the southern bank of the Yellow River, destroyed the Yellow River Bridge and faced the enemy across the river. Thus, the operations of this phase came to an end.

5. Battle of Taiyuan (Early September-Early November, 1937. See Map 6 and Charts 16 and 17)

CHART 16

Chart Showing Japanese Chain of Command during the Battle of Taiyuan

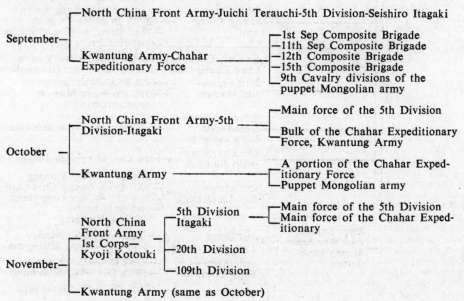

CHART 17

Chart Showing Chinese Chain of Command during Battle of Taiyuan
(After first part of September, 1937)

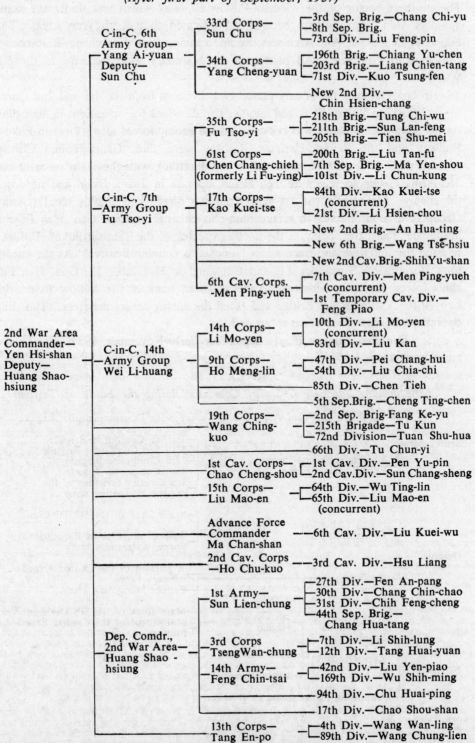

2nd War Area
Commander—
Yen Hsi-shan
Deputy—
Huang Shao-
hsiung

C-in-C, 6th
Army Group—
Yang Ai-yuan
Deputy—
Sun Chu

33rd Corps—
Sun Chu
—3rd Sep. Brig.—Chang Chi-yu
—8th Sep. Brig.
—73rd Div.—Liu Feng-pin

34th Corps—
Yang Cheng-yuan
—196th Brig.—Chiang Yu-chen
—203rd Brig.—Liang Chien-tang
—71st Div.—Kuo Tsung-fen

New 2nd Div.—
Chin Hsien-chang

C-in-C, 7th
Army Group
Fu Tso-yi

35th Corps—
Fu Tso-yi
—218th Brig.—Tung Chi-wu
—211th Brig.—Sun Lan-feng
—205th Brig.—Tien Shu-mei

61st Corps—
Chen Chang-chieh
(formerly Li Fu-ying)
—200th Brig.—Liu Tan-fu
—7th Sep. Brig.—Ma Yen-shou
—101st Div.—Li Chun-kung

17th Corps—
Kao Kuei-tse
—84th Div.—Kao Kuei-tse
(concurrent)
—21st Div.—Li Hsien-chou

New 2nd Brig.—An Hua-ting

New 6th Brig.—Wang Tse-hsiu

New 2nd Cav.Brig.-Shih Yu-shan

6th Cav. Corps.
-Men Ping-yueh
—7th Cav. Div.—Men Ping-yueh
(concurrent)
—1st Temporary Cav. Div.—
Feng Piao

C-in-C, 14th
Army Group
Wei Li-huang

14th Corps—
Li Mo-yen
—10th Div.—Li Mo-yen
(concurrent)
—83rd Div.—Liu Kan

9th Corps—
Ho Meng-lin
—47th Div.—Pei Chang-hui
—54th Div.—Liu Chia-chi

85th Div.—Chen Tieh

5th Sep.Brig.—Cheng Ting-chen

19th Corps—
Wang Ching-
kuo
—2nd Sep. Brig-Fang Ke-yu
—215th Brigade—Tu Kun
—72nd Division—Tuan Shu-hua

66th Div.—Tu Chun-yi

1st Cav. Corps—
Chao Cheng-shou
—1st Cav. Div.—Pen Yu-pin
—2nd Cav.Div.—Sun Chang-sheng

15th Corps—
Liu Mao-en
—64th Div.—Wu Ting-lin
—65th Div.—Liu Mao-en
(concurrent)

Advance Force
Commander
Ma Chan-shan
—6th Cav. Div.—Liu Kuei-wu

2nd Cav. Corps
—Ho Chu-kuo
—3rd Cav. Div.—Hsu Liang

Dep. Comdr.,
2nd War Area—
Huang Shao -
hsiung

1st Army—
Sun Lien-chung
—27th Div.—Fen An-pang
—30th Div.—Chang Chin-chao
—31st Div.—Chih Feng-cheng
—44th Sep. Brig.—
Chang Hua-tang

3rd Corps
Tseng Wan-chung
—7th Div.—Li Shih-lung
—12th Div.—Tang Huai-yuan

14th Army—
Feng Chin-tsai
—42nd Div.—Liu Yen-piao
—169th Div.—Wu Shih-ming

94th Div.—Chu Huai-ping

17th Div.—Chao Shou-shan

13th Corps—
Tang En-po
—4th Div.—Wang Wan-ling
—89th Div.—Wang Chung-lien

The terrain in Shansi Province constitutes a natural barrier in North China. Prior to the War of Resistance, China had constructed defenses at Ladies' Pass, Ping-hsing-kuan and Yen-men-kuan along the Great Wall to effect blockade. During the preliminary phase of the war, Generalissimo Chiang ordered the main force of the 2nd War Area to mass in the eastern sector of the Ping-Sui Railway and to shift timely the main force of the 1st War Area to eastern Shansi in order to consolidate Shansi for sustained operations. In time, the enemy's main force was deployed in the plains of Hopei hoping to drive into southern Hopei in an attempt to destroy our main force north of Shih-chia-chuang and dreaming of bringing Shantung and Shansi to their knees without a fight, so as to realize his dream of achieving the specialization of North China. It was not until the enemy's main force had failed to catch our forces in southern Hopei, and its other units had suffered repeated setbacks, did the enemy realize that his strategic concept was mistaken. Therefore, the enemy changed dispositions and sent reinforcements to Shansi to remedy the situation. Hence, the Battle of Taiyuan broke out.

In early September, the Chahar Expeditionary Force (4 Japanese brigades and 9 puppet Mongolian Cavalry Divisions) of the enemy's Kwangtung Army attacked the western sector of the Ping-Sui Railway from Chahar to invade Mongolia and Sinkiang. The 5th Division of the enemy's North China Front Army made a turning movement from Huai-lai via Wei Hsien and Lai-yuan to Pao-ting to respond to the operations of the main force.

Our 2nd War Area dispatched units to conduct sustained resistance in Wei Hsien, Ping-hsing-kuan, Tien Chen and Yangkao with the main force massing in the vicinity of Ta-tung preparatory to taking decisive actions against the enemy. Between September 3 and 11, after heavy fighting, our 61st Corps was forced to pull back to the south. Thus, the enemy moved into Tatung. At this time, the forces of the 2nd War Zone had not been massed completely, but the terrain of Tatung did not favor us. On October 13, our forces abandoned Ta-tung and withdrew to the prepared positions in the inner Great Wall to stop the enemy.

On September 12, Generalissimo Chiang ordered the 18th Army Group to come under the command of the 2nd War Area, operate in Ping-hsing-kuan and disrupt the enemy's lines of communications in rear areas in order to facilitate the operations of the 2nd War Area. Since mid-September, the enemy's 5th Division was tied down by our 17th Corps and 73rd Division in the area between Wei Hsien and Ping-hsing-kuan, with only a portion of the 5th Division able to make a turning movement to Pao-ting via Lai-yuan. After offering gradual resistance at Wei Hsien, Kuang-ling and Ling-chiu, our 17th Corps and 73rd Division linked up with the 15th Corps (transferred from Shih-chia-chuang) of the 13th Army and withdrew to Pinhsingkuan and Tuan-chen-kou to defend the prepared positions. On September 24, the main force of the enemy's 5th Division was lured into making a major attack. Thus, our forces effected a double envelopment dealing the enemy a heavy blow.

On September 21, a portion of Chahar Expeditionary Force of enemy's Kwangtung Army took Shang-tu and Feng-chen and continued the attack on Chi-ning. In succession, the enemy's main force took Ying Hsien, Shan-yin, Tso-yun, Yu-yi, Ping-lu and Liang-cheng and continued the attack on the line along the inner Great Wall in order to respond to the 5th Division. On September 29, as the enemy broke through Ju-yueh-kou, Gen. Liang Chien-tang, brigade commander of the defense forces, was killed in action. Enemy's capture of Fan-chih threatened the rear areas of our forces at Ping-hsing-kuan. As our forces in Pinghsingkuan were unable to send reinforcement, they had to withdraw to the line along Wutai Shan-Tai Hsien in the night of September 30.

In early October, the main forces of the enemy's 5th Division and Chahar Expeditionary Force advanced toward Kuo Hsien, Yuan-ping and Ning-wu, and the enemy's 1st Corps moved from Pao-ting to Cheng-ting. Having carefully weighed the situation, Generalissimo Chiang resolutely shifted the forces from Peiping-Hankow Railway to consolidate Shansi. On October 2, he directed Gen. Wei Li-huang, commander-in-chief of the 14th Army Group, to move the 14th and 9th Corps, the 85th Division and the 5th Separate Brigade by rail from Shih-chia-chuang to the north of Tai-yuan. In addition, he directed the 2nd War Area to dispatch powerful forces to mass and provide cover for the defense of Kuo Hsien and Yuan-ping. On October 10, Gen. Wei Li-huang's forces massed in the vicinity of Hsin-kou and linked up with the units of the former 2nd War Area. His forces were divided into three armies. Gen. Liu Mao-en, commander of the Right Flank Army, commanded the 33rd, 15th and 17th Corps. Gen. Wang Ching-kuo. commander of the Central Army, commanded the 19th, 35th, 61st and 9th Corps. Gen. Li Mo-an, commander of the Left Flank Army, commanded the 14th Corps, the 85th, 66th and 71st Division. Gen. Wei Li-huang was directed to exercise unified command of these forces, which occupied their positions along the line from north of Hsinkou to Lung-wang-tang, Chieh-ho-pu, Ta-pai-shui and Nan-ku.

The main force of the enemy's 5th Division, attached with the main force of the Chahar Expeditionary Force, captured Kou Hsien and Yuan-ping on October 13. However, our forces stood firm in the positions and repeatedly launched counterattacks. The heavy fighting which lasted until October 18 took the lives of nearly 10,000 Japanese. Gen. Hao Mon-lin, commander of the 9th Corps and Gen. Liu Chia-chi, commander of the 54th Division gave their lives to the country, and the casualties of our officers and men ran high. The fighting became a stalemate, as neither side made any appreciable progress.

On the Hopei front, the main forces of the enemy's 1st Corps and 2nd Corps made a pincers attack against Cheng-ting in early October constituting a most serious threat. Judiciously and resolutely, Generalissimo Chiang directed the 1st War Area to pull out the 1st Army, the 14th Army, the 3rd Corps and the 17th Division for employment in the Ladies' Pass. These forces occupied prepared positions and came under the unified command of Gen. Huang Shao-hsiung, deputy commander of the 2nd War Area, in order to consolidate eastern Shansi. Only minor forces were left along the Peiping-Hankow Railway for sustained resistance and containment of the enemy.

After the capture of Shih-chia-chuang on October 10, the enemy's 1st and 2nd Corps drove south leaving only units of the 20th Division to attack the Ladies' Pass and respond to the offensive of the 5th Division. After October 11, the enemy attacked Ching-ching and Pien-lu-ling. Our 17th Division rose in defense, and both sides suffered heavy casualties. On October 14, when the enemy forces broke through Wei-tze-kuan and Chiu-kuan, they were surrounded by our 26th Route Corps and 3rd Corps. Half of the enemy forces were wiped out, and enemy remnants defended isolated strong points depending entirely on airdrop for their supplies. Unfortunately, our forces lacked the necessary fire-power. Despite the fact that the siege lasted until October 22 and heavy losses were sustained, we were unable to destroy the enemy.

On October 21, the enemy was forced to pull out the entire 20th Division and a portion of the 109th Division from southern Hopei as reinforcements. Later on October 27, the main force of the 109th Division was sent in as reinforcements. When the main force of the 20th Division was committed, the enemy renewed the frontal attack on Ladies' Pass. The enemy's 109th Division advanced from Heng-kou RR Station to Tze-yu Chen and Nan-chang City. As our 3rd Corps had not completed their massing, it suffered reverses. The fact that the flank of our forces at Ladies' Pass was exposed made it necessary for our forces to fall back to Ping-ting. On October 26, the enemy's 20th Division took Ladies' Pass, and on October 30, advanced to the vicinity of Ping-ting. Having reached the vicinity of Hsi-yang, the enemy's 109th Division continued its advance to the west. The situation was so unfavorable that our forces were scattered. With the fall of Ping-ting and Yang-chuan, the enemy pressed against Tai-yuan.

The 2nd War Area directed our forces at Hsin-kou to move to the prepared positions at Blue Dragon Bridge north of Tai-yuan and to join with our forces in eastern Shansi in protecting Tai-yuan. Gen. Fu Tso-yi's forces were directed to hold the city of Tai-yuan. Our forces at Hsin-kou began moving in the night of November 2. Heavy enemy bombing, followed by attacks of the enemy's mechanized units, made it extremely difficult for our forces to maintain a foot-hold. Therefore, our forces moved the positions to the northern outskirts of Tai-yuan. As the fall of Tung-shan, placed the enemy forces in a dominating position, our forces had to cross the Fen River and withdraw to the west.

On November 6, the enemy's 5th Division, attached with the Chahar Ex-peditionary Force, attacked the outskirts of Tai-yuan. On November 7, the enemy forces in northern Shansi and eastern Shansi effected a linkup and con-tinued the attack on Tai-yuan. The fighting became more intense on November 8 when a portion of the enemy forces broke through from the north. With the defenders breaking out toward Hsi Shan, Tai-yuan fell into enemy hands. On November 9, a portion of the enemy forces crossed the Fen River and captured Chiao-cheng. Enemy's main force moved south along the Tung-pu Railway via Yu-tse to Tai-ku and Tung-yang Chen, defeated the advance elements of the 13th Corps from An-yang and halted after taking Chi Hsien and Ping-yao. As our forces withdrew to Tzu-hung Chen, Han-hou-ling, Tue-chiu-ku, this battle came to an end.

In the western sector of the Ping-Sui Railway, since our 35th Corps and 1st Cavalry Corps were transferred to the inner Great wall, 2 infantry brigades, 4 cavalry divisions and 3 cavalry brigades were left behind for disposition in depth and sustained resistance. On October 10, the enemy's Senda Mechanized Corps and 9 puppet Mongolian cavalry divisions attacked Kuei-sui. Another 2 regiments were employed in the attack on the flank of Kuei-sui from Liang-cheng. Our forces which put up piecemeal resistance were greatly under strength. Kuei-sui was abandoned on October 13 and Pao-tou on the 16th, as our forces confronted the enemy at Wu-yuan and Lin-ho. Subsequently, the 8th War Area was activated to exercise unified command of all the forces in the northwestern provinces and to continue the war.

6. Battle of Shanghai (Mid-August-Mid-December, 1937. See Map 7 and Charts 18 and 19)

CHART 18

Chart Showing Japanese Chain of Command during the Battle of Shanghai (After mid-September, 1937)

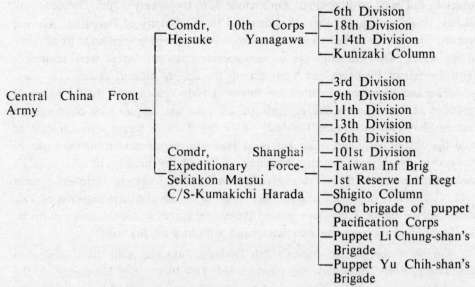

Remarks: In early November, Sekiakon Matsui organized the Central China Front Army by building around it the Shanghai Expeditionary Force and the 10th Corps.

CHART 19

Chart Showing Chain of Command during the Battle of Shanghai
(After the latter part of September, 1937)

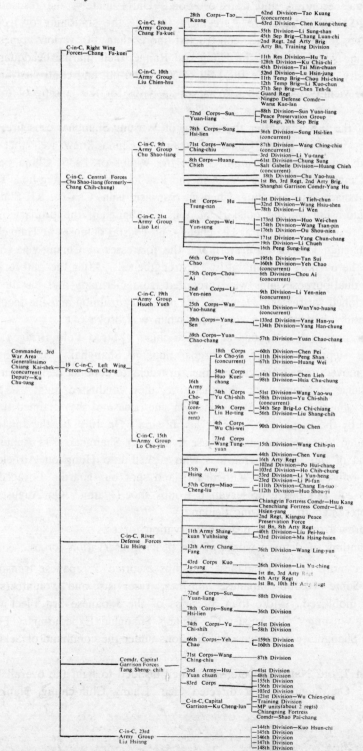

Shanghai was the largest port in East Asia, with Wusung guarding the entrance of Yangtze River and Huangpu River. Shanghai was the most important locality in China's economy and transportation. Unfortunately, the restrictions of the Wusung-Shanghai Ceasefire Agreement forbade the stationing of troops. Nevertheless, the Japanese forces constructed more than 80 various types of emplacements and warehouses at the Hung-kou Range, their marine headquarters and in the vicinity of Kung Ta Textile Mill of Yang-shu-pu, and controlled firmly the areas in the vicinity of Hui-shan Wharves as bases for the landing of major forces.

In view of the fact that after the signing of Wusung-Shanghai ceasefire, the Japanese forces invaded North China increasingly, China knew well that the Japanese would return to East China. Since the winter of 1935, China began construction of many key defense works in the key localities of Lung-hua, Hsu-chia-hui, Hung-chiao, Pei-hsin-ching, Chen-ju, Nan-hsin-tsun, Cha-pei RR Station, Kiang-wan, Miao-hsing on the outskirt of Wusung-Shanghai, the primary positions at Wu-fu, rear area position at Hsi-cheng, and coastal defenses at Hangchow Bay and Hsiang-shan Harbor. Furthermore, the fortresses at Chiang-yin, Chen-chiang and on the outskirt of Nanking were strengthened. After the outbreak of war, scores of dual-purpose guns were procured from Germany and installed in the above-mentioned fortresses. However, the necessary training and the facilities of the gun positions had not been completed when war broke out.

Since their provocative actions at Lu-kou-chiao (Marco Polo Bridge), the Japanese forces stepped up their war preparations in Shanghai. Beginning in mid-July, they moved armed officers and men in trucks to conduct demonstrations and reconnaissance in Kiang-wan. Furthermore, they conducted night exercises on the boundary lines in western Shanghai. On one occasion, they claimed that a Japanese sailor by the name of Miyasaki was missing. On July 20, the Japanese marines demanded that Chinese planes cease flying over Shanghai. On August 9, Lt. Isao Oyama of the Japanese marines who rushed into Hungkou Airfield in an automobile refused to comply with orders and shot our guard. Enraged by this outrageous act, our peace preservation troops shot Oyama. On August 11, the Japanese presented the following demands:

a. Withdrawal of Shanghai peace preservation forces.

b. Dismantling of defense works of the peace preservation forces.

Meanwhile, more than 20 Japanese warships escorted 5 Japanese transports to Shanghai. Some 10,000 Japanese marines, reservists and volunteers in Shanghai were mobilized. More than 30 ships of the Japanese 3rd Fleet were concentrated in Wusung. On August 13, Japan's Shanghai Expeditionary Force was shipped to Shanghai (composed of 2 divisions under the command of Sekikon Matsui).

On August 7, our National Defense Council decided to fight the overall War of Resistance. On August 11, it directed Gen. Chang Chih-chung, Nanking-

Shanghai Garrison commander, to push toward the pre-determined line of siege in Shanghai with the 36th, 87th and 88th Divisions, preparatory to attacking the Japanese in Shanghai. Later, the 55th, 56th and 57th Divisions and the 20th Separate Brigade were directed to push toward Pu-tung and the vicinity of Shanghai. Additionally, the main strength of the Chinese Armed Forces was massed in eastern China. It was hoped that the enemy bases in Shanghai would be mopped up, the landing of enemy forces thwarted, the defense of Wusung-Shanghai insured and the nation's capital consolidated.

On August 13, our forces continued the advance. By nightfall, the 88th Division had occupied such key localities as the Chih Chih University, Wu-chow Cemetery, Pa-tsu Bridge and Pao-shan Bridge. Many casualties including brigade commander Huang Mei-hsing were sustained. On the same day, the 87th Division occupied the Shanghai University and the bank of the Huangpu River to the north. The Chinese Air Force bombed the Japanese marine headquarters, Hui-shan Wharves and Kung Ta Textile Mill which caught fire. Japanese warship Izumo was damaged. Air battles were fought against the Japanese planes resulting in losses on both sides. That night, Generalissimo Chiang ordered the launching of general offensive at dawn on August 14. As heavy street fighting ensued, the enemy made use of well-built houses and defense works to offer strong resistance. Our forces fought from house to house. Heavy fighting lasted until August 19 when our forces pushed to the line from Cha-pei to Hung-kou and Yang-shu-pu. The Japanese continued to send in reinforcements and their naval gunfire and planes coordinated in their actions to hold firmly their positions; however, our forces lacked powerful armor-piercing weapons, and could not effectively neutralize the enemy ships and clear street obstacles. Hence, the advance was delayed. On the Pu-tung front, our 55th Division moved to the eastern bank of the Huang-pu River. Unfortunately, the lack of artillery and the neutralization by enemy planes and artillery rendered our artillery incapable of pushing to the river bank. Thus, the threat imposed on the enemy was limited.

On August 20, our Government designated southern Kiangsu and Chekiang as the 3rd War Area with Generalissimo Chiang acting as the concurrent commander (Initially its commander was Gen. Feng Yu-hsiang who was later assigned to the 6th War Area as its commander). The following operational guidance was published:

a. Principle:

With the consolidation of the national's capital and the maintenance of economic resources as its objectives, the 3rd War Area will swiftly destroy the enemy in the vicinity of Shanghai and break the enemy attempt to land along the coast.

b. Dispositions:

(1) Wusung-Shanghai siege area:

9th Army Group—Gen. Chang Chih-chung, C-in-C

36th Division—Gen. Sung Hsi-lien
56th Division—Gen. Liu Ho-ting (later Gen. Liu Shang-chih)
87th Division—Gen. Wang Ching-chiu
88th Division—Gen. Sun Yuan-liang
20th Separate Brigade—Gen. Chen Mien-wu
Portion of Training Division—Gen. Kuei Yung-ching
Wusung-Shanghai Garrison Units (Peace Preservation Group)
10th Heavy Artillery Regiment
3rd Artillery Regiment
8th Artillery Regiment
2 heavy mortar battalions
2 anti-tank gun batteries
1 light tank battalion

(2) Yangtze River Right Bank Garrison Sector (following units were massed and moved but did not all arrive):
54th Corps—Gen. Huo Kwei-chang
11th Division—Gen. Peng Shan
14th Division—Gen. Chen Lieh
67th Division—Gen. Huang Wei
16th Artillery Regiment (tentatively under the command of the Wusung-Shanghai Siege Area during the siege)

(3) Yangtze River Left Bank Garrison Sector:
57th Corps—Gen. Miao Cheng-liu
111st Division—Gen. Chang En-to
112nd Division—Gen. Huo Shuo-yi

(4) Hangchow Bay Left Bank Garrison Sector:
8th Army Group—Gen. Chang Fa-kuei, C-in-C
61st Division—Gen. Chung Sung
62nd Division—Gen. Tao Liu
55th Division—Gen. Li Sung-shan
57th Division—Gen. Yuan Shao-chang
45th Separate Brigade—Gen. Chang Luan-chi
2nd Artillery Regiment

(5) Eastern Chekiang Garrison Sector:
10th Army Group—Gen. Liu Chien-hsu, C-in-C
16th Division—Gen. Peng Sung-ling
63rd Division—Gen. Chen Kuang-chung
19th Division—Gen. Li Chueh
52nd Division—Gen. Lu Hsin-jung
New 34th Division
37th Separate Brigade—Gen. Chen Teh-fa
11th Provisional Brigade—Gen. Chou Hsi-ching

12th Provisional Brigade—Gen. Li Kuo-chun

13th Provisional Brigade—Gen. Yang Yung-ching

(6) Boundaries: (Omitted)

(7) Wusung-Shanghai Siege Area:

Improve the defense works of the existing key localities. Attack gradually so as to reduce the size of the enemy's defense circle, prevent his reinforcements from increasing and achieve the aim of destroying the enemy. At the same time, construct the defense works at Chen-ju, Ta-chang, Miao-hsing and from Wen-tsao-ping to Wu-sung Chen, in order to consolidate the basis of the siege.

(8) Yangtze River Right Bank Garrison Sector:

Its primary mission is to take aggressive actions so as to destroy the enemy landing forces.

(9) Hangchow Bay Left Bank Garrison Sector:

Its primary mission is to take aggressive actions so as to destroy the enemy landing force. Its main strength will be located in the vicinity of Chia-hsing and Cha-pu. A portion of its forces will guard the key localities along the coast. An infantry-artillery force will be dispatched to the eastern bank of the Huang-pu River to conduct flanking fire against the enemy and respond to the operations of the Wusung-Shanghai area.

(10) Eastern Chekiang Garrison Sector:

Its main strength will be located in the vicinity of Ning-po, Hsiao-shan and Hangchow. A portion of its forces will provide direct security of the coastal areas east of Wusung.

(11) Air Force:

Bomb the enemy troops attempting to make a landing and make every effort to bomb and sink enemy aircraft carriers regardless of sacrifices.

(12) Navy:

Coordinate its actions with the Army. Should enemy ships sail into the lower reaches of the Yangtze River to attempt a forced landing or shift the forces, attack them relentlessly regardless of sacrifices.

Remarks: Yangtze River Left Bank Garrison Sector:

Fragmentary order (omitted).

On August 21, under heavy enemy artillery and naval gunfire, our forces stormed the Hui-shan wharves. Taking advantage of strong defense works and blocking of roads by tanks, the enemy let loose water and set fire to offer stubborn resistance. Gen. Chen, a brigade commander of the 36th Division was seriously wounded, and Maj. Li Tseng, a battalion commander, was killed in action. 300 officers and men of the battalion attempted to break out but failed. All of them were killed in a sea of fire. Later, the commander of the 1st Tank Company was also killed in action. Despite repeated local attacks, our fire power was inadequate and enemy reinforcement poured in steadily. In time, the situation again became a stalemate.

In the night of August 22, the enemy's 3rd and 11th Divisions made a forced landing on the northern flank of Wusung, Chuansha and Shihtzulin, attempting to advance toward Tachang Chen and to hit the left flank of our force laying the siege. Only a nortion of our Yangtze River Right Bank Garrison Force reached the battlefield to defend the line from Wu-sung, Pao-shan, Lo-tien and Liu-ho and to stop the enemy. Subsequently, as our reinforcements from the 15th Army Group (composed of the 11th, 14th, and 98th Divisions with Gen. Chen Cheng as its commander-in-chief) arrived, the counterattack began on August 24. In an area where the field of fire was wide, concealment poor and movement to contact difficult, repeated struggles continued in the net-like river area. Our forces conducted night attacks, whereas the enemy forces conducted daylight counterattacks. The heavy fighting lasted for 14 days with heavy casualties on both sides and no progress. Despite enemy reinforcements from the 13th and 9th Divisions, the superiority of artillery and naval gunfire, high morale and plenty of personnel, our forces fought against the enemy in a stalemate resulting in prohibitive losses.

On September 6, our 3rd War Area ceased the general offensive and promulgated the following second phase operational guidance:

a. Principle:

(1) With the maintenance of economic center, the consolidation of the nation's capital and the prosecution of the protracted War of Resistance as its objectives,[13] this war area, while conscious of the present situation in which the enemy is surrounded, will maneuver superior forces, disrupt the liaison between enemy forces having landed, restrict their development, attack the enemy forces which landed at Shih-tzu-lin and Chuan-sha in order to shatter the enemy attempt of surrounding our forces and achieve defeat of the enemy in detail.

(2) Should the objective of defeating the enemy in detail not be realized, fall back to the areas beyond the range of enemy naval gunfire in accordance with the situation. Capture positions by means of decisive actions and take advantage of the time when the enemy artillery and naval gunfires are not fully coordinated, to develop our spiritual and material power and crush the enemy in one stroke.

b. Dispositions:

(1) Step One: Restrict the enemy development and defeat the landed enemy in detail.

(a) 8th Army Group (Pu-tung Defense Force) continues its previously assigned missions, defend the Pu-tung area and threaten the enemy on the left bank of the Huang-pu River.

(b) 9th Army Group (Wusung-Shanghai Attack Force):

---

13 It was designed to make use of the established positions in the interest of economy of force to await the opportunity to shift to the offensive. After the Battle of Wuhan, such a concept was developed into the full-scale sustained war of "trading space for time and accumulating minor victories into major victories."

i. Strengthen the preparations for the attack on Hung-kou and Yang-shu-pu and block it.

ii. Continue the attack on the enemy at Chang-hua-pin and destroy it. Should the situation not permit such an attack, the line of siege must be protected and the enemy be prevented from linking up with the enemy in Hungkou.

iii. In the Wusung-Paoshan-Kiangwan area, strong points should be defended to prevent the enemy's landed units from further development.

iv. Rear area units should construct strong point defenses at North Station, Heng-pin-kang, Wu-chou Cemetery, Lu-ching-pu, Kiang-wan, Miao-hsing, Ku-chia-chai and along the line from the south bank of Yun-tsao-pin west to Hei-ta-huangchai to stop further enemy development when necessary.

(c) 15th Army Group (Yangtze River Right Bank Defense Force):

i. A portion of its forces will be employed in the area south of Lo-tien and west of Liu-ho to stop the enemy. At the same time, a powerful force will be employed to attack the enemy flanks from Hsin-chen, Tsao-wang-miao and Shen-chia-chiao.

ii. Construct strong point defenses along Liu-chia-hsing, Chia-ting and Liu-ho to stop further enemy development when necessary.

(d) Boundaries: (omitted)

(2) Step Two: Restrict enemy development and make use of terrain and defense works to conduct favorable decisive engagement against the enemy.

(a) 8th Army Group (Right Flank Force):

i. A brigade plus will continue to exercise its original missions in Pu-tung.

ii. A division plus will occupy positions on the right bank of the Huangpu River along a line from the International Settlement via Tsao-chia-tu and North Hsin-ching Chen to Chang-chia-chai (along the right bank of the Soochow River), prevent the enemy from developing to the south, and threaten the enemy's left flank in the area north of the Soochow River, so as to facilitate the operations of our forces on the left flank of the Soochow River.

(b) 9th Army Group (Central Force):

Occupy positions on the left bank of the Soochow River along the line from Fan-chia-chai to Chiangchiao Chen, Nanhsiang, Ma-lu Chen and the southern end of Chia-ting City. The main strength will be disposed in Nan-hsiang and the area north of it. Take full advantage of terrain and defense works to seek a decisive battle against the enemy.

(c) 15th Army Group (Left Flank Force):

Take advantage of the terrain and defense works between Chia-ting, Chou-chia-yuan and Liu-ho to fight a decisive battle against the enemy.

(d) Boundaries: (Omitted)

Between September 7 and 16, as enemy reinforcements gradually arrived, the enemy took Pao-shan and landed at the Chiu-chiang Pier in the International Settlement. Our forces resisted strongly, and the battle line was interspersed.

On September 17, our forces readjusted dispositions by withdrawing to the line from the North Station to Kiang-wan, Miao-hsing, Lo-tien and Shuang-tsao-tun and occupying prepared positions.

At this time, the enemy's 3rd, 11th, 13th, 9th and 101st Divisions, units of the Taiwan Brigade and the puppet Manchurian Army and the Japanese marines totalled more than 100,000 men, 300+ guns (excluding naval guns), 300+ tanks and 200 odd aircraft. These forces constructed landing fields at Ya-wo-sha, the Golf Course and Szechow. Due to heavy losses, our Air Force ceased activities in daytime and was only able to bomb the enemy at night.

Since September 18, our forces defended the positions at the North Station, Yang-hsing, Shih-hsiang-kung Temple and Liu-ho. The fighting was most intense as our forces stopped, assaulted and destroyed the enemy. Repeatedly, the enemy's 3rd and 13th Divisions attacked our forces on Liulo Highway. Our counterattacks resulted in the killing of more than 1,000 troops of the enemy's 3rd Division and crushed the enemy attacks at Chien-chia-chai and Nan-pei-tang-kou. As 3 enemy tanks were destroyed and 1 enemy plane was damaged, the situation turned into a stalemate.

On September 21, our forces increased in strength. Generalissimo Chiang directed the 3rd War Area to make the following adjustment in deployment.

a. The 3rd War Area was divided into the Right Wing, Central and Left Wing Operational Army Corps with Gen. Chang Fa-kuei as commander-in-chief of the Right Wing Army Corps, Gen. Chu Shao-liang commander-in-chief of the Central Army Corps and Gen. Chen Cheng commander-in-chief of the Left Wing Army Corps.

b. The Right Wing Army Corps was composed of the 8th and 10th Army Groups; the Central Army Corps was composed of the 9th Army Group, and the Left Wing Army Corps was composed of the 15th and 19th Army Groups.

c. Gen. Chang Fa-kuei and Gen. Chu Shao-liang acted concurrently as the commanders-in-chief of the 8th and 9th Army Groups. Gen. Liu Chien-hsu, Gen. Lo Cho-ying and Gen. Hsueh Yueh served respectively as commanders-in-chief of the 10th, 15th and 19th Army Groups. For the units under their command, see Chart 19.

By the end of September, enemy reinforcements including the 9th, 13th, and 101st Divisions, Taiwan Brigade, and puppet Manchurian forces under Yu Chih-shan and Li Chun-shan totalling 200,000 men appeared to have arrived. At dawn on September 30, the enemy began the general attack with the main effort directed against Wan-chiao and Liu-hsing and penetrated three kilometers into our positions. Our forces readjusted the line, pulled back to the positions on the south bank of Wen-tsan-pin, Chin-hsing, Kuang-fu and Shih-hiang-kung Temple.

The enemy demanded the United States, Britain, France, Italy, Germany and Holland to move their warships to the lower reaches of the Huangpu River. However, the demand was turned down.

On October 7, enemy main force made a forced crossing of Wen-tsao-pin and broke through our positions on the southern bank. The fighting became most intense as enemy forces continued the frontal attacks against Ta-chang and Nan-hsiang. Meanwhile, our forces resisted gallantly and conducted counterattacks. The battle went on for 18 days. Later, our reinforcements from the 21st Army Group under Gen. Liao Lei arrived and were integrated with the Central Army Corps. In the same night, our forces decided to stage a counteroffensive with the recapture of our positions on the southern bank of Wen-tsao-pin as the objective. The 48th Corps moved from the vicinity of Huang-kang, Pei-hou-chai and Tan-chia-tou to attack the enemy on the southern bank of Wen-tsao-pin. The 66th Corps moved from the vicinity of Chao-chia-chai to attack to the east. The 98th Division moved from the area south of Kuang-fu to attack the enemy along the line from Sun-chia-tu to Chang-chia-chai. The divisions formerly charged with garrison duties organized 1 to 3 raiding parties each to attack the enemy. The counteroffensive began at 1900, October 21. Fierce fighting lasted all night, and little progress was made along the front. In the morning of October 22, the enemy main force, under the support of planes and ships, counterattacked against our 21st Army Group. By October 23, our forces fell back along the line from Little Stone Bridge to Ta-chang, Tsou-ma-tang, Hsin-ching-chiao and Tang-chia-chiao. Our 501st Brigade, 170th Division, commanded by Gen. Pang Han-chen, and 511th Brigade, 171st Division, commanded by Chin Lin, suffered heavy losses. At this time, situation of our positions from Cha-pei to Miao-hsing and north of Chen-hsing remained unchanged.

When our counteroffensive met the reverses, the enemy stepped up his offensive. On October 25, when Ta-chang was lost, Kiang-wan became too exposed. Accordingly, our forces withdrew to the line extending from Chiang-chiao Chen to Little Nan-hsiang on the southern bank of Soochow River and left behind a force to defend the key localities on the northern bank of the Soochow River and the Four-Bank Warehouse. Foreign Press praised the gallantry of our forces and expressed admiration over our orderly shift of positions.

On October 30, the enemy made a forced crossing of the Soochow River at Chou-chia-chai and Yao-chia-chai. Having offered strong resistance, our forces withdrew to the area south of Hsinching Chen to continue the resistance. Meanwhile, 800 gallant fighters of the 88th Division guarding the Four-Bank Warehouse in Chapei who had vowed not to retreat, became an isolated force.[14] Subsequently, our Supreme Command considered that they had already accomplished the mission of providing the necessary cover, and ordered them to withdraw.

---

[14] The Chinese Armed Forces were ordered to withdraw to the west. Lt. Col. Hsieh Chin-yuan, executive officer of the 524th Regiment, 88th Division, led his unit to cover the withdrawal of the major forces. When the mission was accomplished, Lt. Col. Hsieh and Lt. Col. Yang Jui-fu, battalion commander, led their men in the defense of the Four-Bank Warehouse on Kuang-fu Road in Cha-pei vowing to die in the positions.

Upon friendly British advice, these 800 fighters withdrew into the International Settlement. Thus, our advance positions on the north bank of the Soochow River were all abandoned.

On November 5, enemy's 10th Corps (under Gen. Heisuke Yanagawa who commanded the 6th, 18th and 114th Divisions and the Kunizaki Column) landed in the vicinity of Chin-shan-wei on the north coast of Hangchow Bay and attacked the right flank of our main force in Wusung-Shanghai. Enemy forces which had crossed the Soochow River attacked fiercely, placing our forces in a most difficult position. Our 62nd Division and 45th Separate Brigade were ordered to make a converging attack in conjunction with our 79th Division on the enemy forces having landed at Chin-shan-wei. In addition, the 11th Reserve Division was ordered to reinforce the above forces by moving along the Soo-chia Railway. However, the long distances, poor coordinations and ambushes along the way resulted in heavy casualties on our side. As the enemy forces pressed against Sung-chiang, our 67th Corps which had just been transferred from northern Honan and had not been assembled, was defeated in detail by the enemy. Hence, our flanks were seriously threatened. Accordingly, the 3rd War Area formulated the following 3rd Phase Operational guide lines:

a. Operational Objective:

The operational objective of this war area is to crush the enemy attempt to surround us, and to consolidate Nanking. On the Nanking-Shanghai front, take advantage of the prepared positions and economize forces. Draw a portion of our forces for employment on the Shanghai-Hangchow front to stop the enemy and draw another force to consolidate the defense of Nanking. Upon arrival of the follow-up forces, Kuang-teh will be used as the center from which our forces will go into the offense, and press the enemy forces to the Chien-tang River area where they will be destroyed.

b. Guiding Essentials:

(1) On the Nanking-Shanghai front, employ minimum forces to make use of the prepared positions along the line from Wu-cheng Chen—Fu-shan Chen to resist the enemy. When compelled, gradually shift to the line along Wu-hsi-Chiang-yin, and Yi-hsing and Wu-chin positions.

(2) Pull 2 divisions (excluding the 7th Corps) from the Nanking-Shanghai front via Yi-hsing. Chang-hsing and Wu-hsing to be under the command of Gen. Chang Fa-kuei, commander-in-chief of the 8th Army Group, Meanwhile, most of our artillery units are to be shifted to the Shanghai-Hangchow front. Another 3-5 divisions will be pulled for the defense of Nanking.

(3) On the Shanghai-Hangchow front, defend the line from Chung-teh Hsien to Shih-wan Hsiang and Nan-hsun Chen and the line from Lin-ping Chen to Wu-hsing Hsien. Finally, forces of the 10th Army Group under Gen. Liu Chien-hsu will withdraw to the vicinity of Hangchow, and 2 divisions of the 7th Corps to the vicinity of Chang-hsing awaiting the arrival of Szechuan forces to

take the offensive.

(4)   6 Szechuan divisions which arrived by train as follow-up forces were motored from Nanking to Kuang-teh, and those arrived by ship were motored from Wu-hu and Hsuan-cheng to the vicinity of Ning-kuo.   The emphasis was placed on Kuang-teh in the attack on the enemy on the Shanghai-Hangchow front.

On November 8, the 3rd War Area issued the order to move.   On the morning of November 9, our Central Army Corps began the move to the line from Ching-pu to Pai-ho Harbor.   Due to enemy bombing, difficulties in contact, delayed issuance of orders and lack of preparations, there were disorder and confusion during the evacuation.   In the same night, the enemy took Sung-kiang. Gen. Liu, a brigade commander of the 108th Division, was killed during street fighting.   The enemy continued the advance toward the line from Chung-pu to Pai-ho Harbor.   Gen. Wu Chi-kuang, commander of the 174th Brigade, 58th Division, was killed in action.   On November 11, the line was abandoned.   On November 12, the main force of our Left Wing Army Corps had moved west and our Right Wing Army Corps had withdrawn to the vicinity of Soo-Chia Railway and the areas to the west.   On November 13, the enemy forces moving west along the Nanking-Shanghai Railway had arrived in the area southwest of An-ting.   On the same day, the enemy's 16th Division and the Shigito Column which had landed at Pai-mao-kou and Hu-pu, began the attack on Chih-tang, threatening to cut off our highway communications.   In accordance with pre-determined plans, our forces moved in the night to positions along Cha-pu, Ping-hu, Chia-shan, Soochow and Fu-shan.

After November 15, our forces and enemy forces fought bitterly at Hsing-lung-chiao, Fu-shan, Chang-shu and along the Yangtze River.   From dusk until dawn on November 19, enemy forces shelled our positions at Wu-fu line, and his follow-up units greatly increased.   A portion of enemy forces crossed Kun-cheng Lake to attack Soochow.   In conjunction with enemy forces at Hu-pu, enemy forces advancing from Tai-tsang pressed against Chan-shu and Fu-shan.   In order to avoid a decisive battle, our forces moved toward Wu-hsi-Chiang-yin line at night and ordered the 15th and 21st Army Groups to move toward An-chi, Hsiao-feng, Ning-kuo and Hsuan-cheng, southwest of Tai Lake.   On November 25, Wu-hsi fell.   On November 26, our forces ordered the corps along the Nanking-Shanghai Railway to send portions of their force to Chang-chow, and the main force toward the Chekiang-Kiangsi-Anhwei border area.   After a 5-day fierce battle against the enemy from November 27 to December 1, the Chiang-yin Fortress fell into enemy hands as support was cut out and off.   Its defenders, the 103rd and 112nd Divisions broke and moved toward Chen-chiang.

Since the enemy's 10th Corps captured Chin-shan-wei, a portion of the corps moved via Sung-chiang to Ching-pu to take part in the operations along the Nanking-Shanghai Railway, while its main force moved toward Feng-ching and

Chia-shan to attack the positions of our 10th Army Group. Feng-ching, Chia-shan and Chia-hsing fell respectively on November 10, 14 and 19. Enemy forces continued the westward advance along the areas south of the Tai Lake, and took Nan-hsun on November 20. In order to consolidate Wu-hsing, our forces ordered the 7th Corps of the 21st Army Group to occupy the positions along Ling-hu Chen, Sheng-hsien City and Ta-chien Chen. Furthermore, the 23rd Army Group under Gen. Liu Hsiang massed in the vicinity of Kwang-teh, Sze-an and An-chi was ordered to respond to the operations of the 7th Corps. On November 24, the enemy broke through our positions at Sheng-hsien City. On November 26 when Wu-hsing fell, Assistant Division Commander Hsia Kuo-chang of the 173rd Division, 7th Corps was killed in action. The enemy continued the pursuit toward Chang-hsing. Meanwhile, 3 divisions of the 23rd Army Group were employed to attack the enemy forces which had broken through. However, the divisions were not massed completely and did not succeed in the attack. On November 27, the enemy's Akiyama Column sailed in motor boats to the west bank of the Tai Lake to attack our 50th Corps (temporarily organized by the 23rd Army Group). During the attack, Gen. Kuo Hsun-chi, commander of the 50th Corps, was wounded. The enemy forces swung north to Chang-chow in a turning movement. After its capture of Chang-hsing, the enemy's 10th Corps on the southern bank of Tai Lake employed its main force via Yi-hsing, Li-yang and Li-shui, and a portion of its forces via Kwang-teh and Hsuan-cheng, to advance toward Nanking and Wu-hu. Meanwhile, the main force (4 divisions and 1 column) of the enemy's Shanghai Expeditionary Force converged from Wuhsi-Chintan-Tienwang Temple, Wuhsi-Tanyang-Chuyung, Chiangyin-Chenchiang-Chiaotou in an attack on Nanking.

Since the outbreak of the War of Resistance, our Government moved the nation's capital to Chungking and left the National Military Council in Nanking and Wuhan. On November 26, Gen. Tang Sheng-chih was named by special appointment to be the garrison commander of Nanking exercising command over the 72nd Corps (88th Division), the 78th Corps (36th Division), the Training Division and military police units in the defense of Nanking. The 88th Division undertook the garrison from Shui-hsi-men to Chung-hua-men, Wu-an-men and Yu-hua-tai. The 36th Division undertook the garrison of Hsuan-wu-men, Red Mountain, Mu-fu Shan, and Yen-chiang-men; and engaged in coordinated actions with the Mu-fu Shan Fortress. The Training Division undertook the garrison of Kuang-hua-men, Chung-shan-men to Tai-ping-men and Tien-pao-cheng. A portion of the division came under the command of Gen. Shao Pai-chang, commander of the Fortress Command for the garrison of Wu-lung Shan Fortress. The main force of the military police units was located in the vicinity of Ching-liang-shan, undertaking the garrison of Ting-huai-men to Han-chung-men and Ching-liang-shan. Later, the 2nd Army (41st and 48th Divisions), the 66th Corps (159th and 160th Divisions), the 71st Corps (87th Division), the 74th Corps

(51st and 58th Divisions) the 83rd Corps (155th and 156th Divisions), the 103rd and 112nd Divisions were ordered to reinforce Nanking. Subsequently, the 74th and the 83rd Corps were employed to defend the prepared positions in such places on the outskirt of Nanking as Pan-chiao, Shun-hua Chen, Tang Shan and Lung-tan.

Meanwhile, the National Military Council directed the 7th War Area (forces under Gen. Liu Hsiang) to leave powerful forces behind in An-chi and Hsiao-fend awaiting the opportune time to attack the enemy's flanks. Similarly, the 3rd War Area was also directed to leave behind a powerful force in the mountainous area south of Lung-tan and north of Kuang-teh to delay the enemy's advance and destroy the lines of communications in response to the operations in Nanking. However, the fact that all the units were on the move precluded the complete implementation of the plans.

On December 6, the enemy captured the line extending from Hsuan-cheng to Ho-chia-pu, Mo-ling-kuan, Shun-hua Chen and east of Tang Shan. Enemy planes staged heavy bombings preparatory to attacking our primary positions on the outskirt of Nanking. At dawn on December 7, the enemy began the general offensive. Our determined resistance led to heavy sacrifices; however, our lack of firepower ended in the loss of Mo-ling-kuan, Shun-hua Chen and Tang Shan on December 8. Thus, the enemy began the attack on our multiple positions in Nanking. Despite great odds, our forces fought gallantly. In the afternoon of December 12, Gen. Chu Chih, commander of the 262nd Brigade, 88th Division and Gen. Kao Chih-sung, commander of the 364th Brigade, 88th Division, gave their lives to the nation at Yu-hua-tai. During the counterattack at Hsuan-wu Lake, Gen. Yi An-hua, Commander of the 259th Brigade, 87th Division was killed in action. Later, the key localities of Yu-hua-tai and Tze-chin Shan successively fell into enemy hands. As the enemy forces broke through Chung-hua-men, Kuang-hua-men, and Chung-shan-men, street fighting followed immediately. In the meantime, a portion of the enemy forces crossed the Yangtze River at Tang-tu and headed for Pukow via Wu-chiang Chen. Another force crossed the Yangtze River at Chen-chiang and headed for Yang-chow. Seeing that the situation was too far gone, Gen. Tang Sheng-chih, Nanking garrison commander, ordered our forces to break out. As the original plan was to fight to the end, there was no plan to withdraw our forces. Therefore, only the 66th Corps which broke out to the east, safely moved to the Chekiang-Kiangsi border area, and a small force succeeded in breaking out, the bulk of our forces defending Nanking was sacrificed.

On December 13, after the capture of Nanking, enemy forces engaged in indiscriminate killing and burning. Their slaughter of more than 100,000 people of Nanking was typically representative of their brutality. Later, through German Ambassador Trautemann, Japan proposed peace negotiations. Farsighted and determined, Generalissimo Chiang issued "A Message to the People upon Our

Withdrawal from Nanking" on December 17, in which he reiterated our determination to fight to the last. In January, 1938 at the Wuchang Conference, he pointed that the lawlessness and brutality of the Japanese forces would lead to Japan's sure defeat in the end.

7.　Realignment of Our Command Agencies

On January 17, 1938, our command agencies were realigned as follows:

a.　Reorganization of the Supreme Command:

Revising the Organic Outline of the National Military Council (promulgated on January 17, 1938)

Article 1:　In order to facilitate the wartime governing of the people and armed forces, the National Government establishes under it the National Military Council. It delegates the chairman of the Council to exercise the functions stipulated in Article 3 of the Organic Law of the National Government.

Article 2:　The Council has a Chairman and 7-9 members who will be selected by the Central Political Committee and will be specially appointed by the National Government. In addition, the Chief of the General Staff, the Vice Chief of the General Staff, the Minister of War, the Directors of the Boards of Military Operations, Military Training and Political Training and the Chairman of the Military Advisory Council are member of the National Military Council.

Article 3:　For the organizational system of the Council, see attached chart.

Article 4:　The Chairman commands the nation's army, navy and air force and is charged with the responsibility for directing the people in national defense. The members assist the Chairman in planning defense activities.

Article 5:　The Chief of the General Staff, is the chief of staff to the Chairman, directs the activities of the subordinate agencies of the Council and assists the Chairman in the discharge of various activities of the Council. The Vice Chief of the General Staff assists the Chief of the General Staff in the discharge of various activities of the Council.

Article 6:　The military councillors are ready for consultation by the Chairman.

The Military Advisory Council is an agency which engages in military research and makes recommendations.

Article 7:　The Main Office is charged with issuing orders, submission and transmission of documents, general affairs and security.

Article 8:　The Board of Military Operations has the General Affairs Department, the 1st Department and the 2nd Department which handle the following activities:

(1)　Defense preparations, local pacification and the mobilization operations of the Army, Navy and Air Force.

(2) Planning and employment of rear area services.

(3) Collection and evaluation of intelligence and international political information.

(4) Management and employment of staff personnel, the Army War College, the Survey General Bureau and military attaches stationed abroad.

Article 9: The Ministry of War has the General Affairs Department, the Military Affairs Service, the Quartermaster Service, the Ordnance Service and the Medical Service which are charged with the following activities:

(1) Improvement and reconstruction of the Army and the Navy, the maintenance and replacement of personnel and horses, the realignment of transportation and communications and the planning of national general mobilization.

(2) Preparation and distribution of funds, rations, clothing, equipage, materials for barracks repair and other military supplies of the Army and the Navy; construction and management of plants and warehouses; and utilization of pertinent civilian industrial resources.

(3) Preparation and distribution of weapons and ammunition; construction and management of plants and warehouses; and utilization of pertinent civilian industrial resources.

(4) Hygiene and maintenance of health of members of the Army and Navy, and the planning and employment of health organizations.

Article 10: The Board of Military Training has the General Affairs Department and the 1st Department and the 2nd Department which handle the following activities:

(1) Training and revamping of the Army and the Navy and inspection of the Army, Navy and Air Force.

(2) Reconstruction and improvement of military schools.

Article 11: The Board of Political Training has the General Affairs Department, the Secretariat, the 1st Department, the 2nd Department, the 3rd Department, the Steering Committee, and the Planning and Technical Committee which are charged with the following activities:

(1) Political training for the Army, Navy and Air Force.

(2) National guard military training.

(3) Battlefield service, organization of the people and propaganda.

Article 12: The Directorate General of Courts Martial is charged with the maintenance of military discipline and activities pertaining to military law.

Article 13: The Commission on Aeronautical Affairs is charged with the build-up, maintenance, training and command of the Air Force.

Article 14: The Military Personnel Bureau is charged with the evaluation, rating, gratuity and award of personnel in the Army, Navy and Air Force.

Article 15: The organic regulations and internal organizations of the various ministries, boards, commissions and bureau of the Council will be formulated separately.

ATTACHED CHART

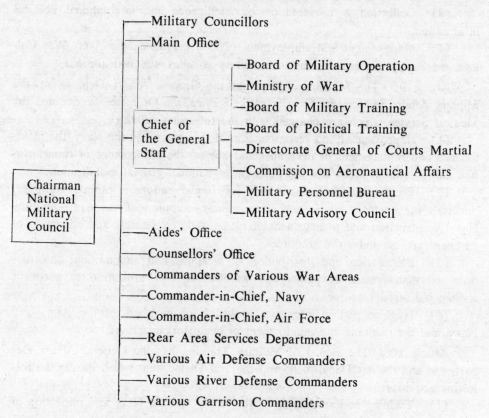

b.   Order of Battle of the Chinese Armed Forces:

Supreme Commander of the Armed Forces and Chairman of the National Military Council—Generalissimo Chiang Kai-shek.

Chief of the General Staff: Gen. Ho Ying-chin.

(1)   1st War Area

Commander: Gen. Cheng Chien

Area of Operations: Along the Peiping-Hankow Railway

Forces:

20th Army Group—Gen. Shang Chen

32nd Corps—Gen. Shang Chen (concurrent)

14th Cavalry Brigade—Gen. Chang Chan-kuei

1st Army Group—Gen. Sung Che-yuan

53rd Corps—Gen. Wan Fu-lin

77th Corps—Gen. Feng Chih-an

181st Division—Gen. Shih Yu-san

17th Division—Gen. Chao Shou-shan

3rd Cavalry Corps—Gen. Cheng Ta-chang

68th Corps—Gen. Liu Ju-ming (directly subordinate)

92nd Corps—Gen. Li Hsien-chou (directly subordinate)

106th Division—Gen. Shen Ke (directly subordinate)

118th Division—Gen. Chang Yen-tien (directly subordinate)

New 8th Division—Gen. Chiang Tsai-chen (directly subordinate)

New 35th Division—Gen. Wang Ching-tsai (directly subordinate)

4th Cavalry Division—Gen. Wang Chi-feng (directly subordinate)

The 1st War Area commanded a total of 25 infantry divisions, 2 infantry brigades, 2 cavalry divisions, excluding other non-infantry units:

(2)   2nd War Area

Commander: Gen. Yen Hsi-shah

Area of Operations: Shansi

Forces:

South Route Commander-in-Chief—Gen. Wei Li-huang

3rd Corps—Gen. Tseng Wan-chung

9th Corps—Gen. Kuo Chi-chiao

14th Corps—Gen. Li Mo-an

93rd Corps—Gen. Liu Kan

15th Corps—Gen. Liu Mao-en

17th Corps—Gen. Kao Kuei-tze

19th Corps—Gen. Wang Ching-kuo

47th Corps—Gen. Li Chia-yu

61st Corps—Gen. Chen Chang-chieh

14th Army—Gen. Feng Chin-tsai

North Route Commander-in-Chief—Gen. Fu Tso-yi

35th Corps—Gen. Fu Tso-yi (concurrent)

New 2nd Division—Gen. Chin Hsien-chang

1st Cavalry Corps—Gen. Chao Cheng-shou

2nd Cavalry Corps—Gen. Ho Chu-kuo

18th Army Group—Gen. Chu Teh

66th Division—Gen. Tu Chun-chi (directly subordinate)

71st Division—Gen. Kuo Tsung-fen (directly subordinate)

33rd Corps—Gen. Sun Chu (directly subordinate)

34th Corps—Gen. Yang Cheng-yuan (directly subordinate)

The 2nd War Area commanded a total of 27 infantry divisions, 3 infantry brigades, and 3 cavalry divisions, excluding other non-infantry units.

(3)   3rd War Area

Commander: Gen. Ku Chu-tung

Area of Operation: Kiangsu-Chekiang

Forces:

10th Army Group—Gen. Liu Chien-hsu

28th Corps—Gen. Tao Kuang

             70th Corps—Gen. Li Chueh

             79th Division—Gen. Chen An-pao

             13th Provisional Brigade—Gen. Yang Yung-ching

             Ningpo Defense Commander—Gen. Wang Kao-nan

                 19th Division—Gen. Chen Teh-fa

             Wentai Defense Commander—Gen. Hsu Chih-chien.

                 12th Provisional Brigade—Gen. Li Kuo-chun

         19th Army Group—Gen. Lo Cho-ying

             4th Corps—Gen. Wu Chi-wei

             18th Corps—Gen. Lo Cho-ying (concurrent)

             79th Corps—Gen. Hsia Chu-chung

             25th Corps—Gen. Wan Yao-huang

             73rd Corps—Gen. Wang Tung-yuan

         23rd Army Group—Gen. Tang Shih-tsun

             21st Corps—Gen. Tang Shih-tsun (concurrent)

         28th Army Group—Gen. Pan Wen-hua

             23rd Corps—Gen. Pan Wen-hua (concurrent)

      New 4th Corps—Gen. Yeh Ting (directly subordinate)

      6th Independent Brigade—Gen. Chou Chih-chun (directly subordinate)

      Guerilla Commander-in-Chief—Gen. Huang Shao-hsiung

     The 3rd War Area commanded a total of 24 infantry divisions, and 6 infantry brigades, excluding other non-infantry and guerilla units.

     (4)   4th War Area

        Commander: Gen. Ho Ying-chin (concurrent)

        Area of Operations: Kwangtung and Kwangsi

        Forces:

        12th Army Group—Gen. Yu Han-mou

             62nd Corps—Gen. Chang Ta

             63rd Corps—Gen. Chang Jui-kuei

             64th Corps—Gen. Li Han-hun

             65th Corps—Gen. Li Chen-chiu

             8th Army—Gen. Hsia Wei

             9th Separate Brigade—Gen. Li Chen-liang

             20th Separate Brigade—Gen. Chen Mien-wu

             Humen Fortress Commander—Gen. Chen Tse

     The 4th War Area commanded a total of 9 infantry divisions, and 2 infantry brigade, excluding other non-infantry and fortress garrison troops.

     (5)   5th War Area

        Commander: Gen. Li Tsung-jen

        Area of Operation: Tientsin-Pukow Railway

        Forces:

        3rd Army Group—Gen. Yu Hsueh-chung

    51st Corps—Gen. Yu Hsueh-chung (concurrent)
    12th Corps—Gen. Sun Tung-hsuan
    56th Corps—Gen. Ku Liang-min
    55th Corps—Gen. Tsao Fu-lin
11th Army Group—Gen. Li Pin-hsien
    31st Corps—Gen. Wei Yun-sung
    4th Columm of the New 4th Corps
21st Army Group—Gen. Liao Lei
    7th Corps—Gen. Chou Tsu-huang
    48th Corps—Gen. Liao Lei (concurrent)
22nd Army Group—Gen. Teng Hsi-hou
    41st Corps—Gen. Sun Chen
    45th Corps—Gen. Teng Hsi-hou (concurrent)
24th Army Group—Gen. Ku Chu-tung (concurrent)
    57th Corps—Gen. Miao Cheng-liu
3rd Army—Gen. Pang Ping-hsun
27th Army Group—Gen. Yang Sen
    20th Corps—Gen. Yang Sen (concurrent)
59th Corps—Gen. Chang Tze-chung
Marines—Gen. Yang Huan-tsai

The 5th War Area commanded a total of 27 infantry divisions, and 3 infantry brigades, excluding other non-infantry units.

(6)   8th War Area
    Commander: Generalissimo Chiang Kai-shek (concurrent)
    Deputy Commander: Gen. Chu Shao-liang
    Area of Operations: Kansu, Ninghsia and Chinghai
    Forces:
    17th Army Group—Gen. Ma Hung-kuei
        81st Corps—Gen. Ma Hung-ping
        168th Division—Gen. Ma Hung-kuei (concurrent)
        10th Cavalry Brigade—Gen. Ma Chuan-chung
        1st Cavalry Brigade—Gen. Ma Kuang-tsung
        Ninghsia 1st Garrison Brigade—Gen. Ma Pao-lin
        Ninghsia 2nd Garrison Brigade—Gen. Ma Teh-kuei
    80th Corps—Gen. Kung Ling-hsun
    82nd Corps—Gen. Ma Pu-fang
    5th Cavalry Corps—Gen. Ma Pu-ching
    191st Division—Gen. Yang Teh-liang
    Advance Force Commander—Gen. Ma Chan-shan

The 8th War Area commanded a total of 5 infantry divisions, 4 infantry brigades, 5 cavalry divisions, and 4 cavalry brigades, excluding other non-infantry units.

(7)   Wuhan Garrison General Headquarters·
Commander-in-Chief—Gen. Chen Cheng
Forces:
2nd Corps—Gen. Li Yen-nien
75th Corps—Gen. Chou Ai
60th Corps—Gen. Lu Han
54th Corps—Gen. Huo Kuei-chang
13th Division—Gen. Wu Liang-shen
185th Division—Gen. Kuo Chan
77th Division—Gen. Peng Wei-jen
49th Corps—Gen. Liu Tuo-chuan
River Defense Commander-in-Chief—Gen. Liu Hsing
    Marines
    57th Division—Gen. Shih Chung-cheng
    One brigade of the 14th Division

The Wuhan Garrison General Headquarters commanded a total of 14 infantry divisions and 1 infantry brigade, excluding other non-infantry and river defense garrison units.

(8)   Si-an Headquarters of the Generalissimo
Director—Gen. Chiang Ting-wen
Forces:
11th Army—Gen. Mao Ping-wen
    37th Corps—Gen. Mao Ping-wen (concurrent)
    43rd Division—Gen. Chou Hsiang-chu
17th Army—Gen. Hu Tsung-nan
    1st Corps—Gen. Hu Tsung-nan (concurrent)
    8th Corps—Gen. Huang Chieh
46th Corps—Gen. Fan Sung-pu
38th Corps—Gen. Sun Wei-ju
21st Army—Gen. Teng Pao-san
    New 1st Corps
    165th Division—Gen. Lu Ta-chang
    86th Division—Gen. Kao Shuang-cheng
1st Provisional Cavalry Division (directly subordinate)
    6th Cavalry Corps—Gen. Men Ping-yueh (directly subordinate)

The Si-an Headquarters commanded a total of 12 infantry divisions, 4 infantry brigades, and 3 cavalry divisions, excluding other non-infantry units.

(9)   Fukien Pacification Headquarters
Director—Gen. Chen Yi
Forces:
80th Division—Gen. Chen Chi
75th Division—Gen. Sung Tien-tsai

Fukien 1st Peace Preservation Brigade—Gen. Chen Pei-yu

Fukien 2nd Peace Preservation Brigade—Gen. Li Shu-tang

Fukien 3rd Peace Preservation Brigade—Gen. Chao Lin

2nd Marine Brigade

The Fukien Pacification Headquarters commanded a total of 2 infantry divisions and 4 infantry brigades, excluding other local and fortress units.

(10) National Military Council Direct Subordinate Forces

    20th Army—Gen. Tang En-po

        52nd Corps—Gen. Kuan Lin-cheng

        13th Corps—Gen. Tang En-po (concurrent)

        85th Corps—Gen. Wang Chung-lien

    2nd Army Group—Gen. Sun Lien-chung

        42nd Corps—Gen. Feng An-pang

        30th Corps—Gen. Tien Chen-nan

    26th Army Group—Gen. Hsu Yuan-chuan

        10th Corps—Gen. Hsu Yuan-chuan (concurrent)

        87th Corps—Gen. Liu Ying-ku

    8th Army Group—Gen. Chang Fa-kuei

        36th Division—Gen. Chiang Fu-sheng

        50th Division—Gen. Cheng Kuang-yao

        92nd Division—Gen. Huang Kuo-liang

        93rd Division—Gen. Kan Li-chu

        167th Division—Gen. Hsueh Wei-ying

The above forces totalled 17 infantry divisions.

(11) Units undergoing reorganization and training and units which had not been shifted:

26 infantry divisions underwent reorganization and training in the rear areas, and 14 infantry divisions and 7 infantry brigades were not shifted in the rear areas.

8. Battle of Hsuchow (Late December, 1937-late May, 1938. See Map 9-1 and Charts 20 and 21)

CHART 20

Chart Showing Japanese Chain of Command during the Battle of Hsuchow
(Latter part of December, 1937)

North China Front Army — Comdr, Northern Sector, Tientsin-Pukow Railway Juzo Nishio —
- 10th Division-Rinsuke Isoya
- 16th Division-Kesao Nakashima (less 30th Brig.)
- 110th Division-Yoshitsugi Tategawa
- 114th Division-Shigeharu Suematsu
- 105th Brig, 113th Div-Shozo Motogawa
- A brig of 111th Div-Yamamoto
- 5th Division-Seishiro Itagaki
- 121st Brig, 105th Div-Itada
- Bulk of Yamashita Army
- A portion of Sakai Army
- A portion of 120th Division

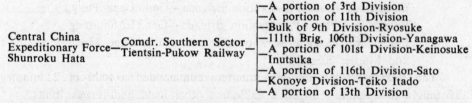

Central China Expeditionary Force—Shunroku Hata — Comdr. Southern Sector Tientsin-Pukow Railway —
- A portion of 3rd Division
- A portion of 11th Division
- Bulk of 9th Division-Ryosuke
- 111th Brig, 106th Division-Yanagawa
- A portion of 101st Division-Keinosuke Inutsuka
- A portion of 116th Division-Sato
- Konoye Division-Teiko Itado
- A portion of 13th Division

Our forces sustained heavy losses in the Battle of Taiyuan and Battle of Wusung-Shanghai. When Nanking fell, the entire nation was alarmed. Fully aware of the overall situation, Generalissimo Chiang assumed full command and established subsequent operational guidance by massing elite forces in Wuhan and Honan-Anhwei border areas for replenishment. Additionally, Powerful forces were drawn from North China and areas south of the Yangtze River to reinfore the forces in central Shantung and areas south of the Huai River in order consolidate Hsuchow and lure the main strength of the enemy forces to the areas along the Tientsin-Pukow Railway so as to delay the enemy forces in their attempt to move westward along the Yangtze River. Meanwhile, efforts were made to defend the key localities north of the Yellow River, northern Honan and southern Shansi, prevent the enemy forces from crossing the Yellow River in a dash toward Wuhan, and launch extensive guerilla operations so as to tie down and wear out the enemy. Taking advantage of the lack of coordination between the enemy forces in Central China and the enemy forces in North China, our forces pulled powerful units from northern Honan and southern Shansi for employment in southern Shantung and defeated the enemy's 2nd Corps at Tai-erh-chuang. As a result, our morale was greatly boosted and international situation changed. The enemy was forced to send reinforcements from the northern and southern ends of the Tientsin-Pukow Railway. Thus, the Battle of Hsuchow erupted.

In North China, in mid-November, 1937, our 3rd Army Group under Gen. Han Fu-chu withdrew from northern Shantung to defend the southern bank of the Yellow River and confronted the enemy's 10th Division across the river. For a while, the situation was very quiet. In mid-December, elements of the enemy's 11th and 13th Divisions in Central China crossed the Yangtze River and took Chiang-tu and Chu Hsien. Accordingly, our 5th War Area readjusted its dispositions by moving the 3rd Army Group, the marines and the 3rd Army to defend the key localities along the Yellow River and the East Sea. The 27th, 11th and 24th Army Groups were ordered to defend the key localities in central Anhwei and northern Kiangsu. The 51st Corps was pulled from Tsing-tao for employment in the vicinity of Pang-pu to stop the enemy from Central China and to assume the offensive at the opportune time.

Since the capture of Nanking in mid-December, the enemy's General Headquarter (activated on November 30) ordered the North China Front Army to seize the areas along the Chiaochow-Tsinan Railway[15] and the left bank on the upper

---

[15] Tsingtao to Tsinan.

CHART 21

Chart Showing Chinese Chain of Command during the Battle of Hsuchow

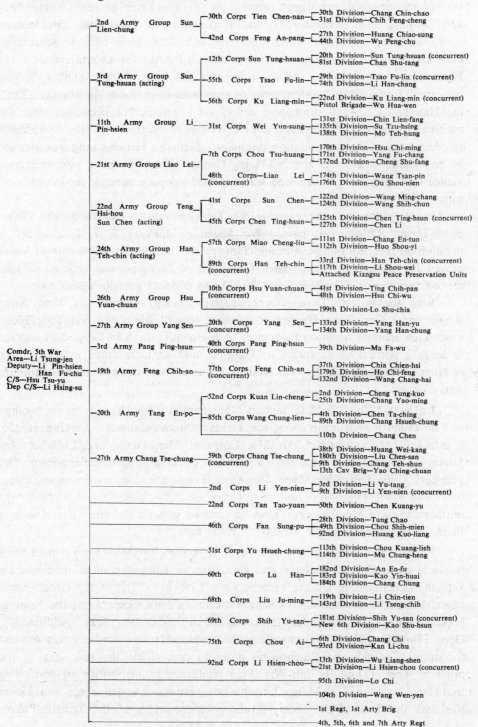

2nd Army Group Sun Lien-chung
- 30th Corps Tien Chen-nan
  - 30th Division—Chang Chin-chao
  - 31st Division—Chih Feng-cheng
- 42nd Corps Feng An-pang
  - 27th Division—Huang Chiao-sung
  - 44th Division—Wu Peng-chu

3rd Army Group Sun Tung-hsuan (acting)
- 12th Corps Sun Tung-hsuan
  - 20th Division—Sun Tung-hsuan (concurrent)
  - 81st Division—Chan Shu-tang
- 55th Corps Tsao Fu-lin
  - 29th Division—Tsao Fu-lin (concurrent)
  - 74th Division—Li Han-chang
- 56th Corps Ku Liang-min
  - 22nd Division—Ku Liang-min (concurrent)
  - Pistol Brigade—Wu Hua-wen

11th Army Group Li Pin-hsien
- 31st Corps Wei Yun-sung
  - 131st Division—Chin Lien-fang
  - 135th Division—Su Tzu-hsing
  - 138th Division—Mo Teh-hung

21st Army Groups Liao Lei
- 7th Corps Chou Tsu-huang
  - 170th Division—Hsu Chi-ming
  - 171st Division—Yang Fu-chang
  - 172nd Division—Cheng Shu-fang
- 48th Corps—Liao Lei (concurrent)
  - 174th Division—Wang Tsan-pin
  - 176th Division—Ou Shou-nien

22nd Army Group Teng Hsi-hou / Sun Chen (acting)
- 41st Corps Sun Chen
  - 122nd Division—Wang Ming-chang
  - 124th Division—Wang Shih-chun
- 45th Corps Chen Ting-hsun
  - 125th Division—Chen Ting-hsun (concurrent)
  - 127th Division—Chen Li

24th Army Group Han Teh-chin (acting)
- 57th Corps Miao Cheng-liu
  - 111th Division—Chang En-tuo
  - 112th Division—Huo Shou-yi
- 89th Corps Han Teh-chin (concurrent)
  - 33rd Division—Han Teh-chin (concurrent)
  - 117th Division—Li Shou-wei
  - Attached Kiangsu Peace Preservation Units

26th Army Group Hsu Yuan-chuan
- 10th Corps Hsu Yuan-chuan (concurrent)
  - 41st Division—Ting Chih-pan
  - 48th Division—Hsu Chi-wu
  - 199th Division—Lo Shu-chia

27th Army Group Yang Sen
- 20th Corps Yang Sen (concurrent)
  - 133rd Division—Yang Han-yu
  - 134th Division—Yang Han-chung

3rd Army Pang Ping-hsun
- 40th Corps Pang Ping-hsun (concurrent)
  - 39th Division—Ma Fa-wu

19th Army Feng Chih-an
- 77th Corps Feng Chih-an (concurrent)
  - 37th Division—Chia Chien-hsi
  - 179th Division—Ho Chi-feng
  - 132nd Division—Wang Chang-hai

20th Army Tang En-po
- 52nd Corps Kuan Lin-cheng
  - 2nd Division—Cheng Tung-kuo
  - 25th Division—Chang Yao-ming
- 85th Corps Wang Chung-lien
  - 4th Division—Chen Ta-ching
  - 89th Division—Chang Hsueh-chung
  - 110th Division—Chang Chen

27th Army Chang Tse-chung
- 59th Corps Chang Tse-chung (concurrent)
  - 38th Division—Huang Wei-kang
  - 180th Division—Liu Chen-san
  - 9th Division—Chang Teh-shun
  - 13th Cav Brig—Yao Ching-chuan

- 2nd Corps Li Yen-nien
  - 3rd Division—Li Yu-tang
  - 9th Division—Li Yen-nien (concurrent)

- 22nd Corps Tan Tao-yuan
  - 50th Division—Chen Kuang-yu

- 46th Corps Fan Sung-pu
  - 28th Division—Tung Chao
  - 49th Division—Chou Shih-mien
  - 92nd Division—Huang Kuo-liang

- 51st Corps Yu Hsueh-chung
  - 113th Division—Chou Kuang-lieh
  - 114th Division—Mu Chung-heng

- 60th Corps Lu Han
  - 182nd Division—An En-fu
  - 183rd Division—Kao Yin-huai
  - 184th Division—Chang Chung

- 68th Corps Liu Ju-ming
  - 119th Division—Li Chin-tien
  - 143rd Division—Li Tseng-chih

- 69th Corps Shih Yu-san
  - 181st Division—Shih Yu-san (concurrent)
  - New 6th Division—Kao Shu-hsun

- 75th Corps Chou Ai
  - 6th Division—Chang Chi
  - 93rd Division—Kan Li-chu

- 92nd Corps Li Hsien-chou
  - 13th Division—Wu Liang-shen
  - 21st Division—Li Hsien-chou (concurrent)

- 95th Division—Lo Chi

- 104th Division—Wang Wen-yen

- 1st Regt, 1st Arty Brig

- 4th, 5th, 6th and 7th Arty Regt

Comdr, 5th War Area—Li Tsung-jen
Deputy—Li Pin-hsien
     Han Fu-chu
C/S—Hsu Tsu-yu
Dep C/S—Li Hsing-su

reaches of the Yellow River west of Tsi-nan.   On December 23, the 10th Division of the enemy's 2nd Corps crossed the Yellow River between Ching-cheng and Tsi-yang.   On December 27, and 31 Tsi-nan and Tai-an fell.   By January 7, 1938, Meng-yin, Ta-wen-kou, Tsi-ning and Tsou Hsien fell in succession. Gen. Han Fu-chu, commander-in-chief of the 3rd Army Group, retreated to Tan Hsien, Cheng-wu and Tsao Hsien in western Shantung without a fight, leaving only small forces on the western bank of the Canal to confront the enemy.   Finding Han hesitating and disobeying orders on a number of occasions since the outbreak of the War of Resistance, our Government ordered that Han be executed in order to straighten our military discipline.   Gen. Yu Hsueh-chung was appointed commander-in-chief of the 3rd Army Group.   (Gen. Yu never assumed command) Gen. Sun Tung-hsuan who was appointed deputy commander-in-chief, became the acting commander-in-chief.

In early January, the enemy's 5th Division moved east along the Chiao-chow-Tsinan Railway.   It passed Wei Hsien on January 8, while elements of the division reached Tsing-tao in mid-January and linked up with the naval forces having landed there.   Mayor Shen Hung-lieh of Chingtao was ordered to lead the marines toward Chu-cheng and Yi-shui to conduct guerilla operations.

With the fall of Tai-an, Generalissimo Chiang ordered the 22nd Army Group under Gen. Teng Hsi-hou to advance toward Lin-cheng and Teng Hsien to stop the enemy's southward advance.   Additionally, the 51st Corps was ordered to leave a portion of its forces in Pang-pu, and its main force in the vicinity of Huang-kou and Tang-shan for security, to respond to the operations of the 3rd Army Group.

In Central China, in late January, the enemy's 13th Division in the vicinity of Chu Hsien moved north along the Tientsin-Pukow Railway.   On January 25, it attacked the positions of our 31st Corps at Ming-kuang and Chih-ho.   On January 31, our forces withdrew to the west of Ting-yuan and Feng-yang.   By February 3, the enemy had taken Ting-yuan, Feng-yang, Lin-huai-kuan and Pang-pu.   The 114th Division of our 51st Corps defending Pang-pu withdrew to the northern bank of Huai River.   Thus, the enemy crossed the Huai River west of Pang-pu to capture the key locality of Huaiyuan.

In order to consolidate the defense of Hsuchow, lure the enemy's main force to the Tientsin-Pukow Railway and gain time to achieve combat readiness for Wuhan, Generalissimo Chiang ordered Gen. Liao Lei's 21st Army Group south of the Yangtze River and Gen. Chang Tse-chung's 59th Corps along the Peiping-Hankow Railway to come under the command of the 5th War Area.   Additionally, Gen.   Tang En-po's 20th Army along the Peiping-Hankow Railway was ordered to control Kuei-teh and Po-chow in order to consolidate the rear area of the 5th War Area.   Thus, the 5th War Area readjusted its disposition by employing the 11th, 21st and 26th Army Groups from Ho-fei, Lao-jen-tsang, and Lo-ho to attack the flank of the enemy in the southern sector of the Tientsin-Pukow

Railway and to hold the enemy south of the Huai River. The 3rd Army Group, the 3rd Army and the marines were directed to defend western and southern Shantung and to conduct guerilla operations so as to tie down the enemy.

On February 4, Generalissimo Chiang directed the 5th War Area to counterattack the enemy in the northern sector of the Tientsin-Pukow Railway. In the night of February 12, the 3rd Army Group attacked the enemy at Tsi-ning and Wen-shang. Fighting was intense, as our troops entered the city. Later, when enemy reinforcements arrived and counterattacked, our forces withdrew to the line from Hsiang-li-chi to Yang-shan-chi and Chu-yeh, occupied positions and dispatched forces to conduct guerilla operations along the Tientsin-Pukow Railway. On February 14, the 22nd Army Group attacked the enemy at Tsou Hsien. As the attack failed, a state of stalemate resulted. On February 26, the 3rd Army and the marines attacked the enemy at Hsin-tai, Meng-yin and Sze-shui, ending in the recovery of Meng-yin.

On February 9, the enemy's 13th Division in the southern sector of the Tientsin-Pukow Railway made a forced crossing of the Huai River in the vicinity of Pang-pu. Our 51st Corps threw its full weight into the fight. Eventually, enemy fire power superiority compelled our forces to fall back to the banks of Wo River and Hui River. The 5th War Area therefore, ordered the 59th Corps, to race to the scene, in conjunction with the 7th Corps of the 21st Army Group and the 31st Corps of the 11th Army Group, in order to attack the flanks of the enemy in the vicinity of Ting-yuan on the southern bank of the Huai River. The main strength of the enemy's 13th Division withdrew from the northern bank of the Huai River to provide assistance. On February 16, our 59th Corps recovered our original positions on the northern bank of the Huai River (except Huai-yuan). Later, the corps was ordered north to Teng Hsien, and the 51st Corps continued to garrison the northern bank of the Huai River. Meanwhile, the enemy deactivated the Central China Front Army and the Shanghai Expeditionary Army, and activated the Central China Expeditionary Army with Gen. Shunroku Hata as the commander. Between March and April, the enemy moved from Kuang-teh to attack our guerilla forces. Meanwhile, the front in the southern sector of the Tientsin-Pukow Railway was quiet.

As to the front along the Chiaochow-Tsinan Railway, the enemy's 5th Division began to move south in early February taking Meng-yin, Yi-shui, Chu Hsien and Jih-chao. Our 3rd Army and marines offered piecemeal resistance. By late February, our forces fell back to Lin-yi, occupied positions and fought bitterly against the enemy. At this time, Generalissimo Chiang directed the 5th War Area to move the 59th Corps from Teng Hsien to Lin-yi. On March 12, the corps reached the northern outskirts of Lin-yi. It launched a counterattack in conjunction with the 3rd Army. After a bloody battle which lasted for 5 days, it broke the back of a brigade of the enemy's 5th Division killing more than half of the men in that brigade. In the night of March 17, enemy remnants retreated toward Yi-shui. Our forces followed up with a pursuit which led to still greater achievements. On March 23, the enemy launched a counterattack after arrival of reinforcements. Accordingly, our forces fell back to the vicinity of Lin-yi to confront the enemy.

As to the northern sector of the Tientsin-Pukow Railway, the enemy poured more reinforcements since early March. The enemy's 10th Division, attached with more than 100 tanks, massed toward Tsou Hsien to respond to the operations of the 5th Division. By this time, the enemy's attempt to attack Hsuchow became quite obvious. Generalissimo Chiang, therefore, directed the 20th Army to reinforce Hsuchow by rail from Kuei-teh, the 3rd Army Group to move toward Yen-chow in a flank attack responding to operations, and Gen. Sun Lien-chung's 2nd Army Group to move from southern Shansi to Hsuchow under the 5th War Area. On March 14, the enemy's 10th Division took Chieh-ho, followed by an attack on Teng Hsien on March 15. The 122nd Division of our 22nd Army Group defended the city of Teng Hsien. On March 16, the advance elements of our 85th Corps, 20th Army reached Kuan-chiao to the north of Lin-cheng to cover the massing of the main force. Another unit of the 85th Corps advanced toward the northeast of Teng Hsien in an effort to break the siege of Teng Hsien. Separated into 2 routes, the enemy forces attacked our positions at Kuan-chiao. Our forces resisted gallantly, and both sides suffered heavy losses. Supported by air planes, heavy artillery and tanks, the enemy took Teng Hsien on March 17. Gen. Wang Ming-chang, a division commander, gave his life to the country after his division suffered prohibitive losses. Subsequently, our positions at Kuan-chiao were penetrated. An advance brigade of the 52nd Corps reached the vicinity of Sha-kou to occupy positions and stop the enemy. On March 18, the enemy broke through the positions. Gen. Tang En-po directed the follow-up units of the 52nd Corps to occupy positions along the Canal line in the vicinity of Han-chuang, and the 85th Corps to occupy Yi Hsien and the high grounds to the northeast and southwest. Later, the 110th Division was ordered to occupy the positions along the Canal line and the 52nd Corps was ordered to advance to the east of Yi Hsien, hoping to gain control of the exterior lines and to envelop the enemy's left flank.

After its capture of Teng Hsien and Kuan-chiao on March 17 and Sha-kou on March 18, the enemy's 10th Division dispatched a force to occupy Han-chuang and its main force to attack Yi Hsien. The bitter fighting lasted until March 19. As all the officers and men of the 23rd Regiment, 4th Division, 85th Corps, including the regimental commander, were wounded or killed, the enemy broke through Yi Hsien with the Setami Brigade moving along the Tai-tsao branch road toward Tai-erh-chuang. Earlier, Gen. Sun Lien-chung's 2nd Army Group had occupied positions along the east-west line of Tai-erh-chuang in an attempt to stop the enemy. Our 20th Army (less 110th Division) faced the enemy east of Yi Hsien and Tsao-chuang. On March 24 when Generalissimo Chiang and

Gen. Pai Chung-hsi, Vice Chief of the General Staff, arrived in Hsuchow and Tai-erh-chuang to direct the operations, morale was greatly boosted. Supported by airplanes, heavy artillery and tanks, the main force of the enemy's 10th Division was gradually committed in Tai-erh-chuang to attack our positions and broke into the ruins of Tai-erh-chuang. Our 31st Division of the 2nd Army Group under Gen. Chih Feng-cheng fought against the enemy in street fighting and stood firm. Meanwhile, repeated hand-to-hand fighting was conducted against the enemy along the east-west line of Tai-erh-chuang. Despite two weeks of bitter fighting, the situation ended in a stalemate. On March 26, in a fierce attack against the enemy at Yi Hsien and Tsao-chuang, our 20th Army killed more than half of the enemy troops. Enemy remnants, though cornered, offered stubborn resistances. Accordingly, our 20th Army shifted its main force and fiercely attacked the enemy's flank northeast of Tai-erh-chuang. The attack progressed smoothly and by March 31, enemy forces in Tai-erh-chuang were completely surrounded and were about to be annihilated. In the meantime, our 55th Corps crossed the lake from western Shantung cutting off the Tientsin-Pukow Railway north of Lin-cheng. Additionally, local people were called upon to thoroughly sabotage the enemy's lines of communications. In Lin-yi, as the enemy's 5th Division failed to succeed in its repeated attacks, it shifted its main forces to the northwestern outskirts of Lin-yi, to attack Chu-chen, southwest of Lin-yi, cover the advance of the Itaka Brigade toward Tai-erh-chuang and hit the rear of our 20th Army in order to break the siege of the 10th Division. On April 1, enemy's advance elements appeared in the vicinity of Hsiang-cheng and Ai-chu. Our 20th Army dispatched a force to meet the enemy. The main force of the 20th Army was directed to the southeast in a counter-turning movement in an effort to open the Tai-Wei Highway. With a portion of its forces defending Hsiang-cheng, the enemy's Itaka Brigade employed its main force toward Cha-ho Chen (east of Tai-erh-chuang) and fell into our trap. Once again, our 20th Army began the siege. Our 75th Corps and 139th Division of the 32nd Corps were deployed along the line east and west of Cha-ho Chen to meet the enemy. Later, the 139th Division was employed in the attack against the enemy in Hsiang-cheng. Our 2nd Army Group also launched a counterattack. Bitter fighting lasted until the night of April 6 when the bulk of the enemy's 10th Division and a portion of the enemy's 5th Division were wiped out. Enemy remnants left behind many tanks, heavy artillery and weapons in their breakout to the north at night. Separated into several routes, our forces attacked the enemy forces which offered stubborn resistance on the high grounds of Hsiang-cheng, Shui-kuo, Tsao-chuang, Yi Hsien and Chiu-shan. The enemy's North China Front Army hurriedly dispatched two divisions as reinforcements to engage our forces. No progress was made by either side.

Meanwhile, having assessed the overall situation, the National Military Council considered that the enemy forces in North China became more scattered as they invaded more territories in northern Honan and southern Shansi in February and March. However, their total strength stood at no less than 12 divisions, and it was relatively easy for them to shift the forces from Manchuria. Other than the fact that they were compelled to shift forces to effect direct rescue of the 2nd Corps, it was possible that they could force a crossing of the Yellow River east of Cheng-chow and cut off the Lung-hai Railway to respond to the operations of the Tientsin-Pukow Railway. Originally, the enemy forces in Central China totalled 9 divisions. After the Battle of Nanking, two and half divisions were shifted to North China. By the end of 1937, the enemy took Hangchow. By the time Pang-pu fell in February 1938, the battlefield was greatly expanded requiring a garrison force of at least 3 divisions and a mobile force of at most 4 divisions. To move forces from Japan and shift forces from Manchuria would require considerable amount of time. For the time being, the enemy lacked the capability to move up the Yangtze River for an attack on Wuhan. However, to respond to the operations in North China and to rescue the 2nd Corps from its predicament, it was necessary to pull sufficient forces for a converging attack on Hsuchow. Having become greatly exhausted from prolonged fighting, the 5th War Area could not sustain much longer. As the situation was unfavorable, it was difficult to withdraw. The plains in eastern Honan and northern Anhwei lacked critical terrain for defense. In spring, as the Yellow River lacked water, there was no possibility of flood. It was feared that the enemy forces in North China and Central China might link up for a drive against Wuhan. Should such a possibility arise, the main strength of our forces would be defeated in detail. Hence, various courses of action were advanced.

Fully aware of the overall situation and determined to achieve victory, Generalissimo Chiang pulled some forces from Wuhan and committed them to the strategic salient—Hsuchow. He sought exploitation of success and controlled elite forces (mostly reorganized divisions under Gen. Huang Chieh, Gen. Kuei Yung-ching, Gen. Yu Chi-shih, Gen. Sung Hsi-lien and Gen. Li Han-huen) in eastern Honan, Kuei-teh and Lan-feng to consolidate the rear of the 5th War Area. He anticipated greater enemy attrition and more time to turn the situation in our favor. Subsequently, Gen. Lin Wei, deputy director of the Board of Military Operations, led a staff corps to Hsuchow to establish contact and exercise supervision with the above-mentioned intention. Gen. Lin was advised that the army in eastern Honan not be committed to the areas east of Hsuchow.

In mid-April, the enemy in Lin-yi again launched an offensive. After bitter fighting for more than a month, our defenders were greatly exhausted. Our attempt to take Chu-chen ended in heavy losses. The 92nd Corps (took part in the fighting at Hsiang-cheng) which had arrived from southern Shansi was isolated by the enemy. On April 17, our forces had to abandon Lin-yi and retreated toward Tan-cheng and Ma-tou Chen so as to respond to the 92nd Corps and stop the enemy.

On April 20, our 46th and 60th Corps arrived from Wuhan to take part in the operations at Tai-erh-chuang. At this time, enemy reinforcements arrived and launched counterattack which led to heavy fighting. On April 24, the enemy in Lin-yi took Tan-cheng. Having lost half of its men, our 3rd Army which had been exhausted was moved to Pei Hsien for replenishment. The 69th Corps which had been transferred from southern Hopei moved via the area east of Tan-cheng to Lin-yi to attack the enemy's rear areas. The 68th Corps moved from Ho-tse to mass in Chin-hsiang, preparatory to crossing the lake for an attack. Later, the corps was transferred to Hsuchow as the reserves of the 5th War Area. The 3rd Army Group continued to execute its original missions. The 1st War Area assigned the 32nd Corps of the 20th Army Group and the 23rd Division for garrison on the bank of the Yellow River in western Shantung in order to prevent the enemy crossing of the Yellow River.

Since the overwhelming defeat suffered by the 2nd Corps at Tai-erh-chuang in early April, the enemy's General Headquarters decided to employ its forces in North China and Central China for a converging on Hsuchow and to annihilate our forces in the 5th War Area. Accordingly, the enemy's North China Front Army dispatched 2 divisions to reinforce the 2nd Corps occupying the line from Han-chuang to Yi Hsien so as to tie down and contain our forces in the 5th War Area. Later, another 3 divisions arrived to attack the line from Kuei-teh to Yung-cheng. The 14th Division of the enemy's 1st Corps crossed the Yellow River from southern Shantung and cut off the Lung-hai Railway east of Lan-feng. The enemy's Central China Expeditionary Army dispatched 2½ divisions which moved north between Pang-pu and Huai-yuan along the Huai River.

Since mid-April, there had been heavy movement of enemy forces from various battlefields to the northern and southern ends of the Tientsin-Pukow Railway. By then, the enemy's design of a converging attack on Hsuchow was quite obvious. In early May, our 26th Army Group under Gen. Hsu Yuan-chuan moved east from Ho-fei to attack the flank of the enemy along the Tientsin-Pukow Railway. However, its forces were scattered and were subjected to enemy counterattacks. As enemy forces captured Ho-fei to cover his left flank, our forces withdrew to the west of Ho-fei to confront the enemy. In early May, the enemy's 13th Division moved north from Pang-pu along the Tientsin-Pukow Railway and from Han-tsun-chi and Chu-hsi-ou. Meanwhile, the enemy's 9th Division and the Iseki Mechanized Forces moved north from Huai-yuan along the Wo River via Meng-cheng. Having resisted the enemy attacks, our 21st Army Group withdrew to the west. As our 51st Corps was transferred to Tai-erh-chuang in the north, the 77th Corps was moved from Hsuchow to Su Hsien to stop the enemy's advance.

At the same time, one enemy brigade moving north from Nan-tung and Chiang-tu captured Yen-cheng and Kao-yu and pressed near Fu-ning and Huai-yin against our 24th Army Group.

On May 9, Meng-cheng fell.   On May 10, the boundary between our 1st and 5th War Areas was changed to the line east of Pochow-Huangkou-Pei Hsien-Hsia Chen.   The 3rd Army Group and the 3rd Army were placed under the command of the 1st War Area.   The 74th and 8th Corps of the 1st War Area massed in Tang Shan and Kuei-teh.   Thus, the operations in western Shantung came under the command of the 1st War Area.

On the morning of May 12, enemy forces from Men-cheng took Yung-cheng. Another force headed toward Tang Shan with its main strength making a right turning movement to attack Hsiao Hsien.   At this time, the enemy force moving north along the railway pressed against Su Hsien and Chu-hsi-kou.

On May 11, the enemy's 111th Division in the northern sector of the Tientsin-Pukow Railway captured Yun-cheng in conjunction with the crossing of the Yellow River by the 14th Division at Pu Hsien for an invasion of Ho-tse.   The enemy's 16th Division crossed the lake at Nan-yang Chen prior to the attack against Pei Hsien.   Having crossed the Canal at Tsi-ning, the enemy's 114th Division took Ching-hsiang and Yu-tai.   Our 3rd Army, 74th Corps, 3rd and 20th Army Group made use of the forts in northern Kiangsu and western Shantung to offer sustained resistance and to delay the enemy on the Lung-hai Railway.   At this time, the enemy forces at Tai-erh-chuang shifted to the offensive.   On May 15, to avoid a decisive engagement against the enemy under unfavorable circumstances, our High Command left the 24th Army Group in northern Kiangsu and the 69th Corps and marines in southern Shantung and central Shantung to conduct guerilla operations.   The main force of the 5th War Area began the breakout to the southwest leaving a small force on the outskirt of Hsuchow to provide cover and delay the enemy's advance.   On May 18, Su Hsien, Hsiao Hsien and Pei Hsien fell in succession.   In the night of May 19, our forces abandoned Hsuchow.   Having been lured by our forces to eastern Honan, Kuei-teh and Lan-feng, the enemy committed mistakes in dispositions, suffered from too wide a front, lacked depth, and made blind turning movement leaving his rear areas exposed.   Accordingly, in late May, our 5th War Area withdrew its forces safely to western Anhwei and southern Honan.

9.   Operations in Northern and Eastern Honan (Early February-Early June, 1938.   See Map 9-2 and Charts 22 and 23).

CHART 22

Chart Showing Japanese Chain of Command during Operations in Northern and Eastern Honan (January, 1938)

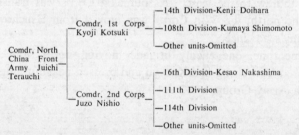

CHART 23

*Chart Showing Chinese Chain of Command during Operations in Northern
and Eastern Honan (February, 1938)*

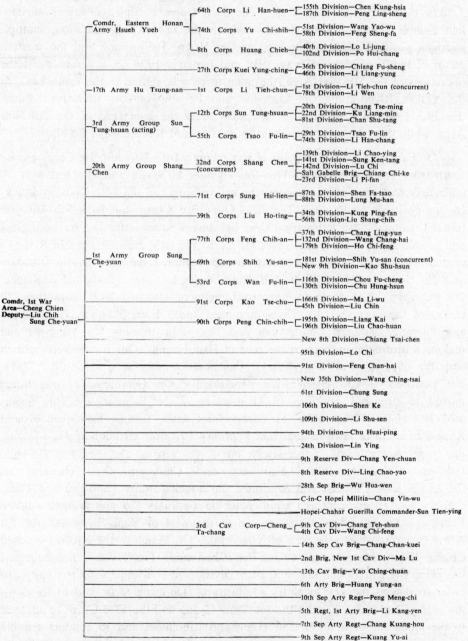

Remarks:
1. On January 27, the 59 Corps was transferred to the 5th War Area.
2. In December, 1937, the 2nd Army was reassigned from the 2nd War Area to the 1st War Area. Later, it came under the command of the 5th War Area.
3. Local militia, partisan forces and guerilla forces are not listed in this chart.

In the winter of 1937, in an effort to insure the safety of the key localities on the north bank of the Yellow River and stop the enemy at Ta-ming and An-yang, the 1st Army Group occupied the line from Lung-wang Temple-Neihuang-Taokou-right bank of Wei River. The 53rd Corps occupied positions at Pao-lien Temple north of Tang-yin to confront the enemy. In addition, multiple alternate positions were constructed at Chi Hsien, Hsin-hsiang and the western sector of the Tao-ching Railway. By mid-January, 1938, in order to assist the operations of the 5th War Area, the main force was shifted to the south bank of the Yellow River along the Lung-hai and Peiping-Hankow Railways. Later, the 59th Corps was ordered to Hsuchow under the command of the 5th War Area, while the 20th Army was held in readiness at Kuei-teh and Po-chow.

On February 7, 1938, a force of the enemy's 14th Division, 1st Corps moved south from Ta-ming and took Nan-loh. Under air cover and attached with 30 tanks and more than 10 heavy guns, the main strength of the 14th Division attack-ed our positions at Pao-lien Temple. Our 53rd Corps and New 9th Division resisted strongly. By February 11, as our forces were outflanked on both sides and counterattacks failed, our forces moved to the right bank of the Chi River to continue resistance. Our 1st Army Group occupied the positions at Tao-kou and Chi Hsien and were disposed in depth hoping to achieve sustained resistance. On February 14, a force (a reinforced regiment attached with more than 20 tanks) of the enemy's 14th Division moved south from Ta-ming via Nan-loh and Pu-yang, captured Chang-yuan and Feng-chiu heading for Yang-wu and making a turning movement to the rear of Hsin-hsiang. Our forces were split to stop the enemy. For several days, the situation was at a standstill. Then, our positions at Chi Hsien were penetrated. On February 15, our forces moved to prepared positions in Hsin-hsiang. On February 16, the enemy took Hui Hsien. Meanwhile, an enemy force made turning movement around Keng-tsun south of Hsin-hsiang. On February 17, after abandoning Hsin-hsiang, our forces moved west. Successively, our forces resisted the enemy at Hu-chia, Hsiu-wu, Chiao-tso, Po-ai, Hsin-yang and Chi-yuan. On February 24, the enemy took Chiyuan and continued the attack toward Yuan-chu and Chin-cheng. The enemy captured Chin-cheng on February 26 and Yang-cheng on February 28. Our 53rd Corps moved to the west of Yang-cheng and the 1st Army Group moved to the west of Yüan-chu. On March 3, these forces reached Chiang Hsien, Mao-chin-tu, Chang-tien Chen and Hsia Hsien. Subsequently, the main strength of the enemy's 14th Division also withdrew to the east. In order to defend the key localities southeast of Tai-hsing Shan and to tie down the enemy, our forces directed the 1st Army Group and the 53rd Corps to advance to the mountainous areas in Lin Hsien and Lin-chuan and to conduct guerilla operations. Later, the 1st Army Group received orders to withdraw to the south bank of the Yellow River for replenisnment. Furthermore, elements of the 95th Division and the garrison force defending the south bank of the Yellow River were ordered to cross the Yellow River and conduct guerilla operations along the Tao-ching Railway[16] in response to the operations of the 53rd Corps.

Since early March, the enemy's 2nd Corps attacked western Shantung and fought bitterly against the forces of the 5th War Area. Accordingly, our 1st War Area pulled the 139th Division of the 32nd Corps, 68th, 69th and 77th Corps to reinforce the 5th War Area. In early April, after the overwhelming defeat of its 2nd Corps at Tai-erh-chuang, the enemy pulled forces from other battle-fields to reinforce the northern and southern ends of the Tientsin-Pukow Railway in an attempt to make a converging attack on Hsuchow. The enemy's 14th Division massed in Pu Hsien and Pu-yang preparatory to an eastward crossing of the Yellow River. Our 94th Division and 10th Cavalry Division which were reinforcements, took active steps to harass the enemy and conduct guerilla opera-tions along the Tientsin-Pukow Railway and Peiping-Hankow Railway. In the meantime, the 23rd Division, 32nd Corps (less 139th Division) and 39th Corps defended the Yellow River against enemy crossing.

In early May, enemy forces in Tsi-ning increased in number. The 1st War Area, therefore, directed the 23rd Division to mass its main strength in Yun-cheng against possible enemy attack from the east. Generalissimo Chiang order-ed the 74th, 8th, 64th, 71st and 27th Corps to move out from Wuhan and mass in Tang-shan, Kuei-teh and Lanfeng. Later enemy forces moving north along the Wo River took Meng-cheng. On May 10, the boundary line between the 1st and 5th War Areas was changed, and all the forces in western Shantung and eastern Honan came under the command of the 1st War Area. On May 11, the enemy from Tsi-ning took Yun-cheng and then swung south. On the same day, our 74th Corps completed its massing at Tang-shan and dispatched a force to Han-tao-kou south of Tang-shan and Feng Hsien for security. Similarly, the 8th Corps completed its massing at Ma-mu-chi and Kuei-teh, and the 64th Corps was moving to Kuei-teh. These 3 corps formed the Eastern Honan Army with Gen. Hsueh Yueh as the commander. The objective of this army was to stop the enemy and cover the Lung-hai Railway so as to facilitate the operations of the 5th War Area.

On May 12, the enemy from Meng-cheng took Yun-cheng. Its main force swung to the right and attacked Hsuchow via Hsiao Hsien. Its fast-moving forces headed for Tang-shan. A force of our 74th Corps engaged the enemy in the vicinity of Han-tao-kou and heavy fighting ensued. On the same day, the enemy's 16th Division at Nan-yang Chen crossed Nanyang Lake for an attack on Pei Hsien. After putting up strong resistance, our 3rd Army was forced to fall to the west on May 16. Seeing the unfavorable situation, the 5th War Area began the move to the southwest on May 15. On May 19, our covering forces abandoned Hsuchow breaking out toward the southwest.

On May 14, the main strength of the enemy's 14th Division in Pu Hsien

---

[16] Nei-huang to Hsin-hsiang.

crossed the Yellow River and captured Ho-tse.   Elements of our 32nd Corps and the 23rd Division suffered heavy losses.   Gen. Li Pi-fan, the division commander, committed suicide.   The 32nd Corps massed its forces for the defense of Tung-ming, Kao-cheng and the bank of the Yellow River west of it.   On May 16, the enemy forces moved south from Ho-tse via Tieh-lu-chai and Ta-huang-chi.   On May 17, more than 2,000 enemy's fast-moving troops reached the vicinity of Yi-feng, east of Lan-feng, and cut off the Lung-hai Railway.   On May 18, the enemy's main force moved south through Ta-huang-chi.   Realizing the gravity of the situation, Generalissimo Chiang personally went to Cheng-chow.   He directed the 27th and 71st Corps at Lan-feng to mop up the enemy in the vicinity of Yi-feng.   Gen. Hsueh Yueh was ordered to take the main force of the Eastern Honan Army to make a converging attack to the west from Kuei-teh on the enemy's 14th Division.   A force was left in Tang-shan and Kuei-teh to delay the westward movement of the enemy's main force.   Additionally, the 20th Army Group was directed to make a flank attack against the enemy in the east.   By May 20, our forces killed many enemy troops in Yi-feng and Nei-huang.   As the enemy's 14th Division was subjected to a converging attack, it crossed the Lung-hai Railway at night and moved to the southwest.   Taking the main force of the 74th Corps, 64th Corps, 27th Corps and the main force of the 71st Corps, Gen. Hsueh Yueh followed up in a pursuit to the southwest.   On May 22, the enemy passed through the south of Yang-ku-chi, and turned to the northwest, capturing Lowang Railway Station. Chu-hsing-chi. and San-yi-chai.   In the vicinity of Yang-ku-chi, our forces attacked the enemy. Meanwhile, our 17th Army had already reached Kai-feng via the Lung-hai Railway, preparatory to mopping up the enemy in the east.   The 39th Corps (formerly garrisoning the Yellow River between Lan-feng and Kai-feng) was ordered to stop the enemy's northward advance. Heavy fighting lasted until May 24 resulting in many enemy casualties. However, the 39th Corps failed to capture the strong points of Lo-wang and Chu-hsing-chi. Meanwhile, an enemy force at Kuantai on the north bank of the Yellow River, crossed the Yellow River at Chen-liu-kou to link up with the main force of the enemy's 14th Division, controlled the crossing site to keep the line of communications open and took Lan-feng.   Thus, the enemy occupied the circular position from San-yi to Lan-feng, Lo-wang, Chu-hsing-chi, and Chen-liu-kou and offered stubborn resistance while awaiting the arrival of reinforcements.   After readjusting dispositions, our forces renewed the attack on the enemy and fought bitterly.   On May 27, with the breakthrough of the enemy's primary positions, our 71st Corps and 64th Corps respectively recovered Lan-feng and Lo-wang and opened the Lung-hai Railway. 42 of our trains were safely evacuated.   Our forces continued to attack enemy remnants at San-yi-chai, Chu-hsing-chi and Chen-liu-kou.   At this time, the 20th Corps of the 3rd Army Group fell back from western Shantung to take part in the operations.   At one time, our forces entered San-yi-chai and pressed near enemy artillery positions at Chai-ho-tan dealing a heavy blow against the enemy. Relying on well-prepared positions, the enemy resisted stubbornly. Due to lack of firepower, our forces failed to annihilate the enemy.

In Tsi-ning, the enemy's 111th and 114th Divisions began the southward advance on May 21. Our 3rd Army Group and a portion of the 74th Corps resisted gallantly at Chin-hsiang, Yu-tai, Feng Hsien and Tang-shan. The bitter fighting lasted until May 24 when our forces withdrew to the west. Enemy's main force followed up in a pursuit along the Lung-hai Railway, while a portion passed Yu-cheng to make a turning movement toward Kueiteh and joined force with the enemy moving south from Chin-hsiang in a converging attack on Kueiteh. Our 8th Corps and a portion of the 3rd Army Group conducted sustained resistance at Ma-mu-chi, Yu-cheng and Kueiteh. On May 28, the Lung-hai Railway was cleared and all trains were evacuated to the West. As the forces of the 5th War Area broke out safely, our forces abandoned Kueiteh and withdrew to Chi Hsien, Chu Hsien and Liu-ho. On the same day, the 68th Corps broke out from Hsiao Hsien and fell back to Po-chow. On the morning of May 30, having repelled the enemy pursuit forces, the corps received orders to withdraw to Huai-yang.

On May 31, in order to avoid a decisive battle against the enemy on the eastern Honan plains, our headquarters ordered the main force of the 1st War Area to withdraw to the west of the Peiping-Hankow Railway and a force (composed of the 32nd and 39th Corps under the command of Gen. Shang Chen) to conduct sustained resistance at Kai-feng and Chung-mu. On June 8, the enemy's firstline troops passed the line from Chung-mu to Wei-shih, and the enemy's cavalry reached the vicinity of Hsin-cheng. As the water in the Yellow River rose, Hua-yuan-kou, east of Cheng-chow, was flooded, and the main outflow followed the Chia-lu River into the Huai River. The enemy's 2nd Corps, finding itself about to be trapped in the flood hurriedly retreated. Our forces took advantage of the opportunity to wipe out enemy remnants west of the flooded area. Since then, the two opposing forces faced each other across the flooded area for six years.

10. Battle of Wuhan (Early June-Mid-November, 1938. See Map 10 and Charts 24 and 25)

Since the fall of Nanking and Shanghai, Wuhan, as the nation's military and communication center, became increasingly important. In early June, 1938, after the Battle of Hsuchow, when the enemy's 2nd Corps was blocked by the flood of the Yellow River, the enemy began to move toward Cheng-yang-kuan and Ho-fei. At the same time, the enemy in the lower reaches of the Yangtze River began to advance toward Ta-tung and An-king. Its attempt to attack Wuhan became more obvious. The National Military Council made an estimate of the enemy's total strength and the size of the battlefield and revealed that the forces which the enemy could employ stood at 12-13 divisions, more than 400

CHART   24

Chart Showing the Japanese Chain of Command during the Battle of Wuhan (Mid-July, 1938)

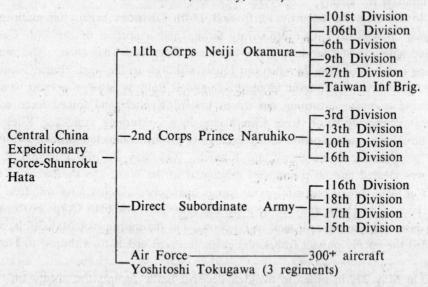

airplanes, necessary naval units (in the summer, ships below 10,000 tons could sail to Wuhan) and marines.   The enemy was capable of staging a converging attack along both banks of the Yangtze River, Pu-hsin Highway and Shang-ma Highway, and of employing a force along the Nan-hsun Railroad in an attack to cover his left flank.   If his strength were sufficient, he would go beyond Hsiu River to seize Nanchang, attack Changsha along the Hunan-Kiangsi Railway to cut off our withdrawal to the south.   In addition, he could employ naval units up the Yangtze River in joint operations.   The time for the attack would be sometime after the first part of July.   Accordingly, in mid-June, our operational plans were prepared.   An outline of the operational plans is stated as follows:

a.   Operational Guiding Principle:

A portion of the Chinese Armed Forces will defend the coast of South China and the present positions in East China and North China, and actively step up guerilla operations to impede enemy shipping in the lower reaches of the Yangtze River, tie down and wear out the enemy.   Another powerful force will support Ma-tang Fortress, force the enemy to deploy east of Poyang Lake and prevent the enemy from moving up the Yangtze River to mass in Kiu-kiang.   Our main force will concentrate on the outskirts of Wuhan and take advantage of the natural barriers of the Po-yang Lake and Ta-pieh Shan, and the hills and swamps on the banks of the Yangtze River, to conduct strategic sustained operations with emphasis on the outer flanks to seek freedom of maneuver.

It is estimated that the operations against the enemy's main force will take 4-6 months.   Every effort will be made to wear out the enemy and shatter his

CHART 25

Chart Showing Chinese Chain of Command during Battle of Wuhan

(Early July, 1938)

```
                                                                        ┌─139th Division-Li Chao-ying
                                              32nd Corps                 ├─141st Division-Tang Yung-liang
                                              Shang Chen                 ├─142nd Division-Fu Li-ping
                          20th Army Group      (concurrent)              └─Salt Gabell Brig-Chiang Yung-ke
                          Shang Chen
                                              18th Corps                 ┌─11th Division-Peng Shan
                                              Huang Wei                  ├─16th Division-Ho Ping
                                                                         └─60th Division-Chen Pei

                                              4th Corps                  ┌─59th Division-Chang Teh-neng
                                              Ou Chen                    └─90th Division-Chen Yung-chi

                                              8th Corps                  ┌─3rd Division-Chao Hsi-tien
                                              Li Yu-tang                 └─15th Division-Wang Chih-pin

                                              66th Corps                 ┌─159th Division-Tan Sui
                                              Yeh Chao                   └─160th Division-Hua Chen-chung

                          9th                 64th Corps                 ┌─155th Division-Chen Kung-hsia
                          Army                Li Han-huen                ├─187th Division-Kung Ke-chuan
                          Group      29th     (concurrent)               └─9th Res Division-Chang Yen-chuan
                          Wu          Army
                          Chi-wei     Li Han-  70th Corps Li Chueh─19th Division-Li Chueh (concurrent)
                                      huen
                                                                         91st Division-Feng Chan-hai

                                                                         6th Res Division-Chi Chang-chien

                                      37th Army   25th Corps             ┌─52nd Division-Tang Yun-shan
                                      Wang        Wang Ching-chiu        └─109th Division-Liang Hua-sheng
     C-in-C, 1st                      Ching-chiu  (concurrent)
  ─ Army Corps─
     Hsueh Yueh                       74th Corps                        ┌─51st Division-Wang Yao-wu
                                      Yu Chi-shih                       └─58th Division-Feng Sheng-fa

                                      29th Corps                        ┌─40th Division-Li Tien-hsia
                                      Chen An-pao                       └─79th Division-Chen An-pao (concurrent)

                                                                        167th Division-Chao Hsia-kuang

                                                                        Po Yang Lake Garrison Comdr.

                                              72nd Corps                ┌─New 13th Division-Liu Juo-pi
                          30th Army Group     Wang Ling-chi             └─New 14th Division-Fan Nan-hsuan
                          Wang Ling-chi        (concurrent)
                                              78th Corps                ┌─New 15th Division-Teng Kuo-chang
                                              Chang Tsai                └─New 16th Division-Chen Liang-chi

                                                                        ┌─20th Division-Chang Tse-min
                          3rd Army Group      12th Corps                ├─22nd Division-Shih Tung-jan
                          Sun Tung-hsuan       Sun Tung-hsuan           └─81st Division-Chan Shu-tang
                                               (concurrent)

                                                                        ┌─23rd Division-Ouyang Fen
                                              13th Corps                ├─89th Division-Chang Hsueh-chung
                          31st Army Group     Chang Chen                └─35th Division-Wang Ching-tsai
                          Tang En-po
                                                                        ┌─82nd Division-Lo Chi-chiang
                                              98th Corps                ├─193rd Division-Li Tsung-chien
  Comdr,                                      Chang Kang                └─195th Division-Liang Kai
  9th War
  Area-                                       52nd Corps                ┌─2nd Division-Chao Kung-wu
  Chen                     32nd Army          Kuan Lin-cheng           └─25th Division-Chang Yao-ming
  Cheng                    Kuan Lin-cheng      (concurrent)
                                              92nd Corps                ┌─21st Division-Hou Ching-ju
     C-in-C, 2nd                              Li Hsien-chou            └─95th Division-Lo Chi
  ─ Army Corps ─
     Chang Fa-kuei         Tienpei Fortress                            ┌─9th Division-Cheng Tso-min
                          Comdr, 11th Army    2nd Corps                ├─57th Division-Shih Chung-cheng
                          Li Yen-nien          Li Yen-nien             └─Tienchiachen Fortress Units
                                               (concurrent)

                          Tiennan Fortress                             ┌─14th Division-Chen Lieh
                          Comdr Huo           54th Corps               └─18th Division-Li Fang-pin
                          Kuei-chang          Hou Kuei-chang

                          Yangtze River North 6th Corps
                          Region Comdr Wan    Kan Li-chu               93rd Division-Kan Li-chu (concurrent)
                          Yao-huang
                                              16th Corps
                                              Tung Chao                28th Division-Tung Chao (concurrent)

                          Yangtze River                               ┌─6th Division-Chang Ying
                          South Region        75th Corps              ├─13th Division-Fang Ching
                          Comdr: Chou Ai      Chou Ai                 └─Huang Ngo Fortress Units

     C-in-C, Wu-          Wuhan Garrison      94th Corps              ┌─55th Division-Li Chi-lan
  ─ han Garrison ─        Comdr Kuo Chan      Kuo Chan                └─185th Division-Fang Tien
     Lo Cho-ying
                                              37th Corps              ┌─92nd Division-Huang Kuo-liang
                                              Huang Kuo-liang         └─(concurrent)

                          Hupei Provincial Air Defense Units

                                                                      ┌─184th Division-Chang Chung
                          30th Army           60th Corps              ├─49th Division-Li Ching-yi
                          Lu Han              Lu Han                  └─102nd Division-Po Hui-chang
                                               (concurrent)

                          26th Army           53rd Corps              ┌─130th Division-Chu Hung-hsun
                          Wan Fu-lin          Wan Fu-lin              └─116th Division-Chou Fu-cheng
                                               (concurrent)
```

(concurrent)

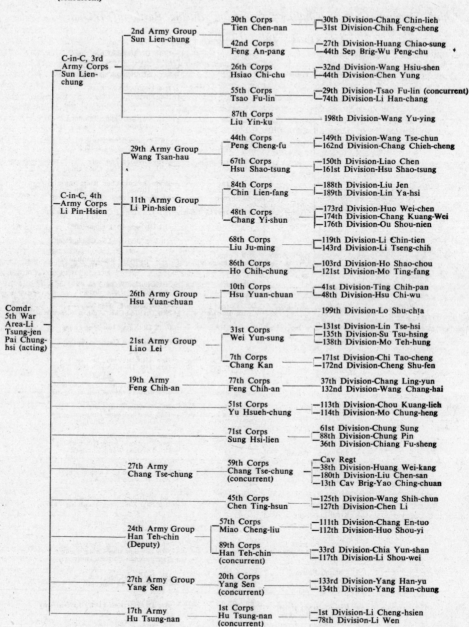

Comdr
5th War
Area-Li
Tsung-jen
Pai Chung-
hsi (acting)

C-in-C, 3rd
Army Corps
Sun Lien-
chung

2nd Army Group
Sun Lien-chung
- 30th Corps
  Tien Chen-nan — 30th Division-Chang Chin-lieh / 31st Division-Chih Feng-cheng
- 42nd Corps
  Feng An-pang — 27th Division-Huang Chiao-sung / 44th Sep Brig-Wu Peng-chu
- 26th Corps
  Hsiao Chi-chu — 32nd Division-Wang Hsiu-shen / 44th Division-Chen Yung
- 55th Corps
  Tsao Fu-lin — 29th Division-Tsao Fu-lin (concurrent) / 74th Division-Li Han-chang
- 87th Corps
  Liu Yin-ku — 198th Division-Wang Yu-ying

C-in-C, 4th
Army Corps
Li Pin-Hsien

29th Army Group
Wang Tsan-hau
- 44th Corps
  Peng Cheng-fu — 149th Division-Wang Tse-chun / 162nd Division-Chang Chieh-cheng
- 67th Corps
  Hsu Shao-tsung — 150th Division-Liao Chen / 161st Division-Hsu Shao-tsung

11th Army Group
Li Pin-hsien
- 84th Corps
  Chin Lien-fang — 188th Division-Liu Jen / 189th Division-Lin Ya-hsi
- 48th Corps
  Chang Yi-shun — 173rd Division-Huo Wei-chen / 174th Division-Chang Kuang-Wei / 176th Division-Ou Shou-nien
- 68th Corps
  Liu Ju-ming — 119th Division-Li Chin-tien / 143rd Division-Li Tseng-chih
- 86th Corps
  Ho Chih-chung — 103rd Division-Ho Shao-chou / 121st Division-Mo Ting-fang

26th Army Group
Hsu Yuan-chuan
- 10th Corps
  Hsu Yuan-chuan — 41st Division-Ting Chih-pan / 48th Division-Hsu Chi-wu
- 199th Division-Lo Shu-chia

21st Army Group
Liao Lei
- 31st Corps
  Wei Yun-sung — 131st Division-Lin Tse-hsi / 135th Division-Su Tsu-hsing / 138th Division-Mo Teh-hung
- 7th Corps
  Chang Kan — 171st Division-Chi Tao-cheng / 172nd Division-Cheng Shu-fen

19th Army
Feng Chih-an
- 77th Corps
  Feng Chih-an — 37th Division-Chang Ling-yun / 132nd Division-Wang Chang-hai
- 51st Corps
  Yu Hsueh-chung — 113th Division-Chou Kuang-lieh / 114th Division-Mo Chung-heng

- 71st Corps
  Sung Hsi-lien — 61st Division-Chung Sung / 88th Division-Chung Pin / 36th Division-Chiang Fu-sheng

27th Army
Chang Tse-chung
- 59th Corps
  Chang Tse-chung (concurrent) — Cav Regt / 38th Division-Huang Wei-kang / 180th Division-Liu Chen-san / 13th Cav Brig-Yao Ching-chuan
- 45th Corps
  Chen Ting-hsun — 125th Division-Wang Shih-chun / 127th Division-Chen Li

24th Army Group
Han Teh-chin
(Deputy)
- 57th Corps
  Miao Cheng-liu — 111th Division-Chang En-tuo / 112th Division-Huo Shou-yi
- 89th Corps
  Han Teh-chin (concurrent) — 33rd Division-Chia Yun-shan / 117th Division-Li Shou-wei

27th Army Group
Yang Sen
- 20th Corps
  Yang Sen (concurrent) — 133rd Division-Yang Han-yu / 134th Division-Yang Han-chung

17th Army
Hu Tsung-nan
- 1st Corps
  Hu Tsung-nan (concurrent) — 1st Division-Li Cheng-hsien / 78th Division-Li Wen

Notes: After the fighting at Ma-tang, the 53rd Division of the 16th Corps, 9th War Area underwent reorganization and training. After its defeat, the 167th Division was deactivated. A new 167th Division was activated by combining the 5th Division and the 95th Division.

ability to continue the offensive (This was the tentative plan of the subcommittee and was never promulgated).

b.   Order of Battle:
      See Chart 25.

c.   Tasks of the Various War Areas:

(1)   The 1st War Area will assign a force to defend the Yellow River and conduct guerilla operations in eastern Honan, western Shantung and northern Honan.   Its main force will occupy prepared positions along the line from Chueh-shan to Szu-shui.   It will place emphasis on the vicinity of Yu Hsien and will assume the offensive at the opportune time.   Additional forces will be left in key localities on the frontline to delay the enemy.   However, the 36th, 45th and 46th Divisions must mass in the vicinity of Pi-yang as the reserves of the war area.   The 24th and 109th Divisions and 7th Reserve Division will move to Tung-kuan under the command of the Generalissimo's Headquarters in Si-an.

(2)   After offering, gradual resistance, the 5th War Area will direct the Huai-pei Army Corps to mass in the vicinity of Shang-cheng, preparatory to attacking the flanks of the enemy heading toward the southwest.   The 26th Army Group of the Huainan Army Corps will mass in Shu-cheng, Tung-cheng, Huo-shan and Lu-an to stop the enemy from moving west.   The 27th Army Group will defend An-king, Wu-wei, and Lu-chiang, preparatory to attacking the flanks of the enemy moving west along the Yangtze River.   Regardless of changes in situation, the security of Ta-pieh Shan base must be insured.   The 24th Army Group will insure the defense of northern Kiangsu and conduct guerilla operations in the southern sector of the Tientsin-Pukow Railway.

(3)   The 3rd War Area will strengthen river defense emphasizing adequate combat readiness between Tung-liu and Ma-tang, and control adequate forces to stop enemy landing or assist the operations in An-king.   Local militia and local labor will be directed to construct defense works along the Hangchow-Ningpo Railway, the Chekiang-Kiangsi Railway, the Hangchow-Anhwei Highway and Nanking-Kiangsi Highway.   Furthermore, adequate forces should be massed in the above-stated lines of communications to attack the enemy.

(4)   The Wuhan Garrison General Headquarters (The 9th War Area was not yet activated.   All the forces on the outskirts of Wuhan came under the command of Gen.   Chen Cheng, commander-in-chief of the Wuhan Garrison General Headquarters) will dispatch its main force to occupy primary positions along the line from Kuangchi to Ping-ching-kuan.   Emphasis will be placed on the vicinity of the highways near Wu-sheng-kuan, Ma-cheng and Kuang-chi, and offensive will be launched at the opportune time.   A force will be dispatched to Hsin-yang, Lo-shan and Su-sung in conjunction with the 5th War Area to delay and wear out the enemy.   However, 6 divisions under Gen. Hsueh Yueh and Gen. Liu Hsing will assume river defense with emphasis on Ma-tang, forcing the enemy's main force to deploy east of Po-yang Lake.   The 52nd and 190th

Divisions under Gen. Wan Yao-hung's corps will be located along the Nan-hsun Railway,[17] 3 divisions of Gen. Hsia Wei's corps will be located in Yang-hsin and Ta-yeh and 2 divisions of Gen. Yeh Chao's corps will be in readiness along the Hunan-Kiangsi Railway.[18] 3 corps under Gen. Kou Chan, Gen. Li Yen-nien and Gen. Chou Ai, totalling 8 divisions will assume the defense of Wuhan. 4 divisions under Gen. Wang Ling-chi's army group massed in Chin-men and Sha-shin, will come under command of the National Military Council.

(5) Gen. Tang En-po, commander-in-chief of the Honan-Hupei Border Area, will mass his forces in Sui Hsien, Hsiang-yang, Fan-cheng and Nan-yang, preparatory to attacking the flanks of the enemy moving south along the Peiping-Hankow Railway, and will assist in the operations of the Wuhan Garrison General Headquarters. However, should the enemy advance from the south of the Lung-hai Railway to the west or southwest, a powerful force will be dispatched to assist the operations of the 1st War Area. Its 28th Army under Gen. Liu Ju-ming and 95th Division under Gen. Lo Chi will occupy the positions in Pi-yang and Chueh-shan in the order of battle of the 5th War Area.

(6) The main strength of our air force will be concentrated in Hankow and Nanchang Airfields, bombing enemy ships in the Yangtze River day and night, and attacking enemy airfields in Nanking, Wu-hu and An-king along the river.

(7) The navy will exert every effort to strengthen the fortresses at Ma-tang (In December, 1937, the Ma-tang blockade line had been completed). Hu-kou, Tien-chia Chen, and Ko-tien along the river.

(8) 2nd, 4th and 8th War Areas: Omitted.

At this time, our Government bought more than 100 airplanes and more than 100 light howitzers, field guns, antiaircraft guns and anti-tank guns. Training was actively conducted. Field works in depth were constructed in Lu Shan, Mu-fu Shan, Tai-pieh Shan, various passes and the vicinity of Wuhan. At the same time, fortresses along the river were strengthened and defense forces designated in preparation for war.

Beginning in early June, 1938, the enemy's 2nd Corps moved south from the Lung-hai Railway and successively took Wo-yang, Feng-tai, Shou Hsien and Cheng-yang-kuan before it massed in the vicinity of Ho-fei. Meanwhile, enemy ships in the lower reaches of the Yangtze River covered the advance of the Tai-wan Infantry Brigade in its advance toward Ta-tung and An-king along the river. The enemy's 6th Division at Ho-fei attacked Ta-kuan via Shu-cheng. Our 21st and 26th Army Group and the 19th Army (77th Corps) of the 5th War Area fell back to the line from Huo-shan to Lu-an and Fu-yang to stop the enemy. The 27th Army Group (20th Corps) garrisoned An-king, Wu-wei and Ta-kuan to stop the enemy's westward advance.

---

[17] Nanchang to Kiukiang.
[18] Nanchang to Chuchow.

On the night of June 11, more than 20 enemy ships covered the landing of 2,000 enemy troops below Anking. After resisting strongly, our defenders withdrew toward Chienshan in the night of June 12. On June 11, the enemy's 6th Division captured Ta-kuan. Our forces fell back to Yuan-tan-pu to continue resistance. On June 15, our forces withdrew to Chien-shan as the enemy continued the attack. Our 20th Corps resisted firmly and fought bitterly against the enemy for 4 days and nights. By June 18, the corps fell back to the vicinity of Hsiao-chih-yi and Tai-hu continuing to stop the enemy. On June 26, our 26th Army Group in Huo-shan attacked the flanks of the enemy at Tai-hu. Heavy fighting continued until June 29 when many enemy troops were killed. The enemy was forced to retreat toward Chien-shan and Wang-chiang. The 26th Army Group occupied the mountainous area west of Chien-shan to Wang-chia-pai-lou and Tien-chu Shan, preparatory to attacking the flanks of the enemy advancing west along the Chien-tai Road. The 31st Corps was located in the vicinity of Tai-hu to respond to the operations of the 26th Army Group. Then, the focal point of the operations had shifted to the right bank of the Yangtze River. The situation on the Chien-tai front was quiet.

Under the support of 1 cruiser and a number of destroyers, the enemy moved along the river to begin the attack of Ma-tang Fortress on June 24. Our 53rd and 167th Divisions fought with the fortress troops against the enemy in Huang-shan and Hsiang-shan in a bitter see-saw battle. Heavy fighting lasted until noon, June 26 when air-ground-navy firepower superiority enabled the enemy to break through a portion of the fortress. Our forces counterattacked from the outskirts killing large number of enemy troops. Our fortress guns damaged 1 enemy cruiser, 2 destroyers and sank 3 motor boats. In the end, the fortress was lost and Gen. Wang Hsi-tao, its commander, missing. Hsueh Wei-ying, Commander of the 167th Division, was executed. On June 29, enemy motor boats with 800 marines on board crossed the Ma-tang blockade line landed in General's Temple in the vicinity of Peng-tze and took it. On July 3, the enemy continued to move west and engaged our forces in the vicinity of Liu-sze-chiao. Meanwhile, the column sailed in motor boats to land in the vicinity of Hu-kou. Heavy fighting lasted for 2 days resulting in the destruction of many gun sites and many casualties to the defenders. Our 26th Division put up final resistance in Hukou City by employing a combination of firepower and counterattacks. By July 5, superior firepower enabled the enemy to take Hu-kou. Later, our 11th and 16th Divisions arrived as reinforcements and counterattacked, inflicting heavy casualties on the enemy. By July 8, the enemy forces were cornered to the area along the river. Unfortunately, the lack of heavy weapons prevented our forces from achieving success.

At this time, our main forces massed in Wuhan. The 9th War Area was activated with Gen. Chen Cheng as the commander in order to facilitate command. It commanded a total of 27 corps built around the 1st and 2nd Army

Corps in Kiangsi west of the Po-yang Lake, southern Hupei, and Hunan for operations in the areas south of the Yangtze River. The 5th War Area was expanded to include northern Honan, southern Anhwei, central Ahwei, northern Anhwei and northern Kiangsu. Built around the 3rd and 4th Army Corps, it had a total of 23 corps under the command of Gen. Li Tsung-jen for operations in areas north of the Yangtze River. However, the defense of Wuhan and the garrison of Tien-chia Chen were placed under the 9th War Area.

In mid-July, the enemy's General Headquarters changed the order of battle of the Central China Expeditionary Army in order to mount an offensive against Wuhan. Gen. Shunroku Hata, commander of the Central China Expeditionary Army, commanded the 2nd Corps (under Gen. Prince Naruhiko and built around 4 divisions), the 11th Corps (under Gen. Neiji Okamura and built around 5½ divisions), Direct Subordinate Army (built around 4 divisions), an air division (under Gen. Yoshitoshi Tokugawa and built around 3 air regiments). The Central China Expeditionary Army moved the 2nd Corps to the vicinity of Ho-fei preparatory to an advance along the west bank of the Yangtze River. The main force of the Direct Subordinate Army was held in the Nanking-Shanghai-Hangchow area, and another force controlled the key localities between the Yangtze River and the Huai River, the lower reaches of the Yangtze River below Hukou.

Our 9th War Area dispatched the 1st Army Corps to garrison Kiu-kiang and the west bank of the Po-yang Lake, and the 2nd Army Corps to garrison the areas on the south bank of the Yangtze River west of Kiu-kiang and the fortresses along the river to stop the enemy. The 5th War Area assigned the 4th Army Corps to garrison Hsiao-chih-kou and the north bank of the Yangtze River west of Huang-mei to stop the enemy landing. The 21st, 26th and 27th Army Groups garrisoned Su-sung, and the line of the mountian foot northwest of Tai-hu and Chien-shan, preparatory to attacking the flanks of the enemy forces which advanced to the west. The 3rd Army Corps garrisoned the north side of Ta-pieh Shan against the enemy.

In mid-July, enemy bombings were intensified and the enemy swept mines in Po-yang Lake. Before dawn on July 23, enemy forces landed in the vicinity of Ku-tang. The 8th, 64th and 70th Corps of the 1st Army Corps were gradually committed. Repeated counterattacks led to heavy fighting. On July 24, the enemy continued to land at Kiu-kiang and the vicinity of Ma-chang Lake. For 3 days, our forces fought bitterly against the enemy's air-ground-naval team near the lake and the lowland along the Yangtze River. As the situation became unfavorable, our forces had to abandon Kiu-kiang on July 26 and withdrew to prepared positions south of Nan-chang-pu and Sha-ho.

As to the north bank of the Yangtze River, on July 25, more than 20 enemy ships and scores of airplanes bombarded Hsiao-chih-kou. The enemy's 6th Division launched attacks against Tai-hu, Su-sung and Huang-mei. Our 68th and

31st Corps resisted strongly.   Heavy fighting lasted until August 5 when our forces moved to the line from the west of Huang-mei to north and south of Ta-chin-pu to confront the enemy.   Thus, the main force and a portion of the enemy's 2nd Corps massed respectively in the vicinity of Kiu-kiang and Huang-mei ready for the attack on Wuhan.

In late August, the enemy's Central China Expeditionary Army began the general offensive.   The enemy's 11th Corps dispatched its main force (9th, 27th and 106th Divisions) moved along Jui-yang Highway and Jui-wu Highway to attack Wuchang, Hsien-ning and Tung-shan.   One force (6th Division) moved along the north bank of the Yangtze River to attack Hankow.   Another force (101st Division) advanced Nan-hsun Railway and on the Po-yang Lake to attack Teh-an and cover its left flank.   The main force of the 2nd Corps (3rd Division, 10th Division and bulk of 16th Division) passed the highway through Lu-an, Ku-shih, Huang-chuan and Hsin-yang to attack Hsinyang.   Another force (13th Division and later portion of the 16th Division) attacked Ma-cheng via Huo-shan and Shang-cheng.   Another force (approximately 7,000 men) moved from Shou Hsien up the south bank of Huai River to attack Huang-chuan.   Meanwhile, enemy fleet (2 cruisers and over 40 destroyers and gunboats) supported the Tai-wan Infantry Brigade and the marines to move up the Yangtze River and land at Po-yang Lake as the secondary attack.   The main strength of the air division (3 regiments) directly supported the ground operations.

As to the Nan-hsun Railway, the 1st Army Corps of the 9th War Area made use of the Lu-shan mountain ranges, Nan-hsun Railway and the highground west of the railway by occupying positions in depth and combining firepower and countterattacks to offer gradual resistance.   Beginning on August 20, our forces fought for more than 80 days against the enemy's 101st and 106th Divisions which had landed at Hsing-tze to make a frontal attack along the Nan-hsun Railway, and the enemy's 27th Division which attacked along the Jui-wu High-way. Our forces dealt the enemy a heavy blow. Especially the Battle of Wan-chia-ling from October 6 to October 10, our 4th, 66th and 74th Corps jointly destroyed 4 enemy regiments and inflicted casualties on half of the 101st Division.   On October 31, our 1st Army Corps gradually fell back to the south bank of the Hsiu River to confront the enemy.

As to the south bank of the Yangtze River, our 2nd Army Corps made use of the Mufu Mountain Range west of Jui-chang and the fortresses along the river by occupying positions in depth and combining firepower and counterattacks to offer gradual resistance.   Beginning on August 22, our forces fought for 2 months against the enemy's 9th Division moving along Jui-yang Highway,[19] the enemy's Taiwan Brigade which landed in the harbor northeast of Jui-chang, and the enemy's 6th Division which moved along the north bank of the Yangtze River to attack our fortress at Tien-chia-chen.   At Wu-shih-chieh and Ma-tou Chen,

---

[19] Jui-chang to Yang-hsin.

northwest of Jui-chang and Tien-chia-chen Fortress, our forces inflicted heavy casualities on the enemy. Especially in middle and late September, during the Battle of Tien-chia-chen, the 57th Division and a portion of the 9th Division, 2nd Corps and the fortress artillery fought a bloody battle against the enemy for 20 days, killing several thousand enemy troops, damaging or sinking scores of enemy ships and motor boats and delaying the enemy's attack on Wuhan. They also supported the operations on the right flank of the 5th War Area contributing greatly to this campaign. On October 25, as the enemy pressed near Wuchang, our forces withdrew to Tung-cheng and Yueh-yang.

On the north bank of the Yangtze River, the 4th Army Corps of the 5th War Area attached with the 26th Corps made use of the hilly terrain on the south side of Ta-pieh Shan and swamps to occupy positions in depth from east and west of Kuang-chi to Hsi-shui in order to stop the enemy. Based on the mountainous terrain north of Kuang-chi, Tai-hu and Chien-shan, our 21st and 27th Army Groups attacked the enemy's flanks to the south. As our forces captured Tai-hu and Chien-shan, the enemy changed his line of communications to Hsiao-chih-kou. On August 28 and 29, our forces continued the attack on Huang-mei killing many enemy troops. On August 30, the enemy's 6th Division began the counterattack. Our forces fought bitterly against the enemy at Kuang-chi and Wu-hsueh. On September 9, the enemy captured Kuang-chi. On September 16, after taking Wu-hsueh (It had several fine jetties), the ememy surrounded the fortress at Tien-chia Chen. Our 26th, 48th and 86th Corps attacked the enemy's flanks in response to the operations of the fortress. For more than 10 days our forces fought against the enemy achieving local victories and killing many enemy troops. Absolute superiority in naval gunfire, bombing and artillery enabled the enemy to capture the Tien-chia-chen Fortress on September 29. Our forces offered gradual resistance on the north side to the mountains and at Chi-chun, Hsi-shui and Pa-ho. On October 24, the enemy broke through our positions at Huang-pi. The main strength of our forces withdrew to the west of Peiping-Hankow Railway leaving a force to conduct guerilla operations in Ta-pieh Shan.

With regard to the north side of Ta-pieh Shan, our 5th War Area employed the 51st and 77th Corps to garrison Huo-shan and Lu-an and the 71st Corps to garrison Fu-chin-shan and Ku-shih. The 2nd Army Group massed in Shang-cheng and Ma-cheng, the 54th Corps in Huang-chuan, the 1st Corps in Hsin-yang, one division of the 31st Corps in Liu-po-tung expecting to fight a decisive battle against the enemy east of Shang-cheng. On August 27, the enemy's 2nd Corps began the attack. After taking Lu-an on August 28 and Huo-shan on August 29, the enemy's 2nd Corps crossed Pei River to advance to the west. Beginning on September 2, our 71st Corps and 2nd Army Group defended strong points at Fu-chin-shan, Ku-shih and Shang-cheng against the enemy for 2 weeks killing 5,000-6,000 enemy troops. However, the enemy's absolute superiority changed our original plans to fight a decisive battle east of Sang-cheng. On September 16, our forces abandoned Shang-cheng and fell back to Ta-chuan-tien and Sha-wo south of Shang-cheng and the various passes in Ta-pieh Shan. For over a month, our forces foought against the enemy's 13th Division and a portion of the 16th Division killing nearly 10,000 enemy troops. Enemy failure shattered his design to move along the Shang-ma Highway,[20] break through Ta-pieh Shan and attack Hankow. The 59th Corps operated in Huang-chuan and Chun-ho-pu to meet the enemy moving along Pu-hsin Highway[21] and the Huai River. The one-week battle ended in the killing of many enemy troops. On September 19, Huang-chuan fell due to superior firepower of the enemy's 10th Division (2 regiments of field artillery and 2 battalions of heavy artillery), air support and indiscriminate gas attack. The enemy took Huang-chuan on September 19 and crossed Loshan on September 21. Our 1st Corps struck the enemy east of Hsin-yang killing over 5,000 enemy troops and forcing the enemy to fall back to Lo-shan City. Later, the enemy's 3rd Division reinforced and counterattacked for 2 days and nights. Our forces fell back to the vicinity of Hsin-yang for sustained resistance. Another enemy force circled around Liu-lin on both sides of the Peiping-Hankow Railway south of Hsin-yang. On October 12, our forces abandoned Hsin-yang. The 31st Corps and 13th Division defended Wu-sheng-kuan to stop the enemy from moving south. The 1st Corps moved to the mountainous area northwest of Hsin-yang to cover the Hsi-ching Highway and seek exterior lines so as to insure freedom of maneuver. In late October, the enemy's 3rd Division advanced toward Ying-shan threatening the withdrawal route of the main force of the 5th War Area.

For nearly 5 months, the Battle of Wuhan raged. Several hundred major and minor combat operations were conducted, over 200,000 enemy troops were killed or wounded, over 100 enemy ships and craft were sunk or damaged and over 100 enemy planes were destroyed. Thus, coupled with the advance evacuation of the people and materiel of Wuhan, the objective of a war of attrition was realized. On October 25, our forces, having abandoned Wuhan, withdrew to the line from Hsiu River to Hsin-chiang River, Sha-yang and Sui Hsien. At this critical moment, instead of increasing his forces for an exploitation of success, the enemy dispersed his forces in search of secondary objectives. On October 21, the 21st Corps (built around 3 divisions) took Canton. As the enemy forces were depleted in their will-to-fight and combat effectiveness, they resorted to sustained operations. By November 12 when the enemy's Central China Expeditionary Army stopped on the line from Teh-an to Yueh-yang and Hsin-yang, this campaign came to an end.

11. Operations in Fukien-Kwangtung (Early May-Mid-December 1938. See Map 11 and 12 and Charts 26 and 27).

---

[20] Shang-cheng to Ma-cheng.
[21] Pu-chiang to Hsin-yang.

CHART 26

Chart Showing Japanese Chain of Command during Operations
in Fukien-Kwangtung Area (Early May, 1938)

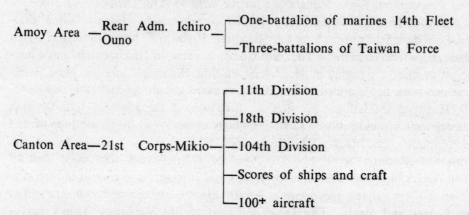

Amoy Area — Rear Adm. Ichiro Ouno

- One-battalion of marines 14th Fleet
- Three-battalions of Taiwan Force

Canton Area — 21st Corps-Mikio

- 11th Division
- 18th Division
- 104th Division
- Scores of ships and craft
- 100+ aircraft

CHART 27

Chart Showing Chinese Chain of Command during Operations in
Fukien-Kwangtung Area (Early May, 1938)

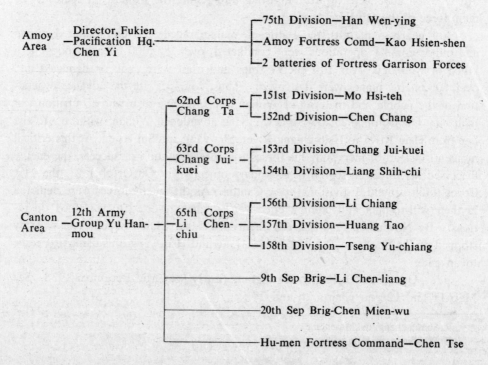

Amoy Area — Director, Fukien Pacification Hq. Chen Yi

- 75th Division—Han Wen-ying
- Amoy Fortress Comd—Kao Hsien-shen
- 2 batteries of Fortress Garrison Forces

Canton Area — 12th Army Group Yu Han-mou

- 62nd Corps Chang Ta
  - 151st Division—Mo Hsi-teh
  - 152nd Division—Chen Chang
- 63rd Corps Chang Jui-kuei
  - 153rd Division—Chang Jui-kuei
  - 154th Division—Liang Shih-chi
- 65th Corps Li Chen-chiu
  - 156th Division—Li Chiang
  - 157th Division—Huang Tao
  - 158th Division—Tseng Yu-chiang
- 9th Sep Brig—Li Chen-liang
- 20th Sep Brig-Chen Mien-wu
- Hu-men Fortress Command—Chen Tse

In the summer of 1938, the enemy made active preparations for an invasion of Wuhan. In an attempt to cut off our overseas supply line, the enemy' 14th Fleet with over 2,000 troops on board and under the command of Rear Admiral Ichiro Ouno invaded Amoy in early May, 1938. Later in mid-September, the 21st Corps was organized (under the command of Gen. Mikio and built around 3 divisions). Beginning in late September, enemy forces were shipped to Ma-kung from Tsing-tao, Shanghai and Dairen. On October 12, under the support of scores of enemy ships and over 100 airplanes, the enemy made a forced land-ing in the vicinity of Ao-tou in Taya Bay, Kwangtung Province, ready to invade Canton.

Our 4th War Area undertook the garrison of the coast of Fukien and Kwang-tung to cover the movement of material to the interior. The 75th Division under-took the garrison of Amoy, while the 12th Army Group undertook the garrison of the coast of Kwangtung.

As to Amoy, at dawn on May 10, 1938, over 30 enemy aircraft repeatedly bombed the coastal positions northeast of Amoy, while enemy ships bombarded Ho-tsu, Ni-chin and Wu-tung to cover the landing of more 2,000 marines. The main force of our 75th Division fought against the enemy suffering heavy casualties. Eventually our positions were overrun by the enemy. Acting division commander Han Wen-ying was wounded, while 2 battalion commanders, Sung Tien-cheng and Wang Chien-chang were killed in action. Thus our forces fell back to the line from Yun-ting-ai to Chin-chi-shan and Chiang-tou to continue resistance. At dawn on May 11, the enemy in Wu-tung was increased in strength and broke through our positions at Chiang-tou and Yun-ting-ai. As the enemy headed for the city of Amoy, our forces fell back the line from Hu-li-shan to Hsi-ku-ling and Hu-tou-shan. In the night of May 12, our forces abandoned Amoy and moved to Sung-yu.

As to Taya Bay, in the morning of October 12, under the cover of scores of ships and more than 100 aircraft, the enemy made a surprise landing at Ao-tou Harbor and the area to the east. As the defenders were weak in strength, the enemy successively took Tam-sui, Hui-yang, Po-lo and Tseng-cheng before head-ing for Canton. An enemy force advanced from Ping-shan to Heng-li, Ping-ling, Pai-tan and Tsung-hua. Another force from Tam-sui cut off the Canton-Kowloon Railway before heading for Shih-lung. Later, it took Pao-an and attacked the rear and flank of Hu-men Fortress. As our water and land transportations were destroyed, it was most difficult for troops to mass. On October 21, Canton was lost. Subsequently, Hu-men Fortress fell on October 23 and Fu-shan and San-shui fell on October 25. Our 12th Army Group was forced to evacuate to the line from Ching-yuan to Heng-shih, Liang-kou and Hsin-feng. Two brigades under Gen. Chen Yao-shu were left in Hui-yang, Tam-sui, Hu-men and Pao-an areas to conduct guerilla operations, tie down the enemy and sabotage his lines of communications. Later, our 12th Army Group readjusted the dispositions of its main forces and launched counterattacks. On November 24, Tsunghua was recovered. On December 9 and 10, Hui-yang, Po-lo, and Pao-an were re-captured. Thus, the enemy abandoned the contact line in Taya Bay and supplied Canton on water via the Pearl River. One division was pulled for employment in North China and was substituted by a composite brigade. The enemy 21st Corp's strength in this area stood at 2½ divisions. With Canton as the center, the enemy switched to the defense. Thus, the enemy and our forces were at a stalemate.

12.　An Account of Guerilla Operations

Since the Manchurian Incident when the Japanese forces attacked our key cities and lines of communications in Manchuria, our patriots organized volunteer corps to conduct guerilla operations against them. People rallied to our cause. In few months, guerillas spread wide in the vast territories of Manchuria greatly harassing the enemy. As Governor Ma Chan-shan of Hei-lung-chiang Province controlled the province politically and militarily, civil-military coordination was greatly facilitated. Governor Ma's forces were built around several infantry and cavalry brigades which distinguished themselves in combat. The forces under Gen. Su Ping-wen, Gen. Ting Chao, Gen. Li Tu, Gen. Feng Chan-hai and Gen. Tang Chu-wu fought gallantly. However, lack of a tight organization and unity of command and poor coordination led to their defeat in detail by the Japanese.

During the Battle of Jehol in 1933, our Generalissimo's Headquarters in Peiping directed former Governor Liu Yi-fei of Chahar Province to exercise unified command over the remaining forces of the Manchurian Volunteer Corps and parti-cipate in the operations in northern Jehol. As his forces were hastily organized, it was difficult to exercise control. Lacking a guerrilla base, it was not possible to continue operations behind the enemy lines. When the situation grew worse, the bulk of his forces withdrew to Chahar. A portion acted on its own to withdraw to central Hopei and became undiciplined. Eventualy, it disintegrated. Gen. Feng Chan-hai's unit was the only one which was reorganized into the 91st Division in advance.

With the outbreak of full-scale war in 1937, our country adopted the strategy of attrition which employed guerilla operations to supplement regular operations as an important means to tie down and wear out the enemy and control the occupied area so as to prevent it from being exploited by the enemy and the puppet regime. Accordingly guerilla warfare manuals were published and guerilla cadres trained. Elements of regular force and local militia were dispatched to conduct guerilla operations. Officials in the battlefield were directed to lead the local forces against the enemy and in self-defense and not to leave their stations at will. Guided by this correct policy, the various war areas were able to control the vast areas behind the enemy lines, lead the people, and tie down and wear out the enemy so to achieve glorious combat results. Had the Chinese Communists not taken advantage of this opportunity to swallow local forces and attack guerilla forces, the effectiveness of our guerilla warfare would have been much greater and victory expidited. An account of guerilla operations in the various war areas during the first phase of the War of Resistance is stated as follows:

a. 1st War Area

Between September and October, 1937, when the 1st War Area was subjected to a pincers attack by the enemy's 1st and 2nd Corps, its main force was shifted to Shansi and a portion withdrew to the Chang River line. Col. Lu Cheng-tsao's regiment (less one battalion) which was the rear guard of the 53rd Corps was cut off by the enemy's 2nd Corps by the Hu-tuo River and remained in central Hopei to conduct guerilla operations. The 1st War Area appointed Col. Lu commander of the 1st Separate Guerilla Column, Col. Li Fu-ho commander of the 2nd Separate Guerilla Column and Col. Sun Kuei-yuan Western Hopei guerilla commander. Gen. Chang Yin-wu was appointed commander-in-chief of Hopei militia by the National Military Council. Meanwhile, 2 peace preservation brigades in Hopei were organized into the 181st Division by Gen. Sung Che-yuan for employment in southern Hopei, leaving a vacuum in central Hopei. So people rose in self-defense, though they were not properly organized nor subordinated. Hence, the forces under Lu Cheng-tsao and Sun Kuei-yuan rapidly developed. Gen. Chang Yin-wu's forces were temporarily stationed in Lin-chuan with cadres undergoing training. As Gen. Chang was highly regarded in Hopei, many people rallied around him. In early November, the 1st War Area began the counterattack against the enemy along the Peiping-Hankow Railway in response to the operations of the 2nd War Area. Repeatedly, the 52nd Corps and Sun Kuei-yuan's forces conducted guerilla operations in Han-tan and Tse Hsien. At one time, they entered the enemy airfield and destroyed many enemy aircraft. In the spring of 1938, Gen. Chang Yin-wu's forces went deep into Central Hopei and defeated one enemy regiment in An-kuo and Po-yeh steadily gaining fame.

On September 2, 1937, the Chinese Communists issued a declaration to meet national crisis disguising themselves as willing to take part in the War of Resistance so as to gain legal status and space for freedom of action. They dispatched party members and fellow travellers to infiltrate the ranks of our troop units, organizations, schools and various levels of the society. Chu Jui was named the Chinese Communist liaison chief in the 1st War Area, to set up radio stations and collect intelligence information, seeking to win over Lu Cheng-tsao and attacking Gen. Chang Yin-wu. By 1938, Lu Cheng-tsao's forces turned Red when Lu was appointed Chinese Communist commander in the Central Hopei Military District. Forces under Chinese Communist Ho Lung and Liu Po-cheng which had been subordinated to the 2nd War Area moved into Hopei in conjunction with Lu Cheng-tsao's forces, forcing Gen. Chang Yin-wu's forces to move south. Thus, the Chinese Communists gained superiority in Central Hopei, commandeered people's weapons, swallowed local forces and escaped the mopping up of the opponent's forces. As they conducted no real fighting, they had no achievements to speak of. The fact that they forced landlords, rich farmers and dissident elements to escape to the cities and seek asylum in the enemy occupied areas was most damaging.

Between February and March, 1938, when the enemy's 14th Division attacked Tao-ching Railway, our 1st War Area ordered the 53rd Corps moving to Ling-chuan and Lin Hsien, to conduct guerilla operations in conjunction with the 4th Cavalry Division, and forces under Gen. Chang Yin-wu, Gen. Sun Kuei-yuan and Gen. Li Fu-ho to defend the key localities southeast of Tai-hsing Shan in the Shansi-Hopei-Honan border area. Later, the 95th Division was ordered north to cross the Yellow River and conduct guerrilla operation against the enemy along the Tao-ching Railway. Efforts were made to go beyond the road to cover the movement of supplies into the Taihang Shan area. For more than 5 years, our forces persisted in guerilla operations contributing greatly to guarding against and tieing down the enemy.

b.   2nd War Area

Between September and October, 1937, the enemy's 5th Division and the Chahar Expeditionary Force of the Kwangtung Army attacked the Great Wall from Ping-hsing-kuan to Ju-yueh-kou in the 2nd War Area. Generalissimo Chiang ordered the 18th Army Group under Chu Teh to be subordinated to the 2nd War Area so as to facilitate the operations of the main forces in the war area in maneuvering in and out of Ping-hsing-kuan and disrupting enemy's line of contact in the rear area. However, the main force of the 18th Army Group was scattered in the vast areas of the Shansi-Hopei-Chahar borders busily establishing bases and seizing areas of influence without executing its assigned missions. Thus, the enemy was able to mass forces and openly attack our primary positions. As enemy forces succeeded in breaking through Ju-yueh-kou, the war situation was affected. The 18th Army Group fabricated guerilla combat results and indulged in propaganda to deceive people at home and abroad.

During the Battle of Taiyuan in October and November, our forces under Gen. Wei Li-huang and Gen. Sun Lien-chung fought for more than 20 days against the enemy in Hsinkou and Ladies' Pass, yet the main force of the 18th Army Group sat idle along the Tungpu Railway and Chengtai Railway. The 18th Army Group actively expanded its bases and made false reports on its combat results.

Between February and March, 1938, the main force (3 divisions) of the enemy's 1st Corps moved south from Taiyuan along the Tung-pu Railway. Another force (2 divisions) moved west along the Peiping-Hankow Railway via Tung-yang-kuan and Po-ai forming a converging attack on our 2nd War Area. The main force of our 2nd War Area was divided into several columns and counterattacked from Han-hou-ling, Shih-kou Chen, Wen-shui and Chiao-cheng. The heavy fighting lasted for more than 10 days, and our forces scored local victories.

However, the Chinese Communist 129th Division under Liu Po-chen opened Tung-yang-kuan and made it possible for the enemy's 108th division to reach Lin-fen—a vital locality in our rear area. Thus, the situation deteriorated rapidly. The 129th Division claimed that it destroyed several hundred enemy quartermaster trucks on the road to Tung-yang-kuan.

c. 5th War Area

In the latter part of December, 1937, the enemy's 2nd Corps moved south to cross the Yellow River, took Tsi-nan and Tsing-tao continued its advance to the south. Mayor Shen Hung-lieh of Tsingtao was ordered to take the marines and local militia to Chu-cheng and Yi-shui where they would wage guerilla warfare. Later, they joined force with Gen. Pang Pin-hsun's 3rd Corps to recover Meng-yin and defend the cities in southeastern Shantung. In January, 1938, the main force of the enemy's 5th Division moved south along the Chiaochow-Tsinan Railway. Our guerilla commander Liu Chen-tung who led his forces in defense of Yi-shui was killed in action. During the enemy invasion of Lin-yi when enemy forces fought bitterly against the forces of Gen. Chang Tze-chung and Gen. Pang Pin-hsun, our guerillas raided the enemy rear areas, tied down enemy forces and harassed the enemy supply lines contributing greatly to our victories in the initial operations at Lin-yi. As the enemy was forced to abandon the Wei-tai Highway supply line and switched to Chufu-Szeshui Road the vast areas in southeastern Shantung, particularly Yi-meng Shan region and the mountainous region northwest of Jih-chao became excellent guerilla bases and were maintained for 6 years.

Between April and May, 1938 and during the Battle of Hsu-chow, Gen. Han Teh-chin's 24th Army Group of the 5th War Area defended northern Kiangsu and eastern Anhwei against the northward advance of the enemy along the Grand Canal and Tung-hai Highway[22] and repeatedly conducted guerilla operations against the enemy in the southern sector of the Tientsin-Pukow Railway to tie down the enemy and relieve the threat to the flanks of the main force in the 5th War Area, contributing greatly to our victory in the Battle of Tai-erh-chuang. During our withdrawal from Hsuchow, they assisted the 51st Corps to cross the Huai River via Wuho and fall back to western Anhwei. In the latter part of April, Generalissimo Chiang ordered the 69th Corps to advance to Lin-yi from the east of Tan-cheng to attack the enemy. Upon termination of the Battle of Hsuchow, these forces were left in southern Shantung to continue the guerilla operations. Later, the 57th Corps of the 24th Army Group was moved from northern Kiangsu to southern Shantung in order to reinforce the guerilla forces there. When Shen Hung-lieh was appointed governor of Shantung, he directed the administrative commissioners in the various districts to lead the local militia in defense against the enemy. Thus, guerilla operations spread throughout the province. In particular, Administrative Commissioner Fan Chu-hsien was most outstanding in de-

---

22 Nan-tung to Hai-an.

fending the neighboring hsiens of Tung-chang (Liao-cheng) against the enemy. Although Commissioner Fan was later killed in action, his outfit killed more enemy troops.

d. 3rd War Area

In December, 1937 after invading the Nanking-Shanghai-Hangchow triangular area,[23] the enemy's Central China Front Army assumed the defensive. It began to construct defense works of the first line along Hangchow, Fu-yang, Yu-hang, Wu-hsing, Chang-hsing, Hsuan-cheng and Wu-hu. Another force operated in the vicinity of Chu Hsien and Chiang-tu. Two divisions and a column were redeployed to North China. In conjunction with the 5th War Area, our 3rd War Area conducted guerilla operations in the enemy's rear areas by raiding small enemy units and lines of communications, impeding their transportation and supply, and harassing them.

In the latter part of January, 1938, the enemy's 13th Division attacked Pangpu from Chu Hsien. Our 3rd War Area ordered the 10th Army Group to conduct guerilla operations between Hangchow and Tai Lake, the 19th Army Group between Hsuan-cheng and Nanking, and the 23rd Army Group between Wu-hu and Kuei-chih. Between February and March, many battles were fought resulting in heavy losses and destruction of the enemy. For a time, Fu-yang, Hai-ning, Hai-yen, An-chi, Li-yang, Yi-hsing, Tang-tu and Hsuan-cheng were recovered and Hangchow was entered. In mid-March, the enemy began to mass his forces from the vicinity of Chin-tan, Wu-hsi, Chang-hsing, Hangchow and Ning-kuo for a 5-pronged attack on Kiangsu-Chekiang-Anhwei border areas. Highly mobile, our forces avoided the enemy's main strength and tangled with the enemy. By mid-April, the enemy was greatly exhausted and halted the attack. Holding the enemy's main strength, and making it not possible for the enemy to pull forces for commitment in the Battle of Hsuchow was the key factor which contributed to our victory in the Battle of Tai-erh-chuang and subsequent breakout of our forces.

In the spring of 1938, our Government reorganized 5,000 Chinese Communist remnants in Kiangsi, Fukien and the border area of Hupei and Anhwei into the New 4th Corps which commanded 4 columns. Subordinated to the 3rd War Area, it was stationed in Tung-ling, Fan-chang, Nan-ling and Ching Hsien in southern Anhwei. It was directed to conduct guerilla operations in Kiangsu and Anhwei south of the Yangtze River. In order to facilitate its operations, the Government designated the area between Tung-ling and Fan-chang for it to garrison. Yet it made use of the slogan of "national united front against Japan" by deceiving the youths, expanding its organizations, threatening the able-bodied males and developing rebellious forces. It scored no achievement insofar as operations against the Japanese were concerned.

------

23 Meaning Nanking-Shanghai-Hangchow area which was the political, economic and cultural center in Eastern China.

Between June and October, 1938, the Battle of Wuhan took place. Our 3rd War Area organized pack howitzers and anti-tank guns accompanied by necessary infantry and engineers into several mobile artillery detachments. These detachments advanced to the bank of the Yangtze River in southern Anhwei and sank or damaged many enemy ships and craft. Furthermore, they tied down the enemy's 116th Division along the Yangtze River and impeded enemy shipping contributing immensely to the Battle of Wuhan.

When the Battle of Wuhan was in progress, the enemy General Headquarters was aware that their forces were being bogged down in the interior of China. Despite the employment of the main strength of their field forces totalling 30 divisions (excluding the Kwantung Army), they were only able to occupy major cities and a 10-km narrow corridor along their lines of communications, while our guerilla forces possessed the vast areas surrounding and harassing them. Besides, the bulk of our forces which was intact could not be conquered by force. Meanwhile, the international situation turned more and more unfavorable to the enemy. After the Battle of Wuhan, the enemy halted the offensive and switched to sustained operations. Already the enemy lost confidence in victory through strategy of annihilation.

An Account of Navy Operations

The main strength of the enemy's navy lay in the 3rd Fleet in Shanghai. Its composition included the following major forces:

1. Fleet Hq.—Warships Izumo and Notoro and Shanghai Special Marines.
2. 1st Task Force—Syake (flagship), 10 gunboats including Tenryu, Hirado, Togiwa, Zushima and 5 destroyers.
3. 3rd Squadron—Naka (flagship), Yura.
4. 1st Torpedo Squadron—Yubari (flagship) and 12 destroyers.
5. 1st Aviation Squadron—Kaga (flagship), Housho and 4 destroyers.

When hostilities broke out in Shanghai on August 13, 1937, the enemy kept the following naval forces afloat in the vicinity of Shanghai.

Main Force—Izumo and 16th Destroyer Squadron.

1st Security Force—11th Squadron.

2nd Security Force—8th Squadron and 1st Torpedo Squadron.

In December, 1928, our Directorate of Navy was established. In June, 1929, it became the Ministry of Navy. Warship "Hsien-ning" was built in 1928, "Yung-sui" in 1929, "Min-Chuan" in 1930, "Yi-hsien" and "Min Sheng" in 1931, and "Ning-hai" in 1932. Between 1933 and 1934, 10 gunboats including "Chiang-ning," "Hai-ning," "Fu-ning," "Sui-ning," "Hsien-ning," "Su-ning," "Chung-ning," "Yi-ning," "Cheng-ning," and "Chang-ning." In 1937, warship "Ping-hai" was built and 12 old ships including "Chung-shan" were converted giving a total of 59 ships and 12 PT-boats. The total tonnage was 51,288 tons. As our navy was newly established and the nation lacked the foundation of heavy industries, we were unable to establish adequate sea defense and powerful fleet so as to engage the enemy in the ocean. Hence, our Navy's operational guidance during the first phase of the War of Resistance was to assist the Army in defending Shanghai, wear out the enemy, guard the nation's capital and cover the evacuation of materials from the coast. A brief account of our naval operations is as follows:

1.   Battle in Defense of the Nation's Capital:

Wusung-Shanghai Area: On August 13, 1937, hostilities broke out in Shanghai. On the same day, our Navy ordered the sinking of transport "Pu-an" to blockade the Tung-chia-tu channel and rushed the manufacture of torpedoes blockading all the waters in the Wusung-Shanghai area. In addition, three lines of defense were constructed on the Huang-pu River to keep the enemy submarines from sneaking in. In the night of August 14, the River Defense Headquarters in the Chiangyin area dispatched 2 camouflaged high-speed boats to Shanghai via inland waters. At 2000, August 16, our high-speed boat Shih No. 102 set out from New Lung-hua, crossed 3 lines of sunk ships and sped past Japanese destroyers and British, French and Italian warships, heading directly for The Bund on Nanking Road. At a distance of 300 m. and an angle of 50° it fired 2 torpedoes on the "Izumo." The torpedoes scored direct hits which rocked the banks of the Huangpu River. As our boat made a sharp left turn the "Izumo" began firing and hit the engine and bottom of the boat. Engine dead and water in, the boat sank in the vicinity of Pukow Wharf at Kiu-kiang Road on the Bund. Despite enemy pursuit, our officers and men dismantled the weapons, threw them over board and took to the water. Heavy damage sustained by the "Izumo" shocked the Japanese Navy. Beginning on August 20, enemy planes bombed our naval installations in Wusung-Shanghai area including Kiangnan Shipyard and Wusung Naval Patrol Station. In the night of September 7, our forces used own-manufactured mines to destroy the enemy's Mitsui Wharf 25, enemy planes bombed our naval shipyard at Kao-chang-miao, our warship "Yung-chien" rose in defense. Unfortunately, it was sunk by enemy planes resulting in heavy casualties. On September 28, our Navy's special troops took mines, sneaked past Chun-chiang Wharf and swam underwater to set off the mines which damaged the "Izumo." Additionally, 4 iron-hull lighters and 2 small steamers were damaged. On November 11, the enemy attacked our Navy's Guard Battalion at Kao-chang-miao resulting in heavy fighting. November 12, our Torpedo School dispatched a high-speed boat Shih No. 181 sailing down the Yangtze at night to attack enemy ships by surprise. At 0430, November 13, our boat discovered enemy ships at Chin-chi-kang. Restricted by hidden sand bars, our torpedoes failed to score hits. Later, our boat was hit and set on fire. Chief training officer Ma Pu-hsiang and Boatswain Yeh Yung-hsiang were killed in action. As our forces were withdrawn from Wusung-Shanghai area, bridges along the Soochow Creek and Fan-wang-tu Bridge were mined in order to delay the enemy advance.

Chiang-yin Area: On August 11, 1937, warships including the "Kan-lu" were sent down river from Chiang-yin to destroy navigational sign and block passage so as to prevent the enemy warships from sailing up river.   Meanwhile, warships "Tung-chi," "Ta-tung," "Tse-chiang," "Teh-sheng," "Wei-sheng," "Chen-tse," and "Su-tse," and 20 ships including the "Chia-ho" and "Hsin-ming" commandeered from the Government-owned China Merchants Steamship Navigation Co. and other steamship companies, totalling 28 ships were sunk to block the passage.   Subsequently, 3 steamships "Kungping," "Wan-hsin" and "Ping-chi" and 4 warship "Hai-chi," "Hai-yung," "Hai-chou" and "Hai-shen" were commandeered and sunk. Altogether, 35 large and small warships and merchant steamships were sunk. Later, 8 enemy lighters from Chen-hai, Wu-hu, Kiu-kiang and Sha-shih were pulled to block the passage.   Rocks, boats, salt boats from Kiangsu, Chekiang, Anhwei and Hupei were used to fill the gaps.   A section of the Yangtze River near Chiang-yin was also mined to form a strong line of blockade.   On August 26, "Chiao-jih," a survey ship, was engaged in destroying navigational signs in the vicinity of Tung-chow when it was attacked by 3 enemy warships.   Just then, enemy planes arrived to join the attack and destroyed "Chiao-jih."   In defense of the nation's capital, our Navy dispatched the warships "Ping-hai," "Ning-hai," "Ying-jui," and "Yi-hsien" to the front line of the Chiang-yin line of blockade in conjunction with other warships.   However, since August 16, enemy planes bombed our ships incessantly.   On August 22, our ship shot down one enemy plane.   The anti-aircraft guns of our squadrons formed an air defense net over the entire Kiang-yin line of blockade.   For more than 30 days, our ships fought against the enemy.   On September 20, enemy planes came in force, damaged our warships "Ping-hai" and "Ying-jui," killing many officers and men. 5 enemy planes were also damaged. On September 23, 60-70 enemy planes attacked our fleet in all directions aiming primarily at "Ping-hai" and "Ning-hai."   As a result, both ships were sunk.   Four enemy planes were shot down.   After the sinking of the two ships, our 1st Squadron Hq. moved to warship "Yi-hsien."   On September 26, 16 enemy planes rotated in bombing "Yi-hsien" which had by then expanded all its ammunition. At a most critical moment, the "Yi-hsien" fired two rounds from its 15-cm. gun in the bow and shot down 2 enemy planes which sank into the river.   The remaining enemy planes fled.   Though the damaged ship went aground, enemy planes continued the bombing until it capsized.   While the "Yi-hsien" was subjected to heavy bombing, other ships including the "Chien-kang" went to the rescue.   While en route, the "Chien-kang" was attacked by more than 10 enemy planes and was sunk.   Later, warship "Chu-yu" was ordered to Chiang-yin as the relief.   On September 28 and 29 after enemy planes seriously damaged the "Chu-yu," it sailed to Tayu Harbor and sank on October 2.   The 1st Squadron Hq. was removed to River Defense General Hq.   Thereafter, enemy continued to bomb the Chiang-yin area destroying the warships "Ching-tien," "Hu-peng" and "Hu-ying" at Lung-shao Harbor, Man-yu-sha, Shih-yu Harbor and Pao-tse-chow.   On October 13, the "Sui-ning" was seriously damaged by enemy artillery at Shih-erh-yu.

During its defense of Chiang-yin, the "Ying-jui" was damaged by enemy bombing. On October 25, when the guns were being dismantled and removed from the ship, at Tsai-shih-chi, enemy planes again bombed the ship. The ship resisted bravely and sustained heavy casualties. 74 officers and men were killed or wounded. Heavy guns were dismantled from the ships being sunk to blockade the channel and were used in organizing artillery detachments. First to be activated was the Navy's Ta-hu Artillery Detachment. The former Chiang-yin Artillery Detachment was augmented to include two details responsible for the gun positions at Wu-shan and Lu-chu-kang. At 0830, November 30, 5 enemy ships sailed up the river to approach Luchukang. Our artillery detachment fired 4 round of which one hit an enemy ship. Enemy ships returned fire and knocked out our No. 3 gun at Wu-shan, and damaged the base plate of our No. 1 gun. The action lasted until 1100 hours. Two enemy ships pulled back, while three enemy ships cruised the area. Our artillery opened fire again and damaged one enemy ship. On December 1, when enemy forces reached Chiangyin City, our artillery detachment at Wu-shan was ordered to destroy the guns. The action lasted until 2000, December 3 when the detachment completed its withdrawal. Subsequently, the Navy's artillery detachments in various areas were successively evacuated to continue the resistance.

Tai Lake-Chapu-Wenchow Area: As enemy craft moved up along the Wu-sung River, they were able to enter the Tai Lake. Our Navy equipped "Ping-ming" and "Chieh-sheng" for patrol of the Tai Lake. In October, a number of gun boats were used in organizing the Tai Lake Squadron to defend the key localities of the lake. Despite enemy occupation of Wu-hsi, "Ning-tai," a small boat, continued to conduct guerrilla operations. For over a year, it fought against more than 20 boats at Chao-kuan Dam sinking many of them.

Guarding the gateway to Hangchow and Chia-hsing, Cha-pu[24] was a key locality in enemy landing. Our Navy, therefore, positioned 2 naval guns in the vicinity of Cha-pu supplemented with artillery detachments. This measure deterred enemy invasion. By November 5, 1937, despite the enemy landing at Chin-shan-wei which brought an end to the Battle of Shanghai, our artillery detachments stood firm at Cha-pu. By the time Chia-hsing fell, the operational importance of Cha-pu was lost. Our detachments destroyed the guns and withdrew to the west. Subsequently, lines of blockade were set up at Fu-yang and Tung-lu in the upper reaches of the Chien-tang River to stop the activities of enemy ships.

After the loss of Hangchow, Wenchow became too exposed. In October, 1938, our Navy moved one artillery detachment for emplacement at Mao-chu-ling near Wenchow. It was attached to the Wenchow Defense Command for operations. On November 6, Ou River was blockaded to stop enemy invasion.

---

24 Hangchow and Chia-hsing, conveniently located were fertile in land and rich in wealth. Cha-pu, a bay more than 10 m. deep, was located to the east. Dr. Sun Yat-sen had planned the Orient's major port here.

2. Battle in Defense of Wuhan:

Matang-Hukou Area: Despite the fall of Chiang-yin, our Navy's line of blockade stood firm rendering the enemy ships incapable of moving west along the Yangtze River. This enabled our Navy to gain time in making dispositions in the upper reaches of the Yangtze River. In June, 1938, when stopped by the Yellow River, the enemy shifted his forces to the invasion of Anhwei-Kiangsi border areas. Ta-tung and An-king fell in succession rendering the situation along the Yangtze River most critical. However, our efforts in establishing the line of blockade at Ma-tang started as far back as December, 1937. In addition to mining the channel between Kuan-chow, Tung-liu and Ma-tang, all the navigational signs between Ti-kang and Kiu-kiang were destroyed. Forts were built between Ma-tang and Hu-kou, stationed with the Navy's fortress garrison units and Marines. Meanwhile, Ning-class and Sheng-class gunboats patrolled near the lines of blockade. On March 27, 1938, 3 enemy planes suddenly dropped bombs on our "Yi-sheng" gunboat which exploded. On June 24, 9 enemy planes dropped more than 40 bombs on our "Hsien-ning" gunboat causing its bottom to leak. In order to strengthen our defense capability, new-type mines were laid in large quantities near Ta-tung sinking or damaging many enemy ships and craft passing through. In Ma-tang, more than 600 mines were laid; in Tung-liu more than 100 mines; and in Hu-kou more mines. On July 2 and 3, "Chung-ning" gunboat was laying mines in Tien-chia Chen when it was bombed by enemy planes and sunk. On July 1, while en route to Wu-hsueh from Tien-chia Chen, "Chang-ning" gunboat fought against the attacks of 7 enemy planes. Upon arrival at Wu-hsueh, it was temporarily docked at Li-chi Wharf. When "Hsien-ning" gunboat was sent to the rescue, it was attacked by 16 enemy planes. Hit fatally in the middle, "Chang-ning" went down. Upon completion of mine-laying at Kiu-kiang and Pei-kang, "Hsien-ning" gunboat sailed via Kiu-kiang to the vicinity of Ta-yen Shan when it came under the attack of 7 enemy planes. Fighting bravely, officers and men continued to sail the boat up the river despite the fact that the ship was on fire and that heavy casualties were sustained. Having downed 2 enemy planes, the boat reached Wu-hsueh and was docked at Jih-ching Company Wharf. As efforts were being made to put out the fire and stop the leaks, 16 enemy planes dropped more bombs. In the end, the boat and the lighter were both sunk. This was a brief account of the missions executed by the above-mentioned ships and craft and their sacrifices.

On June 21, enemy ships invaded Ma-tang. On June 22, enemy ships covered their motor boats in an attack on our fortress. An intense artillery engagement led to one enemy cruiser catching fire after being hit. As two enemy destroyers took to their heels, the remaining enemy ships also fled. On June 26, enemy ground forces approached Ma-tang, our naval forces on land fought for five days and nights against the enemy. Positions changed hands time and again resulting in heavy losses on both sides. Eventually, our forces were ordered to break out.   On uly 4, the enemy approached Hu-kou along Hu-tse Highway,[25] while enemy planes rotated in bombing the fortress and the line of blockade.   Our forces fought bravely to stop the enemy advance and sustained heavy losses. After the fall of Hu-kou, the mines we laid within the line of blockade were still useful.   Quite frequently, as enemy ships sailed up the river, they encountered mines and exploded.   On July 9, small enemy ships appeared in the area.   As the Torpedo School was deactivated, ships and craft of the school which were suitable for operations were turned over to GHQ Navy . A number of high-speed boats were reconditioned.   On July 14, high-speed boat No. 93 fired a torpedo on an enemy medium-size ship berthed at Hu-kou and scored a direct hit.   The mission was accomplished; however, our boat was also damaged and received several hits as it returned to base.   On July 17, two high-speed boats Shih No. 223 and Yueh No. 253 again were to make a night attack on enemy ships in Hu-kou. Unfortunately, while enroute the ships were entangled by the net laid by the Army Supplementary Engineering Division which drifted out of position.   As a result, former was sunk and the latter slightly damaged.   Neither boat accomplished its mission.   On July 21, enemy planes dropped many bombs on the berth area of our high-speed boats in the vicinity of Chi-chun.   Two boats, Wen No. 42 and Wen No. 88, were damaged.   On August 21, Yueh No. 22 was bombed and sunk, while Yen No. 161 was damaged.   Later, the PT-boats were turned over to the Kwangtung River Defense Hq.   This terminated our plans to attack enemy ships in the lower reaches of the Yangtze River below Wuhan.   At this time, all the important channels which did not obstruct our military communications or the interest of third nations were systematically mined.   Between July and August, low-flying enemy planes searched and destroyed more than 10 of our mine-laying boats.   Gunboat "Sui-ning" which had been damaged in Chiang-yin was bombed and sunk by enemy planes at Huang-shih-kang on July 13 when it was executing mine-laying missions.   On August 9, while en route to the frontline, mine-layer "Hu-ying" was bombed and sunk by enemy planes at Lan-hsi.

Poyang Lake Area: Po-yang Lake is an important channel which leads to Nan-chang.   In order to prevent the enemy from entering the hinterland of Kiangsi and crossing to Kuang-lu in the west, our Navy dispatched several Ning-class gun boats and a number of armed steamboats to assume the defense of the lake.   In June, 1937, mines were laid in Po-yang Lake and Ku-tang.   On June 26, while patrolling near Hu-kou and Pai-hsu Chen, gunboat "Yi-ning" was subjected to heavy attacks by 9 enemy planes.   Boat commander Yen Chuan-ching was killed in action, and heavy casualties were sustained.   The hull and the engine of the boat were damaged.   In the same month, gunboats Chang-ning and Chung-ning were sunk respectively at Wu-hsueh and Tien-chia Chen after being bombed by enemy planes at Hu-kou.   After the fall of Hu-kou, Po-yang Lake was isolated. On July 9, it was reported that small enemy ships had reached Tang-ku.   Our

---

25 Hu-kou to Peng-tse.

gunboat "Hai-ning" raced to Ting-chia Shan in the vicinity of Wu-chang to under-take security. On July 14, enemy planes dropped 70-80 bombs on the "Hai-ning" and sank it. Survivors from the gunboat were organized into a mine-laying detach-ment to operate in Po-yang Lake. On September 13, scores of mines were laid in Wu-cheng. In March, 1939, the enemy was anxious to take Nan-chang. GHQ Navy shipped 100 mines for laying in Po-yang Lake and the channels of Kan River to increase defense capability.

Tien-chia Chen-Ko-tien Area: After the fall of Ma-tang and Hu-kou, the de-fense in Wuhan was increasingly threatened. In addition to emplacing naval guns at Tien-chia Chen station on the outskirt of Wuhan during the deployment of forces so as to form a third line of defense on the Yangtze River, more naval guns were emplaced at Ko-tien guarding the entrance to the Wuhan area by artillery detachments. Meanwhile, navigational signs between Kiu-kiang and Hankow were destroyed or removed. Further, mine areas were designated between Tien-chia Chen and Pan-pi Shan, Chi-chun and Lan-tou-chi, Huang-shih-kang and Shih-hui-yao, and Huang-kang and Ou-cheng. Supplementary mine areas were also designated in the vicinity of the main area. The total number of mines which had been laid stood at 1,500. Plans were made to blockade Tuan-feng, Yang-lo and Shen-chia-chi, and ships were stationed in Wuhan. Additionally, 8 ships in-cluding "Yung-chi," "Chung-shan," "Chiang-yuan," "Chiang-chen," "Chu-kuan," "Chu-chien," "Chu-tung," and "Min-sheng" were stationed in Hankow to provide transportation for the National Military Council. While executing mine-laying missions, 10 steamboats including Ping-ming and Yung-ping were lost at Chi-chun, Tien-chia Chen, Hsin-chou, Wei-yuan-ko, Li-chia-chou, Yu-chia-chou, Shih-hui-yao and Tao-shih-fu. A number of minestoring gunboats were sunk. At 2300 hours, September 8, our partisan unit laying floating mines learned that enemy ships had sailed to waters between Wu-hsueh and Ta-lung-ping and shelled Ma-tou Chen, the unit pulled the mines to the mid-stream and returned safely to home base at 0300, September 9. Subsequently, 2 enemy ships hit the floating mines and sank. In the Kuei-chih area which was close to the war area, com-munications were difficult and materials were lacking. Despite these limitations, efforts were made to plant floating mines. Naval personnel hid in mountains and sawed planks and converted civilian boats. Mines were made by hand and planted at night. The mission was accomplished in the night of September 11 after 3 nights of hazardous work. In mid-September, heavy fighting broke out at Tien-chia Chen. Upon capture of Kiu-kiang, enemy ships were active in Erh-tao-kou and Hsin-chou. When they learned that our forces were prepared, they changed their original plans of advancing west along the Yangtze River. Instead they at-tacked Kuang-chi and cut off the communications between Tien-chia Chen and Chi-chun thereby threatening Wuhan. On September 9, Kuang-chi fell, and on September 14, enemy forces landed east of Ma-tou Chen. As our Army forces evacuated, Ma-tou Chen was lost and the mine areas on the south bank at Wu-

hsueh could not be controlled. The situation in river defense was critical. On
September 18, when 2 enemy ships sailed to the vicinity of Shai Shan, our fortress
suddenly opened fire. One enemy ship was hit and fled. On September 20, 6
enemy ships took advantage of rain and fog by covering 11 motor boats in an invasion of our fortress. Our shelling repelled the enemy attack. Subsequently, 2
enemy destroyers and 2 cruisers again attacked our fortress with heavy fire. Our
firing led to the withdrawal of enemy ships. On September 21, 14 enemy motor
boats sailed up the river for mine-sweeping. As they came near, our fortress
began shelling and sank 8 of them. The remaining 6 motor boats hastily withdrew to the lower reaches of the river. On September 22, an enemy shallow water
ship led more than 10 motor boats up the river in an attempt to break through
our fortress positions. Our forces along the river fired light howitzers. Unfortunately, the impact was too widely scattered making it possible for the enemy to
come within 6000 yards. As our fortress began firing, one enemy motor boat exploded and the enemy did not succeed. On September 23, enemy motor boats
at Shang-chao Lake attempted a crossing. Two were sunk by our fortress artillery.
In the same evening, as our defenders on the south bank withdrew, the Fu-chin-
kou Fortress was lost. On September 25, enemy army, navy and air forces invaded the Tien-chia Chen Fortress in strength. Enemy bombing lasted all day
with naval gunfire support. The 1st and 4th Sub-Stations were bombed. By
this time, enemy forces had reached Tsui-chia Shan. As enemy motor boats were
active in Fu-chih-kou, several were sunk by our fortress artillery. On September
26, the enemy launched an attack from Tsui-chia Shan and took Ma-kou. Though
Tien-chia Chen was surrounded on four sides, the defenders were determined to
fight to the end. On September 26, our fortress sank 2 enemy boats which had
penetrated into Huang-lien-chou. At night, more than 10 enemy motor boats
launched an attack on the fortress. The defenders fired on the enemy troops in
close formation with machine guns and killed many of them. On September 28,
the enemy again invaded our fortress. Under air and ground cover, more than 20
enemy motor boats landed in the vicinity of Sheng-tang. Later, they advanced
to Feng-chia Shan and were only several hundred meters from our fortress. Our
fortress personnel defended the positions along the river with machine guns and
rifles. Naval fortifications and artillery positions were totally destroyed. At night,
our forces received orders to withdraw. To augment the defenses at a time when
the situation in Tien-chia Chen was most critical, more than 120 floating mines
were planted. In the Tien-chia Chen sector, over 400 fixed mines were planted.
Though our forces had withdrawn from Tien-chia Chen for 10 days, enemy ships
dared not make the invasion. In mid-October, the enemy adopted the grand turning movement strategy surrounding Ko-tien on three sides. On October 22, enemy
ships which sailed up from San-chiang-kou along Yangtze River hit our floating
mines and led to the sinking of 2 enemy ships. In the afternoon of October 24, 4
enemy motor boats were sunk by our fortress artillery as they attempted to land

at Chao-chia-chi. In the morning of October 25, the enemy converged on our fortress in two columns from the highway between Ting-chiao Chen and Ko-tien. Balloons were used in fire direction against our fortress, while enemy planes rotated in bombing. By 1700 hours, the fortress received instructions to withdraw. At night, after breechblocks were removed, our forces abandoned Ko-tien. On the same day, Wuhan fell. On October 24, enemy planes flew over the area between Chin-kou and Cheng-ling-chi and bombed our ships "Chung-shan," "Chu-tung," "Chu-chien," "Yung-sheng" etc. Three craft, "Chu-chien," "Yung-sheng," and "Hu-fu" escaped, while "Chu-tung" was damaged in the vicinity of Chia-yu. Our ship "Chung-shan" fought hard against the enemy planes. By 3:10 p.m., 6 enemy planes attacked her by rotation. The ship crew resisted with all the fire power they could muster. She was hit first on the port side near the stern, and her boiler exploded. There was more than 4 ft. of water in the ship. As the ship began to capsize to the left, her bow was hit and caught fire. Sa Shih-chun, the Captain, who was on the bridge directing the operations was wounded in the leg and arm. Despite considerable damage, her officers and men fought on. Though seriously wounded, Captain Sa managed to issue an order to run the ship aground. However, mechanical failure, fire in the bow and loss of firefighting equipment made firefighting doubly difficult. Casualties on the ship ran high. Although the ship was out of commission floating aimlessly in water, Captain Sa nevertheless stood fast in the bridge. As the men knew that the ship was about to sink, they forcibly carried him to a sampan. Not far from the ship, enemy planes strafed and killed him. By the time the sampan was sunk, the ship was inclined at 40° angle. Suddenly the bow went up and then the ship went down. Officers and men of the "Chung-shan" gave their lives to the country.

Ching River-Hsiang River Area: As the enemy threw all his forces for the invasion of Wuhan, GHQ Navy, well aware of the importance of Cheng-ling-chi in guarding the entrance to Ching River and Hsiang River, organized Tung-ting Area Artillery Detachments in Lin-hsiang-chi, Pai-lo-chi, Hung-chia-chou, Yang-lin-chi, and Tao-jen-chi. Naval guns were emplaced. Plans were made to lay mines and blockade key localities on Ching River and Hsiang River. In the Ching River area, Chin-kou, Chia-yu, Hsin-ti, Lin-hsiang-chi and Tao-jen-chi were designated as mine areas and defense works constructed. In the Tung-ting Lake area, similar mine area was designated. In addition, ships and craft were stationed in Chin-kou, Cheng-ling-chi, Yueh-chow and Chang-sha to strengthen the defense in rear areas. On July 21, 1938, 27 enemy planes flew over Yueh-chow and heavily bombed our ships. Our ships massed their fire in defense. "Min-sheng" and "Chiang-chen" were seriously damaged. As the ships developed leaks, officers and men on board had to run it aground. Transport "Ting-an" was damaged, and so were 2 gunboats and merchant boats. First Officer Chen Ping-hsin of "Chiang-chen" was killed in action, together with scores of officers and men. On October 21, "Yung-chi" was also bombed by enemy planes at Hsin-ti and lay aground. "Chiang-yuan" was damaged in several places by enemy planes at Yueh-chow and suffered heavy casualties. Nevertheless, it sailed away safely. Later, the enemy in Pu-chi advanced to Lu-kou-pu Station forcing our Army forces to withdraw. Thus, our forces were compelled to destroy the damaged "Min-sheng" and "Chiang-chen" which had lain aground. Similarly, "Yung-chi" was destroyed in Hsin-ti so as not to serve the interest of the enemy. On November 8, enemy ships sailed to Lin-hsiang-chi and were driven away by the fire of our fortress. Later, a number of enemy planes bombed Cheng-ling-chi, Lin-hsiang-chi and Tao-jen-chi causing heavy damage to our gun emplacements. On November 9, enemy planes rotated in bombing Hung-chia-chou. Meanwhile at Pa-chiao Lake behind Hung-chia-chou, enemy troops in rubber boats were discovered attempting to make a landing. Enemy motor boats were also discovered in the vicinity of Tao-jen-chi. Our artillery from the fortress stopped them. Later, the batteries in the fortress received orders to withdraw. Mines were laid in Shih-shou and Ou-chih. On November 11, gunboats "Yi-sheng," Yung-sheng," "Jen-sheng," "No. 6" and "No. 4" carrying mines were trailed and attacked by enemy planes. The boats were bombed and sunk at Ou-chih, and personnel suffered casualties.

3.   Defensive Operations in Fukien-Amoy Area:

As Amoy lay close to Taiwan, the enemy had long had his eyes on it. When the War of Resistance broke out on July 7, 1937, our Amoy Harbor Head-quarters directed the batteries to maintain close surveillance over the enemy. Since September, 1937, enemy planes and ships began attacking the various batteries of the Amoy Fortress and bombing our naval installations. The batteries were bombed and damaged, while our personnel suffered casualties. By October 26 when Kin-men fell, enemy ships began to invade Wu-tung, Ho-tso and Ao-tou. Heavy firing of fortress defenders repelled the enemy. At 1600 hours, May 10, 1938, 11 enemy ships and 18 planes heavily bombarded Ho-tso to cover the landing of enemy troops in more than 20 motor boats in the vicinity of Wu-tung. Ho-tso beachhead and Ho-shan fell in succession. In the morning of May 11, enemy planes again bombed our positions. Additional enemy troops landed in Huang-tso and Ta-tou in the vicinity of Amoy. 3 enemy destroyers and 2 gunboats launched frontal attacks on the fortress. At 1030 hours, when Hu-li-shan and Pan-shih batteries and Pai-shih Fortress were surrounded, our forces suffered heavy casualties. Scores of enemy planes rotated in the bombing. Amoy fell into enemy hands when Army forces completed the withdrawal. Officers and men of Amoy harbor were ordered to Chang-chow to await further instructions. At this time, Yu-tze-wei Fortress on the opposite side of Amoy was still in the hands of our Navy. Bitter fighting lasted until May 13. With the destruction of our ammunition dump and gun emplacement by enemy bombardment, our forces withdrew due to lack of means for defense.

The fall of Amoy instantly threatened the security of the provincial capital Foochow. On May 23, enemy ships bombarded Mei-hua, Huang-chi and Pei-chiao while enemy planes continued to harass our forces. Between May 31 and June 1, our gunboats "Fu-ning," "Cheng-ning" and "Su-ning" defending the blockade line in the estuary of the Ming River were successively bombed and sunk. Meanwhile, our ship "Chu-tai" berthed at Nankang was damaged. Our Navy's Harbor Command, school, barracks, shipyard, hospital and marine barracks at Ma-wei were successively bombed. Our morale became even higher, as personnel formerly on board ship were organized into Ming River Estuary Naval Station to continue the resistance and shatter enemy's aim to capture the fortress at the estuary of the Ming River.

4. Operations in Kwangtung-Kwangsi Area:

Since August 13, 1937, the enemy employed his superior navy to blockade China's coast and waited for the opportunity to land in South China. Apart from blocking the channels and laying mines, the River Defense Command in Kwangtung dispatched ships and craft to various places for security preparatory to counterattacking the enemy. Our Navy's deployment was such that "Shao-ho," "Hai-chou," "Hai-hu" and "Hai-ou" patrolled the area from Ling-ting-yang to Hu-men. "Chien-ju," "Hu-shan," and "Kuang-cheng" defended the area near Tan-chou-kou; "An-pei," "Hai-chi," "Ping-hsi," and "Ching-tung" defended the area near Yai-men. Four high-speed boats were stationed in Heng-men-kou awaiting the opportunity to attack enemy ships. In the morning of September 14, 1937, one enemy cruiser and three enemy destroyers headed for Hu-men from Ling-ting-yang. Our ships "Shao-ho" and "Hai-chou" opened fire. Meanwhile, all the batteries in the Hu-men Fortress massed their fires on the enemy ships. The sea battle lasted for 40 minutes, as both sides exchanged fire. As one enemy destroyer emitted smoke, the remaining enemy ships dared not continue the fight and escorted the damaged destroyer away in retreat. Eventually, the damaged enemy destroyer sank in Ling-ting-yang. "Hai-chou" was hit in the stern during the engagement and suffered many casualties.

After suffering heavy losses inflicted by our naval squadrons, the enemy resorted to the employment of planes to bomb our ships. Despite the fact that only larger ships were equipped with anti-aircraft guns, our officers and men on board ships fought hard against the attacking planes. Since September 25, enemy planes rotated in bombing our ships. One enemy plane was shot down and four enemy planes were damaged by our ships. Unfortunately, our ships were weak in anti-aircraft firepower. As a result, "Shao-ho," "Hai-chou" and "Hai-hu" were sunk between Hu-men and Huang-pu. "Chiang-ta," "Wu-feng," "Hai-wei," and "Chien-ju" (later salvaged and repaired) were sunk respectively in Heng-men, Mo-tao-men, Yai-men and Tan-chou. Scores of our officers and men were wounded or killed in action. At this time, most of the larger ships in the Kwangtung River Defense Command had been damaged. The remaining ships were re-deployed for patrol and security duties. "Kung-sheng," "Chiang-kung" and "Hu-shan" were assigned to the area from Canton to Hu-men; "Ping-hsi" and "Chung-kai" to the area from Tan-chou to Pan-sha-wei; "Chung-yuan" and "Fei-peng" to the area from Heng-men to Hsiao-lan and Tse-ko-tsui; and "Chih-hsin" and "An-tung" to the area from Lei-shih outside of Chiang-men to Hu-keng-kou. Four PT-boats were held in readiness at the Sha-chiao Battery in Humen awaiting an opportunity to attack the enemy. On October 21, 1938, our forces abandoned Canton. Scores of enemy planes fiercely bombed Hu-men Fortress and our ships in the vicinity. On October 22, though the enemy continued the bombing, our PT-boats stood firm in the bombing. In the morning of October 23, enemy planes began attacking our PT-boats. No. 2 PT-boat was hit in the fuel tank and caught fire. No. 1 and No. 4 PT-boats were also hit and sunk. On October 25, No. 3 PT-boat was chased by enemy planes in Shihtzu-yang. It was hit and caught fire. After the fall of Canton, the ships sailed to Hsi River to await further orders. When the "Chiang-kung" sailed in Tzu-ni River in Pan-yu Hsien, it fought for more 2 hours against 40 enemy planes. After damaging 2 enemy planes, it was hit and sunk. Similarly, the "Kung-sheng" encountered more than 10 enemy planes over the Yung-chi River in Shun-teh Hsien and was hit and sunk.

After its withdrawal from Canton, the Kwangtung River Defense Command fell back to Shao-ching near Hsi River for defense of the key locality there. It ordered the ships to defend the Chiangmen-Hsi River-Sanshui-Shaoching line. Later, as the enemy took San-shui, it directed the ships to assemble along the line from Ching-chi near San-shui to Shao-ching. Subsequently, it was reported that enemy armored boats were hiding in Ho-kou and Sze-hsien-hao near San-shui attempting to move west. The command, therefore, directed the ships to conduct that enemy troops were constructing artillery positions on the east bank of Sze-hsien-hao. At 1700 hours on the same day, the "Chih-hsin" led "Chien-ju," "Chung-yuan," "Chung-kai," "Fei-peng," and "Hu-shan" in reconnaissance and attack. Artillery engagement against enemy shore-based artillery broke out as they reached the vicinity of Sze-hsien-hao. Despite heavy enemy fire the ships headed directly for the opening at Sze-hsien-hao and destroyed 4 enemy gun emplacements. The enemy massed the fire on "Chih-hsin" and employed planes in the attack. Though hit the "Chih-hsin" continued the fight. Later, she received several more hits. When her boiler was destroyed, she sank suffering 40 casualties in her officers and men. The ship's commanding officer, Li Hsi-hsi and first officer Lin Chun were both killed in action. Although the "Chih-hsin" was sunk, the other ships fought on. Meanwhile, the enemy shifted the fire against the "Chien-ju" and hit her in two places. As the attack power of our ships became depleted, the ships returned to guard Shao-ching Strait. Meanwhile, our Army forces raced to the scene to confront the enemy at San-shui. This confrontation lasted until September, 1944 when our forces withdrew. Anxious to destroy our ships in the Hsi River, the enemy began sending planes to destroy our ships and craft. A number of anti-aircraft guns on board ships were taken ashore. Under constant enemy bombing, all our ships were sunk except "Ping-hsi."

Kwangtung was filled with interwoven rivers and streams. Since the outbreak of the War of Resistance, many ships were either sunk by the enemy or by ourselves, leaving only a handful of ships afloat. Thus, our Navy in Kwangtung made preparations for mine-laying. Various types of stored mines were re-conditioned and laid in Hu-men, Heng-men, Yai-men, Shih-tze-yang and Ma-yu-kou near Swatow by the mine-laying detachments. There were altogether 11 mine-laying detachments with 12 men in each. More than 10 small motor boats and one hundred civilian boats were hired to move mines and personnel. As enemy planes constantly flew over the delta area, mine-laying was extremely difficult and had to be performed at night. Apart from laying anchored contact mines at the three blockade lines of Hu-men, Heng-men and Yai-men, large number of mines were laid at the blockade lines of Hu-tiao-men, Ni-wan-men, Mo-tao-men, Ta-tao-sha, Tan-sui-ho-kou, Hsiao-hu-shan, San-hu-shan and Tan-chou. Each blockade line had 10 belts. Further, a small number of mines were laid at Hu-men-tou in Taya Bay. Mine-laying was completed on October 20, 1938. In addition to contact mines, timed drifting mines were also laid against enemy ships sailing near the coast. These mines constituted a serious threat to enemy ships as they were hit at San-tsao Island and Hu-men. While laying drifting mines against enemy ships at Hu-men on the morning of November 23, personnel of 11th Mine-Laying Detachment were killed by enemy bombing. Subsequently, the enemy came south in force for an invasion. As all the estuaries in the Pearl River delta were mined, the enemy dared not come in through the estuaries. In the morning of October 12, the enemy made a forced landing at Taya Bay. One enemy ship ran into a mine and sank. The enemy succeeded in the landing. After the fall of Canton on October 21, the enemy sent planes to bomb the mined areas in Hu-men and Tan-chou, followed by mine-sweeping conducted by personnel in motor boats and by landing. On October 22, three enemy motor boats were sunk in Tan-chou River. On October 24, when the enemy landed near Sha-chiao Battery in Hu-men, two fishing boats carrying enemy troops ran into mines and sank.

5. Operations in Yucheng, Shantung Province:

In October, 1937, enemy force and our force confronted each other across the Tu-hai river. Our 3rd Squadron which was stationed in Tsing-tao consolidated the coastal defense of Shantung and assisted friendly forces in their operations. The decision was made to pull artillery detachments from other places in order to increase firepower and strengthen the defense of Chiao-tung. 8 37 mm. guns and a number of machine guns were removed from "Chen-hai," "Yung-hsiang," "Chiang-li" and "Tung-an" and able-bodied officers and men were selected to form an artillery battalion of two batteries. Upon completion of its organization, the battalion moved out from Tsing-tao on October 19. In the same evening, the 2nd Battery reached Yu-cheng and the 1st Battery reached Hui-min. Meanwhile, enemy forces massed in Yu-cheng and Li-chia-chai on the north bank of Tu-hai River preparatory to launching a general offensive against our forces defending the south bank. At 0700 hours, October 21, enemy planes rotated in bombing our positions. At 1600 hours, under the cover of armored cars, the enemy attempted to cross the bridge. Our two trains of railway armored cars were destroyed. As two trains of enemy railway armored cars rushed to the bridgehead on the north bank, our 2nd Battery opened fire. The enemy's locomotive and main turret were destroyed. Enemy armored reinforcements rushed to the scene and met our heavy fire which inflicted heavy casualties on them. The enemy retreated hastily. Since then, the enemy dared no longer make frontal attack.

An Account of Air Force Operations

1. Air Force Operations:

Immediately before the outbreak of hostilities, the enemy had 1,530 army and naval aircraft, while we had only 230 aircraft. The ratio was 7:1, placing our air force in an absolute inferiority. In the preliminary phase, our estimate was that the enemy could employ no more than 600 planes. Fighting on exterior lines, the enemy could not mass and maneuver his forces so easily as our forces which fought on interior lines. Hence, our air operations during the first phase aimed, in principle, at attacking enemy air bases by surprise, bombing enemy ships, and assuming the air defense of major cities. Based on this principle, when the War of Resistance broke out on July 7, 1937, the Chinese Air Force (CAF) planned to employ the bulk of its strength in attacking Tientsin, Fengtai etc. by surprise during the preliminary stage of the operations on the mainland and so destroying the enemy's ground and air bases. Meanwhile, the air defense in Nanking-Shanghai-Hangchow, and coastal reconnaissance, patrol and security were strengthened. The deployment of forces was just completed on August 11 when the Hung-kou Incident took place on August 12. The enemy massed his ships southeast of Chung-ming Island and constructed an airfield in the vicinity of Kung Ta Textile Mills ready to make an invasion. Knowing that Shanghai was located near the nation's capital and that the outcome of the preliminary operations had an important bearing on our morale and international reaction, our Government had to abandon our operational plans in North China and shifted the entire strength of the Chinese Air Force to Nanking-Shanghai area to coordinate with ground and naval operations. On August 14, planes of the Chinese Air Force bombed and destroyed Kung Ta Textile Mills. In a matter of days, the enemy's Shikaya and Kisarazu Squadrons, their elite units, were destroyed. Hence, the enemy air force was frightened during the initial phase of the operations. By the latter part of September, though enemy losses were heavy, our losses in planes and personnel were equally heavy. During the first part of December, as Chinese Air Force acquired a number of new planes, training was conducted in accordance with the development of the war situation to meet the operational requirements. After January, 1938, as Chinese Air Force grew steadily in strength it began to launch air strikes over Hsu-chow, Wu-han, Nan-chang,

Chang-sha and Lo-yang. Fierce air battles took place. In spite of an inferior air force, officers and men of the Chinese Air Force gave their lives to the country and dealt the enemy a serious blow. A brief account of the major air battles is stated as follows:

a. Air Battle of August 14:

When the War of Resistance erupted in Shanghai on August 13, CAF planes flew in several flights on August 14 to attack enemy strong points and ships in Shanghai.[26] On the same day, enemy planes also flew in flights to raid Hangchow and Kuang-teh Airfield. Shortly after arrival at the Chien-chiao Airfield from Chou-chia-kou Airfield, planes of the 4th Group took to the air at once to engage the enemy. Col. Kao Chih-hang led 2 groups totalling 27 planes headed by squadron commanders Cheng Shao-yu and Li Kuei-tan to intercept the enemy. As a result, 3 enemy Model-96 bombers were shot down to begin the first outstanding record of the Chinese Air Force.

b. Battle of Annihilation of the Shikaya and Kisarazu Squadrons:

During the initial operations, the enemy had no air base in Shanghai. Apart from employing the bombers on board ships, the enemy moved his elite Shikaya and Kisarazu Squadrons to Taiwan and Chi-chou Island awaiting the opportunity to hit our primary airfields along the coast and the nation's capital and hoping to cripple CAF in one stroke. On August 15, 60 enemy bombers raided the airfields in Hang-chow, Chia-hsing, Tsao-erh and Nanking. CAF 9th Group shot down 4 enemy Model-94 bombers over Tsao-erh while the 4th Group shot down 16 enemy Model-94 bombers over Hang-chow. The 3rd and 5th Groups and the Temporarily Organized Group of the Air Cadet Flying School, shot down 14 planes over Nanking. On August 16, over 20 enemy bombers again raided these places and were intercepted by the 3rd, 4th and 5th Groups over Hang-chow, Chia-hsing, Chu-yung, Yang-chow and Nanking. 8 of the enemy bombers were shot down. The 3-day intense fighting ended in 42 enemy planes being shot down and the destruction of the Shikaya and Kisarazu Squadrons winning fame for the Chinese Air Force in defeating a numerically superior enemy.

c. Bombing Enemy Headquarters in Shanghai:

When the enemy and our forces faced each other across the Hungkou area, CAF decided to destroy enemy headquarters and barracks in that area in order to assist the general offensive of our ground forces. On August 17, led by Deputy Group Commander Sun Tung-kang and Squadron Commanders Liu Tsui-kang, Tung Ming-teh, Yang Hung-ting and Li Kuei-tan, 17 Hawk planes, 12 Northrop planes and 15 Corsair planes bombed enemy positions at Hungkou inflicting heavy losses on the enemy. One enemy fighter and one bomber were shot down. Intense enemy anti-aircraft fire shot down one of our planes piloted by Yen Hai-wen. By mistake, Yen parachuted into enemy position. Refusing to be captured alive,

---

26 The Chinese Air Force scored its first major victory here on Aug. 14, 1937. Hence, August 14 was designated Air Force Day.

Yen committed suicide after killing several Japanese soldiers who surrounded him. In recognition of Yen's gallantry, the enemy buried him with honors and erected a tablet which read "Tomb of A Gallant Chinese Air Warrior." Even Japanese newspapers at home covered Yen's gallantry with admiration.

d.   Bombing Enemy Ships in Pai-lung Harbor:

In support of the ground operations in Shanghai, the enemy massed his naval forces in Pai-lung Harbor.   Enemy aircraft carriers were active near She-shan outside the estuary of the Yangtze River.   In an effort to wipe out the enemy aircraft carriers and bombers, CAF ordered Kung Yin-cheng and Hsieh Yu-ching of the 2nd Group to lead 7 Northrop planes, under the cover of 7 Hawk's led by Li Kuei-tan, commander of the 4th Group, to conduct bombing of Pai-lung Harbor and Hua-tao Shan on August 19th.   The bombing resulted in the sinking of one enemy cruiser.   Pilot Shen Chung-hui whose plane developed mechanical failure, switched to full throttle, and dived right into an enemy ship.   Both Shen and the enemy ship were destroyed.

e.   Air Battle over the Nation's Capital on September 19:

Since the capture of strong points after landing in early September, the enemy began to construct a new airfield in Chung-ming near Shanghai.   His air strength was greatly increased, as new fighters were added.   Due to difficulties in replenishment, CAF was unable to insure air supremacy over Shanghai.   Despite poor night navigation facilities, CAF continued the night attacks.   In the night of September 18, 24 planes were launched for a large-scale night raid on Shanghai which inflicted heavy losses on the enemy.   On September 19, the enemy retaliated by raiding Nanking with more than 30 ship-based bombers, reconnaissance sea-planes and fighters. 21 of our Hawk and Boeing fighters based in Nanking and Chu-yung led by Squadron Commanders Mao Ying-chu and Hu Chuang-ju, Assistant Squadron Commander Huang Hsin-jui rose to engage them in a fierce air battle.   One enemy plane was shot down, while 4 enemy planes were damaged.   Our pilots Liu Lan-ching and Tai Kuang-chin were killed in action, and pilots Liu Yi-chun, Liu Tsung-wu, Yang Chi-en and Wu Ting-chen were wounded.

f.   Air Battle of Taiyuan:

On September 21, 1937, 14 enemy bombers and 8 fighters raided Tai-yuan. Four of our Hawk's and three of our Hawk's in the Temporarily Organized Group of the Air Cadet Flying School under the command of Squadron Commander Chen Chi-kuang rose to meet the enemy.   One enemy plane was shot down in the vicinity of Tayu.   Major Hirashi Miwa, known as the enemy's "ace fighter" who was wounded was captured and later died.   Our pilot, Liang Ting-fan, was killed in action in this battle.

g.   Air Battle of Nanchang:

As a result of the fierce battles fought in August, September and October, 1937, CAF suffered heavy losses in planes.   By November, CAF was replenished with a number of Russian SB-bombers and E-15 and E-16 fighters.   In December, as CAF grew in strength, the enemy pushed his air bases to Nanking, Wu-hu, and Hang-chow. His fighters were able to reach Nan-chang and Hankow. On December 9, under the cover of 14 fighters, many enemy bombers raided Nan-chang. Squadron Commander Wang Han-hsun of the 26th Squadron, 9th Group led 4 new Hawk's against the enemy and shot down 1 enemy Model-96 fighter. Our pilots Chou Kuang-yi and Kuan Chung-chieh were killed in action. On February 25, 1938, enemy formation of 35 bombers and 18 fighters raided Nan-chang again. 19 of our E-15 planes and 11 E-16 planes totalling 30 planes attack-ed the enemy bombers in 3 waves. As a result of the engagement, one enemy plane was shot down, and so was one of our planes. Four of our planes were damaged and made forced landings.

h. Air Battle of Hankow:

Between January and February, 1938, the combat effectiveness of CAF was greatly increased after replenishment. In addition to supporting ground opera-tions, CAF massed its main strength in bombing enemy airfields and positions in the eastern theater and the southern sector of the Tientsin-Pukow Railway, and enemy ships in the Yangtze River. CAF planes also intercepted enemy planes which attempted to destroy the Canton-Hankow Railway and inflicted heavy casualties on the enemy. On February 18, under the cover of 26 enemy fighters, 12 enemy bombers raided Wuhan. Group Commander Li Kuei-tan of the 4th Group stationed in Hankow and Hsiaokan led his group of 29 E-15 and E-16 planes against them. The fierce air battle ended in 14 enemy planes being shot down. Our Group Commander Li Kuei-tan, Squadron Commander Lu Chi-shun and pilots Pa Ching-cheng, Wang Yi and Li Peng-hsiang were killed in action.

i. Air Battle of April 29:

Between March and May, 1938, CAF supported ground forces in operations at Tai-erh-chuang and Hsuchow. In addition, CAF planes bombed such enemy strong points as An-tse, Ling-shih and Feng-ling-tu north of the Yellow River, and attacked enemy forces in river-crossing. In an attempt to destroy the Chinese Air Force and reduce ground threat, the enemy raided CAF bases in Nanchang, Canton and Wuhan. CAF planes took to the air to meet the enemy. Of all the air battles, the one fought on April 29 was the fiercest and the result most brilliant. The day was the Japanese Emperor's birthday. 39 Japanese planes raided Wu-han. CAF was ready to defend the air over Wu-han with 67 planes on alert. Its de-fensive scheme was to patrol the air over Wu-han with E-16 planes and to attack enemy bombers; and patrol the air space northeast of the outskirt of Wu-han luring the enemy fighters to pull away from the bombers with E-15 planes so that the attack of our E-16 planes would be facilitated. As enemy planes flew over Wu-han, our planes rose to meet the enemy attack. The fighting was most bitter. A total of 21 enemy planes were shot down, while 12 of our planes were lost. Having suffered heavy losses, the Japanese morale and aggressiveness de-clined greatly.

j. Expedition to Japan:

In order to awaken the Japanese militarists and the Japanese people, CAF prepared plans for an expedition to Japan in March, 1938 by dropping leaflets over Japan proper. As CAF lacked the training in flying over ocean and was not properly equipped in communications, such problems as navigation, command, weather and airfield contact must be solved. Furthermore, airplane radio-compass, shortwave radio equipment and ground-to-air radio station must be made available. When all the necessary arrangements were completed, Squadron Commander Hsu Huan-sheng of the 14th Squadron and Assistant Squadron Commander Tung Yen-po of the 19th Squadron, 8th Group flew in two Martin aircraft loaded with pamphlets and leaflets. The planes took off from Hankow at 1523 hours, May 19. They flew via Nan-chang and Chu-chow and landed in an advance base at Ning-po for refueling. At 2348 hours, they left Ning-po for Japan dropping leaflets over Nagasaki, Fukuoka, Kurume, Saga and Kyushu to awaken the self-consciousness of the Japanese people, and to reconnoiter the seaports and airfields of Japan. On May 20, the planes landed separately at Yu-shan and Nanchang. At 1130 hours on the same day, they made a rendezvous over Wu-han and landed in Hankow Airfield, having successfully accomplished their mission.

k. Defense of Wuhan:

Since June, 1938, the enemy took advantage of the time when water was rising to break through our line of blockade in the Yangtze River with its naval forces. The enemy succeeded in his joint army-navy-air force effort to take key localities along the Yangtze River and the Ma-tang Fortress. Its forces advanced along the Yangtze River on water and by land heading for Wuhan. One force moved via Chien-shan to take Hsiao-kan, while another force moved via Yung-hsiu to capture Hsienning. These forces cut off the communications of the Peiping-Hankow Railway and moved to surround Wu-han. In order to assist the Army in the defense of Wu-han, CAF employed its main force to bomb enemy ships in the Yangtze River and enemy airfields in Wu-hu and An-king, destroy enemy landing forces to delay their advance and intercept enemy planes which raided our rear areas. After three months of heavy fighting, CAF inflicted heavy casualties on the enemy. Between September and October, CAF supported the operations of the 17th Army at Lo-shan and Hsin-yang against the enemy. In the five months since its participation in the defense of Wu-han, CAF damaged 67 enemy ships, sank 23 enemy ships, destroyed 16 enemy planes, shot down 62 enemy planes and damaged 9 enemy planes.

All in all, during the first phase of the operations, the enemy employed a total of 450 planes in the China theater. Later, as the theater of war increased in size, the number was increased to 800. Yet, the number of CAF planes never exceeded 300 at any one time. Despite the disparity in strength, CAF personnel fought bravely against overwhelming odds. A total of 627 missions were flown in the northern and southern battlefields including 446 strikes, 66 reconnaissance missions, 115 air defense intercepts. 3,281 sorties were flown and 519 tons of ammunition were expended. 227 enemy planes were shot down and 44 enemy planes were damaged. The elite of the Japanese Air Force, the Shikaya Squadron and Kisarazu Squadron were wiped out, and Maj. Hirashi Miwa, ace fighter pilot, was killed. Of the four aces in the Japanese Air Force, 2 were killed in action and 1 was captured. 140 enemy planes were bombed or destroyed. CAF sank 16 enemy ships, destroyed 98 enemy ships, damaged 60 enemy ships and craft and destroyed 1 enemy aircraft carrier. Enemy airfields, railroads, bridges, wharves, positions, barracks, factories, warehouses, armored cars and vehicles came under the continued attacks of CAF planes. As a result, the enemy suffered prohibitive losses. On our side, 202 planes were lost and 112 planes were damaged. 152 CAF flying officers were wounded, 122 killed in action and 10 missing, 118 non-flying officers and enlisted men were wounded and 115 were killed in action.

2. Air Defense Operations:

Based on the guidance of our high command strategy, our air defense had always employed such tactics as mass, dispersion, and mobility to check the enemy. During the preliminary operations, our mass deployment enabled us to mass superior anti-aircraft fire and inflict heavy losses on the enemy planes. Later, as the theater of war increased in size, our anti-aircraft guns were deployed along the main lines of communication and at strategic localities against enemy raids, With mobility, our anti-aircraft guns attacked the enemy planes by surprise so that the enemy planes dared not fly at low altitude and dive-bomb. Between early July and mid-August, 1937, our emphasis in this regard was in North China. Air defense units were deployed along the Yellow River Bridge, Peiping-Hankow Railway, Tientsin-Pukow Railway and Lung-hai Railway. Between mid-August when hostilities broke out in Shanghai and mid-December, our emphasis was placed on Nanking, Chekiang-Kiangsi Railway and the southern sector of the Canton-Hankow Railway. Between mid-December when our forces abandoned Nanking and late May, 1938, the nation's air defense organizations underwent readjustment. In each province, an air defense command was activated. Air defense units were augmented, field air defense was strengthened, and large-caliber anti-aircraft units were mostly deployed in Wuhan and Canton. Small caliber anti-aircraft units were pulled from other places to defend the Canton-Kowloon Railway and the Canton-Hankow Railway in order to cover our international lines of communications. Between the time after the Battle of Hsu-chow in late May, and late October, 1938, apart from deploying its main strength in such strategic localities as Wuhan and Canton, our air defense forces deployed the small-caliber anti-aircraft guns to the various fortresses and their outskirts. As Canton and Wuhan were abandoned in late October, the deployment of our air defense units also underwent readjustment. An account of our air defense operations is given as follows:

Hangchow Area: Since the outbreak of hostilities at Marco Polo Bridge on July 7, 1937, our 2nd AAA Battery and 4 20mm. AAA guns of the 41st AAA Regiment covered Chieh-chiao Airfield and Chien-tang River Bridge. On August 14, while raiding Hangchow, 3 enemy planes were shot down by our AAA guns. On August 15, 13 enemy bombers dive-bombed Tsao-erh Airfield and fought against 5 CAF planes. Our 2nd AAA Battery took part in the action and damaged 1 enemy plane which was forced to land on water in Hangchow Bay. Later, it sank and its crew of four swam ashore. As they refused to surrender, troops of our 368th Regiment, 62nd Division defending the fortress killed two and captured the other two.

Shanghai Area: In September, 1937, the main strength of our 41st AAA Regiment assumed the air defense of Shanghai. After 4-mo. operations, it shot down many planes. The cover it provided to our Army operations was excellent. As the war situation turned against us, it withdrew to the interior with our Army Forces. On November 27, it moved to the vicinity of Chin-tan. Just then, 3 enemy planes were flying at low altitude in reconnaissance. The guns of the regiment caught the enemy by surprise. One round hit the fuse of a bomb hung underneath the enemy lead plane. The plane was destroyed at once. The other two planes on either side were also destroyed by the explosion. The miraculous fact that one round was able to destroy 3 planes was due to the accurate firing and superior direction of our anti-aircraft artillery. The 12th Battery of the 41st AAA Regiment which had the mission of providing air defense of the Huangpu River blockade line withdrew to the French Concession because of drastic change in situation.

Nanking Area: In August, 1937, the air defense of Nanking was undertaken jointly by the AAA units of the Air Defense School and the Cadet Regiment of the Ministry of War and the AAA units of the Central Military Academy under the command of the local air defense commander. Due to heavy losses, CAF planes could not be pitted against the enemy. Hence, our AAA units undertook the air defense. Adequate peacetime preparations, accurate intelligence transmission, and proper construction of gun positions resulted in timely firing against the enemy. In Nanking, over 10 enemy planes were shot down. Many more were damaged or fell in the rear of the enemy positions after being hit. Our statistics revealed that each 75mm. AAA gun could shot down one enemy plane in 300 round. This was considered as a new record by foreigners. By the latter part of November, the war situation changed drastically and our Government moved to the west. Our air defense forces, nevertheless, continued to assist CAF in dealing a heavy blow against the enemy. In the morning of December 12, as the enemy were approaching the outskirts of Nanking, fighting was most intense. As it was not possible to remove the guns, the decision was made to destroy the guns. Our AAA troops crossed the Yangtze River and withdrew along the Tientsin-Pukow Railway. Of the AAA guns, only 5 guns in Pukow were safely pulled out, while the rest were destroyed.

Hsu-chow Area: In the spring of 1938 when the Battle of Hsuchow broke out, a portion of our Air Defense Training Unit undertook the air defense there. On May 13, many enemy planes raided Hsu-chow. Having fired too many rounds, our AAA positions were discovered by the enemy and destroyed. The damaged guns were thrown into the river. On May 15, the unit was ordered to leave Hsu-chow. Upon arrival in Kaifeng, the 1st Battery (37mm. AAA guns) of the 41st AAA Regiment which was intended to reinforce Hsu-chow could not move forward as the road was blocked. Hence, it remained in Kai-feng to undertake the air defense. It shot down many enemy planes constituting a serious threat to the enemy but also suffered considerable losses. In mid-May, 1938 near Lan-feng, one platoon of the 11th Battery, 42nd AAA Regiment, which was attached to an armored column, was forced to bury one of its two guns and took another gun with it during the withdrawal with other combat units, as the war situation changed drastically. When our forces later recovered the original positions, the gun was dug out. Such loving care for weapons and resourceful spirit were most admirable.

Canton Area: After May, 1938, enemy planes bombed Canton heavily. The 3 batteries of 75mm. anti-aircraft guns, over 20 lesser caliber guns and 4 sets of searchlights under the Kwangtung Air Defense Command which were newly activated failed to take effect as their training, selection of positions and fire direction left much to be desired. Later, the Air Defense School added large-caliber anti-aicraft guns and searchlights to the outskirts of Canton, the Canton-Kowloon Railway, the southern sector of the Canton-Hankow Railway, and the Hu-men Fortress. Since October 15, the situation in Canton became critical. The medium and small caliber anti-aircraft artillery detachments along the Canton-Kowloon Railway and the southern sector of the Canton-Hankow Railway were pulled back to Chu-chiang and Lo-chang for air defense. Two batteries of 76.2mm. anti-aircraft guns of the 45th AAA Regiment defending the city of Canton were not pulled out until too late and were lost. Withdrawing along the Tsung-hua Highway the 3rd Searchlight Detachment lost one searchlight and one set of generator. One battery of 41st AAA Regiment deployed in the Humen Fortress shot down many enemy planes. On November 20, 1938, during a joint invasion of Humen enemy planes rotated in bombing our AAA positions for a whole day. Our anti-aircraft fire was so intense that enemy planes dared not fly at low altitude. Later, as enemy forces pressed near the fortress, our air defense troops pushed guns into the river at 0130 hours, November 21 and withdrew at 0300 hours.

Wuhan Area: During the Battle of Hsu-chow, two of our AAA batteries in Hankow received conversion training before undertaking the air defense mission. After Nanking and Hsuchow were abandoned, many AAA units were concentrated in Wuhan. In order to coordinate the operations, AAA units were deployed with other ground units 3 batteries of 76.2mm. anti-aircraft guns, 1 battery of 75mm. anti-aircraft guns, 1 battery of 37mm. guns and 1 battery of 20mm. guns and 1 searchlight detachment defended Wuhan. Additional batteries of 75mm., 37mm. and 20mm. guns were deployed to Tienchia Chen, Ma-tang and Hu-kou on the outskirts. Two batteries of the 5th Battalion, 44th AAA Regiment were attached to the 9th War Area and provided cover for the field artillery units at Chu-chiang, Ma-tou Chen, Pan-pi-shan and Yang-hsin.

On June 26, 1938, Ma-tang Fortress fell into enemy hands. Essential parts of 2 of our 37mm. anti-aircraft guns deployed there were dismantled and shipped out and other parts destroyed. On July 4, one of our 20mm. guns deployed to Hu-kou was destroyed, and the other was withdrawn. Despite continued enemy raids, our anti-aircraft guns fired relentlessly constituting a serious threat to enemy planes. By the latter part of October, as our objective of wearing out the enemy had been achieved, the main force of our anti-aircraft units was withdrawn to the west along the Wu-chang Highway. One part was left behind in Wu-han. It did not cross the Yangtze River to withdraw along the Wu-chang Highway until the enemy approached the former Japanese Concession. En route, it was bombed by Japanese planes. Scores of casualties were sustained, and 1 76.2mm. anti-aircraft gun, 1 tractor and 1 vehicle were destroyed. The unit marched at night and reached Chang-sha safely to continue its air defense missions.

Nanchang Area: In late March, 1938, the 6th Battery (37mm AA gun) and the 15th Battery (20mm. AW) of the 41st AAA Regiment undertook the air defense of Nanchang. Although enemy planes penetrated the air over the city on a number of occasions, heavy firing of our air defense units forced them to stay high. On September 6, 18 enemy planes flew over the city and indiscriminately bombed Niu-hsing, Chung Cheng Village and New Glass Village. Firing timely and accurately, our air defense units shot down 2 enemy planes.

Changsha Area: In January, 1938, our air defense units withdrawn from Nanking were concentrated in Changsha. Later, they were deployed along the Chekiang-Kiangsi Railway and the Canton-Hankow Railway and in Canton for air defense. 3 batteries of the 45th AAA Regiment, 2 batteries of the 42nd Regiment and the Searchlight Detachment which were deployed in Changsha had been brought back to a state of combat readiness after 10 months. In the morning of November 13, when a big fire broke out in Changsha, our air defense units participated in the fire fighting and suffered no losses.

Summarizing the above, apart from supporting ground and naval operations, enemy air force staged 3,604 air raids and dropped 60,487 bombs throughout China during the preliminary phase of the operations. Our air defense units shot down 83 enemy planes and damaged 90 enemy planes with 10 of our officers and 184 enlisted men killed in action.

An Account of Rear Area Service Operations

In the spring of 1936, the National Military Council activated the Capital Garrison Executive Headquarters which would take charge of national defense matters relating to Japan. The headquarters was divided into 3 sections with the 2nd Section (abbreviated Exec. 2nd Section) responsible for national defense, traffic communications, and wartime supply plans. By the time war broke out on July 7, 1937, the Executive 2nd Section received orders on August 10 to expand and become the Rear Area Services Ministry handling all depot activities including the transportation, storage and supply of rations, uniforms, ammunition and other military items, the commandeering, organization and employment of transportation, the improvement and garrison of lines of communications, and the evacuation and treatment of wounded officers and men.

On August 20, the National Military Council promulgated the following direction plan for the operations of the Chinese Armed Forces: "The Rear Area Services Ministry will come under the direct guidance of the First Ministry. In order to meet the operational requirements of the various war areas, complete facilities for signal communications and transportation, and improve the replenishment of ammunition and equipment, the essentials in storage and transportation must be born in mind. Dispersion, due regard for concealment from the air to avoid being bombed by enemy air force and being shelled by enemy artillery, and timely replenishment of the frontline areas must be stressed."

Upon its expansion and reorganization, the Rear Area Services Ministry complied with the promulgated direction plan governing the operations of the Chinese Armed Forces by implementing the following depot system.

1. Each war area would establish a general depot.

2. Each army group would establish a depot.

3. Each direct subordinate or specially assigned army (corps) would establish a sub-depot.

4. Each division would establish a division depot.

5. Each separate bridge or artillery regiment would establish a bridge (regimental) branch depot.

In accordance with the gravity of the situation, the general depots of the 1st, 2nd, 3rd and 4th War Areas, attached with depot organizations, were established and included in our order of battle to undertake the supply of the various war areas. As war had not spread to the 4th War Area, the general depot of that war area was only organized with 1/4 of the alloted personnel as a preparatory measure. The depots, sub-depots and branch depots and station depots in the other war areas were successively established. In order to maintain contact with the various war areas, the Ministry set up offices in the rear area key locality of each war area. By the time the theater of war was redesignated, the general depots of the 5th and 6th War Areas were established subsequent to the activation of these two war areas. Meanwhile, the Ministry also prepared Installation Plans for the Depots in Various War Areas for the approval of higher headquarters and compliance by the various war areas. On October 1, in accordance with the changes in the war situation, a Supplementary Outline Governing the Installation

Plan of Depots during Operations against Japan was prepared. Later, on October 14 the Second Supplementary Outline Governing the Installation Plan of Depots was formulated prescribing in detail the installation of depot organizations, routes, control areas and pertinent points on supply so as to guide the various depot activities. When the 6th War Areas was integrated into the 1st War Area. The 6th General Depot was also deactivated. On October 22, with the activation of the 7th War Area, the 7th General Depot was also activated. In November, when Kansu and Ninghsia became known as the 8th War Area, a transportation office was established to take charge of transportation and supply.

When the war first broke out, operations centered in the northern sectors of the Tientsin-Pukow Railway and Peiping-Hankow Railway. In order to facilitate direction, offices were set up in Tsinan, Hsuchow, Pao-ting and Shih-chia-chuang by the Ministry. Later, as many units of the 1st War Area were shifted to Shansi Province, the 1st General Depot and the 14th Depot jointly set up an office in Shansi to insure smooth flow of supplies into Shansi. At that time, the Rear Area Services Ministry also handled the operations of the 1st General Depot. As the theater of war increased in size, the 2nd Depot was expanded and reorganized into the 1st General Depot.

With the outbreak of the Battle of Shanghai, General Depot of the 3rd War Area moved from Nanking to Soochow. In November, our Government activated the Nanking Garrison Headquarters for the defense of Nanking. Meanwhile, the Transportation Headquarters was activated to handle the supply matters of the garrison troops. With the fall of Nanking, most of the personnel of the Transportation Headquarters were lost. Only a small number withdrew to the north of the Yangtze River and were integrated into the 24th Army Group. At this time, the Tsi-nan and Hsu-chow Offices of the Ministry had moved to Pang-pu and An-king. Since the supply of the forces north of the Yangtze River was most important, the Tsi-nan Office was redesignated the 24th Depot and was located in Pang-pu responsible for the supply of the 24th Army Group. The 3rd General Depot was evacuated from Soochow to Hsuan-cheng responsible for the supply of forces undertaking the counteroffensive in Nanking and Shanghai. The 7th General Depot was located in Fu-liang responsible for the supply of forces from Szechuan.

Earlier in October, the Rear Area Services Ministry in anticipation of changes in war situation in the future, dispatched a number of people to organize an office in Wuhan and to maintain contact with the key localities along the Peiping-Hankow Railway and other routes along the Yangtze River. Later, in response to facilitating direction in supplying the various war areas and in contact with the National Military Council, the Ministry first moved to Nanchang, then to Changsha.

In February, 1938, the National Military Council established the Wuhan Garrison General Headquarters. On March 1, the Wuhan Garrison General Depot was established. As the 7th War Area was integrated into the 3rd War Area, the 7th General Depot was deactivated. In April, the 4th General Depot was deactivated. After the enemy's overwhelming defeat at Tai-erh-chuang, the center of military operations gradually moved to western and southern Shantung. In order to achieve smooth flow of supplies to these two areas and meet the war situation, the Rear Area Services Ministry reorganized the original depot installations in the 1st and 5th War Areas. The following two areas were designated to facilitate supply operations:

1. Forces operating east of the Tientsin-Pukow Railway (including the Tientsin-Pukow Railway and Tungshan) would be supplied by the 5th General Depot.

2. Forces operating west of the Tientsin-Pukow Railway (excluding the Tientsin-Pukow Railway and Tungshan) and east of Cheng-chow along the Lung-hai Railway would be supplied by the 1st General Depot.

With regard to the chain of command, all the depot installations east of the Tientsin-Pukow Railway came under the command of Gen. Shih Hua-lung, commander of the 5th General Depot, while all the depot installations west of the Tientsin-Pukow Railway came under the command of Gen. Wan Wu of the 1st General Depot. All the rations, ammunition and supplies were handled by the respective depot commanders. The 1st and 5th General Depots maintained close coordination in the 5th War Area. The selection of depot supply routes was as follows:

1. In Yi Hsien and Tsao-chuang area, the Lin-tsao-Tai-chao branch line[27] was used. Between Tai-erh-chuang and Linyi, the Tai-Wei Highway[28] was used as the main line, and the Sze-hu Chen as the alternate line. In the vicinity of Lin-yi, highways linking Hsinan Chen, Tan-cheng and Linyi were used. Railways were used in north front of the Tientsin-Pukow Railway.

2. The Hsinyang-Huangchuan-Kushih-Sanhochien-Chengyangkuan line supplied the areas south of the Huai River.

3. Yencheng-Choukou-Taiho-Woyang formed the supply line in northern Anhwei, and Yencheng-Choukou, Huaiyang-Lou-i-Po Hsien formed the alternate line.

In accordance with the supply requirements of the various forces, the 5th General Depot successively established 3 direct subordinate sub-depots, 12 branch depots, 5 stations, 2 ration warehouses, and 1 small boat yeard. It also directed the activities of 4 depots, 1 sub-depot and organized 1 office. The 1st General Depot successively established 1 sub-depot, 10 branch depots, 3 station depots, 2 ration and clothing warehouses, 6 dumps. It also commanded 2 depots and 4 sub-depots to furnish supplies to the various combat forces.

In July, 1938, the National Military Council felt the area of operations was so large that it was beyond the capability of the Wuhan garrison forces to deal

---

27 Meaning Lin-yi, Tsao-chuang, Tai-erh-chuang and Chao-tun.

28 Tai-erh-chuang to Wei Hsien.

with the enemy invasion forces. As a result, the 9th War Area was activated to exercise command over the combat forces in Hupei, Anhwei and Kiangsi. The Rear Area Service Ministry reorganized the Wuhan Garrison General Depot into the 9th War Area General Depot. Later, 4 direct subordinate sub-depots, 14 branch depots, 10 station depots, 11 warehouses, 1 type-A dump, and 1 boat station were established. It also commanded 8 depots and 8 sub-depots to supply the combat forces of the war area. In compliance with the supply plans governing the operations in Hupei, Anhwei and Kiangsi promulgated by the National Military Council, future operational strategy was worked out. It was noted that operating along the Yangtze River, our forces encountered greater enemy naval and air activities. In order to insure permanent security, the rear area contact lines of the depots must not be overlooked. Should it not be possible to make use of the Yangtze River, the supply and contact with our forces thereafter had to be divided into the areas north and south of the Yangtze River. In the areas north of the Yangtze River, the contact lines from the north to the south or from the northwest to the southeast should be maintained. In the areas south of the Yangtze River, the contact lines from the southwest to the northeast should be maintained. The control areas and supply routes are stated as follows:

1.   Wuhan Area: The Wuhan City Depot would handle the various activities.

2.   Yangtze River South Area: The 3rd and 9th General Depots handled the various activities.

3.   Yangtze River North Area: The 5th and 9th General Depots handled the various activities.

The depot route on the south bank of the Yangtze River used Changsha or Heng-yang as the supply bases. Chao-li-chiao, Chu-chow, Ping-hsiang, Hsui-shui, Wan-tsai were the main bases (Hsiu River and Wan River could be used). The routes are stated as follows:

1.   Chang-sha, Li-ling, Ping-hsiang, Yi-chun, Ching-chiang and Nanchang were the main line.

2.   Chang-sha, Liu-yang, Wan-tsai, Kao-an and Nan-chang were the main line.

3.   Chang-sha, Ping-chiang, Hsiu-shui, Wu-ning, Juo-hsi and Yung-hsiu formed the supplementary line.

On the north bank of the Yangtze River, Hsiang-yang, Fan-cheng, Ching-men, Sha-yang, Hsiao-kan and Hua-yuan formed the primary supply bases. The routes are stated as follows:

1.   Sha-yang, Tsao-shih, Ying-cheng, Chang-chiang-fu and Hsiao-kan formed the main supply line.

2.   Hsiang-yang, Sui Hsien, An-hu and Hua-yang formed the main supply line.

3.   Heng-tien, Huang-pi, Chi-ting, Sung-fu, Ma-cheng, Lo-tien, and Ying-shan formed the supplementary supply line.

In early October, as the situation in southern Kwangtung became critical, the Rear Area Services Ministry ordered the activation of the 4th General Depot on October 16.

By the end of 1938, 6 general depots, 2 transportation departments, 23 depots, 48 sub-depots, 253 branch depots and 148 station depots had been established.

Section 5.   Second Phase Operations (Nov. 1938—Aug. 1945)

Subsequent to the Battle of Wuhan in the fall of 1938, the enemy's first line extended from Paotou to Fenglingtu, Kaifeng, Hsinyang, Yuehyang, Tatung and Hangchow. Furthermore, the enemy occupied Canton and controlled the estuary of the Pearl River, the banks of the Yangtze River and the 10 km.-narrow corridor along the railways in North China and East China. In confronting the enemy's first line units the bulk of our forces remained intact. Another forces which was left in the enemy's rear areas led the people in employing guerilla tactics in conjunction with the strategy of attrition and continued to grow strong. At this time, the enemy had already committed approximately 30 army divisions and 1 air division in Manchuria and Korea against Russia. Apart from 7 divisions in Japan proper and Taiwan, the enemy had no strategic reserves. Continuing her advance would run counter to her national defense policy (the Army's main objective was Russia.) The strategic position was highly unfavorable to Japan. Fully aware of China's determined resistance (The Chinese Government refused peace negotiations, and Chinese soldiers would rather die than be captured) and the unfavorable international situation (On July 1, 1938, the United States announced the embargo of strategic materials to Japan. On November 6, protesting over Japan's so-called establishment of Great East Asia New Order in accordance with the Nine-Power Pact, Soviet Russia started the Changkufeng Incident in July and August.[29] As a result, when one Japanese division was defeated and abandoned Changkufeng, Japan humiliatingly ceased fighting), Japan was compelled to change her operational policy. The changes included the stopping of her advance, mopping up of Chinese guerilla forces in North China and East China, the establishment of puppet organizations[30] to check Chinese with

---

[29] Having learned through intelligence that Japan was unable to solve the China problems, Soviet Russia took advantage of the Battle of Wuhan to occupy Chang-ku-feng in the upper reaches of the Tu-men River on Aug. 2, 1938. Japan tried to recapture it, but was dissuaded by Germany and signed a ceasefire agreement with Soviet Russia instead.

[30] Successively Japan created the puppet Mongolian Frontier Autonomous Governments in Charhar and Suiyuan Provinces and the puppet Provisional Government in Peiping placing Hopei, Charhar, Suiyuan, Honan and Shantung under its jurisdiction. In Nanking, the Japanese set up the puppet Wei-hsin Government placing Kiangsu, Chekiang and Anhwei under its jurisdiction in order to divide China. In March, 1940, they set up the puppet National Government in Nanking by combining the two puppet organizations in the south and in the north so as to realize their objective of checking the Chinese and destroying the Chinese.

Chinese, the milking of resources to continue the way by means of another war, the deployment of mobile forces to the Wuhan front, the launching of limited offensives to weaken our forces and the conduct of counter-attrition warfare by disrupting our international lines of communications and staging strategic bombings.

Generalissimo Chiang's awareness of the overall situation enabled him to formulate the subsequent operational guidance. It included the successive launching of limited offensives and counterattacks to tie down and wear out the enemy, responds to guerrilla forces operating behind enemy lines, stepping up control and harassment in enemy rear areas, turning enemy rear areas into front line areas, forcing the enemy to be confined to points and lines, preventing the enemy from achieving total rule and seizing of war materials, and shattering the enemy attempt to check Chinese with Chinese and to wage war by fighting another war. Meanwhile, units were pulled out by rotation to undergo training, and combat effectiveness was strengthened in preparation for the general counteroffensive.

After the winter of 1938, two of our corps were sent into Shantung and Hopei. The Shantung-Kiangsu and Hopei-Chahar War Areas were organized and guerilla warfare was stepped up. Four offensives were launched in April, July, September and winter of 1939 to deal the enemy heavy blows. Our objectives of tying down the enemy and responding to the operations of guerillas were achieved.

During this period, the enemy repeatedly attempted to mop up our guerilla forces, launched the Battles of Nanchang, Sui-hsien—Tsao-yang, Kiangsi-Hunan (i. e. the First Battle of Changsha) and Southern Kwangsi, and bombed such cities as Chungking, Lan-chow and Si-an. Vast areas, scattered forces and our efforts rendered the enemy incapable of concentrating their forces and achieving local absolute superiority. The enemy's employment of inadequate forces to seek minor tactical victories failed to achieve the result of partial destruction. The morale of our forces became increasingly higher, and our confidence in the final victory remained firm.

In the meantime, international situation underwent major development. On July 26, 1939, the United States abrogated her trade and navigation treaties with Japan dealing the latter a damaging economic blow. On August 23, Soviet Russia signed a non-aggression pact with Germany, as they agreed to divide Poland. Hence, the anti-Communist agreement between Germany and Japan fell apart. With the German invasion of Poland on August 31, the war in Europe broke out. On September 15, the signing of the Nomankan Ceasefire Agreement between Soviet Russia and Japan[31] (Since mid-May, Japan and Soviet Russia had fought there) encouraged the Japanese forces to invade China. Meanwhile, Soviet Russia instigated the Chinese Communists to seek active expansion in Hopei, Shantung,

---

[31] On May 28, 1939, the Japanese and the Soviet Forces fought bitterly at Normankam on the border of Northeast China and Mongolia. The fighting continued until Sept. 15 when a ceasefire agreement was reached.

central Anhwei and northern Kiangsu and attack our guerilla forces, and fanned the New Army in Shansi into staging a mutiny. In order to concentrate her forces in the European theater, Britain closed the Burma Road[32] to pacify Japan. This move severed most of China's links with the outside world. An acute shortage in munitions and civilian supplies ensued constituting the most difficult period in the War of Resistance and led to the climax in the sacrifices and sufferings of our people and armed forces in serving the country.

In the spring of 1940, the enemy harassed the southeastern coast of China, seized materials and blockaded all our ports. In May, the enemy launched the Battle of Tsao-yi and took I-chang, the center of water transportation between Szechuan, Hupei and Hunan. The enemy heavily bombed our cities in the rear areas and threatened Chungking. In late September, taking advantage of the French defeat (Germany had swept Western Europe in April), Japanese forces invaded northern Indo-China to sever China's outlet to the sea. Japan signed the Japanese-German-Italian Alliance hoping to threaten the United States and Britain, tie down Russia and isolate China so as to bring a swift conclusion to the Sino-Japanese War.

Accordingly, China revised her operational policy, and efforts were made to step up the sabotage of communications in the various theaters, modify terrain, construct additional lines of positions, adopt mobile defense and retreating offensive to shatter the enemy offensive, persist in guerilla operations behind enemy lines and tie down and wear out the enemy. In January, 1941, taking advantage of the nation's difficulties, the Chinese Communist New 4th Corps openly mutinied[33] and attacked Government forces. Orders were issued by the government to disband the 4th Corps so as to put an end to the rebellion. In February, the enemy launched the Battle of Southern Honan and in March the Battle of Shangkao. Based on the above-mentioned policy, our forces defeated the enemy and reaped excellent results.

On April 13, 1941, as Soviet Russia learned that Germany was about to launch an attack against her, she signed the Russia-Japanese Non-Aggression Treaty with Japan in order to mass all her strength against Germany. Russia also encouraged the Japanese forces to move south and launch offensives against China so as to facilitate the growth of the Chinese Communists. Through Zhukov, chief of the Soviet Advisory Group in China, the Russians requested our forces

---

32 From Kunming, China to Wanting, Burma.

33 In August, 1940 the Chinese Communist New 4th Corps in southern Anhwei took advantage of the heavy fighting between Gen. Han Ten-chin's forces and the Japanese forces by crossing the river to attack Ju-kao and Tai-hsing. It pursued Han's forces and took Tung-tai. To prevent the incident from worsening, the Government ordered the New 4th Corps to move to the area north of the Yellow River. Defying Government order, the new 4th Corps laid siege to the 4th Division at San-chi on Jan, 5, 1941. Thus, the commander of the 3rd War Area took action to disband the rebellious forces.

to launch counterattacks against I-chang and raid well-fortified enemy positions in order to tie down the Japanese forces. (China pretended to be interested and spent 3 months making plans and preparations in counterattacking I-chang and for logistic support. By July-August, when the Russians learned that the Japanese forces were not determined to attack Russia, Zhukov was recalled. Subsequently, the plans were scrapped.)

On April 19, the National Military Council estimated that the enemy would send in reinforcements to launch local offensives, crush our counter-offensive preparations and retain the main force awaiting the opportunity to move south. Accordingly, our operational objectives were changed. Efforts were made to hold key localities, conduct sustained operations, stabilize the interior, and seek foreign aid. In particular, military administration was streamlined and self-sufficiency achieved, while readying our forces to shift to the offensive, should the enemy move south (For complete text, see Annex).

In May, the enemy in North China massed six divisions and three brigades to initiate the Battle of Chung-yuan (i.e. the Battle of Southern Shansi) and lay siege to Chung-tiao Shan. Meanwhile, the enemy in Central China massed three and a half divisions and moved north from northern Hupei to respond to the operations. Heavy fighting lasted for more than one month resulting in heavy casualties on both sides. In the end, the enemy from Central China withdrew to its original positions. Enemy forces from North China invaded the crossing sites of the Yellow River on the south side of Chung-tiao Shan to weaken our guerilla strength north of the Yellow River. Thus, the Chinese Communists in North China became increasingly rampant.

On June 21, German invasion of Russia gave Japan an excellent opportunity to move north or south or launch major operations against us. However, after four years of war, Japan was exhausted. The main strength of the enemy's ground forces was bogged down in the China theater and was incapable of invading Soviet Russia. As Japan lacked strategic materials, particularly fuels, she had to move south in order to seize these resources. Japan's potentials were weak and her shipbuilding capability fell behind the United States and Britain. Therefore, she hesitated in moving south. In the light of the determined resistance of the Chinese forces and favorable development in China's diplomacy (In October, 1940, Britain re-opened the Burma Road. In March 1941, the United States applied the Lend Lease Act to provide China with weapons. In April, Britain provided US$50,000,000 as the stabilization fund for fapi.), Japan's confidence in armed settlement wavered. Hence, the so-called new national policy decided on July 2 was only a speculative move. She was undecided as to whether she should move north or south. In early and mid-July, to step up combat preparations against Russia, Japan mobilized two divisions and the direct subordinate units of four corps to reinforce the Kwantung Army. In addition, reserve divisions were activated in Korea doubling the total strength of her forces against Russia.   These forces included 16 divisions of 700,000 troops, 140,000 horses and 600 planes.   However, they were numerically inferior to the Russian forces (20 divisions, 2,300 tanks and 1,700 planes) in the Far East.   The Japanese decided to wait until Russia was routed by Germany before making the invasion.   In late July, Japanese forces captured southern Indo-China to seize strategic materials and establish a base for the southward advance.   The United States, Britain and Netherlands immediately froze Japanese assets.   On August 9, as Japan estimated that the Russo-German War would be prolonged, she gave up the attempt to move north within the year, actively prepared for the southward move, and increased her pressure on China.   In August-September, she conducted massive bombing of China's rear areas and factories.   In September-October, she initiated the Second Battle of Changsha.   The result was increased attrition and her gains did not justify her losses.   On December 7, Japan made a surprise attack on Pearl Harbor which led to the war in the Pacific. Hopefully, she waited for her gains in the south to bring China to her knees.

In order to respond to the operations of her allies and to seek a common victory, China revised her operational objectives.   Local offensives and fullscale guerilla operations were conducted to tie down the enemy and prevent him from moving his forces to the south.   Thus, the pressure on the Allied forces reduced. Upon request of Britain, the Chinese Government dispatched expeditionary forces into Burma to assist the British in operations.   Apart from 4 divisions which were secretly pulled out in November, total enemy strength stood at 20 divisions and 20 separate brigades and was tied down by our forces.   The speedy entry of the expeditionary force into Burma enabled the British forces to fall back and protect India.   Although our forces suffered heavily, they contributed greatly to the overall situation.   In late December, the enemy in Wuhan launched the Third Battle of Changsha in response to the enemy operations in Hongkong. On the outskirts of Changsha, enemy forces were surrounded and counterattacked by our forces.   As a result, they suffered serious setbacks which greatly lifted the morale of our troops.

In May, 1942, the enemy initiated the Battle of Chekiang-Kiangsi attempting to break the back of our 3rd War Area and destroy our airfields in Chekiang. Meanwhile, the enemy had already taken the Philippines, Burma, Malaysia and Dutch East Indies.   With the operations in the Pacific coming to an end, the enemy was in the position to shift his forces from other areas with considerable freedom.   Having a complete grasp of the overall situation, Generalissimo Chiang directed the 3rd War Area to avoid a decisive battle and conduct sustained resistance.   For more than 3 months, our forces tangled with the enemy resulting in heavy enemy losses (17,000 enemy casualties).   Meanwhile, efforts were made to strengthen the garrison along the Szechuan-Shensi Highway,[34] Han-Pai High-

---

[34] Chengtu to Pao-chi.

way[35] and the Yangtze River in order to consolidate the gateway to Szechuan.

Since the spring of 1942, the enemy General Headquarters planned to pull 16 divisions and logistic units from Japan proper, Manchuria and the South Seas to reinforce the China Expeditionary Forces. The enemy was prepared to employ a main force (10 divisions) from southern Shansi and another force (6 divisions) from I-chang in the spring of 1943 in a converging attack on Szechuan. In June, the enemy encountered an overwhelming defeat during the naval Battle of the Midway Island. In August, American forces began the counteroffensive in the Solomons and landed at Guadalcanal. The enemy gradually poured in reinforcements but suffered heavy losses. In late September, the enemy decided to postpone the invasion of Szechuan. In November, when the enemy was totally defeated on Guadalcanal, the war situation changed drastically. Having lost the freedom to shift his forces, the enemy ceased all preparations for the invasion of Szechuan.

After the spring of 1943, Allied forces in the Pacific made favorable progress in their offensives. In coordination with Allied offensives to clear the China-India Road, China ordered her forces in India (Originally 2 divisions. Later 4 divisions were airlifted to India) to attack northern Burma in October. Meanwhile, the expeditionary forces in western Yunnan were augmented (6 corps, 1 division and 4 artillery regiments were moved. Gen. Sitilwell's recommendation that the 74th Corps be dispatched to cross the mountains in western Yunnan to attack Myitkyina was vetoed by our Government) preparatory to launching the offensive. In November, the enemy initiated the Battle of Chang-teh to prevent the shifting of our forces. After more than one month of bitter fighting, the enemy was repulsed. Enemy naval and air operations were unsuccessful and transportation difficult, while the Chinese and U.S. air forces which had been gradually strengthened were effective in impeding communications in the enemy rear areas. In an attempt to destroy our airfields, clear the lines of communications on the mainland and obstruct our offensive against Burma, since April, 1944 the enemy began to initiate the Battles of Central Honan, Changsha-Hengyang and Kweilin-Liuchow (known to the enemy as Operation No. 1). Under the instigation of Soviet Russia, the Chinese Communists actively attacked Government forces, undermined the Government's prestige and prepared themselves for open rebellion to reap th fruits of victories. Disregarding enemy obstructions and Chinese Communist smears, Generalissimo Chiang who had the foresight with regard to the overall situation, resolutely ordered the Chinese Expeditionary Forces to begin the offensive in May and to coordinate with the Chinese forces in India. As a result, the enemy's 18th and 56th Divisions and elements of the 2nd, 49th and 43rd Divisions were wiped out. On January 27, 1945, the Chinese Expeditionary Forces linked up with the Chinese forces in India and Allied forces

---

[35] Han-yin to Pai-ho.

at Mongyu to clear the China-India (Ledo) Road. The enemy succeeded in clearing the lines of communications on the mainland and achieved parallel development with the Chinese Communist by defeating our forces in the Hopei-Chahar and Shantung-Kiangsu War Areas, establishing the Communist Central Honan Military District and spreading to the Hunan-Kwangtung-Kiangsi border area. However, with the opening of road to the outside, improved equipment and training, plus recent victories along the Ledo Road, the Chinese forces scored major victories in the Battle of Western Hunan between April and June and launched counteroffensives toward Kwangsi. In view of the unfavorable overall situation, the enemy planned to shorten his battle lines and conduct sustained operations. When the enemy forces began to pull out from Kwangsi in late May, our forces began the pursuit. Liuchow was recovered in late June and Kweilin in late July. As our forces were ready to recapture Leichow Peninsula before attacking Canton, enemy combat effectiveness and will-to-fight were exhausted. On August 10, Japanese announcement of unconditional surrender terminated the War of Resistance against Japan.

Annex:

The following was the estimate of situation and countermeasures prepared by our National Military Council after the signing of the Russo-Japanese Neutrality Treaty on April 13, 1941:

I. Estimate of Enemy Situation (April 19, 1941)

1. Enemy course of action—Throwing his full weight in moving south:

To seek victory, the enemy's established national policy is to annex the Far East, befriend Germany and Italy, defeat Britain and the United States and coerce Soviet Russia. However, in view of powerful U.S. naval and air forces, the closing of the Suez Canal, the strength of the U.S.-British-Dutch military alliance in the Far East and the ability of China to launch counteroffensive, Japan seems reluctant to throw her full weight in the southward move immediately. (However, due to changes in the war in Europe and the deterioration of confrontation between U.S.-U.K. and Japan, it is possible that war may break out at any time.)

2. Enemy course of action—Throwing his full weight in a large-scale invasion:

Going deep into Szechuan and involving too many troops impede the enemy's national policy of making speculative southward move. Conscious of the lessons learned after 4 years of war, Japan has realized the national strength and determination of China. Unless foreign assistance to China is cut off, puppet organizations enlarged and Government-Chinese Communist frictions increased, China cannot be subdued by force. The enemy will not throw his full weight in a large-scale invasion against China.

3. Enemy course of action—Sending a number of reinforcements to launch local offensives, destroy our capability in the offensive, and pool forces awaiting

the opportunity to move south:

The course of action is most probable, as it meets Japan's established national policy, the present situation and the opportunistic nature of the Japanese people.

4. Estimate of the enemy's operational guidance, should he adopt the No. 3 course of action:

The enemy will pull forces (at most 2 divisions) from Manchuria or Japan proper to reinforce their forces in North China or Central China, conduct local offensives, capture Lo-yang-Tung-kuan or Chang-sha-Heng-yang, actively instigate the Chinese Communists to harass Szechuan and Shensi, help set up the puppet organization, step up naval and air war of destruction, and destroy our capability to conduct counteroffensive so as to facilitate the opportunistic southward move of his main force

Justifications:

1. Computation of enemy strength:

Japan maintains a total strength of 23 divisions in Japan proper, Korea, Taiwan and Manchuria (8 Manchurian garrison forces and 6 railway garrison forces can not be pulled out. Available troops in Japan proper can be organized into more than 10 divisions. However, they have not been organized and are, therefore, not included). A minimum of 14-15 divisions are required for garrison duty in Japan proper, Manchuria, Korea, and Taiwan. The most they can pull out is 8-9 divisions. The minimum force required for the southward move is 7 divisions (2 corps of 7 divisions for employment in the Philippines,, Malay and Dutch East Indies is the minimum force required for the first phase during the southward move). Hence, the reinforcements they can send to the China theater, at most do not exceed 2 divisions.

2. Observations in military topography:

a. Lo-yang is the heart of North China and Tung-kuan the key to the northwest. Should the enemy send reinforcements and capture these two cities, he will be capable of crippling the Chinese forces in North China. Such a move will help the enemy achieve the total occupation of North China and instigate Chinese Communist forces to move into the interior. The enemy will achieve greater results, if he makes a deep drive into Si-an. However, it will involve larger forces and cannot be achieved without tacit approval from Soviet Russia. Therefore, the probability is less.

b. Chang-sha and Heng-yang form the heartland and the communication hubs in the vast areas south of the Yangtze River. Enemy capture of these two cities will cripple China, weaken China's capability in future counter-offensive and facilitate the enemy's southward move.

c. At present Kunming is an international communication center. However, upon completion of the Hsi-chan Highway, Kunming's fall into enemy hands will not cut off the communication in that area altogether. Should the enemy make a deep drive into Ta-li, it will require many troops and will run counter to the enemy's objective of an opportunistic southward move. Therefore, this course of action is less probable. (Should the enemy succeed in taking Malay Peninsula in his southward move, he will kill two birds with one stone).

II. Our countermeasures in view of the above-mentioned Estimate of Enemy Situation:

1. Objective:

Defend key localities, conduct sustained operations, stabilize the internal situation, and seek foreign aid. Special emphasis will be given to streamline military administration, achieve self-sufficiency and await the enemy's southward move before shifting to the offensive.

2. Guiding principles:

a. Improve defense works at Chung-tiao Shan and Lo-yang-Tung-kuan and actively conduct training. When necessary, pull forces from the 1st War Area to reinforce Shensi and Kansu. Should the Chinese Communists stage open rebellion, take swift actions to attack them.

b. Assign to the 3rd War Area, the primary missions of conducting guerilla warfare and laying mines along the coast. Do not fight against the enemy over the possession of ground. When necessary, pull a force for determined defense of Chang-sha and Heng-yang.

c. Insure the security of existing guerrilla forces, revamp guerilla operations behind the enemy lines, and tie down and wear out the enemy.

d. Other war areas, especially the Generalissimo's Headquarters in Kunming should intensify combat readiness, conduct active training and be prepared to defeat the invader.

e. Intensify domestic propaganda and calm the people. Special efforts should be made to revamp the armed forces, administration and finances. The pay of enlisted personnel should be increased and military conscription improved to achieve self-sufficiency.

f. Step up propaganda toward Chinese Communists and awaken national consciousness in order to continue the resistance against the enemy. At least, the Chinese Communist forces should be divided, crippled and rendered incapable of open rebellion.

g. Employ diplomacy to rapidly seek greater British and American aid. If possible, continue the seeking of Russian assistance.

h. Intensify military and political espionage and collect intelligence information in various fields.

An Account of Army Operations

1. First Stage Operations:

(After the Battle of Wuhan—March, 1940, See Map 13)

After the Battle of Wuhan, the war entered into a new stage. Generalis-

simo Chiang called military conferences at Nan-yueh and Wu-kung to review
the losses and gains of the First Phase operations and to solicit the views of officers on subsequent operations and recommendations on military administration.
Generalissimo Chiang pointed out that the characteristics of the Second Phase
operations lay in shifting from defensive to offensive, and emphasized the importance of political warfare, propaganda warfare and guerrilla warfare. He urged
the conferences to acquire the spirit of Tseng Kuo-fan and Hu Lin-yi[36] in national
renaissance by persisting in our struggle, adhering to loyalty and harmony, bearing in mind our disgrace and undergoing training for operations and vowing to
take revenge. He personally wrote Implementing Outline of the Four Essentials
in the War of Resistance (1. Uplifting morale, 2. Winning people's support, 3.
Treasuring materials, and 4. Looking after the sick and wounded). He also indicated the essentials in military build-up, operations and education during the 2nd
Phase operations of the War of Resistance.

Based on the above-mentioned opinions, our Government proceeded to reorganize command agencies and abolish the army and division-subordinated brigade
headquarters. The corps was used as a strategic unit in order to reduce the number of command levels and achieve flexibility. The Generalissimo's Headquarters in Canton, Si-an and Chungking were abolished, while the Generalissimo's
Headquarters in Kwei-lin and Tien-shui were activated to assume unified direction of the operations in the northern and southern theaters. The Civil Affairs
Military Government Committee was established and placed directly under the
National Military Council with sub-committees in the enemy's rear areas. People were mobilized to take part in the full-scale War of Resistance, wipe out the
puppet organizations and prevent the enemy from undertaking political, economic
and cultural aggressions. Corps and divisions which had suffered prohibitive
losses were pulled back by rotation and placed under the direct control of the
National Military Council to undergo replenishment and training and to restore
their combat effectiveness before entering combat again. In accordance with
the development of the overall situation, the National Military Council formulated
the operational guidance of the Second Phase operations and revised the order of
battle.

a. Operational Guidance

(1) Operational Objectives:

By successively staging a number of limited offensives and counterattacks,
the Chinese Armed Forces seek to tie down and wear out the enemy, respond to
the guerilla forces behind enemy lines, step up control and harassment of the
enemy rear areas, turn enemy rear areas into frontline areas, force the enemy to
be cornered to points and lines, prevent him from achieving complete rule and
seizing materials and shatter his attempt to check Chinese with Chinese and sup-

---

[36] Both borne during the time of Ching Dynasty.

port the prosecution of war by means of another war. Meanwhile, units will be pulled out to undergo training by rotation and strengthen combat effectiveness in preparation for the general counteroffensive.

(2) Order of Battle:

(a) 1st War Area

Commander: Wei Li-huang

Area of Operations: Honan and part of northern Anhwei

Forces:

> 2nd Army Group—Sun Lien-chung
>> 30th Corps—Tien Chen-nan
>> 42nd Corps—Feng An-pang
>> 58th Corps—Liu Ju-ming
> 40th Corps—Pang Ping-hsun (under direct command of the war area)
> 3rd Army Group—Sun Tung-hsuan
>> 12th Corps—Sun Tung-hsuan (concurrent)
> 76th Corps—Li Tieh-chun (under the direct command of the war area)

The 1st War Area has a total of 12 infantry divisions, 1 infantry brigade, 1 cavalry division, 1 cavalry brigade, excluding other special troops.

(b) 2nd War Area

Commander: Yen Hsi-shan

Area of Operations: Shansi and a part of Shensi

Forces:

> 14th Army Group—Wei Li-huang (concurrent)
>> 14th Corps—Chen Tieh
>> 93rd Corps—Liu Kan
>> 98th Corps—Wu Shih-min
> 4th Army Group—Sun Wei-ju
>> 38th Corps—Chao Shou-shan
>> 96th Corps—Li Hsing-chung
>> 47th Corps—Li Chia-yu
> 5th Army Group—Tseng Wan-chung
>> 3rd Corps—Tseng Wan-chung (concurrent)
>> 15th Corps—Liu Mao-en
>> 17th Corps—Kao Kuei-tse
> 9th Corps—Kuo Chi-chiao (under the direct command of the war area)
> 6th Army Group—Yang Ai-yuan
>> 61st Corps—Chen Chang-chieh
>> 19th Corps—Wang Ching-kuo
>> 1st Cav Corps—Chao Cheng-shou
> 7th Army Group—Fu Tso-yi
>> New 1st Corps—Teng Pao-shan
>> 22nd Corps—Kao Shuang-cheng

　　　　　35th Corps—Fu Tso-yi (concurrent)
　　　　Manchuria
　　　　　Advance Corps——Ma Chan-shan
　　　18th Army Group—Chu Teh
　　　71st Division—Kuo Tsung-fen (under the direct command of the war area)
　　　66th Division—Tu Chun-yi (under the direct command of the war area)
　　　Temporary 1st Division—Peng Yu-pin (under the direct command of war area)
　　　Temporary 2nd Division—Chin Hsien-chang (under the direct command of the war area)

The 2nd War Area has a total of 32 infantry divisions, 14 infantry brigades, 5 cavalry divisions, 3 cavalry brigades, excluding other special and local forces.

(c)　3rd War Area
Commander:　Ku Chu-tung
Area of Operations:　Southern Kiangsu, southern Anhwei, Chekiang and Fukien Provinces.
Forces:
　　　25th Army Group—Chen Yi
　　　　　100th Corps—Chen Chi
　　　　　New 28th Division—Wang Chi-hsiang
　　　10th Army Group—Liu Chien-hsu
　　　　　28th Corps—Tao Kuang
　　　　　91st Corps—Hsuan Tieh-wu
　　　32nd Army Group—Shangkuan Yun-hsiang
　　　　　25th Corps—Wang Ching-chiu
　　　　　29th Corps—Chen An-pao
　　　　　67th Division—Mo Yu-shuo
　　　23rd Army Group—Tang Shih-tsun
　　　　　21st Corps—Chen Wan-jen
　　　　　50th Corps—Kuo Hsun-chi
　　　New 4th Corps—Yeh Ting (under the direct command of the war area)

The 3rd War Area has a total of 22 infantry divisions, 2 infantry brigades, excluding other special units.

(d)　4th War Area
Commander:　Chang Fa-kuei
Area of Operations:　Kwangtung-Kwangsi
Forces:
　　　9th Army Group—Wu Chi-wei
　　　　　65th Corps—Li Chen-chiu
　　　　　4th Corps—Ou Chen
　　　12th Army Group—Yu Han-mou

```
        62nd Corps—Chang Ta
        63rd Corps—Chang Jui-kuei
        66th Corps—Yeh Shao
        83rd Corps—
    16th Army Group—Hsia Wei
        46th Corps—Hsia Wei (concurrent)
        64th Corps—Teng Lung-kuang
```

The 4th War Area has a total of 18 infantry divisions and 2 separate brigades, excluding other special troops.

(e) 5th War Area

Commander: Li Tsung-jen

Area of Operations: Western Anhwei, northern Hupei and southern Honan.

Forces:

Honan-Hupei-Anhwei Border

Area Guerilla C-in-C: Liao Lei

```
        7th Corps—Chang Kan
        48th Corps—Chang Yi-shun
    33rd Army Group—Chang Tse-chung
        55th Corps—Tsao Fu-lin
        59th Corps—Chang Tse-chung (concurrent)
        77th Corps—Feng Chih-an
    11th Army Group—Li Pin-hsien
        84th Corps—Chin Lien-fang
        39th Corps—Liu Ho-ting
    22nd Army Group—Sun Chen
        41st Corps—Sun Chen (concurrent)
        45th Corps—Chen Ting-hsun
    29th Army Group—Wang Tsan-hsu
        44th Corps—Liao Chen
```

The 5th War Area has a total of 26 infantry divisions, 1 cavalry division and 1 cavalry brigade, excluding other special and peace preservation units.

(f) 8th War Area

Commander: Chu Shao-liang

Area of Operation: Kansu, Ninghsia, Chinghai and Suiyuan.

Forces:

```
    17th Army Group—Ma Hung-pin
        81st Corps—Ma Hung-pin (concurrent)
        168th Division—Ma Hung-kuei
```

80th Corps—Kung Ling-hsun (under the direct command of the war area)

82nd Corps—Ma Pu-fang (under the direct command of the war area)

5th Cav Corps—Ma Pu-ching (under the direct command of the war area)

191st Division—Yang Teh-liang (under the direct command of the war area)

2nd Cav Corps—Ho Chu-kuo (under the direct command of the war area)

New 2nd Corps—Lu Ta-chang (under the direct command of the war area)

6th Cav Corps—Men Ping-yueh (concurrently deputy C-in-C of the Army Group)

The 8th War Area has a total of 6 infantry divisions, 9 infantry brigades, 4 cavalry brigades excluding other special and peace preservation units.

(g)   9th War Area

Commander: Chen Cheng (Hsueh Yueh acting)

Area of Operations: Northwestern Kiangsi, southern Hupei (south of the Yangtze River) and Hunan Provinces.

Forces:

19th Army Group—Lo Cho-ying
    79th Corps—Hsia Chu-chung
    49th Corps—Liu Tuo-chuan
    70th Corps—Li Chueh
    78th Corps—Hsia Shou-hsun
    32nd Corps—Sung Ken-tang

31st Army Group—Tang En-po
    13th Corps—Chang Chen
    18th Corps—Huang Wei
    92nd Corps—Li Hsien-chou
    37th Corps—Huang Kuo-liang
    52nd Corps—Chang Yao-ming

74 Corps—Wang Yao-wu (under the direct command of the war area)

Hunan-Hupei-Kiangsi

Border Area Guerilla C-in-C: Fan Sung-pu
    8th Corps—Li Yu-tang
    73rd Corps—Peng Wei-jen

1st Army Group—Lung Yun
    58th Corps—Sung Tu
    New 3rd Corps—Chang Chung
    60th Corps—An En-pu

27th Army Group—Yang Sen
    20th Corps—Yang Han-yu

30th Army Group—Wang Ling-chi
    72nd Corps—Han Chuan-pu
20th Army Group—Shang Chen
    54th Corps—Huo Kuei-chang
    53rd Corps—Chou Fu-cheng
    87th Corps—Liu Ying-ku

The 9th War Area has a total of 52 infantry divisions excluding other special and guerilla units.

(h)   10th War Area

Commander: Chiang Ting-wen

Area of Operations: Shensi Province

Forces:

    34th Army Group—Chiang Ting-wen (concurrent)
    27th Corps—Fan Han-chieh
    90th Corps—Li Wen
16th Corps—Tung Chao (under the direct command of the war area)

The 10th War Area has a total of 9 infantry divisions, 1 infantry brigade, 1 cavalry division, and 1 cavalry brigade, excluding other special and peace preservation units.

(i)   Shantung-Kiangsu War Area

Commander-in-Chief: Yu Hsueh-chung

Area of Operations: Northern Kiangsu and Shantung

Forces:

    51st Corps—Yu Hsueh-chung (concurrent)
    89th Corps—Han Teh-chin
    57th Corps—Miao Cheng-liu
    Guerilla C-in-C—Shen Hung-lieh

The Shantung-Kiangsu War Area has a total of 7 infantry divisions excluding other special and peace preservation units.

(j)   Hopei-Chahar War Area

Area of Operations: Hopei and Chahar

Commander-in-Chief: Lu Chung-lin

Forces:

    99th Corps—Chu Huai-ping
    69th Corps—Shih Yu-san
    New 5th Corps—Sun Kuei-yuan
    Hopei Militia—Chang Yin-wu

The Hopei-Chahar War Area has a total of 5 infantry divisions and 1 cavalry division excluding other special and guerilla units.

b. Battle of Nanchang

(Mid-February-Early May, 1939. See Maps 14 and 15 and Charts 28 and 29)

CHART   28

Chart Showing Japanese Chain of Command during the Battle of Nanchang
(Mid-February-Early May, 1939)

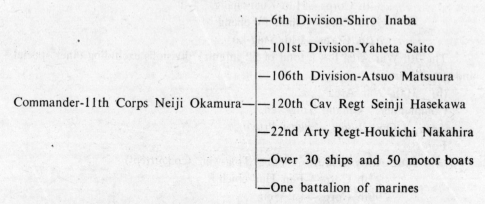

Commander-11th Corps Neiji Okamura—

—6th Division-Shiro Inaba

—101st Division-Yaheta Saito

—106th Division-Atsuo Matsuura

—120th Cav Regt Seinji Hasekawa

—22nd Arty Regt-Houkichi Nakahira

—Over 30 ships and 50 motor boats

—One battalion of marines

Notes: 1. The 9th Division was located in the Yuehyang-Linhsiang area.
2. A portion of the 116th Division took part in this operation.
3. The 3rd, 13th and 16th Divisions confronted our 5th War
Area north of the Yangtze River.

During the Battle of Wuhan in the fall of 1938, the enemy had planned for
the capture of Wuhan simultaneous with the capture of Nanchang. The overwhelming defeat of the enemy's 106th Division at Wan-chia-ling led to the lack
of adequate forces along the Nan-Hsun Railway and to the halt in the vicinity
of Teh-an. Later, the enemy's 2nd Corps Headquarters was demobilized and
returned to Japan. Operations on the Wuhan front were undertaken by the 11th
corps. Its first line extended from Hsin-yang to Chiu-kou, Yueh-yang and Teh-
an, as it confronted our 5th and 9th War Areas. Both sides stepped up replenishment readying themselves for the subsequent operations.

In February, 1939, the enemy's 101st and 106th Divisions massed toward
the area south of Teh-an, the main force of the 6th Division toward Juo-hsi, and
elements of the 116th Division and scores of ships and craft toward the vicinity
of Hu-kou. Enemy attempt to attack Nan-chang and cut off the Chekiang-
Kiangsi Railway gradually became apparent. Our National Military Council
estimated that it would be sometime after March 15 when the enemy would begin
the attack. In an effort to protect Nan-chang and cover the Chekiang-Kiangsi
Railway, Generalissimo Chiang directed the 9th War Area to be prepared to attack the enemy in northern Kiangsi. He had planned to take the initiative by
opening the attack on March 15. As the 9th War Area had not completed its
replenishment and encountered supply difficulties, it repeatedly requested postponement. Since the 9th War Area was unable to check the enemy in advance,
Generalissimo Chiang directed it on March 14 to conduct defensive operations.

CHART 29
Chinese Order of Battle during the Battle of Nanchang (Mid-February, 1939)

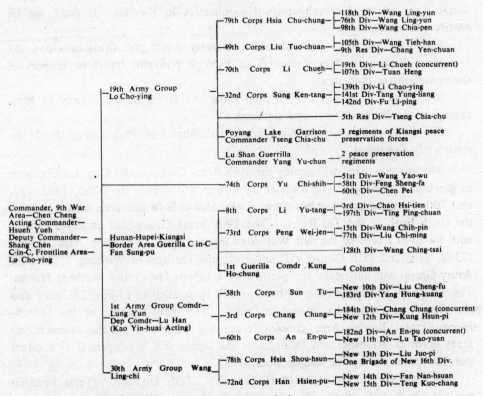

Notes: 1. Units not participating in the Battle of Nanchang omitted.
2. 5 divisions of the 32nd Army Groups, 3rd War Area were committed during the counteroffensive to recapture Nanchang.

Highlights of his instructions are as follows:

(1) Deploy only necessary forces in Wu-ning and maintain powerful forces on the Nan-chang front. Keep the 32nd Corps of the 20th Army Group in the vicinity of Nan-chang under the command of the 19th Army Group.

(2) The employment of the 1st Army Group should be based on the operational plans of the Generalissimo's Headquarters in Kweilin. It must not be hastily committed.

(3) The 3rd War Area should constantly watch the situation along the Nan-Hsun Railway and be prepared to dispatch powerful forces in support of the operations in that area.

(4) Water outlets in the Po-yang Lake and rivers in the vicinity of Nan-chang should be blockaded and guarded.

(5) The highway from Wu-ning to Hsiu-shui and Ping-chiang should be completely destroyed.

The 9th War Area will deploy the 19th Army Group under Gen. Lo Cho-ying to garrison Nanchang. The 19th Army Group will deploy the 32nd, 79th, 49th and 70th Corps to garrison Wu-cheng Chen, Hsu-chia-fu and area to the west on the south bank of the Tiu River. The 19th Army Group will establish contact with the 29th Corps of the 3rd War Area on the right. The 30th Army Group (72nd, 73rd and 78th Corps) will undertake the garrison of Wu-ning. The 31st Army Group will undertake the garrison of southern Hupei and northern Hunan. The 1st Army Group and the 74th corps will be retailed in Li-ling, Liu-yang and the vicinity of Chang-sha as mobile forces. The main strength of the Hunan-Hupei-Kiangsi Border Area guerilla forces will be placed in the mountainous areas north of Wu-ning, and elements of the forces will be dispersed to conduct guerilla operations behind enemy lines.

On March 17, a portion of the enemy's 116th Division, several hundred marines attacked Wu-cheng Chen from the water ways of the Po-yang Lake under the support of more than 30 enemy ships, 50 motor boats and a number of planes. In the meantime, elements of the enemy's 101st Division in Yung-hsiu attacked Tu-chia-fu. Our 32nd corps and the Po-yang Lake garrison forces jointly defended their positions. Heavy fighting lasted until the 23rd, and the enemy failed in the attack. Our 142nd Division under Gen. Fu Li-ping distinguished itself in the defense of Tu-chia-fu.

At dusk on March 18, enemy's main force (bulk of the 101st Division and the 106th Division) between Yung-hsiu and Chang-kung-tu began the attack. Using balloon observations, the enemy conducted heavy shelling for 24 hours with superior artillery (approximately 200 guns). On March 20, the enemy made a forced crossing of the Hsiu River. One division each from our 79th and 49th Corps assumed the firstline defense. Though the front was too wide and our firepower was weak, our defenders gallantly fought on and repeatedly launched counterattacks. Bitter fighting lasted until March 23. As more than half of our troops were wounded or killed, our lines were penetrated by the enemy. The main strength (2 divisions) of the 79th Corps was stopped by the flooding of the Liao River with only advance elements crossing the Liao River to act as reinforcements. One division retained by our 49th Corps rushed to reinforce the area north of An-yi; however, enemy mechanized forces moved swiftly. As our forces were scattered and unable to form well-organized positions, the enemy took An-yi. Later on March 24, the enemy captured Wan-chia-fu and Feng-hsin and swung left with his main force to attack Nan-chang.

At this time, our 3rd War Area had pulled the 102nd Division to defend the highway from Nan-chang to Feng-hsin and stop the enemy. Shortly after arrival, the division was forced by the enemy to retreat toward Feng-cheng. The 19th Army Group directed the 32nd Corps to withdraw from Tu-chia-fu via Lo-hua to Nan-chang. Enemy advance elements made a turning movement from Hsin-chow and Sheng-mi-chieh southwest of Nan-chang and crossed the Kan River. Only 2 regiments of our 32nd Corps arrived in Nan-chang, while elements of the corps fought bitterly against the enemy west of Kan River. The main strength of the corps moved south. On March 27, the enemy made a violent attack against Nan-chang. Our forces fought bitterly against the enemy in street fighting and suffered heavy casualties. At night, when our forces received orders to retreat toward Chin-hsien, Nan-chang fell.

Earlier, the 9th War Area had ordered the 1st Army Group and the 74th Corps to send reinforcements. On March 27, our advance elements arrived at Hsiang-fu-kuan, northeast of Kao-an, and in the vicinity of Hui-fu-chieh and made contact with the enemy's 106th Division. As Nan-chang fell, they occupied positions to confront the enemy in the area southwest of Kao-an. Meanwhile, the 19th Army Group had directed the 70th Corps south of Che-lin to attack the flanks of the enemy at Ching-an so that the 79th Corps could break out to the southwest via Ta-cheng. Then the Corps moved toward Shang-kao. After the 49th Corps withdrew from Shang-kao, it again moved to the area on the south bank of the Ching River and east of Kao-an.

On the Wu-ning front, on March 20, the main strength of the enemy's 6th Division moved from Juo-hsi to attack the positions of our 8th and 73rd Corps northeast of Wu-ning. On March 21, an enemy force crossed the Hsiu River at Chin-kou to attack our 78th Corps. Our forces put up strong resistance and launched counterattacks which led to heavy casualties on both sides. By March 27, in response to the operations in Nan-chang, our 8th Corps was pulled out and advanced along Nan-Hsun Railway and toward Jui-chang to attack the enemy rear areas. The 72nd Corps relieved the 8th and 73rd Corps so that the latter could be replenished and held in readiness. The enemy took advantage of this opportunity to launch violent attacks against our 72nd Corps and the right flank of the 78th Corps. The two corps gradually pulled back. On March 29, they abandoned Wu-ning and fell back to the positions in Pu-tien-chiao and Yen-kang-chieh west of Wu-ning. When the enemy stopped in the vicinity of Wu-ning, the operations came to an end.

In early April, our first phase troop reorganization and training were mostly completed. The various war areas were ordered to launch the April offensives and actively harass and tie down the enemy. The enemy was forced to transfer his 116th Division from Nanchang to the area east of Hukou along the Yangtze River and main strength of his 6th Division from Wu-ning to northern Hunan and southern Hupei. In an effort to tie down and wear out the enemy and re-capture Nan-chang, Generalissimo Chiang directed the 9th War Area on April 16 to dispatch powerful forces to operate along the Nan-Hsun Railway, cut off the enemy's lines of communications and capture Nan-chang. The attack was planned for April 24, under the unified command of Gen. Lo Cho-yin, frontline commander-in-chief of the 9th War Area and concurrently commander-in-chief of the 19th Army Group. Accordingly, Gen. Lo prepared the following attack dispositions:

(1) The 32nd Army Group (7 divisions) employed the 79th and 16th Divisions, 10th Reserve Division and a part of the 5th Reserve Division in the attack on Nan-chang. Other units were retained in a state of readiness in their original positions east of Fu River.

(2) The 19th Army Group employed the main force of the 49th Corps in a state of readiness for the defense of the right bank of Chin River. A portion of the Corps crossed the Chin River in the north to conduct guerilla operations. The main force of the 74th Corps attacked Kao-an. A portion of the corps attacked Wan-shou-kung in Hsi Shan and advanced toward Niu-hsing and Lo-hua to cut off enemy lines of communications.

(3) The main force of the 1st Army Group attacked Feng-hsin. A portion of the army group maintained surveillance over An-yi and Ching-an and advanced toward Lo-hua and Yung-hsiu. Another powerful column was dispatched to advance toward Tan hsi-shih, destroy lines of communications, and cut off enemy reinforcements.

(4) The 30th Army Group employed its main strength to attack the enemy at Wu-ning. A portion of the army group advanced toward Chang-kung-tu and north of Hsiu River.

(5) Min-shan Column actively operated toward Nan-Hsun Railway.

All the above forces were required to complete their preparations by April 21.

To respond to the operations in Nan-chang, our forces in southern Hupei and northern Hunan attacked the enemy forces at Hsin-tan-pu, Tung-shan and Tsung-yang so as to prevent the enemy from shifting his forces.

On April 21, the 19th Army Group began the advance. Elements of the 49th and 74th Corps crossed the Chin River in the north between Shih-tou-kang and Kao-yu-shih, and attacked the enemy at Sheng-mi-chieh, Wan-shou-kung and Ta-cheng. The main force of the 74th Corps attacked the enemy in the vicinity of Kao-an. Heavy fighting continued until April 26. Our forces recaptured such strong points as Shih-tou-kang, Ta-cheng, Sheng-mi-chieh, Kao-an and Hsiang-fu-kuan and entered Niu-hsing. Elements of the enemy's 101st Division fell back to Wan-shou-kung, while the main force of the 106th Division fell back to the high ground in the vicinity of Chiu-ling, northeast of Kao-an. Under the cover of superior artillery, the enemy counterattacked Ta-cheng and Kao-an and were repelled by our forces. Lack of firepower rendered our forces incapable of taking the high ground of Chiu-ling and the strong points of Wan-shou-kung and Niu-hsing.

On the same day, the 1st Army Group dispatched the 184th and New 10th Divisions to attack the enemy in the vicinity of Feng-hsin. The main force of the New 11th Division maintained surveillance over the enemy in Ching-an. Another force moved toward Tan-hsi-shih to harass the enemy's rear areas. Bitter fighting lasted until April 24 when the enemy retreated to Feng-hsin to link up with the enemy reinforcements arrived and began the counteroffensive. Despite 10 days of heavy fighting, the situation remained at a stalemate.

The 30th Army Group employed its main force in launching local attacks against the enemy in Wu-ning. On May 4, another force drove off the enemy at Chang-kung-tu and coordinated with the guerrillas in Min-shan and Lu-shan to sabotage communications and tie down the enemy.

On April 23, the 32nd Army Group began the attack against Nan-chang. The 16th Division and a part of the 10th Reserve Division attacked to the north from the area between Fu River and Kan River. The 79th Division and a part of the 5th Reserve Division crossed the Fu River between Wu-yang-tu and Hsieh-fu-shih to attack to the west. Bitter fighting lasted until April 26. In time, Shih-cha-chieh, Hsin-tsun-hsu and Hsi-liang-shan were recovered, as our forces pressed near the airfield. The attacks continued toward Hsiang-tang, Lien-tang, Hsieh-fu-shih and Nan-chang. Another force sneaked into Nan-chang and killed many enemy troops. On April 27, enemy planes bombed many places and indiscriminately dropped poison bombs. Our offensive encountered a little setback as the enemy pulled the main force of the 101st Division and counterattacked. Later, Gen. Chen An-pao, commander of the 29th Corps led the 26th Division to cross the Fu River in the west and renew the offensive. By May 5, the airfield and Nan-chang Railway Station were recaptured. As our forces penetrated the city defenses in Nan-chang, they were engaged in hand-to-hand fighting against the enemy. Superior artillery fire and air support made it possible for the enemy to motor powerful forces in the counterattack. Our forces suffered heavy casualties. With Gen. Chen An-pao, corps commander, killed in action and Gen. Liu Yu-ching, commander of the 26th Division, wounded, our offensive was frustrated. On May 9, our forces received orders to stop the attacks, and the entire front returned to what it had been.

Due to slowness in reorganization and training, we were not able to check the enemy first in this battle, depend on mobility to compensate the lack of fire power, maintain the organizational integrity or mass the attack where it was most needed.   Consequently, we failed to retake and insure the defense of Nan-chang. However, the blow and tying down we dealt against the enemy contributed greatly to the overall situation.

    c. Battle of Sui-tsao

(Late April-Mid-May, 1939. See Map 16 and Charts 30 and 31)

CHART   30

Chart Showing Japanese Chain of Command during
the Battle of Sui-Tsao

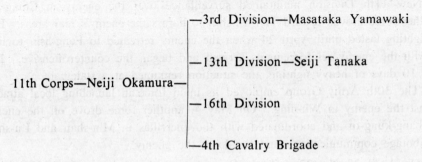

In the spring of 1939, when the Battle of Nan-chang was in progress, our various war areas launched the April offensive to harass and tie down the enemy. The 5th War Area attacked the southern sector of the Peiping-Hankow Railway from the east and west.   Meanwhile, the main strength of the 31st Army Group was shifted from northern Hunan to Tsao-yang to reinforce the 5th War Area. Thus, the enemy was forced to pull 3 divisions and 1 cavalry brigade and mass them in northwestern Hupei preparatory to the counteroffensive and consolidating the outskirts of Wuhan.

In late April, the enemy's 16th Division massed in Chung-hsiang, Yang-tze Chen and Tung-chiao Chen, the 13th Division northwest of An-lu and the main force of the 3rd Division in Ying-shan and north of Hsi-ho Chen.   Another force was located in Hsin-yang, while the 4th Cavalry Brigade was massed in the areas south and north of Hankow-I-chang Highway.

On April 25, Generalissimo Chiang ordered the 3rd War Area to step up the offensive along the Yangtze River and tie down the enemy; he ordered the 9th War Area to continue the attack on Nan-chang, reinforce Tung-shan, exploit success and attack Yueh-yang.

In late April, the 5th War Area ceased the attack and redeployed its forces. The River Defense Force undertook the garrison of Sha-shih, Sha-yang, Ching-men and I-chang.   The Right Army Group undertook the garrison of the banks

CHART 31

Chinese Order of Battle during the Battle of Sui-Tsao (Late April, 1939)

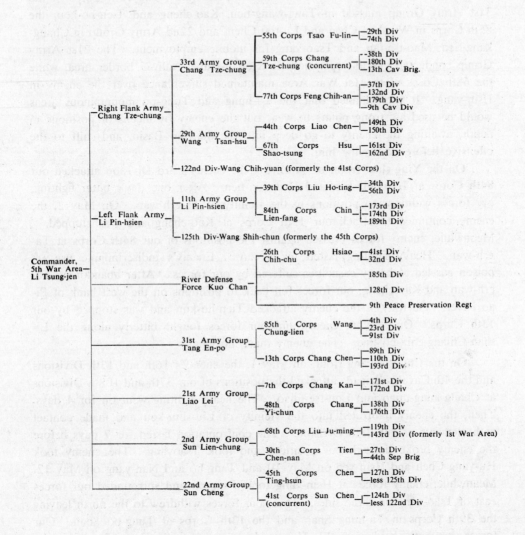

of the Hsiang River north of Chung-hsiang, and the Left Army Group undertook the garrison of Ta-hung-shan, Li-shan and Ta-erh-wan. The 13th Corps of the 31st Army Group massed in Tang-wang-tien, Kao-cheng and Tien-ho-kou, the 85th Corps in Wu-shan Chen and Lu-tou Chen, and 22nd Army Group in Chang-kang-tien, Mao-tse-fan and Tsao-yang for mobile employment. The 21st Army Group conducted guerilla operations in Honan-Hupei-Anhwei border area, while the 68th Corps of the 1st War Area maintained surveillance over the enemy in Hsin-yang. It was planned that the Ta-hung and Tung-po mountainous areas would be used as strong points to wear out the enemy by means of positions in depth, awaiting the enemy to go deep into the Sui-tsao Basin, and shift to the offensive before destroying him.

On the Ying-shan front, on April 30, the enemy's 3rd Division attacked our 84th Corps at Hao-chia-tien and Hsu-chia-tien. After one day's bitter fighting, our forces withdrew to positions in the vicinity of Ta-erh-wan. On May 2, the enemy continued to attack our 13th Corps at Kao-cheng and was stopped. Meanwhile, enemy forces pressed against the positions of our 84th Corps at Ta-erh-wan. Heavy fighting lasted for 4 days. Enemy's indiscriminate use of poison gas led to heavy casualties suffered by our forces. After abandoning Ta-erh-wan and Kao-cheng, our forces fell back to positions on the west bank of Pi-ao River. On May 5, the enemy attacked Tien-ho-kou and was stopped by our 13th Corps. On May 6, enemy and our forces fought bitterly along the Li-shan-Chiang-chia-ho line. The enemy made no gains.

On the Chung-hsiang front, on May 1, the enemy's 16th and 13th Divisions and the 4th Cavalry Brigade attacked the positions of our 37th and 108th Divisions at Chang-kung-miao and Lou-tse-miao. The heavy fighting went on for 4 days. Then, the enemy infiltrated into the vicinity of Liu-shui-kou and made contact with elements of our 38th Division. The confrontation lasted for 7 days before the enemy broke through our positions and took Tsaoyang. The enemy took Hu-yang Chen and Hsin-yeh on May 10 and Tang-ho and Nan-yang on May 12. Meanwhile, enemy forces at Hsin-yang took Tung-po and surrounded our forces east of Tsao-yang on three sides. Thus, our forces withdrew to the north leaving the 39th Corps in Ta-hung Shan and the 13th Corps at Tung-po Shan. Our forces on both banks of the Hsiang River were ordered to intercept the enemy's rear area. Additionally, our 2nd Army Group was ordered from Hsi-hsing-chi and Pao-an-chai to launch a counteroffensive against Tang-ho and Nan-yang. In the face of a converging attack, the enemy hastily retreated and suffered heavy casualties. Successively, our forces recaptured Hsin-yeh, Nan-yang, Tang-ho, Tsao-yang and Tung-po. By May 20, the original frontlines were restored. Subsequently, our 45th and 84th Corps were transferred to the vicinity of Lao-ho-kou, and the 31st Army Group was transferred to Nei-hsiang and Chen-ping for reorganization and training. The main force of the 33rd Army Group was moved to the west bank of the Hsiang River with a portion of the army group deployed to the east bank of the Hsiang River to maintain contact with the enemy. Thus, the Battle of Sui-tsao was brought to an end.

    d.   First Battle of Changsha

    (Early August—Early October, 1939. See Map 17 and Charts 32 and 33)

CHART   32

Chart Showing Japanese Chain of Command during the First Battle
of Changsha (Early September, 1939)

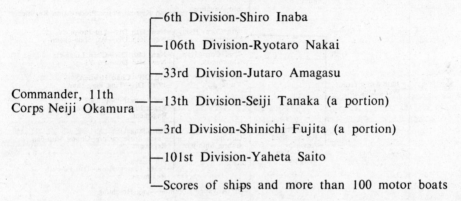

Commander, 11th Corps Neiji Okamura —
- 6th Division-Shiro Inaba
- 106th Division-Ryotaro Nakai
- 33rd Division-Jutaro Amagasu
- 13th Division-Seiji Tanaka (a portion)
- 3rd Division-Shinichi Fujita (a portion)
- 101st Division-Yaheta Saito
- Scores of ships and more than 100 motor boats

Since the spring of 1939, our forces had launched the April and July offensive. In the meantime, the enemy launched the Battles of Nan-chang and Sui-tsao. As both sides suffered heavy casualties and needed replenishments, the situation which was quiet since July became a state of confrontation.

In late August, the enemy's 11th Corps moved its units ready to launch the operations in Kiangsi and Hunan. The enemy had hoped to wipe out the main strength of our 9th War Area in the mountains of northern Kiangsi and Hunan. The main force of its 101st 106th Divisions moved from Nan-chang, Yung-hsiu and Wu-ning to mass in the vicinity of Feng-hsin and Ching-an. His 33rd Division moved from Hsien-ning and Chung-yang to the vicinity of Ta-sha-ping and Tung-cheng, while its 6th Division moved from Tung-cheng and Lin-hsiang to the areas south of Yueh-yang. The Nara Column (built around the 26th Infantry Brigade of the 13th Division) moved from Ching-shan and Tsao-shih via Wu-chang by rail to Yang-lou-sze and Wu-li-pai and then headed south. The Uemura Column (built around the 29th Infantry Brigade of the 3rd Division) moved by ship from northern Hupei via Hankow to mass in Yueh-yang. Enemy ships in the Yangtze River also massed in the lake near Yueh-yang.

On September 12, the enemy deactivated the Central China Expeditionary Force Headquarters and activated the China Expeditionary Force General Headquarters in Nanking with Juzo Nishio as the commander-in-chief and Seishiro Itagaki as the chief of staff exercising unified command of the operations and civil affairs/military government activities of the North China Front Army (1st

CHART   33

Chart Showing Chinese Chain of Command of the First Battle of Changsha
(Early September, 1939)

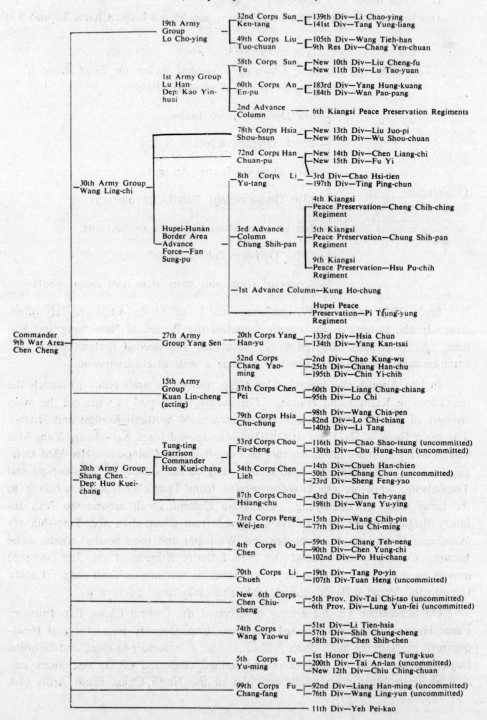

Corps, 12th Corps and Japanese Forces in Mongolia), 11th, 13th and 21st Corps.

At this time, Soviet Russia and Germany signed the non-aggression treaty to carve up Poland, and the war in Europe erupted. As Soviet Russia and Japan signed the Nomanhan Ceasefire Agreement, Britain closed the Yunnan-Burma Road in order to pacify Japan and concentrate on Europe. In the light of the international development, China was aware of the possibility that the enemy might mass his forces for the capture of the Yangtze River area. Accordingly, the Chinese Government directed the various war areas to launch the September offensives and tie down the enemy. The 9th War Area was directed to crush the enemy offensive in accordance with the pre-determined plans (mobile defense). (When the United States abrogated the U.S.-Japanese Trade and Navigation Treaty, Japan was greatly alarmed. With the signing of non-aggression pact between Germany and Soviet Russia, Japan took pre-caution and hesitated. She, therefore, proceeded in accordance with her established policy to conduct anti-attrition warfare against China.)

With a force resisting the enemy in northern Kiangsi, the 9th War Area employed its main force to meet the enemy from prepared positions along Hsin-chiang River, Mi-lo River, Liu-yang River and Yi-su River, banking position in Mu-fu Shan, and multi-layered positions in Chang-sha to resist and wear out the enemy. The main force was timely moved to Mu-fu Shan. Liu-yang, Lu-kou and Chang-sha awaiting the opportunity to conduct flanking attacks and destroy the enemy. Efforts were made to step up harassment, sabotage communications, clear the countryside and strengthen combat readiness.

On the northern Kiangsi front, our 19th, 1st and 30th Army Groups defended the south bank of the Chin River and the positions east of Hsiang-fu-kuan, Hui-fu and Yen-kang-chieh. The 183rd and New 14th Division respectively advanced to Miao-chien-chieh and west of Teh-an to attack the enemy rear area along Nan-hsun Railway.

On September 13, enemy's 106th Division at Ching-an and Feng-hsin began the attack on the positions of our 60th Corps (less 183rd Division). On 15, the enemy's 101st Division south of Feng-hsin began the attack on the positions of our 58th and 32nd Corps at Hsien-ling and Hsiang-fu-kuan. Our forces conducted sustained resistance from positions in depth. The bitter fighting lasted until September 17 when the enemy penetrated our positions in the vicinity of Hui-fu and swung to the left. His advance elements reached Tsun-chien-chieh and seriously threatened the left flank of our 58th Corps. In order to seek the exterior lines, our forces abandoned Kao-an on September 18 and pulled back the 32nd and 58th Corps to the area of Hui-fu, south of Kao-an along the Chin River. Contact was maintained with the 49th Corps on the right to resist the enemy. The 60th Corps (less 183rd Division) broke out toward Yang-kung-hsu and the 51st Division moved to Tsun-chien-chieh to stop the enemy from moving south. The 15th Division advanced from San-tu via Chiu-hsien-yang and the 183rd

Division moved from Miao-chien-chieh to Shang-fu to attack the enemy's rear areas.

On September 21, the enemy left a portion of the 101st Division in Kao-an for defense. The 106th Division and a portion of the 101st Division advanced to Hsiu-shui via Shang-fu attempting to launch a converging attack on our forces with the enemy at Tung-cheng. Accordingly, our forces shifted the offensive against the enemy at Kao-an. After capturing Kao-an on September 22, our forces continued the attack to the northeast and recovered the original positions in the vicinity of Hsiang-fu-kuan. The 49th Corps was assigned garrison duty of Hsiang-fu-kuan and the 32nd Corps was shifted to Tung-ku prepared to intercept the enemy forces which were moving west. The 51st Division advanced toward the Nanshan River-Lichia Shan line, while the 74th Corps (less 51st Division) massed in Sze-hsi and Shang-kao and the 58th Corps in the vicinity of Tang-pu.

At dawn on September 22, our 183rd Division reached Shang-fu and occupied position. Under air support, the enemy's 106th Division moved along Liao River at noon for the attack and broke through Shang-fu shortly afterwards. The division took advantage of the heavily wooded terrain in conducting sustained resistance. After September 23, our 15th and 184th Divisions arrived as reinforcements and were placed under the unified command of the 60th Corps to launch repeated counterattacks and stop the enemy from moving west. The heavy fighting lasted until September 25 when the enemy's main force took Kan-fang and continued its westward advance. A portion advanced toward Fu-chia-fu via Chiu-hsien-tang. Our 15th and 183rd Divisions fell back to the areas northwest of Kan-fang, while the 184th Division made a flanking attack of Kan-fang from the south. On September 26, our 57th Division attacked the enemy's rear areas at Shang-fu and Heng-chiao, while the New 15th Division which had just been transferred to Yen-kang-chieh by the 30th Army Group met the enemy at Fu-chia-fu. On September 27, our 57th Division took Shang-fu. More than 500 enemy troops which returned from Kan-fang for the rescue were defeated by our forces. Our 184th Division took this advantage to attack Kan-fang. As elements of the New 15th Division gradually arrived at Huang-sha-chiao and Fu-chia-fu and encountered the enemy, fighting was intense everywhere. On September 28, the New 10th Division of the 58th Corps occupied positions in the vicinity of Chao-chiao to stop the enemy from advancing west. On October 1, our 57th Division took Heng-chiao and the 184th Division captured Kan-fang. Despite the fact that their rear was threatened, enemy forces attacked to the west. On October 2, they took Chao-chiao and turned to the northeast. Our 32nd Corps followed them in pursuit from Tung-ku and Ta-hsia. Intercepted first by our New 15th Division and later by the New 14th Division, enemy forces at Fu-chia-fu and Huang-sha-chiao began to retreat toward Sha-wuo-li in the morning of October 3, in order to join force with the enemy falling back from Chao-chiao. On October 5, our 51st Division began attacking Chiu-hsien-tang. On October

7, enemy forces at Shawoli retreated toward Chiu-hsien-tang and Shih-men-lou. After a violent attack, our 51st Division took Chiu-hsien-tang and jointly attacked to the northeast with the 57th Division. Heavy fighting which lasted until October 9 resulted in more than 1,000 enemy casualties. More than 300 bodies were left with the remnants fleeing to the northeast. Meanwhile, our 32nd Corps passed Shihmenlou to make the pursuit toward Ching-an. By October 14, enemy forces withdrew to their original positions at Ching-an and Wu-ning.

On the southern Hupei front, our 8th Corps of the Hunan-Hupei-Kiangsi Border Area Advance Force attacked the enemy forces from Yang-hsin and Ta-yeh in the vicinity of Chiu-kung-shan and northeast of Tung-shan. The 20th Corps of the 27th Army Group attacked the enemy forces from Hsien-ning and Chung-yang southwest of Tung-shan. The 79th Corps of the 15th Army Group garrison-ed the line from Wang-ya-chien to Mai-shih, Chiu-ling and Huang-an-shih. On September 19, the 9th War Area estimated that the enemy would mount an offensive and ordered a division of the 20th Corps to move south to Cha-chin and await further orders.

On September 22, the enemy's 33rd Division began attacking the positions of our 140th Division at Wang-ya-chien and Mai-shih. Bitter fighting continued until the night of September 23 when enemy forces infiltrated into our position from both flanks of Wang-ya-chien. On September 24, enemy forces continued the attack to the south. Meanwhile, elements of our 20th Corps gradually arrived at Nan-lou-ling and Tao-shu-kang to offer sustained resistance. Our 79th Corps attacked enemy flanks and rear and killed many enemy troops in the bitter fight-ing. By September 26, enemy forces had taken Nan-lou-ling and Tao-shu-kang. A portion of the enemy force was left behind, while the main force continued to advance to the south.

On September 28, enemy advance elements reached Chu-hsi-chang and Lung-men-chang, elements of our 20th and 79th Corps made a converging attack on the enemy at Tao-shu-kang and Nan-lou-ling, while the main forces pursued the enemy at Chu-hsi-chang and Lung-men-chang. The fighting was most intense. On the same day (September 28), a brigade of the enemy's 13th Division swung east from Weng River and took Ping-chiang. On September 29, the 9th War Area ordered the 79th Corps and the Hunan-Hupei-Kiangsi Border Area Advance Force to come under the unified command of the 27th Army Group. They were directed to destroy the enemy moving south from Lung-men-chang in the area east of Chia-i. Accordingly, the 27th Army Group ordered the main force of the 20th Corps to make a pursuit toward Chang-shou-chieh, and the main force of the 79th Corps to intercept the enemy at Hsien-chung. The 3rd Division of the 8th Corps moved from east of Tung-cheng to attack the enemy at Nan-lou-ling and Tao-shu-kang. On September 30, advance elements of the enemy at Lung-men-chang passed Chang-shou-chieh, while the enemy from Ping-chiang

pressed near San-yen-chiao. Both were heading toward each other in the east
west direction. On October 1, the main force of our 79th Corps fought bravely
against the enemy at Hsien-chung and Fen-pai-ling killing many enemy troops
On October 2, Hsien-chung and Chia-i were recovered.

On October 3, upon link-up in the vicinity of San-yen-chiao of the enemy
forces moving from the east and the west, a portion of the enemy's 13th Division
moved via Ping-chiang to Nan-chiang-chiao. The remainder headed toward
Chang-shou-chieh and Lung-men-chang. The 98th Division of the 79th Corps
and the 82nd Division separately conducted pursuit operations toward Ping-chiang
and Chang-shou-chieh. The main force of our 20th Corps conducted flanking
attacks against the enemy at Chang-shou-chieh. The bitter fighting resulted in
heavy casualties on both sides. At night, the enemy fled toward Lung-men-chang
and Mu-kua-Nan-chiang-chiao.

To respond to the operations of the 106th Division, the main force of the
enemy's 33rd Division at Lung-men-chang and Chu-hsi-chang took Cha-lu in the
east in the night of October 3. Over 200 enemy advance troops reached Ma-ao.
At this time, our 30th Army Group massed forces southeast of Hsiu-shui preparatory to launching a converging attack on the enemy's 106th Division. On
October 4, our New 16th Division and an engineer battalion were hastily pulled
out to reinforce Hang-kou and Hsiu-shui for sustained resistance. On October
5, our forces fell back to the south of Hsiu River and massed forces for the counteroffensive.

Since October 3, our 3rd Division and 140th Division joined force in a converging attack against the enemy at Nan-lou-ling and Tao-shu-kang. The situation
was progressing favorably. On October 6, the 9th War Area ordered the 3rd
Division to move east via Cha-chin and the 20th Corps from the southwest to the
northeast to assist the 30th Army Group in counterattacking Hsiu-shui. Our 98th
Division recaptured Ping-chiang on the same day and Nan-chiang-chiao on October
7. The enemy retreated toward Lin-hsiang. On the same day, enemy in the
vicinity of Nan-lou-ling retreated toward Tung-cheng.

On October 8, the main force of the enemy's 33rd Division moved from
Hsiu-shui and San-tu toward Chiu-kung-shan. On October 9, our 3rd Division
recovered Hsiu-shui and the 197th Division intercepted the enemy at Chiu-kung-
shan killing many enemy troops. By October 14, enemy forces retreated toward
Tung-shan and Yang-hsin.

In northern Hunan, our 52nd Corps (attached with 60th Division) of the
15th Army Group maintained liaison with our 79th Corps on the right, to defend
the positions along the Hsin-chiang River. Our 70th Corps (attached with 95th
Division) garrisoned the positions along the Hsiang River from the Mi-lo River
to the north of Hsiang-yin. Our 73rd Corps (less 15th Division) was the general
reserve (On September 19, it moved west from Hsiu-shui and Cha-chin to Ping-

chiang). Its left boundary with the 20th Army Group was the east bank of the Hsiang River.

On September 18, the enemy's 13th and 6th Divisions began the attack against our security positions on the north bank of the Hsinchiang River. As they approached the bank, they were prepared to cross the river. On the night of September 22, more than 100 enemy ships and craft were moored in the lake off the estuary of the Hsin-chiang River ready for the landing. At dawn on September 23, they began the attack on our positions on the south bank of the Hsinchiang River. Air and artillery support plus balloon observation enable them to make a forced crossing of the Hsin-chiang River (the river could be forded since water was shallow) west of Hsin-chiang. Enemy marines and elements of the 3rd Division, supported by scores of ships, sailed in more than 100 motor boats and landed in the vicinity of Hsin-chiang River and the estuary of the Mi-lo River. Our defenders offered strong resistance and repeatedly conducted counterattacks which led to the killing of many enemy troops. It was not until the bloody fighting continued until noon that our 2nd Division defending the west of Hsin-chiang abandoned strong positions along the bank. Later, the 180th Brigade of the 60th Division arrived as reinforcements to secure the positions along the Hsin-chiang-Hsiang-kung-ling-Pa-tou-po-Chang-chih-ho-Pei-ti-chung-Hsin-wan-tzu line and stop the enemy. At the estuary of the Mi-lo River, our 95th Division sank 20 some steel-hull boats at dawn. After 0500 hours, the division engaged elements of the enemy's 3rd Division which had landed at Tu-hsing-kang, Tui-san-tzu, Li-tou-tzu and Ying-tien. Bloody fighting continued until 1600 hours when the division fell back to Chung-chia-ping-Ou-chia-ping-Ching-chia-ping line to stop the enemy.

After dusk on September 23, Fu-chao-sun, Wang-fang-chieh, Chi-pu-tang and Shuang-ho-yuan on the south bank of the Hsin-chiang River fell in succession. On the Mi-lo River front, the enemy had already established a bridgehead in the vicinity of Ying-tien. Our 15th Army Group modified its dispositions by moving the 52nd Corps to Huang-chen-hsia, Chang-hu-chung and Hsieh-tze-chi south of Yang-lin-chieh on September 24 to delay the enemy. In the night of September 24, the corps fell beck to the Peng-chia-hsia-Hu-shao-pao-Kuan-wang-chiao-Tu-tou-chiao line to occupy flanking positions preparatory to conducting flanking attacks against the enemy. The 60th Division was moved to the south bank of the Mi-lo River in the vicinity of the foot of the bridge, reverting to the organic command of the 37th Corps and strengthened the defense on the upper reaches of the Mi-lo River.

On September 24, the main force of the 52nd Corps was massed in the vicinity of Chang-hu and launched violent counterattacks enemy forces operating near Hsin-chiang River and inflicted heavy casualties on them. Later, our Ta-ching-chieh positions defended by a portion of the 25th Division were penetrated by the enemy. As the positions of our 95th Division at Chung-chia-ping and Ou-chia-ping in the lower reaches of the Milo River were under heavy pressure of superior enemy forces, the division withdrew to Tung-tang and Huang-chia-chiao. At night, after being relieved by the 19th Division, the 95th Division massed toward Pai-shui.

On the night of September 24, our 15th Army Group ordered the 52nd Corps to dispatch a force to occupy flanking positions along the Kuan-wang-chiao-Tu-tou-chiao-Tien-chia-hsia line, its main force to occupy positions along the south bank of the Mi-lo River east of Yen-chia-pu, and the 195th Division to the vicinity of Pai-sha to await further instructions. The 60th Division employed a force to occupy positions on the south bank of the Mi-lo River between Yen-chia-pu and Hsin-shih (both exclusive) and kept the main force in the vicinity of the foot of the bridge. The 70th Corps (attached with the 95th Division) continued to defend the positions along Hsin-shih—Kuei-yi—Huang-chia-chiao—Hsiang-yin line to halt the enemy.

On September 25, Tu-tou-chiao east of Ta-ching-chieh was locked in con-fused fighting. When its positions at Huang-chia-chiao were penetrated by the enemy, the 19th Division fell back to Pai-lou-feng positions. The situation be-came stabilized after elements of the 95th Division arrived as reinforcements and made flanking attacks.

On the morning of September 26, the enemy's main force made a forced cross-ing of the Mi-lo River (Water was deep and unfordable). Our forces resisted bravely. The fighting was so intense that the situation was most complicated. In an effort to lure the enemy into the vicinity of Chang-sha for a decisive battle, our 9th War Area directed the 52nd Corps (less 195th Division and attached with the 60th Division) to leave 2 regiments between Wu-kou and Hsin-shih to delay the enemy. At 1900 hours on September 26, the main force of the corps moved to east of Chin-ching and occupied westward positions north and south of Sha-shih-chieh, to attack the enemy who was invading south. The 70th Corps, at-tached with the 95th Division, left 2 regiments in the positions at Hsin-shih and Pai-ni-chiao to delay the enemy. At 1900 hours on September 26, the main force of the corps moved to Shih-ting, Lu-kou and east of Chu-chow to occupy positions. The 73rd Corps (less the 15th Division and attached with the 195th Division, lay hiding in Fu-lin-pu, Chiao-tou-yi and area to the north to attack the enemy heading south. The 59th Division of the 4th Corps lay hiding in Chang-sha and area to the southeast to attack the enemy who was heading south. The main force of the corps pushed to the area between Chang-shih on the south bank of the Liu-yang River and Tu-tou-shih to occupy positions and respond to the operations there. The 11th Division occupied the Yueh-lu-shan-Chiao-kou line with emphasis on the vicinity of Yueh-lu-shan. Contact was maintained with the 87th Corps on the left.

On September 27, a portion of the enemy's 13th Division moved via Weng-chiang to swing to Ping-chiang. Portions of the 6th and 3rd Divisions south. By September 30, enemy advance elements reached Chin-ching, Shang-shan-shih,

Ching-shan-shih, and Chiao-tou-yi. Later, our 73rd and 52nd Corps lay ambush and killed many enemy troops at Fu-lin-pu, Ching-shan-shih, San-chieh-chiao, Shang-shan-shih and Yung-an-shih. Meanwhile, the main force of the enemy's 11th Corps which was scattered in the vast areas of Kiangsi, Hupei and Hunan showed many weaknesses. High in morale, our forces took advantage of this opportunity to attack the enemy forces at Shang-fu, Heng-chiao, Huang-sha-chiao, Nan-lou-ling, Chang-shou-chieh and Hsien-chung. As a result, the enemy found the situation most difficult to cope with. The arrival of our fresh troops in the vicinity of Chang-sha and the launching of offensives in the various war areas, particularly the 5th War Area, greatly threatened the enemy's rear areas. On October 1, the enemy in northern Hunan began to retreat. On October 2 our 52nd Corps took Shang-shan-shih. On October 3, when it was determined that the enemy's 11th Corps had retreated, our forces began the pursuit in different routes. By October 8, our forces operated in Hsin-chiang River. Later, with the restoration of the original positions, the battle came to an end.

Deploying a force of 5 divisions over a 200 km. front of hilly woods and paddy fields, the enemy executed a major envelopment in a converging attack hoping to destroy the main strength of our 9th War Area in the mountains of northern Kiangsi and Hunan. Scattered strength, lack of strategic depth, unfavorable terrain and supply difficulties rendered the enemy incapable of sustaining our counterattacks. Hastily the enemy retreated. As the enemy exposed his weaknesses in offensive capability, his gains could not compensate his losses. In the end, psychological defeat and deep ramifications resulted.

e. Battle of Southern Kwangsi
(Mid-November, 1939—Late February, 1940. See Map 18 and Charts 34 and 35)

CHART   34

Chart Showing Japanese Chain of Command during the
Battle of Southern Kwangsi

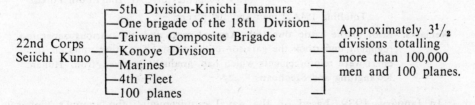

| 22nd Corps Seiichi Kuno | 5th Division-Kinichi Imamura
One brigade of the 18th Division
Taiwan Composite Brigade
Konoye Division
Marines
4th Fleet
100 planes | Approximately 3½ divisions totalling more than 100,000 men and 100 planes. |

Remarks: 1. Enemy commander from November 1939 to January 1940 was Kinichi Imamura who commanded the 5th Division and the Taiwan Brigade.

2. This chart indicates the enemy's chain of command after reinforcing in January 1940.

CHART   35

*Chart Showing Chinese Chain of Command during the Battle
of Southern Kwangsi*

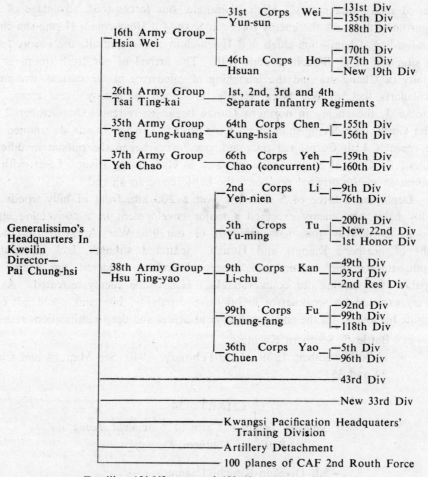

Totalling 154,642 men and 100 planes.

Remarks: Prior to the battle, our 16th Army Group and the various separate
regiment undertook the garrison of Kwangsi. The other units in this
chart were reinforcements which had gradually arrived from Hunan,
Kwangtung and Szechuan.

In January, 1939, based on the naval requirements, the enemy's General
Headquarters directed the 21st Corps to capture Hainan Island in order to seek
a base from which air operations against our southwest and blockade operations
could be conducted. Under the support of the Japanese Navy, the 21st Corps
dispatched the Taiwan Brigade to land at Hai-kou on February 10. Our peace
preservation units which had been defeated and retreated to the heartland of the

island to continue harassing the enemy. In time, the enemy occupied such hsiens in northern Hainan as Chun-shan, Wen-chang, Ting-an, Lo-hui and Cheng-mai. Subsequent enemy occupation of the port of Yu-lin obviously was preparatory to his southward advance. In September when the war in Europe broke out, Britain and France were too deeply involved to look to the east. Thus, the enemy's General Headquarters directed the 21st Corps to capture the vicinity of Nan-ning and cut off the international highway between Kwangsi and Indo-China, and the Japanese naval air force could have a base to conduct air operations against our southwest. In addition, the enemy's General Headquarters attached the 5th Division to the 21st Corps. In early November the enemy's 4th Fleet and air-craft carrier Kago covered the massing of the 5th Division and the Taiwan Brigade in the vicinity of Hai-kou, while enemy planes fanatically bombed our major cities in Kwangsi.

With the purpose of protecting the international communications between Kwangsi and Indo-China, the Generalissimo's Headquarters in Kwei-lin assigned the 46th Corps of the 16th Army Group the mission of defending the coastline from Fang-cheng to Chin Hsien, Ho-pu and Lien-chiang, and the 31st Corps the defense of key localities on the banks of the Hsi River. Positions were prepared in advance and communications were sabotaged in the hope of offering gradual resistance and wearing out the enemy before fighting a decisive battle by the Yung River.

On November 15, under air and naval fire support, the enemy's 5th Division and the Taiwan Brigade made a forced landing on the west coast of Chin-chow Bay. After offering strong resistance, our New 19th Division was forced to fall back to Pan-cheng and Shang-sze. Having taken Chin Hsien, the enemy's 5th Division moved north along the Yung-Chin Highway,[37] and the Taiwan Brigade along Hsiao-tung—Pai-chi—Pu-chin Road. On November 21, the enemy pressed near the south bank of the Yung River to confront a portion of our 16th Army Group across the river. On November 22, our 135th, 170th and 200th Divisions raced to the vicinity of Nan-ning, Lao-tu-kou and Sze-tang as reinforcements. On November 23, the enemy made a forced crossing of the Yu River and captured Sze-tang. After the fall of Nanning on November 24, a portion of our forces withdrew along the Yung-Wu Highway[38] to Kao-feng-ai. Our main force moved along Yung-Pin Highway[39] to fall back to Pai-tang and Kun-lun-kuan. Heavy fighting went on until November 1 when Kao-feng-yi fell. With the capture of Kun-lun-kuan on December 4, the enemy assumed the defense. Our forces massed troops preparatory to the counter-offensive. The deployment of our forces was as follows:

---

[37] Yung-ning to Chin Hsien.

[38] Yung-ning to Wu-ming.

[39] Yung-ning to Pin-yang.

(1)   The 1st Column (170th and 135th Divisions) of the 16th Army Group (West Route Force) will attack the enemy at Kao-feng-ai, operate in Sze-tang and Wu-tang and assist the North Route Force in enveloping and destroying the enemy at Kun-lun-kuan.   Later, it will launch the attack northwest of Nanning.   The 2nd Column (31st Corps less 135th Division) will mass in the vicinity of Suhsu and attack the enemy at Ta-tang, Wu-tsun and Nan-ning.   It will insure the occupation of Wu-tsun and Ting-tzu-hsu to stop the enemy from moving north.

(2)   The 5th Corps of the 38th Army Group (North Route Force) will move from Pin-yang to attack the enemy at Kun-lun-kuan.   Later, it will operate near Nan-ning and assist the East and West Route Forces in an enveloping attack against Nan-ning.   The 99th Division of the 99th Corps will move from Na-ho, Lu-tou, and Ling-li-hsu to attack toward the vicinity of Chi-tang and coordinate with the 5th Corps in enveloping and destroying the enemy in the vicinity of Kun-lun-kuan.   Later, it will move along the Yung-Pin Highway to the high ground south of Erh-tang and Wu-tang and attack the enemy at Pu-miao, Chien-tze-hsu and Liang-ching in order to stop the enemy from moving north.

(3)   The 46th Corps of the 26th Army Group (East Route Force) and the 3rd Advance Column will use Lu-wu and Ling-shan as bases, join force with the local people and undertake the missions of destroying the traffic and signal communications of the Yung-Chin Highway so as to prevent the enemy from sending reinforcements.   The 66th Corps will operate toward Ku-la and Kan-tang and later cross the river between Yung-Chun and Nan-hsiang to attack the enemy east of Yung-Chin Highway, cut off his traffic and signal communications and prevent him from moving his reinforcements to the north.

(4)   The main force of the 99th Corps will be located in the vicinity of Pinyang and Tala as the general reserves.

On December 18, our forces began the attack.   Our air force provided direct support to the ground combat.   On the same day, the North Route Force captured Kun-lun-kuan and Chiu-tang and on December 19 Kao-feng-ai.   On December 20, as the enemy reinforced and counterattacked, Kao-feng-yi, Chiu-tang, and Kun-lun-kuan again fell into enemy hands.   Our New 22nd Division and 92nd Division continued to intercept enemy reinforcements between Wu-tang and Pa-tang on the Yung-Pin Highway.   Disregarding heavy losses, the enemy poured reinforcements to Kun-lun-kuan by airlifting replacements, rations and ammunition so as to hold it.   After December 25, our 159th Division was committed in the operations on the high ground northeast of Kun-lun-kuan.   The close coordination of our combined arms enabled our forces to occupy the high grounds in that vicinity of Kun-lun-kuan and achieve dominating control.   Our air force strafed and bombed the enemy troops at Chi-tang and Pa-tang.   It also provided close air support to ground combat and inflicted heavy casualties on the enemy.   Heavy fighting lasted until December 31 when elements of our New 22nd Division and the 159th Division of the East Route Force finally captured Kun-lun-kuan and

Tien-yin, wiping out 8,000 enemy troops including Nakamura, commander of the 12th Brigade, 5th Division.   Meanwhile, the 1st Column of our West Route Force attacked the enemy at Kao-feng-ai reaping considerable gains.   After routing the enemy force which had fled to Lu-wu, the 46th Corps of our East Route Force relentlessly attacked the enemy along the Yung-Chin Highway.   The enemy became greatly exhausted and suffered heavy attrition.

Immediately before our forces launched the offensive, a portion of the enemy's 5th Division moved from Sui-lu via Hsi-chang-hsu to Lung-chow on December 17.   After resisting strongly, our militia withdrew to the outskirts on December 21 and abandoned Lung-chow.   On December 24, the enemy turned from Lung-chow and was intercepted by the 2nd Column of our West Route Force.   Over 1,000 enemy troops were killed, while the remnants fled to Nan-ning.

On January 4, 1940 when our forces recovered Chiu-tang, the enemy retreated to Pa-tang to defend the critical terrain.   As a result of heavy casualties, our forces underwent replenishment preparatory to continuation of the attack.

With the overwhelming defeat of the enemy's 5th Division, the situation in Nan-ning was most critical.   Hence, the enemy pulled the Konoye Division and a brigade of the 18th Division from Kwangtung as reinforcements.   This and the original strength gave a total of 3 divisions which were organized into the 22nd Corps with Seiichi Kuno as the commander ready to launch the counteroffensive. The corps came under the command of the South China Front Army (commander: Reikichi Ando).

On January 25, one brigade of the enemy's 18th Division and a portion of the 5th Division moved along the Yung-Pin Highway to make a frontal attack on our positions.   The Konoye Division moved along Yung-Yung Highway[40] to make a turning movement against Pin-yang.   Despite heroic resistance, the inferior equipment of our forces failed to stop the enemy advance.   Meanwhile, our 38th Army Group Headquarters at Pin-yang was bombed.   As contact with various forces was cut off, units fought independently.   By February 2, Pin-yang and Sze-lung were captured by the enemy.   However, our forces on the Kun-lun-kuan front (2nd and 36th Corps) and in the west (6th and 99th Corps) did not retreat and fought bitterly for 6 days inflicting heavy casualties on the enemy. Later, as supply was disrupted, our forces fell back to Lung-shan, Tu-an, and Hsin-cheng.   On February 3, the enemy at Pin-yang advanced north to Tsou-hsu and confronted our New 33rd Division across the Ching-shui River.   On February 4, a portion of the enemy force moved from Pin-yang and took Shang-lin.   At the arrival of reinforcements, our forces conducted frontal attacks when the enemy forces were still scattered.   The 64th Corps made a flank attack on Pin-yang from Kuei Hsien.   After three days of heavy fighting, our forces finally repelled the enemy.   Kan-tang and Ku-la were recovered on February 3 and Yung-shun

---

40 Yung-ning to Yung-chun.

on February 4, threatening the lines of contact in enemy's rear areas. On February 9, the enemy force in Pin-yang began the retreat toward Kun-lun-kuan and Nan-ning, while the enemy force which had taken Wu-ning on February, 8, retreated toward Kao-feng-ai and Nanning on February 11. Our forces followed in pursuit and at one time recovered Kao-feng-ai on February 18. Later, one force was employed to maintain surveillance over the enemy, and the main force was as-sembled to undergo replenishment ready to resume the offensive.

After the fighting in Pin-yang, the enemy's 18th Division was transferred to Canton and reverted to the order of battle of the 21st Corps. His 22nd Corps continued to hold Nan-ning, Chin Hsien, Fang-cheng and the strong points on the outskirts and strengthened the defense works. With the ob-jective of recovering Nan-ning, our forces employed the main strength in the areas east of the Yung-Chin Highway and another force to the west to cut off the enemy's rear areas and assist the operation of the units on the north bank of the Yung River. Meanwhile, our forces east of Yung-Chin Highway and the East Route Force (46th Corps of the 26th Army, Group 1st, 2nd and 3rd Separate Regiments, guerrillas, and 64th Corps of the 35th Army Group) employed the main force of the 46th Corps to push to the northeast of Ling-shan. On March 12, the 46th Corps attacked the enemy communications along the Yung-Chin Highway. Our forces on the north bank of the Yung River began the attack on the enemy at Nan-ning. To insure the security of Nan-ning and relieve the threat on its flank, enemy force in Chin Hsien, built around one regiment and attached with cavalry and artillery moved from Niu-kang via Ping-chi to launch the attack on March 14. A portion of the enemy's 5th Division in the vicinity of Nan-ning moved east from Liang-ching to Pu-chin. One route of over 2,000 troops advanced toward Tai-ping, another route of approximately one regiment took Yung-shun. On March 16, as Chiu-chow and Lu-wu fell in succession, the enemy from Yung-shun also reached the area southeast of Sha-ping to engage in heavy fighting with our 64th Corps. With the fall of Ling-shan on March 17, a portion of the enemy force reached the line from Fu-tze-ling to Feng-tang. Our East Route Force resisted continuously resulting in heavy casualties on both sides. On March 20, a portion of our force confronted the enemy northeast of Ling-shan along the line from Lo-feng to Shih-tang, while our main force underwent reorganization and replenishment. On March 21, elements of our 93rd Division crossed the Yung River in the south near Heng-shan and advanced toward Ta-tang, and the enemy retreated to the vicinity of Ling-shan to continue the resistance. At one time, our forces entered Ling-shan on March 22. On March 24 and 25, the enveloping attack of our 156th Division and 46th Corps led to the recovery of Ling-shan. Our 93rd Divi-sion pursued the enemy along the line from Sha-ping to Yen-tun. The enemy hastily fled along the Yung-Chin Highway. Apart from retaining the main strength for reorganization and replenishment, our forces dispatched a powerful unit to continue the attack.

On June 17, enemy on the south bank of the Yung River invaded west along the Yung-Lung Highway[41] and took Sui-lou City at night. Our 135th Division fell back to Pan-li and Lo-pai. On June 23, the enemy took Pan-li and Lei-shih-hsu, the 135th Division again withdrew toward Ming-chiang and west of Chiang-chow. On June 24, after capture of Pei-chiang-hsu, the enemy controlled the Yung-Lung Highway, consolidated his positions and continued his westward invasion. As the enemy took Ming-chiang on June 26, our 135th Division withdrew to the mountainous areas east of Ting-liang to continue the resistance. By June 29, 3,000 enemy troops massed in Ming-chiang with over 100 vehicles moving north, while enemy planes bombed Lung-ching. After heavy fighting which led to heavy casualties, the main force of our 131st Division withdrew to the north bank of the Lung River to assist elements of the 181st Division in occupying the areas north of Lung-chin and stopping the enemy. A force was left behind in Lung-chin to prevent the enemy from crossing the river. At dusk on July 2, the enemy sailed in rafts to cross the Lung River. Despite our ambush, the enemy captured Lung-chin in the end.

With France defeated in Europe, Japan took advantage of this opportunity to exert pressure on Indo-China. In September, the enemy's 5th Division moved into Vietnam, and the Konoye Division and the Taiwan Brigade remained in the original positions. In late September, our forces repeatedly attacked and inflicted heavy casualties on the enemy whose lines of communications in the rear areas were overextended. By October 13, elements of our 188th Division, 31st Corps crossed the Lung River and made turning movement to the south, while its main force moved from the southeast to Wu-teh for the attack. At dawn, it broke through the west gate of Lung-chin. Nevertheless, the enemy made use of defense works and put up stubborn resistance. Bitter fighting continued until 0900 hours when the enemy poured in reinforcements to launch counterattacks. Having suffered heavy casualties, our forces withdrew to the outskirts of the city. At night, after our counterattacks failed, our forces fell back to the line along Kung-mu-shan—Airfield—San-chia Village. At this time, having been surrounded and attacked by our force at Lung-ching and our 46th Corps on the north bank of the Tso River which had crossed the river and mopped up the enemy north of the Ming River, 2,000 enemy troops at Lung-chin, and Ping-hsiang along the Yung-Lung Highway began the southward withdrawal into Indo-China on October 26. Our 31st Corps immediately ordered its units to storm Lung-chin which was recovered on October 28. With the recapture of Nan-ning and the mopping up of enemy remnants in southern Kwangsi as the objective, the 4th War Area directed the 16th Army Group to mop up the enemy remnants along east section of the Yung-Lung Highway and assisted the 35th Army Group in the capture of Nan-

---

41 Yung-ning to Lung-tou.

ning. The main force of the 35th Army Group was directed to move along the Yung-Wu Highway and Yung-Pin Highway, attack the enemy and capture Nan-ning. Another force crossed the Yung River and cut off the enemy route of retreat along the northern sector of the Yung-Chin Highway and assisted the 16th Army Group in a converging attack on the enemy along the northern sector of the Yung-Chin Highway. Fighting courageously, our 64th Corps captured Kao-feng-ai, and San-tang and Chien-tao-hsu on the Yung-Pin Highway on October 29, and continued the advance toward Nan-ning. Our 155th Division crossed the Yung River at Yung-shun to attack the enemy. In the meantime, enemy on the north bank of the Yung River began to retreat toward the Yung-Chin Highway. On October 30, our 35th Army Group recaptured Nan-ning. The enemy's main force of over 20,000 troops massed in the Yung-Chin area. Our forces began the pursuit against the retreating enemy forces in Yung-Chin area, which were chased out altogether by November 17.

Shortly after our forces had recovered Kunlunkuan and the enemy had retreated to Yung-ning for determined defense, Generalissimo Chiang called the Liu-chow Military Conference in late February, 1940 to review the gains and losses of the entire operations. Improvement measures were decided with the hope that our officers and men would be inspired and would distinguish themselves in combat. He gave the following instructions:

(1) Recognize the enemy spirit. Our officers should deepen their self-criticism and alertness.

(2) Describe the enemy's tactical merits and weaknesses.

(a) The enemy's tactical merits:

A. "Speed"—"Attack the enemy where he is unprepared; appear where you are not expected." "Exhibit the coyness of a maiden; afterwards emulate the rapidity of a running hare."

B. "Hardness"—Defend a position at all costs and with perseverance.

C. "Sharpness"—Conical break-in and bold advance.

D. "Secrecy"—Maintain secrecy and keep the enemy guessing.

(b) The enemy's tactical weaknesses:

A. "Minority"—Capable of only small-unit harassing actions.

B. "Shortness"—Capable of only short time combat.

C. "Shallowness"—Capable of only shallow distance attack.

D. "Emptiness"—Lack of reserve force and emptiness in the rear areas.

(3) Tactics and countermeasures our forces should adopt to overcome the enemy and achieve victory.

(a) Tactics to exploit enemy weaknesses—Employ large units to attack small enemy units. Engage the enemy for an extended period of time to defeat the enemy's short attacks. Employ disposition in depth to break the enemy's short-distance harassing attacks. Advance boldly to attack the enemy's empty rear areas.

(b)   Tactics and countermeasures to break the enemy's merits:

A.   Check the enemy's "speed" with "steadfastness."

B.   Check the enemy's "hardness" with "fortitude."

C.   Check the enemy's "sharpness" with "ambush."

D.   Check the enemy's "secrecy" with "rigid discipline."

(4)   Urge senior commander to be determined, responsible and willing to sacrifice. Cultivate the spirit of initiative and capability on the part of subordinates.

(5)   Warn the ranking officers to pay attention to details, emphasize research, and achieve unity, mutual assistance and cooperation.

(6)   Announce the present phase operational objectives—urge the commanders at the various levels to go all-out to seek initiative and to attack actively.

Immediately after the Liu-chow Conference, Generalissimo Chiang flew back to Chungking. Fully aware of the fact that deficiencies in the staff operations of the various units adversely affected combat effectiveness, and that the qualifications of staff personnel concerned not only military build-up but also national reconstruction, he, therefore, called and presided over a nationwide Chiefs of Staff Conference in early March, 1940. First of all, he pointed out the responsibilities and position of chief of staff in a unit, and then described in detail the culture, integrity, knowledge and skills that a chief of staff should have. In addition, he gave instructions on the staff operations in troop units in general, future operational objectives, and improvements to be made. He made the following remarks on revolutionary tactics:

(1)   Strategically we should be persistent and fortitudinous; tactically we should seek decisive and swift operations.

(2)   Advance and attack boldly without regard to the right or left and front or rear. Persist until the objective is reached. Commanders at various levels should cultivate the audacity of conical assault.

(3)   In retreat, adhere to no rigid customary rule of retrograde action but withdraw to the enemy's rear areas.

(4)   Commanders at various level should possess outstanding command ability so as to develop the spirit of "defeating a numerically superior enemy" which is so characteristic of our revolutionary army and to help write glorious war history.

f.   Winter Offensive of 1939
       (Late November 1939—Late March 1940. See Map 19)

During the Battle of Sui-tsao in the summer of 1939 and the First Battle of Chang-sha in the fall of 1939, the enemy retreated hastily before he was dealt a fatal blow. As the enemy was bogged down, his strength was dissipated. If he received no additional reinforcements, he would lack the strength to launch a major offensive. However, since the enemy stood on the interior lines and benefitted from convenient communications, it was possible that he could shift his forces and conduct local offensives to impair our combat effectiveness or mop up our guerrillas. Hence, our forces had to seek the initiative, conduct multiple-front attacks and tie the enemy down. Therefore, they could frustrate the enemy's local offensives and exploit our advantage of fighting on exterior lines.

Meanwhile, most of the enemy's former divisions which were composed of 2 infantry brigades each had been rotated back to Japan for reorganization. There were replaced by a number of 3-regiment divisions and 5-battalion separate brigades. Although 8 brigades were added to the enemy's total strength, their total firepower and mobility were inferior. This was another indication that the enemy had no desire to mount major offensives.

In October, 1939, our forces completed second-phase reorganization and training. Greatly increased in combat effectiveness, our forces formulated the winter offensive operational plans soon after the launching of the autumn offensive, in order to effect a general offensive and increase enemy attrition. The main strength of those forces undergoing reorganization and training under the direct command of the National Military Council were added to 2nd, 3rd, 5th and 9th War Areas and formed the main attack, while the 1st, 4th, and 8th War Areas and the Shantung-Kiangsu and Hopei-Chahar War Areas employed their available forces in feint attacks against the enemy.

The following fragmentary orders were issued to the various war areas:

(1) 1st War Area—Attack Kai-feng and Po-ai to tie down the enemy.

(2) 2nd War Area—Cut off the enemy communications along the Cheng-tai[42] and Tung-pu[43] Railways and mop up the enemy in the triangle formed by southern Shansi and the southern sector of the Tung-pu Railway.

(3) 8th War Area—Employ a force to assist the ʼoperations of the 2nd War Area. The main force will attack the enemy in Kuei-sui and capture it.

(4) 10th War Area—Undertake original river defense mission. Be prepared to dispatch a force to cross the river for exploitation of success in accordance with the progress of the attack on the triangular area in southern Shansi.

(5) 5th War Area—Mop up the enemy between Hsin-yang and Wu-han, in the southern sector of the Peiping-Hankow Railway and then capture Hankow, attack the enemy along the Han-Yi Highway,[44] and cut off the communications of the Hsiang-Hua[45] and Han-Yi Highways.

(6) 9th War Area—Attack the enemy in the northern sector of the Canton-Hankow Railway with emphasis on Pu-chi and Hsien-ning and advance toward Wu-chang. At the same time, attack Nan-chang and Nan-Hsun Railway. Continue the attack to Jui-chang and Kiu-kiang.

---

42 Cheng-ting to Tai-yuan.

43 Tatung to Pu-chow (Yung-chi).

44 Hankow to I-chang.

45 Hsiang-yang to Hua-yuan.

(7)   3rd War Area—Employ its main force of approximately 11 divisions to cut off enemy traffic communications on the Yangtze River. Units which come from Hu-kou, Ma-tang, Tung-liu, Kuei-chih, Ta-tung, Tung-lin and Ti-kang will await opportunity for the attack, operate near the river bank, occupy position, and blockade the Yangtze River with light and heavy artillery and water mines.

(8)   4th War Area—Employ a force to capture Chao-chow and Swatow and the main force to mop up the enemy along the Canton-Kowloon Railway and in Nan-ning.

(9)   6th War Area—Employ a force to attack and tie down the enemy at Yueh-yang and Lin-hsiang.

(10)   Hopei-Chahar War Area—Employ the main force to cut off the enemy's communications between Pao-ting and Hsing-tai, and in the vicinity of Shih-chia-chuang. Employ another force to cut off the enemy's communications in the vicinity of Tsang-chow and Teh-chow in response to the operations in Shansi.

(11)   Shantung-Kiangsu War Area—Launch attacks on a wide front on Tai-an-Lin-cheng, and Tung-shan-Chu Hsien from the east and west in order to respond to the operations along the Yangtze River.

Apart from the 5th and 9th War Areas which were required to complete the operational preparations by November 26, secondary attacks and main attacks of the various war areas must be launched by the end of November and early December respectively.

1st War Area: In compliance with the outlines of the plans, it prepared attack dispositions by ordering the commander-in-chief of the 3rd Army Group to direct the 81st Division and 40,000 guerrillas in the Anhwei-Honan border area to cut off the Lan-feng-Kai-feng sector of the Lung-hai Railway, press against the enemy strong points which outside the Lunghai Railway and lure the enemy. The 2nd Cavalry Corps mass in Lu-yi southwest of Kuei-teh ready to attack it and stop the enemy reinforcements from Hsu-chow. The 36th Army Group launched the attack on Po-ai and Hsin-hsiang. The New 5th Corps attacked and destroyed the enemy north and south of An-yang, while the 9th Corps attacked Po-ai, Hsin-yang, Wu-she and the area between Hsiu-wu and Po-ai south of the western sector of Tao-tsing Railway.

On December 1, 1939, our various corps opened the attack against the enemy. The 3rd Army Group employed guerrillas to cut off the railroad near Lo-wang, Nei-huang and east and west of Lan-feng as well as the highways at Tung-hsu, Huai-yang, and Lu-yi. Elements of the 81st Division attacked Lan-feng, while the main force attacked Kai-feng. The division took Lo-wang RR Station on December 15 and entered Kai-feng on December 16 to mop up the enemy in the city, and set fire to the enemy headquarters and warehouses. In response, our agents also set fire in many places. Meanwhile, a portion of our 2nd Cavalry Corps advanced to the east of Po Hsien, encircled Kuei-teh and took the east gate, 500 drums of gasoline in the enemy airfield were burned, as another force routed enemy reinforcements moving west from Tang-shan.   On December 6, our New 5th Corps reached the north and south of An-yang and succeeded in destroying the bridges along the roads at Chi, Chun, Tang-yin and Pao-lien Temple Station.   As a result, traffic communications was disrupted for several days. Beginning on December 13, our 47th Corps mopped up the southern entrance of Tai-hsing Shan north of the Tao-tsing Railway and took the RR stations at Chang-kou and Po-shan.   Beginning on December 1, the 9th Corps employed its main force to cut off the traffic communications between Hsin-yang and Po-ai and attack the enemy defending the outskirts of Hsin-yang and the strong points of Wu-she. At down on New Year's Day, 1940, a portion of the 47th Division of the corps, attached with a demolition team, broke through Hsin-yang City and spent half a day mopping up enemy troops.   A total of 5130 enemy troops and 180 horses were killed, 106 rifles and 50 machine guns and military supplies were captured.

2nd War Area: In attack disposition, the 40th and 27th Corps maintained surveillance over the enemy at Chang-chih and Chang-tze.   The 14th, 5th and 4th Army Groups moved toward Yi-cheng, Chiang Hsien, Wen-hsi, An-yi and Yun-cheng to join force with the 61st and 34th Corps in western Shansi, in cutting off the southern sector of Tung-pu Railway and mopping up the enemy in the southern Shansi triangle with emphasis on Chu-wu and Hou-ma. The other corps attacked the enemy before them or destroyed communications, to facilitate the success of the main force.

At dawn on December 10, 1939, our forces began the general offensive. At that time, the enemy maintained a force of 6½ divisions in this theater and 10,000 troops in Chung-tiao Shan. Earlier on December 3, enemy attacked our forces at Wen-hsi and Hsia Hsien.   After 9 days of bloody fighting, our forces routed the enemy by killing more than 3,000 enemy troops including battalion commander Enoshima.   The mopping-up operations continued until December 20 when enemy units in minor strong points were wiped out.   Meanwhile, the enemy's major strong points at Heng-ling-kuan, Chen-feng-ta and Yen-chang-chen were encircled and communications on the neighboring highways were completely destroyed.   By late December, areas near Pei-she southeast of Wen-hsi were cleared of enemy troops.   To stop our forces from continuing the attacks, over 2,000 enemy infantry and artillery troops counterattacked from Yen-chang and Hsia Hsien.   By early January, 1940, elements of our 98th Corps and 7th Division repeatedly counterattacked, killing several hundred enemy troops.   A confrontation resulted.   Another force attacked along Tung-pu Railway between Wen-hsi and An-yi and destroyed the enemy's traffic communications reaping excellent results.   Since its launching of the offensive, the 4th Army Group joined force with the 5th Army Group in attacking the enemy strong points in Hsia Hsien and other places.   While the attack of the 14th Army Group against Yi-cheng and Chiang Hsien was in progress, the enemy massed 5,000 troops on

December 15 under air and artillery cover and launched the conteroffensive. The bitter fighting led to heavy casualties on both sides. By December 18, with the enemy from Yi-cheng fleeing west, our forces occupied Lung-hua Chen and continued the pursuit to Yi-cheng. By December 20, enemy forces at Hsiang Hsien suffered nearly 1,000 casualties, and enemy strong points An-kuo Village and Tien-wang Village were occupied by our forces. By mid-January, 1940, the enemy was completely routed.

In eastern Shansi, on December 13 and 14, our 27th Corps successively captured the strong points on the outskirts of Chang-tze and Tun-liu. As a result, enemy troops in Chang-tze and Tun-liu were trapped in our encirclement. To extricate himself from this precarious position, the enemy pulled more than 10,000 infantry, cavalry and artillery troops from the various strong points and began the attacks on our positions at Hsien-wong Temple, Yang-lu Village and Chin-yi Village southwest of Chang-tze on January 1, 1940 under air cover. Our 46th and 8th Reserve Divisions fought against the enemy in see-saw battles which led to heavy casualties on both sides. In the morning of January 3, our main force opened the attack which continued after dark. As the enemy was sandwiched, suffered heavy losses and fled, our forces followed in pursuit and pressed near the outskirt of Chang-tze. Our 40th Corps continued to attack the enemy forces which defended the strong points between Hu-kuan and south of Chang-tze. On January 5, our forces captured Hsiu-shan Village, Ta-shan and Nan-chia Village. On January 22 and 24, our forces recovered such key localities along the Han-Chang Highway[46] as Li-cheng, Tung-yang-kuan, and She Hsien. After capture of Lu-cheng on January 28, another force continued to fight bitterly against the enemy east of Lu-cheng. Yet, the Chinese Communists conducted raids in our rear areas, instigated rebellions, seized food from the people and forbade people to sell food to the Government forces. As a result, supply difficulties greatly affected operations. Since the mounting of the winter offensive in this area, 13,770 enemy troops were wounded or killed, and many booties were captured in this war area.

3rd War Area: In compliance with the winter offensive instructions, the 3rd War Area made the following dispositions.

(1) The 32nd Army Group will step up the attack against the enemy at Nan-chang and harass Nan-chang.

(2) The 23rd Army Group will organize 3 divisions each from the 50th, 21st, 86th and 25th Corps and 2 Divisions from the 18th Corps which had been assigned garrison duties of the Yangtze River, into an attack force on the Yangtze River front. The force will be divided into the Right Flank Army, Central Army and Left Flank Army. The Right Flank Army will operate along the line from Shun-an to Tung-kuan-shan, Tung-chiang Village and Ma-shan to insure

---

[46] Han-tan to Chang-chih.

our security and attack the enemy between Ti-kang and Ta-tung. Another powerful column will be organized to maneuver near Ti-kang, Tung-ling and Ta-tung,
advance to the river bank and attack enemy ships. When necessary, they will
capture Ta-tung and Tung-ling at once. Another powerful force will be sent
to Wan-chih and Wu-hu to harass and tie down the enemy. The Central Army
will move to Ta-tung and Huang-pen to attack the enemy. The main force will
attack the enemy strong points at Tseng-hsing-shan, Cheng-chia-ta-shan and
Hsiang-shan to insure the security along the line from Shan-tan-chow to Chiang-
chia-tzui. Later, it will attack the enemy in the vicinity of Man-tou-shan and
operate along the line from Mei-keng to the upper and lower estuaries of the river,
and Kuei-chih in order to cover the artillery shelling and minelaying. The Left
Flank Army will organize 2 columns (built around one infantry regiment, attached with necessary artillery) to approach the river banks from areas between
Tung-liu and Hsiang-kou, and between Peng-tze and Hu-kou to attack enemy
ships and lay mines. Individual battalions or companies, attached with necessary
anti-tank guns, will be organized into 3 attack teams to infiltrate into the river
banks and attack enemy ships. Two divisions, attached with necessary artillery
and engineers, and the Navy's Mine-Laying Group will form the reserves and
be placed in the vicinity of Tai-ping and Ching Hsien.

On December 16, 1939, the attack began. By December 18, the 144th
Division of the Right Flank Army had taken Cha-shan and Wang-chia-tan, and
the 10th Reserve Division of the Central Army had taken Tseng-hsing-shan, Pai-
fang-shan, Mao-tan and part of Cheng-chia-ta-shan. The 16th Division took
Pu-ling and Hsiang-shan, while the 190th Division captured Tuan-shan, Han-
shan and Shih-tze-shan. The 147th Division of the Left Flank Army captured Hui-
lu-ling and Kang-yao-ling, and push the anti-tank guns to Kuo-chia-kou on the
river bank. These guns fired on and threatened enemy transports sailing up the
river. Unfortunately, the 50th Corps and the 79th Division failed to achieve
coordination with the Central Army. Consequently success was not fully exploited. Both our 10th Reserve Division and 16th Division suffered heavy losses.
On December 20, they were relieved by the 40th and 67th Divisions. On December 23, the enemy poured in reinforcements, while enemy planes bombed for
days. In spite of several days of heavy attack, our forces failed to make any
progress. On December 28, our forces changed the dispositions by employing
the Right Flank Army to hold the existing positions, pulling out the main force,
organizing 2 columns (built around one infantry regiment attached with necessary artillery) and three teams (built around one battalion), and attaching necessary artillery, engineer and minelaying detachments to infiltrate into the river
banks near Ti-kang, Wu-hu and Ta-tung, attack enemy ships and lay mines.
Central Army held the existing positions to insure the security of Ching-yang,
organized columns and stepped up team activities from Ching-yang so as to
advance to the river bank, attack enemy ships and lay mines. The Left Flank

Army held existing positions to insure the security of Pei-mien-shan and Hung-tsao-shan. Furthermore, it massed all the artillery to attack enemy ships, and laid drifting mines.

In the Kan River area, in the morning of November 21, a portion of our 32nd Army Group attacked Nan-chang. At night on December 12 and 18, our plainclothes detachment broke through Nan-chang for harassing attack and sabotage. As a result, the enemy suffered heavy losses.

With regard to the forces on the 10th Army Group front, our 192nd and 62nd Divisions separately took Hang-chow, Fu-yang and Yu-hang in the night of December 13 and set fire to the enemy and puppet organizations and warehouses. Apart from dispatching a force to maintain contact with our forces, the enemy moved one regiment from the vicinity of Hang-chow to invade south on January 21, 1940. At dawn on January 22, the enemy made a forced crossing of the Chien-tang River and landed at Chiu-chia-tou north of Hsiao-shan to engage our 2nd Resistance and Defense Column in Chekiang. The enemy force was divided into 2 routes. One headed for Kan-shan-tou between Hsiao-shan and Shao-hsing; another (the main force) took Hsiao-shan at noon and advanced east to Shao-hsing. On January 25, this force fought bitterly against our 6th Resistance and Defense Column in the vicinity of Ko-chiao, our 8th Resistance and Defense Column at Lin-pu, portions of the 2nd and 5th Columns, and the 3rd District Self-Defense Group in the vicinity of Pai-lu-tang south of Hsiao-shan. On January 27, the enemy reached Lin-pu Chen and confronted our force from Kan-shan, Ya-chien, west of Suo-chien and south of Yueh-ta-chiao to the east of Wen-chia-yen. Later, our fierce counterattacks forced the enemy to fall back and defend Hsiao-shan City.

Throughout the entire period of the offensive, 4 enemy medium-size transports were seriously damaged, 1 large-size and 4 medium-size transports were lightly damaged. A total of 10,321 enemy troops were killed, 190 enemy and puppet troops, 464 rifles, 29 light machine guns and large quantities of military supplies were captured.

4th War Area: On the Kwangsi front, since the enemy began the landing on November 15, 1939 and took Nan-ning, heavy fighting went on for 2 months at Kun-lun-kuan and Kao-feng-ai during the winter offensive. For a detailed account of the operations, see Battle of Southern Kwangsi. In the morning of December 8, the main force (5,000 troops) of the enemy's 104th Division in Kwangtung was divided into several columns at Yin-chan-ao under air cover to invade northern Kwangtung in order to check our forces and relieve the enemy force in Nan-ning. They succeeded in penetrating our positions at Chang-kang and occupied Ta-mao-shan. By December 17, 2,000 enemy troops broke through and reached the east of Yuan-tan. While the enemy force was scattered, our force struck by ordering 2 divisions to attack the enemy. Our 158th Division attacked the enemy at Yin-chan-ao and took it after heavy fighting. Having suffered heavy casualties, the enemy sent 2,000 reinforcements from Chun-tien to launch counterattacks. Despite fierce fighting which lasted until December 19, the enemy still confronted our forces along the line southwest of Yin-chan-ao. By early December, the enemy secretly poured in additional reinforcements. On December 20, the enemy employed elements of the 18th, 104th, 38th and Konoye Divisions totaling 11 regiments to make the northward invasion in 3 routes. The Left Route Force which was composed of elements of the 104th Division moved north along the Canton-Hankow Railway via Yuan-tan. After heavy fighting, it took Yin-chan-ao and Pa-chiang-kou of December 24. On December 2, it made a forced crossing on the North River, and took the estuary of the Lien River on December 27. On December 31, the enemy reached the vicinity of Ying-teh and dispatched a force to Kao-tien to cover the security of its left flank. The Central Force consisted of the 1st Brigade of the Konoye Division and a portion of the 38th Division which moved north from Tai-ping-hsu to Tsung-hua. After its capture of Liang-kou on December 25, it was attacked by our forces at Lu-tien and Niu-pei-chi. After being intercepted by our forces and suffering heavy losses, the enemy no longer made any progress. The enemy's Right Route Force consisted of the main force of the 18th Division which moved north from Tseng-cheng along the tributary of the East River. On December 23, the enemy took Lung-men and Tso-tan-hsu to the west. On December 25, the enemy fought against our forces in the vicinity of Mei-keng southwest of Hsin-feng, as another enemy force moved north to Wong-yuan which they took on December 30. Our forces launched a general offensive upon arrival of the 54th Corps when the enemy force was still scattered. During the general offensive, our 12th Army Group fought against the enemy at Pa-chiang-kou, Liang-kou-hsu, Lu-tien and Mei-keng; the 64th Corps against the enemy who had reached Wong-yuan; and the 54th and the 2nd Provisional Corps against the enemy at Ying-teh. A portion of the 35th Army Group attacked south from Tseng-cheng and Tsung-hua. In addition, Gen. Hsiang Han-ping's forces attacked Lung-men in the west. On January 1, 1940, after routing the enemy force which invaded west from Wong-yuan, our 54th Corps recovered Wong-yuan on January 2, Kuan-tu on January 4, and Ching-tang on January 5. The enemy main force retreated to the vicinity of Sha-tien, while our 54th Corps operated near Fu-kang. On January 3, the 2nd Provisional Corps laid siege to Ying-teh and took it on January 5. It continued the advance to Lien-chiang-kou; however, enemy remnants moving south escaped and took Ching-yuan. Subsequently, portions of our 64th Corps and the 2nd Provisional Corps staged a counterattack and recovered it on January 10. On January 11, our Central Route Force recaptured Tsung-hua. Our 14th Division successively recovered Pa-chiang-kou and Yuan-tan on December 12 and Yin-chan-ao on December 16. In addition to dispatching units to pursue the enemy remnants by the various corps, the main force of the 35th Army Group moved along the west bank of the North River and near Chiang-hsin, and the 54th Corps and a portion of the 12th Army Group moved along the line from Heng-shih, Liang-kou-hsu, Lu-tien and Mei-keng to occupy positions. Since launching the winter offensive, the 4th War Area killed 10,300 enemy troops and captured more than 100 rifles and large quantities of military supplies.

5th War Area: Upon receipt of instructions for the winter offensive, the 5th War Area issued the necessary orders on November 22. A portion of the River North Army (75th Corps less one division, 41st Division, 128th Division and Central Hupei guerrillas) will cross the river east of Sze-kang and attack the enemy at Tien-men and Tsao-shih. The main force of the River North Army will cross the river between Sze-kang and Chiu-kou, attack the enemy west of Pai-ma-miao along the Han-Yi Highway, and operate along the line from Tien-men to Pai-ma-miao and Wu-yen-ling in response to the operations of the Right Flank Army. The Right Flank Army (59th Corps, 77th Corps less one division, 55th Corps less one division, and 29th Army Group less one brigade) will employ a force to cross the river south of Chung-hsiang and attack the enemy west of Ching-shan. Its main force will cross the river north of Chung-hsiang to attack the enemy along the Ching-Chung Highway. Having cut the enemy's lines of communications and occupied enemy strong points, it will operate along the line from Ching-shan to Sung-ho and Ping-pa preparatory to launching subsequent attacks. The Left Flank Army (River East Army) (22nd Army Group and 1st Guerrilla Column of the 39th Corps) will employ a portion of its forces to attack the enemy along the line from Ping-lin-shih to Ma-ping and Hsi-ho, advance to the line along An-Ying Highway and cut off lines of communications behind the enemy lines. Its main force will attack the enemy at Sui Hsien and Kuan-ti-miao, mop up minor enemy strong points and operate in the vicinity of An-lu, Ping-lin and Ying-shan preparatory to launching future offensives. The Southern Honan Army (2nd Army Group, 68th Corps, 92nd Corps and Honan-Hupei Border Area Group Guerrilla Group) will employ a force to attack the enemy north of Ying-shan, Kuan-yin-tang and Hsi-shuang-ho and dispatch a powerful force to advance to the area between Kuang-shui and Hsin-yang and cut off the enemy's lines of communications. Its main force will attack the enemy in the vicinity of Hsin-yang and occupy it. The force will operate along the line from Kuang-shui to Wu-sheng-kuan ready for future offensive. The Eastern Hupei Guerrilla Force will employ a regular force in conjunction with guerrillas to attack the enemy along the line from Kuang-shui to Hsin-yang and cut off the enemy's lines of communications. Its main force will advance to the enemy rear areas at Kuang-shui, Hua-yuan and Hankow to check the enemy movement. Additionally, it will order the 84th Corps, its reserve force, to mass in the vicinity of Taosyang.

On December 12, the various armies began the offensive against the enemy. The 32nd and 49th Divisions of the River North Army moved portions of the divisions to Chien-chiang and Pai-lo-chi, while the 128th Division attacked Hsien-tao. Having crossed the river at Chang-nao-yuan and Hsin-cheng-shih, our 6th,

13th and 41st Divisions mopped up the enemy strong points west of the Yung-lung River. At night on December 15, our 4th Reserve Division crossed the river north of Sha-yang to take part in the operations. On December 16, the divisions recovered such strong points as Nieh-chia-chang, Fu-nan-chang, Wu-hsu-chia-chang, Chou-chia-chang, Tung-hsin-chang, Tuo-chuan-fu and Nan-ho-fu and continued to fight the enemy at Sze-kang and Kung-yi-chang. At dawn on December 17, more than 1,000 enemy infantry and artillery troops of the 116th Regiment with ten tanks from Hsiang-chia-wan and Lin-chia-chi, and 1,000 enemy troops with several tanks from Sze-kang, fought bitterly against our forces in the vicinity of Hsien-tao and Sze-kang. Eventually our forces took both places. On December 18, enemy troops in more than 90 trucks advanced to the southwest via Wa-miao-chi and were intercepted by our forces in the vicinity of Wang-wu-tai and Han-ching-miao. As the enemy's route of withdrawal of 600 infantry and cavalry troops was cut off, some managed to flee to Tuo-pao-wan. On December 22, under the cover of 8 planes, enemy force at Kung-yi-chang attacked our positions at Wang-wu-tai and Lo-chia-tang. Our defenders suffered heavy losses, and the highway from Wang-wu-tai to Tuo-pao-wan was cleared by the enemy. Mean-while, the enemy force at Lin-chia-chi was increased to over 2,000 men, more than 10 guns, 60 tanks. Enemy troops were discovered northeast of Chu-chia-chang and northwest of Tuo-chuan-fu. Having fought against the enemy in see-saw battle for days, our forces suffered heavy casualties. To avoid further losses, our 55th and 13th Divisions were ordered to hold the enemy in Yen-men-kuan. On December 23, our main force was withdrawn to the west of the river, and on December 31 completed its new disposition. On the night of January 11, 1940, a portion of the 32nd Division intercepted several truck loads of enemy troops which moved from Chien-chiang to Yueh-kou, killed one full colonel, 50 enlisted men, and captured large quantities of military supplies.

On the front of the Right Flank Army: On December 12, our 74th Division crossed the river to attack the enemy south of Chung-hsiang. Our 77th and 59th Corps and the 29th Army Group separately crossed the river to capture Chu-pao-ta-chiao and Hsi-hu-shan and attacked Lo-chia-po, San-yan-tien, Wang-chia-pao and Tan-fu-miao. On December 13, they took Ta-hsiao-chen-chung and Chang-chia-wan. On December 18, our forces fought bitterly against several thousand troops at Wang-chia-ling and San-yang-tien. On December 19, our converging attack in conjunction with the 74th Division led to heavy losses on both sides. On December 21, the enemy retreated to the south. On December 22, our forces followed up by attacking Tung-chiao and Huangchiachi and also enemy strong points at Yangtze and Chunghsiang. On December 26, the enemy force in the vicinity of Chung-hsiang was increased to 5,000 with more than 10 guns and 20 tanks. At dawn on December 27, they made a fierce attack along the entire front. On December 28, elements of the enemy force advanced to the vicinity of Chang-shou-tien. A force of our 84th Corps (the corps later came under the command of the Right Flank Army) repelled the enemy. Meanwhile, our 74th Division already reached Yeh-chia-pu and Pai-miao-chang to join force with the 59th Corps in launching a flanking attack against the enemy in the vicinity of Hung-shih-po. By December 31, our forces confronted the enemy along the line from Pu-men-chung to the south of Chang-shou-tien, Tan-chia-ta-shu and Pai-miao-chang. On January 5, 1940, Wang-chia-tien and the high ground in front of the 29th Army Group were for a time, captured by the enemy. However, a counterattack in conjunction with the 55th Division restored our lost positions. On January 17, a portion of our 13th Division fought bitterly against enemy reinforcements at Yeh-chia-chi and Lo-chia-chi on the east bank of the river. From January 9-13, the enemy force at Huang-yang was increased to 3 regiments and began the attack on our forces. The enemy at Yang-tze shelled our forces. On January 14, our forces made a night attack along the line and took the high ground south of Kao-cheng and Shih-ling-szu, and Wang-chia-tai, Sun-chia-tien and Chu-chia-miao. Six days of continuous attack led to 2,000 enemy casualties. A state of confrontation resulted.

On the Left Flank Army (River East Army) front, on December 12, apart from maintaining surveillance over the enemy defending the strong points at Tu-chung-shan, Lei-ku-tun and Kun-shan on the outskirts of Sui Hsien, our forces attacked the area from Lo-yang-tien to Hsu-chia-tien. Another force occupied Wu--li-pu and Shih-li-pu east of Sui Hsien, assisted in destroying Sui Hsien—Hsi-shui traffic communications and engaged the enemy. On December 15, under enemy pressure, the left flank of the 22nd Army Group moved to the line from Chih-cheng-shan to Chi-ku-tien and San-ching-kuan. On December 18, our forces took Tze-pa-kang and Chang-kang to continue the attack against the enemy. On December 28, a portion of our forces took Yun-tan-kang southwest of Ma-ping, while the remainder fought against and beat off enemy reinforcements at Lo-yang-tien, Tze-pa-kang, Tu-chung-shan and Hsu-chia-tien.

On the Southern Honan Army front, on December 12, the army opened the attack. On December 13, our 92nd Corps and another group captured Chuan-kou-tien, Chiang-hsi-tien- and Yang-liu-ho and continued the attack to Hua-shan, Ping-ching-kuan and Feng-chia-chuang. On December 15, Yang-liu-ho fell again into enemy hands. Meanwhile, our 30th and 68th Corps pressed near enemy strong points at Lo-tuo-tien, Yu-ho and Chang-tai-kuan and sent detachments to sabotage the communications between those enemy strong points and Hsin-yang reaping many gains. The enemy force which had advanced north from west of Chang-tai-kuan, was driven off by our forces south of Mu-chu-ho. On the night of December 22, two of our regiments separately advanced toward the northeast and southwest of Hsing-yang to attack the enemy in Hsin-yang. On December 26, our 27th Division was also employed in attacking Hsin-yang. On December 27, our forces repelled enemy reinforcements at Hua-shan and Ping-ching-kuan. On January 5, 1940, more than 2,000 enemy infantry and artillery troops moved from Chang-tai-kuan to attack the 68th Corps. The left flank force of our 30th Corps employed 2 regiments east of Ping-chang-kuan against 2,000 enemy troops. Later, as our 68th Corps withdrew to the rear, the enemy pressed against the left flank of the 30th Corps. On January 8, the enemy fought bitterly against our forces at Hsiao-lin-tien and Kung-chia-fan. The commitment of our 85th Corps enabled our forces to drive away the enemy on January 9, and continue toward Yu-fang-wan, Wu-chia-tien and Ping-chang-kuan to mop up the enemy remnants.

To achieve exploitation of success and deal a heavy blow against the enemy, our forces committed the 31st Army Group. On December 28, the commander-in-chief of the Northern Hupei Army exercised command over the 4 divisions and the 92nd Corps of that Army Group. Its main force was ordered to cross the line from Kao-cheng to Yen-tze-ho and operate near Hua-yuan and Kuang-shui by January 1, 1940. Since January 5, it attacked enemy units at Hsu-chia-tien, Hsin-tien, Yu-chia-tien, Hua-shan, Ta-miao-fan and Ping-ching-kuan. Later, our 23rd Division advanced to the area between Wu-sheng-kuan and Kuang-shui. On January 7 our 4th Division recovered Hua-shan. On January 17, our 4th, 21st, and 142nd Divisions engaged the enemy at Wan-chia-tien, Chien-ting-miao, Lo-han-ting and Hua-shan. On January 22, the enemy and our forces fought at Chiang-chia-ho, Pi-chia-shan, Ku-sao-ling, Chih-shan-ai and Yin-chia-tien. Days of fighting at Hsiao-chia-wan, Tu-men-chung, Shih-men and Kao-cheng ended in the destruction of several thousand enemy troops, more than 10 tanks and large quantities of supplies.

After repeatedly attacking enemy strong points in eastern and northern Hupei and western Anhwei, our guerrilla force in eastern Hupei employed its main force in Huang-an, Ho-kou and Hsia-tien reaping considerable gains.

8th War Area: The objective of the war areas was to tie down the enemy and respond to the operations of the main effort. In launching its attack against Pao-tou and Kuei-sui, it designated the 35th Corps attached with the New 6th Brigade and a portion of the Wu-lin Garrison Brigade as the main force against Pao-tou, and ordered the Advance Force and 6th Cavalry Corps to advance and sabotage the railroad and the area between Kuei-sui and Sa-la-chi, so as to prevent enemy reinforcements from moving west. The 81st Corps assisted the 35th Corps in capturing An-pei, while guerrilla forces attacked and tied down enemy forces scattered in various places. On December 18, our forces participating in secondary attacks launched offensives to check the enemy. In the night of December 19, our forces making the main effort reached the outskirts of and entered Pao-tou at dawn on December 20. After capturing enemy headquarters and warehouses, they continued to engage in street fighting against the enemy. Meanwhile, our 101st Division recovered the key locality of Chien-tzc-kou between Pao-tou and An-pei, continued the advance and encountered 50 enemy trucks and 7 tanks near Mao-kuei-shen-yao-tze. The fighting continued until darkness when 1 enemy tank and 10 trucks were destroyed. Our New 6th Brigade destroyed most of the 200 enemy troops with more than 10 trucks fleeing from An-pei. At Kung-yi-hsing, our guerrilla force destroyed half of enemy 44 odd troops reinforcing Pao-tou from Ku-yang. Elements of our new 32nd and 101st Divisions jointly wiped out the enemy force which had fled to the vicinity of Peihuangtsaoyu. By noon on December 22, our force captured four fifths of the city of Pao-tou driving the enemy remnants to the southwestern corner. From Peiping-Tientsin, the enemy poured in 200 trucks, more than 10 guns, 8 tanks and 2,000 infantry and artillery troops supported by 4 planes. Over half of the enemy reinforcements were annihilated by our forces on the outskirts of Pao-tou. On the night of December 24, additional enemy reinforcements arrived. As the objective of tying down the enemy had been attained, our forces changed disposition to confront the enemy.

Having suffered a heavy blow at Pao-tou, the enemy was actively engaged in bringing reinforcements and replenishment to relieve the threat. In late January, 1940, the enemy moved west to invade Wu-yuan and Lin-ho. The enemy took Wu-yuan on February 3 and Lin-ho on February 4 at which time our forces withdrew to the outskirts awaiting the time to stage the counterattack.

With the objective of taking Wu-yuan in mind, the war area ordered the various units to attack the enemy defending Wu-yuan. On March 16, while the enemy was pressing against our New 4th Division, our 35th Corps, Sui-yuan Guerrilla Force and Wu-lin Garrison Brigade, secretly advanced east along the Wu-chia River. On the night of March 20, our forces entered the city of Wu-yuan by surprise and engaged in all-night street fighting against the enemy. Officers and men of our New 31st Division and Garrison Brigade repeatedly fought over possession of the strong points and finally recovered Wu-yuan at 1600 hours on March 21. The enemy fled to the north along the city walls. On March 22, our forces captured the strong points in the vicinity of Hsing-lung-chang. In an attempt to save the rapidly deteriorating situation, the enemy dispatched 600 troops in 80 trucks as reinforcements to make a forced crossing of Wu-chia River in the vicinity of Ta-tsai-chu (10 km. north of Wu-yuan) via An-pei. For 3 days and nights, they fought against our 101st Division without success. On March 25, the enemy force was increased to over 3,000 and made a forced crossing of the Wuchia River under air and artillery cover. As Wu-yuan again fell into enemy hands on March 26, our forces moved to the banks of Fang-chi-chu to continue the attack against the enemy and fought at Pa-tze-pu, Hsi-shan-tzu, Hsi-chiao and Man-ko-su. Unable to withstand our pressure, the enemy at Wu-yuan retreated to the east on March 30 and 31. Our ambush resulted in the killing of many enemy troops. On the morning of April 1, our guerrilla force and cavalry column recaptured Wu-yuan, and the 11th Provisional Division took Wu-pu-lang-kou. On April 3, as our 3rd Cavalry Division recovered Hsi-shan-tzu, enemy remnants fled east. By this time, the enemy inside of the Ordos Bend was mopped up.

9th War Area: Its attack disposition was to employ elements of the 19th, 1st, 30th, 27th and 15th Army Groups as the advance force against the enemy.

The main forces of these army groups which formed the garrison army made feint attacks against the enemy in their present positions and checked the re-deployment of enemy forces. On December 12, the various forces began the at-tacks. Our 58th Corps and 184th Division of the 60th Corps, 19th Army Group, repeatedly fought against enemy forces at Wan-shou-kung, Ta-cheng and Kulo-pu in the general area north of Shih-tou-kang and Kao-yu-shih and east of Hsiang-fu-kuan, cut off the communications between Nan-chang and Ta-cheng, and be-tween Ta-cheng and Chih-tien-chang, and captured such key localities as Wan-ling, Pu-ling, Hsiao-ling, Man-kang-ling, Chien-chow and Pai-tze-chiao northwest of Feng-hsin. On the night of December 13, our forces burned 2 enemy ware-houses north of Feng-hsin City, while the main force of our 139th Division, 32nd Corps attacked the enemy at Ching-an. On the night of December 21, our forces rushed into the city of Ching-an and set fire to the enemy warehouses. Our 141st Division and a portion of the 131st Division sabotaged the traffic and signal com-munications between Chang-kung-tu-An-yi, and between Teh-an—Juo-hsi, and the railways and telegraph wires between Niu-hsing and Lo-hua, and in the vicinity of Teh-an. These actions led the enemy's 33rd and 34th Divisions to trail the movements of our forces. The 78th Corps of our 30th Army Group attacked the 213th Regiment of the enemy's 33rd Division in the vicinity of Wu-ning and pressed it near Lao-ta-hsia in the southern end and Chapi-ao in the western end of the city. Our 72nd and 8th Corps attacked the enemy's 40th Division near Hsin-tan-pu, Ta-fan, Tung-shan and Nan-lin-chiao and cut off the highway and telegraphic wires from Yang-hsin to Tung-shan and Pai-ni-chiao. Later, our 72nd Corps took Hsin-tan-pu and Tze-kou Chen, and the 8th Corps captured Ni-keng-kou and Shih-hsia. Beginning on December 14, the enemy's 33rd and 40th Divisions employed 2 regiments to begin the counterattack from Yu-chia-fan, Lung-kang and Ta-fan, and fought bitterly against the 72nd and 8th Corps in the area from Shih-men to Shih-pi-hu. By December 19, our forces drove off the enemy and continued to launch pincers attacks against the enemy at Hsin-tan-pu, Tung-shan and Nan-lin-chiao. On January 10, 1940, one regiment of our 72nd Corps cut off the Nan-Hsien Highway, and a portion of our 3rd Division cut off the railway and telegraphic wires in the vicinity of Ting-sze-chiao. Similarly, our 3rd Advance Column sabotaged the enemy's railway and telegraphic wires from Li-ho-nan to Ta-chiao on the Nan-Hsun Railway, and the traffic and signal com-munications in the vicinity of Wang-chia-pu on the Jui-Wu Highway. Our 1st Advance Column sabotaged extensively the enemy's railway and telegraphic wires at Shan-po Ho-cheng-chiao and Tao-lin-pu along the Canton-Hankow Railway. During the entire duration of our offensive, the Nan-Hsun Railway was never cleared for traffic and the Canton-Hankow Railway was cleared only once in the sector between Wu-chang and Pu-chi. On December 12, after recovering Chung-yang, the 20th Corps of our 27th Army Group cut off the telegraphic wires along the highways from Pai-ni-chiao to Chung-yang and Yang-lo-tung, and between

Chung-yang and Shih-cheng-wan. The corps also routed enemy reinforcements at Wu-li-miao, Ta-shih-ling and Kuei-hua-shu inflicting heavy losses on the enemy for the entire duration of the offensive. Since it was committed on December 16, our 73rd Corps began the attacks against the enemy at Shih-cheng-wan, Kuei-kou-shih and Ta-sha-ping for nearly one month. On several occasions, our forces pressed near Kuei-kou-shih and Ta-sha-ping and set fire to most of the enemy barracks reaping many gains. Since December 13, our 70th Corps directed the 3rd and 19th Divisions to attack the enemy at Chung-yang, Kuei-hua-shu, and Shih-cheng-wan areas, mopped up the enemy east of Kuei-hua-shu and captured more than 10 key localities on the outskirts of Shih-cheng-wan. On the night of January 8, 1940, the corps swung to the direction of Yang-lo-tung, Pu-chi and Chao-li-chiao to mop up the enemy there, twice routed enemy reinforcements at Pai-hua-pu, and thoroughly sabotaged the enemy's railway and telegraphic wires at Ting-sze-chiao, Kuan-tang-yi, and Chung-huo-pu. A portion of our 82nd Division, 79th Corps, 15th Army Group took Yang-lou-sze Station, sabotaged enemy communications and cut off enemy liaison and supply. The main force of the division, the 98th and 140th Divisions and 2 replacement regiments of the corps had attacked the enemy at Ta-sha-ping and Tung-cheng, sabotaged enemy communications and blew up the bridge at Tieh-chu-kang, killed and captured many enemies. In succession, our forces captured the key localities of Chiu-kung-shan and Wu-li-pai and pressed near the outskirts of Yueh-yang City. In conjunction with a portion of the 116th Division of the 6th War Area, our 4th Corps attacked the enemy at Lin-yueh, destroyed the enemy's railway and telegraphic wires between Wu-li-pai and Yueh-yang, and the traffic and signal communications to the south, and fought hard against the enemy at Ching-kang-yi, Tang-chia-pai, Kun-shan northwest of Tao-lin, Wu-li-pai and Yun-hsi. Scores of enemy key localities were captured and the liaison and supply of the units of the enemy's 6th Division disrupted so as to isolate the enemy. All in all, from the initiation of the counter-offensive to the end, the 9th War Area wounded and killed a total of 33,913 enemy troops and captured large quantities of military supplies and documents.

Briefly, the operations of the 6th, Hopei-Chahar, and Shantung-Kiangsu War Areas were as follows:

In mid-December, the 6th War Area dispatched a portion of the 116th Division, 53rd Corps to cross the river at Cheng-ling-chi, attacked the enemy at Yueh-yang and Kao-chiao Railway Station, destroyed many enemy trains and killed more than 100 enemy troops. Later, as the enemy was divided into several columns to make an enveloping and converging attack, our forces broke out and massed in the vicinity of Kao-chia.

Hopei-Chahar War Area: Beginning in early December, the war area employed the 69th Corps, New 6th Division and guerrilla forces to attack the enemy's key localities south of Shih-chia-chuang along the Peiping-Hankow Railway, and between Tsang-chow and Teh-chow along the Tientsin-Pukow Railway, destroy railways and cut off communications.

Shantung-Kiangsu War Area: In late December, the war area employed portions of the 51st, 57th, and 89th Corps against the enemy in the vicinity of Tai-an, Teng Hsien and Chu Hsien, sabotaged the southern sector of the Tientsin-Pukow Railway to cut off traffic communications.

During the entire winter offensive which began on November 26, 1939 and terminated at the end of March, 1940, some 77,386 enemy troops were killed, over 400 enemy troops and 2,743 rifles were captured. Although the various war areas did not accomplish all their missions in accordance with the pre-determined plans and did not achieve all the anticipated results, they achieved the objectives of tying down and wearing out the enemy. However, the Chinese Communists took advantage of this opportunity to attack our guerrilla forces, garble up local militia units and enlarge their territories causing heavy losses to our winter offensive.

2. Second Stage Operations
(March 1940-Outbreak of Pacific War. See Map 20)

Our recapture of Wu-yuan in March 1940 marked the beginning of operations in the Second Stage. It was shortly after the Winter Offensive when our guerilla forces went deep into the enemy's rear areas to launch attacks by rotation. To mop up our guerilla forces in the occupied areas and prevent our forces from launching the attacks, the enemy staged large-scale invasion in southern Shansi, central Hupei, southern Kiangsi and northern Hunan.

a. Battle of Tsaoyang-Ichang
(Early May-Late June, 1940. See Map 21 and Charts 36 & 37)

CHART 36

Chart Showing Japanese Chain of Command during the Battle of Tsaoyang-Ichang (Mid-April, 1940)

Commander, 11th Corps—Katsuichiro Enbu

—3rd Division—Masataka Yamawaki

—4th Division—Kenzo Kitano (transferred from Manchuria in May and June)

—13th Division—Seiji Tanaka

—30th Division—Keisaku Muragami

—6th Division—Norimoto Kitano (a portion)

—40th Division—Shojikiro Amaya (a portion)

—20th Separate Brigade

—18th Separate Brigade—Koichi Kayashima

CHART 37

Chart Showing Chinese Order of Battle during the Battle of Tsaoyang-Ichang (Mid-April, 1940)

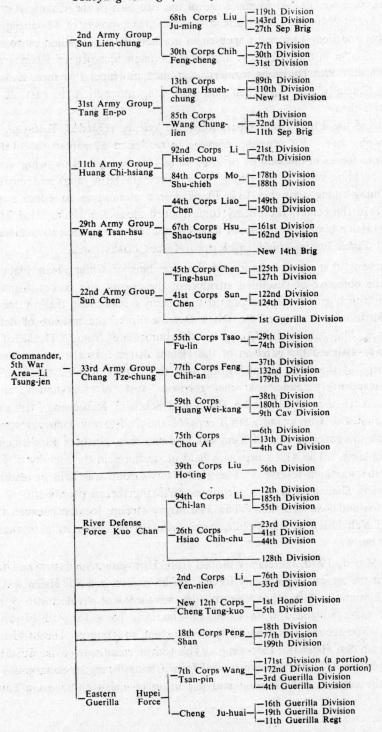

Having been dealt a heavy blow by our forces in the Winter Offensive, the enemy in Wuhan increasingly felt the threat of our forces in Ta-hung Shan and Tung-po Shan.   He was unable to make use of the rice bins of the Chiang-Han Plains. In mid-April, 1940, the enemy abandoned the strong-points of Ma-cheng in eastern Hupei and Feng-hsin and Ching-an in northern Kiangsi, pulled portons of the 6th Division in northern Hunan and 40th Division in northern Kiangsi and the 3rd, 13th and 39th Divisions formerly stationed in Hupei Province, and massed them in Chung-hsiang, Sui Hsien and Hsin-yang attempting, to cast all he had in a single throw.

During the First Phase Operations, the enemy regarded Tsao-yang as his advance objective.   By adopting converging tactics, it attempted to envelop and destroy our forces in the vicinity of Tsao-yang. He had hoped to swing west upon capture of Ming-kang by his Right Flank Force (in Hsin-yang) and move north from Chung-hsiang with his Left Flank Force attempting to effect a pair of pincers.   In the center, the enemy force moved along the Hsiang-Hua Highway from Sui Hsien hoping to draw our forces in the Tsao-yang area so that his Right and Left Flank Forces could envelop our forces in that area.

Knowing that our possession of the rice bins of Chiang-Han Plain would realize the objective of sustained attrition of the enemy, our forces dispatched a force to launch guerilla operations in the enemy's rear areas thereby increasing enemy attrition and assigned the River Defense Force the mission of defending Ching-men, Sha-shih, and I-Chang on the immediate front.   The 33rd Army Group was assigned the garrison of the Hsiang River.   In the central area, the 45th Corps of the 22nd Army Group and the 84th Corps of the 11th Army Group respectively undertook the garrison west of Loyangtien and Sui Hsien, and the area north of Sui Hsien and South of Kao-cheng.   In southern Honan, the 30th Corps and 68th Corps of the 2nd Army Group respectively undertook the garrison east of Tung-po, and the area north of Ping-chang-kuan and Ming-kang.   The 41st Corps was held in readiness in the vicinity of Hsiang-yang as the war area reserves.   The 29th Army Group was held in readiness at the Ta-hung Shan area with a portion undertaking the garrison north of Tung-chiao Chen and San-yang-tien.   The 31st Army Group, located between Chueh-shan and Yeh Hsien as the mobile army, awaited the opportunity to strike the invading enemy.

On May 1, 1940, the enemy moved from Hsin-yang, Sui Hsien and Chung-hsiang for the attack. The enemy force from Hsin-yang and Sui Hsien was divided into 2 routes. Altogether, the enemy's advance was divided into 5 routes. The first route advanced from Chang-tai-kuan via Ming-kang to Pi-yang and Tang-ho. The second route moved from Hsinyang to Tung-po. The third route moved from Sui Hsien to Tsao-yang. The fourth route moved from Sui Hsien to Wu-chia-tien. The fifth route moved from Chung-hsiang to Shuang-kou. On May 1, the enemy's 3rd Division and a portion of the 40th Division advanced from Hsin-yang by several routes and took Ming-kang, Lion's Bridge, and Hsiao-lin-tien; and on May 5, took Pi-yang and Tung-po. Meanwhile, our 31st Army Group which had massed northeast of Pi-yang joined force with the 68th and 92nd Corps in attacking the flanks and tail end of the enemy. Apart from leaving a portion of the forces west of Tung-po to attack the enemy, the main force of our 30th Corps attacked the enemy flanks. On May 7, after capture of Tang-ho, the enemy moved south toward Tsao-yang. On May 8 and 9, our 31st Army Group successively recovered Tang-ho and Hsin-yeh and continued the pursuit. On May 3, the enemy's 13th Division, attacked with more than 20 tanks, 40 planes and artillery and cavalry units moved north from Chung-hsiang and took Chang-shou-tien and Tien-chia-chi. Later, it took Feng-yao and Chang-chia-chi on May 6. Taking advantage of favorable terrain, our 33rd Army Group intercepted the enemy. Our 29th Army Group attacked the flanks and back of the enemy at Changchia-chi and Wang-chia-tien. Our 41st Corps fought hard to stop the enemy. By May 7, enemy advance elements reached Chang-chia-chi on the Tsao-Hsiang Highway, and a portion invaded Shuang-kou. On May 8, enemy's rear cavalry unit took Hsin-yeh. Commander-in-Chief Chang Tze-chung personally led his forces in attacking the enemy along the line from Tien-chia-chi to Huang-lung-tang. Our 29th Army Group also intercepted and attacked the rear of the enemy violently. Awaiting the completion of flanking actions, the enemy's 39th Division and a brigade of the 6th Division from Sui Hsien did not attack our 11th Army Group until May 4. As our positions at Kao-cheng and An-chu were overrun by the enemy on May 5, our forces fell back to the line from Huan-tan to Tang Hsien and north of Kao-cheng. Meanwhile, as our 33rd Army Group encountered reverses in its operations, a portion of the 11th Army Group was dispatched to assist the operations there. Our 175th Division was left in the vicinity of Tang Hsien to stop the enemy advance, and the main force fell back to the vicinity of Tsao-yang. While the army group was in the process of moving, the enemy at Tang Hsien massed its forces for the attack and employed tanks for the envelopment. Our 174th Division found itself engaged in bitter fighting as the Tsao-Hsiang Highway had already been cut off by the enemy. In order to break out, our forces abandoned Tsao-yang. In addition to employing the 173rd Division in sustained resistance to cover up our intention, the main force of the 11th Army Group moved to the west bank of Tang River and Pai River. The enemy took Sui-yang-tien and Wu-chia-tien on May 7 and Tsao-yang on May 8. During the breakout, our 173rd Division suffered heavy casualties including the death of Gen. Chung Yi, its divisional commander.

On May 10, the enemy completed the encirclement with the invading forces massed by the Tang River and Pai River east of Hsiang-tung. However, the encirclement fell through, as our forces on the exterior outflanked the enemy forces on the right and left flanks and pressed against the central area. As a result, the bulk of the enemy forces was surrounded in the Hsiang-tung Plains. Upon completion of the encirclement, our 2nd and 31st Army Groups and 92nd Corps moved south, 39th and 75th Corps moved east and 33rd and 29th Army Groups moved north to attack the encircled enemy. The 94th Corps operated on the Han-Yi Highway reaching deep into Ching-shan, Tsao-shih, Ying-cheng, and Yun-meng to attack the enemy's lines of contact in the rear areas. Meanwhile, our 7th Corps and eastern Hupei guerillas had already occupied such strong points as Chi-kung Shan, Li-chia-chai, and Liu-lin RR Station on the Peiping-Hankow Railway. Our 92nd and 68th Corps successively recovered Tsao-yang, Tung-po and Ming-kang encircling 4 enemy divisions in Hsiangtung Plains. By May 11, the enemy, having suffered heavy casualties, retreated to the east, Pursued by our forces which attacked its flanks and rear, the enemy left many bodies on the battlefield. On May 16, our 31st Army Group recovered Tsao-yang. By May 16, our confirmed reports indicated that 45,000 enemy troops were wounded or killed and 60+ field guns, 2000+ horses, 70+ tanks and 400+ trucks were captured. To destroy the enemy remnants, our 33rd Army Group fought hard to intercept the enemy. As a result, large bodies of enemy troops fled to the vicinity of Nan-kua-tien. Taking personal command of his Guard Battalion and the main force of the 74th Division, Gen. Chang Tze-chung was unfortunately killed in action at noon of May 16. As our pressure on the enemy's left flank was reduced, the enemy staged a counterattack against Tsao-yang on May 17 and took it again. Hence, our forces fell back to Hsin-yeh on the west bank of the Tang-pai River and the area north of the Tang River awaiting the opportunity to launch the counteroffensive.

Subsequent to the termination of operations on the east bank of the Hsiang River, the enemy was engaged in consolidation ready for subsequent operations with I-chang as the objective. The enemy's 4th Division and 18th Separate Brigade were respectively pulled from Manchuria and Wu-ning as reinforcements. The 4th Division took over the Sha-yang, Chung-hsiang area east of the Hsiang River. On the night of May 31, the enemy's 3rd and 39th Divisions crossed the Hsiang River at Yi-cheng and Ou-chia-miao. After taking Hsiang-yang on the night of June 1, its main force crossed the river toward the west and was separated into several columns. On June 3, the enemy captured Nan-chang and Yi-cheng. After attacking the enemy fiercely, a portion of our 41st Corps took Hsiang-yang, as the main force fought bitterly against the enemy in the vicinity of Nan-chang. Meanwhile, our 77th Corps also attacked the enemy in force. On June 4, our forces recovered Nan-chang with the enemy fleeing to the south. At this time, the enemy's 13th Division and a portion of the 6th Division on the Han-Yi Highway made a forced crossing of the Hsiang River in the vicinity of Chiu-kou and Sha-yang to link up with the enemy moving south from Hsiang-yang, for an attack on our forces. Accordingly, our River Defense Force shifted our main force to defend the main positions, and a portion of our forces took advantage of the terrain to stop the enemy moving south and crossing the river. Meanwhile, our 2nd and 31st Army Groups separately chased enemy south. On June 5, our forces were compelled to abandon Sha-yang and on June 6, Ching-men, Shih-li-pu and Shih-hui-chiao were captured by the enemy. Nevertheless, our 77th Corps and river defense units fought hard against the enemy along the line from Ching-men to Chiang-ling. After recovering Yi-cheng, our 2nd Army Group continued to pursue the enemy to the south. At this time, the enemy's main force was massed in the Ching-men-Shih-li-pu area, and Chiang-ling fell into enemy hands. On the morning of June 9, the enemy made a joint air-ground attack against our forces along the line from Tung-shih to Tang-yang and Yuan-an. In the afternoon, as our right flank position was penetrated by the enemy, our forces fell back at night to the line from Ku-lao-pei, Shuan-lien-shih and Tang-yang along the Tsu River to Yuan-an. On June 10, the enemy took Ku-lao-pei and Tang-yang forcing our forces to defend the positions on the the out-skirt of I-chang. The enemy followed up in the attack. After heavy fighting for several days, our forces suffered prohibitive losses and took the initiative to abandon I-chang. Later our 2nd and 31st Army Groups reached the area from Tang-yang to the north of Ching-men. On June 16, our forces launched a general offensive. On June 17, our forces recovered I-chang for a short time, while our 2nd Army Group joined force with the 77th Corps to attack the enemy at Tang-yang. Having cut off the enemy's lines of communications between Tang-yang and Ching-men, our 31st Army Group launched a violent attack against the enemy at Ching-men. Our 5th and 32nd Divisions south of the Yangtze River crossed the river to attack the enemy at Sha-yang and Shih-li-pu. By June 18, the enemy's main force continued to mass in the vicinity of the area from Tang-yang to Hsiang River offering stubborn resistance with its superior equipment. Fighting on the exterior lines, our forces separately reached the line from Chiang-ling to I-chang, Tang-yang, Chung-hsiang, Sui Hsien and north of Hsin-yang to form an encirclement of the enemy and maintain surveillance over the enemy. Thus, the Battle of Tsao-Yi came to an end.

Operations in Central Hupei
(i.e. Operations East and West of the Hsiang River)
(Late November, 1940. See Map 22)
Subsequent to the Battle of Tsao-Yi in the summer of 1940, though the enemy occupied I-chang and Sha-shih, our forces controlled the area east and west of the Hsiang River. Our lines extended from the southwest of Yuan-an via Ching-men, north of Chung-hsiang, and the foothills of Ta-hung Shan to the area northwest of Sui Hsien astride both banks of the Hsiang River. Wu-tang mountains was on the right and Tung-po mountains on the left. In coordina-tion with the guerilla forces in the southeast, our forces repeatedly struck against the enemy forces which had penetrated I-chang. Hence, the enemy forces in I-chang and Shashih were greatly threatened on the flanks, finding themselves

in a most awakward situation. To rid it self of this thorn, the enemy launched a series of attack against our forces in late November, 1940.

Since early November, the enemy actively made attack preparations which included the repair and construction of highways and bridges, defense works and airfields, and the storage of rations, ammunition, iron-bull boats and rubber boats in the vicinity of Chung-hsiang. The enemy pulled 5 regiments to the vicinity of Chung-hsiang and maintained additional forces in the areas east and west of the Hsiang River giving a total strength of over 3 divisions. In addition, the enemy also increased the strength in Sui Hsien along the Hsiang-Hua Highway. Together with the forces which had been there, the enemy maintained the strength of one division. Furthermore, the enemy added artillery and tanks in these areas. All these were indicative of adequate preparations made by the enemy.

By November 23, the enemy had completed his attack preparation with units deployed to the attack positions. Altogether, the enemy maintained the following 5 major forces:

Kayashima Force—composed of the entire 18th Composite Brigade and a portion of the 40th Division. Koichi Kayashima, commander of the 18th Composite Brigade, commanded this force.

Muragami Force—composed of the entire 39th Division and other non-infantry units. Keisaku Muragami, commander of the 39th Division, commanded this force.

Hirabayashi Force—composed of portions of the 17th and 15th Divisions. Morito Hirabayashi, commander of the 17th Division, commanded this force.

Kitana Force—composed of a portion of the 4th Division and the Kususe Armored Force. Kenzo Kitana, commander of the 4th Division, commanded this force.

(In parallel deployment, the 4 above-mentioned forces were stationed in the vicinity of Tang-yang, Ching-men, Chung-hsiang and north of Ching-shan.)

Hanjima Force—composed of the 3rd Division. Fusataro Hanjima, commander of the 3rd Division, commanded this force which was deployed near Sui Hsien on the Hsiang-Hua Highway.

The above disposition indicated the enemy attempt to encircle our forces on both banks of the Hsiang River.

Realizing the enemy's apparent attempt of an invasion and complying with the instructions of the National Military Council, the 5th War Area cabled the River West Army Group (30th and 77th Corps), the Right Army Group (44th and 67th Corps), and the Central Army Group (41st and 45th Corps) to adopt the tactics of checking a rampant enemy by employing the main force to intercept the enemy's outer flanks at the opportune time. The 5th War Area also directed the 59th Corps to push to the Hsiang-Fan area ready to respond to the operations both banks of the Hsiang River.

On the morning of November 25, the enemy force, separated into several routes, began the invasion.

On the Hsiangyang West front, over 1,000 enemy troops in the vicinity of Tang-yang and over 3,000 enemy troops from Ching-men separately invaded Heng-tien and Yen-chih-miao and broke through the positions of our 30th Corps. Meanwhile, the enemy force moving from Chu-chia-fu to Tung-lin-ling was divided into several routes to go deep north into Liang-shui-ching, Hsia-chia-tzu, and Kuai-huo-pu. At night, our River West Army Group swung to the line from Heng-tien to Yen-chih-miao and Kuai-huo-pu. On November 26, the enemy reached Hsien-chu. On November 27, the enemy invaded Liu-hou-chi and Li-chia-tang fighting bitterly for one whole day before his offensive was frustrated. At dusk, our 30th Corps launched a counterattack in force and ordered the 27th and 31st Divisions to dispatch units and raid the enemy's rear areas. Unable to withstand the attack, the enemy retreated toward Ching-men and Chung-hsiang. Our pursuit reaped heavy gains.

Ching-Chung Highway front: The enemy massed more than 3,000 troops in an attack on Chang-shou-tien and Wang-chia-tien and encircled Chang-chia-chi and Sha-ho-tien. Our 149th Division was forced to fall back to the Wang-chia-ho-Wu-lung-kuan line. On November 26, the enemy force was increased to 4,000-5,000. One enemy force invaded San-li-kang, while the main force attacked Pein-chai, Wang-chiaho and Yu-nan-men. The heavy fighting which lasted until dark ended in stalemate. On November 27, the main force of our 44th Corps counterattacked from Wang-chia-ho. Its converging attack with the main force of the 67th Corps to the northwest led to heavy casualties suffered by the enemy. Nevertheless, the enemy fought on.

On the Sui Hsien front: On the morning of November 25, over 2,000 enemy troops, having reached Liang-shui-kou, launched a violent attack against the positions of our 123rd Division at Li-shan. In addition, 2 enemy columns with more than 1,000 troops each advanced west toward Ho-yuan-tien and Ching-ming-pu. By darkness, the number of enemy troops steadily increased. On November 26, the enemy fought bitterly against our 124th and 127th Divisions at Chin-chi Shan and Ching-ming-pu. Another enemy force of 700-800 men moved from Hsi-ho via Lang-ho-tien to Tang chia-fan. Having been attacked by our 41st Corps, the enemy in the vicinity of Ching-ming-pu linked up with the enemy at Chin-chi Shan and moved to the vicinity of Ho-yuantien on November 27. At night, the enemy force near Tang-chia-fan reached the vicinity of Huan-tan Chen to confront our 125th Division.

Since its objective was to break the enemy force which had spread to various places, the War Area directed the subordinate units to insure the possession of key localities and employed the main force to take advantage of the mountainous terrain and conduct ambush so as to stop the invaders. The heavy fighting lasted until November 28 when the enemy retreated. Our forces west of Hsiangyang continued the pursuit against the enemy. The enemy force in front of our Right

Army Group was routed on the same day by our forces. It retreated in several routes. Having been subjected to a converging attack by our forces in the Central Army Group, the enemy forces in the Sui Hsien area which were in Ho-yuan-tien and Huan-tan Chen, fell back to the highground in the vicinity of Ho-yuan-tien and Tang-chia-fan and were encircled by our forces. Again, the enemy pulled 1,500-1,600 infantry troops and cavalry troops from Sui Hsien and Ying-shan via Shang-shih-tien and Sha-tien for a turning movement against our forces hoping to save the worsening situation. Once again, the enemy was ambushed by our forces. Under the cover of planes and armor, the enemy retreated toward Sui Hsien and Hsi-ho, as our forces attacked along the line from Chun-chuan to An-chu, Li-shan, and Kao-cheng. On November 30, our Army Groups recovered their original positions.

The operations resulted in the killing of over 5,000 enemy troops and wounding of 7,000-8,000 enemy troops. Over 1,000 enemy bodies were left on the battlefield. The speedy victory of our forces carried special significance. Firstly, the enemy forces which had penetrated I-chang and Sha-shih were threatened by our forces on the flanks and had no room for development. Secondly, the enemy had hoped to score a major victory at the time of its recognition of traitor Wang Ching-wei's regime so as to dampen our morale. The effect it had hoped to produce turned out to be just the opposite.

Operations in Western Hupei
(Early March—Mid March 1941. See Map 23)

The enemy's entire 13th Division was in I-chang with its 65th Regiment and 19th Artillery Regiment separately stationed in the vicinity of Lung-chuan-pu, Tu-men-ya and Ya-chueh-ling east of I-chang, the 104th Regiment NW of I-chang, and the 17th Cavalry Regiment in Yang-cha-lu-Pai-shan-ao area. Its 58th Regiment which was stationed on the west bank of I-chang along the Yangtze River constructed bridgehead positions between Chao-chia-ling and Shang-wu-lung-kou. In November, 1940, the enemy was defeated in operations in central Hupei. Between late January and early February, the enemy encountered defeat in the Battle of Southern Honan. Again in March, 1941, the enemy attacked western Hupei.

Our 26th Corps which undertook river defense confronted the enemy on the west bank of the Yangtze River at I-chang. The disposition was as follows:

The 41st Division was assigned the defense in the right zone along the line from Mu-chia-tien and Tan-chia-tai-tze to the north of Fan-chia-hu.

The 32nd Division was assigned the defense in the left zone along the line from Mu-chia-tien to Tse-yang and Hsiang-tze-kou.

The 44th Division was the reserve located in the vicinity of Tsao-chia-fan.

On March 6, 1941, the strength of the enemy force on the west of I-chang was increased to more than 3 regiments, plus cavalry and artillery. Beginning at 0530, the enemy artillery started shelling, followed by infantry advance and air support.   Our security positions at Tan-chia-tai-tze and Chao-chia-tien were broken through by the enemy who then continued the attack against our main positions at Chang-kang-ling.   Meanwhile, 600-700 enemy troops attacked our positions at Fan-chia-hu under air and artillery cover.   After heavy fighting, both places fell into enemy hands.   On the morning of March 7, the enemy again relied on the air force to capture our positions at Chien-chia-tai and Wu-chia-pa. Then the enemy continued to attack Chien-chia-chung and Yu-tai-shan, and was repelled.   At this time, the enemy force which has taken Fan-chia-hu fought bitterly and unsuccessfully against our 44th Division in the vicinity of Tai-ping-chiao.   Later, as enemy planes destroyed our positions, the division fell back to the eastern end of the bridge to continue the resistance.   When its positions at Hu-tze-yeh was taken by the enemy from Fan-chia-hu, our 32nd Division withdrew to the line from Tun-tze-chiao to Tu-yen-chung.   Again, the enemy followed up in the attack, but was driven off by our forces.   Meanwhile, the enemy found himself in a conical position.   To launch a converging attack against the enemy, our River Defense Force relieved the force defending the line from Mu-chia-tang-Ying-tze-shan to Chao-tien-kuan with the 103rd Division, 8th Corps, and the new positions at Yu-tai-shan, Pi-chia-shan, Ching-shui-pa, Kuan-kung-ling and Hsiao-ping-shan-pa with the 26th Corps, awaiting the opportune time to destroy the enemy east of the line and recapture original positions.   On March 8, two guerilla columns of the 41st Division separately attacked Chang-kang-ling and Fan-chia-yuan, while another force of the division attacked the enemy east of Pi-feng-chien. Over 2,000 enemy troops in front of the 44th Division attacked our positions from Kao-ling-po and Ta-chiao-pien to Wang-hu-tze-chung.   The resistance of our forces including units of the 41st Division was able to halt the enemy attack ending in a stalemate.   Later, as the enemy succeeded in penetrating the positions of the 32nd Division at Tien-wang-shih, our forces continued to fight against the enemy along the line from Ming-chia-chung to Hei-tan-kou on the outskirt of the Shih-pai Fortress.

On the morning of March 9, our 103rd Division occupied the line from Tu-ti-ling to Shih-tze-nao and was separated into several routes to attack the enemy. A portion of our 44th Division fought bitterly against the enemy on the high-ground on both sides of Kuo-chia-pa and suffered heavy casualties.   Its main force launched a flank attack against the enemy at Tai-ping-chiao and Hsiang-ling-kou.   By dusk, our forces captured enemy strong points at Tu-chiao-pa and Ta-chiao-pien along the highway, destroying many enemy troops.   Our 32nd Division employed its main force to attack the area northwest of Ta-chiao-pien. By noon, heavy fighting was still in progress in the vicinity of Wang-hu-tze-chung. Later, enemy reinforcements were repulsed.   Our 41st Division launched flank attacks against the enemy reaping fruitful gains. On March 10, our 103rd Division recovered the highground at Hsia-wu-lung-kou and north of Tien-tze-po.   The guerillas of the 41st Division still took advantage of gaps to attack the enemy.

As the positions of the 44th Division at Hung-shih-po and Lung-tan-ping were penetrated by the enemy, the division moved to the highground on the western end of Po-mu-ping to face the enemy. At dawn on March 11, having suffered heavy casualties, the enemy laid smoke screen and withdrew to the east in several routes. Our pursuit led to the recovery of Hsiang-ling-kou, Kuo-chia-pa, Kuan-kung-ling, Tien-wang-shih and Ta-chiao-pien. By March 12, the enemy defended the line from the east of Tai-ping-chiao to Hu-tze-ai and Huang-ni-keng. On March 13, our forces launched counterattacks against the enemy. Unable to sustain our counterattacks, the enemy fell back to his original positions. The confrontation returned to what it had been.

This engagement lasted 8 days. The enemy did not launch large-scale attacks, and we dispatched only a portion of our forces which routed the enemy. The fact that the enemy suffered 4,000-5,000 casualties was ample evidence which frightened the enemy and ended the enemy's design to move west.

b. Battle of Southern Honan
(Late January—Early February, 1941; See Map 24 and Charts 38 and 39)

CHART 38

Chart Showing Japanese Chain of Command during the Battle of
Southern Honan (Early January, 1940)

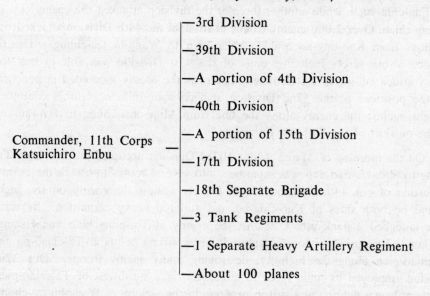

Commander, 11th Corps
Katsuichiro Enbu

—3rd Division

—39th Division

—A portion of 4th Division

—40th Division

—A portion of 15th Division

—17th Division

—18th Separate Brigade

—3 Tank Regiments

—1 Separate Heavy Artillery Regiment

—About 100 planes

CHART 39

*Chart Showing Chinese Order of Battle during the Battle of
Southern Honan (Early January, 1940)*

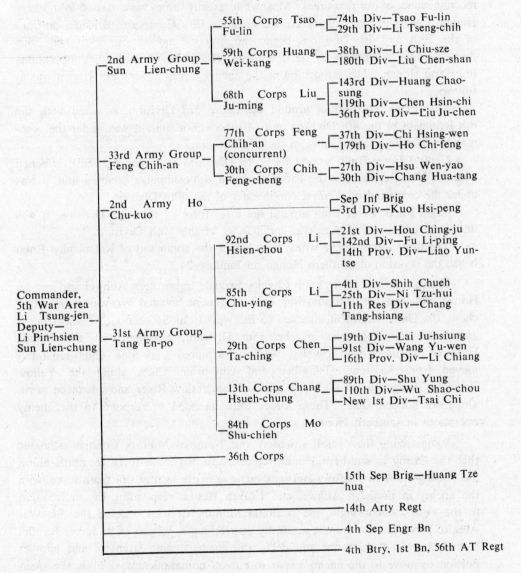

After the operations in central Hupei in November, 1940, enemy forces were
immobilized in the Ching-Hsiang Plains. In late January, 1941, the enemy
massed 7½ infantry divisions, 1 separate cavalry brigade, 3 separate armored
regiments and 1 separate artillery regiment totalling over 150,000 infantry troops,
8,000+ cavalrymen, 550+ guns, 300+ tanks and 200+ armored cars. In addi-

tion, 100+ planes were massed in An-yang, Hsin-hsiang, Huai-yang and Hsin-yang. Since early January, the enemy began to move ammunition and equipment to Hsin-yang from the lower reaches of the Yangtze River and conducted air reconnaissance of our rear areas. Meanwhile, enemy forces were massed in southern Honan. At noon on January 20, the enemy's 18th Composite Brigade, portions of the 39th and 4th Divisions began the invasion against our 29th and 33rd Army Groups attempting to tie down our forces and facilitate their operations in central Honan. The disposition of the enemy forces in southern Honan was as follows:

Left Flank Force-Built around the entire 3rd Division, attached with the 8th Regiment of the 4th Division and Mizuno armor unit, it was under the command of Hanjima, commander of the 3rd Division.

Central Force-Built around the 17th Division (less one regiment), attached with the 67th Regiment of the 15th Division and Yoshimatsu armored unit, it was under the command of Amaya, commander of the 40th Division.

Right Flank Force-Built around the main force of the 40th Division, it was under the command of Ameaya, commander of the 40th Division.

The three forces above which were under the command of Katsuichiro Enbu began the invasion of southern Honan on January 24.

In addition, the enemy's 4th Cavalry Brigade in northern Anhwei and eastern Honan, attached with Hirabayashi Tank Regiment invaded Wo-yang from Hao-chow, the Ouda Regiment attacked to the west from Suo-chow, and the Uguchi and Kobayashi Regiments of the 35th Division, attached with the Tarada Envineer Regiment and cavalry, artillery, armored and atnk units separately moved from Kaj-feng, Tung-hsu and Chu-hsien Chen along the Yellow River to Chengchow on the north bank of the Yellow River and advanced north along the flooded area. These forces were intended to respond to the enemy operations in southern Honan.

Summarizing the overall situation, our National Military Council estimated that the enemy in southern Honan would mass his main force to north along the Peiping-Hankow Railway and seek decisive battle against our main force, with the enemy in northern Anhwei and eastern Honan responding by an invasion to the west. Accordingly, the National Military Council ordered the 5th War Area to avoid decisive frontal action by dispatching a portion of its forces to offer frontal, sustained resistance and delay the enemy's main strength, and another portion to move to the enemy's rear to cut off communications, while the main force would conduct flank attacks against the enemy and destroy it. In compliance with the above instructions, the 5th War Area deployed only one division in the vicinity of Hsi-ping along the Peiping-Hankow Railway, while the main force lay in hiding on both sides of the enemy's anticipated route of advance, to be disposed in depth and maintain its mobility ready to maneuver to the flanks and rear of the enemy and destroy him should he divide his forces and advance toward Ju-nan, Yen-cheng and Wu-yang.

As a result of adequate disposition, the various forces were able to maneuver themselves into favorable positions, encircle and strike the enemy during the entire operation.

In the morning of January 25, the enemy in southern Honan was divided into 3 routes to make the invasion. Its Left Flank Force was deployed along the line from Hsiao-lin-tien to Ku-cheng and Cha-shan. Its Central Force attacked north from the vicinity of Ming-kang. Its Right Flank Force was deployed between Huai-chiao Chen and Cheng-yang and made a forced crossing of the Huai River for the attack. Meanwhile, the enemy air force also assisted the ground operations by violently bombing our positions. In accordance with our pre-determined plans which called for the aversion of needless sacrifices in the initial phase, our forces employed only small strength to lay ambush and launch flank attacks, while the main force was held in readiness. On January 26, the enemy reached the line from Pi-yang to Kao-yi, Hsing-tien and Chueh-shan. On January 27, as the enemy reached the line from Chun-shui to Sha-ho-tien and Chu-ma-tien, our 13th Corps of the 31st Army Group in the north headed toward the vicinity of Hsiang-ho-kuan and the main force of the 85th Corps toward the viciniay of Shang-tsai to launch an enveloping mobile attack. The 68th Corps of the 11th Army Group attacked the enemy's rear south of Hsiang-ho-kuan, the 55th Corps moved from Tang-ho to Pi-yang, and the 59th Corps of the 33rd Army Group advanced toward Nan-yang. On January 29, our 13th Corps attacked the enemy's Left Flank Force in the vicinity of Chieh-kuan-ting and Hsiao-shih-tien south of Wu-yang, while our 85th Corps attacked the enemy's Right Flank Force in the vicinity of Ju-nan, SE of Shang-tsai. Enemy Central Force moved north along and to the west of the Peiping-Hankow Railway. As our forces had already withdrawn to the north, the enemy failed to trap them. Having been subjected to the attacks of our superior forces, the enemy's two columns on the extreme right and left suffered 3,000+ casualties and the destruction of 6 tanks during operations in the vicinity of Chieh-kuan-ting. On January 31, to save its right and left columns, the enemy readjusted its disposition by having the Central Force make turning movement to the two flanks. A portion of its 15th Division turned right from Sui-ping via Shangtsai, attempting to launch a converging attack with the enemy force moving north from Ju-nan against our 85th Corps. The main force of its 17th Division, divided into two columns, moved from Sui-ping via Hsi-ping for a left turning movement toward Wu-yang. The main force of the enemy's 3rd Division on the left flank and a portion of the 4th Division also headed for Wu-yang attempting to join force with the main strength of the 17th Division for a a converging attack against our 13th Corps in the vicinity of Chieh-kuan-ting and Hsiao-shih-tien. Before the enemy completed the encirclement, our 13th and 85th Corps separately fell back to the area north of Yeh Hsien and the areas between Yen-cheng and Shang-shui, and north of

Sha-ho.   Failing to find our force after the enemy's breakthrough of Wu-yang and Shang-tsai, the enemy turned back.   Meanwhile, our main force in western Honan which was composed of the 59th, 55th and 68th Corps separately moved from Tangho and Pi-yang and the area to the north, to attack the enemy's rear area at Wu-yang.   On January 29, our 84th Corps and guerillas in western Anhwei recovered Cheng-yang and followed through in pursuit.   While trying to trap our main force, the enemy not only failed to mass superior strength at the desired place and exercise complete control of the battlefield, but also was intercepted by our forces, finding himself greatly threatened by our 68th, 55th and 59th Corps.   Bitter fighting against our forces for days exhausted the enemy who became isolated as his liaison in the rear had been cut off.   On the night of February 2, the enemy retreated to the south.   Apart from leaving his remnants in Wu-yang and Pao-an-chai to tie down our 13th Corps, the main force of the enemy's 3rd Division moved from Fangcheng to invade Nan-yang and Chen-ping. Our 13th Corps took advantage of this opportunity to launch the counteroffensive and recovered Pao-an-chai and Wu-yang before pursuing the enemy toward Fang-cheng.   On February 3, the enemy moved south in columns from Ta-shih-chiao and Chen-ping north of Nan-yang to attack Nan-yang which it captured in the night of February 4.   Our 59th Corps fell back from the line along Pai-ho to defend the west bank of Liao-ho west of Nan-yang.   Meanwhile, the main force of our 13th Corps operated in Fang-cheng and attacked the enemy's rear.   Our 55th Corps also advanced along the south flank of Nan-yang.   At dawn on February 6, the 38th Division of our 59th Corps launched the counteroffensive and recaptured Nanyang with the enemy fleeing east toward Tang-ho.

At night on February 2, when the enemy's main force reached Nan-yang, the main force of his 17th Division, portions of his 15th and 4th Divisions had already moved south from Wu-yang via Hsiang-ho-kuan to invade Pi-yang.   The enemy attempted to link up with the enemy force moving east from Nan-yang for a converging attack on our 68th, 55th and 29th Corps. As the enemy force reached the vicinity of Hsiang-ho-kuan, our 68th Corps attacked fiercely and inflicted heavy casualties on the enemy who left large quantities of military supplies behind.   The enemy force was struck by our 29th Corps and suffered still greater casualties as it reached the vicinity of Pi-yang.   Trapped in a siege, a portion of the enemy retreated along the Tang-ho-Pi-yang Highway in the night of February 7, while its main force retreated along the Tung-po-Hsin-yang Highway toward Hsin-yang leaving many bodies behind.   Our 85th Corps moved south and trailed the enemy toward the southeast. Portions of our 13th, 29th, 55th and 59th Corps pursued the enemy toward Hsin-yang and recovered the original positions before the fighting.

In response to the battle in southern Honan when the enemy force there was making an invasion (in the morning of January 25) to the west, the enemy force in northern Anhwei and eastern Honan was divided into 4 columns to invade west.   One column which was composed of the Ouda Regiment of the

21st Division invaded the west from Suchow. Another column which was composed of the 4th Cavalry Brigade, attached with the Hirabayashi Tank Regiment, was divided into 3 routes at Po-chow to invade Wo-yang, Shan-ho-chi and Shuang-chiao in the west and fought bitterly against our cavalry division in the vicinity of Shih-tze-ho and Ni-chiu-chi. The third column which was composed of the Uguchi Regiment of 35th Division moved from Tung-hsu and Chu-hsien Chen to invade the flooded area and fought against Gen. Ho's division. The fourth column which was composed of the Kobayashi Regiment advanced along the Yellow River near the north bank of Cheng-chow for the westward invasion. Meanwhile, in the vicinity of An-yang, enemy air force stepped up its activities by bombing such cities as Chou-chia-kou, Cheng-chow, Yen-cheng, Yeh Hsien, Hsiang-cheng, Wu-yang and Lo-yang and our firstline positions. On January 29, the enemy advanced to the vicinity of San-ta-chi and suffered heavy casualties as a result of our attack. Threatened on the left flank by the enemy in the vicinity of Huai-yang, our two corps fell back to the line from Fu-yang to Tai-ho and Chieh-shou. Later on February 5, enemy's attack led to the fall of Tai-ho and Chieh-shou. In the morning of February 6, as our two corps counterattacked and recovered both Tai-ho and Chieh-shou, the enemy retreated to the northeast.

This battle which began on January 25 and ended on Feb. 10 lasting 17 days, resulted in 9,000+ enemy casualties. When the enemy retreated from Nan-yang, 300+ military vehicles were burned. Our forces captured large quantities of military supplies and suffered less casualties than the enemy.

    c. Battle of Shangkao

    (Mid-March, 1941—Early April, 1941. See Map 25 and Charts 40 and 41)

CHART 40

Chart Showing Japanese Chain of Command during the Battle of Shangkao (Early March, 1941)

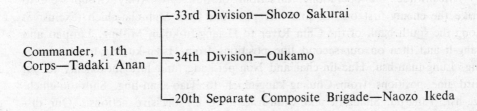

Commander, 11th Corps—Tadaki Anan
- 33rd Division—Shozo Sakurai
- 34th Division—Oukamo
- 20th Separate Composite Brigade—Naozo Ikeda

CHART 41

Chart Showing Chinese Order of Battle during the Battle of Shangkao

Dep Comdr, 9th War Area and concurrently C-in-C, 19th Army Group Lo Cho-ying Dep C-in-C Liu Ying-ku

49th Corps Liu Tuo-chuan
- 26th Division—Wang Ke-chun
- 105th Division—Wang Tieh-han
- 5th Res Division—Tseng Yu-chu

70th Corps Li Chueh
- 19th Division—Tang Ying-po
- 107th Division—Sung Ying-chung
- 9th Res Division—Chang Ying-chung

72nd Corps Han Chuan-pu
- New 14th Division—Chen Liang-chi
- New 15th Division—Fu Yi

74th Corps Wang Yao-wu
- 51st Division—Li Tien-hsia
- 57th Division—Yu Cheng-wan
- 58th Division—Liao Ling-chi

2nd Advance Column—Kang Ching-lien

Since its defeat at the First Battle of Chang-sha, the enemy in Hunan and Kiangsi was in a state of stalemate against our forces. Our forces took advantage of this opportunity to undergo reorganization and training and increase their combat effectiveness. In early March, 1941, the enemy ordered his 14th Separate Brigade to take over the defense from both banks of the Kan River to Juo-hsi in order to crush our field forces and impede our preparations for the counter-offensive. His main force was pulled out and divided into the Southern, Central and Northern Route Forces. The Northern Route Force was composed of the main force of the 33rd Division and was massed in the vicinity of An-yi and Kan-chou-chieh. The Central Route Force which was composed of the 34th Division was massed in the vicinity of Hsi-shan and Wan-shou-kung. The Southern Route Force which was composed of the 20th Separate Composite Brigade was massed north of Shih-cha-chieh in the vicinity of Hou-tien-chieh ready to make a converging attack on Shang-kao and crush our field forces.

Meanwhile, the operational directions of our 19th Army Group were to strike the enemy first on our first line positions from Shih-cha-chieh (exclusive) along the south bank of the Chin River to Hsiang-fu-kuan, Mi-ling, Lai-pao and Tang-li and then on our second line positions from Hsien-ku-ling to Lao-keng-ling, Lung-tuan-hsu, Hua-lin-chai and Nan-pei-kang, and lure the enemy to our third line positions from Chuang-kang-chieh to Tiao-shan-ling, Shih-tou-chieh, Sze-hsi, Tang-pu, Shang-fu and Chiu-hsien-tang for decisive actions. Our disposition called for the 49th Corps to defend the line from Lo-she-tu, Liang-chia-tu and crossing the Fu River to Yeh-tze-shan and Shih-cha-chieh; the 70th Corps from Shih-cha-chieh exclusive along the Chin River to Shih-tou-kang, Ta-cheng, Chih-tien-chang, Feng-hsin to Ching-an; the 74th Corps to be located by Ying-kang-ling, Szehsi and Tang-pu for reorganization and training; the 78th Corps to garrison Wu-ning, Kuan-tsai-shan and Ta-chia-ho; and the 72nd Corps to employ a portion of its forces for the garrison of Yen-hsia, Heng-shih-tan, and Pao-shih-kuan, and its main force in mobile readiness at San-tu and Liao-tien.

At dawn on March 15, the enemy in the north route at An-yi attacked Feng-hsin, took it by noon and continued the westward advance. Our 70th Corps made use of the highground on both banks of the Liao River to offer gradual resistance and lure the enemy. By March 18 and 19, the enemy was lured to Ku-chu-ao and Hua-men-lo, intercepted and pursued by one of our forces. The enemy suffered 2,500+ casualties, while our forces also suffered heavy losses. By March 19, the enemy's 33rd Division was forced to turn back to An-yi from the vicinity of Shang-fu-tsun along the Liao River.

At noon on March 15, the enemy in the south route launched the attack, where the Kan River and the Chin River met and was repulsed. At night, after succeeding in the forced crossing, the enemy moved from the area north of Tu-cheng for a westward invasion along the south bank of the Chin River. The resistance offered by our 107th Division and a portion of the 51st Division stopped the enemy along the line from Lai-chun-ling to Chu-tou-shan. On the night of March 20, the main force of the enemy's 20th Separate Composite Brigade crossed the Chin River via Hui-fu to link up with the enemy's Central Force. A portion of the enemy force was stopped and destroyed by our forces.

On March 16, the enemy's 34th Division of the Central Route Force advanced toward Kao-an along the Hunan-Kiangsi Highway for the westward invasion. The division attempted to coordinate with the South and North Route Forces for the defeat of our 70th Corps and laid siege to our 74th Corps defending the third line positions on the Hunan-Kiangsi Highway[47] in three columns. In accordance with pre-determined plans, our 74th Corps, dispatched a portion of its force to the area east of the Tang-pu River to delay the enemy advance, and the main force for the defense of the third line positions from Sze-hsi and Kuan-chiao to Tang-pu. Apart from directing the 70th Corps to exert pressure on the enemy's flanks in the south, our forces pulled the 26th Division and the main strength of the 105th Division, 49th Corps on the east bank of the Kan River, to cross the Kan River and engage the enemy south of the Chin River. On the left flank, the 72th Corps was ordered to operate in the vicinity of Ta-hsia and south of Kan-fang to respond to the operations. On March 20, the enemy attacked our positions at Sze-hsi and Kuan-chiao. Apart from leaving behind a force for security on the south bank of the Chin River, the main force of 20th Composite Brigade crossed the Chin River to link up with the Central Route Force in attacking our positions. The enemy hoped to penetrate our positions by means of conical attack so as to exploit the success. On March 21, as the enemy reached the vicinity of Shang-chi-chia, the 57th and 58th Divisions of our

---

[47] Changsha to Nanchang.

74th Corps fought hard to stop the enemy by holding the nucleus positions on the outskirt of Shang-kao at all costs. Enemy remnants on the south bank of Chin River were encircled and destroyed by two divisions of our 49th Corps.

From March 22 to 25, the enemy and our forces were engaged in a bloody battle at Shih-hung-chiao and Pai-mao-shan. Despite enemy air superiority which enabled him to conduct low-altitude bombing in inclement weather, our officers and men fought on gallantly. Key localities changed hands many times. Finally, the enemy was stopped along the line from Shih-hung-chiao to Hsia-po-chiao and Shang-chung. Earlier, after achieving defeat in detail of the enemy of the South and North Route Forces, our forces ordered the various units to move from the north and south to encircle the enemy's Central Route Force. By March 24, our 49th Corps advanced to Yang-kung-hsu and Shih-tou-chieh and continued the advance toward the enemy's rear at Sze-hsi. Our 70th Corps reached Kuan-chiao and Nan-cha-lo, while the New 15th Division of the 72nd Corps reached the southeast of Shui-kou-hsu. At this time, the enemy was trapped in our ring of encirclement which extended approximately 10 li's (one li is about one third of a mile) north to south, and 30 li's east to west. At great risk, the enemy advanced taking full advantage of his air and artillery firepower and attempting to penetrate the positions of our 57th Division on the eastern outskirt of Shang-kao. As our defense works were destroyed, hand-to-hand fighting continued at Nieh-chia and Hsia-po-chiao. The enemy sent plainclothes detachment to harass the outskirt of Shang-kao. Determined to defend the positions at Shang-kao at all costs, our 74th Corps destroyed the enemy plainclothes detachment on the outskirt of Shang-kao. Our various corps gradually tightened our ring of encirclement destroying many enemy troops who were trapped in our sea of fire. A portion of the enemy forces succeeded in breaking out to the east, but were intercepted by a division of our 49th Corps in the vicinity of Hui-fu. With half of the force destroyed, the enemy was compelled to turn back. On March 25, the enemy's 215th Regiment which was the reinforcement from the North Route Force rushed to Kuan-chiao and Tang-pu from Wu-chiao-ho via Tsun-chien-chieh. Meanwhile, the enemy's 34th Division, encircled in the area NE of Shang-kao, broke out to the northeast. The encirclement line of our 70th Corps was forced to yield making it possible for the enemy forces of the two routes to link up in the vicinity of Kuan-chiao. At night, Gen. Lo Cho-ying, commander-in-chief of the 19th Army Group, took swift actions to effect a second encirclement of the enemy forces which had linked up, and continued the violent attack. On March 26, our 74th Corps took Sze-hsi and pressed the enemy near Kuan-chiao and South Cha-lo in conjunction with the 19th Division and the 72nd Corps. In the night of March 26, the enemy launched counterattacks aginst the boundary of our 107th and New 15th Divisions greatly shaking our positions and affecting our destruction of the enemy. In the night of March 27, enemy remnants fled to the east. At the key localities of Tsun-chien-chieh, Yang-kung-hsu, Lung-tuan-hsu and Kao-an and in the vicinity of highways, our forces laid ambush to attack and kill many enemy troops. On March 28, our 74th Corps took Kuan-chiao forcing enemy remnants to flee to the east. Later, the enemy remnants were intercepted by our 105th Division at Lung-tuan-hsu and the 26th Division in the vicinity of Yang-kung-hsu. The fighting was most intense. After wiping out the enemy remnants at Lung-tuan-hsu, Yang-kung-hsu and Tsun-chien-chieh, our 49th Corps (less 5th Reserve Division), attached with the New 15th Division, moved along the Hunan-Kiangsi Highway via Kao-an to continue the pursuit to Ta-cheng and Niu-hsing. The 70th Corps led the pursuit to Feng-hsin and Wan-chia-fu via Tsun-chien-chieh and Wu-chiao-ho. Our 49th Corps recovered Kao-an and Hsiang-fu-kuan on April 1 and Hsi-shan. Wan-shou-kung and Chih-tu-chieh on April 2. The 70th Corps recovered Tsun-chien-chieh on March 31 and Feng-hsin on April 2. Later on April 8 and 9, it recovered the strong points on the outskirt of An-yi and then halted the attack.

During this battle, the enemy committed two and half divisions. The attack began on March 15 and ended on April 2 lasting 19 days and nights. Our forces first repelled the enemy's 33rd Division of its North Route Force and then timely formed a ring of encirclement around the enemy's main force which consisted of the 34th Division and the 20th Separate Brigade, dealing a fatal blow against the enemy. 15,000 enemy troops including Maj. Gen Iwanaka became casualties, and 10 guns and 1000+ rifles and machine guns were captured. This battle marked the first unprecedented tactical victory in the first four years of the War of Resistance and reflected the increasing combat effectiveness of the Chinese Armed Forces.

    d. Battle of Southern Shansi
       (Early May—Early June, 1941. See Map 26 and Charts 42 and 43)

CHART 42

Chart Showing Japanese Chain of Command during the Battle of Southern Shansi (Early May, 1941)

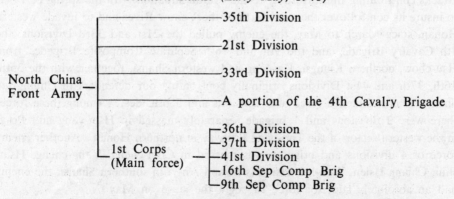

Remarks: 1. The enemy's 3rd Air Force assisted in this battle.
        2. The Japanese named this battle the Battle of Chung-yuan.

CHART 43

Chart Showing Chinese Order of Battle during the Battle of
Southern Shansi (Early May, 1941)

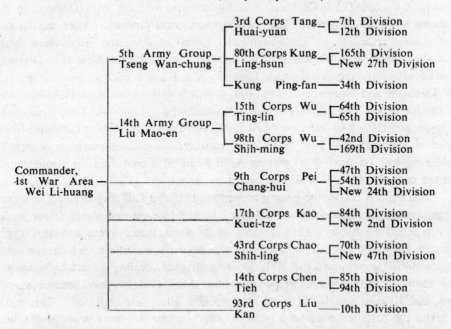

Remarks: The 43rd Corps was formerly in the order of battle of the 2nd War Area.

As Chung-tiao Shan is connected with Tai-hang Shan in the northeast and Lu-liang Shan in northwest, it dominates northern Honan and southen Shansi, screens Lo-yang and Tung-kuan, and forms a key locality on the north bank of the Yellow River. Since 1938, our 1st and 2nd War Areas joined force to defend Chung-tiao Shan and repeatedly repulsed the enemy's enveloping attacks contributing immeasurably to the overall situation. In the spring of 1941, to insure its control over the area north of the Yellow River and to invade western Honan, since March to May, the enemy pulled the 21st and 33rd Divisions, the 4th Cavalry Brigade, and the 9th and 16th Separate Composite Brigades from Hsu-chow, northern Kiangsi, Kai-feng and western Shansi, together with the 35th, 36th, 37th and 41st Divisions originally confronting our defenders in Chung-tiao Shan, and constituted a force of 6 divisions and 3 brigades. Among these forces there were 2 divisions and 1 brigade separately massed in Hsin-yang and Po-ai in the western sector of the Tao-tsing Railway in northern Honan. Another enemy force of 4 divisions and brigades was massed in Chin-cheng, Yang-cheng, Hsin-shui, Chiang Hsien, Wen-hsi, Hsia Hsien and An-yi in southern Shansi, the enemy had an absolutely superior force to begin the siege on May 7.

With the objective of insuring the defense of the strategic localities in southern Shansi, our 1st War Area deployed its main strength (9th, 15th, 98th, 43rd, 17th,

3rd and 80th Corps) in the Chung-tiao Shan area which was 170 km. wide and 50 km. deep. In took advantage of the precipitous mountain passes in the front, the fast-flowing Yellow River in the rear and the well-fortified defense works to stop the enemy advance. A portion of our forces moved stealthily to the vicinity of the enemy strong points to launch surprise and lay ambushes in order to delay the enemy movement, increase enemy attrition and frustrate his offensive. Meanwhile, our various corps in Ta-hang and Lu-liang Shan areas were to respond to our operations and strike a heavy blow against the enemy.

Beginning on May 7, enemy forces on the outside of Chung-tiao Shan began the attack from the north, east and west.

On the afternoon of May 7, the enemy's 35th Division at Chin-yang and Po-ai on the western section of Tao-tsing Railroad in northern Ho-nan, 21st Division and a portion of the 4th Cavalry Brigade moved in two routes to attack Meng Hsien and Tsi-yuan. The enemy's indiscriminate bombing led to heavy losses on our 9th Corps. At noon on May 8, the corps abandoned Meng Hsien and Tsi-yuan and withdrew to prepared positions at Feng-men-kou. Then enemy poured additional reinforcements in the violent attack. The bitter fighting began on the morning of May 9 and ended on the morning of May 10. Later, as our positions at Feng-men-kou and Lung-wan-wo were captured by the enemy, our forces withdrew to both sides of the Tsi-yuan-Yuan-chu Highway for a converging attack on the enemy. The fighting continued until May 11. As our defense on the south bank of the Yellow River was weak, the 9th Corps was ordered to dispatch the 47th Division and a portion of the 42nd Division for a southward crossing of the Yellow River at Kuang-kou. The remainder was left in the area north of the western sector of the Tao-tsing Railway and Tsi-yuan mountain area for guerilla operations. On the morning of May 12, a portion of the enemy forces moved west via Hung-yang and Mao-tien to blockade the river crossing sites along the Yellow River, while his main force moved west along Feng-men-kou to the vicinity of Shao-yuan in order to link up with the enemy force moving east from Yuan-chu.

In the afternoon of May 7, the main force of the enemy's 33rd Division at Yang-cheng in southern Shansi attacked our 98th Corps along the line cast and west of Tung-feng. Despite heavy fighting which lasted until May 12, our positions remained intact. The enemy committed one battalion to invade Hsuehshan southeast of Tung-feng and failed as the battalion was wiped out. On May 13, the enemy poured in additional reinforcements to launch a counterattack and captured Tung-feng. Our forces gradually fell back to the area southeast of Heng-ho Chen.

Adopting the tactics of central breakthrough, the enemy's 41st Division and 9th Separate Brigade at Chiang Hsien and Heng-ling-kuan in southern Shansi moved toward Yuan-chu, and launched a violent attack against the west flank of the Heng-Kao Highway on the afternoon of May 7. Fighting bitterly against the enemy until 0200 hours, May 8, our 43rd Corps was penetrated in the center. Despite several counterattacks, our forces were unable to recover the lost positions.

Later, our forces were compelled to fall back to the vicinity of Wan-hsien-chuang. At dusk on May 8, as Yuanchu fell, our forces withdrew to the area on both sides of Yuan-chu. Meanwhile, our forces in Chungtiao Shan were cut into two. With communications cut, our forces were unable to achieve coordinated shifting of the offensive. On May 9 and 10, the enemy force was divided into columns to move to the east and west. On May 12, the enemy column moving to the east reached Shao-yun to link up with the enemy moving to the west from Tsi-yuan. On May 11, the enemy moving to the west took Wu-fu-chien and gained control of the river crossing sites on the north bank of the Yellow River.

At 1600 hours on May 7, the main force of the enemy's 36th Division, and portions of the 37th Division and 16th Separate Brigade at southeast of Wen-hsi and Hsia-hsien in southern Shan-hsi, launched a violent attack against our forces east of Chang-tien-chen. Heavy fighting continued until dusk when the boundary of our 3rd Corps and 80th Corps were penetrated. Our forces fell back to the line from Sze-chiao River to Wang-yuan to continue the resistance. By the afternoon of May 9, the enemy offensive was intensified and our forces were forced back to defend Tai-chai-tsun to continue the fight. Division commander Wang Chun, assistant division commander Liang Hsi-hsien and chief of staff Chen Wen-szu of the New 27th Division gave their lives to the country.

Since May 12, our 5th and 14th Army Groups fought bitterly against superior enemy forces in the various mountain passes of Chung-tiao Shan. Various units had to conduct independent operations. In view of the inadequate supply in the mountains, the 1st War Area directed the corps to leave a force in Chung-tiao Shan to continue the resistance and the main force to attack the enemy's rear area. On May 13, the main forces of our corps began to break out. On May 18, 19 and 20, our 93rd and 17th Corps separately reached Chi-shan and Hsiang-ning, two divisions of the 98th Corps reached north of Hsin-shui, and the 15th Corps reached the area north of Tsi-yuan. With the response of the 13th and 27th Corps, our forces linked up with the 43rd Corps in a converging attack which frustrated the enemy offensive. By May 27, the operations ended. Readjusting the disposition of our forces in Chung-tiao Shan by shifting them to Tai-hang Shan and Lu-liang Shan, the 1st War Area established guerilla bases ready for the counteroffensive.

During this battle, as the enemy succeeded in pulling and shifting his forces to form absolute local superiority, he was able to score swift, tactical victories. Should the enemy use the same method and gradually lay siege in zones, our forces would find the situation most difficult to handle. However, the enemy did not learn the lesson of this battle. As hostilities between Germany and Soviet Russia broke out, the enemy poured additional forces into Manchuria, moved into Saigon and increased his pressure on China. He was prepared to speculate; however, he was indecisive and his forces were scattered. Since the enemy would not give up an inch of the ground that it gained in the China theater, his did not pull its forces for redeployment to seek local superiority. With inadequate forces to conduct indecisive operations, the enemy invited final defeat.

With the main force in Chung-tian Shan, our 1st War Area, with the enemy and the Chinese Communists in the front and the Yellow River in the rear, found it difficult to maintain mobility, and suffered heavy losses. In October, the enemy forced the crossing of the Yellow River and took Chung-mou and the bridgehead of the Yellow River Bridge. Thus, our defense along the Yellow River showed a major weakness. As our isolated force in Tai-hang Shan could not last long, the Chinese Communists were able to wrest superiority in the Japanese-occupied areas. This led to many deep ramifications later.

e. Second Battle of Chang-sha

(Early September—Early October, 1941. See Map 27 and Charts 44 and 45)

CHART 44

Chart Showing Japanese Chain of Command during the Second Battle of Changsha (Mid-August, 1941)

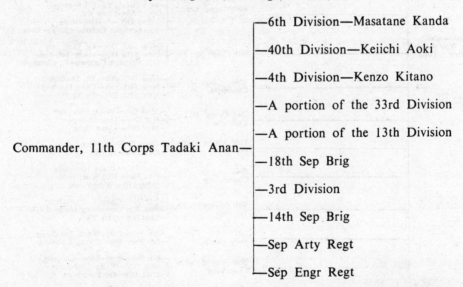

Commander, 11th Corps Tadaki Anan—
—6th Division—Masatane Kanda
—40th Division—Keiichi Aoki
—4th Division—Kenzo Kitano
—A portion of the 33rd Division
—A portion of the 13th Division
—18th Sep Brig
—3rd Division
—14th Sep Brig
—Sep Arty Regt
—Sep Engr Regt

After the fighting in Chung-taio Shan in May, 1941, there had been no major actions in the various theaters. By early June, when the war between Germany and Russia broke out, Japan sent reinforcements to Manchuria in early and mid-July ready for her venture to the north. In late July, she took the southern part of Indo-China ready for her venture to the south and stepped up her war efforts against China. In August, she conducted massive bombings of China's cities and factories in the rear areas and launched the Second Battle of Chang-sha attempting to destroy China's capability for the counteroffensive and relieve herself of worries when she moved south.

CHART 45

Chart Showing Chinese Order of Battle during the Second Battle of Changsha
(Late August, 1941)

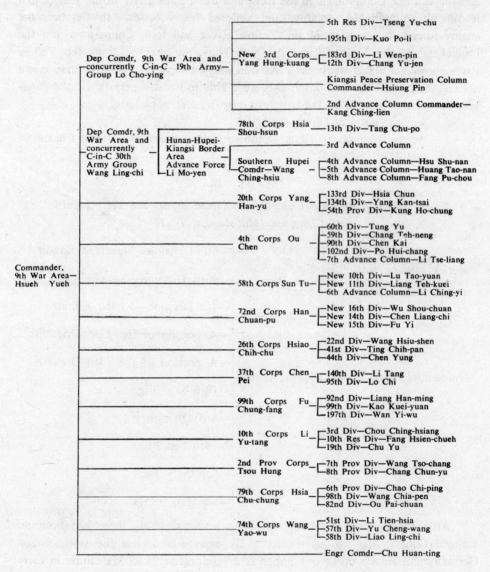

Commander,
9th War Area—
Hsueh   Yueh

Dep Comdr, 9th War Area and concurrently C-in-C 19th Army-Group Lo Cho-ying

New 3rd Corps Yang Hung-kuang

5th Res Div—Tseng Yu-chu
195th Div—Kuo Po-li
183rd Div—Li Wen-pin
12th Div—Chang Yu-jen
Kiangsi Peace Preservation Column Commander—Hsiung Pin
2nd Advance Column Commander—Kang Ching-lien

Dep Comdr, 9th War Area and concurrently C-in-C 30th Army Group Wang Ling-chi

Hunan-Hupei-Kiangsi Border Area Advance Force Li Mo-yen

78th Corps Hsia Shou-hsun
13th Div—Tang Chu-po
3rd Advance Column

Southern Hupei Comdr—Wang Ching-hsiu
4th Advance Column—Hsu Shu-nan
5th Advance Column—Huang Tao-nan
8th Advance Column—Fang Pu-chou

20th Corps Yang Han-yu
133rd Div—Hsia Chun
134th Div—Yang Kan-tsai
54th Prov Div—Kung Ho-chung

4th Corps Ou Chen
60th Div—Tung Yu
59th Div—Chang Teh-neng
90th Div—Chen Kai
102nd Div—Po Hui-chang
7th Advance Column—Li Tse-liang

58th Corps Sun Tu
New 10th Div—Lu Tao-yuan
New 11th Div—Liang Teh-kuei
6th Advance Column—Li Ching-yi

72nd Corps Han Chuan-pu
New 16th Div—Wu Shou-chuan
New 14th Div—Chen Liang-chi
New 15th Div—Fu Yi

26th Corps Hsiao Chih-chu
22nd Div—Wang Hsiu-shen
41st Div—Ting Chih-pan
44th Div—Chen Yung

37th Corps Chen Pei
140th Div—Li Tang
95th Div—Lo Chi

99th Corps Fu Chung-fang
92nd Div—Liang Han-ming
99th Div—Kao Kuei-yuan
197th Div—Wan Yi-wu

10th Corps Li Yu-tang
3rd Div—Chou Ching-hsiang
10th Res Div—Fang Hsien-chueh
19th Div—Chu Yu

2nd Prov Corps Tsou Hung
7th Prov Div—Wang Tso-chang
8th Prov Div—Chang Chun-yu

79th Corps Hsia Chu-chung
6th Prov Div—Chao Chi-ping
98th Div—Wang Chia-pen
82nd Div—Ou Pai-chuan

74th Corps Wang Yao-wu
51st Div—Li Tien-hsia
57th Div—Yu Cheng-wang
58th Div—Liao Ling-chi

Engr Comdr—Chu Huan-ting

Since mid-August, the enemy secretly pulled the 3rd and 4th Divisions, the 116th Regiment of the 13th Division, three battalions of the 18th Separate Brigade, a portion of the 33rd Division in northern Kiangsi, three battalions of the 14th Separate Brigade, and two separate artillery and engineer regiments to mass in Lin-hsiang and Yueh-yang. These forces together the 6th Division formerly garrisoning northern Hupei and the 40th Division (less 235th Regiment) formerly garrisoning southern Hupei, 20+ ships, 200+ motorboats, and 100+ planes, gave a total strength of over 120,000 men under the command of Tadaki Anan, commander of the 11th Corps, with 100,000+ local forced laborers, ready to invade Chang-sha for the second time.

Generalissimo Chiang ordered our 3rd, 5th and 6th War Areas to attack and tie down the enemy. In accordance with pre-determined plans, the 9th War Area deployed its main force between the area south of the Hsin-chiang River and Chang-sha and made use of prepared positions to offer gradual resistance and lure the enemy's main force to the bank of Lao-tao River. Our main force was timely shifted to the area between Ping-chiang, Liu-yang, and Chu-chow to attack the enemy's flank and rear and destroy the enemy.

Before the battle began, the disposition of our 9th War Area was as follows:

(1) The 19th Army Group garrisoned the line in the vicinity of Liang-chia-tu, Shih-tou-kang and Ching-an. The 74th Corps massed in the vicinity of Hsin-yu and Fen-yi for reorganization and training.

(2) The 30th Army Group garrisoned the line from Wu-ning to Chiu-kung-shan. The 72nd Corps massed in the vicinity of San-tu for reorganization and training.

(3) The 20th Corps of the 27th Army Grop garrisoned the line from Yang-ku-lin to Tung-cheng. Its 134th Division massed in Tao-shu-kang for reorganization and training.

The 58th Corps garrisoned the line from Chiu-ling to Huang-an-shih. Its New 10th Division massed in Shang-ta-shih for reorganization and training.

The 4th Corps garrisoned the south bank of Hsin-chiang River and along the Hsiang River from Lou-chiao to Lei-shih-shan, and Ta-yu-shan advanced positions. Its 59th Division massed in Kuan-wang-chiao for reorganization and training.

(4) The 99th Division, 99th Corps garrisoned the line from Kuei-yi to Ying-tien and Hsiang-yin. The 92nd Division massed in the vicinity of Shang-pin-shih for reorganization and training.

The 37th Corps massed in the vicinity of Chang-lo-chieh and Weng-chiang for reorganization and training.

The 26th Corps massed in the vicinity of Liu-yang and Chin-ching for reorganization and training.

The 10th Corps massed in the vicinity of Heng-shan for reorganization and training.

On September 7, 1941, to cover the massing and the deploymant of its main force, the enemy employed two regiments of the 6th Division to attack Ta-yun-shan from Chung-fang and Hsi-tang. The main force of our 4th Corps and the 58th Corps repelled the invaders. However, the fighting in the vicinity of Kang-kou on the southwest side of Ta-yun Shan became intense on September 16. Meanwhile, 20+ enemy ships and 3 battalions of the enemy's 14th Separate Brigade and marines sailing in 200+ motor boats and several hundred junks were active near Shang-hsia-ching-shan at the Tung-ting Lake threatening western Hunan.

At dawn on September 17, the enemy main force separately made forced crossing of the Hsin-chiang River at Kang-kou, Hsi-lu-fang, Tung-hsi-chieh and Hsin-chiang-shih. A portion of our 4th Corps offered sustained resistance, while the main force of the corps joined force with the 58th and 20th Corps to be deployed along the line from Yang-lin-chieh to Pu-hsien-chiao and Hung-yuan-tung and attack the enemy flanks and rear. On September 19, the enemy reached the bank of the Mi-lo River. On September 20, the enemy made a forced crossing of the Mi-lo River at Huang-tang, Wu-kou, Chang-lo-chieh, Wu-kung-shih, Hsin-shih, Lo-kung-chiao and Kuei-yi. The attacks launched by our defenders, the 37th Corps and reinforcements, the 10th and 26th Corps and 92nd Division, inflicted heavy losses on the enemy. On September 21, a portion of the enemy force moved via San-chiao-tang east of Weng-chiang to make a turning movement against our right flank and then headed toward Chin-ching. Meanwhile, the enemy on our front attacked our main positions at Fu-lin-pu, Lo-chiao and San-chieh-chiao. After offering gradual resistance, our forces fell back to the areas near Lao-tao River and Liu-yang River to lure the enemy and seek decisive battle. By the morning of September 26, the enemy's right force made a turning movement from San-shih-chieh to the southeast of Chang-sha. Another enemy force made a turning movement from Chun-hua Shan to the east of Chang-sha, while the main force launched a violent attack on Chang-sha. Our forces offered strong resistance. At 1600 hours on September 27, enemy plainclothes detachment entered the city of Chang-sha, and another fast-moving unit and plainclothes detachment moved to Chu-chow via Tu-tou-shih. Meanwhile, enemy airborne troops having landed in the rear of our firstline positions were wiped out. At this time, our 4th, 20th, 58th, 72nd, 26th, 74th, 37th, 10th, 2nd Provisional, and 79th Corps which had arrived at the battlefield were successively committed. Despite heavy casualties on both sides, our forces succeeded in encircling the enemy between the Lao-tao River and the Liu-yang River. In response to the operations in Chang-sha, our 3rd, 5th and 6th War Areas launched extensive offensives against the enemy rendering him incapable of shifting his forces. Although heavy losses were sustained, the attack on I-chang by the 6th War Area greatly threatened the enemy. As the enemy's lines of communications to the rear were cut off by our 4th, 20th, and 58th Corps, his supply situation became most difficult. At 1600 hours on September 30, enemy forces began to break out to the north. Our 79th Corps pursued the enemy toward Chang-lo-chieh and Hsin-shih, while the 72nd Corps and 58th Corps raced to intercept the enemy at Yang-lin-chieh and Kuan-wan-chiao respectively. The main strength of our 4th, 20th and 99th Corps intercepted the enemy at Chin-ching, Ma-feng-tsu, Ching-shan-shih and Ma-an-pu. Our 26th, 74th and 2nd Provisional Corps mopped up the battlefield between Liu-yang River and Lao-tao River. Our pursuit forces crossed Mi-lo River on October 5 and Hsin-chang River on October 8. Our 4th, 20th, 58th and 72nd Corps separately attacked the enemy at Yang-lo-sze and Lin-yueh. Greatly threatened in the rear, the enemy fell back to his original positions. Thus, our foces scored a major victory in the Second Battle of Chang-sha.

During this battle, over 40,000 enemy troops were casulties, and 1,347 rifles, 38 machine guns, 6 field guns, 9 infantry guns, 871 mules and horses, 8 armored cars and 269 men were captured. 3 enemy planes were shot down and 7 enemy motor boats were sunk. In addition, large quantities of supplies were captured.

In view of the failure of his grand encirclement strategy during the First Battle of Chang-sha, the enemy switched to frontal attack in this battle. He made use of such tactics as gap penetration, infiltration, and partial encirclement to rush to Chang-sha. However, the enemy did not pull large forces from other theaters. As his 11th Corps did not have sufficient strength, his gains did not justify his losses. In mid-October, 1941, Generalissimo Chiang called the Third Nan-yueh Military Conference to review the gains and losses of this battle. At described the way to success and great career for ranking officers:

(1) He hoped that the ranking officers would realize that the key to victory in the War of Resistance lay in the maintenance of our national spirit of righteousness and the development of the traditional spirit of our Revolutionary Army.

(2) He cited Gen. Tseng Kuo-fan of the Ching Dynasty as an example and described the way to success and great career for ranking officers:

(a) Take the initiative, study hard to improve themselves, fear no difficulties and remain firm and loyal.

(b) Seek promising people, improve the staff, and be open-minded in accepting criticism and seeking improvement.

(c) Emphasize moral culture, alertness, constant improvement and performance of duty.

(3) In accordance with operational strategy and the principles of construction of defense works, he stated our weaknesses in the Second Battle of Chang-sha and our future improvements:

(a) Operational strategy—Gain time, seek sustained operations, crush enemy offensive, and destroy the enemy in an opportune moment.

(b) Essence of construction of defense works—Construct defense works in accordance with strength. Begin from the interior to the exterior and from small to large.   Consolidate the nucleus first.

(4) Future employment and deployment of forces in the various war areas:

(a) Strategywise—All bases and key strongpoints constituting major targets to the enemy must be heavily guarded and defended.

(b) Tacticwise—Prior to an estimate of the enemy situation and terrain, mass and control major forces and await the opportunity to attack the enemy.

(5) Points requiring our immediate attention: Such as the strength and utilization of defense works, organization and training of non-infantry units, air defense and gas defense facilities, tightening communication security, implementation of pao-chia interlocking system, straightening marksmanship discipline, improving bayonet training, studying field manuals, and training personnel in street fighting, communication and espionage.

(6) Items requiring our attention in the future: Such items as education, training and management should be improved by means of competition; reception and administration of recruits should be revamped; training measures for the wounded be implemented; and personnel in rear areas are strictly forbidden to violate military discipline, disclose classified military information or engage in smuggling.

(7) Reaffirm Generalissimo Chiang's instructions in previous military conferences in the hope that ranking officers will study and abide by them. Additionally, Generalissimo Chiang gave the following instructions:

(a) Ranking officers should emphasize moral culture.

(b) Use those who are capable, improve staff organizations, and emphasize propaganda in enemy rear areas and espionage.

3. Third Stage Operations

(Outbreak of Pacific War—V-J Day. See Maps 28 and 29)

On December 8, 1941, as the Japanese attacked Pearl Harbor to open the Pacific War, China's War of Resistance entered into a new phase. China moved from fighting the war alone to fighting shoulder to shoulder with her Allies. Her objective was to respond to the operations of the Allies and seek common victory. Accordingly, she launched successively attacks to tie down the enemy and dispatched expeditionary forces to Burma to render direct assistance to the British forces. Later, she did her best to stop the enemy from clearing his lines of communications, destroying our airfields and threatening our wartime capital. Meanwhile, our expeditionary forces were strengthened, the China-India Road cleared and U.S. assistance sought in preparation for the general counteroffensive.

a. Third Battle of Chang-sha

(Late December, 1941—Mid-January, 1942. See Maps 30 and 31, Charts 46 and 47)

CHART 46

Chart Showing the Japanese Chain of Command during the Third Battle of Changsha (Mid-December, 1941)

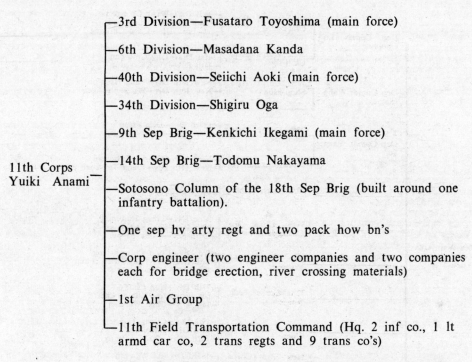

11th Corps
Yuiki Anami

—3rd Division—Fusataro Toyoshima (main force)

—6th Division—Masadana Kanda

—40th Division—Seiichi Aoki (main force)

—34th Division—Shigiru Oga

—9th Sep Brig—Kenkichi Ikegami (main force)

—14th Sep Brig—Todomu Nakayama

—Sotosono Column of the 18th Sep Brig (built around one infantry battalion).

—One sep hv arty regt and two pack how bn's

—Corp engineer (two engineer companies and two companies each for bridge erection, river crossing materials)

—1st Air Group

—11th Field Transportation Command (Hq. 2 inf co., 1 lt armd car co, 2 trans regts and 9 trans co's)

Remarks: 1. The 34th Division and 14th Sep Brig along the Nanhsun Railway each pulled one battalion for employment in northern Hunan.

2. The 13th and 19th Divisions, one brigade of the 3rd Division, and the main force of the 8th Sep Brig operated in northern Hupei.

CHART 47

Chart Showing Chinese Order of Battle during the Third Battle of Changsha (Mid-December, 1941)

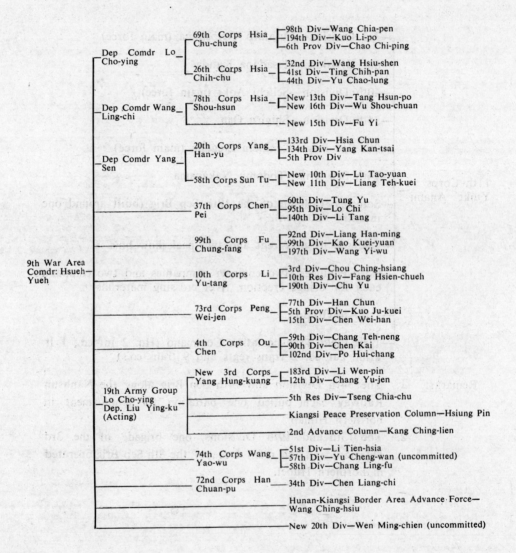

9th War Area Comdr: Hsueh-Yueh

Dep Comdr Lo Cho-ying

- 69th Corps Hsia Chu-chung
  - 98th Div—Wang Chia-pen
  - 194th Div—Kuo Li-po
  - 6th Prov Div—Chao Chi-ping
- 26th Corps Hsia Chih-chu
  - 32nd Div—Wang Hsiu-shen
  - 41st Div—Ting Chih-pan
  - 44th Div—Yu Chao-lung

Dep Comdr Wang Ling-chi

- 78th Corps Hsia Shou-hsun
  - New 13th Div—Tang Hsun-po
  - New 16th Div—Wu Shou-chuan
- New 15th Div—Fu Yi

Dep Comdr Yang Sen

- 20th Corps Yang Han-yu
  - 133rd Div—Hsia Chun
  - 134th Div—Yang Kan-tsai
  - 5th Prov Div
- 58th Corps Sun Tu
  - New 10th Div—Lu Tao-yuan
  - New 11th Div—Liang Teh-kuei

- 37th Corps Chen Pei
  - 60th Div—Tung Yu
  - 95th Div—Lo Chi
  - 140th Div—Li Tang
- 99th Corps Fu Chung-fang
  - 92nd Div—Liang Han-ming
  - 99th Div—Kao Kuei-yuan
  - 197th Div—Wang Yi-wu
- 10th Corps Li Yu-tang
  - 3rd Div—Chou Ching-hsiang
  - 10th Res Div—Fang Hsien-chueh
  - 190th Div—Chu Yu
- 73rd Corps Peng Wei-jen
  - 77th Div—Han Chun
  - 5th Prov Div—Kuo Ju-kuei
  - 15th Div—Chen Wei-han
- 4th Corps Ou Chen
  - 59th Div—Chang Teh-neng
  - 90th Div—Chen Kai
  - 102nd Div—Po Hui-chang

19th Army Group Lo Cho-ying Dep. Liu Ying-ku (Acting)

- New 3rd Corps Yang Hung-kuang
  - 183rd Div—Li Wen-pin
  - 12th Div—Chang Yu-jen
- 5th Res Div—Tseng Chia-chu
- Kiangsi Peace Preservation Column—Hsiung Pin
- 2nd Advance Column—Kang Ching-lien
- 74th Corps Wang Yao-wu
  - 51st Div—Li Tien-hsia
  - 57th Div—Yu Cheng-wan (uncommitted)
  - 58th Div—Chang Ling-fu
- 72nd Corps Han Chuan-pu — 34th Div—Chen Liang-chi
- Hunan-Kiangsi Border Area Advance Force—Wang Ching-hsiu
- New 20th Div—Wen Ming-chien (uncommitted)

With the outbreak of the Pacific War on December 8, 1941, Generalissimo Chiang directed the various war areas to conduct all-out guerilla warfare on December 9 and designated units to take turns in attacking and checking the enemy. The 4th War Area was directed to attack the enemy in Canton and respond to the operations of the British Forces in Hong Kong. The 5th, 6th, and 66th Corps were shifted from Kwangsi and Szechuan to Yunnan ready to enter Burma. The 4th and 74th Corps moved from Hunan to reinforce Kwangtung and Kwangsi.

In mid-December, to stop our forces from reinforcing Hong Kong, Kowloon and Burma, the enemy's 11th Corps launched the Third Battle of Chang-sha. Its dispostion was as follows:

The 6th Division massed on the right bank of the lower reaches of the Hsin-chiang River on December 20 ready to cross the river for the attack.

The main force of the 40th Division massed in the area east of Keng-kou on December 21 ready to attack our forces.

The main force of the 3rd Division massed in the vicinity of Lung-wan-chiao ready for the attack. Sawa Column (built around one infantry battalion of the 14th Separate Brigade) massed at Yueh-yang by December 24.

The GHQ of the enemy's Expeditionary Forces pulled the 9th Separate Brigade from North China to be subordinated to the 11th Corps. The 1st Air Force assisted in the operations of the 11th Corps.

During the initial phase of the battle, the 11th Corps ordered the 34th Division and the 14th Separate Brigade to attack from the Nan-Hsun Railroad in response to the operations of the main force in northern Hunan. The enemy's forces on the north bank of the Yangtze River, having completed combat readiness stopped our forces in the counteroffensive. During the final phase of the battle, the Sotosono Column (built around one infantry battalion of the 18th Separate Brigade) and the Nokuchi Column (built around one infantry battalion of the 34th Division) reinforced northern Hunan to cover the retreat.

Prior to the battle, the disposition of our 9th War Area was as follows:

The 19th Army Group employed the 5th Reserve Division, Kiangsi Peace Preservation Column, New 3rd Corps and 2nd Advance Column to guard the line from Liang-chia-tu to Shih-cha-chieh, Hsiang-fu-kuan, Feng-hsin and Ching-an. The 194th Division was kept in Ching-chiang for reorganization and training.

The 30th Army Group employed the New 13th Division and 34th Division to garrison Wu-ning and Chiu-kung-shan respectively. The remaining forces were held in readiness in the vicinity of San-tu and Hsiu-shui for reorganization and training.

The 27th Army Group employed the 20th Corps to garrison the line from Tou-mi-shan to Mai-shih, Chiu-ling, Fang-shan-tung, Tsao-hsieh-ling, Kan-tien, Yang-lin-chieh, Sze-lu-fang, Tung-hsi-chieh, Hsin-chiang, Lu-chiao, and Lei-shih-shan as well as the advance strong points at Tung-cheng and Pei-kang. The 58th Corps was held in readiness in the vicinity of Huang-an-shih for reorganization and training.

The 37th Corps which was directly subordinated to the 9th War Area garrisoned the strong points at Chang-lo-chieh, Wu-kung-shih and Hsin-shih with its main force in Weng-chiang, Pu-tang, Li-shan-hsiang and Ta-chiao for reorganization and training. The 99th Corps undertook the river and lake garrison of Kuei-yi, Ying-tien, Hsiang-yin, Lu-lin-tan, Lu-hsing-shan, Lin-tze-kou, Yuan-chiang and Han-shou. Its 92nd Division was held in readiness at San-chieh-chiao for reorganization and training. The 26th Corps was held in readiness at Liu-yang, Tung-yang-shih, Pu-chi-shih and Hua-chiao fo rreorganization and training. The 10th Corps garrisoned Chang-sha with its 190th Division held in readiness at Chu-chow and Lou-kou for reorganization and training. The New 20th Division was held in readiness at Heng-yang for reorganization and training.

All the above-mentioned first-line corps dispatched attack forces to attack the enemy, sabotage enemy signal and traffic communications and trains, and collect information.

On December 19, the enemy in northern Hunan began the attack on the advance positions of our 20th Corps on the east bank of Yu-kang River and conducted reconnaissance in force on the south bank of the Hsin-chiang River to cover the massing of its main force. The enemy along the Nan-Hsun Railway also reinforced An-yi and Juo-hsi to respond to the operations of its main force.

On December 20, the 9th War Area estimated that the enemy would invade Chang-sha for the third time. It decided to employ a force to stop the enemy coming from Nan-Hsun Railway, by massing all the forces in northern Hunan and luring the enemy's main force to the area between Liu-yang River and Lao-tao River for envelopment and destruction. The disposition of the 9th War Area was as follows:

Deputy Commander Yang Sen of the 9th War Area was stationed in Ping-chiang directing the 20th and 58th Corps. The first step was to offer strong resistance from prepared strong-point positions, and wear out and delay the enemy. The second step was to stand by for orders to move to flanking positions at Kuan-wang-chiao and San-chiang-kou and attack from the northeast to the southwest and pursue the enemy force which was moving south.

The 37th Corps offered strong resistance from prepared positions on the south bank of the Mi River to wear out and delay the enemy. Later, it would move to the mountainous area between She-kang-shih, Ken-ku-tai and Chin-ching, and coordinate with the 78th Corps in attacking the enemy from the northeast to the southwest when the enemy should attack Chang-sha.

The first step taken by the 99th Corps was to insure the security of the prepared strong point positions at San-chieh-chiao, Luo-kung-chiao, Kuei-yi, Ying-tien and Hsiang-yin and the defense of the south bank of the Tung-ting Lake. The second step was to employ two divisions from the northwest to the southeast to attack the enemy, and one division in lake defense, should the enemy invade Chang-sha.

The 10th Corps would defend Chang-sha, and the prepared strong points at Yueh-lu-shan and Shui-lu-chow. Three days after the enemy's attack on Chang-sha, it moved from the west to the east for the counterattack.

Deputy Commander Lo Cho-ying of the 9th War Area moved from Shang-kao to Liu-yang to direct the operations of the 26th and 79th Corps and the 194th Division. The first step the 26th Corps took was to insure the security of our present positions in Liu-yang. It then counterattacked from the east to the west when the enemy attacked Chang-sha. The 79th Corps moved one division from Heng-yang to Chu-chow, and another force to occupy prepared strong point positions at Tu-tou-shih and Tung-shan. The 194th Division moved from Ching-chiang to Li-ling and counterattacked from the south to the north when enemy attacked Chang-sha.

Deputy Commander Wang Ling-chi of the 9th War Area led the 78th Corps and New 15th Division from Hsiu-shui to Ping-chiang. First of all, the 78th Corps insured the security of Ping-chiang, San-chiao-tang and Chiang-chia-tsun. Then, when the enemy invaded Liu-yang and Chang-sha, it was ready to coordinate with the 37th Corps and move from the northeast to the southwest to attack the enemy's flanks.

The 73rd Corps moved to Ning-hsiang and Yi-yang as the reserves of the war area.

In northern Kiangsi, the war area employed the available forces to defend our positions at Kao-an and Wu-ning, stop the enemy and cover the right flank of the main force in the war area.

On December 23, a portion of the enemy's 40th Division attacked the positions of our 133rd Division at Wang-koting and Mei-shu-tan east of Yu-kang River and was stopped by our forces. On December 24, the enemy's 6th Division attacked the positions of our 134th Division near Hsin-chiang River. By noon, it reached the south bank and captured several strong points. It night, the enemy's main force crossed the river and headed south.

On December 25, our 20th Corps relied on prepared positions on the south-western flank of Ta-yun Shan, and the well-scattered independent strong points south of Hsin-chiang River to offer determined resistance. Our forces and the enemy both suffered heavy losses. The enemy's 40th and 6th Divisions employed their main forces to infiltrate the gaps at Kuan-wang-chiao and Ta-ching-chien, leaving a force to encircle our independent strong points and cover the rear, while the main force of the enemy's 3rd Division closely followed the 6th Division. At night, our 20th Corps received orders to defend the strong points south of the Hsin-chiang River with a force and to move its main force to line from Kuan-wang-chiao, to Chen-chia-chiao, San-chiang-kou and Yang-chiao-ling. Our 58th Corps operated along the line from Ta-ching-tang to Hung-yuan-tung and attacked the flanks of the enemy moving south.

On December 26, the enemy's 40th Division launched a violent attack on the positions of our 20th Corps.   Heavy fighting which lasted all day resulted in the fall of Kuan-wang-chiao and Chen-chia-chiao.   Meanwhile, the enemy's 6th Division surrounded and attacked our strong points at Huang-sha-chieh and Lung-feng-chiao, but our forces held the positions.   In the evening, the main force of the enemy's 3rd Division operated on the north bank of Mi River in the vicinity of Kuei-yi.

On December 27, the main forces of the enemy's 40th and 6th Divisions massed in the vicinity of Chang-lo-chieh and Hsin-shih respectively, ready to cross the Mi River.   The main force of the 3rd Division took our two strong points at Nan-tu and Ho-chia-tang before forcing a crossing of the Mi River.   Operating near Kuan-wang-chiao, the enemy's Sawa Column took over the missions of portions of the 40th and 6th Divisions to cover the flanks of its main force.   Our 9th War Area directed the 20th and 58th Corps of the 27th Army Group, to attack the enemy at Chang-lo-chieh, and the main forces of the 37th and 99th Corps to defend the positions along the Mi River and stop the enemy from crossing the river.

On December 28, the enemy's 40th and 6th Divisions made a forced crossing of the Mi River between Chang-lo-chieh and Hsin-shih and was stopped by our 37th Corps.   The main force of the enemy's 3rd Division crossed the Mi River west of Kuei-yi.   The main force of our 99th Corps was forced to fall back to the lines from Li-chiao to Pai-lou-feng and from Hsin-kai-shih to Ta-niang-chiao to continue the resistance.   The 9th War Area directed the 140th Division to race from Chin-ching to the area north of Hsin-kai-shih and stop the enemy from moving east.

On December 29, the main force of the enemy's 3rd Division swung east from Paishui Station to attack our 140th Division greatly threatening the left the flank of 37th Corps.   The enemy's 40th and 6th Divisions took advantage of this opportunity to erect pontoon bridges east of Chang-lo-chieh and Hsin-shih and cross the Mi River for the southward advance. By night, our 37th Corps held the line from Tan-tou-pu to Yu-chia-tung, Hsiu-shui-hsia, Yen-chia-pu, Wu-kung-shih, Ya-po-chien, Shuang-chiang-kou and Hsin-kai-shih fighting bitterly against the enemy. Along the line from Ta-niang-chiao to Lu-tang-pu, and Ying-tien, the main force of our 99th Corps faced a portion of the enemy's 3rd Division.   On the same day, our 73rd, 74th, and 4th Corps received Generalissimo Chiang's orders to race to Ning-hsiang, Heng-yang, and Chu-chow from Hupei, Kwangsi and Kwangtung.   Our 1st Artillery Brigade (150) mm howitzers) arrived in Yueh-lu-shan from Heng-yang and occupied positions.

On December 30, the enemy's main force launched a general offensive against the positions of our 37th Corps and fought bitterly against the corps for a whole day in the area south of Chang-lo-chieh and east of Shuang-chiang-kou and Hsin-kai-shih. The main force of our 37th Corps moved east to the line from Wu-kou to Ya-chien, Sun-chia-shan, Wang-hu-chien, and Hsia-mo-ling. Its 140th Division moved southwest to Ming-yueh-shan. The enemy's 40th and 6th Divisions continued to attack the positions of our 37th Corps at Ya-chien and Sun-chia-shan. The 3rd Division swung south to Ching-shan-shih and pressed near Chang-sha. Meanwhile, the enemy moved the 9th Brigade from Yueh-yang to Kuan-wang-chiao and directed the Sawa Column to cover the flanks of its forces.

On the same day, Deputy Commanders Lo Cho-ying, Yang Sen and Wang Ling-chi of the 9th War Area led their forces to designated locations near Liu-yang and Ping-chiang ready to attack the enemy flanks. Generalissimo Chiang cabled the following operational instructions:

In fighting a decisive battle in the vicinity of Chang-sha, the 9th War Area should forestall the enemy employment of a portion of its forces to tie down our forces in Chang-sha, and of its main force to press our second-line forces for a decisive engagement before laying siege to Chang-sha. The 9th War Area should place the second-line forces in remote area of the theater and maintain favorable position on the exterior lines so as to insure freedom of maneuver and permit the enemy to attack Chang-sha first. When the enemy attacks are frustrated, every effort will be exerted against the enemy by taking the initiative and grasping every opportunity. In the night of December 30, the 9th War Area directed Deputy Commander Yang Sen to lead the 58th Corps from Chang-lo-chieh via Li-shan-kang-Ching-shan-shih-tao to An-sha. The 20th Corps was directed to move from Ching-shiang-kou-Fu-lin-pu-Wen-chia-hsia-tao to Shih-ase-pu, search and attack the enemy. The first line to reach was San-tuo-chiao-An-sha-Tai-chia-yuan; the second line to reach was Fu-chia-chung-Chou-po-tang. Deputy Commander Wang Ling-chi directed the 37th Corps (less 140th Division) which moved from Weng-chiang via Tuo-chia-tien-Shang-pin-shih Chih-shih-ho-tao to Wang-hsien-chiao. The 78th Corps moved from San-chiao-tang and Keng-ku-tai via Chin-ching-Lu-kou-yu-Chun-hua-shan-Huang-hua-shih-tao to Chang-chiao to search and attack the enemy. The first line to reach was Tai-chia-yuan-Chun-hua-shan-Tung-lin-shih; and the second line to reach was Ta-wan-kang-Chang-chiao. Deputy Commander Lo Cho-ying directed the main force of the 26th Corps which moved from Tung-yang-shih via Yung-an-shih-Yang-feng-pa-tao to Lang-li-shih to search and attack the enemy. A portion of the corps moved from Chiang-hua-chiao via Yung-an-shih to assist in the attack of the main force. The 79th Corps, attached with the 194th Division, employed its main force from Chin-tan via Ma-ying to the south of Huang-hua-shih to search and attack the enemy. Pending the development of the situation, it would swing to Lang-li-shih for the attack. A portion moved from Tu-tou-shih to Tsuo-shan-chiao to search and attack the enemy. Pending the development of the situation, it would swing to Tung-shan for the attack. The 4th Corps employed its main force from Lung-tu-pu via Tiao-ma-chien-Pai-tien-pu, and a portion from Tan-chia-pa via Shui-kou-shan-Hsi-tang-chung to the area south of Chang-sha to search and attack the enemy. The first line for the corps to reach was Tung-lin-shih-Lien-tang-Tsuo-shan-chiao-Feng-shu-ho-Pai-tien-pu-Ta-tuo-pu; the second line was Lang-li-shih-Tung-shan-Chin-pen-ling. The 10th and 73rd Corps defended Chang-sha and Yueh-lu-shan respectively. A portion undertook the garrison of the line from Kuan-yin-kang via Ying-wan-shih to Pai-sha-chow on the west bank of the Hsiang River. When the forces reached the vicinity of the second line, our counteroffensive began. The 197th Division of the 99th Corps held the west bank of the Hsiang River and the south bank of the Tung-ting Lake. The 92nd Division moved from San-chieh-chiao via Chiao-tou-yi and the 140th Division from Li-chiao via Kuan-chiao to Lao-tao River to search and attack the enemy. The first line of objective extended from Chiao-tou-yi on the east bank of Pai-sha-chow to Kuan-chiao; the second line was in the vicinty of Lao-tao-shin. The 99th Division defended the key localities of Shuang-shih-tung, Liu-shi-chiao, Hua-shih-ai, Hsiang-yin and Ying-tien. A powerful force moved from Ming-yueh-shan and Shuang-shih-tung to Li-chiao and Fu-lin-pu to attack the flanks of the enemy forces and cut off the enemy supply routes. The time to launch the attack was stipulated separately.

On the morning of December 31, the enemy's 40th Division fiercely attacked the positions of our 37th Corps at Ya-chien. The heavy fighting lasted until noon when our 37th Corps (less 140th Division) moved to the mountainous area northeast of Chin-ching. The enemy's 40th Division left a portion in the vicinity of Ya-chien, while its main force advanced toward Chin-ching. The enemy's 6th Division advanced toward Lang-li-shih. At night, the 3rd Division made a forced crossing of the Liu-yang River in the vicinity of Mo-pan-chow. As the enemy pressed near the area of decisive engagement, the 9th War Area ordered the various army groups and corps to begin the advance at mid-night on January 1 and reach the first line of objective by the night of January 4.

At dawn on January 1, 1942, the main force of the enemy's 3rd Division began to attack the outlying positions southeast of Chang-sha. Our 10th Reserve Division offered strong resistance and launched counterattacks. After one-day heavy fighting, the division succeeded in repelling the enemy forces which had broken through Tso-chia-tang, Chun-chu-ku and Lin-tse-chung. However, several hundred enemy troops which had broken through Pai-sha-ling fought on stubbornly although they were cornered. At night, Deputy Commander Wang Ling-chi led the 78th Corps from the vicinity of Chih-ma-tien to Chun-hun-shan and ordered the main force of the 37th Corps to advance from the mountainous area northeast of Chin-ching to Chih-shih River via Tuo-chia-chiao.

On January 2, the enemy deployed the 6th Division on the northeastern outskirt of Chang-sha. With the support of the 3rd Air Force, it joined force with the enemy's 3rd Division to attack Chang-sha. A portion of the enemy's 40th Division defended the defile north of Chin-ching, while its main force massed in the vicinity of Chin-ching to protect the flanks. In addition, the enemy ordered the 9th Separate Brigade to mope from the vicinity of Kuan-wang-chiao to Ma-lin-shih. Our 10th Corps defended the positions on the outskirts of the city. Support from our heavy artillery at Yueh-lu-shan enabled our forces to crush repeated enemy attacks and destroy the enemy force which had entered Pai-sha-ling. The 9th War Area ordered the 77th Division of the 73rd Corps to cross the Hsiang River and reinforce the 10th Corps in the defense of Chang-sha. On the night of January 2, Deputy Commander Lo Cho-ying led the 26th Corps from Liu-yang to Huang-hua-shih and Shih-kung-wan, the 79th Corps from Tu-tou-shih to Tsuo-chan-chiao and Mo-pan-chow, and the 4th Corps from Chu-chow and Lung-tu-pu to the southeastern outskirts of Chang-sha. At Hua-men-lo and Tuo-chia-tien, the main force of the 37th Corps confronted the enemy's 40th Division.

On January 3, the enemy continued the violent attack against Chang-sha. The fact that the enemy air-dropped supplies revealed its lack of ammunition and its destined failure in storming our fortified positions. Leaving thousands of bodies, the enemy was frustrated in the offensive. As our counter-envelopment made the situation most difficult, the enemy decided to withdraw. His disposition was as follows:

On the morning of January 4, the 40th Division would leave a portion of its forces in the vicinity of Chin-ching to cover its flanks and rear, while its main force would advance to Chun-hua-shan. The 9th Separate Brigade would advance to Ma-lin-shih while the Sotosono Column would advance from Yueh-yang to Chieh-tou-shih on January 6 to coordinate with the withrawal of the main force. On the night of January 4, the 3rd and 6th Divisions would cross the river in the vicinity of Lang-li-shih and would then withdraw to the line along the Mi River via Ma-lin-shih.

On the same day, our 10th Corps and a portion of the 73rd Corps held the outskirts of Chang-sha. The fighting was most intense in the northeast. Our combination of firepower and counterattacks killed many enemy troops. Despite heavy sacrifices, our key localities in the primary positions stood firm and our troops were confident in the final victory. At night, our 26th Corps reached the line from Huang-hua-shih to Shih-kung-wan; the 79th Corps reached the line from Tsuo-shan-chiao to Mo-pan-chow; and the 4th Corps reached the vicinity of Pai-tien-pu and Ta-tuo-pu. Our 78th Corps pressed near Chun-hua-shan, while the main force of the 37th Corps confronted the enemy's 40th Division in the vicinity of Chin-ching. The main force of the 99th Corps, attached with the 140th Division, advanced to Lao-tao River via San-chieh-chiao. The advance elements of the 20th and 58th Corps reached the vicinity of Fu-lin-pu. A portion of our forces confronted the enemy's 9th Separate Brigade in the vicinity of Chang-sha. As the stage was set to destroy the enemy's main force, our 9th War Area ordered the various corps to reach the second line of objective by the night of January 4. Meanwhile, Generalissimo Chiang urged our officers and men to develop the spirit of aggressiveness, encircle and destroy the enemy forces on the battlefield.   The morale of our troops was high, as they marched onto the road of victory.

At dawn on January 4, the enemy expended every effort to launch attacks along the entire line.   Eenemy artillery conducted indicriminate shelling, while scores of enemy planes flew at low altitude to support the operations.   In addition, the enemy used poison gas in its final struggle.   Having determined that the enemy lacked food and ammunition and was about to withdraw, our defenders fought gallantly in repeated close combat and repelled the enemy.   Our heavy artillery in Yueh-lu-shan massed first to neutralize enemy artillery and stop the enemy's advance.   These were key factors which led to our victory.   On the morning of January 4, the 26th Corps reached the line from Hsi-tang to Tsao-chia-ping, and the 79th Corps pressed near Lang-li-shih and Tung-shan.   In the afternoon, the 4th Corps recovered Yu-hua-ting, Lin-tse-chung, Chin-pen-ling, and Huang-tu-ling to establish contact with the defenders of Chang-sha.   Our defenders attacked and broke the enemy's left flank.   With the intention of destroying the enemy in the area south of Mi-lo River and north of Lao-tao River, the 9th War Area made the following dispositions.

Deputy Commander Lo Cho-ying was the commander-in-chief of the South Pursuit Force exercising command over the 26th, 4th, and 73th Corps which began the pursuit at dawn on January 5.   The 26th Corps began the pursuit from Pai-lou-feng to Chang-lo-chieh and Wu-kung-shih via Feng-lin-kang, Ma-lin-shih, Liang-chia-chiao, Ma-feng-tzu, Li-shan-kang and Chang-lo-chieh-tao.   The 4th Corps began the pursuit from Ah-mi-ling and Tso-chia-tang to Hsin-shih and Lan-shih-ho via Tung-tun, Po-shih-tze, Ching-shan-shih, Fu-lin-pu, Li-chia-hsia and Shuang-chiang-kou-tao.   The 73rd Corps led the pursuit from Chang-sha to Luo-kung-chiao and Kuei-yi via Shih-tze-pu, Ma-an-pu, Hsin-chiao, Li-chiao, Wu-chang-miao and Luo-kung-chiao-tao.

Deputy Commander Yang Sen was the commander-in-chief of the North Intercepting Force exercising command over the 20th and 58th Corps and moving from north to south to intercept the enemy at Hsiang-pi-chiao, Fu-lin-pu and Lichiao.

Deputy Commander Wang Ling-chi was the commander-in-chief of the East Intercepting Force exercising command over the 37th and 78th Corps which moved from the east to the west to intercept the enemy in the area north of Feng-lin-kang and south of Chang-lo-chieh.

Fu Chung-fang was the commander of the West Intercepting Force exercising command over the main force of the 99th Corps which moved from the west to the east to intercept the enemy in the area north of Shih-tze-pu and south of Hsin-shih.

Li Tang was the advance commander directing the 140th Division to attack and intercept the enemy at Huang-sha-chieh and Hsin-chiang.

At dawn on January 5, the enemy's 3rd Division withdrew to the vicinity of

Tung-shan and Mo-pan-chow to force a river crossing and breakout. Hovever, the enemy force was crushed by our 79th Corps which succeeded in killing over 1,000 enemy troops including a regimental commander named Shin Ishii. Enemy remnants were forced to flee along the dikes to Lang-li-shih, follow the 6th Division and cross the river by means of pontoon bridges. By mid-night, the enemy reached the north bank of the Liuyang River.

At dawn on January 6, over 2,000 enemy troops moved from Chang-chiao to launch counterattacks against the positions of our 26th Corps and cover its main force in crossing the Lao-tao River. As the enemy troops were routed, our forces recovered Chang-chiao. Our 79th Corps moving north from Tung-shan caught up with the enemy in the vicinity of Li-chia-tuo and Ping-shan killing many enemy troops. In addition, over 500 enemy troops were drowned in the Liu-yang River. In the afternoon, Lang-li-shih was recovered with enemy remnants fleeing to thes northeast. Our 78th Corps intercepted the enemy remnants along the line from Ku-kang northwest of Huang-hua-shih to Hou-chia-lung killing many enemy troops. In the evening of January 6, the main force of the enemy's 40th Division from Chinching reached the area west of Chun-hua-shan to tie down our 78th Corps. Earlier in the morning of January 6, the enemy's 9th Separate Brigade reached the area north of Ku-hua-shan and Fu-lin-pu and attacked our 20th Corps there. On the same day, the enemy's Sotosono Column advanced south from Yueh-yang attempting to open the line of retreat for the enemy's main force.

On January 7, the enemy's 6th Division fell back to the areas south of Fu-lin-pu. Later, the enemy's 40th Division withdrew to the north from Ma-lin-shih to thearea southeast of Fu-lin-pu. Meanwhile, the enemy's 9th Brigade attacked from the north to the east sandwiching our 20th and 58th Corps. Subjected to the raids of scores of enemy planes, our key points in the vicinity of Fu-lin-pu were lost and then recaptured by our New 10th Division in the evening, resulting in the killing of many enemy troops.

On January 8, Fu-lin-pu again fell into the hands of the enemy who launched a violent attack against the positions of our 58th Corps at Yinchushan. Repeated wrestling of positions led to the killing of more than 1,000 enemy troops. Meanwhile, our 26th and 4th Corps pursued and killed many enemy troops. At this time, the enemy had repaired the highway from Hsinchiang to Tachingchieh and massed 500 vehicles. The 9th War Area ordered the 78th and 37th Corps to move from Chin-ching to Chang-lo-chieh and Tai-ching-chieh via Wu-kou for the pursuit.

On January 9, our 20th and 58th Corps fought bitterly against the enemy's 9th Separate Brigade and 3rd Division in the vicinity of Yingchushan reaping many gains.

On January 10, under air cover, the enemy fell back to the north in several routes from the vicinity of Fu-lin-pu. Defending the area in the vicinity of Chang-ling, our 37th Corps intercepted the enemy. A portion of the 73rd Corps advanced to Li-chia-hsia and Hsin-kai-shih to intercept the enemy.

Between January 11 and 12, our 37th Corps killed over 1,000 enemy troops in Chang-ling including Toshikatsu Tomonari, commander of the 13th Regiment, 6th Division and captured over 100 troops before continuing the pursuit to Yen-chia-pu. On the morning of January 11, the 26th Corps recovered Fu-lin-pu. On the night of January 11, the 20th and 58th Corps continued the pursuit to Hsin-chiang River Via Huang-po-hsia and Hsin-kai-hih.

On December 13, our 78th Corps recovered Chang-lo-chieh and Tai-ching-chieh; the 4th and 73rd Corps reached Wu-kung-shih and Hsin-shih in the pursuit; and the 140th Division attacked the enemy flanks from Huang-sha-chieh. Having suffered heavy casualties, the enemy crossed the Mi River and retreated to the north.

On January 14, our 37th, 4th, and 73rd Corps mopped up the enemy remnants on the south bank of the Mi River, while our 78th Corps continued the pursuit toward Yang-lin-chieh and Hsin-chiang.

On January 15, enemy remnants retreated to the north of the Hsin-chiang River. Our 78th Corps routed the Sotosono Column, the enemy's rear guards at Chen-chia-chiao and Kuan-wang-chiao. Our 58th and 20th Corps reached Hsin-chiang River, and our 54th Provisional Division and 140th Division attacked Chung-fang and Tao-lin-Yi-tang respectively reaping considerable gains.

On January 16, as the battle came to an end, the 9th War Area readjusted its dispositions.

On the northern Kiangsi front, since the initiation of holding attacks from the vicinity of An-yi and Juo-hsi on December 25, the main forces of the enemy's 34th Division and the 14th Separate Brigade took Kao-an and Wu-ning. Between January 3-6, 1942, forces of our 19th and 30th Army Groups counterattacked, repelled the enemy and restored our original positions.

On the northern Hupei front, as the enemy left more forces than he did during the Second Battle of Chang-sha and our forces committed fewer troops, there had been no major combat.

During this battle, the enemy was late in launching the attack (the enemy crossed the Hsin-chiang River on December 24) and failed to respond timely to the enemy operations in Hong Kong-Kowloon (the operations in Hong Kong were terminated on December 25). Inadequate strength, narrow front, lack of depth, mistaken estimate on our strength and dispositions, blind attacks on our fortified positions in Chang-sha led to enemy defeat. Had the enemy not had air superiority and excellent equipment, he would have been destroyed. Taking full advantage of the lessons learned during the Second Battle of Chang-sha, our forces accurately chose the time and the battlefield for the decisive battle. Our massing of superior strength to seek local superiority and over-run the enemy, enabled our forces to win glorious victories which contributed immensely to the overall situation. Over 50,000 enemy troops including 4 regimental commanders were killed or wounded, 139 enemy troops were captured together with 1,138 rifles and carbines, 115 machine guns, 11 guns, 26 pistols, 20 grenade launchers, 9 radios and large quantities of military supplies.

    b. Battle of the Yunnan-Burma Road

        (Mid-March—Early June, 1942. See Map 32 and Charts 48 and 49)

CHART 48

*Chart Showing Japanese Chain of Command during the Battle of
the Yunnan-Burma Road (Late February, 1942)*

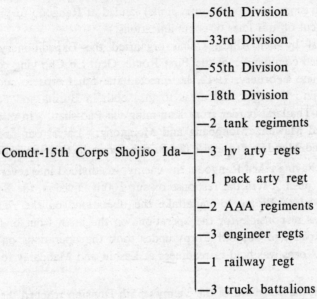

- —56th Division
- —33rd Division
- —55th Division
- —18th Division
- —2 tank regiments
- Comdr-15th Corps Shojiso Ida— —3 hv arty regts
- —1 pack arty regt
- —2 AAA regiments
- —3 engineer regts
- —1 railway regt
- —3 truck battalions

CHART 49

*Chart Showing Chinese Order of Battle during the Battle of
the Yunnan-Burma Road (Late February, 1942)*

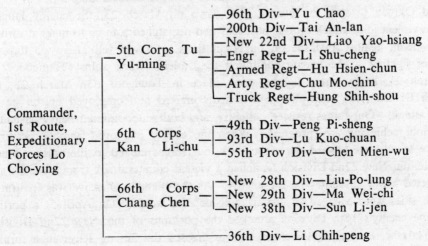

Commander,
1st Route,
Expeditionary
Forces Lo
Cho-ying

5th Corps Tu Yu-ming
- —96th Div—Yu Chao
- —200th Div—Tai An-lan
- —New 22nd Div—Liao Yao-hsiang
- —Engr Regt—Li Shu-cheng
- —Armed Regt—Hu Hsien-chun
- —Arty Regt—Chu Mo-chin
- —Truck Regt—Hung Shih-shou

6th Corps Kan Li-chu
- —49th Div—Peng Pi-sheng
- —93rd Div—Lu Kuo-chuan
- —55th Prov Div—Chen Mien-wu

66th Corps Chang Chen
- —New 28th Div—Liu-Po-lung
- —New 29th Div—Ma Wei-chi
- —New 38th Div—Sun Li-jen

—36th Div—Li Chih-peng

Yunnan Province extends to Indo-China on the south and Burma on the west.   The Yunnan-Indo-China Railway extended from Kun-ming to Ho-kou, and the China-Burma Road extended from Kun-ming to Lashio.   Since the Japanese occupation of Indo-China, the China-Burma Road became the most important international road during China's War of Resistance.

Since the Japanese initiation of the Pacific War on December 8, 1941, the Japanese captured Maly Peninsula, and Thailand became subjugated to Japan. The enemy's 15th Corps (under Shojiro Ida who commanded the 33rd, 55th, 56th and 18th Divisions and non-infantry units) landed at Rangoon to push north and attempted to cut off our lines of communications.

Upon request by her Allies, China organized the Expeditionary Forces. Having been named commander of the First Route, Gen. Lo Cho-ying commanded 3 corps.   In late February, 1942, he directed the 5th Corps to move from western Yunnan into Toungoo and areas to the south in Burma and 6th Corps to push to Burma-Thailand border from Kun-ming via Pao-shan.   In mid-March, our forces reached Mawchi, Mongpang and Mongtong.   Later, our 66th Corps reached Lashio and Mandalay to assist the British forces in their operations.

At this time, having taken Rangoon, the enemy was divided into several routes for the northward push.   Wth the response of our 200th Division, the British 1st Army was deployed in Prome to undertake the operations on the right flank. Our 5th Corps was responsible for the operations on the main front of the Rangoon-Mandalay Road and our 6th Corps under took the operations on the left flank.   Our 60th Corps was held in readiness at Lashio and Mandalay for mobile employment.

On March 18, the vanguard of the enemy's 55th Division reached the vicinity of Tachiao approximately 12 miles south of Pyu and gained contact with the security elements of our 5th Corps.   In the morning of March 20, the enemy main force began the attack.   In accordance with prd-determined plans, our forces held Oktwin to stop the enemy.   At dawn on March 23, the enemy launched a violent joint attack on our positions and dispatched a force to make a turning movement against Yedashe on our right flank.   Oktwin fell after two days of bitter fighting.   The enemy continued the violent attack aginst Toungoo.   By March 26, heavy street fighting took place in Toungoo.   On March 28, the 56th Division, the enemy's reinforcements arrived and employed poison gas in the attack.   Our forces resisted gallantly, and both sides suffered heavy casualties without achieving any progress.   When the enemy employed another powerful force to advance toward our right flank, our forces moved to the north.   Meanwhile, our New 22nd Division launched a violent counterattack from Yedashe and inflicted heavy casualties on the enemy.   As the enemy's offensive was frustrated, both sides were engaged in constructing defense works.   On April 5, a portion of the enemy's 18th Division attacked the positions of our New 22nd Division at Yedashe, as over 1,000 enemy troops crossed the Sittang River in a turning movement agains tthe flanks and rear of our forces. The heavy fighting lasted until April 8 when our forces fell back to the north bank of the Szuwa River to continue the resistance. By April 10, artillery and air cover enabled the enemy to make a forced crossing of the Szuwa River for the northward invasion. Our New 22nd Division continued to hit the enemy. On April 16, our forces fell back to main positions at Pyinmana. On April 17, the enemy launched a violent attack against the positions on our right flank at Liehna and was repulsed by our 96th Division. On April 18, the British forces on the right flank withdrew. As our positions were too exposed, our forces abandoned Pyinmana with the 200th and New 22nd Divisions moving north and the 96th Division delaying the enemy's advance. On April 20, the enemy took Pyinmana and continued to fight against our forces at Kyidaunggan. Our forces resisted gallantly. By May 1, our forces fell back to Mei-yin River to continue the resistance.

On April 1, the enemy's 33rd Division broke through the positions of the British and Indian forces. After capturing Prome, the enemy continued his attack to the north and on April 5, took Thayetmyo and Kyaukpadaung. Despite continued resistance, the British forces were unable to stop the enemy's offensive. After taking Allanmyo on April 6, the enemy invaded Okpo, Magwe and Satthwa on April 12. On April 14, the enemy's main force crossed the river to capture Magwe, as the British and Indian forces withdrew to Yenangyaung. By April 16, the enemy also took Yenangyaung trapping the British 1st Division and tank battalion in the area north of Yenangyaung. This seriously threatened the right flank of our forces. Accordingly, a portion of our New 38th Division defending Mandalay raced to reinforce the British forces. Another force was sent to cover the frontal operations of our force. Our forces racing to reinforce the British fought hard against the enemy for two days in the vicinity of Yenangyaung before routing the main force of the enemy's 33rd Division. As Yenangyaung was recaptured, the enemy fled south leaving over 1,200 bodies. Having broken the siege in which over 7,000 British troops were encircled, our forces also saved over 1,000 horses, and 500+ British prisoners and American missionaries and correspondents. This marked the first time that Chinese forces distinguished themselves on foreign soil since the middle of the Ching Dynasty.

Subsequent to the capture of Toungoo, the enemy employed the main force of the 18th Division and a portion of the 56th Division to invade Mawchi and Yato and fought bitterly against our 93rd and 55th Provisional Divisions. Our forces then fell back to Naba to continue the resistance. On April 17, the enemy continued the violent attack which lasted all day and resulted into the fall of Bawlake. This made our positions at Naba most unfavorable. As a result, our forces withdrew to Hopong, Mongpang and Mongtang. On April 20, the enemy took Loikaw and continued to invade Hopong. Another enemy force made a turning movement against Taunggyi. Our 200th Division operated in Hopong to stop the invading enemy. Heavy fighting continued until April 24 when our forces recovered Taunggyi. The enemy's main force then attacked and took Loilem, Mongnawng and Konghaiping on April 25 before advancing toward Lashio in two routes. Our 66th corps intercepted it in several routes, both sides took heavy and casualties. On April 28, the enemy captured Hsi-pao and Nan-ma, continued its advance toward Lashio. Bitter fighting lasted for one day and one night. To maintain flexibility in subsequent operations, our forces gave up Lashio and took up defense in Hsenwe. The enemy continued the advance to the north and captured Hsenwe on May 1, Wan-ting on May 3, and also Lungling. His main force advanced via Bhamo to take Myitkyina on May 8. On May 10, the enemy at Bhamo crossed the river above Katha and engaged our forces. With the purpose of disengaging themselves from the enemy, our forces fell back to the line from Mongnawng to Taro. As the monsoon made the the mountain roads extremely slippery and dangerous, both personnel and horses moved with great difficulties. By May 23, when our 200th Division travelled on the Hsipaw-Mogok Highway to swing to northern Burma, they were intercepted by the enemy. The heavy fighting which ensued took the life of Gen. Tai An-lan, commander of the 200th Division. From then on, the 200th and the 96th Divisions passed Teng-chung and We-hsi and headed for the east bank of the Salween River. Other units reached Ledo in East India via Singkalilng, Tarao and Shing-bwiyang around August 3 eventually. Many officers and men died along this march due to supply difficulties.

After the enemy captured Lashio and Wan-ting they headed north to relieve the threat on their flanks and rear. They met with no opposition. Our forces demolished the Hui-tung Bridge, a key locality on the Burma Road. On May 4, a portion of our 36th Division moved south from Pao-shan to the east bank of the Hui-tung Bridge. On May 5, the enemy force reched the west bank of the Hui-tung Bridge and faced our forces across the Salween River. On May 6, a portion of the enemy forced a crossing of the Salween River to attack our forces. The heavy fighting lasted for several days before the enemy was finally routed. On May 9, our powerful force crossed the Salween River from the upper reaches and seriously threatened the enemy flanks and rear. On May 11, the enemy attacked Teng-chung. On May 13, a portion of the enemy force attacked to the north. At that time, our 2nd Reserve Division had already crossed the Salween River and reached the area south of Malipa to meet the enemy. In the night of May 19, our main force continued to cross the Salween River along the upper reaches north of the Hui-tung Bridge and attacked the enemy's left flank, while the 88th Division crossed the river south of the Hui-tung Bridge and harassed Chen-an-chieh, Meng-chang-chieh and Lung-ling destroying highways in the enemy rear, disrupting enemy communications, and cutting off enemy reinforcements. Since May 23, our forces, having crossed the river, launched extensive attacks against the enemy, captured many key localities and inflicted heavy casualties on the enemy. On May 29, unable to withstand our attacks, the enemy poured large reinforcements from Wan-ting and launched a counterattack. Having achieved the objective of striking the enemy, our forces assumed the defensive on May 31 and halted the enemy attacks by making use of positions already constructed. The 2nd Reserve Division was then sent to the enemy rear to conduct guerilla operations, and the remaining forces began to move back to the east bank of the Salween River. By June 6, our 36th and 88th Divisions withdrew to ferry points on the east bank and dug in facing the enemy across the Salween and making preparations for future counterattacks.

Due to the lack of a concrete agreement on Allied combined operations, after the enemy capture of Rangoon, the British main force was shifted to the west of the railway. Our forces had to defend the railway front. Our entry into Burma for military operations was so hasty that we had insufficient time to mass our forces and fully develop our combat effectiveness. Despite the all-out efforts of our officers and men, we were on the passive from the beginning to the end. It was most regrettable that our efforts failed to turn the tide of a critical situation. During the retreat, our forces went into the jungle and experienced much hardship. Their indomitable spirit fully reflected the performance of truly revolutionary soldiers.

    c. Battle of Chekiang-Kiangsi
       (Mid-May—Early September, 1942. See Map 32 and Charts 50 and 51)

CHART 50

Chart Showing Japanese Chain of Command during the Battle of Chekiang-Kiangsi (Late April, 1942)

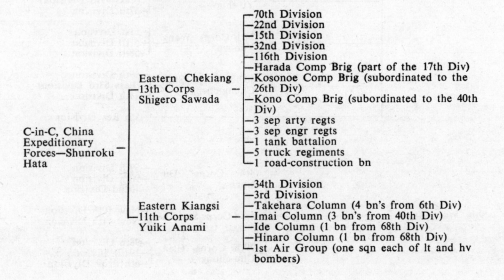

CHART 51

Chart Showing Chinese Chain of Command during the Battle of
Chekiang-Kiangsi (Late April, 1942)

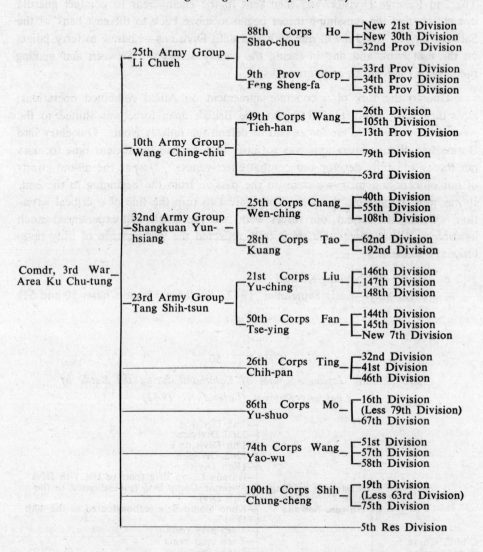

```
                                                                ┌─New 21st Division
                                              88th Corps Ho ───┼─New 30th Division
                                              Shao-chou         └─32nd Prov Division
                           25th Army Group ─┤
                           Li Chueh           ┌─33rd Prov Division
                                              9th Prov Corp ───┼─34th Prov Division
                                              Feng Sheng-fa     └─35th Prov Division

                                                                ┌─26th Division
                                              49th Corps Wang ─┼─105th Division
                                              Tieh-han          └─13th Prov Division
                           10th Army Group ─┤
                           Wang Ching-chiu   ──────────────────── 79th Division

                                            ──────────────────── 63rd Division

                                                                ┌─40th Division
                                              25th Corps Chang ┼─55th Division
                           32nd Army Group    Wen-ching         └─108th Division
                          ─Shangkuan Yun- ──┤
                           hsiang             28th Corps Tao ──┬─62nd Division
                                              Kuang             └─192nd Division

                                                                ┌─146th Division
                                              21st Corps Liu ──┼─147th Division
                                              Yu-ching          └─148th Division
                           23rd Army Group ─┤
                           Tang Shih-tsun     ┌─144th Division
                                              50th Corps Fan ──┼─145th Division
                                              Tse-ying          └─New 7th Division

Comdr, 3rd War ─┤
Area Ku Chu-tung                                                ┌─32nd Division
                                              26th Corps Ting ─┼─41st Division
                                              Chih-pan          └─46th Division

                                                                ┌─16th Division
                                              86th Corps Mo ───┼─(Less 79th Division)
                                              Yu-shuo           └─67th Division

                                                                ┌─51st Division
                                              74th Corps Wang ─┼─57th Division
                                              Yao-wu            └─58th Division

                                                                ┌─19th Division
                                              100th Corps Shih ┼─(Less 63rd Division)
                                              Chung-cheng       └─75th Division

                                            ──────────────────── 5th Res Division


                                                                ┌─59th Division
                                              4th Corps Ou ────┼─90th Division
                                              Chen              └─102nd Division

9th War Area ─────────────────────────────┤  58th Corps Sun Tu ┬─New 10th Division
                                                                └─New 11th Division

                                                                ┌─98th Division
                                              79th Corps Hsia ─┼─194th Division
                                              Chu-chung         └─6th Prov Division
```

On April 18, 1942, the planes of U.S. aircraft carriers raided Tokyo and Nagoya before they landed in Chekiang Province. The raid greatly terrified the Japanese people and created social unrest. In order to prevent the U.S. planes from conducting shuttle bombing, the enemy Supreme Headquarters ordered the China Expeditionary Forces to occupy the airfields in Chekiang as soon as possible. Accordingly, the China Expeditionary Forces launched the operations in Chekiang-Kiangsi. In mid-May, the main force of the 13th Corps began to attack the eastern sector of the Chekiang-Kiangsi Railway with the response of a portion of the 11th Corps which began its operations from Nan-chang area by the end of May. The strength and the massing of the forces were indicated as follows:

In Chekiang:

Main force of the 13th Corps (Having been massed in Chang-hsing, Wan-chih, and Ti-kang, it was prepared to attack our 32nd Army Group in Kuang-teh and Hsuan-cheng. It changed its operation plans on April 22).

Main force of 70th Division moved from Ning-po and Shao-hsing to mass in Feng-hua and Hsi-kou.

22nd Division moved from Chang-hsing to mass in Yu-yao and Shang-yu.

15th Division moved from Wan-chih to mass in Hsiao-shan.

Main force of the 116th Division moved from Ti-kang to mass in Fu-yang and Yu-hang.

Kono Composite Brigade (subordinated to the 40th Division) moved from Tikang to mass in Shao-hsing.

On May 13, the above-mentioned 4 divisions and 1 brigade completed their massing.

32nd Division massed in Hang-chow.

Harada Composite Brigade (subordinated to the 17th Division) massed in Hang-chow.

Kosonoe Composite Brigade (subordinated to the 26th Division) massed in Hang-chow.

On May 23, the above-mentioned division and 2 brigades completed their massing.

In Nanchang:

A portion of the 11th Corps

Imai Column (built around 3 infantry battalions of the 40th Division) moved from southern Hupei to mass in Wan-she-chieh.

Ide Column (built around 1 infantry battalion of the 68th Division) moved from northern Kiangsi to mass in Wan-she-chieh.

Hinaro Column (built around 1 infantry battalion of the 68th Division) massed in Nan-chang.

The main force of the 3rd Division moved from northern Hupei to mass in Sha-fu-tan.

The main force of the 34th Division moved from northern Kiangsi to mass in Hsieh-fu-shih.

By May 27, the above-mentioned divisions and 3 columns massed on the left bank of the Kan River and advanced toward the above-stated places immediately before launching the attack.

1st Air Regiment

2 reconnaissance fights, 2 reconnaissance squadrons and 1 fighter flight. Additionally, 1 light bomber flight and 1 heavy bomber flight each were added and arrived in Central China at the end of April.

Since the Battle of Wusung-Shanghai, as our 3rd War Area insofar as the overall strategy was concerned was secondary in importance, it switched to guerilla operations. In April, 1941, with signing of the Russo-Japanese Neutrality Treaty, our National Military Council estimated that the enemy would move south. Since the enemy was going to place emphasis on this area, the National Military Council pulled the 49th Corps and 19th Division from the 9th War Area and shifted them to the 3rd War Area. In December, with the outbreak of the Pacific War and after the 3rd Battle of Changsha, the 26th and 74th Corps were pulled from the 9th War Area and shifted to the 3rd War Area in order to augment the strength and step up attacks against the enemy. Efforts were made to protect the airfields in Chekiang and Kiangsi and draw the enemy's main strength so as to reduce the pressure on Shensi and Hunan and insure the security of Szechuan.

In late April, 1942, the enemy sent reinforcements to the east and west of the Chekiang-Kiangsi Railway. The operational guidance of our 3rd War Area was to dispose minimum force along the western sector of the Chekiang-Kiangsi Railway for sustained resistance, mass the main strength along the eastern sector of the Chekiang-Kiangsi Railway make use of constructed positions to conduct sustained resistance, harass the enemy rear areas, and delay and tie down the enemy. Fortified positions were constructed in Chinhua and Lanhsi to offer resistance and seek decisive battle eventually against the enemy around Chu-chow.

The War Area Headquarters disposed the 25th Army Group in southern Chekiang with its headquarters in Chinyun; the 10th Army Group south of the Chien-tang River with its headquarters in Chin-hua, responsible for the garrison of Chin-hua and Lan-hsi and the defense of the south bank of the River; the 32nd Army Group, north of the Chien-tang River with its headquarters in Shu-nan, responsible for operations in the area; the 100th Corps (less the 63rd Division), responsible for operations along the western sector of the Chekiang-Kiangsi Railway; the 26th and 74th Corps in Chu-chow. All the above forces should complete massing and deployment by mid-May, and were ready to attack the enemy. The 23rd Army Group responsible for garrisoning the line Ning-kuo-Kuei-chih-Tu-chang, laid mines to interrupt enemy transportation along the Yangtze River. In time of need, the 23rd Army Group would place 2 divisions in Shou-chang and Yin-tan to participate in the operations along the Chekiang-

Kiangsi Railway.

With 4½ divisions on the first line, the enemy's 13th Corps was deployed along the line from Feng-hua to Yu-yao. On May 15, the enemy began the advance, while his follow-up force of 1 division and 2 brigades massed in the vicinity of Hang-chow.

Our 9th Provisional Corps, 88th Corps and a portion of the 28th Corps offered resistance from previously constructed positions along the line from Chen-chao-shih to Chang-lo-chieh, Hsin-chang, San-chieh-chen, An-hua-chieh, Wang-sha-hsi and Hsin-teng and the line from Tung-yang to Yi-wu, Pu-chiang and Tanglu. Afterwards, a portion of our forces conducted guerilla operations in the enemy's rear areas, while our main forces fell back to the east-west line from Chin-hua to Lan-hsi and massed the forces ready to strike the enemy.

On the night of April 24, the enemy's 22nd Division operated along the mountain line north of Wu-yi; the Kono Composite Brigade in the area southeast of Chin-hua; the 70th Division in the area west of Hsiaoshun; the 15th Division in the area north of Lanhsi; and the 116th Division in the area on the southern flank of Chienteh with the follow-up 32nd Division deployed abreast on its right heading toward the southwest. At this time, the enemy estimated that our forces in Chin-hua and Lan-hsi began to withdraw and had no intention to offer resistance. The enemy, therefore, decided to pursue to Chu-chow in one stroke forcing our forces to fight a decisive battle.

On April 25, the enemy's 22nd Division and Kono Composite Brigade made a turning movement from the south of Chin-hua to Tang-hsi and Ku-fang. The main force of our 40th Division and the 13th Provisional Division intercepted the enemy. The enemy's 70th Division and 15th Division opened the attacks against Chin-hua and Lan-hsi respectively. Our 79th and 63rd Divisions defended our previously constructed positions at Chin-hua and Lan-hsi strongly and killed many enemy troops.

On April 26, the enemy captured Tang-hsi. Our forces offered resistance along the railway and in the area to the south. In the afternoon, the enemy's 22nd Division and Kono Brigade continued to advance to Lung-yu and pulled 2 battalions to assist the 70th Division in its attack on Chinhua. Later, the enemy's follow-up unit, the Kosonoe Brigade arrived in the area south of Tung-yang. At night, the enemy's 116th Division reached the area northwest of Lan-hsi. The 32nd Division attacked Shou-chang, while the Harada Composite Brigade garrisoned the rear area along the Fu-chun River. Our 192nd and 5th Reserve Division launched flank attack against the enemy at Chien-teh and Tung-lu. Our 146th Division and a portion of the 40th Division intercepted the enemy northeast of Shou-chang.

On April 27, as the enemy took Lung-yu, our defenders in Chin-hua and Lan-hsi (Chin-lan) became more isolated. Accordingly, our defenders fell back to Pei-shan after abandoning Chin-lan on April 28 and conducted guerilla operations in the enemy's rear areas in conjunction with the 88th Corps. After the capture of Chin-lan, the enemy assigned the 70th Division to garrison it and the area along the Chekiang-Kiangsi Railway to the east.

On April 29, the enemy's 15th Division moved west along the railway. On April 30, the enemy's 22nd and 15th Divisions and the Kono Brigade massed in Lung-yu and the area to the south. After capturing Shou-chang, the 32nd Division established contact with the 116th Division on its left and operated in Hsia-kou, Tu-tse and Lien-hua-shih on the north bank of the Chu River, with the Kosonoe Brigade moved toward Lung-yu. The enemy gradually completed his preparations for the attack on Chu-chow. Our 13th Provisional Division made contact with the Kono Brigade at Ling-shan Chen and then fell back to Pei-chieh-chen. After offering resistance south of the railway, our 40th Division withdrew to Ta-chow Chen and Shih-pao-chieh. With our 74th Corps in Hu-shan Chen, Hsi-kou-chieh, and Huang-tan-kou, the 49th Corps in the vicinity of Chao-hsien Chen west of Chu-chow, the 86th Corps in Chu-chow, the 26th Corps in Fu-ho-tsun and Fang-tsun Chen northwest of Chu-chow, and the 25th Corps in Shih-kan-tou, Ta-tung Chen and Shan-fang Chen west of Shou-chang, ready to encircle and destroy the enemy forces which were about to attack Chu-chow. Adequate preparations and high morale stimulated the desire of our troops to serve the nation and distinguish themselves like they did during the Third Battle of Changsha.

On May 31, a portion of the enemy's 11th Corps in Nan-chang, approximately 2 and a half divisions crossed the Fu River to attack to the southeast in an attempt to launch a converging attack on our forces along the Chekiang-Kiangsi Railway. With an insight into the overall situation, Generalissimo Chiang directed the 3rd War Area to avoid a decisive battle against the enemy in the vicinity of Chu-chow. Accordingly, the 3rd War Area ordered the 86th Corps (less 79th Division) on June 3 to garrison Chu-chow and draw the enemy, while the main force of the 3rd War Area avoided the main front along the railway and withdrew to the mountainous areas on both flanks. When the enemy advanced along the railway, our main force intercepted the enemy in sectors. To gain time for the War Area to make re-disposition, our 86th Corps held Chu-chow at all costs and fought for 4 days and nights against an enemy vastly superior in strength. Finally on June 6, the corps broke out from the south.

After the enemy's seizure of Chu-chow on June 7, his 116th Division and Kono Brigade remained in Chu-chow. His 22nd, 15th and 32nd Divisions continued to move west. On June 11, the 22nd Division took Chiang-shan. On June 12, the 32nd Division took Yu-shan. On June 14, the 22nd Division took Kuang-feng. After its capture of Shang-yao on June 15, the enemy continued his westward advance. On June 24, the Kosonoe Brigade advanced from Lungyu to capture Lishui. On July 1, a portion of the enemy's 22nd Division and the enemy moving east from Nan-chang joined force to take Heng-feng. Having cleared the Chekiang-Kiangsi Railway, the enemy shifted to the defensive, and engaged in destroying airfield, dismantling railways and seizing materials. Since mid-June, the main force of our 3rd War Area was shifted to the lines between Hsia-kou and Hsien-hsia-kuan, Kuang-feng and Shang-yao, and from the south bank of the Hsin River to Wang-erh-tu. A portion of our forces was shifted to the area on the north flank of the Chekiang-Kiangsi Railway to continue attacking the enemy flanks. Especially during the actions at Shan-hsi and on the banks of Hsin River, 3 enemy regiments were routed.

On the Nan-chang front, since mid-May, Generalissimo Chiang estimated that the enemy's 11th Corps would launch the attack from the western sector of the Chekiang-Kiangsi Railway in response to the operations of the 13th Corps. Accordingly, on May 16, he directed the 9th War Area to pull the 79th Corps and mass it within one week in Fen-yi and Ching-chiang ready to operate in eastern Kiangsi and respond to the operations of the 3rd War Area. On May 21, the 79th Corps was ordered to push to Lin-chuan by June 4, and the 9th War Area was ordered to transfer the 4th Corps for operations in eastern Kiangsi. In addition, the 9th War Area was ordered to move the 58th Corps from Shang-kao to Feng-cheng prepared to launch flanking attacks against the enemy.

On the night of May 31, the enemy's 34th and 3rd Divisions and Imai and Ide Columns advanced from Hsieh-fu-shih-Sha-fu-tan-Wan-she-chieh line to the right bank of the Fu River and attacked the positions of our 75th Division and the Peace Preservation Column between the Fu River and the Kan River. At this time, our 19th Division was committed in Shang-yao, while a portion of our 75th Division conducted sustained resistance. The main force of the 75th Division fell back to the previously constructed positions west of Yingtan for joint defense with the 147th Division. Our Kiangsi Peace Preservation Column shifted a portion of its forces to the line from Kao-kung-ling to Kuang-fu-yu, and San-hsien-hu. Its main force continued resistance in Hu-toufeng and Ta-kang-kou.

On june 3, the enemy reached the Tung-yuan-yu-Li-chiatu-Chin-hsien line. The 6th Provisional Division of our 79th Corps encountered and attacked the enemy's Imai Column in a meeting engagement in the vicinity of Tung-yuan-yu and Chan-ping-hsu. Greatly threatened on the right flank, the enemy shifted the main force of the 34th Division to the left flank of the Fu River in conjunction with the Takehara Column which turned to the area on the southern flank of San-chiang-kou. The Iwanaka Column (built around 3 infantry battalions of the 34th Division) advanced to Tung-hsiang along the Chekiang-Kiangsi Railway, while the main force of the 3rd Division advanced to Lin-chuan.

On June 4, despite heavy downpour and floods, our 79th Corps made the advance. At night, a portion of the 79th Division entered Linchuan and engaged the advance elements of the enemy's 3rd Division in an all-night street fighting. On the same day, a portion of the New 11th Division, 58th Corps reinforced the Kiangsi Peace Preservation Column and fought bitterly against the Ide Column at Hu-tou-feng and Ta-kang-kou.

On June 5, the main force of the enemy's 3rd Division reinforced Linchuan. A portion of our 98th Division withdrew to the Yeh-chia-chiao-Chi-li-tien line on the outskirts of Lin-chuan facing the enemy. Meanwhile, our 58th Corps ordered the Kiangsi Peace Preservation Column to launch attacks against the enemy at Li-chia-tu and San-chiang-kou and reaped many gains. On June 6, the 9th War Area directed the 79th Corps to counterattack Lin-chuan and check the enemy. On the same day, the main force of the enemy's 34th Division reached San-chiang-kou and ordered the Ide Column to join force with the Takehara Column in counter-attacking our 58th Corps. On June 7, as the enemy advanced to the Tao-sha-yu-Tu-chia-wei-Pai-ma-chai line, the 58th Corps fell back to the line from Hsiu-tsai-fu to Feng-cheng. On June 8, a portion of the enemy's 34th Division took Chung-jen, and on June 9 Yi-huang. In an effort to seek the exterior lines, our 79th Corps directed the 194th Division to fall back and defend Nan-cheng on June 10, while its main force massed in the vicinity of Tseng-fang, Huang-chia-yuan and Nan-yuan-kang south of the city. The enemy's 3rd Division and Takehara Column advanced to Nan-cheng; the 34th Division massed east of Lin-chuan; the Imai Column was disposed in Lin-chuan; and the Ide Column was disposed in the vicinity of San-chiang-kou to protect their flanks, rear and water route. On June 11, over 2,000 troops of the enemy's advance elements fiercely attacked Nan-cheng. Our 194th Division, attached with the Corps Dual-Purpose Gun Battalion halted and repelled the enemy in the vicinity of Miao-chien west of Nan-cheng. On June 12, the enemy's 34th Division was shifted from the vicinity of Lin-chuan to the main front of the Chekiang-Kiangsi Railway to team up with the Iwanaka Column in an attack on Ying-tan. After capturing Nan-cheng, the enemy's 3rd Division turned to Chin-hsi leaving the Takehara Column to garrison Nan-cheng. Later, our 194th Division moved to Hsiao-shih for reorganization.

On June 12, with the purpose of first destroying the enemy in Yi-huang, Chungjen and Lin-chuan before attacking Tung-hsiang and Chin-hsien, our 9th War Area ordered the 4th Corps to attack Yi-huang, Chung-jen and Lin-chuan from the southwest, the 58th Corps to attack Chung-jen and Lin-chuan in the southwest, and the 79th Corps to attack Yi-huang and Lin-chuan from the southeast. The 3rd War Area employed the main force of the 100th Corps to attack Lin-chuan and Huwan from Chin-hsi. On June 13, our 79th Corps counterattacked Nan-cheng. On June 15, the 90th Division recaptured Chung-jen. On June 16, the 59th Division recovered Yi-huang, both reaping considerable gains. The two divisions continued the attack to Lin-chuan. On the same day, after the enemy's 34th Division captured Ying-tan and Kuei-hsi, the Iwanaka Column continued the advance to Heng-feng. Meanwhile, in conjunction with the Japanese Navy, the Hirano Column landed at the estuary of Chin River on June 15, took Jui-hung, and sailed up the Chin River in a joint attack on Kuei-hsi to control the water communications. Despite all-out resistance, our garrison forces in the

Po-yang Lake withdrew to the flank to continue harassing the enemy.

On June 21, our 4th Corps repelled the enemy along the line from Tung-chia-ling on the southern outskirts of Lin-chuan to Yeh-chia-chiao and the highground of Chi-li-chiao, and captured Wu-li-tang and Lo-hsi-chiao to approach the city. The enemy's Imai Column set fire to civilian houses ouside the city, inundated the neighboring area and stubbornly defended the city.

On June 23, over 1,000 troops of the Imai Column attacked Nan-shih-li and Fei-lu-feng to the south in order to tie down our 79th Corps. Another enemy force of over 3.000 troops advanced near the right flank of our 4th Corps. Meanwhile, the enemy's 3rd Division moved south from Chin-hsi and Hu-wan to Mao-pai. Our 9th War Area estimated that the enemy attempted to attack our 4th Corps so as to break the siege of Lin-chuan. Accordingly, it directed the 79th Corps to dispatch a force and pursue the enemy moving west from Nan-cheng. The 4th Corps threw the full weight in destroying the invaders from Nan-cheng and Hu-wan. On June 24, the corps swiftly moved to the north-south line from Mao-pai. On June 25, the enemy forces in Nan-cheng, Huwan and Lin-chuan separately attacked the front and flanks of our 4th Corps. The heavy fighting lasted until June 28 when our two key localities of Yuan-kou on the right flank and Li-hsi on the left flank were broken through by the enemy. Another enemy force of over 1,000 troops crossed Yu-huang River at Lung-ku-tu and sped to Tan-fang-Yi-huang Highway. Meanwhile, the 98th Division of our 79th Corps was deployed along the line from Fu-yung-shan to Tsai-fen-shan and attacked the enemy's left flank to the west. The New 10th Division of the 58th Corps moved east via Pai-lu-tu and Hsi-ching-tu to attack the enemy's right flank. On June 29, over 1,000 enemy troops attacked Yi-huang via Yung-hsing-chiao, while the enemy from Lin-chuan advanced to Chung-jen. Our 98th Corps pursued the enemy to the line from Yuan-kou to Kang-kou. A portion of our Ney 10th Division pressed near Hsi-ching-tu and Yang-pai-shih but was unable to establish direct coordination with the 4th Corps. Our 9th War Area, therefore, directed the 4th Corps to turn and mass in the mountainous areas south of Yi-huang and Feng-kang-yu. With Lo-an as the base, it turned northwest to attack the enemy's flanks and rear. The 79th Corps employed the 6th Provisional Division in attacking the enemy remnants at Nan-cheng, while the main force of the corps moved west from Yuan-kou and Kan-kou to pursue the enemy. The 58th Corps employed a portion of its forces in launching a feint attack toward Lin-chuan-Li-chia-tu and San-chiang-kou, while the main force of the corps massed in Pan-chiao and Hsiu-tsai-fu and then occupied positions to the east ready to meet the enemy from Chung-jen. On June 30, after capturing Yi-huang and Chung-jen, the enemy massed forces ready to attack our 58th Corps and relieve the threat on his flanks and rear.

On July 1, the main force of our 79th Corps moved west to the Chu-ling-Tang-yin line repelling over 1,000 enemy troops. The corps pressed near Yi-huang on July 2 and took Kao-hua-shan (on the eastern outskirts of Yi-huang) on July 3. The enemy moved the bulk of his forces west to Chung-jen leaving 500-600 troops in the defense of Yi-huang. By this time, our 4th Corps had completed its massing toward the mountainous areas from Hsing-fang and Feng-kang-yu. On the morning of July 4, our 90th Division and 79th Corps jointly attacked and captured Yi-huang destroying many enemy troops.

On July 4, the enemy's Takehara Column at Chung-jen advanced toward Pai-pi (southwest of Hsiu-tsai-fu); the 3rd Division advanced to Hsiu-tsai-fu and Pai-ma-chai (north of Hsiu-tsai-fu); and the enemy's Ide Column at San-chiang-kou advanced toward Pai-ma-chai, to lay siege against our 58th Corps from 3 sides. Our advance elements conducted sustained resistance. On July 5, more than 10 enemy planes supported the enemy's continued attack on the main positions of our 58th Corps at Ta-kang-ling, Pan-chiao, and Hsiu-tsai-fu. The fighting was most intense. The 9th War Area ordered the 58th Corps to cross Fu River in the west and fall back to the mountainous areas southwest of Ho-hu-yu (30 km. southwest of Hsiu-tsai-fu) before turning back to attack the enemy flanks; the 4th Corps to attack the enemy rear at Ma-an-yu, Pai-pi and Chiao-keng; the 79th Corps to employ the 98th Division in attacking the enemy rear at Chung-jen and Pan-chiao; and the 194th Division to control Yi-huang and the 6th Provisional Division to attack Nan-cheng.

On July 6, a portion of our 58th Corps withdrew to the vicinity of Ho-hu-yu and encountered the Takehara Column. After bitter fighting for one day and one night, our forces succeeded in killing over 600 enemy troops with the remnants retreating north to Tien-hsia-chieh. On July 7, our 58th Corps occupied positions along the Le-shan-Ping-shan-Mo-pan-shan line. Meanwhile, the enemy north of Tien-hsia-chieh took Chang-shu. While crossing the Kan River in the west on July 7, the enemy was stopped by our New 12th Division and New 20th Division. Another enemy force took Yung-tai and Shih-kou in the south. On July 8, the 58th Corps shifted the unit in the vicinity of Le-shan on the right flank to the area northwest of Ho-hu-yu and attacked the enemy there killing and wounding several hundred enemy troops. On the same day, our 79th Corps recovered Chung-jen and on July 9, it recovered Nan-cheng. As our Kiangsi Peace Preservation Column took Yung-tai and Chang-shu, the enemy retreated to the line from Hu-wan to Lin-chuan, San-chiang-kou and Fu-ho. Our 9th War Area directed the 79th Corps to dispatch one division pursuing toward Lin-chuan and Hsu-chia-tu, and the main force of the Corps to stand by in the vicinity of Chung-jen; the 58th Corps to dispatch one division pursuing toward Li-chia-tu and San-chiang-kou with the main force of the Corps held in readiness in the vicinity of Ho-hu-yu; and the 4th Corps to mass in the area west of Chung-jen. By July 13, the 79th Corps reached the vicinity of Tung-chia-ling and Shang-tun-tu on the southern flank of Linchuan. The 58th Corps reached the vicinity of San-chiang-kou and Ta-kang-kou reaping considerable gains. When order was received from Generalissimo Chiang to halt the attack, the corps ended their actions.

As to the eastern sector of the Chekiang-Kiangsi Railway, since early July when our 3rd War Area launched local offensives, the enemy found it difficult to look after everywhere. Consequently, he was forced to abandon Fu-chun River depot line on mid-July, and mass the Harada Composite Brigade in Lung-yu. In succession, our forces recovered Hsin-teng, Tung-lu, Chien-teh, Heng-feng and Yi-yang. The enemy continued to pull the Nara Column (built around 3 infantry battalions) from northern China and attach it to the 13th Corps. Later, it became subordinated to the 70th Division and deployed in Li-shui. On July 7, the Kosonoe Brigade moved east from Li-shui and took Wen-chow on July 11. On July 12, over 1,000 enemy marines in more than 10 ships landed at Wen-chow. Taking Jui-an on July 13, the enemy plundered. The Harada Brigade moved south from Lung-yu on July 28 and took Sui-chang on August 1. On August 2, it joined force with the main force of Nara column from Li-shui to take Sung-yang and continued to move south. At this time, our 88th Corps which had just been pulled back from Pei-shan-hou to Yun-ho coordinated with the 9th Provisional Corps in a converging attack on the enemy from the north and south. Fighting took place in Shih-tsang-yuan and San-ma-pai. In the meantime, the enemy's Kono Composite Brigade and a portion of the 15th Division respectively moved from Chiang-shan and Pa-tu to attack Hsien-hsia-kuan and Pu-cheng. On August 8, the enemy took Hsien-hsia-kuan and responded to the enemy in Sung-yang. The counterattack of our 105th Division, 49th Corps led to the recovery of Hsien-hsia-kuan on August 9 and pursuit toward Chiangshan and Pa-tu. With the recovery of Shih-tsang-yuan by our 88th Corps on August 10, the enemy fell back to Sung-yang. On August 9, a portion of the enemy's 32nd Division at Yu-shan invaded Chu-chuan Chen in the west. Another enemy force from Chang-shan moved north to invade Hua-fu and engaged our 145th Division. The enemy's 22nd Division at Shang-yao moved north to invade Cheng-chia-fang and engaged our 146th Division. The enemy assumed the offensive instead of the defensive in order to cover the destruction of the airfields and the evacuation of railroad and other seized materials, and to facilitate subsequent withdrawal. Our 26th Corps south of Shang-yao, successively inflicted heavy casualties on the enemy at Shang-kuan-chiao, Leng-tan and Keng-kou forcing the enemy to fall back to Shang-yao. On August 15, our 33rd Provisional Division recovered Wen-chow forcing the Kosonoe Brigade to withdraw. to Li-shui.

On July 28, the enemy's Supreme Headquarters ordered the China Expeditionary Force to end the operation in Chekiang and insure the security of the vicinity of Chin-hua. It also instructed that the transfer to take place in the middle of August. Hence, the China Expeditionary Force decided to begin the transfer on August 19. The transfer of the 13th Corps was divided into two phases. In Phase One, all the forces west of Chu-chow were massed in the vicinity of Chu-chow. In Phase Two, forces were massed in the vicinity of Chin-hua leaving the 22nd Division behind in Chin-hua, Wu-yi and Tung-yang and the 70th Division in the area north of Hsin-chang and Feng-hua. The enemy's 11th Corps which began to withdraw on August 19, massed in the vicinity of Nan-chang on August 27.

During the period of the enemy withdrawal, our force followed up in pursuit. By the end of August, with the exception of a corner of Chin-lan in eastern Che-kiang, the pre-battle posture was restored.

During this battle, the enemy, feeling conceited, massed over 9 division to conduct operations for the destruction of airfields in Chekiang, clearing the Chekiang-Kiangsi Railway, and plundering war materials. Nevertheless, when an important crisis of the Pacific War came to an end, the enemy wasted 4 months of precious time to undertake such secondary operations. Though small in size and concentrated in industries, Japan was exceedingly sensitive to the threat of air raid. But at that time, the American force lacked the capability to launch massive air raids over Japan proper. Insofar as her overall strategy was concerned, Japan was mistaken in launching this operation. Having a complete grasp of the overall situation and knowing the enemy and ourselves, Generalissimo Chiang resolutely ordered the 3rd War Area to avoid a decisive engagement in Chu-chow. Thus, our forces were able to conserve our strength and continued to harass the enemy, forcing him to fall back to his original positions. Generalissimo Chiang's decision was outstanding, as he caused the enemy to waste strength and time and enabled our forces to tide themselves over the most difficult period.

    d.   Battle of Western Hupei
        (Early May—Mid-June, 1943. See Map 34 and Chart 52 and 53)

CHART 52

Chart Showing Japanese Chain of Command during the Battle of
Western Hupei (Late April, 1943)

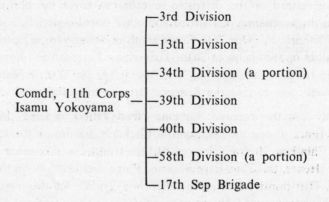

Comdr, 11th Corps
Isamu Yokoyama

- 3rd Division
- 13th Division
- 34th Division (a portion)
- 39th Division
- 40th Division
- 58th Division (a portion)
- 17th Sep Brigade

CHART 53

Chart Showing the Chinese Chain of Command during the Battle of Western Hupei
(Late April, 1943)

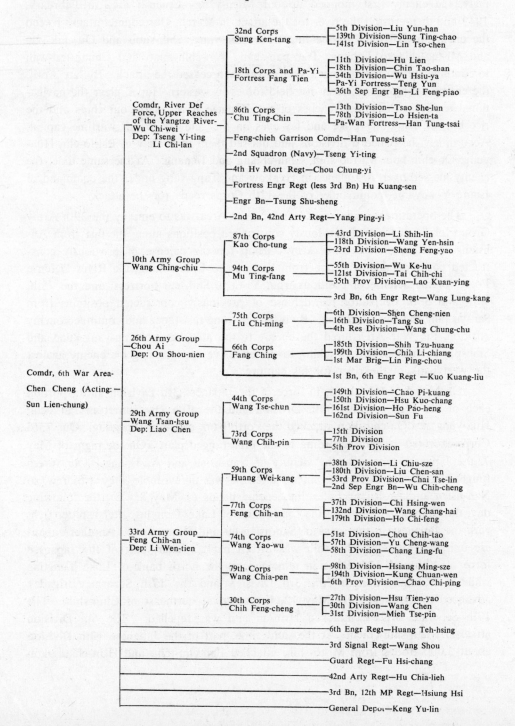

Since his occupation of I-chang in 1940, the enemy was subjected to our flanking attacks on the upper reaches of the Han River in the north and the checking of our Mien-yang—Chien-li area in the south. Later, our counterattack operations against I-chang placed the enemy in an unfavorable position. Accordingly, the enemy first mopped up our Mien-yang—Chien-li area in February, 1943 and then crossed the river for the attack in March. Our counterattacks forced the enemy to fall back to the line from Hua-yung, Shih-shou and Ou-chih-kou and Mi-tuo-shih to I-chang, Tien-pao-shan, Yen-chih-miao and Chuan-tou-wan to continue stubborn resistance. Our forces then ceased the attack. By late April, the enemy attempted to crush our field forces in western Hupei, clear the navigational traffic in the upper reaches of the Yangtze River, seize our ships and the rice bins of Tung-ting Lake and lay eyes on the gateway to our wartime capital. Accordingly, he pulled 6 divisions and massed them separately in Pai-lo-chi, Hua-yung, Ou-chih-kou, Mi-tuo-shih, Chih-chiang and I-chang. At the same time, the enemy massed over 100 planes in Hankow and Tang-yang under the command of Isamu Yokoyama, commander of the 11th Corps ready for the attack.

The operational guidance of our 6th War Area was to employ the 29th Army Group for the defense of previously constructed positions along the line from An-hsiang to Kung-an; the 10th Army Group for the defense of previously constructed positions along the line from Kung-an to Chih-chiang; the River Defense Force for the defense of positions from Yi-tu to Shih-pai Fortress; and the 75th, 77th and 59th Corps for the defense of previously constructed positions from San-yu-tung to Chuan-tou-wan. By offering strong resistance and continued enemy attrition, the War Area lured the enemy to the area between Yu-yang-kuan and Shih-pai Fortress before switching to the offensive and pressing the enemy against the west bank of the river for his capture.

On May 5, 1943, the main force of the Japanese 3rd Division and a portion each of the 17th Brigade, 34th Division and the 40th Division from Pai-lochi, Hua-yung and Ou-chih-kou attacked the north bank of Lake Tung-ting. Our 73rd Corps executed a delay according to the prearranged plan. On the night of May 7, the Japanese arrived at the vicinity of Nan-hsien and An-hsiang. Our forces fought bloodily for 24 hours. Since the terrain was unfavorable, they withdrew, so Nan-hsien and An-hsiang fallen into enemy hands on May 8. On the following day, the Chinese withdrew to the south bank of Lake Tungting after a bitter fight with the Japanese in the areas of San-hsien-hu and Hung-miao. Another Japanese unit that attacked Chin-shih was driven back. Later, part of the Japanese force of 40th and 34th Division remained on the north bank of Lake Tungting while their main strength (the 3rd Division and the 17th Separate Brigade) advanced to the west. By May 12, it massed at northeast of Chin-shih. The 17th Separate Brigade attacked Hsin-an and was repelled. The 6th Division attacked Nuan-shui-chieh. At the same time, part of the Japanese 13th Division about 3,000 troops from Mi-to-shih, attacked Pan-chu-tang and Hsin-chiang-kou while the main strength veered westward after a successful crossing of the river between Yang-chi and Chih-chiang. By May 15, both sides stood opposite each other along the Ta-yen-tang-Nu-an-shui-chieh-Liu-chia-chang-Cha-yuan-chih-Chih-chiang line. During that time, units of our 10th Army Group suffered heavy casualties in several battles.

Meanwhile, the Japanese 3rd Division moved northwestward. The Japanese military strength at I-chang and Ku-lao-pei was being increased. Apparently, the Japanese were planning an attack on our River Defense Force. The War Area, therefore, decided on the following: Control the northern area of Shih-men with the 79th and 74th Corps, continue to delay the enemy in the southern area of Ching-chiang with the 10th Army Group and consolidate the Shih-pai Fortress with the River Defense Force in order that Shih-pai could be used as a base for our counteroffensive. On the morning of May 21, the Japanese 13th Division from Cha-yuan-chih, after taking Wang-chia-fan, converged on our 67th Division with about 3,000 men and part of their 58th Division from Chih-chiang. On the night of May 21, these two groups of the Japanese force crossed the Hsi-yang River at Nieh-chia-ho and Miao-tan. At the same time, the main strength of the Japanese 39th Division was fighting furiously with our 13th Division after crossing the Yangtze River at Hung-hua-tao north of I-tu. On May 22, Yu-yang-kuan was lost. Our 87th Corps withdrew to the Chuan-hsin-tien-Lung-tan-ping line. On the same night, the Japanese broke through our position manned by our 13th Division at Ta-hsiao-sung-shan and Chang-ling-kang. The 13th Division shifted to the Pi-pa-chih-Mo-shih-Yen-chia-to-Hsien-jen-chiao line. Under cover of artillery and air the Japanese continued to advance. Our 86th Corps moved its position to the areas of Ma-an-shan (south of Chang-yang), Pan-chiao-pu and Wu-kuei-shan. On May 24, the Japanese concentrated their 3rd and 39th Divisions on the outskirts of Chang-yang, which fell in the late afternoon after bitter fight. Meanwhile, our 139th Division, the spearhead of the 32nd Corps, arrived in the area between Chin-yang-kou and Tu-chen-wan. Therefore, both sides stood opposite each other along the Chang-yang-Ching-chiang-Feng-huang-shan line.

On May 24, the main strength of the Japanese 3rd and 39th Divisions situated on the bank west of I-chang fell on our 18th Division. Their advance was immediately blocked. On the following day, the Japanese overwhelmed our position under cover of their air force. Part of their force dashed into the area between Pien-yen and Chin-yang-kou, but they were attacked by our forces from the south and the north and suffered heavy losses. At that time, enemy forces on the banks of the Ching River and attacking Shih-pai totalled 60,000 men, and appeared ready to take our first line fortress in one stroke and threaten En-shih and Pa Hsien. However, our forces were adequately prepared. Our Supreme Commander indicated that the Shih-pai Fortress was our Stalingrad and called upon the commanders of the River Defense Force to consider this an excellent

opportunity to destroy the enemy.   Upon receipt of the instructions, our commanders were determined to defend the fortress at all costs and took advantage of
favorable terrain to fight a decisive battle against the enemy.   The battle was to
be fought on June 1 along the Tzu-chiu-Mu-chiao-hsi-Tsao-chia-fan-Shih-pai line.
The 79th Corps advanced from Shih-men towards Yu-yang-kuan, the 74th Corps
from Tao-yuan to assemble in Shih-men and the 27th Division to advance towards
the southeast of Lang-shu-tien.   Between May 26 and 27, the River Defense Force
was committed to a hard battle, especially the action in Man-tou-tsui, Chiao-ting-
shan and Pi-chien-feng fought by the 5th and 18th Divisions.   Here, the Japanese
had to pay dearly for every inch of ground they gained.   Fighting gallantly, the
officers and men of our 18th Division killed or wounded 3,000-4,000 enemy troops.
About 4,000-5,000 troops of the enemy's 13th Division from Yu-yang-kuan which
had reached Tien-chu Shan and crossed the Ya-tse River were intercepted by our
forces. Bitter fighting ensued and resulted in heavy casualties on the enemy.   On
the night of May 27, the River Defense Force confronted the enemy along the
Tac-tsao-ping-Kao-chia-yen-I-chia-pa-Tsao-chia-fan-Shih-pai line while the main
force of 94th Corps, 10th Army Group defended the vicinity of Tzu-chiu to cover
the right flank of the River Defense Force.   On May 28, our counterattack slowed
down the enemy offensive.   Continuous bombings of our air force caused the
enemy serious difficulties in sending reinforcements.   On the following day, our
118th Division from Wu-feng and Tzu-chiu recovered Yu-yang-kuan.   By then,
we had cut off the rear of the Japanese 3rd and 13th Divisions.   This gave the
signal for the all-out counterattack of our various corps which began on May 30.
At this time, the Japanese opposing our River Defense Force concentrated the
full strength of their infantry, artillery and air and assaulted Tsao-chia-fan and
the Shih-pai Fortress and turned their force towards Mu-chiao-chi from Tien-
chu-shan.   Our 11th Division held steadily in Shih-pai and inflicted very heavy
casualties upon the enemy.   One enemy group of over 1,000 men that attacked
San-kuan-yen and Szu-fang-wan was almost wiped out.   However, our 18th
Division at Tsao-chia-fan was committed to a bitter battle for many days.   Its
right flank was overrun by the enemy as a result of heavy casualties.   After the
counterattack of our 13th Division. the enemy advance was brought to a stop east
of Lo-pu-tang.   At the same time, the enemy that had turned towards Mu-chiao-
chi was also held back by our 32nd Corps.   As a result of heavy casualties, the
Japanese fled to the east in confusion on May 31, leaving many horses and supplies behind.   Their covering force occupied positions in Li-shu-yao, Nieh-chia-
ho, Hua-chiao, Chang-yang, Wu-chia-to and Ta-chiao-pien to cover their escape,
while their 13th Division and part of their 17th Separate Brigade were encircled
on the outskirts of Mo-shih and I-tu by our 23rd, 55th, 98th and 121st Divisions.
Chinese and American planes bombed and strafed the fleeing invaders, destroying
enemy equipment and personnel.   On June 2, the bombings on enemy's 3rd and
39th Divisions and a portion of the 58th Division fleeing and crossing the river

to I-chang were most successful. As a result, many enemy troops were drowned. By 3 June, the River Defense Force had advanced smoothly and recaptured all those positions held before the battle. The 29th Army Group and the 74th Corps pressed on the Kung-an-Mo-pan-chou line after they recovered An-hsiang, Hsin-an, Wang-chia-chang and Nu-an-shui-chieh. Over 1,000 troops of the enemy's 40th Division and 3,000 troops of the puppet 11th Division fled separately to Shih-shou, Ou-chih-kou, and Kung-an. After bitter fighting, the enemy under siege in the vicinity of I-tu and Mo-shih suffered prohibitive losses. On June 5, our forces recovered Mo-shih having wiped out most of the enemy forces there. However, enemy remnants offered stubborn resistance on the high ground in the vicinity of Tao-chia-po southeast of Mo-shih. As our pursuit forces reached the outskirts of I-tu, our air force had destroyed the river-crossing materials. The enemy had to find other river-crossing sites. Knowing that the enemy in Mo-shih desperately needed reinforcements, the enemy on the outskirts of I-tu counterattacked. On June 6, the enemy took a chance and broke out through the fronts of our 194th and 98th Divisions. As its follow-up units had not yet arrived, the 194th Division had to bear the brunt of the enemy's main attack. Greatly outnumbered, the division's front was penetrated. By the time the 6th Provisional Division raced to the scene, the enemy had reached the vicinity of Hsiao-shih-yen and Nieh-chia-ho. Meanwhile, the enemy at Sung-tzu turned toward Yang-hsi and Chih-chiang to attack the flank and rear of our 118th Division. With a strength of only four battalions, the division had to fall back to the vicinity of Yuchiachiao. On June 7, enemy remnants southeast of Mo-shih used poison gas and broke out under cover of his air force. After uniting with the enemy at Nieh-chia-ho, both groups fled eastward in confusion. At night on the same day, our 6th Provisional Division raided the headquarters of the enemy's 13th Division. Tsutomu Akashika, the division commander, was missing. Between June 6 and 8, to respond to the enemy force which tried to break out from I-tu, the enemy increased his reinforcements to over 3,000 and fought against our 74th Corps in the vicinity of Chieh-ho-shih, Hsi-chai, and Pao-ta-shih. The fighting which continued for three days and three nights led to heavy casualties on both sides and the downing of one enemy plane. On 8 June, our 121st Division recovered I-tu. On the following day, the 121st and 85th Divisions recaptured Chih-chiang. The enemy remnants fled to the east. On the night of June 11, the 6th Provisional Division retook Yang-chi. and Sung-tze. On 12 June, the 194th Division recovered Mo-pen-chou and Hsin-chiang-kou. On 17 June, the 74th Corps recaptured Che-chia-tsui and Shen-ching-tu, while the 194th Division retook Pan-chu-tang and Mi-chi-tai. Subsequently, our forces advanced to the river bank and took Tou-hu-ti to attack the enemy forces which had retreated to the Hua-yung-Shih-shou-Ou-chih-kou-Mi-to-shih line. The situation on both sides had returned to that of 5 May.

    e. Battle of Northern Burma and Western Yunnan (Late October, 1943— Late March, 1944. See Maps 35, 36 and 37, and Charts 54-1, 2, 3, and 55).

CHART 54-1

Chart Showing Japanese Chain of Command during the Battle of
Northern Burma-Western Yunnan (Late October, 1943)

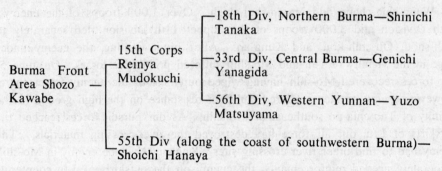

Burma Front Area Shozo — Kawabe

15th Corps — Reinya Mudokuchi —

- 18th Div, Northern Burma—Shinichi Tanaka
- 33rd Div, Central Burma—Genichi Yanagida
- 56th Div, Western Yunnan—Yuzo Matsuyama

55th Div (along the coast of southwestern Burma)— Shoichi Hanaya

Remarks: 1. The Burma Front Army was activated on January 15, 1943. In October, 1943, Shozo Kawabe was relieved by Heitaro Kimura and Seikachi Katamura assumed command of the 15th Corps.
2. The 5th Air Wing assisted in the operation.

CHART 54-2

(Mid-January, 1944)

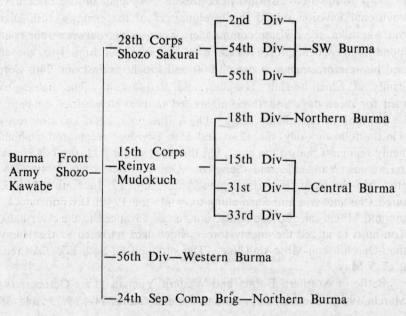

Burma Front Army Shozo— Kawabe

28th Corps Shozo Sakurai —

- 2nd Div —
- 54th Div —SW Burma
- 55th Div —

15th Corps —Reinya Mudokuch —

- 18th Div—Northern Burma
- 15th Div —
- 31st Div —Central Burma
- 33rd Div —

—56th Div—Western Burma

—24th Sep Comp Brig—Northern Burma

CHART 54-3

(Early April, 1944)

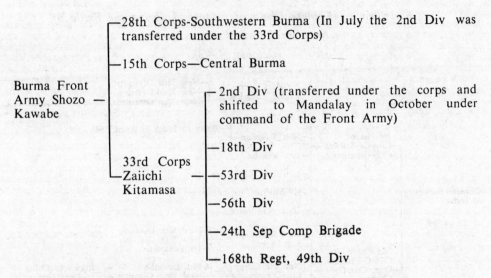

Burma Front Army Shozo Kawabe

— 28th Corps-Southwestern Burma (In July the 2nd Div was transferred under the 33rd Corps)

— 15th Corps—Central Burma

33rd Corps Zaiichi Kitamasa

— 2nd Div (transferred under the corps and shifted to Mandalay in October under command of the Front Army)

— 18th Div

— 53rd Div

— 56th Div

— 24th Sep Comp Brigade

— 168th Regt, 49th Div

This operation, a part of the Allied counteroffensive operations in Burma, was conceived in the Casablanca Conference in January, 1943 and gradually took shape at the Washington Conference in May, the Quebec Conference in August, and the Cairo Conference in November. Since the spring of 1943, China made active preparations to augment the Chinese Forces in India and the Expeditionary Forces providing them with all the U.S. weapons and ammunition. They were also given first priority in personnel replacement. China withstood inadequate supplies in the other war areas in order to seek a common victory in Burma with the Allied forces and to clear the China-India international thoroughfare:

(1) First Phase Operations of the Chinese Forces in India:

The enemy occupied Burma and western Yunnan to consolidate the left flank of the Mainland battleground, cut off China's link to her allies and instigated India's defection from Britain. Politically and strategically speaking, these moves carried great significance. In September, 1943, the enemy's Burma Front Army employed the main forces of the 15th Corps to push toward western Burma preparatory to attacking Imphal. The main force of his 18th Division massed in Myitkyina and Mawngkwan and conducted sustained operations against our forces in India to the north. The enemy's 56th Division and a portion of the 18th Division attacked a portion of our expeditionary forces on the west bank of the Salween River in order to seize our strong points there. Later, the enemy's 56th Division alone resisted the counteroffensive of our expeditionary forces. In late October, 1943, the New 22nd and New 38th Divisions of our forces in India launched counterattacks from Ledo against the enemy in northern Burma, in the hope of destroying the enemy there, recovering Myitkyina and linking up with our ex-

CHART 55

Chart Showing Chinese Chain of Command during the Battle of
Northern Burma-Western Yunnan
(October, 1943)

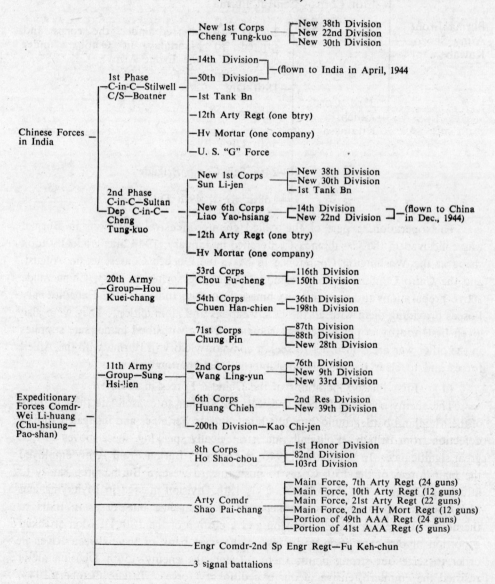

peditionary forces and the British and Indian forces so as to clear the traffic communications between China and India.

At the end of October 1943, the 112th Regiment of the New 38th Division moved from Tagaplung Ga via Shing-bwiyang towards Taro, Yupang and Ningpien. In early November, these troops seized Lachiasu, Shingbwiying and Ningpien, but a portion of the enemy 18th Division resisted stubbornly at Yupang. With the arrival of reinforcements, the enemy launched a counterattack and besieged a portion of our troops for over one month. With only bananas to ward off starvation, these troops held their positions firmly. In the last 10 days of December, the 114th Regiment of our New 38th Division rushed to the scene as reinforcements and wiped out one enemy battalion. The victory won at Yupang was the first of our victories in Northern Burma. In early January 1944, the enemy in the area west of the Tarung River were wiped out completely. By this time, all units of our New 38th Division had reached the area west of the Tarung River, and traffic on the Sino-Indian Highway was open to Shingbwiyang. The 65th Regiment of the New 22nd Division, as right flank, now moved through the thick forests along the Taro River toward Taro. For one week they pushed forward, encountering much hardship along the way, and then besieged the surprised Okada Battalion at Wanankuan and Lachiasu; the enemy was annihilated. On 31 January, these troops captured Taro. The main force of the New 38th Division, as the left flank, attacked and captured Taihapa Ga on February 1. At this time, all the troop units of the New 22nd Division had reached the area near Shingbwiyang. They launched an attack towards Maingkwan in two columns. The right column, consisting of the New 22nd Division, sent part of its 65th Regiment over the Wantokoshan, while the main force of the division crossed the river at Kantau and attacked Yangpangchia. The left column, consisting of the main force of the New 38th Division, after pursuing the enemy in the area southeast of the Tawang River, engaged the main force of the 18th Division for a decisive battle. The enemy made use of the many streams and embankments along the Tanai River for defensive positions and blocked the road intersections with superior artillery fire in an attempt to contain our troops in the valley on the north bank of the Tanai River. The main force of our New 22nd Division captured Yangpangchia on February 21 and recovered Lachengka on February 23. The enemy left flank was completely crushed. At this time, our New 38th Division detoured to reconnoiter the enemy right flank. This pincer attack inflicted heavy losses upon the enemy 18th Division. All the strategic points surrounding Maingkwan were now in our hands. Then, our victorious troops of the New 22nd Division launched a frontal attack against Maingkwan and the New 38th Division attacked the enemy on the north bank of the Tanai River. The 1st Tank Battalion, combined with one battalion of the 66th Regiment, skirted to the enemy rear from west of Maingkwan to cut off his contact. After fighting for 10 days, our New 38th Division captured Makaw and Lashuka and wiped out all the enemy on the north bank of the Tanai River. Our New 22nd

Division assaulted and captured Maingkwan on March 5. The tank battalion, which had skirted to the enemy rear, advanced under great hardships through virgin forests and finally reached Ningkuka. The battalion killed over 1,400 enemy troops along the way and crushed the main force of the enemy 18th Division.

When the Battle of Maingkwan reached the decisive stage, the enemy tried to shift his troops to the Walawbum area and concentrate his main force for a counterattack. Enemy orders to this effect were captured and with lightning speed, our troops relentlessly pursued the enemy along several routes. At this time, an American unit also reached the area northeast of Walawbum and attacked the enemy on March 4. The enemy counterattacked furiously and forced the American troops to pull back eight miles. In order to support our allies and capture Walawbum swiftly, the 113th Regiment of our New 38th Division marched on the double for two days and nights. On arriving at the scene, the regiment attacked the enemy and sent part of its force to cut off the retreat. The main force of the New 22nd Division moved south along the highway, while part of its force attacked southward from Panni, and the tank battalion pursued the enemy from Ningkuka. On March 8, the tank battalion reached the area northwest of Walawbum and encountered the enemy. After a bloody fight, many of the enemy were killed or wounded and on March 9, the 113th Regiment captured Walawbum. The New 22nd Division and the tank battalion then chased the enemy southward. On March 15, Tingkawk Sakan was recaptured. The Hukawng Valley was now cleared of the enemy. However, the enemy mustered all the troops of his 56th Regiment and deployed them in the mountain pass of Chienpushan and along a line stretching east to west, intending to prevent our troops from marching south. The mountain range divides the Hukawng Valley from the Mogaung Valley. The distance from Tingkawk Sakan, north of the mountain pass, to Shaduzup, south of the pass, is approximately 10 miles. One highway winds through the waist of the mountain and the enemy had already constructed fortifications on the hill tops on either side of this highway. To make a detour was impossible due to the thick forests. By this time, enemy reinforcements had already arrived with 30 large guns of various calibres. To launch an attack uphill would be extremely difficult, so the main force of our New 22nd Division was ordered to launch a frontal attack while the 113th Regiment of our New 38th Division was sent to cut a way through the hilly land east of the highway. This regiment moved laboriously for 10 days and finally reached Lapan, south of Shaduzup on March 28. It then turned north. At this time, the New 22nd Division had already broken through Kaoluyang of Chienpushan and rushed south. The enemy was under attack from both south and north. On March 29, our troops captured Shaduzup. The enemy dead covered the battleground. After seizing the strategic places in North Burma, our troops proceeded toward the Mogaung Valley to fight the enemy.

The Mogaung Valley is about 75 miles long and less than seven miles wide with the Mogaung River winding through it. Making use of this long valley, the enemy resisted our attacks step by step and with the arrival of the 146th Regiment of their 56th Division and about two infantry battalions of the 2nd Division as reinforcements, their fighting strength became even stronger. Our troops pushed on along several routes. By the end of April, the New 22nd Division moving along the highway had reached Malakao and the New 38th Division moving along the hilly land east of the highway had already captured Kaoli, Malan and Manping. On 3 May, under air cover dispatched by the Allied Force, our tank battalion broke through enemy positions with longitudinal depth at Yingkokantao. The enemy fled south in disorder. In late May, the monsoon season in North Burma began. In order to restore traffic along the Sino-Indian Highway as soon as possible, our troops launched an attack against Kamaing in bad weather. The 112th Regiment of our New 38th Division cut a road through the thick forests and skirted to the south of Kamaing. On May 27, these troops crossed the swift current of the Mogaung River and captured Hsimu, cutting off the Kamaing-Mogaung Highway for a length of four kilometers. In early June, our New 22nd Division, with the 149th Regiment of the 50th Division attached, launched a frontal attack against the enemy. The enemy mustered their troop units under the direct command of the 18th Division and portions of the 56th and 2nd Divisions, under fire cover, counterattacked and were repelled. The 65th Regiment of the New 22nd Division skirted the enemy positions at Malakao and pushed forward, cutting a road through the hilly land to the west of the enemy. On June 1, the roads west of Kamiang were cut off by this detachment. The main force of the New 22nd Division, with the 149th Regiment of the 50th Division attached, broke through the enemy positions at Malakao and headed for Kamaing. The New 38th Division sent its 114th Regiment to secretly skirt south along the Mogaung Mountains towards Mogaung and sent its 113th Regiment southwest from Manping. By this time, the enemy at Kamaing were surrounded by several layers of our troops. On 16 June, our troops captured Kamaing. The enemy 18th Division commander, leading about one thousand of his remaining troops, climbed Hsuehpangshan and fled hastily southward. On 18 June, the 114th Regiment reached the area northeast of Mogaung. At that time, Mogaung was defended by units of the enemy 2nd, 18th and 53rd Divisions. Frightened by the valor of our troops, the enemy hid behind fortifications and dared not engage our troops. However, they attacked furiously the 500 British soldiers who had just arrived at a place two miles south of Mogaung. In order to support our allies, our 114th Regiment crossed the swift current of the Mogaung River and launched an attack against the enemy. Beginning on June 20, the bloody battle lasted for three days and two nights. Finally, our troops captured the strategic points outside of Mogaung and encircld the city. They then broke into the city and street fighting ensued for two days and two nights. On June 25, the enemy were completely crushed and the city was in our hands. At this time, the 113th Regiment also encountered enemy reinforcements totalling about 600 men, northwest of Mogaung. After fighting for two days and two nights, most of the enemy were annihilated.

When the main force of our troops was engaged with the enemy in the Mogaung Valley, the 88th Regiment of our New 30th Division, the 150th Regiment of our 50th Division, one company of the artillery regiment and two American battalions were organized into a commando unit to capture Myitkyina. In early April, this unit moved out of the Hukawng Valley, through the Kumon Mountain Range across cliffs and thick forests. In a little over one month, this lone army penetrated over a hundred miles into the enemy rear and reached the vicinity of Myitkyina on May 15. The enemy who was completely taken by surprise thought these troops must have come from the sky, and fought back desperately. In one attack, we seized Myitkyina Airfield and covered the landing of our airborne troops. Gen. Stilwell personally led the main force of the New 30th Division and parts of the 14th and New 22nd Divisions which had arrived as reinforcements. Some British troops at Sumprabum also moved south to render help. On May 17, our troops launched the attack against the city. Over 3,000 enemy troops, comprising the main force of the 114th Regiment of the 18th Division, engineer troops, airfield garrison unit, military police and a battalion of the enemy 56th Division which arrived in late June, fought back desperately behind well-constructed buildings and fortifications. The battle raged for two months and the enemy still refused to retreat. When Kamaing and Mogaung were captured, the 149th Regiment of our 50th Division rushed to Myitkyina as reinforcements. Finally, on 3 August, the enemy was wiped out and Myitkyina was recovered.

(2)   Second Phase Operations of the Chinese Forces in India:

In the first week of August 1944, part of the enemy 2nd Division rushed from Southern Burma to reinforce Namhkam. Later, a detachment was organized with a reconnaissance regiment as the basic unit and one battalion each of the 2nd and 18th Divisions and 10 tanks attached, all under the command of Colonel Hara Yoshizo, commander of the reconnaissance regiment. The detachment rushed to Bhamo as a garrison force, arrived in the city on August 13 and sent part of its force of over one battalion to defend Myothit and the hilly ground on either side of Myothit, in an attempt to hold Bhamo firmly, stop our troops and wait for the arrival of their 18th Division to counterattack. The enemy 2nd Division moved towards Mangshih on August 20 to reinforce their 56th Division. Later, since the enemy 33rd Corps had mistakenly estimated that the Allied Force would send its main force to attack Mandalay by way of Mongmit, it ordered the 18th Division to turn and head for Mongmit. The 2nd Division began to push towards Mandalay on October 10.

In order to restore traffic on the Sino-Indian Highway as early as possible, our expeditionary force in India, after replenishment during the monsoon, was reorganized into the New 1st Corps and the New 6th Corps. In mid-October, they moved in two columns from Kamaing and Myitkyina southward. The east column, consisting of the New 1st Corps with the 2nd Company of the Artillery

Regiment attached, moved along the Myitkyina-Bhamo Highway and the west column, consisting of the New 22nd Division (less the Artillery Battalion) of the New 6th Corps, moved toward Shwegu via Hopin. The 14th and 50th Divisions of the New 6th Corps were appointed as the general reserve force. They were each ordered to dispatch part of their forces to cover the flanks.

The New 1st Corps sent the New 38th Division towards the area between Tanpangyang and Napao and placed the New 30th Division in the vicinity of Waingmaw to wait for further orders. The attack was launched on October 21. By October 27, the man force of the New 38th Division had reached Ta-li on the north bank of the Taping River and part of its force had reached Yalupen. The main force of the New 30th Division moved into the Tanpangyang area and took up garrison duty. On October 29, the advanced detachment of the main force of the New 38th Division attacked and captured Myothit and mopped up the enemy on the north bank of the Taping River. On 3 November, it captured the line stretching north of Pai-keng to the Taping River. The main force of the New 38th Division, placing part of its force on the north bank of the Ta-ping River to launch a diversionary attack, moved secretly from the area north of Ta li towards the hilly ground on the left flank and crossed the river by steel-cable to the Pulantan-Sinlumkaba line, skirting towards Bhamo and Mansi. The New 30th Division continued to push towards Tali. On November 6, the main force of the New 38th Division captured Sinlumkaba. On November 8, it reconnoitered in and out of the hilly ground and captured all the strategic points north of Momauk to Myothit, on the east side of the highway. On November, 9 our troops on the north bank of the Taping River crossed the river and charged along the Myitkyina-Bhamo Highway. On November 11, these two units linked up, wiped out enemy remnants and moved south to lay siege to Momauk. Meanwhile, the 113th Regiment moved from the mountain path east of Momauk toward Mansi. It captured Shawang-chiatang on November 14, cutting off the only communication line leading to Bhamo. Part of the enemy force at Mansi attacked our 113th Regiment. Our troops attacked from both sides. The battle raged for three days. We crushed the enemy and captured Mansi. Bhamo was completely encircled by our troops. Momauk was captured by our troops on November 14 and the enemy fled in disorder towards Bhamo where they were besieged by our troops in the forest north of Momauk and completely wiped out on November 19. From then on the enemy at Bhamo stayed within the city walls and resisted desperately. On November 30, the main force of the New 38th Division joined the siege of Bhamo, leaving part of its force to defend Mansi. Airplanes were dispatched to help. The battle lasted until December 15, when Bhamo fell to our troops. Colonel Hara, the enemy garrison commander, was killed, and all the troops annihilated except for sixty to seventy men who escaped by swimming across the river at night.

On November 1, the New 22nd Division of the New 6th Corps moved to the area on the north bank of the Irrawaddy River. On the 2nd, it captured Chiaochih and Moshou. On the 3rd, the main force moved into Tingpafoyin. With river-crossing equipment supplied by the American force, it crossed the Irrawaddy on the 5th and crushed the combined enemy force, consisting of part of the enemy 2nd Division and puppet Burmese troops. On the 7th, it attacked and captured Shwegu. The remnants of the enemy force broke out and headed for Kaichih, then turned and fled toward Bhamo in disorder. In order to help the Allied troops capture Bhamo, intercept enemy reinforcements and cut off the enemy route of retreat, our New 22nd Division left its 64th Regiment to defend Shwegu and moved in two columns towards Mantha and the hilly ground northwest of Mantha on November 11. The left column, consisting of the 65th Regiment, crushed the enemy at Hsiman and captured Mantha on November 12. On November 14, the right column also reached Mantha. Part of this force attacked and captured Sikaw while another part of the 65th Regiment moved towards Bhamo. The latter linked up with the 113th Regiment of the New 38th Division at Kungmaha on the southern suburbs of Bhamo. It took part in the attack against that city and then returned to its parent organization.

In order to gain the strategic initiative, the 1st Corps sent the main force of the New 30th Division to detour and launch an attack against Namhkam without waiting for the fall of Bhamo. This division (less the 89th Regiment) moved in three columns along the Bhamo-Namhkam Highway and the hilly ground on either side of the highway at the end of November. On December 2, the advance units encountered the enemy along the line running from northwest of Kangma to the hilly ground near Nanyu. On December 4 and 5, the enemy attacking our left flank were repulsed and the High Ground 5338 on either side of the Bhamo-Namhkam Highway was captured. On Dec 9, the main force of the New 30th Division encountered an enemy composite detachment (consisting of parts of the 18th, 49th and 56th Divisions, and artillery, engineer and transportation battalions, commanded by Colonel Yamazaki, Commander of the enemy 55th Regiment) near Nanyu on its way to reinforce Bhamo. The battle raged until December 11. As the enemy had made no gains, they infiltrated through gaps in our lines and harassed our units. But all the infiltrators had been wiped out on 14 December. At this time, our 89th Regiment at Hsiman was transferred to the frontline and the 112th Regiment (reinforced) of the New 38th Division was transferred to serve as the left flank independent detachment to skirt far to the right flank of the enemy. On December 15, the enemy moved his main force to the right flank and assaulted High Ground 5338; they were completely crushed by our troops.

Before this, in order to annihilate the enemy along the front and to gain the initiative, our 88th Regiment of the New 30th Division, with one pack howitzer battery and some engineer troops attached, was ordered to launch an attack from the left flank towards Machih on December 13. This regiment crushed the enemy resistance and captured Machih on December 17. It proceeded south and helped by the assault of the frontal and flank units, captured Katiko and Kalung on 19 December. The enemy fled southward. On December 21, it captured Pangcha. On 22 December, the main force of the Left Flank Independent Detachment crossed the Nanwang River and reached the vicinity Lak'ang where it confronted the enemy with part of its force, while another part rushed south along the west bank of the Nanwang River. On 23 December, the Bhamo-Namhkan Highway was cut up and the enemy in the vicinity of Nankai were surrounded by our troops. From Dec. 23 to 25, our frontal attack troops and the troops cutting off the Bhamo-Namhkan Highway attacked the enemy in the vicinity of Nankai from both sides, repulsed two reinforcing enemy companies and captured Nankai. On 26 December, our Left Flank Attack Force captured Manchiehmu and Manwing. On December 27, our Left Flank Independent Detachment rushed along both banks of the Nanwang River and captured Laochih and the airfield. On December 28, this detachment attacked and captured Pangkhan. The attacking units of our New 30th Division also pushed forward along the highway and to the right of the highway. By January 4, 1945, these units had captured enemy defensive points on the west bank of the Juili River and continued to attack Maotang, the last defensive point of the enemy. At this time, we learned through intelligence reports that the enemy was going to make use of the strategic points on the hilly ground southeast of Namhkam for a sustained defence. Therefore, we decided to avoid a frontal attack against the fortifications and instead adopted round about tactics for a surprise attack. The New 30th Division was ordered to assign part of its force to launch a frontal attack to detain the enemy troops along the front, while moving its main force in a wide detour to the southwest of Namhkam. On January 5, the 89th Regiment of the New 30th Division and the 114th Regiment of the New 38th Division marched through the thick forests and narrow paths of the Kutang Mountains and reached the vicinity of Hsilang on January 7. It rained heavily for three days, and the water poured off the mountains, flooding the streams; the men and horses plodded on regardless of the danger. This force crossed the Juili River near Hsilang and moved towards mountains to the west of Namhkam. While part of our force launched an attack against Maotang. The main force of the 90th Regiment of the New 30th Division headed south along the river. It also crossed the Juili River under cover of fog at dawn on December 11 and moved south of the enemy from the northeast. At 1100 hours on December 15, our troops attacked and captured Namhkam. The enemy on the east bank of the Juili River and on the mountainous area along the west bank fought back hastily. Attacked by our troops from both south and north, the enemy was almost completely wiped out.

The New 22nd Division of the New 6th Corps turned over its defensive duty to a portion of the 50th Division on November 14, 1944. It then placed part of its force at Mantha and moved its main force along the Mantha-Tangkua road. On November 21, this force captured Tangkua and continued to head south. On

November 28, the New 6th Corps was given the mission of cutting off the highway between Lashio and Wanting. It ordered the New 22th Division, with the 148th Regiment of the 50th Division attached, to rush towards Kuei-chieh and skirt to the rear of the enemy at Ho-hsi, to prevent the retreat of enemy troops from West Yunnan and Namhkam and intercept enemy reinforcements from Lashio. On 29 November, the advance unit of this division crossed the Juili River at night and captured Lahsi and Mangka. While the main force was marching on the double, it was ordered to concentrate on December 1 and wait for further orders. On December 7, enemy troops launched a counterattack towards Tangkua and Molai. They were repulsed by our 66th Regiment. The defence of Tangkua was then turned over to the American troops. Our New 22nd and 14th Divisions were ordered to return to China by air to be placed under the direct command of our Army GHQ.

On December 28, the 50th Division assigned its 148th Regiment to defend the line stretching from Siu to Mangka and on January 1, 1945, its main force struck southward from Sikaw and Siu. On January 8, it encountered the enemy near Wanhao and a fierce battle ensued. The enemy sent parts of their 18th and 56th Divisions, a little over 800 men, as reinforcements and held their positions firmly. By January 12, our troops had cut the enemy into three sections and besieged their main force near Wanhao. The battle raged until January 14, when Wanhao was captured by our troops and the remnants of the enemy fled toward Molo. Our troops pursued and mopped up the enemy on the north bank of the Juili River.

After capturing Namhkam, our troops continued the assault against the enemy, in order to restore traffic on the Sino-Indian Highway as early as possible. On January 16, the main force of the New 22nd Division moved out along the Mongyu Highway and the main force of the New 30th Division besieged the enemy in the Laolungshan area. On January 17, after mopping up the enemy remnants at the bend of the river northeast of Namhkam, the main force of the New 38th Division pushed on along the highway. In order to facilitate the main assault, part of this force was sent to move secretly to the hilly land on the left flank of the enemy and push on eastward. On January 19, this force captured Shelan and Panho. At this time, the enemy troops south of Namhkan were unable to withstand the incessant attacks launched by the main force of our New 38th Division and retreated to their central positions in the Lao-lung-shan area, where they continued to resist stubbornly.

On January 21, the main force of the New 22nd Division captured Nao-yang, Manweiyin and Miaohsi and secured contact with the 116th Division of our Expeditionary Force. Meanwhile, the troops charging from Panho towards the hilly land northeast of Panho also captured Nanla and Hill 4561 on the same day. By now, all the natural barriers southwest of Mongyu were in our hands. The enemy hastily assembled their troops and sent three columns against Hill 4561 and our positions nearby. The battle lasted for a day and a night beginning on Jan 23.

Finally, our troops repulsed the enemy, captured Tangpashan, pushed on towards the highway and cut off the communications line in the enemy rear, seriously threatening the enemy at Mongyu. However, at this time, the remnants of the enemy 56th Division pulled back to Mongyu from West Yunnan and joined the enemy at Mongyu in an attempt to hold Mongyu firmly. Without waiting for the capture of Lao-lung-shan, our 114th Regiment infiltrated through the gap near Namhpakka to cut off the retreat of enemy troops at Mongyu. This regiment then sent part of its force south along the newly-constructed Namhkam-Namhpakka Highway while its main force out its way through the forests. On January 24, a part of the New 22nd Division captured Mot'ang and its main force captured Mongyu on January 27. These troops thus linked up with our troops from West Yunnan. The traffic of the Sino-Indian Highway was completely restored.

The enemy defending the Lao-lung-shan area were finally and completely annihilated, after five days of incessant attacks by the main force of our New 38th Division. At this time, part of our 114th Regiment also captured K'angshu and the 82-mile highway marker and encircled the remnants of the enemy 56th Division. On January 28, 1945, the enemy sent the 411th Regiment of their 2nd Division, with several field guns and tanks attached, to assault our troops at the 82-mile highway marker in an attempt to relieve the besieged remnants of the enemy 56th Division. Our troops fought back bravely and repulsed the enemy on January 29. Taking this opportunity, our troops marching south launched an assault. A bloody battle raged for five days and the remnants of the enemy 56th Division were completely annihilated, with the exception of the division commander Matsuyama Takezo, who alone escaped. On January 28, our troops captured Namhpakka. The enemy retreated to Kueichieh, Hsenwi and to the hills on either side of the highway. In order to safeguard Lashio, they tried to halt the advance of our troops by using natural barriers for fortifications. On Feb. 11, the main force of the New 30th Division marched south from Namhpakka to capture Hsenwi and advance to Lashio. It forced a crossing of the Nankai River and engaged the enemy in a furious battle. On February 12, the division captured Nengshu while the 88th and 90th Regiment captured Panni and Hollao respectively. On February 13, the 88th Regiment captured Taohsiao. On February 14, the main force of the New 30th Division captured Kueichieh and rushed to the south end of the pass at Nan-yueh-wen on February 15. By this time, the attacking units on both flanks had already captured Manai and Manwen. These units swiftly crossed the Nantu River on February 17, and captured Lopan and Hsiwu. On February 18, the Left Flank Attacking Force moved west from Hsiwu, crushed enemy resistance and reached the suburbs of Hsenwi. On February 19, our central troops broke through the main enemy positions and at dawn on February 20, all the enemy were annihilated and Hsenwi fell into our hands.

The enemy sent the reconnaissance regiment of their 56th Division as reinforcements to defend the hills south of Hsenwi at Naoheng. The 148th Regiment of the 56th Division and some artillery troops were sent to Mangli and the main force, with a tank unit attached, was sent to the delta area at Manmu. These troops dug in behind natural barriers or along river banks, trying to stop our troops. At Lashio, the 146th Regiment, artillery battalion and tank unit of the 56th Division constructed strong fortifications as the last defensive line.

On February 23, our force mopped up the area north of Sha-kao. But from Hsin-wi to Lashio, it was rugged ground, the valley was narrow and steep, favored to the defenders. So the main force of our New 38th Division moved south along the highway while parts of our New 30th and 38th Divisions advanced from both sides of the highway. On February 26, the central column captured Naoheng and approached Lahsiu. The 113th Regiment of the New 38th Division to the west reached Ka-kand-mu. On 27 February, after capturing Nantao the 113th Regiment swiftly crossed the Nanla River. On February 28, it captured Man-ti-mu and turned right. The enemy fought back fiercely. On the east side of the highway, the 88th Regiment of the New 30th Division captured Hantu. The central column, helped by tanks and heavy artillery, captured Lashiu and Mangli.

On March 2, our central column captured Penglang and Wenta; on March 3, it captured Manmu and advanced rapidly to the banks of the Nanyu River. On the night of March 5, the main force secretly crossed the river at Tapang and headed west. On the morning of March 6, this force captured Laolashio. By this time, our attacking units on both flanks had already crossed the Nanyu River and approached Yinai and Huiyueh, completing the encirclement of Lashio. On March 7, our central column captured the Lashio railway station; on March 8, all enemy troops defending the city were annihilated and Lashio fell into our hands. Our troops then marched respectively east and west. The New 38th Division moved swiftly towards Hsipaw and on 24 March, linked up with the 50th Division there. On 27 March, the New 30th Division captured Mongyin.

After capturing Monghkak and Lasi, the 50th Division launched an attack against Nantu in two columns. Nantu was captured on February 23 and Hsipaw on March 16. The 50th Division then headed southwest and linked up with the British troops at Kywaikong on March 30. After this mission was completed our troops pulled back to the vicinity of Lashio for replenishment.

(3) Operations of Expeditionary Forces in Western Yunnan and Northern Burma:

On April 8, 1944, the enemy activated the 33rd Corps Headquarters with Zaichi Kitamasa as the corps commander exercising command over the 18th, 53rd and 56th Divisions and the 24th Separate Composite Brigade. The corps undertook operations in northern Burma and western Yunnan and against the British airborne force. The 56th Division occupied fortified strong point positions in Teng-chung, Sungshan (on the west flank of Lamang), Mangshih, Lungling and Pingchia to stop the westward advance of our expeditionary forces, and massed reserves in the vicinity of Chenanchieh and Bhamo ready to launch counterattack at any time.

To assist the Allied forces in counterattacking Burma and respond to the Chinese Forces in India to clear the China-India Highway, the decision was made by our expeditionary forces to mop up the enemy in western Yunnan first. In early May, the 20th Army Group was employed as the attack force crossing the Salween River between Li-chai-pa and Shuang-hung-chiao before attacking Teng-chung. The 11th Army Group was employed as the River Defense Force responsible for the defense of the east bank of the Salween River. The 39th, 76th and 88th Division dispatched one reinforced regiment each to cross the Salween River and respond to the operations of the attack force.

On May 11, 1944, a reinforced regiment of the New 39th Division crossed the Salween River from the vicinity of Hui-jen Bridge and took Chiang-mu-shu on May 12. One reinforced regiment each from the 76th and 88th Divisions crossed the river from the south and north of San-chiang-kou to attack Ping-chia-chieh. On May 13, the bulk of the enemy forces retreated toward Mang-shih leaving a portion (one infantry battalion and one artillery battery) for the defense of Ping-chia-chieh.

On May 12, the 198th Division on the right flank of our attack force crossed the river at Li-chai-pa. On May 16, its 593rd Regiment took Ma-mien-kuan and Chiao-tou, while the main force laid siege to Pei-chai-kung-fang. As the enemy's 148th Regiment relied on the critical terrain for defense at all costs, a stalemate resulted. The 36th Division on the left flank crossed the river in the vicinity of Shuang-hung-chiao to reinforce and captured Ta-tang on May 14. Triumphantly, it crossed the Kao-li-kung-shan to reach the line east of Wa-tien and Chiang-chu-chieh to confront the enemy.

On May 22, to achieve exploitation of success, our expeditionary forces crossed the river to take part in the operations. The 20th Army Group which commanded the 53rd and 54th Corps and the 2nd Reserve Division was the right flank force with Teng-chung as its objective. The 11th Army Group which commanded the 6th, 71st and 2nd Corps was the left flank force with Lung-ling and Mang-shih as the objectives.

After crossing the Salween River in early June, our 2nd Reserve Division of the right flank force, relieved the 198th Division so that the latter could launch and attack against Pei-chai-kung-fang. On June 9, the main force of the enemy's 56th Division was shifted to this front for counterattacks. The enemy succeeded in breaking through our positions at Ma-mien-kuan and Chiao-tou and in Pei-chai-kungfang. A portion of our 36th Division maintained surveillance over Wa-tien, while the main force attacked Chiao-tou in the north. By June 14, our 198th Division, the main force of the 36th Division and the 2nd Reserve Division jointly captured Pei-chai-kung-fang and took Ma-mien-kuan and Chiao-tou on June 16. Enemy remnants retreated to Tengchung via Ming-kuang and Wa-tien. Later, the 2nd Reserve Division which captured Ming-kuang and Ku-tung-chieh, the 36th

Division which captured Wa-tien, and the 53rd Corps which took Chiang-chia-chieh successively reached the vicinity of Teng-chung by the end of June ready for the attack. By early July, our 116th Division and 2nd Reserve Division attacked the city of Teng-chung, as the enemy offered stubborn resistance from fortified positions. This stalemate lasted until early August when our 116th, 36th, 198th and 130th Divisions entered the city and fought from house to house against the enemy. By September 14, our forces recaptured Teng-chung and wiped out the main force of the enemy's 148th Regiment, 56th Division.

On June 1, our 71st Corps of the left flank force, attached with the New 39th Division crossed the Salween River. On June 4, our New 28th Division encircled Sungshan after its capture of La-meng-chieh. As the enemy positions were strongly fortified, our division laid five sieges in more than 3 months supplemented by 9 continuous attacks launched by the main force of the 8th Corps mobilizing a total strength of 3 divisions before our forces succeeded in destroying the enemy's nucleus fortress and wiping out the enemy defenders (built around one infantry battalion and one artillery battalion). After crossing the river, a portion of the 87th Division recovered Chen-an-chieh on June 9. On June 10, the main force of the division and the 88th Division reached the vicinity of Lung-ling and took such strong points on the outskirts as Huang-tsao-pa, Pang-miao, and Fang-ma-chiao. Subsequently, the enemy's 56th Division sent over 3,000 reinforcements from Teng-chung and Mang-shih. On June 16, our 71st Corps withdrew to Huang-tsao-pa and Chang-kang-ling for redeployment. Our New 28th Division moved south from Lung-chiang-chiao to cover the right flank of the corps. Meanwhile, the main force of our 1st Honor Division and New 39th Division successively arrived as reinforcements. On June 28, our forces renewed the attack making rapid progress. After crossing the river in early June, our 2nd Corps (less 33rd Division) took Hsiang-ta and Fang-ma-chiao respectively on June 24 and early August.

In mid-August, our 71st Corps, 1st Honor Division and New 39th Division laid siege on Lung-ling and captured all the key localities on the outskirts. Earlier in last June the enemy's Burma Front Army, conscious of its unfavorable situation in Burma and western Yunnan, decided to assume the defensive at the Chindwin River and Mogaung Valley. It actively launched counterattacks in western Yunnan by reinforcing the 33rd Corps with the 2nd Division and a portion of the 49th Division. The enemy's 33rd Corps dispatched the main force of the 2nd Division to reinforce Mang-shih on August 28 and deployed it on the left flank of the 56th Division. The bloody battle continued for over a week, as the enemy repeatedly counterattacked. Most of the key localities fell into enemy hands. The situation did not become stabilized until the main force of our 9th Division arrived as reinforcements. By early September, our 200th Division arrived from Kun-ming as reinforcements. Our 36th Division which moved south from Teng-chung joined force with the 1st Honor Division in a converging attack against the enemy. After bloody fighting for 3 days and 3 nights, the enemy was disorganized and retreated along the same route as they had come. His Ping-chia garrison force also took to its heels. Our persistent pursuit cost the enemy heavy casualties. Having restored the lost positions, our forces continued the attacks against the enemy. Beginning on October 29, the close infanty-artillery coordination of our forces and heavy fighting for 5 days and 5 nights led to our encirclement of the enemy forces on three sides. To avoid total annihilation, the enemy hastily retreated to Namhkam on the night of November 2. On the morning of November 3, our forces entered the city of Lung-ling.

On November 19, our 53rd Corps (attached from the 20th Army Group) made a turning movement from the right flank and captured the key localities north of Che-fang. Our 71st Corps, attached with the 1st Honor Division, pursued the enemy toward Mang-shih in the southeast. Our 6th Corps pursued the enemy on the main front of the Yunnan-Burma Road and took Mang-shih at dawn on November 20 and Che-fang on Dec. 1. The main force of the enemy's 2nd Division and a portion of the 53rd Division covered each other in the withdrawal and massed in Wan-ting attempting to fight a large-scale decisive battle on the China-Burma border. With Wan-ting in the center, Lung-chuan River on the north, Hui-lung Shan on the east and Yi-ku-hsiang highground on the south, the enemy was well dug-in. By December 26, our 11th Army Group (Left Flank Force) employed the 53rd Corps and swung from the west bank of Lung-chuan River to the south of Wan-ting. Our 6th Corps attacked Wan-ting from the northwest, the 2nd Corps attacked Wan-ting from the southeast, and the 71st Corps was the reserve. Subsequently, other than the 87th Division which was attached to the 2nd Corps, the main force of 71st Corps was placed between the 6th Corps and the 2nd Corps. The units began the attacks on December 27. After 25 days and 25 nights of bitter fighting, repeated enemy counterattacks and night attacks were repelled. On January 15, 1945, our forces in India captured Namhkam and advanced south. To avoid total destruction, the enemy broke out and fled to the southwest. On January 19, our forces recovered Wan-ting. On January 21, our pursuit forces crossed the national boundaries to continue the attack with the enemy fleeing. At noon on January 22, a portion of our 53rd Corps and the New 38th Division of our forces in India linked up at Muche. Our morale was never higher, as our forces pressed against Mongyu in a pincers attack. At 0700, January 27, our expeditionary forces and our forces in India and Allied forces linked up at Mongyu. Thus, the Sino-Indian Road was cleared.

Up until the link-up at Mongyu, our forces killled 48,850 enemy troops, captured 647 troops, 11,644 rifles, 601 light and heavy machine guns, 160 guns, 12 tanks, 3 aircraft, 606 trucks and 1,430 horses. Despite difficult terrain and foul weather, our steadfastness prevailed through the battle clearing the Sino-Indian Road and winning fame at home and abroad.

f.   Battle of Chang-teh

(Early November—Late December, 1943, See Map 38 and Charts 56 and 57)

CHART 56

Chart Showing the Japanese Chain of Command During the Battle of Chang-te (End of October, 1941)

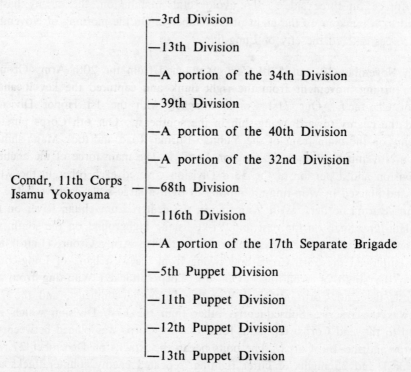

Comdr, 11th Corps
Isamu Yokoyama

—3rd Division

—13th Division

—A portion of the 34th Division

—39th Division

—A portion of the 40th Division

—A portion of the 32nd Division

—68th Division

—116th Division

—A portion of the 17th Separate Brigade

—5th Puppet Division

—11th Puppet Division

—12th Puppet Division

—13th Puppet Division

Since the Battle of Western Hupei, the enemy and our forces faced each other for more than four months. By October, our forces pulled 7 corps for re-deployment in Yunnan and India ready to assist the Allied Forces in the counteroffensive in Burma and to clear the China-India Highway. In the Pacific, the attacks of superior U.S. forces caused the enemy to fall back gradually. On the European front, in early August, 1943, Italy requested the Allies for a cease-fire, while the German forces were bogged down on the Ukraine battlefield. On October 23, the foreign ministers of the United States, Britain and Soviet Russia conferred in Moscow. The Allied forces were firmer than ever to fight to the end. In the face of many threats, the enemy initiated the Battle of Chang-teh in order to stop the continued re-deployment of our forces to Yunnan and India and crush our counteroffensive operations. Portions of the enemy's 40th and 13th Divisions which had been stationed in Hua-yung, Shih-shou, Ou-chih-kou and Mi-tuo-shih covered the massing of their main forces. By October 31, the enemy's 39th Division massed in the area west of Ching-chow (exclusive), the

CHART 57

Chart Showing Chinese Chain of Command during the Battle of Chang-te
(End of October, 1943)

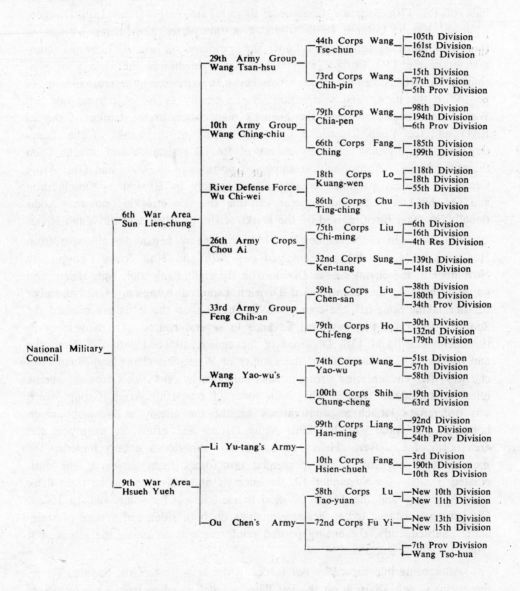

13th Division in Ching-chow and the area to the southeast, the 3rd Division in Huo-hsueh and the area to the northwest, the 116th Division in the area north of Shih-shou, and the 68th Division in Chien-li and the area to the west. In addition, the Sinnosuke Column (built around a portion of the 34th Division) massed in rear of the 3rd Division and the Miyawaki Column (built around the bulk of the 17th Separate Composite Brigade) in rear of the 13th Division, while the Karabe Column (built around a portion of the 32nd Division) was on the way. All these forces came under the command of Isamu Yokoyama, commander of the 11th Corps, (stationed in Kuan-yin-shih in the vicinity of Sha-shih). In early November, these forces began the advance in several columns.

With the luring and destruction of the enemy as its objectives, our 6th War Area expected to draw the enemy's main force to the banks of the Li River and the Yuan River and press the enemy to the banks of the Tung-ting Lake for his destruction by means of frontal resistance and attacks from the outer flanks. Accordingly, it employed portions of the 29th and 10th Army Group to conduct sustained resistance respectively in Hua-yung—Ou-chih-kou and Ou-chih-kou—I-tu and to wear out the enemy's attacking power. Additionally, its main force massed on the banks of the Li River and the Yuan River.

On the night of November 2, 1943, the enemy began the offensive from Hua-yung to Mi-tuo-shih and engaged our 29th and 10th Army Group. By November 3, the enemy's 68th Division on the right flank took Nan Hsien, and on November 4, the enemy's 3rd Division captured Kung-an. On November 5, after taking Sung-tsu, the enemy's 39th Division on the left flank crossed the Sung-tzu River for the westward advance in several routes. On November 8, the enemy's 3rd and 13th Divisions in the center, attached with the Sinnosuke and Miyawaki Columns reached the vicinity of Wang-chia-chang and Nuan-shui-chieh. After encountering strong attacks launched by our 79th Corps the enemy offensive subsided a little. The main force of our 10th Army Group which was ordered to launch a counterattack against the enemy at Nuan-shui-chieh hoped to join force with the 29th Army Group and crush the enemy in the area north of Li River. Heavy rains coupled with floods greatly impeded the movement of our forces and prevented our forces from achieving the anticipated results. By November 10, the enemy's 68th Division on the right flank took An-hsiang and the 116th Division pressed near Ching-shih and Li Hsien. Our strong resistance led to heavy casualties on both sides and a state of stalemate. Subsequently, the enemy poured reinforcements to renew the attack, but failed to achieve success.

After being intercepted by our forces in the area west of the Sungtzu River, the enemy's 39th Division on the left flank reached the line from Chih-hsi River to Chih-chiang on November 10. Further attacks by our forces forced the enemy to shift to the offensive in order to protect his right flank and rear. The enemy's 3rd and 13th Division swung south from Wang-chia-chang and Nuan-shui-chieh

to respond to the enemy's 116th and 68th Divisions from Pin-hu in storming
. our positions at Li River. Our 10th Army Group pursued the enemy from the
north, while our 73rd Corps at Shih-men and 44th Corps at Li Hsien struck,
inflicting heavy casualties on the enemy. On November 11, under air cover,
the enemy directed his attack against Shih-men. As a result of the heavy fighting which continued until November 15, the enemy took Ching-shih, Li Hsien
and Shih-men in succession and crossed the Li River to move south. Having
suffered heavy losses, 73rd Corps fell back to the area west of Tsu-li and the
44th Corps withdrew to the south. Meanwhile, our 6th War Area decided to
lure the enemy to the vicinity of Chang-teh and destroy him. Accordingly, it
ordered the 57th Division of the 74th Corps to defend Chang-teh and the 44th
Corps to defend Tai-yang-shan, Tai-fu-shan and Pan-lung-chiao. The main
forces of the 100th and 74th Corps were directed to operate between the area
northwest of Tao-yuan and launch a right flanking attack against the enemy.
The 10th Corps and portions of the 4th, 58th and 72nd Corps were pulled from
the 9th War Area to reinforce Chang-teh in succession. The 18th Corps was
directed to advance from San-tou-ping to Ching Li and attack the enemy's rear.
On November 21, the enemy's 3rd Division turned south of Chang-teh and dispatched a force to assist his airborne force in capturing Tao-yuan. His 116th
Division took Pan-lung-chiao and his 13th Division reached the area south of
Tzu-li. Our 100th, 44th, 74th and 73rd Corps counterattacked. On November
24, the main forces of the enemy's 40th, 116th and 3rd Divisions were gradually
committed in the attack on Chang-teh. Taking advantage of previously constructed positions on the outskirts to offer strong resistance, the 57th Division of
our 74th Corps succeeded in killing many enemy troops. Meanwhile, our 73rd
Corps had taken Tzu-li. On November 26, as our 18th, 79th, 73rd, 74th and
100th Corps completed the encirclement of Chang-teh and Tao-yuan, the ring
was gradually tightened. On November 27, our 100th Corps captured Tao-
yuan. On November 30, despite great odds, our 10th Corps advanced bravely
to take Teh-shan and the South Station at Chang-teh, and mopped up the enemy
remnants on the south bank of the Yuan River. The enemy employed the main
forces of his 3rd and 68th Divisions to sandwich our 10th Corps, poured reinforcements to attack Chang-teh covering the entire city of Chang-teh in a sea
of fire. Furthermore, the enemy employed large quantities of gas. Despite
heavy odds, our defenders (57th Division) were determined to survive or die
with the city. Every inch of ground was fought over in the bitter battle. The
bitter fighting on the outskirts continued for 5 days, and the street fighting lasted
for 7 days. The opposing forces fought over every house. In the end when
our forces ran out of food and ammunition and suffered heavy casualties, only
500 men were left. These men defended several strong points in the southwestern corner of the city tenaciously. By December 3, at one time Chang-teh
fell into enemy hands. Meanwhile, the reinforcements of our 9th and 6th War

Areas gradually arrived and attacked the enemy at Chang-teh. A fierce see-saw battle took place on the outskirts of Chang-teh. Having suffered great casualties, the enemy was greatly depleted in strength. However, the enemy continued to supply his forces in Chang-teh by using over 100 motor boats and junks to sail up the Yuan River from the Tung-ting Lake. Meanwhile, our forces on the outskirts of Chang-teh continued the violent attack on December 8, the New 11th Division of our 58th Corps entered Chang-teh causing the enemy to retreat hastily. By December 22, our forces recovered Nan Hsien, An-hsiang, Ching-shih, Li Hsien, Wang-chia-chang, Chih-chiang and Kuan-an. By December 30, all our former positions were restored.

During this battle, Chinese and U.S. air forces, with En-shih, Chih-chiang, Heng-yang, Pai-shih-yi and Liang-shan as the bases, massed over 100 bombers and fighters of various types and dispatched a total of 280 bomber sorties and 1,467 fighter sorties to bomb and strafe enemy personnel, horses, materials, warehouses, wharves, ships and other military installations in Chang-teh, Ou-chih-kou, Shih-shou, and Hua-yung inflicting heavy casualties on the enemy. During the air battles, 25 enemy planes were shot down, 14 enemy planes were probably shot down, 19 were damaged and 12 were destroyed on the ground.

During the course of the battle, ground and air, the fighting was most intense. The gallantry of our officers and men led to the killing and wounding of over 20,000 enemy troops. Three of our division commanders, Hsu Kuo-chang, Peng Shih-liang and Sun Ming-chin were killed in action, so were most of the officers and men of the 57th Division. Similarly, our 10th and 73rd Corps also suffered heavy losses. Due to the re-deployment of several elite corps to Yunnan and India, our strength in this battle was inadequate. However, our forces, having succeeded in defeating a stubborn enemy and shattered the enemy objective to capture Chang-teh and keep our forces from clearing the China-Burma Highway, contributed immensely to the overall situation.

g. Battle of Central Honan
    (Mid-April—Mid-June, 1944. See Map 39 and Charts 58 and 59)

With the objective of undermining the efforts of our field forces in Ho-nan, to clear the Peiping-Hankow Railway, the enemy began to re-establish the Mang-shan-tou strong points, rush the repair of the Yellow River Bridge and repaired the northern sector of the Peiping-Hankow Railway from Hsiao-chi to the north bank of the Yellow River in January, 1944. By early April, the enemy pulled four divisions, four separate brigades, one tank division and one cavalry brigade from Manchuria and North China totaling over 150,000 men under the command of Neiji Okamoto. The main force of the enemy's 12th Corps was massed between Kai-feng and Hsin-hsiang, while a portion of the 1st Corps was deployed on the north bank of the Yellow River in southern Shansi. In addition, the Central China Front Army dispatched a portion of its forces to the area between Hsin-yang in southern Honan and Cheng-yang-kuan in western An-

CHART 58

Chart Showing the Japanese Chain of Command During the Battle of Central Honan (Early April, 1944)

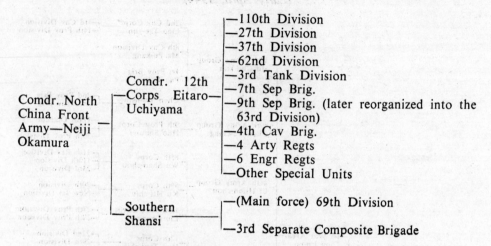

Comdr. North China Front Army—Neiji Okamura

Comdr. 12th Corps Eitaro Uchiyama
- 110th Division
- 27th Division
- 37th Division
- 62nd Division
- 3rd Tank Division
- 7th Sep Brig.
- 9th Sep Brig. (later reorganized into the 63rd Division)
- 4th Cav Brig.
- 4 Arty Regts
- 6 Engr Regts
- Other Special Units

Southern Shansi
- (Main force) 69th Division
- 3rd Separate Composite Brigade

Southern Honan—11th Sep Inf Brigade
Western Anhwei—A portion of the 65th Division
5th Air Force directly assisted in this Battle

hwei. This force attacked central Honan in several routes seeking to capture our key positions and clear the Peiping-Hankow Railway.

In formulating our operational guidance to fight a decisive battle against the enemy in the vicinity of Sung-shan, our 1st War Area envisaged the employment of the garrison forces in Fu-kou, Szu-shui, and Hsi-ho to stop the enemy from crossing the river. Should the enemy succeed in crossing the river, our forces at Szu-shui and Hsi-ho would wear out the enemy from the strong point fortifications at Hsu-chang, Chang-ko, Wei-chuan, Hsin-cheng, Cheng-chow and Ying-yang. Meanwhile, a portion of Tang En-po's army and the 4th Army Group were to form a defensive belt from Mi Hsien to Szu-shui in the mountainous area north of Mi Hsien and Teng-feng, and an offensive belt from Hsiang-cheng, Yu Hsien, Mi Hsien, Teng-feng, Lin-ju, Pao-feng and Yeh Hsien. The 78th and 89th Corps were directed to defend the 4 strong points of Sui-ping, Hsu-cheng, Yen-cheng and Wu-yang, and the 12th, 13th and 29th Corps were secretly massed in the offensive zone. All these forces were placed under the command of Deputy commander Tang En-po of the 1st War Area for a decisive battle against the enemy.

Before dawn on April 18, the enemy's 37th Division in the vicinity of Kai-feng and the 7th Separate Brigade crossed the river at Chung-mu for the invasion and were violently attacked by our defenders along Hsi-ho and Szu-shui. The bitter fighting continued until April 19 when the enemy penetrated the position

CHART 59

Chart Showing Chinese Chain of Command during the Battle of Central Honan
(Early April, 1944)

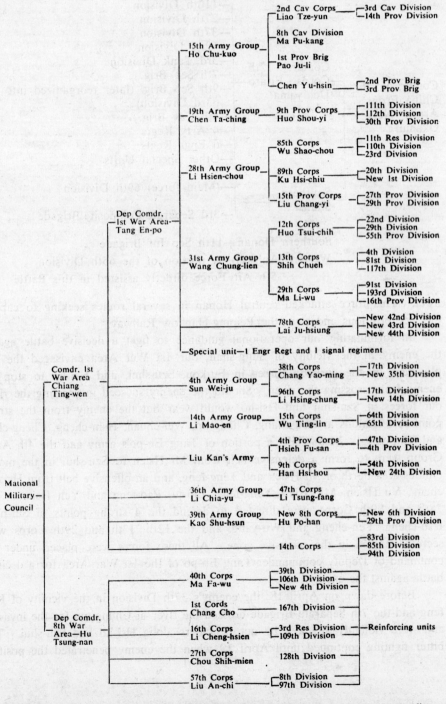

Remarks: Six divisions. advance columns and Hopei militia form the 5th War Area directly responding
to the operations in this battle are not included in this chart.

of our 15th Provisional Corps and pushed toward Wei-shih, Wei-chuan, Hsin-cheng and Cheng Hsien in several columns with his main force heading toward Mi Hsien. Thus, the enemy engaged units of our 28th Army Group in various places. Wei-shih and Hsin-cheng were captured by the enemy on April 21, and Cheng Hsien and Wei-chuan fell into enemy hands on April 22. With the fall of Chang-ko on April 23, our 15th Provisional Corps and 2nd and 3rd Provisional Brigades, fell back to the areas northwest of Yen-ling and Hsu-chang. As Mi Hsien fell on April 24, a portion of our 85th Corps held the northwestern mountainous areas to stop the enemy.

On the morning of April 19, the enemy's 110th and 62nd Divisions and 9th Separate Brigade attacked the positions of our 85th Corps at Mang-shan-tou. After penetrating our positions along the river on April 21, the enemy captured Kuang-wu and Szu-shui. On April 22, Ying-yang was captured by the enemy. On April 24, the enemy's 101st Division and the enemy invading westward from Kai-feng jointly took Mi Hsien before advancing to the west. Our 4th Army Group held the line from Ma-chu-ling to Hu-lao-kuan to stop the westward advance of the enemy's 63rd Division. Beginning on April 26, Deputy Commander Tang En-po of the War Area directed our forces to launch counter-attacks against the enemy. Our 23rd Provisional Brigade seized Wei-shih, while our 13th and 29th Corps attacked Mi Hsien. Ma-chu-ling was lost and re-captured. Eventually, our forces pressed the enemy in the area northwest of Mi Hsien and in the vicinity of Sung-shan so hard that the enemy switched to the defensive. Heavy fighting continued until April 30 when the enemy's 27th Division, 3rd Armored Division and 4th Cavalry Brigade massed in Hsin-cheng and swiftly attacked Hsu-chang, Yu Hsien and Hsiang-cheng fighting bitterly against our 28th and 31st Army Groups. Hsu-chang and Lin-yin fell on May 1 and 2 respectively. Meanwhile, the enemy pushed toward Hsiang-cheng and Chia Hsien with the 3rd Armored Division and the 4th Cavalry Brigade. Employing over 10,000 infantrymen in the siege, the enemy captured Yu Hsien and Chia Hsien on May 3, and Hsiang-cheng and Lin-ju on May 4. On May 5, a portion of the enemy's advance force reached the vicinity of Lung-men south of Lo-yang. After days of bitter fighting against the enemy having been subjected to turning attacks by the enemy armored units, our positions were mutilated making control most difficult. By May 6, Pao-feng, Lu-shan and Teng-feng fell in succession. Although our 4th Army Group and 9th Corps dealt heavy blows against the enemy's 63rd Division, our forces were outflanked by the enemy on the right and had to fall back to Yen-shih. On May 7, the enemy moving south from Hsu-chang took Yen-cheng and Lo-ho. On the same day, the enemy's 11th Separate Brigade moving north from Hsin-yang took Sui-ping. On May 8, in a converging attack from the north and south, the enemy took Hsi-ping. For a time, the enemy succeeded in cleaning the southern sector of the Peiping-Hankow Railway. After capturing Yi-chuan, the enemy headed toward Lung-men in force.

Earlier, to crush the enemy heading toward Lung-men, our 1st War Area directed Liu Kan's army to rush to Sung Hsien, Yi-chuan and Lung-men for defense and shift to the offensive when appropriate. The War Area directed the 15th Corps, attached with the 94th Division, to defend Lo-yang, and the 13th and 85th Corps of Tang En-po's army at Lin-ju to pursue, sandwich and destroy the enemy in the vicinity of Lung-men. Subsequently, our forces engaged the enemy in bitter fighting in the vicinity of Lung-men-chieh. On May 9, the enemy's 1st Corps, 3rd Separate Brigade and 59th Infantry Brigade from Yuan-chu in southern Shansi crossed the Yellow River at Nan-tsun and Pai-lang to attack Mien-chih to stop our reinforcements. Thus, the enemy broke through a portion of the Lung-men position. Having only limited mobility, Tang En-po's west bound forces failed to achieve the effectiveness of a converging attack. Greatly threatened, our major forces in Yen-shih, Lo-yang and the area to the south readjusted their battle lines. With the 15th Corps, attached with the 94th Division, defending Lo-yang, the War Area directed the 4th Army Group to mass in Han-cheng—Ouchih area, and Liu Kan's army in the area from the north of Yi-yang to Shih-ling ready to attack the flanks of the enemy forces which moved from Mien-chih to invade Lo-yang and Lo-ning. On May 13, the enemy forces from Yen-shih, Lung-men and Mien-chih converged in the Tzu-chien area. Despite gallant interceptions, Liu Kan's army was caught in the middle and had to move to the southwest. Our 36th Army Group in the vicinity of Mien-chih moved west to the vicinity of Lu-shih. Meanwhile, our defenders at Lo-yang, though isolated, fought on grimly. Just when our forces were in the process of moving, the enemy was divided into 3 routes with one route along the Sung Hsien—Lu-shih Highway, another route along the Lo-yang—Lu-shih Highway and a third route along Lung-Hai Railway for the west. After taking Lo-ning on May 17 and Shen Hsien on May 18, the enemy pressed near Ta-ying. On May 20, Lu-shih was abandoned. In order to save the war situation and crush the enemy offensive, powerful forces of the 5th and 10th War Areas joined force with Tang En-po's army to launch a counteroffensive against the enemy, successively recovered Sui-ping, Lo-ho, Lu-shan, and Sung-hsien, pressed against Pao-feng and cut off the Peiping-Hankow Railway to inflict heavy losses on a stubborn enemy. Meanwhile, our defenders at Lo-yang continued to fight bitterly against the enemy. Greatly threatened on the flanks and in the rear, the enemy dared not go in too deeply. Our continued counter-attacks caused the enemy moving west to abandon Lu-shih and fall back on Lo-ning. The enemy's main force was pulled to the east in order to protect his line of contact in the rear. On May 22, the enemy employed the 63rd Division, the 3rd Armored Division and the Yazae Force in a violent attack on Lo-yang. Our 15th Corps and 94th Division fought over every inch of ground against the enemy. The heavy fighting continued into the night of May 25 when our defenders broke out in several columns. Thus, Lo-yang was lost.

In the end of May, to prevent our forces from using the mountainous areas of western Honan for the counterattacks, the enemy constructed defense works along the line from Lu-shan to Sung Hsien, Lo-ning and Shen-chow for defense. On June 2, the forces of our 1st and 8th War Areas launched counteroffensives against the enemy. By June 4, progress was achieved in the various routs. In an attempt to shatter our counteroffensive plans, the enemy massed over 6,000 infantry and cavalry troops and 60+ tanks to storm Han-ku-kuan. After taking Ling-pao on June 10, the enemy reached Kuo-lueh-chen. On June 11, the enemy captured Wen-hsiang. On June 12, portions of our 16th and 40th Corps launched violent attacks and repelled the enemy. After taking Wen-hsiang and Kuo-lueh-chen, our forces recovered Ling-pao on June 15.

On June 5, they enemy at Lu-shan invaded south. Meanwhile, enemy forces at Wu-yang, Pao-feng and Yeh Hsien also launched attacks against our forces and engaged in heavy fighting against units of our 78th and 89th Corps and 2nd Army Group. The enemy's repeated attacks against Pi-yang and Fang-cheng were repulsed by our forces. By January 19, our forces were still able to insure the security of the line from Wu-yang to Lu-shang and south of Yeh Hsien (exclusive) and to confront the enemy in a stalemate.

Between May 1 and May 8, the enemy forces on the front of the Peiping-Hankow Railway and Hsin-yang succeeded in clearing the Peiping-Hankow Railway, our forces along the railway, the 55th Corps and the Southern Honan Advance Force launched a converging attack against the enemy. By May 19, Lo-ho, Hsi-ping, Sui-ping, Chueh-shan and Shang-tsai along the railway line were recovered. In early June, the enemy along the Peiping-Hankow Railway again made the invasion. On June 16, the enemy took Ju-nan and then Shang-tsai. On June 17, the enemy moving north from Ming-kang joined force with the enemy moving south from Hsu-chang to clear the Peiping-Hankow Line for the second time. On June 18, a portion of the enemy forces took Shang-shui and actively rushed the repair of the Peiping-Hankow Railway so as to insure the flow of traffic communications in Central China and North China.

In mid-April, the enemy's 65th Division in western Anhwei massed more than 2,000 troops to respond to the operations in central Honan and took Ying-shang on April 27. On May 8, while trying to capture Fu-yang, the enemy was repelled by powerful forces of our 15th Army Group. In time, our forces successively recovered Ying-shang and Fu-yang forcing the enemy to fall back to the original strong points in Cheng-yang-kuan and Shou Hsien.

During this battle, the enemy took full advantage of superior fast-moving tank and cavalry units to operate at will in the plains of central Honan. Attacking our forces from the north, east and south, the enemy was in a most advantageous position. Lack of tanks placed our forces in an unfavorable position. Despite bitter struggles and heavy losses, our forces failed to stop the enemy from clearing the Peiping-Hankow Railway. However, our forces inflicted heavy losses on the enemy and retained the bulk of our strength and the key localities in western Honan and western Anhwei. Our continued harassment rendered the enemy incapable of effectively utilizing the Peiping-Hankow Railway.

h. Battle of Changsha—Hengyang
(Late May—Early August, 1944. See Map 40 and Charts 60 and 61)

CHART 60

Chart Showing Japanese Chain of Command during the Battle of Changsha-Hengyang (Mid-May, 1944)

Comdr, 11th Corps Isamu Yokoyama
- 3rd Division—Mitsuo Yamamoto
- 13th Division—Richi Akashika
- 27th Division—Jinkuro Ochiai
- 34th Division—Yoshio Ban
- 40th Division—Seiichi Aoki (replaced by Seizo Miyagawa on August 2, 1944)
- 58th Division—Suchiro Mari
- 68th Division—Sukuma (replaced by Mikio Tsutsumi on July 1, 1944)
- 116th Division—Iwanaka
- 64th Division
- 109th Inf Regt
- 5th Sep Brig
- 7th Sep Brig
- 17th Sep Brig
- 12th Sep Brig
- 1st Fld Rpl Detachment
- 2nd Fld Rpl Detachment
- 5th Air Force

Since the Allied forces launched the counteroffensive in the Pacific, rapid progress was achieved. Realizing the increasing danger in sea communications, the enemy attempted to open mainland lines of communications in order to insure the overland communications on the Indo-China Peninsula. Accordingly, in April, 1944, the enemy initiated the Battle of Central Honan in order to clear the southern sector of the Peiping-Hankow Railway. Moreover, in May the enemy launched the offensive in northern Hunan attempting to crush our field forces in central Hunan and clear the Canton-Hankow Railway. Since February, 1944, the enemy increased his activities in troop movement in northern Hunan, and pulled nearly 170,000 troops from Kwangtung, North China and coastal areas massing them in Chung-yang, Yueh-yang and Hua-yung. Initially, the forces were divided into two lines. The first line of 5 divisions was deployed abreast the line from Hua-yung to the south of Yueh-yang and Chung-yang. The enemy's 40th Division was deployed west of the Hsiang River, while the 116th, 68th, 3rd and 13th Divisions were deployed east of Hsiang River. His second line of 3 divisions was so deployed that the 58th Division was massed in

CHART 61
Chart Showing Chinese Chain of Command during the Battle of Changsha-Hengyang
(Mid-May, 1944)

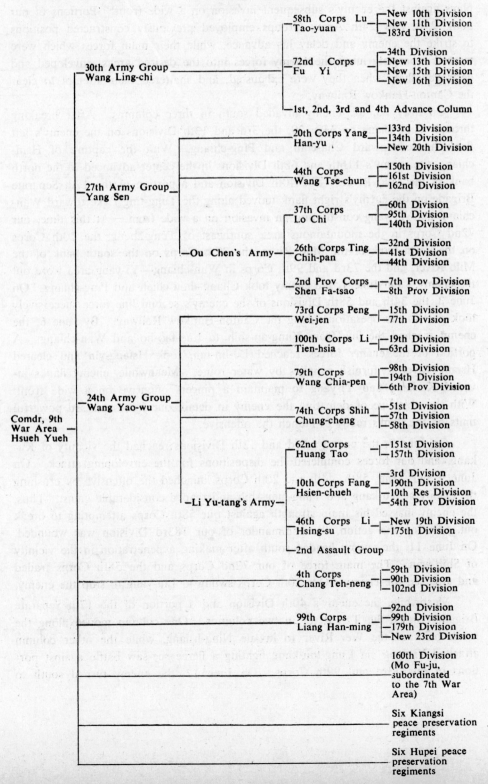

Chien-li, the 34th Division southwest of Pu-chi and the 27th Division in the vicinity of Chung-yang. In the latter part of May, the enemy began the push.

After the 3rd Battle of Changsha, our 9th War Area prepared the operation plans against the enemy's subsequent invasion on a wide front. Portions of our 30th, 27th and 24th Army Groups employed previously constructed positions to strike the enemy and delay his advance, while their main forces which were massed separately lured the enemy forces into the desired areas, enveloped and destroyed them when they were exhausted, and shattered their attempt to clear the Canton-Hankow Railway.

On May 26, the enemy invaded south in three columns. After breaking through Tung-cheng on May 29, the 3rd and 13th Divisions on the enemy's left flank headed toward Cha-chin and Ping-chiang. With the capture of Hsin-chiang, the enemy's 116th and 68th Divisions in the center advanced to the north bank of the Milo River. The 40th Division and a portion of the 17th Separate Brigade on the enemy's right flank moved along the Tung-ting Lake toward Wan-chiang and Yi-yang constituting an invasion on a wide front. At this time, our 72nd Corps in the mountainous area southeast of Tung-cheng, the 20th Corps on the north bank of the Milo River, the 37th Corps on the south bank of the Milo River, and the 73rd and 99th Corps in Wan-chiang—Yi-yang area wore out the enemy. On June 1, the enemy took Chang-shou-chieh and Ping-chiang. On June 3, the 34th and 58th Divisions of the enemy's second line force successively took part in the operations along the Canton-Hankow Railway. By June 6, the enemy reached the line from Yung-an-shih to Lao-tao-ho and Wan-chiang. A portion of the enemy forces reached Lu-lin-tan, took Hsiang-yin and cleared Hsiang River to furnish supplies by water route. Meanwhile, enemy flanks invaded Ku-kang and Yi-yang to maintain a pincers offensive on a wide front. With the objective of defeating the enemy in detail, our forces massed powerful units on the flanks ready to launch the offensive.

On June 7, the enemy's 3rd and 13th Divisions reached the vicinity of Ku-kang, and our forces completed the dispositions for the enveloping attack. On June 9, our 72nd, 58th, 44th and 20th Corps launched the offensive by crushing the enemy at Ku-kang and Tung-men-shih and reaped considerable gains. Thus, the enemy massed his main strength against our 58th Corps attempting to break out. During the action, the commander of our 183rd Division was wounded. On June 11, the enemy headed south after making a penetration in the vicinity of Shih-wan. The main force of our 72nd Corps and the 58th Corps trailed and attacked the enemy. Our 20th Corps swung to Liu-yang to stop the enemy.

Meanwhile, the enemy's 40th Division and a portion of the 17th Separate Brigade crossed the Tzu River in two columns. One column moved along the south bank of the Wei River to invade Ning-hsiang, while the other column attacked Yi-yang cia Lung-tou-kang fighting a fierce see-saw battle against portions of our 73rd and 99th Corps. On June 12, the enemy turned south to link up with the enemy moving west along the Wei River in a joint attack on Ning-hsiang. On June 14, our 19th Division coordinated with the 77th Division in the pursuit after mopping up the enemy remnants in the city of Yi-yang. At the same time, our 24th Army Group completed the envelopment of the enemy in Ning-hsiang and then opened the attack. Four days of continuous bitter fighting resulted in the destruction of many enemy troops who were unable to escape. With the fall of Changsha on June 19, the enemy succeeded in obtaining the support of the enemy in Pai-Juo-pu and broke out to the south.

On June 6, 68th and 116th Divisions, the enemy's main force, invaded Chang-sha—Liu-yang. With superior strength, the enemy invaded Liu-yang. For nine days and nine nights our 44th Corps fought bitterly against the enemy. Greatly depleted in strength, the corps withdrew to the outskirts of Liu-yang City on June 14. After crossing the Lao-tao River on June 9, the enemy's 34th and 58th Divisions on the north bank of the river reached the south bank of the Liu-yang River on June 12 and headed for Lu-shui and Changsha. On June 17, Huang-tu-ling and Hung-shan-tou on the outskirts of Changsha fell. Similarly, our main position at Yueh-lu-shan was penetrated. On June 18, the remainder of our defenders at Changsha broke out to Yung-feng where they were received.

Powerful in strength, the enemy's second line force kept the 27th and 64th Divisions and the First Field Replacement Detachment which were not yet committed. Hence, our plans which called for decisive battles against the enemy in Changsha and Liu-yang were not implemented. Our forces, therefore, lured the enemy deep into Heng-yang and launched counterattacks, while the enemy was exhausted. In addition, Ou Chen's army wore out the enemy on the banks of Lu-shui, as two corps were pulled from the 4th and 7th War Areas ready to fight a decisive battle against the enemy on the outskirts of Heng-yang. On June 20, our forces successively abandoned Li-ling, Chu-chow, Lu-kou and Hsiang-tan shifting the battlefield to the south bank of Lu-shui to stop the enemy invasion. However, the enemy infiltrated through the gaps and went rampant along the east bank of the Hsiang River. On June 23, the enemy reached the outskirt of Heng-yang, contacted our 10th Corps, invaded Yu Hsien in the east and captured Hsiang-hsiang in the west. The enemy then continued to invade south in order to tie down our forces on the outskirt and isolate Heng-yang. Since then, our defenders in Heng-yang were surrounded and fought bitterly.

As to the east bank of the Hsiang River, the enemy moving south via Li-ling took Yu Hsien on June 24 and headed for An-jen. Hurriedly, our 20th, 26th, 37th and 44th Corps raced to the areas north and south of Cha-ling to meet the enemy. On July 2, having completed disposition of forces for attack to the west, our forces began the attack. On July 8, our forces recovered Yu Hsien and Kuan-tien and surrounded the enemy at Lei-yang. Meanwhile, our 58th Corps also recovered Li-ling and pressed near Cha-ling. Unable to hold out any longer,

the enemy committed the 27th Division which it held. On July 10, the enemy
took Li-ling again before moving south to capture Cha-ling and Lei-yang. On
July 29, the enemy at Cha-ling moved east to take Ping-hsiang and headed toward
Lien-hua in the south. Renewing the offensive, our forces recaptured Ping-hsiang
to press near Li-ling and Lien-hua and reached Cha-ling and An-jen. Efforts
were made to intensify the siege against the enemy in the vicinity of Lei-yang. A
portion of our forces crossed the Lei River to respond to the operations on the
outskirt of Heng-yang.

As to the west bank of the Hsiang River, after the enemy at Ning-hsiang
turned south, our 24th Army Group followed in pursuit and dispatched the 79th
Corps to intercept the enemy at Heng-pan-chiao via Yung-feng. On July 1, our
forces completed the disposition with the 73rd Corps garrisoning the Ning-yi area,
and the 100th Corps massing in Yung-feng to meet the enemy forces which
invaded west. Our 62nd Corps controlled Wen-ming-pu in response to the
operations in Heng-yang. On July 2, the enemy attacking Yung-feng and our
100th Corps fought bitterly, as the city changed hands several times. By July
10, driven out of the outskirt, the enemy was forced to adopt the defensive. Accordingly, our 100th Corps moved its main force to the south and committed it
in Heng-yang. Meanwhile, our 79th Corps attacked the enemy at Chin-lan-shih
and Heng-po-chiao, and the 62nd Corps took offensive actions from Pai-ho-pu.
On July 15, our 62nd Corps reached the area southeast of Lu-tang and infiltrated
through gaps to reach the outskirt of Heng-yang on July 19. However, the
progress of the 79th Corps was slow. By the time it crossed the Cheng River,
the 62nd Corps was sandwiched and suffered heavy casualties and disruptions in
supply. On July 22, it withdrew to the area south of Tieh-kuan-pu for replenishment. Hence when the 79th Corps reached the northwestern outskirts of Heng-
yang, the enemy could pull superior forces for the counterattack. On July 29, the
79th Corps was forced to withdraw to the area west of the bridge. Meanwhile,
the 46th Corps was pulled from the 4th War Area and was moved by rail as
reinforcements. On August 2, various columns achieved progress, as our forces
renewed the offensive. In the night of August 7, the main force of our 46th
Corps, the general reserve, was committed in the general offensive. It headed
toward the city of Heng-yang seeking to press the enemy against the Hsiang River
and destroy him so as to lift the siege of Heng-yang. In the morning of August
8, when our forces advanced to the vicinity of Wu-li-pai, the offensive was somewhat frustrated. Having fought bitterly for 48 days and repeatedly repelled the
enemy's general offensive, our defenders of Heng-yang under Fang Hsien-chueh
suffered prohibitive losses and our positions were totally destroyed. On the same
day, Heng-yang fell into enemy hands. This battle lasted altogether two and half
months resulting in heavy casualties on both sides.

   i. Battle of Kweilin—Liuchow
      (Early September-Mid-December, 1944. See Map 41 and Charts 62
      and 63)

CHART 62

*Chart Showing Japanese Chain of Command during
the Battle of Kweilin-Liuchow (Mid-Aug. 1944)*

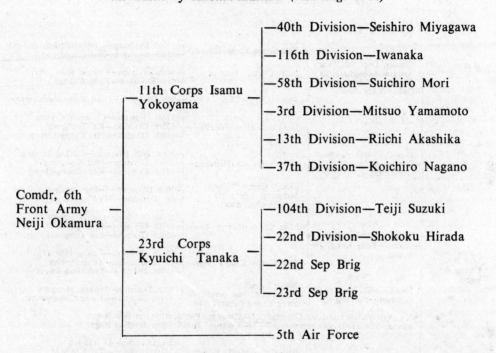

Comdr, 6th Front Army Neiji Okamura

11th Corps Isamu Yokoyama
—40th Division—Seishiro Miyagawa
—116th Division—Iwanaka
—58th Division—Suichiro Mori
—3rd Division—Mitsuo Yamamoto
—13th Division—Riichi Akashika
—37th Division—Koichiro Nagano

23rd Corps Kyuichi Tanaka
—104th Division—Teiji Suzuki
—22nd Division—Shokoku Hirada
—22nd Sep Brig
—23rd Sep Brig

—5th Air Force

After his capture of Heng-yang, the enemy initiated the Battle of Kwei-lin—Liu-chow with the objectives of clearing the main lines of communications and destroying our air bases in the southwest. The 3rd, 13th, 40th and 58th Divisions of the enemy's 11th Corps totalling over 100,000 troops were massed along the Hunan-Kwangsi Railway and the area to the south. Meanwhile, on the Hsi River front, the enemy's 23rd Corps massed the 104th and 22nd Divisions and the 22nd Separate Brigade totalling over 30,000 troops. On the Lei-chow Peninsula front, the enemy massed 3,000-4,000 troops of the 23rd Separate Brigade ready to make a converging attack against the Kwei-lin—Liu-chow area.

Due to inferior strength, our 4th War Area made plans to fight on the interior lines. On the Hunan-Kwangsi Railway front, the terrain was complicated. The decision was made to assume the defense by deploying a portion of our forces there to delay the enemy's advance. The Hsi River area was designated as the offensive area since traffic communications were convenient, and air-ground liaison was easy. Therefore, our main force was employed there to defeat the enemy in detail. Later, the National Military Council felt that since the enemy's main force was employed along the Hunan-Kwangsi Railway, the enemy there should be crushed first in order to insure the defense of Kwei-lin and Liu-chow.

CHART 63

Chart Showing Chinese Chain of Command during the Battle of Kweilin-Liuchow
(Mid-Aug. 1944)

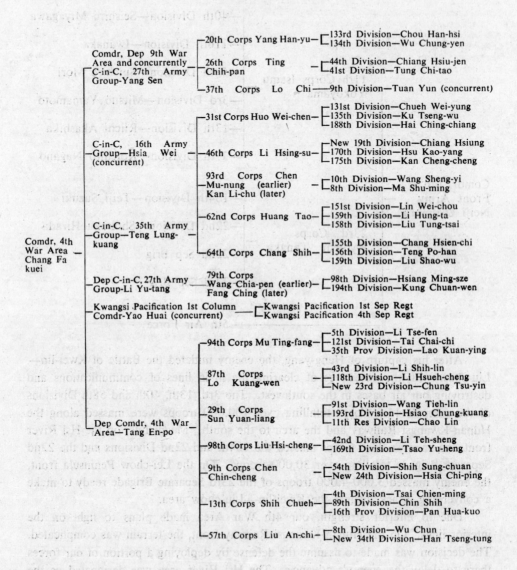

Comdr, 4th War Area — Chang Fa kuei

- Comdr, Dep 9th War Area and concurrently C-in-C, 27th Army Group-Yang Sen
  - 20th Corps Yang Han-yu
    - 133rd Division—Chou Han-hsi
    - 134th Division—Wu Chung-yen
  - 26th Corps Ting Chih-pan
    - 44th Division—Chiang Hsiu-jen
    - 41st Division—Tung Chi-tao
  - 37th Corps Lo Chi
    - 9th Division—Tuan Yun (concurrent)

- C-in-C, 16th Army Group-Hsia Wei (concurrent)
  - 31st Corps Huo Wei-chen
    - 131st Division—Chueh Wei-yung
    - 135th Division—Ku Tseng-wu
    - 188th Division—Hai Ching-chiang
  - 46th Corps Li Hsing-su
    - New 19th Division—Chiang Hsiung
    - 170th Division—Hsu Kao-yang
    - 175th Division—Kan Cheng-cheng
  - 93rd Corps Chen Mu-nung (earlier) Kan Li-chu (later)
    - 10th Division—Wang Sheng-yi
    - 8th Division—Ma Shu-ming

- C-in-C, 35th Army Group-Teng Lung-kuang
  - 62nd Corps Huang Tao
    - 151st Division—Lin Wei-chou
    - 159th Division—Li Hung-ta
    - 158th Division—Liu Tung-tsai
  - 64th Corps Chang Shih
    - 155th Division—Chang Hsien-chi
    - 156th Division—Teng Po-han
    - 159th Division—Liu Shao-wu

- Dep C-in-C, 27th Army Group-Li Yu-tang
  - 79th Corps Wang Chia-pen (earlier) Fang Ching (later)
    - 98th Division—Hsiang Ming-sze
    - 194th Division—Kung Chuan-wen

- Kwangsi Pacification 1st Column Comdr-Yao Huai (concurrent)
  - Kwangsi Pacification 1st Sep Regt
  - Kwangsi Pacification 4th Sep Regt

- Dep Comdr, 4th War Area—Tang En-po
  - 94th Corps Mu Ting-fang
    - 5th Division—Li Tse-fen
    - 121st Division—Tai Chai-chi
    - 35th Prov Division—Lao Kuan-ying
  - 87th Corps Lo Kuang-wen
    - 43rd Division—Li Shih-lin
    - 118th Division—Li Hsueh-cheng
    - New 23rd Division—Chung Tsu-yin
  - 29th Corps Sun Yuan-liang
    - 91st Division—Wang Tieh-lin
    - 193rd Division—Hsiao Chung-kuang
    - 11th Res Division—Chao Lin
  - 98th Corps Liu Hsi-cheng
    - 42nd Division—Li Teh-sheng
    - 169th Division—Tsao Yu-heng
  - 9th Corps Chen Chin-cheng
    - 54th Division—Shih Sung-chuan
    - New 24th Division—Hsia Chi-ping
  - 13th Corps Shih Chueh
    - 4th Division—Tsai Chien-ming
    - 89th Division—Chin Shih
    - 16th Prov Division—Pan Hua-kuo
  - 57th Corps Liu An-chi
    - 8th Division—Wu Chun
    - New 34th Division—Han Tseng-tung

The 4th War Area decided to deploy the two corps formerly stationed in Kwei-lin and Liu-chow along the Hunan-Kwangsi Railway in order to stop the enemy's advance, and to employ the local militia to defend southern Kwangsi and delay the enemy's advance. In addition, the 93rd Corps which was transferred from Chi-chiang advanced to Chuan-chow on September 13, 1944 for deployment. On the Canton-Hankow Railway front, the 27th Army Group was moved to Tao Hsien via Ning-yuan and Cha-ling in order to stop the enemy invasion from the flanks and be prepared to participate in the decisive battle in Kwei-lin—Liu-chow. The 62nd and 79th Corps of Li Yu-tang's army fought delaying actions against the enemy along the Hunan-Kwangsi Railway. After luring the enemy to the vicinity of Chuan Hsien, our forces hoped to swing north to the mountainous areas in northern Hunan and attack the flanks of the enemy moving from Hsin-ning to Tzu-yuan in order to protect the left flank of our defenders at Chuan Hsien. In addition, our 31st and 46th Corps were held in readiness in Kwei-lin to construct defense works on the outskirts. The 175th Division was held in readiness in Liu-chow ready to meet and attack the enemy.

After the enemy's capture of Heng-yang, Li Yu-tang's army turned to the mountainous areas in western Hunan from Tung-an in early 1944. By early September the enemy's newly activated 6th Front Army Headquarters' with Neiji Okamura as the commander, commanded the 11th, 23rd and 34th Corps. Later, the 20th Corps was transferred from Manchuria and came under the command of the 6th Front Army. On September 8, the 58th Division of the enemy's 11th Corps operated in Huang-sha-ho, and the 32nd Separate Brigade of the enemy's 23rd Corps in Kwangtung reached Huai-chi. Between September 11 and 14, as our 93rd Corps did not complete its massing, it successively abandoned the key localities of Huang-sha-ho and Chuan Hsien. The enemy at Huai-chi headed for Wu-chow via Hsin-tu to assist the 104th Division at San-shui to move west along the river. On September 22, the enemy's 23rd Separate Brigade in Leichow Peninsula reached Yung Hsien southwest of Wu-chow from the Kwangtung-Kwangsi border to assist in the enemy's capture of Wu-chow. The 35th Army Group of our 7th War Area in Hsi-chiang became subordinated to the 4th War Area. Commander-in-Chief Teng led the 64th Corps and local militia to intercept the enemy from Hsi-chiang and the south. Our 62nd Corps was ordered to mass in Liu-chow as the mobile force. Weak in strength in southern Kwangsi, our forces directed the 93rd Corps to delay the enemy north of the Ta-yung River, and the 135th Division of the 31st Corps to operate in Ping-nan, and the 155th Division to trail the enemy moving north from Lien-chiang. It was hoped to sandwich the enemy from the north and south and delay him while awaiting the arrival of reinforcements.

In late September, the 27th Army Group which were shifted from the 9th War Area and the 64th Corps from the 7th War Area gradually moved into Kwangsi from Kwangtung and Hunan. After the Battle of Changsha and Heng-yang, our forces were greatly depleted in strength being only a quarter of the T/O strength. In early October, the enemy's 58th Division along the Hunan-Kwangsi Railway massed in the area south of Hsin-ning and operated in Hsing-an. His 40th and 13th Divisions massed in areas south of Chuan Hsien. The 3rd Division massed in the Tao Hsien area. On the Pao-ching front, the enemy's 37th Division moved toward the Hunan-Kwangsi Railway. On the Hsi-chiang front, the enemy's 104th and 22nd Divisions teamed up with the 22nd Separate Brigade in Huai-chi, and the 23rd Separate Brigade in Lei-chow Peninsula to press near Ping-nan and Tan-chu hoping to effect a converging attack on Kwei-lin and Liu-chow from the north and south. Our forces, therefore, deployed the 1st and 2nd Columns from Kwei-sui and the 155th and 135th Divisions in the vicinity of Ping-nan and Kuei-ping to stop the enemy. Our 93rd Corps fought delaying actions against the enemy near Kung-cheng and Ta-yung-chiang to protect the front of Kuei-lin. Additionally, the 27th Army Group and the 46th Corps (175th and 188th Divisions) massed in Ping-loh, Li-pu and Yang-suo hoping to fight and destroy the enemy at Lung-hu-kuan first.

In mid-October, the first line of the enemy forces along the Hunan-Kwangsi Railway remained in the vicinity of Hsing-an. The enemy did not seem to have completed his preparations. Our 93rd Corps still faced the enemy in the vicinity of Ta-yung-chiang. Traffic communication convenience facilitated the capture of Tan-chu Airfield by the enemy from Hsi-chiang on September 28. On October 11, the enemy took Ping-nan and Kuei-ping. In order to insure the security of Liu-chow and cover the Kweichow-Kwangsi Railway, our forces readjusted dispositions and decided to crush the enemy in Ping-nan first. On October 21, the offensive began. After eight days and eight nights of bitter fighting, our forces dealt the enemy a heavy blow and recovered such key strong points on the outskirts of Kuei-ping as Meng-yu and Ma-ling. Meanwhile, the 11th Corps, the enemy's main force on the front of the Hunan-Kwangsi Railway, began the advance and dispatched a force to make a turning movement against Sung-kou on the left flank of Ta-yung-chiang. On October 18, one enemy battalion was wiped out. Later, the enemy's 58th, 40th, 37th, 13th and 3rd Divisions advanced abreast and broke through our positions on the outskirts of Kwei-lin and operated in the eastern outskirts of Kwei-lin and the vicinity of Ping-loh and Yang-suo. On the Hsi-chiang front, our left flank was penetrated. To avert an unfavorable situation, our forces moved to the outskirts of Kwei-lin and Liu-chow to mass our strength for decisive battle against the enemy.

The defense of Kwei-lin was undertaken by the 131st Division and the 170th Division of the 46th Corps. Beginning on Oct. 29, the enemy employed the 58th, 40th and 37th Divisions to conduct reconnaissance in force on the outskirts. On November 4, the enemy used poison gas on our Chi-hsing-ai positions in the southern end of the city resulting in heavy losses on both sides. Our positions fell on November 5, as our forces were completely isolated. On November 6, the enemy shelling of the city of Kwei-lin caused many fires and the destruction of many houses. On November 7, the enemy attempted forced crossings of the Li River at Ting-kuei-men, Chung-cheng Bridge and Ma-wang-chou. At Ting-kuei-men, the enemy failed. Three of our bridgeheads at Chungcheng Bridge were lost and later recaptured. On November 9, the enemy poured many reinforcements and engaged our forces in bitter street fighting. On November 11, as our forces received orders to break out, Kwei-lin fell, Kan Wei-yung, commander of the 131st Division; Chen Chi-yuan, chief of staff of the Defense Command; Lu Tan-meng, chief of staff of the 31st Corps; and Hu Hou-chi, assistant division commander of the 170th Division, were all killed in action.

On the Liu-chow front, a portion of our forces was ordered to occupy positions along the Hung-shui River and the Liu River to stop the enemy from crossing the rivers. Our main force which was massed in the vicinity of Liu-chow would crush the enemy, while the enemy was crossing the river to operate in Liu-chow. During the deployment, it rained continuously for days making it impossible for our airplanes to operate. The enemy, therefore, took advantage of this opportunity to exert pressure on our 16th Army Group rendering it incapable of shifting its positions. On November 14, our positions at Yung-fu between Kweilin and Liu-chow were penetrated by the enemy's 13th Division. Our 93rd Corps and 19th Division were locked in bitter fighting. As our 20th Corps was engaged in heavy fighting against the enemy's 3rd Division in the vicinity of Hsiu-jen, it was unable to disengage itself. Consequently, our 16th and 27th Army Groups failed to complete their dispositions on schedule. Thus, the enemy was able to move south by dispatching the 13th Division to head for Liu-cheng from Chung-tu and threaten the left flank of Liu-chow. To insure the security of the flanks and rear of Liu-chow, our forces shifted to Liu-cheng the 188th Division which was held in readiness. By this time, the enemy moving along the West River had reached the south bank of the Hung-shui River and the west bank of the Liu River. A portion of the enemy forces succeeded in crossing the river in the vicinity of Hsiang Hsien and on the east side of Liuchow. Beginning on November 6, heavy fighting took place along the line from Chien-chiang to Liu-chow and Liu-cheng. On November 9, the enemy penetrated our strong points at Liu-cheng. Liu-cheng fell after two regiments of our 26th Corps were surrounded by the enemy and suffered heavy losses. One powerful enemy force advanced to the west from the north of Liu-cheng. In an effort to protect Yi-shan and cover Kweichow and Kwangsi Provinces, our forces realigned their dispositions on November 11. On November 12, our 35th Army Group reached the designated line from Pei-sze to Ta-tang. Our 16th Army Group fought bitterly against the enemy along the line from Li-miao to Lo-tung. Our 27th Army Group resisted and gradually shifted its positions to Lung-chiang River. Meanwhile, over 3,000 enemy troops moving west from Liu-cheng advanced rapidly for the attack and were stopped by our 20th Corps north of Yi-shan. Our 46th Corps on the front moved to the area southeast of Yi-shan. On November 15, Yi-shan fell. On November 16, the enemy pressed near Huai-yuan, while 3,000-4,000 enemy troops from Hsin-cheng attacked our positions at Pei-wang. Efforts of our 8th Engineer Regiment, 4th War Area, frustrated the enemy attempt. Accordingly, the enemy shifted his main force and took An-ma on November 18 and continued his invasion to the west. Meanwhile, one enemy regiment from Pei-wang captured Chin-cheng-chiang. One enemy division crossed the river at Chiu-tu-hsiang and headed for Tu-an. As our 62nd Corps bravely intercepted the enemy, both sides suffered heavy casualties. At this time, a portion of our 97th Corps completed its occupation of positions along the line from Ta-chang to Che-ho and Pa-yu southeast of Nan-tan to cover the operations of our follow-up units. On November 22, the bulk of our 97th Corps defended the positions at Che-ho, and the main force of our 16th Army Group assisted the 97th Corps in attacking the flanks of the invaders in the areas southeast of Na-ti-yu. Another force stopped the enemy moving west from Pao-ping-yu. Our 27th Army Group stopped the enemy at Sze-en and Tu-yu. When it could no longer hold the enemy, it would make every effort to defend Li-ming-kuan. Our 35th Army Group resisted the enemy with its main force and dispatched a force to operate in Yung-tien in order to stop the enemy moving from Nan-ning to Yung-tien Road. To protect the nation's wartime capital,[48] Generalissimo Chiang directed the 6th War Area to pull the 94th and 87th Corps, assemble them in Huang-ping and Chen-yuan and attack the left flank of the enemy force which invaded southern Kweichow; and the 1st and 8th War Areas to pull the 29th, 98th, 9th, 13th and 57th Corps to assemble in Kwei-yang, Ma-chang-ping, Tu-yun and Tu-shan hoping to crush the enemy in Kweichow in one stroke and insure the defense of Kwei-yang. All our forces in Nan-tan and Ho-chih came under the command of Gen. Tang En-po, deputy commander of the 1st War Area. By this time, the enemy's 23rd Corps had taken Wu-ming and Nan-ning attempting to open the communication line to Indo-China.

On November 21, the enemy's 13th Division which had taken Ho-chih advanced along the Kwangsi—Kweichow Road[49] to attack the security positions of the 97th Corps. At drawn on November 24, our force withdrew to Che-ho after bitter fighting. On November 25, the enemy again fell on Ta-chang and Che-ho with full force and was stopped. On November 27, the enemy tied down our defenders on the front with a part of his force, and advanced to the area between Che-ho and Ta-tang with a powerful force. On November 28, as the enemy took Nan-tan, a portion of our 188th Division and the Guard Regiment of the 4th War Area were ordered to occupy positions in the vicinity of Lu-chai; the 27th Army Group to defend Li-ming-kuan; and the 35th Army Group to

---

[48] Meaning Chungking (also known as "Yu").

[49] Kweilin to Hsien-ning in northwest Kweichow Province.

insure the security of the area east of Tien-tung and stop the enemy's westward advance. On November 30, one battalion of the enemy's 3rd Division skirted around Hei-shih-kuan and reached the eastern end of San-ho attempting to make a turning movement against Tu-yun. Having fought for an extended period of time, our 27th Army Group withdrew to the north for replenishment. On December 1, the enemy's 13th Division made contact with our 91st Division. The fighting continued until December 3 when the enemy poured in more than 5,000 reinforcements and succeeded in entering Tu-shan in the morning of December 5. Subsequently, as the enemy withdrew, our 91st Division recovered Tu-shan and dispatched one regiment to skirt around the area south of Tu-shan and attack the flanks of the enemy forces which retreated to the south. Meanwhile, our 169th Division launched counterattacks against Pa-chai. On December 5 and 6, it successively recovered Pa-chai and San-ho. Further, it assisted the 91st Division in the pursuit toward Shang-sze and Hsia-sze. After Nan-tan and Che-ho were recaptured on December 12 and 13 respectively, the 91st Division joined force with the 46th Corps in laying siege against the enemy at Ho-chih. In the night of December 14, the enemy poured in more than 2,000 reinforcements for the counterattacks which led to having casualties on both sides. A stalemate resulted, as our forces, having fought too long, needed replenishment. Thus, the Battle of Kweilin—Liuchow came to an end.

j. Operations in Hunan—Kwangtung—Kiangsi Border Areas
(Mid-January-Mid-February, 1945. See Map 42 and Charts 64 and 65)

CHART 64

Chart Showing Japanese Chain of Command during Operations in Hunan-Kwangtung-Kiangsi Border Areas (Early January, 1945)

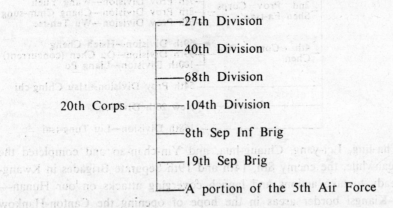

Subsequent to the Battle of Kweilin—Liuchow, the enemy was active in resupply and realignment. Meanwhile, enemy forces in Kwangsi separately massed in southern Hunan and northern Kwangtung. By early January, 1945, the enemy deployed the 27th, 68th, 40th, and 104th Divisions respectively in the

CHART 65

Chart Showing Chinese Chain of Command during Operations in
Hunan-Kwangtung-Kiangsi Border Areas
(Early January, 1945)

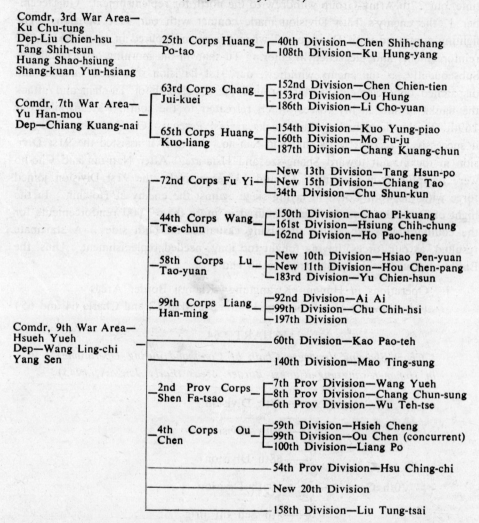

Comdr, 3rd War Area—
Ku Chu-tung
Dep-Liu Chien-hsu
Tang Shih-tsun ——— 25th Corps Huang—┌40th Division—Chen Shih-chang
Huang Shao-hsiung   Po-tao   └108th Division—Ku Hung-yang
Shang-kuan Yun-hsiang

                          63rd Corps Chang_┌152nd Division—Chen Chien-tien
Comdr, 7th War Area— ┌   Jui-kuei   ├153rd Division—Ou Hung
Yu Han-mou   │   └186th Division—Li Cho-yuan
Dep—Chiang Kuang-nai —
                      │   65th Corps Huang_┌154th Division—Kuo Yung-piao
                      └   Kuo-liang   ├160th Division—Mo Fu-ju
                                           └187th Division—Chang Kuang-chun

                      —72nd Corps Fu Yi—┌New 13th Division—Tang Hsun-po
                                        ├New 15th Division—Chiang Tao
                                        └34th Division—Chu Shun-kun

                      44th Corps Wang┌150th Division—Chao Pi-kuang
                       Tse-chun   ├161st Division—Hsiung Chih-chung
                                       └162nd Division—Ho Pao-heng

                      58th Corps Lu┌New 10th Division—Hsiao Pen-yuan
                       Tao-yuan   ├New 11th Division—Hou Chen-pang
                                      └183rd Division—Yu Chien-hsun

                      99th Corps Liang┌92nd Division—Ai Ai
                       Han-ming   ├99th Division—Chu Chih-hsi
                                        └197th Division

Comdr, 9th War Area— ————————————————60th Division—Kao Pao-teh
Hsueh Yueh   —
Dep—Wang Ling-chi   ————————————————140th Division—Mao Ting-sung
Yang Sen
                      2nd Prov Corps┌7th Prov Division—Wang Yueh
                       Shen Fa-tsao   ├8th Prov Division—Chang Chun-sung
                                      └6th Prov Division—Wu Teh-tse

                      4th Corps Ou┌59th Division—Hsieh Cheng
                       Chen   ├99th Division—Ou Chen (concurrent)
                                      └100th Division—Liang Po

                      ————————————————54th Prov Division—Hsu Ching-chi

                      ———————————————— New 20th Division

                      ———————————————158th Division—Liu Tung-tsai

vicinity of Cha-ling, Lei-yang, Chiang-hua, and Yin-chan-ao and completed the massing. Meanwhile, the enemy 8th, 14th and 19th Separate Brigades in Kwangtung were ready to take actions and launch coverging attacks on our Hunan—Kwangtung—Kiangsi border areas in the hope of opening the Canton-Hankow Railway.

After the disruption of the Hunan—Kwangsi Railroad, the 3rd, 7th, and 9th War Areas were isolated from our base of the War of Resistance. The resupply was handicapped. It was the great efforts of the commanders of all levels that made the unit replenishment possible. By early January, 1945, the strength of the 9th War Area were up to seventy per cent. The 7th, sixty per cent. Therefore, the National Military Council ordered them to carry out sustained operations, to stop the enemy from the opening of the Canton-Hankow Railroad.

Along the Canton-Hankow Railway: On January 11, the enemy's 40th Division assigned the 235th Regiment to advance from the vicinity of Chiang-hua toward the key localities of Loh-chang and Ping-shih along the Canton-Hankow Railway. On January 13, it took Lan-shan and Lin-wu. By January 17, several enemy columns reached the areas west of Loh-chang and Ping-shih. Our 59th, 60th, 102nd and 160th Divisions separately attacked the enemy columns. Meanwhile, the enemy's 104th Division at Yin-chan-ao attacked northern Kwangtung with its main force on the west bank of the North River and another force at the estuary of the Pa River. A portion of our 9th Separate Brigade assisted the 154th Division to rise in resistance. On January 19, Ching-yuan fell. Meanwhile, the enemy's 68th Division at Lei-yang moved southward along the bank of the Lei River to form a converging attack from the north, west and south against the southern sector of the Canton-Hankow Railway. Our 2nd Provisional Corps and the 99th Corps offered resistance to the north, as the enemy from Lei-yang continued to move south. On January 21, our 2nd Provisional Corps repelled a portion of the enemy's 68th Division which attacked Yung-hsing, and forced it to cross the Lei River and retreat to the west. The enemy, therefore, ordered his main force to move south along the railway. Our 99th Corps halted the enemy with all its strength. Having advanced east between Hsin-tien and Ning-yuan, the enemy in the Tao Hsien area was stopped by our New 20th Division and 54th Provisional Division between Liu-hsia-tu and Hsin-tien. Later, the main force of the enemy's 40th Division reinforced in the attack forcing our force to fall back to the south. The enemy, then, advanced toward Chen Hsien.

On January 22, the enemy's 68th Division joined force with the main force of the 40th Division in attacking Chen Hsien and Liang-tien. Defending the cities, our forces were engaged in heavy street fighting against the enemy. A portion of the enemy's 40th Division captured Loh-chang and Ping-shih. After taking Ying-teh, the enemy continued to move ahead along the North River. Bitter fighting ensued along the entire railway. Defending Chu-chiang, Pin Hsien, Yi-chang and Chiu-feng on the one hand, our forces underwent re-deployment on the other. The main force of the 7th War Area was shifted to the line from Shih-hsing—Sze-chien—Pa-tzu to prevent the enemy from moving to the east. Force of 9th War Area aggressively attacked the enemy along the railway. On January 24, when the enemy's advance elements from the North River reached the outskirt of Chu-chiang, our 187th Division rose in defense. On January 26, our 99th Corps withdrew from Pin Hsien and moved to the east to continue resistance. On January 27, after the capture of Yi-chang and Chiu-feng, the enemy's 40th

Division which had invaded Liang-tien, Loh-chang and Ping-shih dispatched a force to the south to respond to the 104th Division in the latter's attack on Chu-chiang. Despite courageous intercepts by our forces, Chu-chiang fell into the hands of superior enemy. At this time, our forces abandoned the 450 km railway lines under their control and moved into the mountainous areas on the flanks awaiting the opportunity to strike again.

On January 29, our militia in Hunan Province mopped up the enemy remnants in Hsin-tien, Kuei-yang, Ning-yuan, Lin-wu, Lan-shan, Chia-ho, Yung-ming and Chiang-hua and exercised control over these areas. At this time, our 9th War Area had completed its dispositions for a converging attack on the enemy along the railway line. On January 30, our 60th Division recovered Chiu-feng and pressed against Loh-chang. The main force of the enemy's 40th Division separately advanced to the east from Chu-chiang and Loh-chang to engage in bitter fighting against our forces. On February 2, our New 20th Division re-captured Liang-tien and pressed north against Chen Hsien. On February 3, our 54th Provisional Division recovered Yi-chang and assisted the main force of the 4th Corps in laying a siege against Ping-shih. Key localities along the railway were recaptured; however, the enemy's 68th Division at Chen Hsien had massed its main force for the eastward advance. From February 1-6, the enemy, having been halted by our 99th Corps and a portion of the 2nd Provisional Corps in Tung-chiang and San-tu, was unable to make any progress. On February 9, taking advantage of the southward move of the main force of our 2nd Provisional Corps, the enemy's 68th Division captured Yung-hsing. On February 10, over 3,000 enemy troops took Liang-tien again. After taking Yi-chang and Ping-shih on February 12 and 14 respectively, the enemy controlled the entire railway line. Nevertheless, our force continued to counterattack along the railway inflicting heavy casualties on the enemy.

On the Sui-chuan—Kan-hsien front: On January 12, the enemy's 27th Division at Cha-ling began the eastward advance with the 1st Regiment. Our 58th Corps swiftly raced to the vicinity of Kao-lung to meet the enemy. By January 17, the enemy was halted there. Later, when the enemy's main force was committed, our force gradually shifted to the vicinity of Lien-hua. Meanwhile, another enemy force moved south from Cha-ling and An-jen. Our 44th Corps courageously intercepted and placed the enemy in check. After the fall of Lien-hua on January 17, a portion of our 58th Corps offered piecemeal resistance, while the main force of the corps was shifted to the area north to Ning-kang to continue the resistance so as to protect the bases of the main forces of the 9th War Area. On January 22, after capturing Yung-hsin, some 3,000 troops of the advance elements of the enemy's 27th Division continued the attack on Sui-chuan. The main force (34th and 15th Divisions) of our 72nd Corps which had been shifted to Li-ling advanced toward Yung-hsin. Our 183rd Division in Hsin-kan operated in the area southeast of Sui-chuan, while the main force of our 58th

Corps attacked to the east from Lo-fu. On January 25, enemy and our force were engaged in bitter fighting. On January 28, disregarding our resistance, the enemy continued his southward advance. In time, its spearhead reached the northern outskirt of Sui-chuan. Apart from destroying the airfield, our 40th Division intercepted the enemy. However, the enemy gradually increased his forces and attempted to force the crossing of the river in columns but was repelled. On January 31, Sui-chuan fell. Meanwhile, the enemy's 40th Division at Chu-chiang and Loh-chang attached with a portion of the 104th Division attacked to the east along the Chen River. The enemy took Shih-hsing and Nan-hsiung on February 1 and 3 respectively. Our 63rd Corps offered strong resistance to cover the entry of the 7th War Area units into their bases and violently attacked the enemy's rear. Paying no head to rear area liaison, the enemy advanced toward Ta-yu and was stopped by our 90th Division in the vicinity of Mei-kuan.

On February 4, the enemy's 27th Division penetrated the lines of resistance of our 40th and 183rd Divisions and raced to the northwestern outskirt of Kan Hsien. Our 72nd Corps trailed the enemy in the attack, motored a portion of the 102nd Division from Lin-chuan to hold Kan Hsien and destroyed the airfield. On February 5, after crossing the Chang River, the enemy was engaged in bitter street fighting with our forces. In the meantime, the enemy's 40th Division took Tayu in the north and attacked Hsin-cheng. Our 90th Division continued to attack the enemy flanks, and our 63rd Corps recovered Shih-hsing. On February 6, the enemy's 27th Division took Kan Hsien. On February 6, the enemy advanced east to Mao-tien and was repelled by our 108th Division. Meanwhile, to respond to the operations of the 40th Division, the enemy at Kan Hsien advanced to the west. By February 8, the enemy force from opposite directions linked up at Hsin-cheng. Launching an attack against Ta-yu, our 90th Division entered the city on February 10 and engaged the enemy in street fighting. Due to numerical inferiority, the division failed to achieve success and withdrew to the outskirts in a state of stalemate against the enemy. Another portion of the enemy's 27th Division which moved from Yung-hsin and Sui-chuan to Tai-ho was routed by the main force of the 72nd Corps. On February 13, the enemy's 40th Division was routed by our 63rd Corps at Cheng-chiang and fled to the west. Our forces continued the pursuit against the enemy.

Along the coast of Kwangtung: On January 13, as the enemy's 8th Separate Brigade invaded east from Tseng-cheng and Chang-mu-tou, our 20th Separate Brigade and two advance columns jointly met the enemy. The enemy took Po-lo and Tan-shui on January 15 and Hui-yang on January 16. Our forces gradually withdrew to the east and stopped the enemy between Heng-li and Ping-shan.

On January 23, enemy marines landed at Ping-hai and Hsin-cheng. Meanwhile, the enemy's 19th Separate Brigade moved west from Chao-chow and Swatow to respond to the fighting in Hui-chow—Po-lo. Our garrison force at

Hai-lu-feng and 186th Division fought gallantly.   On January 24, the enemy
captured Hai-fang and Chieh-yang.   On January 25 when Lu-feng fell, our
garrison forces moved to the north to continue resistance.   On January 26, as the
enemy's 19th Separate Brigade reached Tang-keng in the north, our 186th Division massed its main force for the counterattack.   On January 27, the division
drove off the enemy at Tang-keng and pressed against Chieh-yang.   With the
enemy pouring additional reinforcements to offer resistance, the situation become
stalemated.

On February 2, the enemy began to strengthen his coastal defense along
Hui-lai and shifted forces to defend the various strong points, our forces continued to attack and wear out the enemy resulting in heavy gains.

    k.   Order of Battle of Our Forces in the Winter of 1944

Commander-in-Chief of the Army, Navy and Air Force and concurrently
Chairman of the National Military Council—Chiang Kai-shek.

Chief of the General Staff: Ho Ying-chin.

    (1) 1st War Area

        Commander: Hu Tsung-nan (acting)

        Forces:

        28th Army Group—Li Hsien-chou

           89th Corps—Ku Hsi-chiu

             20th Division—Tan Nai-ta

             New 1st Division—Huang Yung-tsan

             62nd Prov Division—Pao Ju-feng

        31st Army Group—Wang Chung-lien

           85th Corps—Wu Shao-chou

             23rd Division—Huang Tzu-hua

             110th Division—Liao Yun-chou

             55th Prov Division—Li Shou-cheng

           18th Corps—Lai Ju-hsiung

             New 42nd Division—Tan Yu-lin

             New 43rd Division—Huang Kuo-hsu

             New 44th Division—Yao Ping-hsun

      4th Army Group—Sun Wei-ju

           38th Corps—Chang Yao-ming

             17th Division—Shen Chi-chih

             New 35th Division—Kung Tsung-chou

           96th Corps—Li Hsing-chung

             177th Division—Li Chen-hsi

             New 14th Division—Chen Tzu-chien

      Director, Shang-nan Command Post—Kuo Chi-chiao

           27th Corps—Hsieh Fu-san

             47th Division—Li Chi-heng

             64th Prov Division—Pien Kuang-han

4th Prov Division—Ma Hsiung-fei
Honan Province Garrison Commander-in-Chief—Liu Mao-en
    15th Corps—Wu Ting-lin
        64th Division—Liu Hsien-chieh
        65th Division—Li Chi yun
34th Army Group—Li Wen
    1st Corps—Lo Lieh
        1st Division—Kao Chun-yung
        78th Division—Hsueh Min-chuan
        167th Division—Wang Lung-chi
    16th Corps—Li Cheng-hsien
        109th Division—Chu Kuang-chih
        1st Res Division—Feng Lung
        3rd Res Division—Chen Chu-lu
    90th Corps—Yen Ming
        28th Division—Wang Ying-tsun
        53rd Division—Yuan Chieh-san
        61st Division—Teng Chung-mei
37th Army Group—Ting Teh-lung
    36th Corps—Li Shih-lung
        15th Prov Division—Li Chia-ying
        52nd Prov Division—Ho Chi
        59th Prov Division—Sheng Wen
    80th Corps—Yuan Pu
        165th Division—Ho Fan
        New 23rd Division—Yen Ying-kao
        New 37th Division—Hsu Pao
    New 7th Corps—Chi Chang-chien (acting)
        24th Prov Division—Sung Tzu-ying
        25th Prov Division—Liu Ying
        26th Prov Division—Li Shu-chen
38th Army Group—Tung Chao
    3rd Corps—Lo Li-jung
        7th Division—Li Yung-chang
        12th Division—Chen Tzu-kan
        New 3rd Division—Chiu Kai-chi
    3rd Cavalry Corps—Huo Kuang-chien
        9th Cav Division—Shih Chien-kang
        New 7th Cav Division—Pai Hai-feng
Directly subordinate and special units:
    17th Corps—Kao Kuei-tzu
    40th Corps—Ma Fa-wu

5th Prov Corps—Li Han-chang
New 34th Division—Han Tseng-tung
2nd Prov Cav Division—Ma Lu
11th Arty Regt.—Lo Chih-yun
3rd Hv Mort Regt.—Tu Chien
52nd AT Gun Regt.—Chou Yu-huan
3rd Engr Regt.—Hsu Kai-chang
7th Engr Regt.—Sung Yao-hua
13th Engr Regt.—Fang Sung-ling
14th MP Regt.—Chao Tsan

(2) 2nd War Area
Commander: Yen Hsi-shan
Forces:
6th Army Group—Yang Ai-yuan
    19th Corps—Shih Tze-po
        68th Division—Kuo Tien-hsin
        37th Prov Division—Yang Wen-tsai
        42nd Prov Division—Yen Chun-hsien
    23rd Corps—Hsu Hung-lin
        40th Prov Division—Wu Shih-chuan
        46th Prov Division—Kuo Yung
        47th Prov Division—Wang Wei-chen
7th Army Group—Chao Cheng-shou
    33rd Corps—Yu Chen-ho
        71st Division—Wei Yu-kun
        38th Prov Division—Wen Tung-sheng
        41st Prov Division—Tien Shang-chih
    34th Corps—Kao Cho-chih
        73rd Division—Hsi An-jen
        44th Prov Division—Wang Chi
        45th Prov Division—Ma Ju-kuei
8th Army Group—Sun Chu
    43rd Corps—Liu Hsiao-tseng
        70th Division—Chen Chi-chou
        39th Prov Division—Chou Chih-jen
        43rd Prov Division—Chang Ching-shun
    61st Corps—Liang Pei-huang
        69th Division—Chou Chien-chih
        72nd Division—Kuo Tang-hsien
        48th Prov Division—Tsao Kuo-chung
13th Army Group—Wang Ching-kuo
    83rd Corps—Sun Fu-lin

66th Division—Li Pei-yin

49th Prov Division—Chang Hung

50th Prov Division—Lei Yang-tang

1st Cav Corps—Shen Jui

1st Cav Division—Han Chun-sheng

2nd Cav Division—Lu Hung-sze

4th Cav Division—Yen Teng-pang

18th Army Group—Chu Teh

115th Division—Lin Piao

120th Division—Ho Lung

129th Division—Liu Po-cheng

Directly subordinate and special units:

196th Brigade—Chia Hsuan-tsung

23rd Arty Regt.—Hou Tien-cheng

24th Arty Regt.—Li Han-chi

27th Arty Regt.—Yen Tso-lin

28th Arty Regt.—Cheng Yi

1st Engr Regt., Taiyuan Pacification Hq.—Cheng Chi-tsung

2nd Engr Regt., Taiyuan Pacification Hq.—Jen Hsiu-lin

Cav Regt., Taiyuan Pacification Hq.—Chang Tso-han

(3) 3rd War Area

Commander: Ku Chu-tung

Forces:

32nd Army Group—Li Mo-an

88th Corps—Liu Chia-shu

New 21st Division—Lo Chun-tung

11st Prov Division—Li Chi-meng

Assault Group

1st Detachment—Lo Chueh-yuan

2nd Detachment—Wei Jen-chien

25th Army Group—Li Chueh

49th Corps—Wang Tieh-han

26th Division—Tsao Tien-ko

105th Division—Liu Han-yu

5th Res Division—Wang Ho-hua

79th Division—Tuan Lin-mao

23rd Army Group—Tang Shih-tsun

28th Corps—Tao Liu

26th Division—Liu Hsun-hao

52nd Division—Chang Nai-hsin

192nd Division—Wang Yu

50th Corps—Tien Chung-yi

148th Division—Liao Ching-an

New 7th Division—Huang Po-kuang

21st Corps—Liu Yu-ching

    145th Division—Ling Chien-hsien

    146th Division—Tai Chuan-hsin

Directly subordinate and special units:

    70th Corps—Chen Kung-ta

    25th Corps—Huang Po-tao

    1st Egnr Regt—Ku Kuan-yun

    16th Engr Regt—Li Yu-hsu

    8th MP Regt—Fang Ti-hsia

    15th MP Regt—Chang Mu-tao

    23rd MP Regt—Shen Wan-chien

(4) 5th War Area

Commander: Li Tsung-jen

Forces:

2nd Army Group—Liu Ju-ming

    55th Corps—Tsao Fu-lin

        22nd Division—Shan Yu-feng

        29th Division—Jung Kuang-hsing

        74th Division—Li Yi-chih

        81st Division—Ko Kai-hsiang

    68th Corps—Liu Ju-chen

        119th Division—Liu Kuang-hsin

        143rd Division—Huang Chiao-sung

        36th Prov Division—Tsui Kung-shen

22nd Army Group—Sun Chen

    45th Corps—Chen Ting-hsun

        125th Division—Wang Hsia-feng

        127th Division—Wang Cheng-hsi

    47th Corps—Li Tsung-fang

        104th Division—Yang Hsien-ming

        178th Division—Kang Chuang

Directly subordinate and special units:

    41st Corps—Tseng Su-yuan

    1st Prov Division—Li Tsai-kuei

    16th Arty Regt—Liu Shun

    57th AT Gun Regt—Chu Shih-chin

    4th Engr Regt—Wu Chung-hsiang

    17th MP Regt—Liu Chia-kang

(5) 6th War Area

Commander: Sun Lien-chung

Forces:

Commander-in-Chief, River Defense Force,
Upper Reaches of the Yangtze River—Wu Chi-wei
39th Corps—Liu Shang-chih
56th Division—Kung Hai-kun
51st Prov Division—Shih Hung-hsi
30th Corps—Lu Chung-yi
27th Division—Hsu Wen-yao
30th Division—Wang Chen
31st Division—Mieh Tzu-pin
2nd Naval Squadron—Tseng Yi-ting
10th Army Group—Wang Ching-chiu
66th Corps—Sung Jui-ko
185th Division—Li Chung-hsin
199th Division—Peng Chan-tsun
92nd Corps—Hou Ching-ju
21st Division—Kuo Hui-tsang
142nd Division—Liu Chun-ling
26th Army Group—Sung Ken-tang
32nd Corps—Tang Yung-liang
139th Division—Sun Ting-chao
141st Division—Lin Tso-chen
33rd Army Group—Feng Chih-an
59th Corps—Liu Chen-san
38th Division—Li Chiu-sze
180th Division—Tung Sheng-tang
35th Prov Division—Chai Tzu-feng
77th Corps—Ho Chi-li
37th Division—Chi Hsing-wen
131st Division—Wang Chang-hai
179th Division—Hsu Chang-lin
Directly subordinate and special units:
9th Prov Corps—Fu Li-ping
86th Corps—Chu Ting-ching
8th Arty Regt—Chang Hsin-ku
4th Hv Mort Regt—Yang Yun-ku
6th Engr Regt—Huang Teh-hsing
17th Engr Regt—Ma Ju-hsiang
(6) 7th War Area
Commander: Yu Han-mou
Forces:
12th Army Group—Yu Han-mou (concurrent)

63rd Corps—Chang Jui-kuei
    152nd Division—Chen Chien-tien
    153rd Division—Ou Hung
    186th Division—Li Cho-yuan
65th Corps—Huang Kuo-liang
    154th Division—Kuo Yung-piao
    160th Division—Mo Fu-ju
    187th Division—Chang Kuang-chun
9th Sep Brig.—Chen Shih
20th Sep Brig.—Chiang Wu
Signal Regt.—Tseng Fei-shih
Training Regt.—Hsieh Yi
Directly subordinate and special units:
    Commander-in-Chief, Fukien-Kwangtung-Kiangsi Border Area—
    Hsiang Han-ping (commanding the 8th Peace Preservation Regt
    and Self-Defense Forces, etc.)
    Chun-Ai Garrison Commander—Wang Yi (Commanding four
    regiments of Peace Preservation Garrison Forces)
    11th Engr Regt.—Shen Cheng-chi
    16th MP Regt.—Chou Chih-hsiang

(7) 8th War Area
Commander: Chu Shao-liang
Deputy Commander: Fu Tso-yi
Forces:
    Commander-in-Chief. Shansi-Shensi-Suiyuan Border Area—Teng
    Pao-shan
    22nd Corps—Kao Shuang-cheng
        86th Division—Hsu Chih-chia
        Cav Division—Hu Ching-tung
    67th Corps—Ho Wen-ting
        New 26th Division—Ho Wen-ting (concurrent)
        7th Cav Division—Chang Shao-cheng
        New 11th Division—Tsao Han-chieh
    Northeast Advance Force—Ma Chan-shan
        New 5th Cav Division—Mu Hsin-ya
        New 6th Cav Division—Lu Chi-hua
    Shansi-Chahar-Suiyuan Border Area Advance Force—Chang Li-
    sheng (Commanding one infantry brigade and one cavalry
    brigade)
    35th Corps—Tung Chi-wu
        101st Division—Kuo Ching-yun
        New 31st Division—An Chun-shan

New 32nd Division—Li Ming-ting

3rd Prov Corps—Sun Lan-feng

    10th Prov Division—Wang Tsan-chen

    11th Prov Division—Wang Tzu-hsiu

    17th Prov Division—Chu Tzu-shun

4th Cav Corps—Yuan Ching-yung

    New 3rd Cav Division—Liang Li-chu

    New 4th Cav Division—Wang Hsien-chang

    25th Arty Regt.—Liu Chen-heng

Above-mentioned units were under the command of Gen. Fu Tso-yi, Deputy Commander of the 8th War Area.

17th Army Group—Ma Hung-kuei

    11th Corps—Ma Tung-ching

      16th Division—Ma Kuang-tsung

      6th Prov Division—Lu Chung-liang

      31st Prov Division—Ma Sai-lin

      1st Cav Brig.

      2nd Cav Brig.—Ma Yi-chung

    81st Corps—Ma Hung-pin

      35th Division—Ma Shun-ching

      60th Division—Ma Hsien-wen

      Cav Regt.—Ma Pu-jen

      3rd Arty Regt—Meng Yuan

3rd Army Group—Chao Shou-shan

    91st Corps—Wang Chin

      58th Prov Division—Yeh Cheng

      10th Cav Division—Liu Yu-ching

      New 4th Division—Chou Hsu-lung

29th Army Group—Li Tieh-chun

    42nd Corps—Yang Teh-liang

      191st Division—Chen Hsi-ping

      7th Res Division—Li Yu-hsiang

    New 2nd Corps—Li Tieh-chun (concurrent)

      New 45th Division—Hsieh Yi-feng

      New 46th Division—Hsu Ju-cheng

40th Army Group—Ma Pu-fang

    5th Cav Corps—Ma Cheng-hsiang

      5th Cav Division—Ma Cheng-hsien

      1st Prov Cav Division—Han Yu-wen

    82nd Corps—Ma Chi-yuan

      100th Division—Tan Hsiang

      New 8th Cav Division—Ma Pu-luan

61st Prov Division—Ma Chuan-yi
Directly subordinate and special units:
    128th Division—Liu Cheng-hsin
    3rd Prov Division—Tang Chih-chuan
    11th Cav Division—Wu Hsi-chih
    12th Cav Division—Chang Hsi-liang
    New 1st Cav Division—Tsui Yin-chun
    New 2nd Cav Division—Wang Ling-yun
    22nd MP Regt.—Tsao Shu-hsi

(8) 9th War Area
Commander: Hsueh Yueh
Forces:
Deputy Commander-in-Chief, 1st Army Group—Sun Tu
  58th Corps—Lu Tao-yuan
    New 10th Division—Hsiao Pen-yuan
    New 11th Division—Hou Chen-pang
  New 3rd Corps—Yang Hung-liang
    183rd Division—Yu Chien-hsun
    New 12th Division—Tang Yu-tsung
30th Army Group—Wang Ling-chi
  72nd Corps—Fu Yi
    34th Division—Chu Shun-kun
    New 13th Division—Tang Shun-po
    New 15th Division—Chiang Tao
    16th Prov Division—Wu Shou-chuan (directly under the command of the army group)
Directly subordinate and special units:
    4th Corps—Ou Chen (concurrent)
    99th Corps—Liang Han-ming
    44th Corps—Wang Tse-chun
    2nd Prov Corps—Shen Fa-tsao
    5th Engr Regt.—Huang Ke-hu
    14th Engr Regt.—Wen Shih-wei

(9) 10th War Area
Commander: Li Pin-hsien
Forces:
21st Army Group—Li Pin-hsien (concurrent)
  7th Corps—Hsu Chi-ming
    171st Division—Li Mao-tsung
    172nd Division—Chu Nai-jui
    173rd Division—Liu Fang
  48th Corps—Su Tsu-hsing

138th Division—Li Ying-chun
176th Division—Li Pen-yi
84th Corps—Chang Kuang-wei
174th Division—Tan Ho-yi
189th Division—Chang Wen-hung
15th Army Group—Ho Chu-kuo (concurrent)
2nd Cav Corps—Liao Yun-tse
3rd Cav Division—Hsu Chang-hsi
51st Corps—Chou Yu-ying
14th Prov Division—Li Hung-tzu
113th Division—Li Yu-tang
114th Division—Li Pu-ching
8th Cav Division—Ma Pu-kang
2nd Prov Brig.—Chang Ching-hsiu
3rd Prov Brig.—Li Chuan-huai
19th Army Group—Chen Ta-ching
1st Prov Corps—Wang Yu-wen
33rd Division—Tuan Hai-chou
29th Division
12th Corps—Huo Shou-yi
111th Division—Sun Huan-tsai
112th Division—Yu Yi-fan
Shantung Advance Force—Li Yen-nien
12th Prov Division—Chao Lu-yuan
New 36th Division—Liu Shih-ming
(10) Hopei-Chahar War Area
Commander-in-Chief: Kao Shu-hsun
Forces:
New 8th Corps—Hu Po-han
New 6th Division—Fan Lung-chang
29th Prov Division—Yin Ying-chou
(11) Chinese Forces in India
Commander-in-Chief: Daniel T. Sultan
Deputy Commander-in-Chief: Cheng Tung-kuo
Forces:
New 1st Corps—Sun Li-jen
New 30th Division—Tang Shou-chih
New 38th Division—Li Hung
Directly subordinate and special units:
50th Division—Pan Yu-kun
4th Arty Regt.—Chiang Kung-chuan
5th Arty Regt.—Liu Tso-yi

12th Arty Regt.—Hou Chih-hsing

Hv Mort Regt.—Hsu Ma-hsi

Tank Commander—Po Lang (commanding 1st and 2nd Tank
  Battalions)

10th Engr Regt.—Li Loh-chung

12th Engr Regt.—Liang Ko-fa

(12) In order to establish contact with Allied forces and shift to the offensive, our government activated General Headquarters, Chinese Army in Kunming
in the winter of 1944 to be responsible for the unified command and training of
all the forces in the various war zones of the southwest. Gen. Ho Ying-chin who
was Chief of the General Staff was concurrently Commander-in-Chief, General
Headquarters, Chinese Army. He exercised command over a total of 28 corps
(86 divisions) excluding other special units. These forces included the Expeditionary Forces under Wei Li-huang, Tang En-po's forces in the Kweichow—
Kwangsi—Hunan Border Area, Chang Fa-kuei's in the 4th War Area, Lu Han's
forces in the Yunnan—Indo-China Border Area and the two army groups under
Tu Yu-ming and Li Yu-tang. Meanwhile, the China—Indo Road (renamed
Stilwell Road) had opened permitting large quantities of U.S. weapons and war
materials to arrive in China. It was anticipated that 36 infantry divisions would
be able to receive U.S. weapons and equipment including adequate artillery. The
logistic facilities for the forces to undertake the counter-offensive were vastly improved, and morale was greatly uplifted. In order to meet the operational requirements in the future counteroffensive, all the forces under the command of GHQ
Chinese Army were reorganized into four front armies as follows:

(a) 1st Front Army

Commander: Lu Han

Forces:

　　　60th Corps—An En-pu

　　　　182nd Division—Yang Hung-yuan

　　　　184th Division—Tseng Tse-sheng

　　　2nd Route Corps—Chang Chung

　　　　20th Prov Division—An Chun-san

　　　　21st Prov Division—Chiu Ping-chang

　　　　22nd Prov Division—Yang Ping-lin

　　　52nd Corps—Chao Kung-wu

　　　　2nd Division—Liu Yu-chang

　　　　25th Division—Liu Shih-mao

　　　　195th Division—Chang Ming-hsin

　Directly subordinate and special units:

　　　18th Division—Hsu Yi-chun

　　　Pack How Regt, Generalissimo's Headquarters in Kunming

　　　Engr Regt, Generalissimo's Headquarters in Kunming

(b) 2nd Front Army
   Commander: Chang Fa-kuei
   Forces:

        46th Corps—Li Hsing-su
          188th Division—Hai Ching-chiang
          175th Division—Kan Cheng-yu
          New 19th Division—Chiang Hsiung
        64th Corps—Chang Chih
          131st Division—Huang Ping-chi
          156th Division—Liu Chen-hsiang
          159th Division—Liu Shao-wu
        62nd Corps—Huang Tao
          151st Division—Lin Wei-chou
          95th Division—Tuan Yun
          157th Division—Li Hung-ta
          158th Division—Liu Tung-tsai

(c) 3rd Front Army
   Commander: Tang En-po
   Forces:

27th Army Group—Li Yu-tang
        20th Corps—Yang Kan-tsai
          133rd Division—Chou Han-hsi
          134th Division—Wu Chung-yen
        26th Corps—Ting Chih-pan
          41st Division—Tung Chi-tao
          44th Division—Chiang Hsiu-jen
          149th Division—Chen Chun-lin

The above forces were subordinated to Li's 27th Army Group.

        94th Corps—Mou Ting-fang
          121st Division—Chu Ching-min
          43rd Division—Li Shih-lin
          5th Division—Li Tse-fen
        13th Corps—Shih Chueh
          4th Division—Tsai Chien-ming
          89th Division—Wang Kuang-han
          54th Division—Shih Sung-chuan
        71st Corps—Chen Ming-jen
          87th Division—Huang Yen
          91st Division—Yu Teh-lin
          88th Division—Hu Chia-chi
Special Units:
        1st Arty Brig.—A portion of Peng Meng-chi's force

51st Arty Brig.—Li Tao-kung

(d) 4th Front Army
     Commander: Wang Yao-wu
     Forces:
             73rd Corps—Han Chun
                15th Division—Liang Chih-lu
                77th Division—Tang Sheng-hai
                193rd Division—Hsiao Chung-kuang
             74th Corps—Shih Chung-cheng
                51st Division—Chou Chih-tao
                57th Division—Li Yen
                58th Division—Tsai Jen-chieh
             100th Corps—Li Tien-hsia
                19th Division—Yang Yin
                63rd Division—Hsu Chih-hsiu
             18th Corps—Hu Lien
                11th Division—Yang Po-tao
                18th Division—Chin Tao-shan
                118th Division—Li Hsueh-cheng

(e) Kunming Defense Command
     Commander: Tu Yu-ming
     Forces:
             5th Corps—Chiu Ching-chuan
                45th Division—Hu Chang-ching
                96th Division—Huang Hsiang
                200th Division—Lo Yu-lun
             8th Corps—Li Mi
                166th Division—Wang Chih-yu
                103rd Division—Liang Hsiao-chai
                1st Honor Division—Wang Po-hsun
             Directly subordinate units:
                48th Division—Cheng Ting-chi
                19th Prov Division

(f) Directly Subordinate Units, GHQ Chinese Army:
             54th Corps—Chueh Han-chien
                36th Division—Li Chih-peng
                8th Division—Wu Chun
                198th Division—Liu Chin-kuei
             6th Corps—Liao Yao-hsiang
                14th Division—Lung Tien-wu
                New 22nd Division—Li Tao
                207th Division—Fang Hsien-chueh

2nd Corps—Wang Ling-yun
  9th Division—Chen Ke-fei
  76th Division—Liu Ping
  2nd Res Division—Ku Pao-yu
53rd Corps—Chou Fu-cheng
  116th Division—Liu Jun-chuan
  130th Division—Wang Li-huan
  2nd Honor Division—Tai Chien
93rd Division—Lu Kuo-chuan
169th Division—Tsao Yu-heng
5th Arty Regt.—Lin Lu-sheng
13th Arty Regt.—Huang Yu-mien
41st Arty Regt.
49th Arty Regt.
6th Signal Regt.
20th MP Regt.—Wei Chih-chao

(13) Local Pacification Forces
  22nd Corps—Liu Wen-hui
    136th Division—Liu Yuan-hsuan
    137th Division—Chen Kuang-tsao
  56th Corps—Pan Wen-hua
    163rd Division—Chen Lan-ting
    164th Division—Peng Huan-chang
  95th Corps—Huang Yin
    136th Division—Hsieh Wu-chi
    9th Division—Yang Shai-hsuan
  New 15th Division—Liu Shu-cheng
  New 1st Brigade—Peng Pin
  23rd Prov Division—Pan Suo-tuan
  2nd Sep Inf Brig.—Lung Sheng-tsu
  14th Corps—Yu Chin-yuan (Chungking Garrison Force)
    10th Division—Ku Ping-kuei
    83rd Division—Shen Hsiang-kuei
    85th Division—Wang Ching-yuan
  New 25th Division—Li Ken-ku (Chungking Garrison Force)

(14) Directly Subordinate Units, National Military Council
  79th Corps—Fang Ching
    98th Division—Hsiang Ming-sze
    6th Prov Division—Chao Chi-ping
    194th Division—Kung Chuan-wen
  76th Corps—Liao Ang
    24th Division—Liu Ching-chih

57th Division—Chu Hsia-nien
69th Corps—Mi Wen-ho
181st Division—Chang Yu-ting
28th Prov Division—Cheng Kuang-jan
2nd Prov Division—Shih Tsu-teh
54th Prov Division—Hsu Ching-chi
Garrison Brigade—Lou Ping-kuo
32nd Training Dept.—Han Wen-yuan

1. Battle of Western Honan and Northern Hupei (Late March-Late May, 1945. See Map 43 and Charts 66 and 67)

CHART 66

Chart Showing Japanese Chain of Command during the Battle of Western Honan-Northern Hopei (Mid-March, 1945)

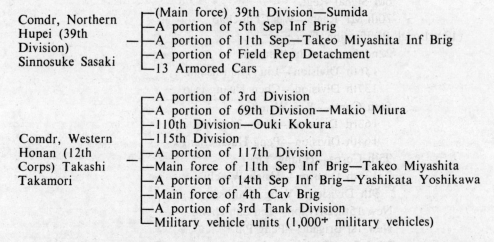

Comdr, Northern
Hupei (39th
Division)
Sinnosuke Sasaki
— ┌─(Main force) 39th Division—Sumida
├─A portion of 5th Sep Inf Brig
├─A portion of 11th Sep—Takeo Miyashita Inf Brig
├─A portion of Field Rep Detachment
└─13 Armored Cars

Comdr, Western
Honan (12th
Corps) Takashi
Takamori
— ┌─A portion of 3rd Division
├─A portion of 69th Division—Makio Miura
├─110th Division—Ouki Kokura
├─115th Division
├─A portion of 117th Division
├─Main force of 11th Sep Inf Brig—Takeo Miyashita
├─A portion of 14th Sep Inf Brig—Yashikata Yoshikawa
├─Main force of 4th Cav Brig
├─A portion of 3rd Tank Division
└─Military vehicle units (1,000⁺ military vehicles)

In order to impede our air raid and air transportations and make preparations for the general counteroffensive, the enemy massed the main force of his 12th Corps (built around the 110th and 115th Divisions, 3rd Tank Division, and 4th Cavalry Brigade totalling over 70,000 troops and more than 100 tanks) in the vicinity of Sui-ping, Yeh Hsien and Lu-shan in the spring of 1945.   On March 22, the enemy began the converging attack on Nan-yang by employing a fast-moving force against Lao-ho-kou Airfield and another force in the vicinity of Lo-ning against Lu-shih to threaten eastern Shensi.   A portion (built around the 39th Division) of the 34th Corps began the attack against Hsiang-fan on March 21 to respond to the overall operations.

To shatter the enemy attempt, Generalissimo Chiang directed the 5th War Area to conduct sustained resistance first at Pi-yang, Fang-cheng and Nan-yang, and timely withdraw to the area between the Tuan River and the Tan River for a decisive battle against the enemy.   The 1st War Area was directed to intercept the

CHART 67

Chart Showing Chinese Chain of Command during the Battle of Western Honan-Northern Hupei (Mid-March, 1945)

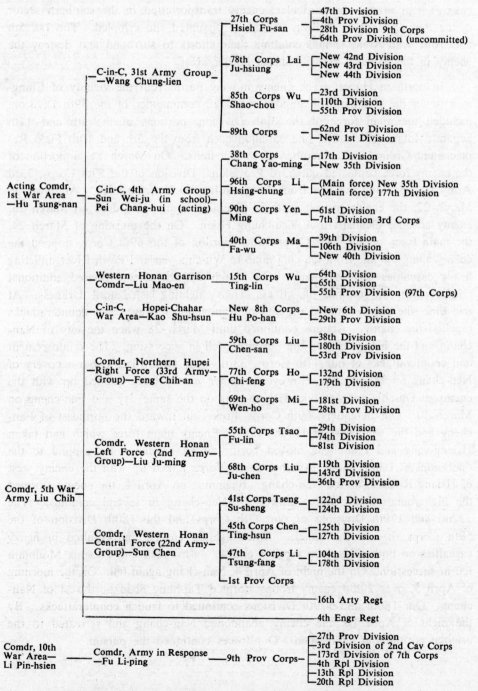

The above forces total 148,000 men and 4 groups of air force.

enemy along the line from Nan-chao to Li-ching-tien in order to crush the enemy offensive. The 10th War Area was directed to attack the enemy in the southern sector of the Peiping-Hankow Railway and sabotage enemy traffic communications. Our air force units in the bases in western Honan and southern Shensi were ordered to step up the bombing of the lines of communications in the enemy's rear areas. In particular, enemy transportation in the southern sector of the Peiping-Hankow Railway should be disrupted and crippled. The 1st, 5th and 10th War Areas should combine their efforts to surround and destroy the enemy in the Honan—Hupei—Shensi border areas.

In northern Hupei: The enemy moving north from the vicinity of Ching-men under the command of Sinnosuke Sasoki, commander of the 39th Division, included the main force of the 39th Division, portions of the 5th and 11th Separate Infantry Brigades, one battalion each from the 5th and 10th Field Replacement Groups and a number of special units. On March 21, a portion of the enemy force contacted our 53rd Provisional Division of the 59th Corps, 33rd Army Group along the line from Tung-mu-ling to Yenchih-miao. At dawn on March 22, the enemy moved north in several columns. By dusk on March 23, enemy advance elements took Tzu-chung Hsien. On the morning of March 24, the main force of our 59th Corps and a portion of the 69th Corps stopped the enemy along the line from Ou-chia-miao to Wu-chia-yen and Pa-tu River inflicting heavy casualties on the enemy. On March 26, the enemy poured additional reinforcements to continue the attack. Heavy fighting lasted until darkness. At one time, the enemy entered the city of Nan-chang; however, our counterattacks repelled the enemy. Actions continued until March 28 when the city of Nan-chang and the highground to the northwest fell in succession. The reinforcement and counterattacks of our 77th Corps, 33rd Army Group led to our recovery of Nan-chang on March 29. However, another enemy force teamed up with the enemy at Ou-chia-miao to take Hsiang-yang on the same day and Fan-cheng on March 30. Our defenders, 69th Corps, broke out toward the northeast of Fan-cheng and the southwest of Hsiang-yang. Enemy main force which had taken Hsiang-yang and Fan-cheng moved north toward Ku-cheng to respond to the operations at Lao-ho-kou. Another enemy force linked up with the enemy west of Hsiang River to attack Nan-chang. Beginning on April 2, the enemy stormed the highgrounds south and southwest of Nan-chang in several columns. The 132nd and 179th Divisions of our 77th Corps and the 180th Division of the 59th Corps rose to the attack. Bitter fighting ensued and resulted in heavy casualties on both sides. On April 3 and 4, Yu-hsi-shan and Phoenix Mountain fell in succession. On the night of April 4, Nan-chang again fell. On the morning of April 5, over 2,000 enemy troops stormed Tai-hung Shan northwest of Nan-chang. Our 180th and 179th Divisions continued to launch counterattacks. By the night of April 10, the enemy abandoned Nan-chang and retreated to the original positions at Ching-men. Our forces continued the pursuit.

On April 7, over 4,000 enemy troops in the vicinity of Hsiang-yang moved west along the Hsiang River. At 1400 hours on April 8, a portion of our 69th Corps abandoned Tzu-ho-shih, but the enemy continued his attack on Ku-cheng. Our 22nd Army Group employed the 124th Division to offer frontal resistance and the 48th Division to attack the enemy flanks at Tzu-ho-shih. By 1500 hours, April 12, our forces recovered Tzu-ho-shih. Meanwhile, over 2,000 enemy troops, having reached the south of Ku-cheng were dealt a heavy blow by our forces and fled in disorder. Our 5th War Area ordered the pursuit. On April 13, having pursued the enemy to Tzu-ho-shih, the main force of our 41st Corps joined force with the 38th and 132nd Divisions and the 28th Provisional Division to continue the pursuit toward Hsiang-yang and Tzu-chung Hsien. On April 15, our 179th Division recovered Wu-chia-yen, and portions of the 38th and 132nd Divisions recovered Ou-chia-miao and Hsiao-ho-chen. On the morning of April 16, the main force of our 38th Division recovered Hsiang-yang, while portions of our 179th and 132nd Divisions took Tzu-chung and trailed the enemy in pursuit. On the morning of April 18, elements of our 38th Division captured Fan-cheng; the main force of our 179th Division and a portion of our 37th Division pursued the enemy to Liu-hou-chi. By this time, pre-battle status was restored in the area west of the Hsiang River.

On the western Honan front: On March 21, under the command of Takashi Takamori, commander of the 12th Corps, the enemy's 115th and 110th Divisions, 11th Separate Brigade, 4th Cavalry Brigade and 3rd Tank Division separately advanced from Sha-ho-tien, Wu-yang, Yeh Hsien and Lu-shan. On March 22 and 23, the enemy left route attacked the positions of our 55th Corps west of Hsiao-shih-tien and Chun-shiu; the enemy central route attacked our 68th Corps between Pao-an-chai and Tu-shu Chen; the enemy right route attacked our New 8th Corps at Nan-chao and Li-ching-tien. On March 24, our forces abandoned Hsiang-ho-kuan, She-chih Chen, Fang-cheng, Nan-chao and Li-ching-tien and withdrew to Nan-yang. On March 25, a portion of the enemy force maintained surveillance over Nan-yang, while the main force continued the westward advance from the north and south of Nan-yang. At dawn on March 26, over 2,000 fast-moving enemy toorps reached the vicinity of Lao-ho-kou and Kuang-hua via the area between Teng Hsien and Hsin-yeh and fought bitterly against our 125th Division. Meanwhile, over 2,000 enemy troops moving south from Li-ching-tien linked up with the main force of the enemy's 110th Division which had reached the northern outskirt of Nan-yang from Nan-chao, and swung to Chen-ping, Nei-hsiang and Hsi-chia-kou for the attack. Our New 8th Corps offered piecemeal resistance. On the night of March 26, a portion of the enemy force passed Nei-hsiang to attack the main force of our 15th Corps, and the Western Honan Garrison Force. On March 27, heavy fighting broke out as the enemy launched violent attack against Lao-ho-kou and Nan-yang. On March 28, over 6,000 enemy troops invaded Teng Hsien and Wen-chu-chi via the area southwest of

Nanyang. After intercepting the enemy, our 22nd Division turned to the north-west. After the fall of Li-kuan-chiao, Chen-ping and Nei-hsiang also fell in succession. On the morning of the same day, our 2nd and 22nd Army Groups launched converging attacks against the enemy at Lao-ho-kou and Teng Hsien succession. In the morning of the same day, our 2nd and 22nd Army Groups and was halted by our 47th Corps. The enemy's 110th Division and 3rd Tank Division in the vicinity of Nei-hsiang separately invaded Hsi-chuan and Hsi-chia-kou. The main force of our 68th Corps and portions of our New 8th, 15th and 85th Corps engaged the enemy resulting in heavy casualties on both sides. Over 4,000 enemy troops attacked Hsi-chuan on March 30 and captured it on April 1. The main force of our 89th Corps stopped the enemy in the area southeast of Hsing-tzu-kuan, and our 68th Corps launched flanking attacks. Having suffered heavy losses as a result of bitter fighting against superior enemy forces for one week, our 143rd Division garrisoning Nan-yang broke out to the southeast of the city and continued its attack against the enemy.

Beginning on March 28, the enemy laying siege on Lao-ho-kou launched violent attacks but were repelled suffering heavy casualties. However, since March 29 when Hsiang-yang and Fan-cheng both fell, the flanks of Lao-pai-lu were threatened. On April 2, apart from leaving the 127th and 1st Provisional Divisions behind in the area northeast of Lao-ho-kou to harass the enemy, our main force was shifted to the vicinity of Ku-cheng to consolidate the front of Lao-pai-lu.

On the Hsi-chia-kou front: Since March 29, our 31st Army Group employed the main force of the 85th Corps and a portion of the 78th Corps to offer piecemeal resistance at Hsi-chia-kou and Kuei-men-kuan. By the afternoon of April 3, over 5,000 enemy troops detoured to Chung-yang-tien. Accordingly, our forces repelled repeated enemy attacks. At dawn on April 5, our forces went into the offensive by flanking actions against the enemy. Bitter fighting continued into the night of April 7 when our forces recovered Kuei-men-kuan killing over 4,000 enemy troops including a regimental commander of the enemy's 110th Division. With the fall of Lao-ho-kou on April 8, our 125th Division broke out toward Tsao-tien. Since early April, continued pressure exerted by our ground and air forces caused a portion of the enemy's 34th Corps to withdraw to its original positions in Ching-men. The enemy's 12th Corps was in a state of stale-mate against our forces at Hsi-chia-kou. A portion of the enemy forces continued to offer stubborn resistance at Hsi-chuan and Lao-ho-kou. Additional forces were pulled and withdrew to Teng Hsien and Nan-yang in order to consolidate the rear areas. On the night of April 12, portions of our 41st and 45th Corps attacked Lao-ho-kou and Kuang-hua, while another powerful force teamed up with the main force of our 55th Corps and a portion of the 69th Corps in the vicinity of Teng Hsien to launch a converging attack against the enemy there. On April 13, the 47th Corps employed its main force to mop up the enemy in the vicinity of Tang-tsei-kou, while a portion of the corps attacked the enemy at Li-kuan-chiao. Bitter fighting lasted until April 15 when the enemy's 115th Division which had returned to the vicinity of Teng Hsien dispatched a powefrul force to the vicinity of Li-kuan-chiao and Lao-ho-kou to respond to the enemy at Hsi-chuan and Hsi-chia-kou. On April 27, with the enemy's capture of Hsin-yeh, the main forces of our 55th and 69th Corps were shifted to the area north of Tsao-yang. On April 28, at one time, units of our 22nd Army Group entered Lao-ho-kou. Still facing the enemy across the river by May 1, our forces fought bitterly against the enemy at Hsi-chia-kou with both sides pouring in reinforcement. A state of stalemate remained by the end of May.

In Lo-ning, on March 23, over 4,000 troops of the enemy's 110th Division attacked Chang-shui Chen and were engaged by the main force of our 38th Corps and a portion of our 96th Corps, both of the 4th Army Group. For more than 10 days, the enemy and our forces fought back and forth on the eastern flank of Ku Hsien. By April 9, our forces outlanked and repelled the enemy. After April 10, the enemy shifted over 3,000 troops for employment in Hsi-chia-kou. By the end of April, our forces confronted the enemy in the vicinity of Chang-shui Chen.

In order to respond to the operations at Hsi-chia-kou, our forces dispatched a portion of the 40th Corps to attack the enemy in Shen Hsien inflicting heavy casualties on the enemy. Between May 16-22, about 5,000 troops of the enemy's 69th and 114th Divisions attacked Kuan-tao-kou and Ling-pao. On May 24 and 25, the converging attacks of our 4th Army Group and 40th Corps repelled the cnemy inflicting heavy casualties. By May 29, the original situation was restored.

Since late March, our 10th War Area attacked the enemy in the southern sector of the Peiping-Hankow Railway reaping considerable gains. In April, one force crossed the Peiping-Hankow Railway to take the key localities of Chun-shui and Niu-ti. Enemy troops which were cornered in the major strong points too frightened to be active.

From March 21 to May 31, this battle witnessed the killing and wounding of 15,000+ enemy troops, the capture of 6 enemy prisoners of war, 92 light and heavy machine guns, 556 rifles, 4 mortars and large quantities of military supplies.

    m. Battle of Western Hunan (Early April-Early June, 1945. See Map 44 and Charts 68 and 69)

CHART 68

Chart Showing Japanese Chain of Command during the Battle of Western Hunan (Early April, 1945)

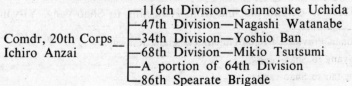

```
                              ┌─116th Division—Ginnosuke Uchida
                              ├─47th Division—Nagashi Watanabe
        Comdr, 20th Corps ─── ├─34th Division—Yoshio Ban
        Ichiro Anzai          ├─68th Division—Mikio Tsutsumi
                              ├─A portion of 64th Division
                              └─86th Spearate Brigade
```

CHART 69

Chart Showing Chinese Chain of Command during the Battle of Western Hunan

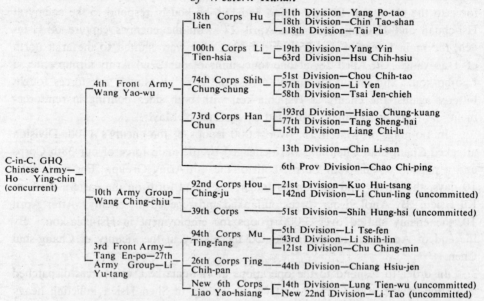

With the objectives of capturing Chih-chiang Airfield,[50] consolidating the traffic communications of the Hunan-Kwangsi and Canton-Hankow Railways and undermining our counteroffensive preparations, the enemy launched the Battle of Western Hunan. Since late March, 1945, the enemy actively undertook the construction of the Heng-Shao Highway[51] and the Tang-Shao Highway[52] and stored rations, ammunition, weapons and equipment in and near Shao-yang. The main force of the 34th Division was massed between Hsing-an and Chuan Hsien; the 58th Brigade of the 68th Division between Tung-an and Ling-ling; the 116th Division in the vicinity of Shao-yang; a portion of the 40th Division between Heng-yang and Heng-shan; the 47th Division between Shao-yang and Yung-feng; and a portion of the 64th Division, and the puppet 2nd Division of the Peace Army between Ning-hsiang and Yi-yang. By early April, the enemy had massed 70,000-80,000 troops under Ichiro Anzai, commander of the 20th Corps, with headquarters in Shao-yang. The enemy attempted to launch a converging attack, surround and destroy our field forces, operate in An-chiang and Hung-chiang and capture our air base in Chih-chiang.

Accordingly, our National Military Council directed the 4th Front Army to dispatch a force to defend the line from Hsin-ning to Shao-yang, Yi-yang, Tung-

[50] In Hunan Province, by the Hunan-Kweichow Railway.

[51] Heng-yang to Shao-yang.

[52] Hsiang-tan to Shao-yang.

ting Lake and its west bank; use the prepared positions to offer piecemeal resistance; and employ the main force for decisive battle against the enemy between Wu-kang and Hsin-hua. The 27th Army Group of the 3rd Front Army dispatched a force to garrison the key localities of Lung-sheng and Cheng-pu and insure the halting of the enemy on the Kweichow-Kwangsi Road and Kwei-Sui Road[53] so as to facilitate the decisive actions of the main force. Additionally, the 94th Corps and 20th Army Group were ordered to operate in the areas east of Wu-kang and east of Hsinhua respectively, and the main force of the New 6th Corps was airlifted to Chih-chiang as the general reserves hoping to destroy the enemy between Wukang and Hsinhua and insure the defense of our air base at Chih-chiang.

On the Hsin-ning front: In early April, the main force of the enemy's 34th Division, and the 58th Brigade of the 68th Division separately moved from Chuan Hsien and Tung-an against our forces. On April 16, after taking Hsin-ning, these two forces continued the attack. The main force of the enemy's 34th Division reached Tzu-mu Shan on April 21 and Chen-liang on April 22. On April 23, a portion of the enemy force reached Mei-chiang to continue the invasion against Chang-pu-tzu and met the piecemeal resistance of a portion of our 44th Division, 26th Corps. In the night of April 24, the enemy attempted to force the crossing of the Wu River and was repelled. On April 25, when the enemy's main force reached Shui-tung and Kuan-hsia, a portion of our 58th Division intercepted. On April 27, the enemy reached Chu-yu-shan and engaged in bitter fighting against the main force of our 58th Division. At night, the enemy laid siege against Wu-yang and detoured to attack Wan-fu-chiao. The enemy took Pai-chia-fang on April 29 and Wu-yang in the afternoon of the same day. One company of the defenders died for the country. On April 30, the enemy launched a violent attack against Wa-wu-tang but failed. On May 1, the enemy invaded Shui-kou. On May 2, with the assistance of our air force, the main force of our 58th Division, and the 193rd Division launched counterattacks against the enemy and wiped out the 217th Regiment of the enemy's 34th Division. In the afternoon, enemy remnants retreated to the area southeast of Cha-shan. Our forces followed up in pursuit and inflicted heavy casualties on the enemy. Moving north along the Wu-Hsin Highway, the 58th Brigade of the enemy's 68th Division reached Hsiao-mai-tien and Hsia-shan-kou on April 19, Shih-men, Sze-chieh-pai on April 20, An-hsin-kuan and Wu-li-pai on April 22, and Tsai-chia-tang and Lung-tan-pu on April 25. In the morning of April 27, the enemy pressed near the outskirt of Wu-kang on three sides. After inflicting heavy casualties on the enemy, a portion of our 58th Division withdrew to the city in defense.

On the Shao-yang front: The enemy's 47th and 116th Divisions began the invasion in four routes. His first route of over 3,000 troops made a forced

---

53 Kweilin to Canton.

crossing of the Tzu River at Chiu-kung Bridge on April 13 and took Ai-shan-pu on April 17. On April 18, it attacked Kuei-hua-ping from both flanks and was intercepted by a portion of our 19th Division. The enemy was divided into several columns for the attack to the west on April 19 and took Kao-sha-shih and Shih-hsia-chiang on April 21. In the morning of April 23, the enemy reached Chu-kao-tang and invaded Tung-kou on April 26. After dealing the enemy a heavy blow, our 58th Division moved to prepared positions at Tung-kou to continue striking the enemy.

The enemy's second column of over 4,000 troops attacked Hsiao-tang from Shao-yang on April 11, reached Shan-hsi on April 12 and Li-shan-pu on April 13. After being intercepted by portions of our 19th and 63rd Divisions, the enemy's advance elements of 800 troops reached Pai-ma-shan on April 16 where it was halted by a portion of our 57th Division. On April 17, elements of the enemy force infiltrated through gaps to reach the vicinity of Fang-tung, followed by the enemy's main forces. Having fought gallantly, our 51st Division inflicted heavy casualties on the enemy and frustrated the enemy attack. Later, the main forces of our 63rd and 19th Divisions arrived to surround and destroy the enemy in the vicinity of Fang-tung.

The enemy's third route of 4,000 dispatched a force on April 12 to invade Shih-ma-chiang northwest of Shao-yang. On April 15, the enemy reached Chu-kou-pu and Shun-shui Bridge, as our 63rd Division offered piecemeal resistance. On April 16, the enemy moved west to Wu-shu-hsia, Lung-hui-sze and Sai-shih. The enemy then swung to Shan-men on April 24, Pan-chiang-feng on April 26, Shang-cha-ping in the night of April 28 and Kan-hsi and Hsien-chiang on April 30. The interceptions by the main force of our 57th Division and a portion of our 6th Provisional Division frustrated the enemy offensive.

The enemy's fourth route which was composed of the Hiroshige Column organized by the 47th Division had about 4,000 men. On April 9 over 1,000 enemy troops made the invasion from Hei-tien-pu and reached San-kou-kuan on April 11. After being intercepted by a portion of our 15th Division, it turned to the west and linked up with the main force of 3,000 troops of the division to invade Hsiao-hsi, force the crossing of the Tzu River and attack Li-tang on April 13. On April 16, the enemy force reached Han-pu-ao and on April 28 swung to Wei-shan in the west and then to Yueh-lao-shan in the north. Our 77th Division conducted piecemeal interceptions against the enemy. On April 29, the enemy reached the vicinity of Yang-hsi-chiao. Violent attacks made by the main force of our 73rd Corps inflicted heavy casualties on the enemy and frustrated the enemy offensive.

On the Ning-hsiang and Yi-yang front: On April 14, an enemy force of 2,000 invaded Yi-yang from Wan-chiang and fought bitterly against elements of our 18th Division. By April 17, the enemy invaded Tao-hua-chiang in the west. On April 19, another enemy force of 800 invaded Shu-tang and skirted

Tao-hua-chiang forcing our defenders to move to the southwest of Tao-hua-chiang to stop the enemy advance. On April 21, our reinforcements arrived to begin the counterattacked which routed the enemy and forced him to retreat to the city of Yi-yang and face our forces across the river. At one time, an enemy force of 1,000 from Ning-hsiang reached Ta-cheng-chiao and was repelled by elements of our 18th Division.

Since the beginning of the enemy offensive, our units had offered steady resistance from point to point, slowly drawing the enemy into areas suitable for decisive battles. Our forces conducted strong interceptions on the front. Meanwhile, our 18th Corps was ordered to race south from Chang-teh and Tao-yuan; the main force of our 94th Corps swiftly advanced to Wu-yang and Wu-kang from the Hunan-Kweichow border; and the main force of the New 6th Corps was massed in Chih-chiang. In early May, our units had reached the designated areas ready to launch converging attacks against the invaders.

On the Hsin-ning front: On April 30, the main force of our 94th Corps (5th and 121st Divisions) began the attack from Chang-pu-tzu to the northeast against the enemy at Wa-wu-tang. On May 1, our 5th Division recovered Wu-yang. On May 3, the enemy was reinforced and counterattacked fighting bitterly against our 5th Division along the line from Ta-ho-chung to Lung-yen-shan. The battle raged violently. On the morning of May 5, the enemy weakened and retreated to Lo-chia-pu in the southeast. Meanwhile, the main force of our 58th Division, and the 193rd Division also attacked the enemy violently. Most of the enemy troops retreated in disorder to the north of Wu-kang, and a portion to Hua-yuan-shih, as our 5th Division led the pursuit along the main road north of Wu-kang. On May 9, the division attacked the enemy west of Huang-chiao-pu. After crushing the enemy force which offered stubborn resistance east and west of Yang-tu-chai, our 121st Division recovered Kao-sha-shih on May 12. On the same day, after routing the enemy south of Wa-wu-tang, our 58th Division reached Kao-sha-shih, 3,000 enemy remnants fled to the east; however they were intercepted by our 5th Division. Consequently, they turned back to Ma-an-shih, crossed the river and retreated to the south. Our 94th Corps encircled and attacked the enemy inflicting heavy losses. On the morning of May 14, enemy remnants broke out to the east and were pursued by elements of our 94th Corps. Meanwhile, the main force of the corps surrounded and destroyed the enemy in the vicinity of Feng-shen-ai and Cha-pu-tzu. By May 16, our forces wiped out the surrounded enemy.

Having crushed the enemy force which had forced the crossing of the Wu River, on April 29 at noon, elements of our 44th Division headed separately for Hsin-ning, Kuan-hsia and Wu-kang in pursuit of the enemy. On the morning of May 4, one of our forces pressed near Shih-shih and captured Hsiao-mai-tien at night. On May 6, the city of Hsin-ning was recovered. On May 16, to save its doomed fate, 3,000 troops of the enemy's 34th Division continued the attack on Hsin-ning. As they reached Yao-tzu-ling northwest of Hsin-ning on May 18, they were stopped by the main force of our 43rd Division, 94th Corps. On May 23, due to lack of rations and ammunition, our defenders in Hsin-ning fell back to the vicinity of Huang-pu-kang and teamed up with the main force of the 43rd Division to defeat the enemy along the Ma-tou-chiao Line. In addition, elements of our 44th Division raced to Chang-chia-sai on May 5 and to the area southwest of Wu-kang on May 6 where they linked up with the defenders of the 58th Division in launching a converging attack against the enemy. At noon on May 7, with over half of its men killed or wounded, the enemy fled to Mi-shan-up in the northeast. As the enemy at Wu-kang collapsed, our forces headed to the east in pursuit on May 9.

On the Shaoyang front: On April 27, the enemy force which had reached the vicinity of Tung-kou launched violent attacks against our positions, while the enemy force invading Kan-hsi and Hsien-chiang continued to engage in bitter fighting against our forces. On May 2, an enemy column of over 1,000 troops attacked Tieh-shan violently and continued the attack on Ching-ai on May 4. Meanwhile, the main force of the enemy's 116th Division in the area east of Chiang-kou which had been increased to 6,000 was engaged in bloody and intense fighting against our forces. Our 57th Division fought gallantly, and a portion of our 51st Division moved south to attack the flanks of the enemy at Shang-cha-ping. The bitter fighting which lasted until May 6 led to heavy enemy casualties and frustrated the enemy offensive. On May 8, the main force of our 4th Front Army began the offensive along the entire front. At this time, our 11th Division took Shan-men, while our 118th Division recovered Sai-shih, Lung-tan-pu and Shih-hsia-chiang in succession. On May 10, the main force of our 57th Division and elements of our 6th Provisional, 13th and 5th Divisions operated along the line east of Ta-wan, Fu-men-shan and Pan-chiang-feng. On May 11, 3,000 enemy remnants fled toward Ling-chiao-tien, Chu-kao-tang and Chni-lung-chai. The main force (11th and 118th Division) of our 18th Corps, a portion of the 74th Corps (elements of the 57th and 58th Divisions), a portion (193rd Division) of the 73rd Corps, and portions of the 6th Provisional and 13th Divisions joined force in the attack. In the night of May 13, our 193rd Division captured Mao-pu. Our 58th Division took Chu-kao-tang on May 16; our 6th Provisional Division captured Ai-shan on May 18; and our 11th and 193rd Divisions recovered Ta-huang-chiu and Chin-lung-chai on the same day. As the enemy remnants retreated to the vicinity of Heng-ting-tzu, they were again surrounded and attacked by our forces. On May 19, more than 1,000 enemy remnants broke out to the east; however, they were intercepted by our 193rd and 118th Divisions between Lung-tan-pu and Heng-ting-tzu. On May 20, the enemy retreated to Ta-lung-shan and Tiu-chiang-pu. As the enemy continued to flee to the east on May 22, the main forces of our 6th Provisional and 193rd Divisions of 18th Corps and our defenders at Ho-shang-chiao and Fu-yung-shan respectively trailed and intercepted the enemy inflicting still heavier casualties on the enemy. By June 7, the situation was restored to that before the battle was fought.

Having been subjected to the encircling attacks of our 51st Division and the main force of our 100th Corps, the enemy at Fang-tung suffered heavy losses. By May 8, 700 enemy remnants, having broken out to the vicinity of Wang-hsiang-shan in the southeast were surrounded by our forces. Our 11th Division also arrived timely to destroy the enemy. On May 12, 400 enemy remnants broke out to the vicinity of Chiao-ling and were completely annihilated by May 16.

After being subjected to violent attacks by our 77th and 15th Divisions for days, 2,000 enemy troops southeast of Yang-hsi-chiao suffered heavy casualties. On May 1, they retreated to the line east and west of Yueh-lao-shan. On May 5, elements of our 77th Division detoured and captured Chu-kou-pu in the enemy's rear area, and our 18th Division operated in the vicinity of Ta-chiao-pien to attack the enemy's left flank. On May 8, our forces engaged another enemy column in bitter fighting in the vicinity of Shun-shui-chiao. On May 16, having been routed, the enemy columns merged and retreated to Shang-hsia-mao-ping and Ying-kuan-chiao. Our 18th Corps and the main force (5th and 77th Divisions) of the 73rd Corps launched a converging attack against the enemy respectively from the southwest and the northeast. Having suffered prohibitive losses, the enemy fled back to original strong points. On June 6, the situation prior to the battle was restored.

During this battle, 28,174 enemy troops were killed or wounded, 17 officers and 230 enlisted men, 374 horses, 24 guns of various calibers, 100 light and heavy machine guns, 1,333 rifles and 20 tons of war materials were captured.

n. Counteroffensive Operations in Kweilin-Liuchow
     (Late April-Late July, 1945. See Map 45 and Charts 70 and 71)

CHART 70

Chart Showing Japanese Chain of Command during the Counter-Offensive Operations against Kweilin—Liuchow (Late April, 1945)

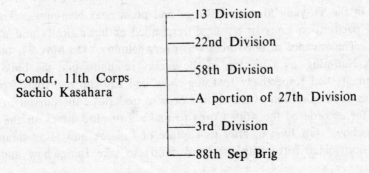

Comdr, 11th Corps
Sachio Kasahara

- 13 Division
- 22nd Division
- 58th Division
- A portion of 27th Division
- 3rd Division
- 88th Sep Brig

CHART   71

Chart Showing the Chinese Chain of Command during the Counter-Offensive

Operations against Kweilin-Liuchow (Late April, 1945)

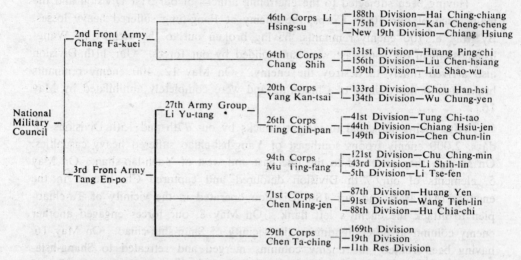

During the Battle of Western Hunan in April, 1945, the enemy was already aware that his depleted strength precluded his effective control of China's vast areas. He therefore, attempted to shorten his battle lines and abandon secondary localities so as to concentrate his forces and cope with our counteroffensive.

Our National Military Council was conscious of the high morale of our forces and the declining will-to-fight of the enemy in the Battle of Western Hunan. In order to effect the speedy recovery of Kweilin—Liuchow and to pave the way for the general offensive, it directed the GHQ, Army to order the 2nd Front Army to dispatch a force for operations in Tu-yang Mountain Ranges and the capture of Nan-ning: the 3rd Front Army to dispatch a force along the Liu-chow— Yi-shan Highway for the capture of Liu-chow; and the main force to advance along the Kuei-Sui Road and cross the Yueh-cheng-ling Mountain Range for the capture of Kwei-lin and the subsequent destruction of the enemy in Kwangsi.

On April 27, 1945, subsequent to its employment of the 175th Division, 46th Corps to capture Tu-an, the 2nd Front Army dispatched its main force to operate in the Tu-yang Mountain Range and press near Nan-ning. The local militia and pacification units in Kwangsi responded enthusiastically and attacked the enemy. The advance of our forces was overwhelming. On May 27, our 64th Corps took Nan-ning, as a portion of the enemy remnants and the bulk of the enemy remnants fled respectively to Lung-chow and Liu-chow. Apart from dispatching the 156th Division of the 64th Corps to undertake the pursuit to Lung-chow, our forces ordered the 46th Corps to make a turning attack to the southeast of Liu-chow. On June 6, after its capture of Loh-sze and Ming-chiang, our 156th Division joined force with the local militia to take Lung-chow and Ping-hsiang in succession on July 3 and drove the enemy out of China's territory. During its attack on Liu-chow, our 46th Corps was assisted by the pacification units of Kwangsi and swiftly mopped up the enemy on the south bank of the Hsi River. Progress was speedy as our forces captured Kwei-ping and Wu-hsuan. On June 29, our 175th Division reached La-pao and pressed near Lin-chiang.

In early May, a portion (29th Corps) of the 3rd Front Army began the attack on Ho-chih and Li-ming-kuan. After capturing Tien-ho, the main force of the 11th Reserve Division of the corps advanced along the mountainous area on the north flank of the Liu-chow—Yi-shan Highway in order to respond to the operations in Liu-chow and Yi-shan. The main force of the 29th Corps recovered Ho-chih on May 19 and Teh-sheng on May 23 before attacking Yi-shan. Meanwhile, our 11th Reserve Division had recovered Li-ming-kuan on May 21, Sze-en on May 23 and Yi-shan on June 6. Despite heavy losses, the enemy on the Liu-chow and Yi-shan front poured reinforcements from Liu-chow to wrest Yi-shan. By June 14, our forces once again recaptured Yi-shan setting enemy remnants fleeing toward Liu-chow. By June 23, the enemy on the west bank of the Yung River was mopped up by our forces. With the capture of Liu-cheng on June 27, our forces converged in the attack on the enemy at Liu-chow. On June 29, as our 46th Corps captured Liu-chow, the enemy retreated in disorder toward Kwei-lin. Divided into three routes in the attack on Kwei-lin, the right route was composed of the 91st Division of the 71st Corps advancing on the right flank of the Kwei-lin—Liu-chow Highway; the central route was the 29th Corps which advanced along the Kwei-lin—Liu-chow Railway; and the left route was composed of the 133rd Division of the 20th Corps which moved from Yung Hsien via Pai-shou to Kwei-lin. In the meantime, the 4th Front Army attacked the enemy at Pao-ching and Heng-yang to respond to the operations of our forces in Kwei-lin. The various forces stepped up their push and were required to recover Kwei-lin by the end of July.

On July 7, the 169th Division of our 29th Corps along the Kwei-lin—Liu-chow Railway recovered Lo-yung on July 7, Chung-tu on July 12 and Huang-mien on July 17. The enemy retreated to Yung-fu to continue his stubborn resistance. Our forces employed the 11th Reserve Division in the frontal attack and the 169th Division in a turning movement against the enemy's left flank. The bitter fighting continued until July 25 when our forces captured Yung-fu and opened the southern gateway to Kwei-lin. Our 91st Division which advanced along the Kwei-lin-Liu-chow Highway recovered Li-pu on July 7 and attacked Ma-ling on July 19 which the enemy defended at all costs. Our main force, therefore, turned to the northwest of Yang-suo forcing the enemy to fall back and defend Yang-suo and dispatch a force to reinforce Pai-sha. Our forces took Pai-sha on July 24 and Yang-suo on July 25 pressing near the outskirt of the city of Kwei-lin. Meanwhile, our 133rd Division also took Pai-shou. On July 27, our three major forces reached the outskirt of Kwei-lin from the southwest.

After the main force of the 3rd Front Army crossed the Yueh-cheng-ling Mountain Range, our 94th and 26th Corps respectively advanced toward Yi-ning, and the area between Chuan Hsien and Hsin-an. On July 10, the 121st Division of our 94th Corps operated in Lan-tien-pao and captured Nan-yu. On July 18, one of our forces took Chang-she-ling (12 km. north of Kwei-lin) exercising dominating control over the highway and railway between Hunan and Kwangsi. Greatly threatened, the enemy pooled over 1,000 troops of the 13th Division from Kwei-lin and Lin-chuan for the bitter fighting which followed. Earlier, the 43rd Division of our 94th Corps took Ting-ling-ao on July 11 and Hui-yuan-yu on July 13. The enemy reinforced from Ling-chuan and counter-attacked resulting in heavy casualties on both sides. Having attacked violently the enemy force which had taken Yi-ning, the main force of our 94th Corps recovered Yi-ning on July 26 and continued to push toward the outskirt of Kwei-lin hoping to lay siege against the city with friendly forces.

On July 19, after capturing the key localities of Wang-chi-ling and Chieh-shou on the north flank of the Hunan-Kwangsi Railway, our 26th Corps cut off the traffic communications between Hunan and Kwangsi. In an attempt to save the only line of communications in the rear of Kwei-lin, the enemy pooled forces from Chuan Hsien and Hsing-an to attack our 26th Corps. After receiving repeated heavy blows, the enemy was routed. At this time, the enemy in the vicinity of Kwei-lin was mopped up. On July 28, our forces recovered Kwei-lin. With the enemy fleeing in all directions, our gains were considerable.

o. Operation Plans in Counteroffensive against Canton

In the spring of 1945, the Supreme Commander, China Theater formulated the general counteroffensive plans, code names Ice Man and White Pagoda, to meet the development of the military situation and coordinate the operations of adjacent theaters. The decision was made to launch resolutely general offensive against the Japanese forces in China in the fall of the year. First, seaports on the southwest coast of China would be captured in order to increase the material supply to the ground and air forces in the China Theater and make maximum contributions in the final phase of the war against Japan.

In June, 1945, all organized resistance of the German forces in Europe had ceased. Due to losses in the various operations in the Pacific, Japan was depleted in the strength of her navy and air force. By this time, the pipe lines on the Stilwell Road had reached Kun-ming. The war materials brought in from India rose to more than 60,000 tons each month. The 36 infantry divisions of the Alfa Force authorized by GHQ Chinese Army during the past six months had completed their organization and training. Equipped with U.S. weapons, these units were vastly superior to the comparable Japanese units in personnel and fire power. In early July, GHQ Chinese Army, to fulfill the important missions assigned by the Supreme Commander, developed the operation plans for the counteroffensive against Canton, in accordance with the China Theater General Counter-

Offensive Plans, and completed all the dispositions. In early August, the advance elements of the 2nd Front Army reached the area west of Wu-chow. Forces of the 3rd Front Army moved along the Ho-Lien Highway and reached the vicinity of Ho Hsien. The army which advanced along the Hunan—Kwangsi Road reached the vicinity of Chuan Hsien. Follow-up armies pushed ahead in accordance with planes. At this time, General Ho Ying-chin, Commander-in-Chief, Chinese Army, flew to the frontline key localities to supervise the execution of orders. GHQ Chinese Army moved forward to Liu-chow with its command post in Nan-ning. Morale was greatly boosted. Had Japan not announced her unconditional surrender on August 15, our forces would have achieved complete destruction of the enemy in accordance with our plans. The highlights of this massive offensive plans were as follows:

(1) Estimate of the situation on the enemy force distribution (by July 14, 1945):

(a) Indo-China: Four divisions and two composite brigades totalling 90,000 men with main force located in northern Indo-China.

(b) Lei-chow Peninsula: One brigade and one battalion totalling 8,000 men.

(c) Hainan Island: Three garrison units and two guard regiments totalling 20,000 men.

(d) Areas in the vicinity of Kweilin and Chuan Hsien: One division and one brigade totalling 17,000 men.

(e) Canton and neighboring areas: Three divisions, four brigades and the Hong Kong Defense Force totalling 90,000 men.

(f) Chu-chiang—Kan-chow area: One division totalling 13,000 men.

(g) Heng-yang and neighboring areas: Two divisions, and one brigade totalling 27,000 men.

(h) Chang-sha: One division totalling 17,000 men.

(i) Han-kow and neighboring areas: One division, five brigades and two field replacement units totalling 50,000 men.

The above enemy forces totalled 332,000 men.

(2) Operational guidance of our forces:

With the objective of opening the seaports of Kwangtung, Chinese Armed Forces dispatched powerful forces to capture Kwei-lin, take Lei-chow Peninsula, then separately attack Heng-yang and Chu-chiang, and tie down the enemy in northern Indo-China, while the main force advanced along the Hsi (West) River area for the capture of Canton.

(3) Operational direction of our forces:

(a) 1st Front Army which commanded the 52nd, 60th and 93rd Corps and 93rd Division should defend original positions in southern Yunnan, stop the enemy spoiling attacks from northern Indo-China and protect the security of our forces operating to the east. The 53rd Corps would be located in the Lu-nan—

Mi-le—Kai-yuan area as the second line force.

(b) 2nd Front Army would dispatch one corps to capture and insure the defense of Lei-chow Peninsula and use it as a supply base. The forces along the Kwangsi—Indo-China border should strengthen their defense and maintain contact with the enemy. Later, the main force would attack the western front of Canton from Wuchow. Located in Nan-ning, the 54th Corps would be the second line force on that front.

(c) Should the enemy in northern Indo-China attempt to undermine the operations of our forces to the east and employ its main force to attack Yunnan in the north, our 2nd Front Army should move the first and second line forces into Indo-China, attack the flanks and rear of the enemy, and head for and capture Hanoi and Haiphong. However, should the enemy employ his main force to attack Nan-ning in the east or Nan-ning and Pei-se both, then the 1st Front Army should move its main force (52nd and 60th Corps) into Indo-China to attack the flanks and rear of the enemy and link up with the main force of the 2nd Front Army for the destruction of the enemy and the capture of Hanoi and Haiphong.

(d) The 3rd Front Army should capture Kwei-lin by the end of July. Late, one corps would launch a converging attack on Heng-yang from Chuan Hsien, Ling-ling and Heng-yang. In accordance with the progress of the offensive, it would protect the right flank of the 4th Front Army. Another Corps would attack Chu-chiang from Ho Hsien and then move south to attack the enemy at Canton. At this time, the 27th Army Group would advance toward the line from Loh-chang to Yi-chang and Chen Hsien and cut off the enemy's north-south traffic communications so as to facilitate the operations of our forces in Heng-yang and Chu-chiang.

(e) The 4th Front Army would employ its main force of two corps to advance along the Pao-ching-Heng-yang Road and the areas on both sides of the road. It would attack Pao-ching and then Heng-yang. Another corps moved from Hsin-hua to attack Yung-feng, Hsiang-hsiang, and Hsiang-tan and tie down the enemy in Chang-sha in order to facilitate the capture of Heng-yang. Later, it would assist the 9th War Area in the latter's continued advance to the north. It would capture Chang-sha, operate along and insure the defense of the line from Mi-lo River to Hsiu River so that our forces attacking Canton and Hong Kong would not be threatened in the north.

(f) The 3rd, 7th and 9th War Areas dispatched powerful forces to jointly mop up the enemy in Kan-chow, Chu-chiang and Wong-yuan. Additionally, the 9th War Area dispatched a powerful force to assist in the capture of Heng-yang. The 3rd, 7th and 9th War Areas each pulled one corps and massed it in the vicinity of Chang-sha. When these corps were properly equipped with air-lifted weapons, they would push toward Mei Hsien, Hsing-ning and Wu-hua. Another powerful force would select a vulnerable area somewhere between Swatow, Lu-feng, Hai-feng and Nien-shan to capture a port which could reach the inland. Upon receipt of equipment brought in by U.S. submarines and increase in combat effectiveness, it would employ a portion of its force to capture Swatow and the main force to advance toward the line from Lung-nan to Ho-yuan in order to exert pressure on the area east of Canton.

(g) To insure success in the attack on Canton, the 3rd War Area should conduct holding attack against the enemy in Nan-chang during the attack on Canton. The 1st, 2nd, 5th and 6th War Areas should attack the enemy in the respective areas and prevent the enemy from shifting his forces.

(h) The main forces of the Chinese and American air forces should assist ground operations and seek air supremacy over the battlefield A portion of the forces should bomb enemy ships and craft at sea.

(i) Simultaneous with the attack on Lei-chow Peninsula, Canton and Hong Kong, it was hoped that the U.S. Navy would assist in the operations and stop enemy reinforcements so as to facilitate the operations.

4. An Account of Guerrilla Operations

Subsequent to the Battle of Wuhan, the enemy reached the Pao-tou-Feng-ling-tu-Kai-feng-Hsin-yang-Yueh-yang-Ta-tung-Hang-chow line, took Canton and blockaded our seaport. Due to vast areas and scattered strengths, the enemy could control only points and lines, but not areas. In view of the increasingly unfavorable international situation, the enemy stopped the offensive and switched to counter-attrition warfare by actively mopping up our guerrilla forces in North China and East China, deploying powerful forces in Wu-han to strike our field forces by means of limited operations, and resorting to such measures as strategic bombings and severing international exits to wear out our will-to-fight and combat effectiveness. Simultaneously with the launching of the peace offensive, the enemy issued the so-called Konoye Statement on December 22, 1938 advancing the three principles of neighborliness, joint defense against communism and economic cooperation to lure our wavering elements, expand the puppet organizations, and squeeze our natural resources so as to check Chinese with Chinese and to fight a war by means of another war.

In order to cope with the enemy's strategy, Generalissimo Chiang directed that political efforts outweigh military efforts, guerrilla warfare outweigh conventional warfare, enemy's rear areas be turned into frontline areas. And one third of our efforts be placed in the enemy's rear areas at the First Nan-yu Conference in the winter of 1938. Accordingly, the various war areas were directed to divide a number of frontline areas into guerrilla areas and assign units to conduct guerrilla warfare. In the spring of 1939, with the revision of the order of battle, the Hopei-Chahar War Area and the Shantung-Kiangsu War Areas were added. The 51st Corps was directed to advance to Shantung and the 69th, New 8th and 99th Corps were directed to advance to Hopei to step up guerrilla warfare. The operational guidance of the Chinese Armed Forces was revised by successively launching limited offensives and counterattacks to tie down and wear out the enemy and respond to the extensive guerrilla operations behind the enemy lines, strengthening control of the occupied areas, turning the enemy's rear areas into frontline areas, forcing the enemy to be cornered in the strong points and preventing the enemy from achieving total rule and exploiting our materials so as to shatter his attempt to fight a war by means of war.

Based on the above operational guidance, our forces successively launched a number of limited offensives in April, July, September and December, 1939. Despite heavy losses, our forces succeeded in wearing out the enemy and tying down his main force so that he was unable to pull his forces for mopping-up operations Accordingly, our guerrilla forces established many bases in the enemy's rear areas, controlled the entire area, encircle the enemy's points and lines and caused the enemy to be bogged down unable to advance or withdraw. Unfortunately, our anti-Communist propaganda efforts were unsatisfactory and our knowledge of and preventive measures against the Chinese Communists were inadequate. As a result, many of our guerilla forces were absorbed by the Chinese Communists. Approaching the final phase of the War of Resistance, the Chinese Communists gained superiority in the Japanese-occupied area, hampered the war effort, usurped political power and caused serious consequences. An account of the guerrilla operations in various war areas is stated as follows:

a. Hopei-Chahar War Area

With the activation of the Hopei-Chahar War Area in March, 1939, Lu Chung-lin was named commander-in-chief and concurrently governor of Hopei Provincial Government, to exercise unified command over the guerrilla forces and local militia in Hopei and Chahar in order to step up guerrilla warfare. In view of the rapid progress achieved by the Hopei militia forces under Chang Yin-wu and the 1st Guerrilla Column under Lu Cheng-tsao in guerrilla operations in the central Hopei and their repeated crushing of the Japanese and puppet mopping-up actions which proved the possibility of guerrilla operations in the plains, the Chinese Communist forces under Ho Lung and Liu Po-cheng crossed the boundaries and entered into the plains of Hopei from Tai-hang Shan area. Our guerrilla force under Lu Cheng-tsao was communized, as Lu was named commander of the Central Hopei Military District by the Chinese Communists. In May, 1939, the Chinese Communist forces under Ho Lung, Liu Po-cheng and Lu Cheng-tsao were massed and broke Chang Yin-wu's force forcing it to fall back gradually to the south from the area north of Hu-tuo River. Having been subjected to the continued converging attack of the Japanese and the Chinese Communists, Chang's force was weakened and transferred to Honan for replenishment. The guerrilla force under Sun Kuei-yuan, Western Hopei guerrilla commander, retained the Hopei—Shansi—Honan border area and distinguished itself by hitting the Japanese and Chinese Communist forces. Subsequently, it was reorganized into the New 5th Corps. Unable to withstand the enemy's mopping-up actions and converging attack, Commander-in-Chief Lu's newly organized local militia forces could no longer remain in the plains of Hopei, and the General Headquarters withdrew to Lu-lo Chen west of Hsing-tai. The situation was most precarious. Generalissimo Chiang directed the 69th Corps under Shih Yu-san and the New 8th Corps under Kao Shu-hsun to move to central Hopei from southern Shantung via northern Shantung, and the 99th Corps under Chu Huai-ping to reinforce western Hopei from northern Honan. In January, 1940, while the forces under Shih and Kao were exhausted after long marches, the Chinese Communists crushed them successively at Nankung, Chingho, Wei Hsien and Puyang forcing them into a corner in southern Hopei. Eventually they were forced to the Hopei-Shantung-Honan border area. Although Chu Huai-ping's corps advanced safely to Lu-lo Chen, it was too late. The Chinese Communists had had already controlled the area south of Lu-lo Chen, cut off supplies, and sealed off foods making our forces unable to survive. In mid-March, the General Headquarters of the Hopei-Chahar War Area and the 99th Corps were forced to pull out of Hopei Province. Later, as Shih Yu-san was pressured by the Chinese Communists to betray the nation, he was executed. Sun Liang-cheng was appointed commander-in-chief of the 39th Army Group exercising guerrilla operations in Hopei-Shantung-Honan border area. Subsequently, when Sun Liang-cheng was captured and Lu Chung-lin was relieved, Kao Shu-hsun was appointed commander-in-chief of the Hopei-Chahar War Area and concurrently commander-in-chief of the 39th Army Group. With Pu Hsien in western Shantung as the base, our forces continued to conduct guerrilla operations. As the vast areas in in Hopei and Chahar War Area existed in name only. As the Japanese and puppet forces lay hidden along the key points and lines, they and the Chinese Communist forces refrained from attacking each other. In the autumn of 1940, Japan formed the Axis alliance with Germany and Italy. Fearful of the Japanese attack, Soviet Russia instigated the Chinese Communists to launch the so-called Battle of One Hundred Regiments by attacking the Japanese lines of communications in North China. Through the Russian Advisory Mission, Soviet Russia urged our forces to counterattack I-chang and claimed that our forces would launch counteroffensives to tie down the Japanese forces. In the winter of the year, Japanese forces launched the mopping-up operations in central and western Hopei. As the Chinese Communists excelled in evasive tactics, the Japanese efforts were fruitless. In April, 1941, Soviet Russia and Japan signed a neutrality which enable Japan to move south. The understanding between the Chinese Communists and the Japanese permitted the Japanese forces to construct the Teh-Shih Railway[54] and highway nets in the various hsiens and municipalities and exploit materials, while the Chinese Communists tightened their control over the people and completed the tunnel nets in the plains of Hopei to facilitate evasion. From then on until the end of the War of Resistance, there was no major combat in Hopei and Chahar.

54 Teh-chow to Shih-men.

In late April, 1942, the enemy pulled portions of the 32nd and 35th Divisions and 4th Cavalry Brigade and massed them in Yun-cheng, Nan-loh, Hua Hsien and Ho-tse. Beginning on April 29, they laid siege on our 39th Army Group in the vicinity of Pu Hsien. Our forces deployed a portion of the New 8th Corps between Ching-feng and Pu Hsien, and between Pu-yang and Tung-ming, and the main force in the Old Ordos Bend of the Yellow River southwest of Pu Hsien. The 69th Corps was deployed between Pu Hsien and Chuan-cheng leaving a small force behind in the original strong points in Pu Hsien and Liu-hsia-tun. It was anticipated that when the enemy failed to catch our main force in Pu Hsien and Liu-hsia-tun, the corps would turn back, counterattack, encircle and destroy the enemy. At dawn on April 29, the enemy launched violent attacks again at Liu-hsia-tun and the strong points to the west. Meanwhile, the enemy at Ho-tse used more than 200 trucks to motor his troops for the attack on Wen-miao near Liu-hsia-tun. Our forces counterattacked in force and the fighting was most intense. The enemy relied on planes, artillery and poison gas for the support, and both sides suffered heavy losses. The bitter fighting continued until May 14 when our main force moved to the area between Ho-tse and Chuan-cheng and the general headquarters of the army group moved to Hou-che east of Ting-tao. When the 181st Division of the 69th Corps reached Ta-chu-tan east of Pu Hsien, it encountered over 4,000 enemy infantry and cavalry troops with more than 10 tanks and repelled them. It then continued to move to Tan Hsien, while one brigade of the 28th Provisional Division moved to the area between Fan Hsien and Pu Hsien to engage the enemy. A portion of the New 8th Corps shifted to the southwest of Pu Hsien, while the main force of the corps headed for the west of Ting-tao after penetrating the enemy's blockade line on the Ho-Chi Highway. On May 15, over 5,000 enemy troops attacked Hou-chi and Liu-lou east of Ting-tao where the general headquarters of our 39th Army Group was located. The fighting lasted until dusk when the enemy was repelled. On May 25, our 181st Division reached the area southeast of Tan Hsien, while the remaining forces successively arrived at the area southeast of Ching-hsiang. On June 1, the enemy massed over 3,000 troops from Ching-hsiang, Yu-tai, Cheng-wu, Tan Hsien and Feng Hsien with more than 10 tanks and 200 trucks and attacked 28th and 29th Provisional Divisions at Tsao-ma-chi east of Tan Hsien in three columns. The heavy fighting continued until dusk when the enemy was finally driven off. Meanwhile, the enemy which attacked our New 6th Division along the line from Tang-shan to the southeast of Hsin-yang-miao was also repelled. Over 1,000 enemy troops were killed or wounded and 4 tank and 20+ trucks were destroyed, while our casualties stood at 1,500+. In the night of June 3, a portion of our forces crossed Lunghai Railway for the south via the the area west of Yang-chi RR Station. At 0800 hours on June 4, this force encountered enemy troops riding in 100+ trucks in the vicinity of Chien-fu-koh near Hsia-yi. The heavy fighting which continued into darkness resulted in 300+ enemy casualties and the destruction of scores of enemy trucks. The enemy retreated toward Hsia-yi, while our casualties numbered at 1,100+ including one brigade commander. Later, our forces left the 181st Division in Tan Hsien-Feng Hsien border area and directed the local militia in western Shantung and in Tang-shan and Feng Hsien in northern Kiangsu to continue guerrilla operations in western Shantung. All the remaining forces were instructed to cross the Lunghai Railway via the area west of Yangchi RR Station and head for Wo-yang and were subordinated to Commander-in-Chief Tang En-po attacking the enemy along the Lunghai Railway and responding to the shifting of the main force of the 39th Army Group. By June 29, the general headquarters of the 39th Army Group and the various corps arrived at Wo-yang for reorganization and training. During the battle, 50+ major and minor engagements were fought and 4,000+ enemy troops were killed or wounded, while our casualties numbered at 9,000+.

b. Shantung-Kiangsu War Area

In March, 1939, the Shantung-Kiangsu War Area was activated with Yu Hsueh-chung as the commander-in-chief who led the 51st Corps from southern Honan to Yi-shan area in Shantung. Additionally, the 57th Corps moved from northern Kiangsu to the mountain areas northwest of Jihchao in southern Shantung. These corps came under the direct command of Commander-in-Chief Yu. Governor Han Teh-chin of the Kiangsu Province who was commander-in-chief of the 24th Army Group was appointed concurrently the deputy commander-in-chief of the war area. In April, the Deputy Commander-in-Chief Headquarters of the war area was activated in northern Kiangsu to exercise command over the guerrilla operations of the 89th Corps and the peace preservation militia in northern Kiangsu. Governor Shen Hung-lieh of Shantung Province was also named deputy commander-in-chief of the war area to direct the operations of the New 4th Division (also known as peace preservation division) and peace preservation militia in Shantung.

With headquarters in Tsi-nan, the enemy's 12th Corps commanded the 5th, 21st, 32nd, 114th Divisions and the 5th, 6th and 7th Separate Brigades which were stationed along the Chiao-chow-Tsi-nan, Tientsin-Pu-kow and Lunghai Railways. In addition, the 12th Separate Brigade of the enemy's Central China Expeditionary Force was stationed along the north bank of the Yang-tze River between Chiang-tu and Nan-tung. Our forces which controlled the vast areas in the interior continued to conduct guerrilla operations, tie down and wear out the enemy. Meanwhile, the enemy constructed strong point fortifications and outer trenches along the railways and forced the inhabitants along the railways to organize railway protecting village. Furthermore the enemy gradually enlarged occupied areas to include important cities and chens in the interior. As a result, our guerrilla operations and the enemy's mopping-up operations led to countless large or small-scale combats. Major actions are stated as follows:

On the Shantung front: During the spring offensive of 1939, our guerrilla forces in Shantung dealt a heavy blow against the enemy. In early June, the enemy massed portions of the 5th, 21st and 114th Divisions and laid sieges against our guerrilla base in southern Shantung via Chiao-chi, Lunghai, and Tientsin-Pukow Railways. On June 3, the Kitagawa Regiment of the enemy's 21st Division moved north along the Lunghai Railway via Lin-yi. The 111th Division, 57th Corps and the 112th Division stopped the enemy respectively at Tang-tou Chen and Ko-kou northeast of Lin-yi, and the area on the north flank of Fei Hsien. After launching flank attacks and ambushes to wear out and deal fatal blows against the enemy on June 7 and 8, our forces moved to the mountain areas east of Chu Hsien and southwest of Fei Hsien. Meanwhile, the enemy's 114th Division moved east along the Tientsin-Pukow Railway and was intercepted by the 114th Division of our 51st Corps at Meng-yin. The intense fighting resulted in heavy casualties on both sides. Subsequently, our forces withdrew to the mountain areas north of Yi-shui and Meng-yin. The enemy took Meng-yin on June 8 and Tan-fu where our general headquarters was located on June 10. The main force of the enemy's 5th Division moved along the Chiao-chow-Tsi-nan Railway, Chu-cheng, An-chiu and Lin-chu. After intercepting the enemy in the areas southwest of Chu-cheng and north of Yi-shui, the 113th Division of our 51st Corps and the New 4th Division withdrew to the mountain areas between Lin-chu and Yi-shui. On June 9, the enemy took Chu Hsien and Yi-shui, and then Tung-hsin-tien, (northwest of Yi-shui) the seat of the Provincial Government of Shantung. During this battle, the enemy captured the three cities of Chu Hsien, Yi-shui and Meng-yin, having suffered 5,000+ casualties. As the enemy went deep into the mainland, he was glued to points and lines unable to look after everywhere. Scattered in the mountain areas of Yi-shan, Fei Hsien and Jih-chao and geared to the local militia of the various hsiens, our forces still controlled the overall situation and made use of air planes and ground routes to provide supplies through gaps and maintain contact with the rear areas.

In 1939, portions of the Chinese Communist 115th and 129th Divisions infiltrated into Shantung via Hopei to drive a wedge between our military and political organizations and pretended to be friendly to Government forces by calling off hostile actions. Meanwhile, the Chinese Communists concentrated their forces in wiping out our local peace preservation units, seizing political power, controlling people and isolating and weakening Government forces. In 1939 and 1940, having been subjected to converging attacks by the Japanese and the Chinese Communists, our peace preservation units in the various administrative districts in Shantung lost half of their strength, and our Peace Preservation Division (also known as the New 4th Division) was forced to surrender to the enemy. In August, 1940, Lu-tsun in the Chishan area, seat of the provincial government was taken by enemy. Governor Shen Hung-lieh was recalled and replaced by Mou Chung-heng, commander of the 51st Corps. However, the rampaging Chinese Communists were active everywhere. Governor Mou was there in name only, and the situation deteriorated drastically.

On August 4, 1942, Wan Yi, a brigade commander of our 111th Division 57th Corps, mutinied under the instigation of the Chinese Communists, threatened Chang En-tuo, the division commander, and surrounded the General Headquarters of the War Area. Fortunately, most of our officers and men knew what was right. The mutiny was soon suppressed, but our losses were heavy. The Chinese Communists became more vociferous than ever. In the same year, the Chinese Communists and Japanese forces coordinated to surround and destroy our 12th Provisional Division at Lai-yang.

In early May, 1943, the enemy's 32nd Division and the 5th and 6th Separate Brigades were massed in Kao-mi, Po-shan, Lai-wu, Hsin-tai, Meng-yin and Yi-shui and began the siege on our Yi-meng Shan area on August 12. Taking advantage of the terrain and prepared positions, our 51st Corps met and attacked the enemy from different routes resulting in heavy casualties on both sides. Heavy fighting continued until August 15, when a portion of our forces in the vicinity of Yi-shui was forced to break out to the south. Later, our defenders northeast of Meng-yin also broke out to the south. Divided into several columns, the enemy intercepted out forces. Our counterattacks resulted in 1,000+ enemy casualties. On May 19, the enemy's main force withdrew to original positions. During this battle, the enemy suffered 3,000+ casualties, while our forces suffered 2,000+ casualties. The Chinese Communists took advantage of this opportunity to capture Yi-meng Shan area making the position of the General Headquarters of our War Area untenable. Subsequently, the Chinese Communists launched night attacks on our Southern Shantung Headquarters at An-chiu, killing Director Chin Chi-yung of the Headquarters. Ho Sze-yuan succeeded Mou Chung-heng as the governor as the latter resigned. The provincial government had only a corner of Shou-kuang Hsien under the cover of two peace preservation regiments commanded by Chang Ching-yueh. This situation remained until the Japanese surrender.

On the northern Kiangsu front: In early 1939, other than the key localities of Chiang-tu, Nan-tung and Hsu-chow and along the railway which had fallen to the enemy, our 24th Army Group under Han Teh-chin controlled the interior. In February, 1939, the enemy's 5th and 21st Divisions took Hai-chow and Huai-yin from the sea and land. Nevertheless, our forces still controlled the canal and the highway leading to the sea and with Hsing-hua as the center established a base to continue guerrilla operations in northern Kiangsu. In April, Han Teh-chin was promoted and became deputy commander-in-chief of the Shantung-Kiangsu War Area with headquarters in northern Kiangsu to continue the execution of original missions. With the activation of the 6th Separate Brigade and several provincial and hsien peace preservation brigades, our strength was greatly augmented seriously threatening the enemy.

In early October, 1939, the enemy forces in North China and Central China teamed up in a major siege against our base in northern Kiangsu. A portion of its 21st Division moved south via Fu-ning, and his main force moved south along the Canal from Huai-yin in 40+ motor boats. A portion of the enemy's 15th Division rode in a number of motor boats and moved north from Chen-chiang via Chiang-tu, and a portion of the enemy's 13th Brigade which rode in 40+ motor boats moved east along the Huai River from Pang-pu. In a converging attack, the enemy forces came from the north, south and west. With the objective of sustained operations in mind, Deputy Commander-in-Chief Han directed the 117th Division of our 89th Corps to stop the enemy from Huai-yin in the vicinity of Tou-han-tung and Ching-ho Chen, the 5th and 6th Salt Gabelle Regiments to halt the enemy from Fu-ning in the area north of Yen-cheng, the 3rd Peace Preservation Brigade to stop the enemy from Chiang-tu at Kao-yu, and the 6th Separate Brigade and the Peace Preservation Regiment to halt the enemy from Pang-pu at Hsu-yi. Heavy fighting took place from August 1-4 at the enemy forces successively linked up at Chieh-shou and Chiang-pa, and our forces fell back to Tsao-tien and Ma-yi-tien east of Huai-an and later attacked the enemy's rear areas. On August 4 and 5, our forces at one time, recovered Kao-yu and Pao-ying. On August 7, our 6th Separate Brigade recovered Chiang-pa and Hsu-yi. On August 11, elements of our 117th Division recaptured Chieh-shou after repelling the attacking enemy at Wang-huo-chiao. Meanwhile, the Kabei Regiment of the enemy's 21st Division continued to move east and responded to the enemy's Kitagawa Regiment moving south from Fu-ning in the capture of Yen-cheng. The 33rd Division of our 89th Corps coordinated with our guerrillas in attacking the enemy's rear areas. For a time on August 19, the enemy was forced to pull out of Fu-ning. Our gallant pursuit resulted in considerable gains. During this battle, although the enemy succeeded in restoring the traffic in the Canal and the highway leading to the sea, our forces still controlled the vast areas on the flanks and continued guerrilla operations. As the enemy strength was widely scattered, his gains did not justify his losses.

In the same year, elements of the Chinese Communist New 4th Corps under the command of Lo Ping-hui and Chang Ai-ping took advantage of the cover provided by Sheng Tzu-chin (a follower of Chang Nai-chi) special commissioner in Sze Hsien, Anhwei Province, crossed the boundary of the 3rd War Area by arbitrarily crossing the Yang-tze River and infiltrating into Chuan-chiao, Tien-chang and Sze Hsien. In the spring of 1940, after attacking the local units of Sheng Tzu-chin's forces, the Chinese Communists disarmed and reorganized them. They then established the Hung-tze Lake base and spread to northern Anhwei and northern Kiangsu steadily increasing in strength. Meanwhile units of the New 4th Corps under Chen Yi, with Kuan Wen-wei's regiment as the spearhead crossed the Yangtze River for latent activities at Ta-chiao of Chiang-tu Hsien in the fall of 1939. In the summer of 1940, Chen Yi led nine regiments under Lo Ping-hui and Kuan Wen-wei, reached the border of Chiangtu and Tai Hsien and attacked the 4th

Peace Preservation Brigade of Kiangsu at Huang-chiao and the 6th and 9th Peace Preservation Brigades at Chiang-yen inflicting heavy losses on our forces. On October 1, our 89th Corps between Hai-an and Chu-tang was forced to fight the Communists. Heavy fighting which continued until October 5 cost the lives of Li Shou-wei, a corps commander, and Wong Ta, a brigade commander. Our casualties stood at 5,000+, as our forces suffered prohibitive losses. Chen Yi therefore, took advantage of this opportunity to expand rapidly in northern Kiangsu. The Chinese Communist Lung-hai Eastward Column in North China under Huang Ke-cheng sped east to the area between Huai-yin and Hai-chow to respond to Chen Yi. The situation in northern Kiangsu became increasingly serious. Meanwhile, the main force of the New 4th Corps south of the Yang-tze River openly mutinied. Our Government ordered the deactivation of the New 4th Corps and directed the 3rd War Area to disarm the corps, apprehend Yeh Ting, the corps commander, and take him to Chungking where he was court-martialled. Chen Yi, a column commander of the Chinese Communist remnants, named himself commander of the New 4th Corps. He actively expanded and reorganized his force into 7 divisions with 20,000+ men in each division and operated in northern Kiangsu and central Anhwei. On December 4, Chen Yi led two divisions under Su Yu and Lo Ping-hui to lay a siege against our 89th Corps under Ku Hsi-chiu. Heavy fighting which continued until October 17 ended in Chen Yi's forces in a rout and the killing of 7,000+ Chinese Communist troops. Unfortunately, our forces were checked by the Japanese and ran short on ammunition. Though our forces failed to wipe out the Communists, Communist arrogance subsided slightly after this battle. In March, 1941, the enemy at Kao-yu and Pao-ying took the city of Hsing-hua where the Kiangsu Provincial Government and the General Headquarters of the Deputy Commander-in-Chief were located. Our non-combatants and trains withdrew to Huai-tung via Sha-kou and Ta-tsung lake. Chinese Communist forces under Su Yu intercepted our forces at Sung-chuang north of Yen-cheng. Our losses in personnel and supplies were heavy. February, 1943, a portion of the enemy's 17th Division and the main force of the enemy's 12th Separate Brigade were massed in the area east of Huai-an and Pao-ying. On February 14, under the support of 20+ planes, the enemy attacked our forces at Feng-ku-tsun and Che-chiao. The one-week bitter fighting ended in heavy casualties on both sides. Later, our forces fell back to Huai-sze to continue the fighting for more than a month. The fighting was most intense. More than 10 regiments of the Chinese Communist forces under Peng Hsueh-feng and Huang Ke-cheng launched surprise attacks against our General Headquarters of the Deputy Commander-in-Chief, the 6th Separate Brigade and the 3rd Peace Preservation Column killing Li Chung-huan, commander of the 6th Separate Brigade and Wang Tien-hua, commander of the 3rd Peace Preservation Column. Our casualties rose to more than three thousand. By mid-March, our forces moved into Fu-yang, then the entire area of northern Kiangsu fell into the Communist hands.

c. 1st, 2nd, and 8th War Areas

Since the spring of 1938 when the enemy captured Hsin-hsiang and opened the Tung-Pu Railway, and Ping-Sui Railway,[55] our 1st, 2nd and 8th War Areas used Tai-hang Shan, Chung-tiao Shan, Lu-liang Shan and Wu-yuan Ordos Bend as bases to continue guerrilla operations in the fore bank of the Yellow River forcing the enemy to defend the narrow bands along the various railways. Having been subjected to the continued attacks of our forces, the enemy suffered heavy attritions. In the spring of 1939, the enemy invaded Tse-lu twice and Chung-tiao seven times attempting to remove the threat. Due to insufficient strength, he was defeated in each attempt. In early April, our various war areas launched the spring offensive. At one time, the 4th Army Group captured the enemy strong points of Hsia Hsien and Hsieh Hsien, while the 5th Army Group separately attacked Wen-hsi, Heng-ling-kuan, and Chiang Hsien. The 14th Army Group laid a siege against Yi-cheng and Fu-shan, as a portion of the Army Group fought bitterly against the enemy force which was moving south from Tai-ku along the Pai-chin Highway. The enemy relied on well-fortified positions and nullified our repeated attacks. Heavy fighting which lasted until April 16 ended in 3,000+ enemy casualties and 4,000+ our casualties. Accordingly, a small force was left behind to maintain surveillance over the enemy, while our main force was pulled back to original positions in Chung-tiao Shan.

In April, 1939, as our 1st War Area launched the spring offensive, the 3rd Army Group was ordered to dispatch forces for the attack on Kai-feng. On the morning of April 11, one brigade of the 12nd Corps was ordered to employ its main force in the capture of Kai-feng Railway Station, while a portion of the brigade broke through Kai-feng. As the enemy defended the city, bitter street fighting ensued. By noon, too exposed in the daytime, our forces withdrew to the vicinity of Ta-ti, 5 km south of the city. During the fighting, over 100 enemy troops were killed and 120 were captured. Our another force which was composed of two infantry battalions and two engineer companies destroyed the Pien-Hsin Railway which the enemy had just repaired and the gap-blocking construction of the Yellow River at San-liu-chai. On the morning of April 12, our forces again entered Kai-feng and engaged in street fighting against the enemy. Threatened by enemy reinforcements in the east, our forces pulled out of the city in order to lure and destroy the enemy. 300-400 enemy troops were used in the spoiling attack and were ambushed by our forces at Ta-ti south of the city. Later, enemy reinforcements violently attacked our right flank forcing our forces to fall back to the line between Hsien-jen-chuang and Pai-mou-kang and confront them. Afterwards, our forces were scattered to conduct guerrilla operations.

In the latter part of May, 1939, the enemy's 1st Corps employed the main forces of the 20th and 37th Divisions which advanced south separately from

---

[55] Peiping to Kwei-sui.

Yun-cheng, Hsieh Hsien and Chang-tien Chen. In his 8th attack on Chung-tiao Shan, the enemy, at one time took the city of Ping-lu and Mao-ching river-crossing site. A turning movement and flanking attack by our forces route the enemy force which fled to north. By the middle of July, the enemy again massed the 110th, 35th, 108th and 36th Divisions which moved separately from Han-tan-Tung-yang-kuan, Hsin-yang-Chin-cheng, Chiang Hsien-Chin-cheng, Chiang Hsien-Kao-ping Fu-shan-Kao-ping, and Tai-ku-Chang-chih Roads to lay sieges against our base in the Shang-tang area. To avoid a decisive engagement, our 14th Army Group opened the Chi-Chin Highway,[56] Po-Chin Highway,[57] Hung-Tun Highway[58] and Pai-Chin Highway[59] as well as the cities and chens along the lines, while our main force fell back to the mountain areas nearby. As the enemy moved along the highways to the cities and chens in southeastern Shansi, our forces launched flanking attacks along the entire line and cut off the enemy's lines of contact inflicting heavy losses on the enemy and forcing the enemy to turn back. In late July, our forces successively recovered Tun-liu, Hsiang-yuan, Wu-hsiang, Hsin-yuan, Yang-cheng and Hsin-shui. In late August, Chin-cheng and Kao-ping were recaptured. Enemy casualties totalled 20,000+.

In early October, 1939, the enemy's 108th Division was divided into 4 routes to attack our Lu-liang Shan area. By the latter part of October, the Inoue Regiment which moved west from Fen-cheng via Niu-wang-miao captured Ning-hsiang. A portion of the enemy force reached the outskirts of Chi Hsien. The enemy's 105th Regiment which moved west from Lin-fen via Hei-lung-kuan took Pu Hsien, Wu-cheng Chen, Ta-ning and Kan-tang. The enemy's 117th Regiment which moved west from Fen-hsi via Ching-hsiang Chen captured Ke-cheng Chen, Hsi Hsien and Peng-men. Then enemy's 32nd Regiment which moved west from Ling-shih via Shuang-chih Chen reached the area east of Shih-lou. Forces of our 2nd War Area separately intercepted and inflicted heavy attrition on the enemy which frustrated the enemy offensive. Meanwhile, our 14th and 5th Army Groups in Chung-tiao Shan dispatched forces to attack the enemy south of Lin-fen in response to the operations in western Shansi. The 6th Army Group of our 2nd War Area directed the 34th Corps in the attack on the enemy at Ning-hsiang and Chi Hsien, while the 70th and 73rd Divisions were pulled from Chung-yang, Li-shih, and Lin Hsien to race to the south and launch flanking attacks. On November 12, as our forces began the counteroffensives, Ning-hsiang, Ta-ning, Wu Chen, Pu Hsien, Hsi Hsien, Shih-kou Chen and Niu-wang-miao were recovered. By November 18, most of the enemy forces attacking Lu-liang Shan were repelled. Our forces took advantage of the situation to attack the enemy at Fen-cheng, Hei-lung-kuan and Fen-hsi reaping considerable gains.

---

56 Chi Hsien to Chin-cheng.

57 Po-ai to Chin-cheng.

58 Hung-tung to Tun-liu.

59 Pai-kuei to Chin-cheng.

In mid-April, 1940, the enemy employed three and a half divisions in a siege against our mountain base in southeastern Shansi. The enemy's 37th Division moved from An-yi and Yun-cheng against Ping-lu and Mao-ching-tu; the 41st Division from Yi-cheng and Fu-shan against Yang-cheng and Chin-cheng; the 36th Division from Chang-chih and Hu-kuan against Kao-ping and Ling-chuan; and a portion of the 35th Division from Po-ai against Chin-cheng. Our 1st and 2nd War Areas jointly stopped the enemy. On April 17, after stopping the enemy's 37th Division at Chang-tien and Tsung-shan, our 4th Army Group open-ed the Chang-Mao Road. Leaving a force behind in the area west of the road, the main force of the army group moved to the east of the road. By April 21, the enemy successively took Ping-lu, Mao-ching, Pai-nan Chen and Jui-cheng before turning east. Our forces began the counterattacks, and the possession of these places changed hands for more than 10 times. Meanwhile, the main force of our 5th Army Group struck Wen-hsi and Hsia Hsien. By early May, after taking many casualties, the enemy retreated toward the original strong points at Anyi and Yun-cheng. Our forces recovered Maoching, Ping-lu and Jui-cheng. On April 17, our 14th Army Group, after heavy fighting for several days and nights against the enemy's 41st Division in the areas east of Yi-cheng and Fu-shan, left a force behind to conduct guerrilla operations behind the enemy lines, while the main force which was composed of the 93rd and 14th Corps moved to the areas north of Hsin Hsien and Tuan-shih Chen and south of Yang-cheng and Tung-feng Chen ready to launch a converging attack against the enemy which had moved in. On April 21, a portion of the enemy from Yi-cheng captured Chang-ma and Chung-tsun Chen. Another enemy force which linked up with the enemy invading the southeast from Fu-shan jointly took Hsin-shui on April 21 and then continued the attack on Chin-cheng. Heavy fighting lasted until April 25 when Yang-cheng and Chin-cheng fell in succession. A portion of our forces withdrew to the southwestern outskirts of Yang-cheng, as another force stopped the enemy at Tuan-shih Chen. Meanwhile, three brigades of our 5th Army Group and the 15th Corps launched extensive attacks to wear out the enemy. The enemy's 36th Division invading south from Chang-chih and Hu-kuan took Kao-ping on April 21 and Ling-chuan on April 22. After counterattacking violently, our 27th Corps recovered Ling-chuan on April 24 with the enemy fleeing to the southwest and northwest. The fighting continued until April 27 when our forces restored original positions and continued the attack against the enemy at Kao-ping. A portion of our 47th Division pursued the enemy force which retreated in disorder to the southwest of Ling-chuan. On April 25, our forces captured Fu-cheng Chen and continued the attack on Chin-cheng. Earlier, 5,000-6,000 enemy troops fought bitterly against our 71st Corps in the area west of Kao-ping. The fighting was so intense that most of the enemy forces were wiped out and enemy remnants retreated to the northeast. On April 24, the enemy at Kao-ping was reinforced and counterattacked our 71st Corps. Another enemy force which invaded south from Kao-ping was intercepted by elements of our 47th Corps. On April 25, this enemy force linked up with the enemy force fleeing to the southwest from Ling-chuan at Chin-cheng. Meanwhile, a portion of the enemy's 35th Division at Po-ai invaded north and linked up with the enemy from Yang-cheng and Chin-cheng on the Chin-cheng—Po-ai Highway. Elements of our 9th, 47th and 97th Corps attacked and wore out the enemy on the Chin-cheng—Po-ai Highway. By April 28, the enemy which counterattacked 71st Corps from Kao-ping rose to 10,000+, and the enemy at Tuan-shih also invaded the northeast. Our 73rd Corps and 10th Division of the 93rd Corps temporarily moved to the area on the northern flank of the Kao-ping—Tuan-shih Road which was the enemy's outer flank. These forces combined their efforts to intercept the enemy. The bitter fighting continued until May 1. As the enemy casualties in the Kao-ping area rose to 3,000+, the enemy turned back and fled. On May 11, our 71st Corps also moved to the area southeast of Yang-cheng for replenishment. In response to the operations on that front, our National Military Council directed the 90th Corps to attack the enemy at Fen-cheng, Hou-ma and Wen-hsi from Shensi Province via Ning-hsian in April. In early May, after sabotaging most of the southern sector of the Tung-Pu Railway, our forces at one time took Hou-ma and Nan-kuan Chen forcing the enemy to pour in reinforcements from various places in southern Shansi. On May 10, the enemy massed several thousand troops to attack Ning-hsiang from Chi-shan and Ho-ching. For four days and nights, our 90th Corps and elements of our 1st Reserve Division fought bitterly against the enemy resulting in heavy casualties on both sides. On May 15, the enemy took Ning-hsiang. The counterattack launched by our 6th Army Group and 34th Corps in conjunction with the 90th Corps against Ning-hsiang forced the enemy to retreat in disorder to the southeast two days later. With the recovery of Ning-hsiang, our 1st and 2nd War Areas realigned their dispositions and launched the general offensive on May 20. As a result of heavy fighting for half a month, the enemy suffered heavy casualties and his lines of communications were cut off. Other than one or two strong points in Chin-cheng, the original posture was restored. In summary, the enemy's casualties stood at 20,000+ during this battle, and our forces still controlled southeastern Shansi. By March, 1941, the enemy massed a strength of 6 divisions and 2 brigades to launch the so-called Battle of Chung-yuan (also known as the Battle of Southern Shansi). After 3 months of bitter fighting, the enemy finally succeeded in taking our Chung-tiao Shan base (for details, see the Battle of Southern Shansi). Thus, our base in Ta-hang Shan became isolated.

In response to the Battle of Southern Shansi, our 8th War Area attacked the enemy between Suiyuan and Pao-tou reaping satisfactory gains. On June 30, our 30th Corps and the Northeastern Advance Force launched the attacks against the enemy in three routes. One route attacked the enemy at Yin-chiang-yao-tzu southeast of Sa Hsien. Another route attacked the enemy at Chou-chu, Wo-yang-tai, Hsi-shan-tsui, Erh-teng and Ta-lai-tien west to Pao-tou. The third route attacked the enemy at Tai-liang southeast of An-pei and at Chi-fen-tzu northeast of Tai-liang. The attacks of the various routes progressed satisfactorily. On the night of July 1, our forces captured the strong points at Chou-chu and Shih-erh-ching and destroyed 6 enemy pillboxes forcing the enemy remnants to retreat to the east. At dawn on July 2, our forces attacked the enemy at Ta-nu-chi-kou forcing the enemy to retreat toward Kung-yi-ming. At dawn on July 3, our forces captured Wo-yang-tai. At night, our forces destroyed more than 10 km of the road southeast of An-pei and east of Wu-lan-hu-tung. At noon on July 4, the enemy force which confronted our forces across the river at Tui-shui-chu crossed the river for the attack. When it was astride the river, our forces attacked killing many enemy troops. Over 20 enemy trucks loaded with troops returned to An-pei from Tai-liang and were ambushed by our forces in the vicinity of Nao-pao-kou and Tung-tien resulting in many enemy casualties. In the attack against the enemy at Wu-lan-pan-chia, our forces forced the enemy to return to Ku-yang and Nao-kou. On July 5, our forces destroyed many enemy wires and telegraphic poles in the vicinity of Lung Hsien railway station and cut off the Suiyuan-Pao-tou Railway. On the same day, our forces engaged the enemy at An-pei, Cho-erh and Mien-kou inflicting heavy casualties on the enemy. The Ku-An Highway[60] was destroyed by our forces in many places. At night, our forces again attacked Wu-lan-hu-tung southeast of An-pei reaping many gains. On July 7, the enemy across the river from Tui-shui-chu again attempt a forced crossing and was repelled.

At the end of November, 1941, the enemy in the northern sector of the Peiping-Hangkow Railway, the southern sector of the Tao-Ching Railway, the Chang-Kao Highway[61] and the Chin-Po Highway commandeered civilian labor. There was much troop movement. Altogether, the enemy massed elements of the 35th and 36th Divisions, and the 1st Separate Brigade totalling 10,000+ troops. Beginning on December 9, the enemy laid siege against our base in the vicinity of Lin-chuan. In order to draw and destroy the enemy, our forces dispatched a portion to offer sustained resistance and shifted the main force to the exterior lines before turning back to launch counterattacks. On December 9, the enemy attacking Ling-chuan from Kao-ping and Ching-cheng was engaged by the main force of our 27th Corps. The bitter fighting continued until the night of November 13 when the enemy was stopped along the line from Niu-chia-chuan to the north of the river confronting our forces. At this time, 2,000+ enemy troops from Chin-cheng made a turning movement against our left flank at East and West Yao-chuan and Tuo-huo Chen. On December 12 and 13, 2,000+ enemy troops from Hui Hsien and Hsiu-wu advanced toward Wang-mang-ling and East

---

[60] Ku-yang to An-pei.

[61] Chang-chih to Kao-ping.

and West Shihmen via Huang-shui-kou. On the night of December 14, the enemy detoured to our rear at Ling-tung. On the night of December 14, our 27th Corps fell back to the line from Shu-chang to Yeh-tou and Ma-yuan. After taking Ling-chuan on December 15, the enemy continued his eastward advance and fought bitterly against our forces along the line from Shu-chang to Yeh-tou and Ma-yuan. In an effort to draw the enemy and seek the possession of exterior lines, a powerful force was left in the vicinity of Wu-cheng Chen and Tuo-huo Chen for flanking attacks to contain the enemy, while our main force fell back to Tzu-yuan-tung, Kan-ma-chia, Oh-wu-ling and San-chiao-kou. On the Peiping-Hankow Railway front, 1,000 enemy troops from Wu-an, Shui-yeh and An-yang and 300+ enemy troops from Miao-kou advanced to the west on December 12, 13 and 14 but were routed by our 24th Army Group (commanding the 40th and New 5th Corps). On December 17, our 27th Corps launched violent attacks against the enemy east of Ling-chuan killing many enemy troops. On the same day, our force under Chang Chiao-ling took Ling-tung and Wang-mang-ling. Elements of the 24th Army Group timely arrived as reinforcements. On December 19, the enemy gradually weakened, as our forces increased the pressure on the enemy's flanks. At dawn on December 20, our forces began the general offensive destroying many enemy troops and recovering Ling-chuan. Enemy remnants fled toward Hu-kuan, Kao-ping and Chin-cheng.

A small enemy force was destroyed in the mountain area southeast of Ling-chuan. By December 21, the original status was restored. All in all, during the 12-day battle, the enemy and our casualties were respectively 1,000+ and 700+.

In early June, 1942, enemy strengths along the Peiping-Hankow, Cheng-Tai, Pai-Chin and Tao-Ching Railways totalled 30,000+ and massed in Wu-an, An-yang, Tang-yin, Hui Hsien, Hsiu-wu, Chin-cheng, Kao-ping, Chang-chih, Pin-shun and She Hsien. Beginning on June 11, scores of enemy planes attacked Tai-hang Shan area. Our 40th Corps in Lin Hsien and Tung-yao-chi, New 5th Corps in Lin-chi Chen and 27th Corps in Ling-chuan offered resistance by a combination of frontal halt, flanking attacks and ambushes to deal the enemy a heavy blow. Bitter see-saw battles took place at the above-mentioned strong points and led to the killing of many enemy troops. The enemy at one time captured these strong points and went deep into Ho-chien Chen and San-chiao-kou. Awaiting the time when the enemy strength was scattered, our forces enlisted the assistance of the mountain people and took advantage of favorable terrain to shift to the offensive in early July. As the enemy was hit in the head and tail, it could not take care of both. Traffic communication difficulties and supply inconvenience forced the enemy to withdraw. By July 15, the original status was restored.

In early April, 1943, the enemy's 35th and 36th Divisions and 4th and 8th Separate Brigades totalling 50,000 men surrounded and attacked our base at Tai-hang Shan. With the 40th Corps of our 24th Army Group deployed in the vicinity of Lin Hsien, the New 5th Corps in the area southeast of Lin-chi Chen, and 27th Corps in Lin-chuan, our forces achieved mutual support ready to engage the enemy. On April 11, under the support of 30+ planes, the enemy attacked in several routes. As a result, our outer strong points fell in succession. The attack launched by the main force of the enemy's 36th Division and a portion of the 35th Division from Kao-ping and Hsiu-wu on the positions of our 27th Corps led to the fall of Ling-chuan on April 17. However, the main force of the Corps still retained the area east of Ling-chuan to continue the interception. Between April 18-20, our various corps and the enemy fought violent major battles. The enemy captured Lin Hsien on April 22 and the strong points of Lin-chi Chen on April 23. Meanwhile, the enemy from Lin-chuan also moved in to encircle our forces. Beginning on April 23, our forces infiltrated the exterior lines. Restricted by terrain and difficulties in coordination and liaison, scattered melees took place. On the night of April 23, while moving in the area west of Lin-chi Chen, Sun Kuei-yuan, commander of the New 5th Corps was ambushed and captured. The ranks of the units in his corps, were also broken. Determined to defend Tai-hang Shan to the last man, our 27th and 40th Corps fought courageously against overwhelming difficulties. On April 26, during its breakout, the ranks of the General Headquarters of the 24th Army Group were broken. As the contact between Pang Ping-hsun, commander-in-chief of the army group, and his forces was lost, the situation deteriorated drastically. On April 28, the last strong point of the 27th Corps at Tuo-huo Chen was lost. On April 30 the 40th Corps was forced to abandon Tung-yao-chi which it had defended for many days. By this time, our major forces were broken into small units to conduct guerrilla operations behind enemy lines. Greatly exhausted after protracted fighting, the enemy left a force to continue searching the mountain area, while his main force gradually pulled back. Wounded in the leg, Commander-in-Chief Pang Ping-hsun escaped to East Chia-nao west of Linchi Chen where he went into in hiding. Unfortunately, the enemy learned of his whereabout on May 6, took him to Hsin-hsiang and coerced him to urge the 40th Corps to surrender. However, Pang had secretly instructed the officers and men of the 40th Corps through courier to link up with the 27th Corps and continue the fight. In late May, the enemy massed 5,000+ troops and continued the attack on the 27th Corps south of Ling-chuan. After more than 10 days of bitter fighting the enemy was finally repelled. Summing up this battle, the enemy suffered approximately 6,000 casualties. Apart from the New 5th Corps, our forces suffered 4,000+ casualties.

In early July, 1943, the enemy massed units from the 25th and 36th Divisions totalling 10,000+ men to lay siege on our forces at Tai-hang Shan. As our 40th Corps had already been transferred to Honan for replenishment, Liu Chin, commander of the 27th Corps, was appointed the Guerrilla Commander-in-Chief in Tai-hang Shan. The 8th Reserve Division operated between Ping-shun and Hu-kuan north of Ling-chuan, while the main force of the 27th Corps was deployed on the outskirts of Lin-chuan to defend the key localities of the various passes. On the night of July 9, the enemy attacked in several routes rampaging everywhere. Confusion reigned until July 10 when Gen. Liu, the concurrent corps commander, led his forces in a breakout and attacked the enemy's rear areas. Being sandwiched between the Japanese and the Chinese Communists, our 8th Reserve Division broke out to the west from the area east of Hu-kuan on the night of July 10. On July 13, as the division fell back to the vicinity of Ku Hsien west of Kao-ping, it was ambushed by the Chinese Communists. As a result, the division was slowed down in its movement and was surrounded. The bitter fighting which continued into darkness ended in division commander Chen Hsiao-chiang's being wounded and captured. Yi Hui, commander of the 2nd Regiment, was also captured, and more than one half of the division was lost. Accordingly, the division was ordered to cross the Yellow River in the south for replenishment. On the night of July 10, Gen. Liu led the 46th Division from Agate Mountain via the vicinity of Tuo-huo Chen to head for the west. Since July 15, the division which was active in Kao-ping, Yang-cheng, Chin-cheng, and Tien-ching-kuan was continuously harassed by the Chinese Communists. Particularly Chinese Communist forces under Tang Tien-chi intercepted our forces at will. Fully aware of the fact that the 27th Corps had fought alone for a long time and that reinforcement and supply were difficult, the National Military Council ordered the Corps to pull back to Honan. On August 5, the main force of the Corps began to withdraw from the area south of Ling-chuan and was attacked on August 7 by the Chinese Communist force under Tang Tien-chi north of Chi-yuan losing 1,000+ men. On August 19 and September 8, it separately completed the crossing of the Yellow River at Meng-ching and Wen Hsien. By this time, Tai-hang Shan was separately occupied by the Japanese and the Chinese Communists.

On July 19, 1944, with the mopping up of the enemy on the south bank of the Yellow River at Pao-tou as its objective, our 8th War Area attacked the enemy at Tzu-teng-chao, Ta-shu-wan, Hsin-cheng and Kao-ho-tang in three routes with the 35th Corps and the Northeast Advance Force. Hastily, elements of the enemy's Cavalry Division and 26th Division engaged our forces and were crushed. At dawn on July 20, our advance force recovered Hsin-cheng and later at night took Shih-chia-ying-tzu. As the enemy retreated in disorder toward Sun-kai and Chi-tan our forces pursued with vigor. On the night of July 24, our forces recovered Sun-kai and Chi-tan reaping considerable gains. On July 25, our forces continued to conduct guerrilla operations in the vicinity of Lang-erh-pan west of Chao-chun's Tomb. On July 28, the enemy's strong points and artillery positions were destroyed and Lang-erh-pan was captured. On July 29, despite repeated enemy reinforcements, our flanking attacks and ambushes forced the enemy to pull back. Thus, all the enemy's key strong points south of Pao-tou were captured by our forces.

d. 3rd, 5th, 6th and 9th War Areas

Since the Battle of Wuhan in 1938, the enemy's Central China Expeditionary Forces depended on the Yangtze River as the main supply route and Nanking and Shanghai as the main bases. The enemy assigned the main force of his 13th Corps in the Nanking-Shanghai-Hangchow triangle and another force between Wu-hu and Hu-kou to construct defense works in key localities, launch limited offensives, and land in the ports in Fukien and Chekiang so as to realize his objective of cutting off our overseas supply route. Our 3rd War Area employed its main force to tie down and wear out the enemy's 13th Corps by dispatching a force to garrison the coast of Fukien and Chekiang and stop the enemy landing. Limited in equipment, our forces were only able to conduct guerrilla-type war of movement or guerrilla warfare. Apart from the winter offensive of 1939 and the Battle of Chekiang and Kiangsi which had already started, some of the major engagements are described as follows:

In mid-October, 1940, the 147th Division of our 23rd Army Group, with the objective of disrupting the navigation of the Yangtze River and attacking on enemy ships in mind, launched bold attacks against enemy strong points in the vicinity of Ma-tang on the night of October 11. At midnight, our forces secretly approached the objective area and engaged the enemy in hand-to-hand fighting. By the morning of October 12, as a portion of the enemy's Sonota Garrison Force was nearly wiped out, our forces captured Matang and set fire to enemy headquarters and ammunition depot. Our artillery moved into positions, began firing on enemy transports in the Yangtze River and covered our naval units in mine-laying, sinking and damaging many enemy ships and inflicting heavy losses on the enemy in personnel and materiel. Later, when the enemy poured in major forces for the counterattack, our forces timely withdrew.

In mid-March, 1941, elements of the enemy's 22nd and 15th Divisions from Hangchow and Nanking totalling 10,000+ men massed toward Chang-hsing and Shang-hsing-fu respectively. Beginning on March 20, they launched converging attacks on our forces between Sze-an and Li-yang. The enemy's 14th Infantry Regiment, attached with 100+ cavalrymen and 4 field guns moved from Chang-hsing and Hung-hsi-chiao to attack our forces at Lin-cheng-chiao before moving west to invade Sze-an. The 62nd Division of our 28th Corps under Liu Hsun-pei intercepted the enemy in the mountain area east of Sze-an. After his capture of Sze-an on March 22, the enemy was subjected to the converging attacks of our forces. On March 23, our 62nd Division recovered Sze-an. 2,000+ enemy troops fled to Chun-hua-tan-shih and were intercepted by our forces. A number of enemy troops were destroyed, and remnants fled east toward Ho-hsi. On March 29, our force recovered Lin-cheng-chiao and pressed near the outskirts of Chang-hsing. On March 20, a portion of the enemy's 15th Division moved east from Shang-hsing-fu and was engaged by our forces in the vicinity of Ching-lung Shan west of Li-yang. On March 21, the enemy took Li-yang and fled south to Tai-fu, Shan-liao-chiao, and Tung-kuan-li. Employing a small force to confront the enemy, our main force turned against the enemy's rear and captured Nan-tu-chiao and strong points in the vicinity. On March 24, a powerful force was employed in our attack on Chang-chu Chen. The enemy, therefore, fled from Shan-liao-chiao and Tung-kuan-li to Chang-chu Chen and Li-yang. Our forces launched converging attacks against the enemy. The heavy fighting lasted until 0800 hours on March 25 when our forces recovered Li-yang and Chang-chu Chen before pursuing the enemy, and reaped many gains.

In April 1941, the enemy's South China Front Army employed the 48th Division and elements of the 18th Division in the invasion on Foochow under the support of 30+ ships, 70+ motor boats and 30+ planes. With the objective of protecting the estuary of the Min River in mind, our 3rd War Area assigned 100th Corps of the 25th Army Group and the local militia in Fukien to guard the coast in the estuary of the Min River and to stop the enemy landing. Additionally, second line positions were constructed in Po-ping, Tai-yun and Tung-kung Shan for sustained resistance, while awaiting the opportunity to stage the counteroffensive and annihilate the enemy. On April 18, under the cover of planes and ships, 1,000+ enemy troops made a forced landing at Chang-kang on the right bank of the Min River. Another 2,000+ enemy troops landed at Ta-hsiao-ao, Pai-sheng, Tung-tai and Pu-kow. 1,000+ enemy marines landed on the islands of Fu-tou and Lang-chi. At night, the enemy in Fu-tou took Chang-men and headed for Kuan-tou. As the enemy from Pu-kow took Lien-chiang, our marines fell back to Min-an Chen. A portion of our 75th Division withdrew to the highground northwest of Lien-chiang, while the main force moved to Lo-lun and Pan-tu. Meanwhile, the enemy on the right bank of the Min River captured Chang-lo and continued to press near Ying-chien. With the enemy invading Hai-kow after landing at Sung-hsia, a portion of our 75th Division fell back to the outskirt of Fu-ching. On April 20, Hai-kow, Ying-chien, Min-an Chen and Kuan-tou fell in succession. An enemy force from Lien-chiang attacked Kuan-hsi and was repelled. The enemy main force of 1,000+ troops attacked Yang-ling and fought against our 80th Division in the vicinity of Huang-shan and Pei-ling-tou. By April 22, our forces defending the line from Kuan-yin Shan to Pei-ling-tou fought bitterly against the enemy. At night, a group of enemy forces infiltrated through the North Gate of Foochow and was engaged in street fighting against our forces. After days of fighting which resulted in heavy casualties, our forces abandoned Fu-ching and Foochow and fell back to Po-lan, Hsi-kou, Tung-kou, Hu-ting Shan, Shan-hsia-Chih-chiao, Ling-tou, Yen-wo Shan where they underwent replenishment for the counteroffensive. On April 23, as the enemy took Shang-hsia-chih-chiao and Ling-tou, our forces withdrew to Tsai-ling and Yen-wo Shan. Later, the enemy and our forces fought fiercely in the areas north and west of Foochow. Greatly weakened, the enemy fell back to Fu-ching, Chang-lo and Lien-chiang on June 1 where he constructed defense works. After the latter part of August, our forces continued to attack the enemy and recovered

Fu-ching at one time. On August 31, our guerrillas, in disguise, entered Foo-chow and Nan-tai for harassing action and destruction. Our 80th Division sur-rounded and attacked Foochow. On September 3, it captured Hu-ting-shan, Ling-tou, and Hung-shan-chiao outside west gate of Foochow city in succession. The enemy was routed. In time, our force recovered Foochow. On August 29, our 107th Division attacked Lien-chiang and took it on September 3. Enemy forces boarded ships and fled. On September 4, all the enemy units along the coast were mopped up.

In the autumn of 1944, the Japanese and the puppet forces captured Foo-chow in order to prevent Allied and our forces from land, maintain sea naviga-tion along the coast, and use Foochow as an alternate base for their ships and craft. On September 24, the 62nd Composite Brigade of the enemy's 13th Corps sailed in six transports from Shanghai under naval cover and reached the waters in the vicinity of Foochow at midnight on September 26. Before day-light on September 27, the enemy's main force made surprise landings between Pu-kow and Ta-hsiao-ao, and another force landed at Chang-men and Kuan-tou in the estuary of the Min River. The landing was completed on September 28. Our 80th Division and Marines which undertook the garrison of Foochow offer-ed sustained resistance in the area from the coast to Foochow. On October 4, our forces abandoned Foochow and moved to the outskirts to confront the enemy. On October 5, the enemy force which had landed at Chang-kang took Chang-lo. Subsequently, our forces continued to attack and wear out the enemy. By April, 1945, when the enemy's 13th Corps massed its forces in Shanghai and Ning-po, there were indications that his 62nd Composite Brigade might with-drew. On May 6, our 80th Division, Marines and local militia separately at-tacked the enemy positions on the outskirts of Foochow, while another force at-tacked the enemy at Chang-lo on the right bank of the Min River. The enemy took advantage of key terrain to offer stubborn resistance, and the fighting was most intense. On April 12 and 13, the enemy launched two counterattacks and were stopped. On April 17, our forces launched general offensive along the entire line inflicting heavy casualties on the enemy and chased the enemy into the city. After capturing the strong points on the outskirts of Foochow, our forces continued the attack toward the city. As a result, the enemy fled toward Lien-chiang and Chang-kang. Having captured Foochow on May 18 and Chang-lo on May 19, our forces continued the pursuit. When our forces recovered Lien-chiang on May 22, 2,000+ enemy remnants fled to the border of Che-chiang Province via Lo-yuan, Ning-teh, Hsia-pu and Fu-ting. Our repeated inter-cepts cost the enemy many casualties. On June 6, when the enemy was inter-cepted by our peace preservation units, still greater casualties resulted. Earlier, to respond to the 62nd Composite Brigade, 3,000 enemy troops from the Nashioka Column at Yung-chia and Lo-ching moved south via Jui-an and Ping-yang on May 26. On June 9, the two enemy forces linked up in the vicinity of

Chiao-tun-men. Attacked violently by our forces, the enemy forces fled north across the Fei-yun River. On June 18, the enemy withdrew from Yung-chia and fled north after crossing the river. On July 23, our forces recovered Lo-ching. Meanwhile, our New 21st Division was committed and launched flanking attacks against the enemy recovering Huang-ai and Hai-men. The enemy fled in ships.

The Ta-pieh Shan area, as one of our most important guerrilla bases, was garrisoned by the 21st Army Group of our 5th War Area since the Battle of Wuhan. Our forces repeatedly attacked the enemy forces in the southern sector of the Peiping-Hankow Railway, on the north bank of the Yangtze River and in central Anhwei. On May 4, 1939, the main force of Gen. Ou Shou-nien's 176th Division, 48th Corps and Gen. Lin Shih-chen's column launched a surprise attack on An-king and entered the city in one stroke. Meanwhile, puppet forces under Hao Wen-po defected and responded to our forces by jointly launching a converging attack against the enemy. For several hours, our forces engaged the enemy in street fighting and destroyed enemy barracks, warehouses and supplies before withdrawing with ease.

In the spring of 1941, Gen. Mo Teh-hung's 138th Division, 31st Corps held the hilly areas east of Ho-fei for guerrilla operations. Repeatedly, it attacked and destroyed the enemy forces along the Huai-nan and the Tientsin-Pukow Railways. The enemy massed the 13th Separate Brigade and elements of the 15th Division totalling 5,000+ troops and attached with 30+ guns. On March 2, they began the siege on our 138th Division on six routes from Chu Hsien, Chuan-chiao, Ho Hsien, Chao Hsien, Ho-fei and Ting-yuan. The enemy from Chuan-chiao and Ho Hsien and the enemy from Chao Hsien respectively reached Ku-ho-chi and Tuo-kao Chen on March 3 and 5 to respond to the enemy forces from the other directions in launching a coverging attack on our forces at Liang-yuan Chen. Our 138th Division coordinated with local militia in intercepting and attacking the enemy flanks. In the night of March 6, the 172nd Division of the 7th Corps crossed the Huai-Nan Railway to the east from the north of Ho-fei and advanced to Tsao-miao-chi to respond to the operations. Additionally, the 171st Division crossed the Huai-Nan Railway from the south of Ho-fei to pursue the enemy force which was moving west. On March 6 and 7, bitter fighting took place in the vicinity of Liang-yuan Chen. Having suffered increasing casualties, the enemy was gradually weakened. On March 10, the enemy retreated to Lo-chi along the Huai-Nan Railway. In time, our guerrilla bases were recovered.

On December 8, 1942, Tsukata, newly appointed commander of the enemy's 11th Corps, and 9 senior officers who accompanied him, on way of their flight from Nanking to Hankow, were shot down by our 138th Division over Mi-tuo Temple in Tai-hu Hsien. To retrieve their remains and to retaliate, the enemy began to mass forces on the south side of Ta-pieh Shan ready to invade our Ta-pieh Shan area. The main strength of his 3rd Division massed in Huang-pi,

Sung-fu and Hsin-chow. Elements of the enemy's 14th Separate Brigade massed in Huang-kang and Lan-hsi, while elements of the enemy's 116th Division
massed in Wang-chiang and An-king. On December 20, elements of the enemy's
44th Division moved toward Shih-hui-yao, and elements of the enemy's 68th
Division massed in Chi-chun and Kung-lung. Our 21st Army Group dispatched
the 39th Corps to garrison Huang-mei, Ying-shan, Lo-tien and Ma-cheng; the
48th Corps to garrison Chien-shan and Tai-hu; and the 7th Corps to garrison
Huo-chiu and Lu-an. The 171st Division and the 173rd Division of the 7th Corps
respectively conducted guerrilla operations east of the Huai-Nan Railway and
garrisoned Lo-shan. The 84th Corps which had originally been held in readiness
at Ju-nan and Cheng-yang-kuan for reorganization and training was transferred
to Shang-cheng for garrison duties on December 25. In eastern Hupei, on December 23, the main force of the enemy's 3rd Division began the advance toward Li-
huang and Shang-cheng via Lo-tien and Ma-cheng. Meanwhile, a portion of the
enemy's 14th Separate Brigade at Lan-hsi advanced to the north via Hsi-shui and
Ying-shan. Our 39th Corps, 2nd, 16th and 17th Columns and 84th Corps offered gradual resistance at Hsi-shui, Ying-shan, Lo-tien, Ma-cheng, Li-huang and
Shang-cheng. Later, the main force of the 7th Corps was employed against the
enemy's rear and flanks killing many enemy troops. On January 2, 1943, the
enemy captured Li-huang. The main force of our 7th, 39th and 84th Corps assisted in the counter-offensive. Heavy fighting took place on the outskirts of Li-
huang on January 3, 4 and 5. Greatly weakened, the enemy fled north in several
routes. On January 5, divided into two columns, the enemy's main force moved
west via Yeh-chia-chi. On January 6, elements of the enemy force took Ku-
shih. The bulk of the enemy force teamed up with the enemy moving north
from Ma-cheng to take Shang-cheng. A portion of the enemy's 14th Separate
Brigade fled to the southeast via Ying-shan. Our 39th and 84th Corps were
employed in the counteroffensive against Shang-cheng. Meanwhile, the 143rd
Division of our 68th Corps advanced toward Huang-chuan along the Peiping-
Hankow Railway to respond to the operations. After bitter fighting, the enemy
abandoned Shang-cheng and Ku-shih and fled west via Kuang-shan and Huang-
chuan. Our 84th Corps followed in pursuit. On January 8, 1,000+ enemy
troops from Hsin-yang moved east to Lo-shan and joined force on January 11
with the main force of the enemy's 3rd Division which moved west. On January 12, the enemy fled to Hsin-yang. Along the Yangtze River, beginning on
December 20, some 2,000-3,000 troops of the enemy's 68th Division at Chi-
chun and Kung-lung took Kuang-chi with a small force, while its main force advanced to the east via Huang-mei. By December 26, it had captured Su-sung,
Tai-hu and Chien-shan. The counteroffensive undertaken by the main force of
our 48th Corps led to the recovery of Chien-shan and Tai-hu. Meanwhile, another enemy force moved to the east via Ying-shan and Mi-tuo-shih and took
Tai-hu again on January 2, 1943 before continuing its advance to the northeast.

The main force of our 48th Corps offered piecemeal resistance in the various mountain passes north of Tai-hu and Chien-shan. Heavy fighting continued until January 5 when the enemy was weakened and began to retreat to the south. Beginning on December 27, a portion of the enemy's 116th Division in An-king moved north via Lien-tan and Kao-ho-fu and captured Tung-cheng, Ching-tsao-keh and Yuan-tan-pu on January 4. A portion of our 48th Corps fell back to San-shih-li-pu north of Tung-cheng, and Yu-fang-chieh northwest of Yuan-tan-pu. On January 6, the enemy retreated to the south via Tung-cheng. By January 12, original status was restored along the entire line. In the winter of 1944, to step up guerrilla activities in Ta-pieh Shan, our 10th War Area was activated with Li Pin-hsien as the commander-in-chief and conducted guerrilla operations until the Japanese surrender.

The triangle with Mien-yang in the center which was interspersed with lakes, swamps, rivers and streams was strategically most important. It was the most important guerrilla base of the 6th War Area garrisoned by Gen. Wang Ching-tsai's 128th Division and 9 brigades of the expanded guerrilla forces. These forces had the strategic functions of organizing people, seeking materials, tying down the enemy and protecting western Hunan. Repeated frontal attacks launched by the enemy's 11th Corps from the north were repelled. Subsequent to the operations at Ta-pieh Shan in January, 1943, the enemy again made preparations to lay another siege. In early February, the main forces of the enemy's 40th and 13th Divisions respectively massed in the vicinity of Yueh-yang and the area southeast of Sha-shih. The main force of the enemy's 58th Division was deployed along the line from Yueh-kou Chen to Hsien-tao Chen and Sha-hu Chen to confront our 128th Division. On February 15, with its main force crossing the Yangtze River, the enemy's 40th Division advanced toward Chu-ho-shih and Chien-li. On the same day, the main force of the enemy's 13th Division advanced separately toward the northern and southern flanks of Pai-lu Lake with emphasis on Hao-hsueh. Elements of our 29th and 10th Army Groups advancing along the left bank of the Yangtze River and a portion of our 128th Division fought gallantly to stop the enemy. Bitter fighting continued until February 21 when superior strength and air superiority enabled the enemy to capture our advance positions at Hao-hsueh, Hsin-kou and Chien-li thus isolating our 128th Division. By dispatching a force to defend the banks of the Yangtze River to prevent our forces from launching the counteroffensive, the enemy moved the main force of the 40th Division to the vicinity of Feng-kou along the flanks of Hung Lake; the main force of the 13th Division to the vicinity to Fu-chang from the area east of Pai-lu Lake; and the main force of the 58th Division to the vicinity of Mien-yang for a converging attack. In addition, the enemy's 44th Air Squadron supported the ground operations. Our 128th Division took advantage of prepared positions to offer strong resistance. Bitter fighting continued until February 24 when superior equipment enabled the enemy to capture our strong points successively. Having suffered great losses, our forces were broken into small units to conduct guerrilla operations behind enemy lines.

As the guerrilla base of our 9th War Area, Lu Shan, Min Shan, Chiu-kung Shan and Ta-yun Shan contributed greatly to our efforts in checking and wearing out the enemy during the Battle of Nan-chang, the 1st, 2nd and 3rd Battles of Chang-sha, and the Battle of Chang-sha—Heng-yang subsequent to the Battle of Wu-han. Limited in scale, their activities are not covered here.

e. 7th War Area

Hai-nan Island was garrisoned by the 11th and 15th Peace Preservation Regiments, seven companies of the Self-Defense Group and the Able-bodied Male Garrison Unit under the command of Wang Yi, Peace Preservation Commander, who was assigned by the 4th War Area. The main force undertook the garrison of Hai-kow, Fu-cheng, Hsiu-ying Fortress and Tien-wei Harbor. A portion of the force undertook the garrison of the other ports. In January, 1939, acting on the request of the Japanese Navy, to seek a base for bombing and blockading southwestern China (actually it was the first step in the enemy's southward advance), the Japanese High Command ordered the 21st Corps to capture Hai-nan Island. At dawn on February 10, under the support of its Navy, the enemy's Taiwan Composite Brigade landed in the vicinity of Haikow and Tien-wei Harbor. On February 12 and 14 and April 16, the enemy landed in the vicinity of Hsin-ying Harbor, Yu-lin Harbor and Po-ao Harbor. Our peace preservation units rose in defense and fought against the enemy until May 6 when all our key localities along the coast were lost. Accordingly, our forces were compelled to fall back to the hinterland of the Five Finger Mountain where a powerful force was organized to conduct guerrilla operations behind the enemy lines, obstruct the enemy efforts to improve the harbor and build airfield, and continue to strike and wear out the enemy until his surrender.

Located in the estuary of the Han River, Swatow had a deep and wide port could accommodate large ships. Chao-chow to its north was a key locality in eastern Kwangtung. Since the fall of Canton, Chao-chow-Swatow became an important link to the outside world. On June 21, 1939, the Kondo Column (built around the 137th Brigade of the 104th Division) of the 21st Corps, under the support of 40+ enemy ships and a number of planes, landed in the vicinity of the airfield east of Swatow. Meanwhile, enemy infantry men sailed up the Han River from Hsin-ching Harbor in 10+ motor boats and landed at Mei-hsi. Our defenders consisting of Hua Chen-chung's brigade and local militia offered strong resistance. The coordinated attack of the enemy's armed forces which enabled the enemy to have absolute superiority in firepower forced our forces to abandon Swatow and fall back to the line from Yen-fu to Mei-hsi. The heavy fighting which took place on June 23 resulted in the killing of many enemy troops. Subsequently, the enemy poured in additional reinforcements which landed in the vicinity of the water works. On June 24, our forces abandoned Yen-fu leaving a portion of the 5th Peace Preservation Regiment in Sang-pu-shan for guerrilla operations, while our main force moved to Liu-lung, Tsai-tang and Fu-yang-shih. The enemy followed in pursuit. On June 25 and 26, elements of the enemy forces landed in Lung-hu-shih and Yun-pu-shih, to encircle our forces from the flanks and rear. A portion of our forces defended Chao-an, while our main force was shifted to the mountain area northwest of Chao-an. On the morning of June 27, the enemy entered the city from the west. After bitter street fighting, our forces pulled out of Chao-an City. Later, our 2nd and 4th Peace Preservation Regiments and the Training Regiment reinforced, and the 5th Reserve Division and the 1st Advance Column respectively massed in the vicinity of Hsing-ning and Chieh-yang. Units were dispatched to the enemy's rear area to conduct guerrilla operations, sabotage the enemy's traffic and signal communications, force the enemy to defend strong points, and continue to hit the enemy.

After the capture of Canton, the enemy defended the key locality on the outskirts of Canton with his 21st Corps and controlled the estuary of the Pearl River. Gen. Yu Han-mou's 12th Army Group of the 4th War Area (In the winter of 1944, the 7th War Area was activated with Gen. Yu as the commander) confronted the enemy and repeatedly launched guerrilla operations to harass the enemy. During the Battle of Southern Kwangsi in the winter of 1939, the enemy in Kwangtung invaded north along the Canton-Hankow Railway and from the area east of the railway to respond to the operations in southern Kwangsi and then withdrew. Additionally, the enemy pulled one and a half divisions to reinforce southern Kwangsi. In February, 1940, the enemy activated the South China Front Army to direct the operations in Canton and Nan-ning. In early May, in order to increase the number of strong points on the outskirts of Canton and wage counter-attrition warfare, the enemy pulled 20,000+ troops and scores of tanks from Chiang-men, Fu-shan and San-shui and massed them in Shen-kang and Tai-ping-chang. With the support of 30+ planes, the enemy again invaded northern Kwangtung. Our 12th Army Group employed elements of the 63rd and 65th Corps to meet and attack the enemy at Tsung-hua, Chieh-kou, Chilung-kang and Hua Hsien hoping to draw the enemy to Mi-she and Liang-kou areas so as to surround, attack and crush the enemy. On May 13, the enemy's 13th Division, attached with scores of tanks, moved from Shen-kang to Tsung-hua and Chieh-kou. On May 14, it reached Chi-lung-kang. The counter-attacks in columns, launched by our 63rd Corps, led to our recovery of Chi-lung-kang, Tsung-hua and Chieh-kou on May 16. On the same day, a portion of the enemy's 104th Division in Hua Hsien made the invasion from Yu-lung and Hsiang-shan. Hua Hsien changed hands several times. Later, as the enemy reinforced and attacked violently, our forces fell back to Fu-yuan, Shui-hua and Chieh-ting. On May 17, when the enemy at Tsung-hua was reinforced and counterattacked, the Hsien city was lost. On May 18, another enemy force reached

Mang-chai, Pai-shih-shan and San-fu-tien. On May 19, the enemy launched a violent attack on our forces at Li-chai-ting and Shih-liu-hua-ting. Heavy fighting continued until May 20, when the enemy penetrated our positions at Li-chai-ting and then took Liang-kou. By May 22, the enemy captured Shih-liu-hua-ting and the highground north of Liang-kou. On May 24, elements of our forces counterattacked the eastern and western flanks of Mi-she and Liang-kou. At one time, our forces entered Liang-kou and dealt a heavy blow against the enemy. Bitter fighting lasted until May 27 when the enemy at Shen-chen and Fu-yung-ting weakened and fled to Mi-she. On May 28 and 29, the enemy was again reinforced and counterattacked resulting in heavy casualties on both sides. On May 30, the enemy captured Kou-erh-nao and Wei-nao-ting. May 31, the enemy took Pai-shih-nao and Fu-yung-chang. On the same day, elements of the enemy's 18th Division at Tseng-cheng and La-pu attacked our positions at Pai-tan. Our strong resistance stopped the enemy at Ho-ta-tang and Ling-shan. Meanwhile, the enemy force which had gone deep into Liang-kou was hit repeatedly and was extremely exhausted. Being separately intercepted by our forces, the enemy forces from Hua Hsien and Tseng-cheng failed to achieve coordination and were surrounded by our forces. In order to destroy the enemy, our forces employed the 63rd and 65th Corps to attack the enemy's eastern and western flanks from Mi-she to Liang-kou and Chi-lung-kang. Piecemeal resistance offered by elements of our 65th Corps drew the enemy to the vicinity of Shui-tou where the enemy was hit badly and suffered heavy casualties. On June 1, the enemy began to waver as his forces in Tung-tung and Fu-yung-chang withdrew to the south. On the same day, our forces recovered Hua Hsien. On June 2 and 3, being surrounded and attacked by our forces, the enemy at Tsung-hua took heavy casualties and retreated in disorder to the south. On June 3, with our recovery of Liang-kou and Pai-tan, the enemy fled to Tseng-cheng and Fu-ho. On June 4, 2,000 enemy troops at Hua Hsien, in an attempt to hold our forces, made an invasion and was repelled on June 5. On the same day, in the Tsung-hua area, our forces pursued the enemy to Tsung-hua, Chieh-kou and Kuan-tsun where the enemy was ambushed. In order to respond to the enemy remnants in the retreat, a portion of the enemy's 104th Division in Canton invaded north and confronted our forces between Hei-shan and Kuan-tsun on June 7. On June 11, our forces recaptured Ho-mu and continued the violent attack. On June 12, our flanking attack at Hei-shan set the enemy fleeing to the south of Shen-kang. As the original situation was restored, the enemy attempt to increase the number of strong points on the outskirts of Canton was shattered.

In the first part of May, 1941, the enemy's South China Front Army (built around the 18th, 38th and 104th Divisions and one brigade of the Konoye Division) pulled the main force of the 18th Division, a portion of the 38th Division and Marines totalling 9,000+ troops from Tseng-cheng, Shih-lung, Shen-

chen and Nien-shan and attacked Hui-yang and Po-lo along the Ta-peng Bay—
Tseng-cheng line. Taking full advantage of favorable terrain, our forces offered
piecemeal resistance, drew the enemy deep into our territory and awaited
the opportune time to counterattack and destroy the enemy. On the morning of May 8, after capturing Cheng-kou, the main force of the enemy's
18th Division continued to invade Tieh-shan-kuan-men, was repelled by our
135th Division and fled back to Cheng-kou. On May 9, the enemy's main force
captured Heng-ho and continued to invade Heng-kang and Lu-hsi. On May
11, the enemy reached the vicinity of Hsiang-shui-yu. At noon on May 10,
after fighting bitterly against our 2nd Separate Column, 5,000+ troops of the
enemy's 18th Division at Tseng-cheng advanced along the Tseng-cheng-Po-lo Highway to Lung-hua west of Po-lo. Having offered sustained resistance, our 160th
Division and 9th Separate Brigade gradually fell back to the vicinity of Po-lo.
In the morning of May 11, 2,000+ troops of the enemy's 38th Division attack
Po-lo. Meanwhile, 1,000+ enemy Marines in scores of motor boats and commercial boats sailed up the East River under low flying air support and joined
force with the enemy from Lung-hua and Hsiang-shui-yu to storm the city of
Po-lo. Jointly, a portion of our 9th Separate Brigade and 2nd and 3rd Columns
intercepted the enemy. The heavy fighting continued into the afternoon when
a portion of the enemy forces broke into the city. After bloody street fighting,
our forces fell back to Pei-hsia and Shen-shan to launch flanking attacks against
the enemy. At this time, 2,000+ troops each from the enemy's 38th Division
at Shen-yu and 18th Division at Nien-shan invaded Ching-hsi and Ping-shan on
the morning of May 11 in order to respond to the enemy's attack on Po-lo, and
fought bitterly against our 160th Division. Hsi-tieh-ling changed hands three
times with both side suffering heavy casualties. As the enemy's indiscriminate
bombing destroyed all of our positions, our forces withdrew to Liang-hua. Meanwhile, an enemy force from Shih-lung which had advanced to Shih-ma was intercepted by our 6th Hai-ting Column. However, the column withdrew to Ta-wo
Shan in order to avoid a converging attack by the enemy from Ching-hsi. On
May 12, the enemy forces which had taken Ping-shan and Po-lo jointly captured
Hui-yang. On May 13, after re-aligning the dispositions, our forces issued orders
for attacks on the enemy. On May 17, the enemy retreated en masse. By
May 23, our forces had retaken Hui-yang and Po-lo. Hence, the original situa-
tion was restored.

Earlier on May 5, 1941, our guerrilla forces at Chung-shan Hsien shot
down an enemy plane in the vicinity of Ta-chih-kan killing Adm. Outsuno, newly
appointed commander of the enemy's Combined Fleet and members of his party
and capturing many important documents.

An Account of Naval Operations

Having been subjected to the attacks of the Japanese naval and air forces during the First Phase operations, many of our ships ~~and craft~~ were destroyed or damaged. Sea supremacy fell into enemy hands. In accordance with the development of the situation, our Navy withdrew the remaining ships and craft to the inland rivers for blockade, gap stopping and surprise attacks against the enemy. In addition, the naval raiding tactics were invented. Taking advantage of the enemy's extended lines of communications, our naval forces sneaked behind enemy lines and laid drifting mines in the navigational channels of the Yangtze River, the Kan River, the Pearl River, the Ming River, and the Chien-tang River to launch surprise attacks against the enemy, wear out his forces and materials, and disrupt his communications. Meanwhile our naval mine-laying teams laid fixed mines to blockade the lakes, swamps, harbors and rivers which the enemy might use for an invasion. Drifting mines were laid in the upper reaches where enemy ships operated to crush his attempt of sea-ground coordinated operations. During this phase of our operations, our Navy ably assisted the Army in achieving glorious combat results. An account of our naval operations is given below.

1. Operation in defense of Ching River

After our withdrawal from Wu-han and Yueh-yang, our Navy organized 7 mine-laying detachments to stop the enemy invasion. Under the command of Tseng Yi-ting, commander of the Second Fleet, these detachments controlled drifting mines at Chien-li, Hao-hsueh, Sung-tzu, Yi-tu and Ping-shan-pa, and fixed mines at Ou-chih, Sha-shih, Tung-shih, Yi-tu and Hung-hua-tao. A sunken ship blockade line was established at Shih-shou, and all important channels were divided into mined areas where mines were laid. While shipping torpedoes our craft "Yi-sheng," "Yung-sheng," and "Jen-sheng," and No. 4 and 6 barges were sunk by enemy planes at Ou-chih-kou. By May, 1939 when enemy ships operated in the vicinity of the estuary of the Ching River, our forces sank more barges to strengthen the original blockade line at Shih-shou. In September, enemy motor boats operated stealthily in the vicinity of Chuan-chiao. Accordingly our forces laid 50 mines at Ta-shih-yi to deal a heavy blow against the enemy. In October, enemy motor boats were active in the vicinity of Chih-pa-kou. Our forces employed obstacles and drifting mines at Shih-shou against the enemy. In March, 1940 when 2 enemy ships were discovered at Yang-lin-shan, our forces laid 30 drifting mines at Erh-chou-tzu to frustrate the enemy offensive and broke the enemy's iron chain defense net at Kuan-yin-chou thereby crushing the enemy attempt to enter Ching River. In June, as the enemy made a turning movement against I-chang, our Navy laid drifting mines at Chuan-chiao. Later, 1,900 fixed mines were laid at Shih-shou, Ou-chih, Hao-hsueh, Tai-ping-kou, Chiang-kuo, Pai-li-chou, Tung-shih, Sung-tze, Pai-yang, Yi-tu and Hung-hua-tao, while 50 drifting mines were laid at Hung-hua-tao to deal the enemy a heavy blow. On June 29, when the enemy at I-chang forced the crossing of the Wu-lung River, our Navy pressed near Tzu-yang opposite I-chang on the Yangtze River the next morning to lay 40 drifting mines and shatter the enemy offensive. Since the fall of I-chang and Sha-shih, our forces had controlled the Ching River from Sung-tzu to Hung-shui Harbor area. In April, 1941, the enemy attempted to reopen the traffic between Sha-shih and Yueh-yang on the Yangtze River. Our forces therefore, laid 180 fixed mines at Hung-shui Harbor, Shih-shou, Ou-chih, Heng-ti-shih, Tou-hu-ti and Tai-ping-kou, to crush the enemy attempt. In October, during the counterattack of our forces against I-chang, our Naval Drifting Mine Team successively laid 44 drifting mines at Huang-kung-miao and assisted the Army in taking I-chang on October 10 thus dealing a heavy blow against the enemy.

2. Mine-Laying Defensive Operations at Tungting Lake

As the gateway to Hunan Province, Tung-ting Lake is vast and interwoven with coves and harbors. Since the fall of Yueh-yang, the enemy operated at will in the lake and posed a threat to Chang-sha in the south. Our Navy, therefore, organized seven mine-laying detchments at Chin-chiwang, Pai-yu-chi, Ying-tien-wan and Lao-hu-chia and laid 190 mines. Gunboat "Shun-sheng," steamers "Chang-ping" and "Yu Ta-yu," No. 2 and 10 barges, and a number of civilian junks were sunk along the line from the vicinity of Ying-tien-tan to Chang-sha in the south and Chang-teh in the west stop the enemy. Later, 400 mines were laid, east at Lu-chiao, south to Hsiang-tan, north to Ching River and west to Chang-teh. In January, 1939, the enemy increased the number of ships in the Yangtze River at Yueh-yang to attempt an invasion to the south. At Lu-chiao, our Navy's Mine-Laying Detachment laid 50 drifting mines inflicting heavy casualties on the enemy ships. Between March and April, 1939, scores of enemy ships and craft appeared in the lake between Lu-chiao and Chiu-ma-tsui. Our Mine-Laying Detachment again laid 70 drifting mines at Lei-shih Shan which attacked and forced the enemy ships and craft to take to their heels.

In September, 1939, the enemy massed powerful forces in an attempt to invade northern Hunan, and open the Canton-Hankow Railway by a three-pronged attack on Chang-sha from Hsin-chiang, Yang-lin and Tung-cheng. Enemy motor boats in Tung-ting Lake were most active. Scores of enemy ships and motor boats, and hundreds of civilian junks were massed at Yueh-yang. On Septembes 22, 300+ enemy motor boats loaded with troops saild from Yueh-yang, detoured to enter the Ho-yeh Lake, passed Chia-kang and crossed the Hsiang River. The next morning the enemy force pressed near Ying-tien. Busily engaged in laying mines at Lei-shih Shan, our Mine-Laying Detachment, when told of the enemy encirclement, accomplished its mission and destroyed motor boat "Ping-hai," mine layer "Yun-sheng" and empty barges so that the enemy could not make use of them. On September 25, despite great risks, the detachment continued to lay mines for blockade at Lao-cha-kou. Having laid mines from Hsu-chia-chou to Lu-yi Harbor, our mine layer "Chiang-an" was trapped in Hsu-chia-chou. Unable to pull it out, our detachment destroyed it.

Upon accomplishment of their missions, 5 mine layers were surrounded and attacked by the enemy. Two were destroyed and three were missing. However, our overlapping mine fields succeeded in preventing the enemy from massing his forces, disrupting enemy liaison and supplies. Hence, our ground forces were able to intercept the enemy achieving unprecedented victories. After the fighting had terminated, our mine-laying detachments conducted mine-sweeping operations south of Hsiang-yin and between Chang-sha and Chang-teh in order to restore navigation. They also piloted ships in the various mine fields. By October our Navy had laid mines at Ying-tien-tan and Pai-yu-chi in order to increase our biockade capability and stop further enemy invasion.

In early September, 1941, the enemy again attempted to capture Chang-sha. Our Navy, therefore, alerted our various mine-laying detachments. On September 13, our mine-laying detachment stopped the enemy at Chu-tzu-kou. On September 17, enemy navy and army moved out with the army forcing the crossing of the Hsin-chiang River and the navy rushing to the vicinity of Lu-chiao. This was the situation before the outbreak of the Second Battle of Northern Hunan. On the same day, our forces stepped up the mine-laying at Lei-shih Shan tying down the enemy forces. With the enemy reaching Ching Shan at Ho-yeh Lake, our forces laid 120 mines at Yu-kung-miao, 92 mines at Lu-lin-tan and 60 mines at Wu-lung-tsui to stop the enemy invasion. On September 19, the enemy's army reached Chang-lo-chieh, as his vanguard went beyond Hsiang-yin. All day long, enemy planes fiercely bombed Ying-tien. Fortunately, our blockade line which was strong was not destroyed. With his navy being halted north of Lu-chiao, the enemy's navy and army failed to achieve coordination in their operations. On September 20 and 21, our mine-laying detachments continued to lay 272 mines between Liu-chia-wan-Lin-tzu-kou-Yuan-tan and between Pien-tan-chou and San-cha River near Hsiang-yun. On September 22, the situation became more critical, as enemy ships were discovered at Lu-lin-tan. Our detachments took great risks to lay mines between San-cha River and Lao-cha-kou near Hsiang-yin and kept enemy craft from sailing into the Hsiang River. On the Yuan River front, our forces actively laid mines. A total of 192 mines were laid at Chiao-kou, and White Horse Temple on September 23 and 24. On September 25, enemy forces broke through Fu-lin-pu and Kao-chiao and pressed near Chang-sha. However, our well-scattered mine fields near Hsiang-yin consolidated our river defense. On September 28, one enemy mine-sweeper hit our mines and sank at Ying-tien. As our forces laid 4,000 mines in Hsiang River and Wan River, we were able to stop the enemy. With enemy ships and craft incapable of heading toward Chang-sha, our friendly forces had time to make dispositions. On Sept. 29, when Chu-chow fell, fighting broke out on the outskirts of Chang-sha. Our forces further laid 200+ mines at Hsiang-tan, Yang-liu-hu, and Shen-tung-yuan. Mine-laying detachments were held in readiness at Nan-hu-chow and Yi-su, River ready to lay mines. With water channels blocked and the shipment of military supplies and reinforcements clogged, the enemy found himself in a hopeless situation. With the defense of Chang-sha secured, our forces scored a major victory in the Second Battle of Northern Hunan.

After our victory in the Second Battle of Chang-sha, our Navy's Hsiang River Mine-Laying Detachment took actions to re-align the mine fields and strengthen blockade so as to prevent further enemy move. In December, 1941, the enemy massed powerful forces ready to invade Chang-sha for the third time. Our forces again laid 200+ mines at Hsia-yi Harbor, Lao-tao River, Lou-yang River, Chiao-kou, Ching-kang and Shih-hu-pao. Furthermore, the security of the various mine fields was stepped up. Hence, during the initial phase of the battle, despite of the fact that the enemy's army made a little progress, his navy was stopped by our mine fields, unable to achieve coordination with the army actions. In time, the enemy's supply was cut off and his morale was low. The counter-offensive of our forces routed the enemy and led to our victory in the 3rd Battle of Chang-sha.

3. River Defense in Szechuan

Subsequent to the Battle of Wu-han, our Government designated Chung-king as the nation's wartime capital. Chung-king became the nerve center in our command. In order to stop the enemy from further advance and consolidate the gateway to our wartime capital, the I-chang-Pa Hsien Fortress was established. The fortress commanded the 1st and 2nd Battalions of two batteries each. At the gun positions of Shih-pai, Miao-ho, Hsieh-tan and Niu-kou, 55 ship guns and field guns were emplaced. A direct-subordinate battery was stationed at Hung-hua-tao with 4 ship guns. In October, the Pa Hsien-Wan Hsien Fortress was established. The 3rd and 4th Battalions which commanded five batteries respectively located at Wan-liu, Ching-shan-tung, Wu-shan, Feng-chieh and Yun-yang. 47 ship guns and field guns were emplaced. Additionally, five smoke-generating teams were attached to the the 1st, 2nd 3rd Battalions. The River Drifting Mines Team of 6 detachments was attached to the forces at Shih-pai, Miao-ho, Hsieh-tan, Niu-kou, Wu-shan and Wan Hsien, while our ships and craft were stationed at I-chang, Pa-tung, Wan Hsien and Chung-king.

Despite the fall of I-chang in June, 1940, our mine field in Ching River was so strong that the enemy was unable to effect a breakthrough. Hence, our river defense was not threatened. However, our Shih-pai Fortress was subjected to enemy bombing. On August 22, one enemy plane was shot down in the vicinity of Pa-tung. The crew of our survey ship "Kan Lu" captured two enemy fliers. On September 3, enemy planes bombed and sank the "Kan Lu" at Tai-tzu-wan near Pa-tung and then bombed our warship, "Chiang-kun" and "Chiang-hsi." Later, enemy planes flew along the Yangtze River to bomb our fleet. On September 4, our PT boat "Hu-chun" was damaged and on September 14, No. 7 barge was sunk.

In February, 1941, the enemy employed his forces at I-chang and Sha-shih for the westward invasion. On March 5, the enemy advanced in three columns. A portion of the enemy force from I-chang crossed the river to reach the south bank. In the night of March 9, our River Drifting Mine Team laid more than 30 drifting mines at Shih-pai dealing a heavy blow against the enemy astride the river. On March 10, when the enemy attacked Ping-shan-pa, our ground forces had already pulled out. Lingering in the estuary of the Ching River, the enemy's navy was unable to achieve coordination with friendly forces. On March 11, the enemy abandoned Ping-shan-pa and withdrew to I-chang. On August 24, our warships "Chiang-kun" and "Chiang-hsi" fought against enemy planes and were sunk at Tai-tzu-wan near Pa-tung.

In February, 1943, the enemy invaded western Hupei and captured and then lost I-chang. Enemy ships at Sha-shih and Yueh-yang increased in number. On February 15, as the enemy force on the north bank of Ching River took Chu-ho, our forces sighted enemy troops at Shang-hsia-che-wan. With the fall of Chien-li on February 16, the enemy shelled the base of our mine-laying detachment at Yang-kung-ti. Despite heavy enemy fire, the detachment laid 150 mines at Shih-shou and Ku-chang-ti. Meanwhile, though enemy ships were active at Yueh-yang, they hesitated to advance. They placed copper wire nets supported by iron bars at the estuary of the Ching River against our drifting mines. On February 28, our detachment laid 20 drifting mines at San-chih-chiao which destroyed enemy defense works and sank one enemy surveillance craft. Later, the detachment laid 50 drifting mines at Kuang-hsing-chow to harass moving enemy ships. In five routes, enemy forces sailed in rubber boats with sails to cross the river at Tai-ping-kou, Yao-tou-fu, Heng-ti-shih, Tiao-hsuan-kou and Huang-kung-miao. As our forces were on the south bank unable to stop the enemy from making a forced crossing, both banks of the Ching River fell into enemy hands. Thus, our forces lost control of the mine fields. Continuous bombings of the base of our mine-laying detachment led to the sinking of two of mine-laying boats and 18 mine barges. In May, the enemy from western Hupei pressed near San-tou-ping and attempted to detour to the flanks and rear of the I-chang-Pa-tung Fortress at Shih-pai. Though their line of retreat was greatly threatened by the enemy, the officers and men of the fortress were determined to live or die with the fortress. As they held the fortress at all costs, enemy ships were unable to advance. By May 31, our mine-laying detachment had laid 50 drifting mines in the vicinity of Ping-shan-pa and had sunk one enemy ship in the lower reaches of the Yangtze River at I-chang. On June 6, after another 30 drifting mines were laid, enemy ships took to their heels and enemy ground forces withdrew. In November, the enemy massed 100,000 troops in western Hu-pei attempting to capture the strategic localities of Chang-teh and Tao-yuan in one stroke so as to move south to Chang-sha and coordinate with the enemy forces from northern Hunan and southern Kwangtung in opening the Canton-

Hankow Railway. The detachments of our Navy's 1st and 3rd Mine-Laying Groups laid another 624 mines in the vicinity of Chin-shih, Nan-pei-kou, Ling-kuan-tsui, Hsiao-po Chen, Liu-hua-kou, Mao-chia-pu, Ya-tzu-kang, Hsi-kang, Niu-pi-tan and Chih-shan-tao, severing all the water navigation in the vicinity of Chang-teh and Tao-yuan. Greatly crippled, the enemy's navy lost its effectiveness. On November 20, fighting in the vicinity of Chang-teh broke out. On November 25, as the enemy ground forces broke into the city of Chang-teh, bitter street fighting ensued. Blockaded as a result of the mines laid by our mine-laying detachments, the enemy's navy was unable to render any support. On December 9, the combined operations of Sino-U.S. air forces and our ground forces routed the enemy and shattered the enemy's objective of capturing Chang-teh and Tao-yuan. Indeed, the contributions of our Navy's mine-laying detachments were unforgettable.

4. Naval Operation in the Fukien Area

In April and May, 1939, the enemy planes indiscriminately bombed our fortresses along the coast of Fukien. The enemy's navy looted our ships and Allied ships and operated near our blockade line at Chang-men and Fu-tou, but were repelled by our fortress guns. On June 27, the enemy raided Chuan-shih Island. On June 29, the enemy invaded Fu-tou and was driven off by our marines. Due to failures in his repeated invasions, the enemy resorted to laying mines at Sha-cheng and Fu-ting-wan to conduct counter blockade. Enemy shelling from Chuan-shih against our positions at Fu-tou was unsuccessful. On April 18, 1941, as 20 enemy ships and 10+ motor boats were moored at the estuaries of the Ming River and Lienchiang, and enemy ship patrolled near Chuan-shih blockade line, tension mounted. At dawn on April 19, under naval and air cover, enemy ground forces landed at Fu-tou and Lang-chi Islands. Our Marines stationed on these islands rose in resistance. Our fortress guns at Tien-kuang Shan, Yen-tai Shan and Chin-pai continued to press the enemy at Chuan-shih in order to prevent him from sending reinforcements. Our company which had fought bitterly against the enemy on Fu-tou Island for 3 hours nearly lost all its men. Similarly, the fighting on Lang-che Island was intense. Our fortress guns at Tien-kuang Shan opened fire to render assistance. However, the enemy's ground forces which had already landed at Lien-chiang and Chang-lo, outflanked our fortress. Defending the area near Hsia-chi, our marines fought bitterly insure the security of Chang-men Fortress. Meanwhile, three enemy destroyers headed for Chuan-shih and Pa-chiao-wei, and 4 enemy motor boats also sailed from Chuan-shih. Our fortresses withheld their fires until the enemy ships came within the effective range of our fortress guns and damaged one enemy destroyer and sank two enemy motor boats. After the fall of Lien-chiang, the enemy at Hsia-chia pressed near Chang-men. At night, the enemy from Lien-chiang reached Kuan-tou. At dawn on April 20, our Marines counterattacked and fought bitterly against the enemy. Massed along the line from Ma-wei to Ming-an Chen, our forces engaged the enemy from several directions. The enemy was unable to make any progress. Meanwhile, the enemy from Lien-chiang had taken Foo-chow. Surrounded by the enemy, our naval forces had to break out and fall back. Thus, the port of Ma-wei which our Navy had built for decades fell into enemy hands. On July 6, our Navy laid 11 fixed mines at Chen-tai-kung to stop the enemy's westward invasion and assisted the ground forces in repeated attacks on the enemy at Foochow. Unable to withstand the pressure, the enemy began the withdrawal at the end of August. Our Navy drove away the enemy remnants at Ma-wei on September 5 and recovered Chang-men on September 6. On the night of October 5, our Navy captured Lang-chi and Chin-sha. Our naval forces captured Chia-teng Island on October 6 and mopped up enemy remnants at Hu-chiang on October 25. After our recovery of Chuan-shih Island on October 26, the enemy forces fled in ships.

5. Eastern Chekiang Operations

During the period between the spring and summer of 1939, our Navy blockaded the Chiao River, Ching River and Fei-yung River. Our fortresses at Mao-chu-ling, Yung-chia successively repelled the invading enemy ships and damaged two enemy cruisers. In March 1940, our forces laid 50 mines at Shih-tzu, Hu-chua Shan and Chi-hsien Shan below Pu-yang River and 20 mines in Tsao-oh River. In June, 30 mines were laid between Lo-ku Shan and Chang-shan in the Fu-chun River. On August 10, another 20 mines and 10 drifting mines in the water channel south of Ou River to attack the enemy ships. In October, 25 mines were laid to Chen-hai. On October 17, as enemy ships re-connoitered Pu-yang River, one of their ships hit a mine at Hsia-shih-tzu and sank. On October 18, two enemy ships hit mines in the vicinity of Chi-hsien Shan and sank. The enemy was slightly frustrated. In March, 1941 our forces laid 20 mines between Hu-chua Shan and Hsin-chien and strengthened the defense in the Fei-yun River area. In April, the enemy launched the southward invasion operating ships and craft at the estuary of Chen-hai. Once again, our Navy's mine laying detachment rushed more mines in the channels of the Ou River and Fei-yun River to stop the enemy. On April 16, enemy motor boats, loaded with several hundred troops, landed at San-chiang City in an attempt to attack Shao-hsing. Despite bombings by enemy planes, our mine-laying detachment there took great risks to lay mines at key localities near Chang-chia-tu and successfully accomplished its mission. On April 18, a small enemy steamer pulled several civilian junks loaded with provisions and military supplies and sailed up the Pu-yang River. When it passed Hu-chua Shan, it hit a mine and sank. As the civilian junks hurriedly sailed away, the enemy swiftly swept the mines. However, the number of mines which had been swept was limited and the mine field still retained its effectiveness. On April 23, a large-size enemy motor boat with scores of troops aboard passed the Hu-chua Shan channel and struck mines again. The entire boat was destroyed leaving only one survivor. Meanwhile, enemy forces at Yung River and Chiao River were active. Our forces laid scores of mines at Ling-chiao to attack the enemy ship. Since the capture of Jui-an, the enemy continued to push toward Yung-chia which it took on April 20. As the enemy continued the attack Hai-men, our Ou-chiang Fortress was surrounded. Orders were given to bury the guns and assemble the men in designated areas. Blockaded by our mine field, the enemy's navy was unable to operate. Due to supply difficulties, the enemy's ground forces were isolated. Our ground forces took advantage of this opportunity to counterattack and recovered Yung-chia on May 2. Our Navy's Ou-chiang Fortress was also recaptured swiftly. Another 10 mines were laid at Tung-fu near Ching-chiang-tu and 25 mines were laid at Hsiao-ho-kou near Fei-yun River to stop the enemy activities.

In May, 1942, the enemy launched the Battle of Chekiang-Kiangsi. As our mine fields in the various rivers along the coast of eastern Chekiang were properly laid, the enemy's army and navy were unable to achieve coordination in their advance. From eastern Chekiang and western Chekiang, the enemy's ground forces invaded Chin-lan. In order to stop the enemy ships from sailing up the river, our Navy began to lay 54 fixed mines at Chiao River, Tung River, Ou River and Lan-hsi. As Chin-hua and Li-shui fell in succession, our mine-laying detachment was unable to execute its missions. Order was issued for the detachment to assemble at Chien-yang leaving one drifting mine detachment at Lo-ching and Tung-shan-fu for mine-laying at the opportune time. Our officers and men remained at Ou-chiang Fortress to maintain surveillance over enemy ships. On July 9, 10 enemy large and small motor boats, loaded with troops, invaded Ou-chiang and were repelled. On July 11, the enemy from Li-shui reached the vicinity of Yun-chia and surround our fortress again. Our officers and men, therefore, buried the gun carriages and withdrew to designated areas. Restricted by our mine fields, enemy ships had not been able to operate and had withdrawn after some patrolling.

6. Mine-Laying Operations in the Kan River

In order to prevent the enemy ships from invading the Kan River after the fall of Hu-kou, our Navy laid mines in the vicinity of Wu-cheng and blockaded the estuary of the river to deal a heavy blow against the enemy. In March, 1939, after the capture of Nan-chang, the enemy's ground forces used water buffalo teams to destroy our mine fields. It was not until our Navy gallantly rushed the laying of mines at the delta near Wu-cheng and sank one enemy ship, was the enemy offensive slightly frustrated. In order to strengthen river defense, our Navy laid 52 fixed mines at Chang-yi-shieh, Chiao-she and Chu-cha. In June, 20 more fixed mines were laid at Ta-hsiao-kang-kou and Lung-tou Shan. Therefore, drifting mines were laid from time to time to attack the enemy.

In April, 1940 our forces laid 20 mines in the vicinity of Shih-cha-chieh and Yao-fen-ling. In May, 20 mines were laid at Shuang-kang and Fu-chia-tang. In August, as enemy ships were active in Po-yang Lake, 10 were laid at

Niu-chiao-shan. In December, 30 drifting mines were laid in the vicinity of Lung-wan-maio north of Shih-cha-chieh in order to deal a heavy blow against the enemy ships and craft in the Po-yang Lake. These mines inflicted heavy casualties on the enemy ships and crushed his invasion attempt.

In March, 1941, our Navy laid a total of 60 mines in the vicinity of Lung-tou-shan, Ta-kang-kou and Chnag-chia-shan to restrict the activities of enemy ships. In May, our mine-laying detachment laid 30 drifting mines below Chiao-she and sank one enemy shallow-water motor boat, setting the remaining enemy ships on their heels.

In June, 1942, the enemy invaded our Chekiang-Kiangsi Railway line. In order to stop the enemy forces from responding to each other from the east, and the west, our Navy laid 40 fixed mines at Feng-kang-kang, Nan-tsun, Nian-yu-shan, Lu-meng-tu, Kuan-ti, and Lao-hu-miao in order to crush the enemy attempt of a coordinated sea-ground attack.

7. Mine-Laying Operations in Kwangtung-Kwangsi Area

After our withdrawal from Canton in 1939, our Navy laid visual-detonating mines near the Shao-ching Gorges. By the time the enemy was well established in San-shui, most of our ships and craft were lost. The decision was made to blockade the Hsi-chiang (West River) from Shao-ching Gorge to San-shui so as to the enemy's westward advance. By the summer of 1939, the blockade lines at Yung-an, Sha-pu and Tao-hsi had been completed. Additional water mines were laid in the frontline areas. The mine areas were readjusted and replenished. Between the summer of 1939 and the fall of 1940, GHQ Navy dispatched mine-laying personnel to Shao-ching to assist in minelaying in the West River. Apart from the above-mentioned places, surveys were made on the main channels of Ta-ting-chia, Kung-wan and Lu-pu of Kao-yao Hsien, Yueh-cheng, Chiu-kuan and Ma-hsu of Teh-ching Hsien, Nan-chiang-kou, Lo-pang of Yu-nan Hsien, and Feng-chuan Hsien. Mines were laid in advance so as to effect blockade when necessary. For 5 years, our forces confronted the enemy forces along the line from West River to Kao-yao and San-shui. Despite several harassing actions taken by the enemy from San-shui against Kao-yao, the enemy ships never invaded our mine fields.

As the main tributary of the Pearl River delta the Hsin-chang River flows through En-ping, Kai-ping, Tai-shan and Hsin-hui Hsiens. Steamboats and motor boats were navigable in the waters. As the lower reaches of the Hsin-chiang River were captured by the enemy, our forces laid mines at Chi-pao, Chen-chung, Shih-tzu, Niu-wan and Tan-mu-kou to stop the enemy's westward invasion. In the spring of 1944, the enemy attacked San-fu in an attempt to seize war materials. Moving west along the Hsin-hui-Kai-ping Highway from Hsin-hui, the enemy force reached Tan-shui-kou in Kai-ping Hsien and attempted to open the Hsin-chang River in order to ship the war materials from San-fu. Large number of enemy ships and craft sailed to Chen-chung mine field to shell our forces along the coast on the one hand and undertook mine-sweeping on the other. One enemy ship hit mines and sank. Personal effects found on the ship indicated that one enemy captain and 40+ officers and men were killed by our mines. The enemy spent two days in mine-sweeping. By the time the enemy reached San-fu, the materials of the people of San-fu have already been dispersed. Finding no war materials, the enemy returned. Once again, our forces laid mines for blockade. By the end of September, the enemy again invaded San-fu by launching a pincers attack on the ground. The enemy moved along the Hsin-hui-Kai-ping Highway on the north bank to capture Tan-shui-kou in the north, stealthily landed at Kuang-hai (in Tai-shan Hsien) in the south, raided the city of Tai-shan and launched a converging attack on San-fu. By the time the enemy sailed west, his ships and craft were intercepted by our detachment guarding the mine fields at Ma-shan (strong point in the vicinity of Chen-chung field) and yere unable to effect a breakthrough to conduct mine-sweeping. After San-fu had fallen into enemy hands and our forces were surrounded by the enemy from the rear, our detachment then abandoned the strong points and broke out.

Pei-chiang (North River) flows through Chu-chiang, Ying-teh, Ching-yuan, Sze-hui and San-shui Hsiens. Key localities along the river included Kuan-yin-ai, Mang-tzu-hsia, Tan-tzu-chi and Ta-miao-hsia (all were in Ying-teh Hsien), Heng-shih, Fei-lai-hsia, and Shih-chiao (all were in Ching-yuan Hsien) and Huang-tang (in San-shui Hsien). In addition to laying mines near the Japanese-occupied area at Huang-tang, Shih-chiao and Huang-kang near Sui-chiang (a main tributary of the North River) and Chang-tang-wan (in Sze-hui Hsien), our Navy surveyed and laid mines in strong points along the river. Mine-laying detachments were dispatched to Heng-shih, Lien-chiang-kou and Huang-kang ready to operate. As Huang-tang and Shih-chiao had fallen into enemy several times, the mine fields there had also been swept several times. Consequently, our forces laid mines several times. In September, 1940, the enemy from Canton invaded Ching-yuan and Ying-teh in the north. Having arrived in Ching-yuan Hsien City from San-shui and Hua Hsien, the enemy swept the mines at Shih-chiao and made use of water transportation. On September 28, one enemy ship loaded with troops, moved north and hit a mine before it sank. 30-40 enemy troops on board were killed. The enemy's follow-up ships dared not advance.

As Hui-yang, Po-lo and Tung-kuan Hsiens at the lower reaches of Tung-chiang (East River) were close to the front-lines, our Navy's Drifting Mine Detachment which was stationed there, laid mines at Ta-tien-pa, Lung-ho (in Hui-yang Hsien), Chi-shih and Tieh-kang (in Tung-kuan Hsien). In December, when the enemy invaded Hui-yang, enemy ships blindly entered our Ta-tien-pa mine field. One enemy armoured motor boat hit a mine and sank. In eastern Kwangtung, other than laying visual detonating water mines at Ma-yu-kou, Swatow, during the preliminary period of the War of Resistance and contact mines at the entrance of Chien-chiang-kou in Chieh-yang Hsien, after the fall of Swatow in the autumn of 1940, our Navy sent mine-laying teams to Han River and Tuo River to survey mine-laying area and await the opportune time for blockade so as to prevent the enemy forces from moving deep along these two rivers. Subsequently, mines were laid along the blockade line between Shih-ching and Ching-Jen at the lower reaches of the Tuo River. October 1942, mechanical contact mines were laid in Tien-yang River in the lower reaches of the Tuo River. As a result, several enemy garrison craft were sunk. In the autumn of 1944, the enemy began the invasion of Chieh-yang but could not advance along the river due to mine blockade. Accordingly, the enemy made a detour on land and captured Chieh-yang.

On the Yung River front, since the enemy landed at Chin-chow Bay on November 15, 1939 and later captured Nanning, our Navy's Mine-Laying Detachment effected blockade of the upper and lower reaches of the Yung River. Mines were laid in the lower reaches of the river at Chien-li-sha, Heng-chow, Yen-tzu-sha, Shih-chow, and Lu-wu, and obstacles were placed at Fu-po-tan in Heng Hsien to prevent the enemy from sweeping down on Kuan Hsien. Effective results were achieved. In addition, water mines were held in readiness at Lung-ling, Lung-an and at Chang-mu-tang, Shih-men and Kuei-ping of Yu-chiang and alternate mine fields were surveyed. During the Battle of Southern Kwangsi, our Navy stationed personnel at the headquarters of the War Area to maintain liaison. At the end of February, 1940, when the enemy withdrew from Nan-ning, our Mine-Laying Detachment was ordered to sweep mines and restore traffic on the Yung River. In mid-November, as traffic was restored, the mine-laying detachments in Kwei-lin were transferred to Kwangtung.

In mid-September, 1944, when the enemy moved into Kwangsi from Kuang-ning, and the enemy on the south bank of Hsi-chiang (West River) was restive, our defense force on the main front of Hsi-chiang withdrew from Shao-ching. However, it did not withdraw to Lu-pu (in Kao-yao Hsien) until friendly forces had been withdrawn. Our command directed that both the Kung-wan, and Lu-pu were mined and blockade. Our defender's covering force continued to defend the strong points on the eastern and western ends of the south bank in Shao-ching Strait. It then covered the withdrawal of our mine-laying detachment and the units guarding the western end of the south bank. Our officers and men fought gallantly against the enemy. Company commander Liu Jen-feng and 30+ officers and men were killed in action. By the time Wu-chow was critical, the defense force effected blockade along the river. Our mine-laying detachment laid mines at Yueh-cheng, Chiu-kuan, Ma-hsu (in Ten-ching Hsien), Nan-chiang-kou, Lo-pang (in Yu-nan Hsien) and Panlung (in Feng-chuan Hsien). Shortly after moving west, the enemy moved along the Fu River to Wu-chow from the north. Our mine-laying detachment installed mine fields in key localities along the Hsun River. Meanwhile, the enemy had taken the airfields at Ping-yang and Tan-chu. In early October, the enemy took Kuei-ping. Our force assigned the mine-laying detachment in Kwangsi Province to work in the west route area. A portion of the detachment undertook the mining and blockade of Liu River, and another portion undertook the mining and blockade of Yung River. The Yung River mine-laying detachment laid mines at Hsia-wan, Tung-ching, and Lo-pu-wan between Kuei-ping and Kuei Hsien. In October, as our counteroffensive against Kuei-ping failed, our forces moved to western Kwangsi. In late November, our Liu River mine-laying detachment was ordered to western Kwangsi.

Mobile mine-laying was one of the major efforts of our Navy in Kwangtung during the War of Resistance and reaped considerable gains. On December 24, 1939, the enemy's Jakukyo Maru, a 1,000-ton transport loaded with weapons, was destroyed in Chou-chun River in Hsin-hui Hsien. On March 22, 1940, two enemy transports were sunk in Tien River. On April 5, 1941, enemy transport Kaikou Maru was seriously damaged San-niang-miao. On January 11, 1942, enemy transport Kaiuon Maru was damaged near Ma-ning in Shun-teh Hsien. In November, enemy transport Nawkai Maru was seriously damaged in Tien River. On January 24, 1943, enemy gunboat No. 609, was destroyed near Ma-ning. On March 19, puppet ship "Chiang-chuan" was destroyed. On March 27, puppet ship "Hsieh-li" was destroyed and Vice Adm. Sa Fu-chou, puppet commander of the port of Canton and 7 key puppet officers were captured. On March 19, 1944, the enemy transport "Nawkai Maru" was destroyed near Li-chia-sha in Shun-teh Hsien. On April 18, one large-size enemy motor boat was destroyed in Heng River in Chung-shan Hsien.

8. Mine-Laying Guerilla Operations in the Yangtze River

After the enemy occupation of Wu-han, the lower reaches of the Yangtze River were under enemy control. Enemy relied on the lower reaches of the Yangtze River for shipping equipment, supplies and materials. In order to synchronize with our guerilla operations along the Peiping-Hankow and Tientsin-Pukow Railways and crush the enemy hope of making use of the Yangtze River for navigation, our Navy delineated the area between Hu-kou and Wu-hu as the 1st Mine-Laying Area. The Mine-Laying Group of 5 companies was activated to coordinate with the guerillas of the 3rd War Area in penetrating gaps reaching the banks of the Yangtze River and laying mines in water. From January, 1940 to V.J Day, drifting mines were laid at Kuei-chih, Liang-ho-kou, Fan-chang, Yung-ho-chow, Cheng-te-chow, Nan-kang near Chiang-hsin-chow, Hu-kou, Shih-pa-chia near Kuei-chih, Niu-tou-shan in the upper reaches of An-king, Pang-hsieh-chi in the vicinity of Wu-hu, Huang-ku-tun in the upper reaches of Peng-tse, Lung-chia-tsui, Mao-lin-chow in the upper reaches of Tung-liu and Tang-chia-ho. These mines sank many enemy ships and craft and cost the enemy dearly in personnel, horses and materiel. Greatly threatened, the enemy had to suspend navigation on several occasions and conducted mopping-up operations against oure mine-laying bases in order to protect navigation. The enemy, furthermore, placed his ships and craft in the upper reaches of the Yangtze River beyond Chiu-chiang. Despite difficulties and sacrifices, our mine-laying personel operated in the vicinity of enemy strong points and blockade lines to lay drifting mines. In an effort to strike a heavy blow against the enemy and disrupt his navigation, our Navy organized the Hsun-hu Area Mine-Laying Detachment by delineating the area between Ao-cheng and Chiu-chiang as the 2nd Mine-Laying Area with 4 mine-laying detachments; and the area between Chien-li and Huang-chi as the 3rd Mine-Laying Area with 2 mine laying detachments. The detachments of the 2nd Mine-Laying Area pushed toward the mine-laying guerilla areas from Hsiu-shui in several routes. In June, again mines were laid in Chang-pu Harbor and Ma-tou Chen south of Huang-sang-kou in the upper reaches of the river at Wu-hsueh, Kuan-yin Harbor in the vicinity of Ao-cheng and Hsia-chao Lake. Scores of enemy ships, and merchant ships were sunk. Greatly enraged, the enemy repeatedly mopped up our mine-laying guerilla base. However, gallant and swift actions of our officers and men rendered the enemy incapable of preventing our detachments from laying mines. Altogether, the various detachments of our 3rd Mine-Laying Area laid 80+ drifting mines at Li-jen-kou near Hsin-ti, Fan-lo-hsu, Sung-chia-fu and Kung-chia-tai, sinking more than 10 enemy ships, killing 100+ enemy troops and rendering the enemy incapable of operating in that area. Later, as there was little enemy ship activity in that area, our Navy integrated its mine-laying activities into the 2nd Mine-Laying Guerilla Area.

9. Employment of Marines

The Canton-Hankow Railway was the main communication artery in the rear area of wartime China. In the summer of 1939, three regiments of our 1st Separate Marine Brigade were assigned 700+ li garrison mission from Chih-fang near Wu-chang to Pai-shih-tu. Though many of our marine officers and men were killed as a result of enemy bombing, their covering mission was successfully accomplished. In May 1939, the brigade assigned its 1st and 2nd Regiment to protect the Hu-nan—Kwei-chow Highway; the 3rd Regiment to protect the Canton-Hankow Railway. In October, the 3rd Marine Regiment was transferred to protect the Heng-yang-Pao-chin Highway. In May, 1940, a portion of the regiment was transferred to Chang-teh for special assignment. In September, the 3rd Regiment undertook the defense of En-shih, In 1941, the 2nd Marine Regiment took over the defenseof Chen-hsi. Thus, the brigade was assigned missions on land and at sea.

Along the coast of Fukien, pirates who were most active were lured by the enemy to harass our rear areas. In October, 1940, while on patrol, our Navy's Ming River Patrol Group sighted a pirate ship in Lang-chi Harbor and immediately gave chase. The pirates abandoned the ship and took to their heels on land. A portion of the 4th Regiment of our 2nd Separate Marine Brigade laid siege to Lang-chi Island and captured many pirates. Japanese flags of the rising sun, pirate flags and munitions were captured. In January, 1941, several pirate ships were sighted in the vicinity of Chen-tang Harbor in Yuan-fu Hsiang of Chang-lo Hsien. Our 4th Marine Regiment drove away the pirates. In June, pirates were again sighted in Yu-hsi and were later mopped up by the 4th regiment. Subsequently, apart from intercepting pirate ship, the regiment undertook the pacification of the area. During the entire period of the War of Resistance, the pirates were unable to do any harm.

An Account of Air Operations

1.   Air Force Operations

In October, 1939, the enemy maintained 10 air forces, 4 fighter groups and 29 separate fighter squadrons totalling 300+ planes of various types in China. His naval air consisted of the 11th, 13th, 14th, 15th and 16th Air Forces, 3 aircraft carriers ("Kago," "Ryujo," and "Souryo") 5 seaplanes tenders ("Notoro," "Jini," "Reikyu Maru," "Jensen Maru" and "Chitose") totalling 300+ planes of various types. During this phase, the enemy air operations were primarity political bombings, supplemented by strategic bombings. Important cities and cultural and commercial centers in China were generally bombed in an attempt to destroy our people's will-to-fight. By the autumn of 1940, the enemy suddenly increased the number of his planes to over 800 and employed his elite units to intensify the bombing, by raiding Sze-chuan Province and our domestic and international lines of communications. This was intended to break our people's will-to-fight and off our material supply. Preparing himself for the Pacific War in September, 1941, the enemy pulled his air units out of China and transferred them to Indo-China. Thus, the number of his planes in China was reduced to 750. In 1942, the enemy further pulled all his elite air units out of China, Shortly before the end of the War of Resistance, the enemy had only 300+ planes in China. Other than the conduct of fatigue bombing against our rear areas in 1943, all his planes in China were employed for the defense of frontline areas.

As a result of the Battle of Wuhan, the Chinese Air Force suffered heavy losses. Apart from stationing a portion of its forces for air defense in southern Kiangsi and eastern Szechuan for air defense, the bulk of the Chinese Air Force was pulled back for reorganization and training. Since the reorganization and training in 1939, the combat units of the Chinese Air Force included 7 groups, 1 separate squadron and 4 volunteer grops, totalling 135 aircraft. After replenishment, the number was increased to 215. There were 1 district headquarters and 3 route headquarters. By 1940, other than the 1st District Headquarters which was renamed the 4th Route Hearquarters, the original 1st, 2nd and 3rd Route Headquarters still retained their original designations. Of the combat units, the 7 groups were kept, but the Russian Volunteer Group was de-activated. There was a total of 160 pursuit planes to support ground operations, protect the nation's wartime capital and key air base, and cover international lines of communications. Continued combat attrition reduced the number of aircraft to 65. In early 1941, Soviet Russia provided 100 bombers and 148 pursuit planes. However, the preformance of the Russian pursuit planes was vastly inferior to the enemy's Zero fighters.   In April, the Air Command was activated to be responsible for operations and training. In May, the 5th Route Headquarters was organized in Kun-ming.   In June, 100 P-40 pursuit planes were purchased from the United States.   Later, with the formation of the American Volunteer Group (AVG), our combat units still stood at 7 guops (the 11th and 12th Groups and one separate squadron which had undergone training for the whole year were not included). By the end of the year, there was a total of 364 planes of various types of which 100 P-40's were turned over to AVG. Since March, 1942, U.S. replacement aircraft gradually arrived.   Personnel from various combat units were pulled and sent to the United States and Karachi, India to receive training and new aircraft.   After July when training was completed, these personnel flew back to China. By the end of 1942, 19 A-29 bombers, 27 P-40 pursuit planes, 41 P-43 pursuit planes, 82 P-66 pursuit planes were received. Of the combat units, there were still 7 groups (1st, 2nd and 8th Groups were, bomber groups; 3rd, 4th 5th, and 11th Groups were pursuit groups. The 12th Group which underwent training for the whole year was not included), 1 reconnaissance squadron and 1 American Volunteer Group totalling 337 aircraft of various types. By 1943, the 5 rounte headquarters were still retained. In September, 1943, there were still 7 groups (1st, and and 12th Groups were bomber groups; 3rd, 4th, 5th and 11th Groups were pursuit groups) and 1 composite group (reorganized from the 8th Group with 2 pursuit squadrons and bomber squadrons each). Later the 1st, 3rd and 5th Groups were integrated into Sino-U.S. Composite Wing.   During this year, most of the time was spent in new aircraft training. The principles of mobility and mass were observed in order to strike a heavy blow against the enemy's air force. In 1944, the combat units consisted of only the 1st, 2nd, 3rd, 4th, 5th and 11th Groups (4 pursuit groups and 2 bomber groups). Prior to the end of the war in 1945, the 2nd Route Headquarters was deactivated. Of the combat units, there were the 1st, 2nd, 3rd, 4th, 5th, 8th and 11th Groups and the direct-subordinate 12th Squadron. With the receipt of additional B-25, P-40 and P-51 planes, the strenght of our air force was greatly increased.   In equipment, performance and speed, our planes were vastly superior to the enemy planes. Apart from three squadrons of the 8th and 2nd groups which were in the United States for training, all the other units participated in actions. Some of the CAF major activities are stated as follows:

a. Bombing Yun-cheng

Since January, 1939, using Yun-cheng as the base, the enemy massed 40+ aircraft to raid the northwest, in order to harass our international line of communications and cut off our material supply. On February 5, 10th Squadron commander Liu Fu-hung led 4 Vortee aircraft each carrying 20 14kg bombs to bomb the enemy planes on the Yun-cheng Airfield.   When our planes arrived over the airfield, 20-30 enemy planes were parked. As a result of our bombing, 10+ enemy planes were destroyed. The enemy planes did not take to the air to fight our planes. Our planes suffered only minor damage from the enemy's anti-air-craft artillery fire. Again on April 11 and 29, the 1st Group commander Kung Yin-cheng led 9 S-B aircraft and the 2nd Group commander Chin Wen led 6 S-B aircraft to bomb the base. No enemy aircraft was discovered on the airfield. In addition to destroying the base, our planes bombed the Tung-pu Railway and the railway station.

b. Air Battle of Lan-chow

On February 20, 1939, 20 enemy planes in 3 flights raided Lan-chow. 15 E-15 and E-16 pursuit planes of our 15th and 17th Squadrons and 14 E-15 and E-16 pursuit planes of the Russian Group took to the air to engage the invaders and shot down 9 enemy planes. On February 23, 12 enemy planes again raided Lan-chow. 31 planes of our 15th and 17th Squadrons and the Russian Group took to the air and shot down 6 enemy planes. In the two air battles, 15 enemy planes were short down.

c. Bombing Nan-chang

Between March and April, 1939, the enemy captured Nan-chang. To assist our ground forces in the counteroffensive, 5 SB IV planes of our 1st Group bombed enemy position on the outskirts of Nan-chang on May 4 and inflicted heavy casualties on the enemy.

d. Bombing Han-kow

In late September, 1938, the enemy in northern Hunan massed 100,000 troops for an invasion of Chang-sha. On October 3, 9 D.B.3 planes of our Volunteer Group bombed Han-kow Airfield to respond to our ground operations and destroy-ed 24 enemy pursuit planes and more than 10 enemy planes under repair. On October 14, 20 D.B.3 again bombed the Han-kow Airfield. 3 enemy planes were shot down and 50+ enemy planes were destroyed.

e. Battle of Southern Kwangsi

In mid-November, 1939 when the enemy invaded Nan-ning. 251 enemy planes of various types were massed to cut off our southwestern international exit, block the flow of strategic materials into China and threaten our southwest. In December, to assist our Army operations in that area, our Air Force massed the 3rd, 4th, 5th and 6th Groups, the 18th Squadron and the Soviet Volunteer Group in Hunan and Kwangsi totalling 115 planes of various types. Col. Chang Ting-meng, commander of the 1st Route and Col. Hsing Chan-fei, commander of the 2nd Route were respectively stationed in Liu-chow and Kwei-lin to com-mand the units there. In late December, the attack began. By mid-January, 1940, 12 strikes were made to bomb enemy positions, airfields and warehouses destroying 15 enemy planes. 18 air battles were fought and 11 enemy planes were shot down. On 6 occasions, air cover was provided in bombing and strafing enemy positions and reconnoitering enemy situations.

f. Battle of Tsao-Yi

In 1940, the enemy made use of traitor Wang Ching-wei hoping to reap political gains. Little did the enemy realize that when Wang was installed, our common hatred for the enemy was intensified and our confidence in the outcome of the War of Resistance became firmer than ever. Our forces maintained superior strength at Ta-hung Shan on the outskirts of Wu-han and seemed ready to head straight for Wu-han. In order to relieve the threat, the enemy transferred the main strength of his forces in northern Hunan and northern Kiangsi and the forces originally stationed in Hupei Province between May and June, 1940 and massed them in Ching-shan, Chung-hsiang, Sui Hsien and Hsin-yang. These forces were divided into 3 routes in the attack on Hsiang-yang readying themselves for the capture of I-chang. To assist in the ground operations, our Air Force employed portions of the 1st, 6th and 8th Groups to bomb Sui Hsien, Tsao-yang, Chung-hsiang, Ching-men, Tang-yang and I-chang (including the I-chang Airfield). Altogether 284 sorties were dispatched during the entire duration of the battle.

g. Exploding Enemy Planes in the Air

In 1940, taking advantage of the clear autumn weather in Szechuan, the enemy resorted to his old tactics a year ago by organizing his elite air units to raid Szechuan. Since April, the enemy raided the nation's wartime capital, our air bases and resources in Szechuan Province around the clock in an attempt to destroy our war materials, break our people's will-to-fight and put an end to our air force. The air battles over Chung-king and Cheng-tu were most violent. On August 11, 90 enemy planes raided Chung-king. Led by Col. Cheng Shao-yu, commander of the 4th Group, 27 E-15 and E-16 planes and Hawk II planes and 2 E-16 planes of the 3rd Group in several flights intercepted the enemy. 6 of our planes carried bombs which were dropped over enemy planes to break their formation. Our planes then attacked shooting down 2 enemy planes and damaging many.

h. Air Battle of Pi-shan

On September 13, 1940, 36 enemy bombers, under the cover of 30 pursuit planes raided Chung-king. Under the command of Col. Cheng Shao-yu, 34 E-16 and E-16 planes of the 3rd and 4th Group in 4 flights rose to meet the enemy in the vicinity of Pi-shan. During the battle, the enemy was equipped with Zero and Model 97 fighters which were superior to our planes in performance. Despite the fact that Col. Cheng Shao-yu was wounded in action, our air force fought gallantly against superior enemy strength and suffered heavy losses. Our losses included 13 planes destroyed, 11 damaged. 10 officers were killed and 8 were wounded in action.

i. Bombing I-chang

In order to expand his outlying areas, the enemy occupying the area on the west bank of the Yangtze River opposite I-chang attempted to seize our strong points. On March 6, 1941, 20,000 enemy troops crossed the river for the westward invasion and penetrated our positions. On March 9, Col. Chen Chiashang, commander of the 8th Group, led 6 D.B.3 planes in bombing the enemy troops at the river-crossing site near I-chang to stop the enemy's westward advance, and inflicted heavy casualties on the enemy.

j. Air Battle of Cheng-tu

On March 14, 1941, 12 enemy Zero pursuit planes raided Cheng-tu. Led by Col. Huang Hsin-jui, commander of the 5th Group, Lt. Col. Chin Tse-liu, deputy commander of the 5th Group, and Chou Ling-hsu, commander of the 28th Squadron, 3rd Group, with 11 E-15 planes of the 3rd Group and 20 E-15 planes of the 5th Group had been alerted and adopted overlapping disposition tactics. At 1153 hours, our planes encountered the enemy ever Chung-ching and Shuang-liu. Bitter fighting which ensued lasted 30 minutes. 6 enemy planes were downed; 4 of our officers including Col. Huang and Col. Chin were killed in action.

k. Battle of Chang-sha

In September, 1941, the enemy massed 110+ planes, 200+ ships and craft and 100,000 troops to attempt a second invasion of Chang-sha. To assist in the Army operations, our Air Force dispatched 8 S.B. III planes of the 1st Group, and 9 S.B. III planes of the 2nd Group, led by Lt. Col. Chiang Hsien-hsiang, deputy commander of the 2nd Group to bomb enemy ships and craft in Tung-ting Lake on September 23. On September 23, 6 S.B. III of the 1st Group and 8 S.B. III of the 2nd Group respectively led by Lt. Col. Chen Han-chang, deputy commander of the 1st Group and Lt. Col. Wang Shih-tuo, deputy commander of the 2nd Group, bombed enemy troops north of Chang-sha. On October 2, our ground forces attacked the enemy at Ching-yi in response to the operations in Chang-sha, 3 S.B. III of our 1st Group staged a night raid of enemy airfields.

1. Air Battles of Chang-lo and Wu-shih-kou

In late December, 1941, the enemy in northern Hunan launched the Third Battle of Chang-sha and encountered the piecemeal resistance of our ground forces. In January, 1942, our forces succeeded in drawing the enemy to our nucleus positions in Chang-sha where bitter fighting took place and lasted 3 days before the enemy offensive was frustrated. Our major forces from different directions surrounded and attacked the enemy. Greatly weakened, the enemy fled in disorder. Unfavorable weather in Hunan and Szechuan prevented our Air Force from assisting the Army in its operation. The weather did not improve until January 8 when 9 S.B. III planes, led by Col. Chin Wen, commander of the 2nd Group, flew to Chang-lo-chieh, Hsin-shih and Wu-shih-kou in northern Hunan to bomb the retreating enemy. Between Chang-lo-chieh and Wu-shih-kou, our planes encountered 8 enemy pursuit planes. One enemy plane was shot down and 2 were damaged. 2 of our planes were shot down and 3 officers were killed in action.

m. Bombing Enemy Airfields in Indo-China

In the winter of 1941, to step up the preparations for the capture of the areas in the South Seas, the enemy massed the 12th, 27th, 75th and 60th Groups of the army air force and the 5th, 6th, 13th and Shikaya Air Forces of the naval air force totaling 450 aircraft in Saigon and other bases in Indo-China. The enemy's main base was Chia-lin Airfield. When informed, our air force decided to crush the enemy's attempt. Accordingly, on January 22, 1942, 18 S.B. III planes of the 1st and 2nd Groups, led by Lt. Col. Yang Chung-an, deputy commander of the 1st Group, flew to Indo-China to bomb the Chia-lin Airfield. 9 P-40 fighters of the AVG provided the air cover. Upon arrival over the target area, all the targets were covered by cloud formation. Hence, the results of the bombing were unknown. On January 24, Lt. Col. Yang again led 18 S.B. III planes, under the cover of 8 P-40 fighters provided by AVG, in bombing the airfield by rotation. As the target area was still covered by thick clouds, time bombing was used. Nevertheless, it was not possible to ascertain the results of the bombing. During the 2-day bombing, enemy planes did not intercept. There were anti-aircraft artillery bursts below our planes. This marked the first time that the Chinese Air Force bombed Hanoi and also the first time that time bombing was used. Other than two incidents involving the French capture of our pilot Shao Jui-lin when the latter made a forced landing in Indo-China, and the capture of bombardier Ho Chien-sheng who parachuted into enemy territory when the engine of No. 1763 aircraft developed mechanical failure, all our planes returned safely to bases.

n. Battle of Western Hupei

In late April, 1943, the enemy air force massed 6 fighter Groups and 1 separate squadron in Han-kow and 1 fighter Group in Ching-men totalling 248 aircraft of various types ready to render assistance to 100,000 army troops. In early May, the enemy moved from Hua-yung and Ou-chih-kou to harass the area north of Pin-hu. The 1st, 2nd, 4th and 11th Groups of our Air Force and the U.S. 14th Air Force employed a total of 165 aircraft of various types (44 bombers and 121 fighters) to assist in the Army operations. Beginning on May 19, 326 fighter sorties and 80 bomber sorties were dispatched to attack relentlessly Han-kow, Ching-men, Sha-shih and I-chang downing 41 enemy planes, destroying 6 enemy planes, 5 airfields, many positions, 6 military installations, 23 enemy ships and craft and vehicles and killing many enemy troops and horses. By June 7, the river defense at I-tu and I-chang was stabilized.

o. Air Battle of Liang-shan

On June 6, 1943, 13 of our P-40 planes, led by Col. Li Hsiang-yang, attacked the enemy at Nieh-chia River. On the return fight, more than 10 enemy planes were sighted over Feng-chieh. Just as our planes were landing in Liang-shan for refueling in accordance with predetermined plans. Col. Yang Ho-hsiao, commander at Liang-shan, seeing that the enemy planes were approaching, instructed our pilots to engage the enemy. Meanwhile, 8 enemy planes were over the airfield dropping bombs. Squadron Commander Chou Chih-kai of the 4th Group did not even have time to wear his parachute and took off while enemy planes were still dropping bombs. He single-handedly attacked enemy formation several times and sent the enemy fleeing to the east. Squadron Commander Chou did not relent and shot down 3 enemy bombers and damaged several planes over Fen-shui-ling, Huang-tu-kan, Yun-yang, Hsin-hsia-hsiang, Pa-tung and Kuan-tu-kou establishing a record of glory and gallantry in air battle.

p. Battle of Chang-teh

In late October, 1943, the enemy in an attempt to undermine Allied offensive preparations in Southeast Asia, massed 100,000 troops in Hua-yung, Shih-shou, Ou-chih, Sha-shih and Chiang-ling and 253 aircraft (6 Groups and 3 separate squadrons) of various types in Hankow and I-chang. Beginning on November 2, the enemy launched a general offensive against our 6th War Area. Our Air Force assigned the 1st, 2nd, 4th and 11th Groups and the Sino-U.S. Composite Wing in coordination with the U.S. 14th Air Force totalling 200 bombers and fighters to assist in the Army operations. From November 10 to Dec. 16, our air units continuously pounded the enemy at Chang-teh, Ou-chih-kou, Shih-shou and Hua-yung dispatching 280 bomber sorties and 1,467 fighter sorties. As a result of the air battle, 25 enemy planes were shot down, 14 were possibly shot down, 19 were damaged and 12 were destroyed on the ground. In addition, many enemy ships and craft and military facilities were destroyed and many troops and horses were killed.

q. Battle of Central Honan

In April, 1944, when the Battle of Central Honan began, the enemy's air strength stood at 4 fighter groups totalling 156 aircraft of various types. Additionally, 114 aircraft were massed in the northern theater to check our forces. In an effort to wrest air supremacy in the central Honan theater and reduce the air threat on our Army, our air force deployed 156 aircraft (36 bombers and 120 fighters) of the 2nd and 4th Groups, the Sino-U.S. Composite Wing and the U.S. 14th Air Force in Chung-king, Liang-shan, Cheng-tu, Nan-cheng and An-kang and placed these units under the direct command of Commission on Aeronautical Affairs. Col. Chang Ting-meng of the 1st Route commanded the air units in the Pai-shih-yi area in Chungking, and Col. Wang Shu-ming of the 3rd Route commanded the air units in Cheng-tu, An-kang and Nan-cheng. Deputy Commander Chiang Yi-fu in Liang-shan and U.S. Col. Morse jointly commanded the Sino-U.S. Composite Wing. The U.S. air units were commanded by Maj. Gen. Claire L. Chennault, commander, U.S. 14th Air Force. This disposition included 3 bomber squadrons of 12 B-24, 12 B-25, and 12 B-29 bombers and 10 fighter squadrons of 120 P-40 fighters. During the period of operations, apart from bombing important bridges and river-crossing sites to stop the enemy offensive, assisting the ground forces in operations and attacking enemy occupied areas in order to protect Si-an, our air force conducted raids against enemy airfields at Yun-cheng, Lin-fen, An-yang, Hsin-hisang, Kai-feng and Hsin-yang. Between April 22 and August 20, 1944, our air force dispatched 1,646 fighter sorties and 272 bomber sorties, downing 87 enemy planes, destroying 79 enemy planes on the ground, bombing enemy airfields at Yun-cheng, Cheng-chow and Han-kow 13 times, Cheng-chow and Lo-yang Cities 8 times, and the Yellow River Bridge 13 times, and destroying 79 enemy vehicles.

r.   Battle of Chang-sha—Heng-yang

Threatened by superior U.S. and British navies in his battlefield supply in Southeast Asia, the enemy dreamed of opening the mainland traffic communications in order to link up with the South Seas in 1944. He, therefore, massed 5 squadrons totalling 168 aircraft of various types in the Wu-han area to gear to the operations of the enemy's army in launching a large-scale offensive in northern Hunan and opening the Canton-Hankow Railway. With 68 bombers (20 B-24's and 48 B-25's) and 113 P-40 fighters of the 1st, 3rd, 4th, 5th and 11th Groups, the Sino-U.S. Composite Wing and the U.S. 14th Air Foce, our Air Force seized air supremacy over the battlefield, supported Army operations and directly attacked enemy naval and air forces. Between May 27 and September 6, 3,978 fighter sorties and 545 bomber sorties were dispatched. 70 enemy planes were shot down, 29 were probably shot down, 17 were damaged, 52 were destroyed on the ground, and more than 10 were probably destroyed on the ground. Enemy airfields were bombed 30 times, enemy occupied cities 41 times, and enemy headquarters 16 times. In addition, 50 enemy positions and 1,360 enemy ships of various sizes were destroyed, and 2, 584 enemy troops and 685 horses were killed.

s.   Battle of Kwei-lin-Liu-chow

Actively supporting the operations of ground forces by destroying enemy railway bridges and disrupting enemy traffic communication in order to crush the enemy attempt of attacking Kwei-lin-Liu-chow and insure the defense of western Hunan, our Air Force continued to employ the original strength and command agencies in the Battle of Chang-sha-Heng-yang. Our Air Force used Kwei-lin and Chih-chiang as the primary air bases, Shao-yang and Ling-ling as the advance bases, and En-shih and Lao-ho-kou as the supplementary bases. The U.S. air force used Kwei-lin, Liu-chow and Kun-ming as the primary bases, Liang-shan, Cheng-tu, Chih-chiang and Pai-shih-yi as the supplementary bases. During the battle which lasted from August 22 to November 9, 1944, our Air Force dispatched a total of 1,386 sorties of which 1,246 were fighter sorties and 140 were bomber sorties. As a result of the air battle, 34 enemy planes were downed, 14 were probably downed, 10 were damaged, 6 were destroyed on the ground. 400 enemy vehicles, 578 junks of various sizes, 50 enemy positions, railway stations, depots and headquarters and 11 bridges were destroyed 4,550 enemy troops and 258 horses were killed.

t.   Air Battle of Tung-ting Lake

On July 23, 1944, 21 P-40 fighters of the Sino-U.S. Composite Wing and the

3rd Group provided the air cover for 6 B-25 bombers of our 1st Group in bombing Yang-lou-sze Railway Station and enemy depots. Upon accomplishment of their missions and while flying over the outskirts of Yang-lou-sze and over Yueh-yang in southern Tung-ting Lake, our planes encountered 40 enemy Zero II and III fighters. The results of the air battle indicated that 10 enemy planes were shot down of which 2 were downed by our B-25 machine gunner Li Hsien-ho. Our planes suffered no losses and returned safely to bases.

u. Battle of Western Honan-Northern Hupei

In order to insure the traffic in the southern sector of the Peiping-Hankow Railway and destroy our air bases in southern Shensi, western Honan and northern Hupei, Takashi Takamori massed more than 4 divisions in Honan and Hupei and 106 aircraft of various types (18 bombers, 48 fighters, and 40 reconnaissance planes) for the westward invasion. In northern Hupei, the enemy took I-cheng, Nan-chang, Kucheng and Hsiang-fan in succession. In southern Honan, the enemy took Fang-cheng, Nan-chao, Nan-yang, Teng-hsien, Nei-hsiang and Hsin-hsiang in succession before heading separately for Hsi-chia-kou and Lao-ho-kou. Beginning on March 22, our air force employed the total strength of the 1st, 3rd, 4th and 11th Groups and the Sino-U.S. Composite Wing to assist the ground forces of the 1st and 5th War Areas in stopping the invading enemy. Deputy Director Wang Shu-ming of the Commission on Aeronautical Affairs established a command post at Nan-cheng to direct the air operations against the enemy. Attacking the enemy's rear areas, the Sino-U.S. Composite Wing and U.S. air units distinguished themselves in combat over Hsin-hsiang, Cheng-chow, Hsu-chang and Nan-yang by inflicting heavy damage on the enemy's traffic communications. Our 4th and 11th Groups directly supported the Army forces in operations. When the fighting was intense at Hsi-ping and Hsi-chia-kou, planes of the 11th Group often flew low altitude to strafe the enemy in valleys and ditches despite heavy enemy fire. Other groups also scored many gains over Ma-teng-pu, Chung-pu-tan, Tou-fu-tien, Ying-chua-shan, Ting-ho-tien, Ma-tou-shan, Hung-shih-yen and Kuan-tao-kou and greatly helped friendly ground forces. By May 31, 1,047 sorties were dispatched of which the 1st Group dispatched 393 B-25 sorties, the 3rd Group 460 P-40 and P-51 sorties, the 4th Group 89 P-40 sorties, and the 11th Group 105 P-40 sorties.

v. Battle of Western Hunan

During the final phase of the Battle of Western Honan-Northern Hupei, the enemy in Hunan and Kwangsi attempted to undermine our counteroffensive preparations and sabotage our Chih-chiang Air Base in the southeast by massing more than 4 divisions in Chuan Hsien, Tungan, Shao-yang and Hsiang-tan and 135 aircraft of various types. In early April, enemy forces separately invaded western Hunan. With the 5th Group in Chih-chiang and the 4th Squadron of the 1st Group as the main force, and supplemented by the 9th Squadron of the 2nd Group at Lu-liang and a portion of the 3rd Group at Liang-shan, our Air Force assisted the ground forces in attacking the enemy. In conjunction with the U.S. Air Force, our Air Force attacked such key localities behind the enemy lines of communications as Hankow, Yueh-yang, Hsiang-hsiang, Shang-sha, Hsin-shih, Kuei-yi, Shao-yang, Heng-yang, Yang-lou-sze, Hsin-ming, Hsiang-yin, Yung-feng and Ling-ling, warehouses, bridges, air bases, transportation and supply installations in order to crush the enemy attempt to seize Chih-chiang. Having wrested air supremacy, our Air Force destroyed more than one enemy regiment and an artillery between Shao-yang and Fang-tung. Enemy forces invading Fang-tung, Shui-kou and Wu-kang were also wiped out by the joint efforts of our Army and Air Force. During the period from April 9 to May 11, despite intense enemy fire, our Air continued to launch strikes against and pursue the enemy, inflicting heavy casualties on the invaders. The 5th Group alone dispatched 942 P-40 and P-51 sorties which far exceeded previous operations. The 1st Group dispatched 113 B-25 sorties, the 2nd Group 58 B-25 sorties and the 3rd Group 18 P-40 and P-51 sorties.

During this period, the U.S. 14th Air Force continued to assist our Air Force in raiding enemy lines of communications to stop his transportation. As a result, enemy forces had to stay away from the highways and took to rugged mountain roads and dense forest for the invasion so as not to expose themselves and make it difficult for our Air Force to discover them. However, during the battle at Fang-tung, the maximum coordinated actions of our Army and Air Force resulted in the destruction of one enemy regiment and considerable artillery. A review of the operations revealed the following 4 causes which attributed to our victory:

(1) During the operations, our Air Force dispatched flying officers to ta distance of approximately 1,000 yards from the frontlines and set up mobile air-ground radio stations to indicate to our aircraft in the air the ground targets to be attacked and adjust the deviation.

(2) Frontline Army units were swift and accurate in laying panels and other signals for contact.

(3) The dropping of napalm bombs were most effective against enemy troops in concealed forest.

(4) Seizure and insurance of air supremacy by our Air Force.

2. Operations of Ground Air Defense Forces

Since our forces abandoned Wu-han and Canton in early October, 1938, our anti-aircraft arillery units underwent re-deployment in accordance with the changes in situation with emphasis on Chungking, Kewi-lin and Heng-yang. Accordingly, the bulk of the caliber 75 mm. and 76.2 mm. antiaircraft guns was emplaced in the above cities. Later, additional AAA was deployed to Kwei-yang, Kun-ming and Tze-liu-ching. AAA units also accompanied our field forces on the Yung-Lung Road and in the 3rd War Area. As the theater of war rapidly expanded in size and the terrain became more complicated, the enemy shifted his strategy of "seeking a quick decision" to that of "fighting a war by means of another war." The enemy shifted the targets to be bombed by his air force from destroying our military power to indiscriminate bombing and burning of our cities in the rear areas. After May, 1939, Chungking, Chengtu, Kun-ming, Kwei-lin, Kwei-yang, Si-an, Lan-chow, and Chu-chiang were subjected to extensive bomb-ings. Of the air raids, the "May 3" and "May 4" raids of Chungking which were most extensive led to the killing of many soldiers and civilians and heavy losses in materials. Having suffered heavy losses in aircraft from combat and encountered difficulties in resupply, our Air Force was compelled to take defensive measures. Hence, we relied heavily on our air defense units scattered in various places. In summary, in the year of 1939, there were 2,603 air raids, 14,138 enemy sorties. 60,174 bombs dropped, 28,463 deaths, 31,546 injuries, and 138,171 houses destroyed. The losses far exceeded the previous years. Altogether 31 enemy planes were shot down by our AAA units over Heng-yang, Chung-king and Lan-chow.

In 1940, the enemy's bombing was primarily political and secondarily strat-egic. Having suffered overwhelming defeat in southern Kwangsi and northern Kwangtung between January and February, the enemy raided our international lines of communications in the southwest by bombing the Yunnan-Indo-China Railway. In March and April, the enemy attempted to destroy the lines of com-munications in Chekiang and Kiangsi. After May, the enemy's air force went all out in raiding Chung-king. When the British reopened the Yunnan-Burma Road in mid-October, the enemy heavily bombed the road to prevent supplies from reaching China. However, due to heavy losses sustained through the years, the enemy's air force showed signs of weakening. The number of aircraft being employed each month was 120 less than a year ago. Improvements in our air defense and closely-knit dispositions placed emphasis on defense against low-altitude attack and on strengthening provincial air defense, surveillance and dis-persion. As a result, losses from enemy air raids were reduced. During the whole year, the enemy staged a total of 2,069 air raids over China, dispatching 12,767 sorties, dropping 50,118 bombs, killing 18, 829 persons, wounding 21,830 persons and destroying 107,750 houses. 15 enemy planes were shot down by our air defense units, while the casualties of our air defense units which were less than previous years included 2 officers and 18 enlisted men who were killed in action.

In 1941, the number of planes used by the enemy's air force averaged 749 each month and was slightly less than that of the previous year. The targets being bombed were more political in nature. Hoping to create a state of terror, waver our determination to continue the war, destroy our materials in the rear area and construction by means of indiscriminate bombings, the enemy conducted the so-called "blockade bombing" and "fatigue bombing." All our defended cities and cultural areas were bombed. Even remote and desolate places like Sungpan and Chung Hsien in Szechuan Province were not spared.   On June 5, the fatigue bombing conducted by the enemy air force led to the tragic deaths of many people in the air defense tunnel in Chung-king.   In early August, the city of Chung-king was raided day and night for air raids over the cities, our authorities moved 20 76.2 mm. anti-aircraft guns and 30 40 mm. automatic weapons which had just arrived in Chungking, Chengtu, Kunming and Lanchow from abroad to strengthen the air defense over the important lines of communications.   The 48th and 49th Artillery Regiments were activated and equipped with the 12.7 mm. automatic weapons which had newly arrived from the United States.   The 48th AAA Regiment was stationed in Szechuan and Hupei, and the 49th AAA Regiment was stationed along the Yunnan-Burma Road.   Despite the enemy's indiscriminate bombings, the augmentation of our air defense firepower and the improvement in air defense greatly reduced our losses over the previous year.   Our reduction in losses reflected the fact that the enemy's air force was going downhill. In the year of 1941, the enemy's air force staged a total of 1,858 raids dispatching 12,211 sorties, dropping 43,308 bombs, killing 14,121 persons, wounding 16,902 persons and destroying 97,714 houses.   14 enemy aircraft were shot down by our air defense units which lost 1 officer and 8 enlisted men in action.

Subsequent to the enemy's attack of Pearl Harbor which led to the outbreak of the Pacific War, the enemy's air strength in China was greatly reduced in 1942. According to our intelligence from various sources, the enemy maintained an average of 273 aircraft in the various airfields in China.   At most, the number stood at 300+ which was less than the number one year ago.   Realizing that its political bombing achieved little results and failed to dampen our people's will-to-fight, that the theater of operations had expanded making it difficult to properly assign the aircraft, and that the Allied air forces gradually gained superiority, the enemy felt compelled to revise his strategy by abandoning his former political bombing and by adopting a new strategy which was primarily strategic and secondarily political.   As a result, the intensity of the enemy's raids over our cities was sharply reduced.   Between January and March, enemy harassed our frontline areas for a number of times.   On April 18, Allied aircraft bombed Tokyo for the first time and shocked the nation.   As the Allied aircraft took off from our airfields in Chekiang and Kiangsi, the enemy, in self defense, pooled his aircraft and heavily bombed our major airfields in Chekiang and Kiangsi. Hence, 40+ cities and chens in Chekiang and Kiangsi were bombed.   Between May and June, to cope with our air strikes, the enemy pooled 100+ aircraft from various places to reinforce Canton, raid our major air bases in Hunan and Kwangsi and destroy our water and land traffic communications.   However, the enemy rarely raided our cities and chens in the rear areas which had no military significance.   Our wartime capital was not bombed, and not one bomb was dropped over the entire Szechuan Province.   While stepping up field air defense on the one hand, our air defense units spread fire nets over railways, highways and various places throughout the country to engage the invading planes. Altogether, 8 enemy planes were shot down. However, our investigations revealed that the enmey lost 1,800+ aircraft during the year. By this time, the enemy's air force had reached the end of the rope. In the year of 1942, the enemy staged 828 raids dispatching 3,279 sorties, dropping 12,435 bombs, killing 6,718 persons, wounding 3,853 persons and destroying 17,609 houses, Chekiang, Kiangsi and Kwangtung Provinces suffered heavy losses, followed by Yunnan and Kwangsi Provinces.

Having been repeatedly dealt heavy blows by the Allied forces in the Pacific theater in 1943, the enemy's air force found its strength incapable of operating over the Pacific Ocean and defending Japan proper. His air strength averaged 353 aircraft per month which fell short of his strength one year ago. The month of July registered the largest number of planes, and the month of February registered the least number of planes. In terms of areas, the southern theater had more planes, followed by the airfields in Wuhan. Like the year before, his operational strategy was primarily strategic and secondarily political in assisting army operations. Targets in the enemy's bombings were mostly in the vicinity of the theater. Only small-scale destructive bombing was conducted against our water and land traffic communications. As our air defense units were scattered throughout the country, difficulties in command and control arose. To facilitate command, movement, control and training, the nation was divided into 5 regions. With headquarters in Chungking, the 1st Region commanded all the AAA units in Szechuan. With headquarters in Pa-tung, the 2nd Region commanded all the AAA units in Hupei and western Hunan. With headquarters in Kwei-lin, the 3rd Region commanded all the AAA units in Canton-Hankow Railway, Hunan, Kwangsi, Fukien and Kiangsi. With headquarters in Kunming, the 4th Region commanded the AAA units in Yunnan and Kweichow. With headquarters in Si-an, the 5th Region commanded the AAA units in Shen-si, Kansu, Ninghsia and western Honan. In time, the Allied air forces in China grew in strength and seized air supremacy. Thus, the enemy's air force was only capable of harassing against our cities in the rear areas such as Chungking, Kunming, Kweilin and Liuchow. In the year of 1943, the enemy staged 664 raids dispatching 3,543 sorties, dropping 13,642 bombs, killing 2,333 persons, wounding 3,406 persons and destroying 14,161 houses. 13 enemy planes were shot down, and 1 officer and 24 enlisted men of our air defense units were killed in action.

In 1944, the enemy's air force which had become further weakened was incapable of launching large-scale strikes. It could only employ a small number of bombers and fighters to harass our airfields in the rear areas and attempted to prevent our aircraft and Allied aircraft from launching strikes. The enemy dispatched more sorties during operations in Honan, Hunan, and Kwangsi; less sorties in Kiangsi, Hupei, Fukien and Shensi Provinces, and again less sorties in Szechuan, Yunnan, Anhwei and Chekiang Provinces. As the enemy bombings were inaccurate, they were only able to inflict minor damages on our cities. In the year of 1944, the enemy staged 917 raids dispatched 2,071 sorties, dropping 17,266 bombs, killing 557 persons, wounding 766 persons and destroying 1,173 houses. 7 enemy aircraft were shot down and 5 damaged, 1 officer and 33 enlisted men of our air defense units were killed in action.

By the beginning of 1943, the enemy's overall situation was such that he showed signs of imminent collapse. During this year, the enemy air raids fell far short of those of previous years. Consequently, the damage was minor. In the year of 1945, the enemy staged 49 raids dispatching 131 sorties, dropping 3,718 bombs, killing 84 persons, wounding 91 persons, and destroying 151 houses.

The Second Phase Operations which began in 1939 and ended in the Japanese surrender in August, 1945 indicated that the enemy staged 8,988 raids, dispatched 48,140 sorties, dropped 197,661 bombs, killed 71,105 persons, wounded 78,394 persons and destroyed 376,729 houses. Losses in materials and properties were uncountable. Indeed, the damage inflicted on us by the Japanese bombings was heavy. However, 88 enemy planes were shot down by AAA. This number did not include the enemy aircraft which were damaged or shot down over enemy held areas but were unconfirmed.

An Account of Rear Area Service Installations

Since entering the Second Phase Operations, our forces re-aligned depot installations. On January 3, 1939, the Rear Services Board, in a cable message, stipulated the following:

1. This Board maintains its main office in Chung-king. Offices are also maintained in Tien-shui and Kwei-lin where the Generalissimo's regional headquarters are located so as to direct the depot operations of the various war areas north and south of the Yangtze River (The logistic command of the 5th War Area is still subordinated to the Board). The former 2nd, 3rd, 4th and 5th Offices are re-designated as branch offices, with the 2nd and 4th Branch Offices and the 3rd and 5th Branch Offices respectively under the direction of the Tien-shui and Kwei-lin Offices. Four direct subordinate logistic commands were established. Other than the 2nd Logistic Command at Yuan-ling and the 3rd Logistic Command at Kwei-yang which are directly subordinated to the Board, the 1st Logistic Command at Han-chung and the 2nd Logistic Command at Kwei-lin are under the Tien-shui and Kwei-lin Logistic Offices.

2. Sub-logistic commands of the army groups in the various theaters of war direct the subordinated depot organizations to handle the supply of various units in the army groups. However, those army group commands only 4 divisions, the sub-logistic commands then handle the supply. No sub-depot is established for the army group which has less than 4 divisions. No depot is established for guerrilla units. In principle, these units are paid temporary transportation

expenses.

3. Of the depot organizations of various levels in the war areas, only the 1st, 2nd, 3rd, 4th, 5th and 9th General Logistic Commands and the 8th War Area Transportation Office remain unchanged. The Transportation Office of the Generalissimo's Headquarters in Si-an is re-named the Transportation Office of the 10th War Area, while the Shantung—Kiangsu War Area and the Hopei-Chahar War Area in which no depot is maintained, transportation supplementary allowances are paid. In addition, a logistic command has been activated in the upper reaches of the Yangtze River. The deactivated units include 7 logistic commands, 21 sub-commands, 30 depots, 34 stations, 14 waerhouses and 10 dumps.

As the operations of the various logistic organizations were increased, the Tien-shui and Kwei-lin Offices were unable to meet the requirements. In May, 1939 permission was granted to expand these two offices to River North and River South Logistic Command to control and exercise command over the logistic organizations north and south of the Yangtze River.

The functions of these two logistic commands are briefly described as follows:

1. In organization, the logistic command is subordinated to the Generalissimo's Headquarters. In logistic channel, it is under the supervision and direction of the Rear Services Board.

2. The River South General Logistic Command commanded the logistic commands of the 3rd, 4th and 9th War Areas. The River North General Logisic Command commanded the logistic commands of the 1st, 2nd and 5th War Areas and the 8th and 10th Transportation Offices. Both commands handle the logistic operations in thier respective areas.

3. The primary functions of a general logistic command are:

a. To direct all the logistic operations of the logistic commands in the various war areas.

b. To review and make recommendations on the storage, locations and quantity of provisions, ammunition, POL, and equipment in the various war areas.

4. On the delineations of the areas of responsibility for transportation, the Rear Services Board is responsible for the area from Nan-cheng in the north to Kwei-lin in the south, and the General Logistic Command would be responsible for the transportation from the various logistic commands to the General Logistic Command. The transportation for the frontline areas would be the responsibility of the various logistic commands and the logistic subcommands concerned.

5. After the activation of the General Logistic Command, the various transportation offices of the Generalissimo's regional headquarters and the Kwei-lin and Si-an Transportation Offices of the Rear Services Board will be deactivated.

During the Second Phase Operations, the primary logistic installations were as follows:

1.   Ammunition replenishment and transportation:

a.   In the northwest, other than the available rifle ammunition, other ammunitions were replenished and stored.   800 tons and 1,600 tons of the urgently needed ammunitions would be moved by water and trucks respectively and would be stored in Pao-chi, Han-chung, Pai-ho and An-kang.   Considerations would be given to the less urgently needed ammunitions, after completion of the movement of the above-mentioned ammunitions.

b.   In the southwest, other than the available rifle ammunition in Kwei-lin and Liu-chow, the ammunition to be replenished should be made available from Yung Hsien and Liu-chow.   Should shortage occur, it would be made up by allocations from western Hunan and Chung-king.

2.   Preparations for the storage of provisions for one year:

Calculated on the basis of 3 million men combat forces, procurement of 3-mo. provisions for the war theaters were made by the Ministry of War.   Procurement of 3-mo. provisions for the rear areas which totalled 1,170,000 bags of rice, 1,800,000 bags of flour and 20,000 bags of cereals (2nd War Area prepared only 1/3), and procurement of 6-mo. provisions for the rear area general depot which totalled 3.6 million bags of rice (It was planned that the procurement of rice be cut by 1,000,000 bags, and 5,000,000 bags of flour be bought from the areas north of the Yangtze River instead), were jointly handled by the Ministry of War, the Board of Military Operations and the Ministry of Economic Affairs. The number and locations of storage areas were determined by the populations in the various war areas taking into consideration the military situation and traffic communications.   Those which pertained to the rear areas in the war areas were handled in coordination with the commanders of the war areas concerned.   A brief account of the operations is given below:

a. Making funds available: The funds required for the storage of provisions were large.   Apart from $7,000,000 which was made available by the four banks (The Central Bank, the Bank of China, the Bank of Communications, and the Farmers' Banks) as directed by the Ministry of Finance, and $3,000,000 advanced by the Ministry of War, the balance of the funds required for the storage of provisions in the rear areas was borne jointly by the Central Government and the local governments (each paying one half of the funds).   The funds required for the storage of provisions by the Rear Area General Depots were borne by the Central Government and the local governments (each paying one fourth of the funds).

b.   Organizing Provision Procurement Committee: All the provinces in the various war areas organized Provision Procurement Committees to handle provision storage.   As a result, the said committees were gradually organized.

c.   Organizing Provision Supervising Committees: Senior officials were dispatched by the Ministry of the Interior, Ministry of War, Ministry of Economic Affairs and Rear Services Board to serve as members of the committee.   The chairman of the Rear Service Board and the general manager of the Agriculture Bureau, Ministry of Economic Affairs were respectively chairman and vice chairman of the committee. Officials of the Ministry of War, the Rear Services Board and the Ministry of Economic Affairs worked in the committee on a full time basis.

d. Prescribing time limits: Originally, it was required that the 3-mo. stored provisions for the rear areas in the theater of war be made available by the end of June, 1939 and the stored provisions for the rear area general depot be made available by the end of September, 1939. Later, postponement was granted when it was reported that it was not possible to meet the deadline for the stored provisions in the theater of war. With regard to stored provisions in the rear area general depot, 5,000,000 bags of wheat were bought in Shensi and Kansu and additional procurement would be made when the newly-harvested grains became available.

e. Making available grinding tools and gunny bags: It was stipulated that the bulk of the provisions for the 3-mo. storage in the rear areas of the war areas and the 6-mo. storage in the rear area general depot be grains and wheat in order to facilitate storage. Grinding tools were properly located to grind the rice into rice flour. It was estimated that 3 million large gunny bags each holding 100 kg. of rice would be needed. Should they be replaced by small gunny bags, then 15 million small gunny bags would be needed. Plans were made to make available 60% of the total number of bags needed for stored provisions in the rear areas of the war areas. Of the 60%, 30% would be procured by the provincial governments and 30% would be procured from the various troop units. The gunny bags needed by the rear area general depot would be procured by the Quartermaster Service and the Agricultural Bureau. As to flour bags, 6,840,000 were needed. Apart from entrusting the Food Administration Department in the 10th War Area to make them in Shensi, the National Military Council cabled the agencies concerned to turn in the used bags.

f. Transportation: Instructions were given to the provincial governments asking them to direct the hsien governments to rally the people into moving the provisions. The transportation charges would be paid in accordance with the provisions governing substitute military shipping. When necessary, the various war area headquarters and depot organizations would render assistance.

3. Checking and turning in automobiles attached to the war areas:

a. Commandeered vehicles which were attached to the war areas were in poor conditions as they had been used for a long time. Their loading capacity was decreased, and the supply of spare part and gasoline could not keep up. In May, 1939, the various war areas were instructed to make a careful check. The following stipulations were made:

(1) Vehicles which were more than 50% worn out were eliminated and turned over to factories nearby where they were dismantled and parts were kept

as spare. Of the drivers who had become excess personnel after reorganization, selected drivers were sent back to the rear areas where they underwent training so that they might be ready when the new vehicles arrived.

(2) Vehicles which were too few in number, not of popular makes or of early models were eliminated.

(3) Should the number of vehicles be too few to be organized into a detachment, the funds needed for the maintenance of these vehicles would be made available from the contingency funds of the unit. Necessary accompanying personnel could be retained. Apart from the Truck Regiment and the 2nd Provisional Regiment which were handled separately by the Ministry of War, all the vehicles attached to the various war areas would be checked and organized in accordance with these stipulations. Altogether 576 vehicles were commandeered of which 130 were eliminated and 1 was replaced. Presently, 447 vehicles were on hand.

b. Withdrawing vehicles from guerilla forces in the various war areas: As most of the highways in the guerilla areas of the war areas had been destroyed, it was not possible for vehicles to travel on them. Moving military supplies from the rear areas was difficult. A request was made and permission was granted to instruct the war area commanders to withdraw the trucks from the guerilla forces in the war areas except those in Shansi and Suiyuan. Those trucks located north of the Yangtze River were received by the Generalissimo's Headquarters in Tien-shui, and those trucks located south of the Yangtze River were received by the Kwei-lin Traffic Control Headquarters.

4. Realignment and improvement of highways and river-crossing sites:

Since the abandonment of Wu-han and the fall of Canton, rail and water transportations were stopped. All the accesses leading to the ocean were blockaded. Since then, the flow of materials in the inland, the transportation of goods and the liaison and supply between the frontline areas and the rear areas had to depend on highways. The Rear Services Board spared no effort to re-align and improve the highways through the years. Major improvements are stated as follows:

a. Northwest Highway: It divided into two sections, namely the Si-Lan (Si-an-Lanchow) Sector and the Kan-Hsin (Lanchow-Hsingshing-chia) Sector. The total length was 1,900 km. The Si-Lan Sector had a dirt surface. After the outbreak of the War of Resistance, the Northwest Highway Transport Administration of the Ministry of Communications made improvements by laying gravel surface (most of the road was finished) and reinforcing the bridges. Vehicles could travel freely. The Kan-Hsin Sector was widened in the winter of 1937 and improved in the spring of 1939. Traffic moved smoothly.

b. Chen-Tang Highway: Since the enemy's capture of Canton when the materials from Hong Kong were diverted to Haiphong, the highway from Chen-nan-kuan to Tatang became an important line in military transportation. This highway had 4 river-crossing sites with poor facilites. In October, 1938, agencies concerned were instructed to make improvements which included the widening of the road base, the reinforcing of the bridges, the reduction of slopes and curves and the construction of parking area. The construction of the above was actively put into force.

c. Yunnan-Burma Road: The road which began at Kun-ming and ended at Wanting on the Yunnan-Burma border totalled 970+ km. Mountainous along the entire line, the engineering was a tremendous feat. The erection of the two bridges at Kung-kuo and Hui-tung was most difficult. As the area near Lu Hsien was plagued with malaria, many workers refused to go. Although the line was open long ago, traffic never moved on the road. After the outbreak of the War of Resistance, the Highway Division of the Economic Commission dispatched large number of technicians to improve the road. In 1938, the Ministry of Communications established the Yunnan-Burma Road Transport Administration to take charge of the engineering. Traffic began moving in March, 1939.

d. Southwest Highway: The river-crossing sites at Huai-yuan, San-chiang and Wu-chiang on the Kwei-lin-Kwei-yang Sector and the Kwei-yang-Chungking Sector had poor facilities and few ferry boats. As many vehicles waited to be ferried, the river-crossing sites became congested. In addition to dispatching capable personnel to supervise the easing of the congestion, the Rear Services Board cabled the Kwangsi-Kweichow Traffic Control Headquarters to take remedial actions and improve facilities so as to maintain the flow of traffic.

e. Hunan-Kweichow Highway: The road began at Chang-sha and extended to Kwei-yang via Chang-teh and Yuan-ling. There were many spiral ridges, soft bridge culverts, and narrow and winding roads. Traffic moved freely after the road had been widened and bridge culverts reconstructed.

f. Szechuan-Shensi Highway: It began at Chung-king and extended to Si-an via Cheng-tu totalling approximately 1,000 km. Originally built by troop labor, the engineering was poor. After the War of Resistance broke out, the Ministry of Communications appropriated funds for the repair of this highway. However, the progress was slow, and traffic was interrupted during the rainy season. In July, 1939, steps were taken to improve the engineering of the road in Shensi Province. Plans were made to contract local builders to repair the road in Szechuan Province. It was expected that traffic would move freely in the near future.

g. Lao-Pai Highway: The road was an important liaison line between Hupei and Shensi. As war was waged in Honan and Hupei Provinces, military transportation was heavy. However, the road surface had not been repaired for a long time. Despite repair work later, the road base continued to cave in and bridges were damaged after rains. Repair work which was performed whenever there was the need managed to keep the traffic moving.

h. Chang-Ping Highway: The road was the main liaison line between Honan and Shensi. Apart from the Chang-an-Shang Hsien Sector which was fair, the road base of the remainder of the road was badly damaged, and many of the bridge culverts were not repaired. In dry spell, traffic moved on river beds. When the river water rose, traffic was disrupted.

i. Chang-Lo Highway: The road ran parallel to the Lunghai Railway. Since the enemy occupation of the north bank of the Yellow River, the Lunghai Railway was often subjected to the threat of enemy artillery fire. As a result, traffic was frequently stopped. As the road became increasingly important, the rugged mountain road from Hua-yin to Wen-ti-chen was repaired and improved by the Rear Services Board. Consequently, traffic moved without difficulty.

j. Hsien-Yu Highway: It was the only supply line in the 8th War Area; however, it was poorly built. The grading was too steep; road span too narrow and bridges rickety. Whenever it rained, traffic was disrupted. After funds were appropriated and repair was made, traffic was restored.

5. Preparations for animal traffic:

The Rear Services Board planned to procure enough draft horses to organize 17 battalions. Each battalion commanded 5 squadrons of 100 draft horses each. The war areas south of the Yangtze River were attached 7 battalions and the war areas north of the Yangtze River 10 battalions. Two draft horse regiments were activated and located separately north and south of the Yangtze River to facilitate command and control. By the end of 1939, all the battalions had been activated and had begun undertaking transport work.

6. Surveying and utilizing water transportation:

a. Surveying and making available ships for the lines in Szechuan:

The Rear Services Board directed the Szechuan Provincial Ship Group to survey and make a report on the number of ships, tonnage and distribution of the ships in all the lines in Szechuan. In July, 1939, when it was learned that the Kuang-yang Sector in the upper reaches of the Chia-ling River could be utilized, the Board built 100 wooden junks each with a load of 30,000 catties. By the end of November, all the junks had been built.

b. Surveying the channel and making available ships in the Han River: To navigate in the Han River both in the flood and dry periods was hazardous. The sector between Han-chung and Pai-ho was shallow and swift. There were few ships and the load was light. In order to supplement the shipping, the 5th Administrative District of Shensi Province was entrusted the task of building 100 junks at An-kang each with a 20,000 catty load for sailing in the Han-chung-Pai-ho sector. 100 serviceable old junks were also rounded up to facilitate shipping.

7. Establishing wounded soldiers' stations:

Realizing that it was difficult to achieve satisfaction in the evacuation, medical treatment, feeding and housing of wounded soldiers since the hospitals were scattered, the Rear Services Board established a wounded soldiers' station every 30 li's along the line of evacuation of wounded soldiers in the various war areas. The number of such stations depended on the requirements of the various war areas. 24 wounded soldiers' station each were set up in the 1st, 2nd and 3rd War Areas; 48 each in the 4th, 5th and 10th War Areas; 6 in the 8th War Area; and 72 in the 9th War Area totalling 294. The supplementary food needed in taking care of the wounded soldiers was issued by the logistic command concerned. The Medical Aid Committee of the Red Cross was asked to dispatch medical and teams to render assistance in medical treatment. To facilitate command and employment, 4 stations were organized into a company; 3 companies into a battalion; and 2 battalions into a regiment.

8. Training logistic command cadres and medical personnel:

a. Training logistic command cadres:

In order to improve the operations of the junior cadres of the logistic command, the Rear Services Board directed the various general logistic commands to establish cadre schools. Each class admitted 40-60 students for a period of 4 weeks until all the training for all the junior cadres in the war area was completed. In compliance with this provision, the war areas began the training on August 1, 1939 and achieved excellent results.

b. Training of wartime medical personnel:

To promote medical services in the logistic commands of the various war areas, the Rear Services Board recommended the establishment of a short-term medical personnel training school in 1938. The Ministry of War, the Ministry of the Interior, the Medical Aid Committee of the Red Cross in China and the Rear Services Board jointly dispatched personnel to organize a training committee in Kwei-yang and established the Medical Personnel Training School to train the surgeons and nurses from the hospitals in the rear areas south of the Yangtze River. The 2 month training turned out 500 students. Training began in March, 1939 and proved most successful. Due to difficulties in transportation, a Medical Personnel Training Branch School was established in Han-chung to provide training for medical personnel in the rear areas of the war areas north of the Yangtze River. On September 1, 1939, the school began its training.

By 1942 when the war entered into the Third Stage of the Second Phase, the responsibilities in rear area services became increasingly heavy. A brief description on the status of supply and transportation is stated as follows:

1. Supply of military provisions: Every soldier received one kilogram of rice each day. The Military Provisions General Bureau of the Ministry of War and the Military Provisions Bureaus of the various war areas were responsible for the rice supply. In areas where transportation was both difficult and limited, combat provisions were stored in advance in the rear areas of regions where it was expected that the main battles would be fought. Should a unit hold a locality at all costs, provisions would be air-dropped to that unit.

2. Ammunition supply: Each soldier carried 1.5 basic loads. Major luggage was 2.5 basic loads and ammunition train was 5 basic loads. The total was 9 basic loads. Immediately before or after every battle, ammunition was reple-

nished in accordance with the provisions of Feld Service Regulations-Operations.

3. Medical installations: Based on the casualty ratio in previous battles, the number of stretchers in the medical teams was determined. Casualties were evacuated to the field hospitals and later to the station hospitals. After 1944, 7 Army hospitals in key areas (such as Chung-king, Kwei-yang and Kun-ming) were improved to admit wounded or sick officers and men.

a. Transportation:

(1) Vehicles: Vehicles in all the truck battalions were re-adjusted and attached to the various logistic commands to undertake military transportation. The 2nd Truck Regiment was attached to the River South Theater; the 4th Truck Regiment and the 8th Separate Truck Battalion were attached to the Northwest Theater. The 1st and 3rd Truck Regiments were attached to the Szechuan-Kwangsi, Szechuan-Yunnan, and Szechuan-Shensi trunk lines; the 6th Truck Regiment was attached to the Chinese Expeditionary Forces in India. 600 trucks from the 5th Truck Regiment and the Yunnan-Burma Road were distributed to the logistic command of the Expeditionary Forces in order to facilitate military transportation.

(2) Railways: Railway transportation was handled by the district headquarters along the various railways.

(3) Shipping: Military shipping in the Yangtze River and the Szechuan River was handled by the Ship Administration. In addition to the ships on hand, commercial shops and wooden junks were chartered.

(4) Fuels: The 4th Fuel Supply General Station which was located in Lan-chow had 9 substations in the northwest. The 5th Fuel Supply General Station which was established on the Szechuan-Yunnan West Highway had 6 substations in Lo-shan, Fu-lin, Lu-ku, Hui-li, Tayao and Chen-nan to supply liquid fuel:

(5) Manual and animal labor: Based on the number of units in their areas, the logistic commands of the war areas organized transporation regiments and draft-horse battalions. Due to complicated terrain, the logistic command of the Expeditionary Forces organized 18 transportation regiments and 9 draft horse battalions.

b. Signal:

In 1942, in addition to the 6 signal regiments and 4 separate signal battalions, the Ministry of War activated 3 separate signal battalions and attached them to the Expeditionary Forces and its logistic command. In 1943, plans were made to extend the signal capability of the Chinese Armed Forces to the battalion level. In 1944, the signal capability reached the company level.

In preparation for the protracted War of Resistance and in anticipation of future development in the war situation and transportation, the Rear Services Board established 3 storage areas in the war areas south of the Yangtze River and 2 storage areas in the war areas north of the Yangtze River to store provisions, ammunition, POL, medical, signal and transportation equipment. Necessary transportation capability was retained to maintain supply flexibility and facilitate operations.

In the spring of 1945, Minister of War Chen Cheng was concurrently commander-in-chief of the Rear Service. In order to seek flexibility in supply operations and eliminate the past malpractices of package deal system or a system which was close to it, the "Program Governing the Realignment of Army Supply System" was prepared. Highlights of this program are listed as follows:

1. To insure the production, preparations, transportation and supply of Army combat military items, the supply system has been implemented in accordance with the following 3 levels so as to clearly delineate authority and responsibility.

a. The Ministry of War would be responsible for the production, preparation, storage and packaging of military items.

b. The GHQ Rear Services would be responsible for the transportation of military items.

c. The units concerned would be responsible for the supply of military items.

2. According to the afore-mentioned Para. 1.a., the Military Affairs Bureau, the Quartermaster Bureau, the Medical Bureau, the Ordnance Bureau and the Procurement Committee of the Ministry of War would, in accordance with their individual responsibilities, take charge of production and insure timely supply of the needed military items.

3. According to the afore-mentioned Para. 1.b., the Materiel Division, the Transportation Division, the Quartermaster Division, the Ordnance Division and the Medical Division of the GHQ Rear Services should timely forward the supply items to the various supply district headquarters, was area general logistic commands, logistic commands or logistic sub-commands so that these items might arrive at the final destinations and meet the requirements of the frontline units.

4. According to the afore-mentioned Para. 1.c., the various troop units wou!d organize supply agencies to receive the supply items forwarded by the logistic terminal stations, and would be responsible in supplying their respective subordinate units.

5. The command channel and supply channel of strategic units such as corps or divisions were clearly delineated. The corps commanders, division commanders or regimental commanders would be responsible for operations, command and training only. The supply operations were handled by their deputies. Hence, the supply stations of corps, divisions, regiments, battalions and companies were respectively headed by the deputy corps commanders, assistant division commanders, regimental executives, battalion executives and company executives. In addition, quartermaster, medical, ordnance and political personnel participated in organizing the quartermaster committees to handle the supply

operations.

6. The munitions bureaus established by the Ministry of War in various places, the traffic communications branch offices, and the offices and warehouses cf the Medical Service were integrated into the supply district headquarters or general logistic commands.

On September 1 of the same year, Chief of the General Staff Chen Cheng, in a cable message, directed the following to the various logistic commands:

"In order to carry out the supply district system, various supply district commanders will act in accordance with the Army Supply Outline and Implementing Procedures. Beginning on September 1, other than urgent cases which will be reported to the General Headquarters with copies of report sent to the supply districts, the various general logistic commands and the logistic commands will conduct their normal operations through the supply district commanders. Reports to the General Headquarters which bypass the supply district commanders will not be answered." Generally speaking, the Army Supply Outline and the above-mentioned re-adjustment program were similar. However, Article 3 of the outline which divided the nation into the Southwest, Northwest and Southeast Supply Districts was the main theme during this re-adjustment.

The highlight of that article is stated as follows:

The transportation and supply missions of the Rear Services General Headquarters are handled by the Materiel Division, the Transportation Division, the Quartermaster Division, the Ordnance Division and the Medical Division. The following supply agencies at various levels are established to execute the missions:

1. The Supply District Headquarters, while maintaining the status quo, is divided into the Southwest, Northwest and Southeast Supply Districts.

The Southwest Supply District Headquarters undertakes the supply of troop units, organizations and schools in the theater of operations of the Expeditionary Forces, the Yunnan-Indo-China border, the Kweichow-Kwangsi-Hunan border area and the 4th War Area.

The Northwest Supply District Headquarters undertakes the supply of the troop units, organizations and schools in the 1st, 2nd, 5th, 8th and 10th War Areas.

The Southeast Supply District Headquarters undertakes the supply of the troop units, organizations and schools in the 3rd, 7th and 9th War Areas.

The supply of the troop units, organizations and schools in the 6th War Area was handled by the General Logistic Command of the 6th War Area under instructions of the Rear Services General Headquarters.

2. General logistic commands: The various war areas and border areas established general logistic commands. In addition, logistic commands, logistic sub-commands, and depots were established in army groups and along supply routes to supply the troop units, organizations and schools in their respective areas.

3. Depots, shops, hospitals and units: In order to meet the requirements, the Rear Services General Headquarters and supply district headquarters and administrative districts established ordnance, clothing, ration, transportation, communications, equipment, fuel and medical supply depots, repair shops, rear area hospitals and manual and animal labor and truck units. These agencies were either subordinated to the individual supply district headquarters or to the Rear Service General Headquarters. Field depots, repair shops, hospitals and quartermaster units were set up in the various war areas to undertake the supply and transportation operations of the troop units, organization and schools in the areas.

Subsequently, upon recommendation of American advisors, the entire nation was divided into 10 supply districts to be responsible for the provisions, uniforms, weapons, ammunition and medicine of each district. On May 1, 1946, the Rear Services General Headquarters was reorganized into the Combined Services General Headquarters and was subordinated to the Ministry of National Defense. Greatly Headquarters provided supplies to troop units, organizations and schools in time of war and peace. Flexible employment was achieved, as its responsibilities were clearly delineated. The past malpractices such as shirking responsibilities and foot dragging were wiped out. Troop unit commanders were not only concerned with training and operations, but also supply. This marked a major improvement in logistics in the Chinese Armed Forces.

CHAPTER SEVEN

An Account of Chinese Communist Sabotage of the War of Resistance

On September 18, 1931, when the Mukden Incident broke out, the Japanese forces occupied Manchuria. In order to resist the Japanese aggression, our Government moved its southern forces to the north. Taking advantage of the Japanese aggression, the Chinese Communists instigated students in various places to meet in the nation's capital and stage mass demonstrations under the pretext of petitioning to the Government. But they were out to embarrass and smear the Government. Meanwhile, the Chinese Communist forces stepped up their armed rebellions and grew in strength. The Chinese Communist troops coordinated their rebellion with the quickening pace of the Japanese aggression. This was tantamount to a pincers movement against the Government from within and without.

After the Shanghai Incident which broke out on January 28, 1932, the Chinese Communists began to enlarge their Soviet areas in Hunan, Kiangsi, Kwangtung and Fukien provinces. They set up a so-called Soviet Provisional Central Government at Jui-chin in Kiangsi and extended their occupation over numerous districts on the Honan-Hupei-Anhwei borders and in central, western and southern Hupei. Their roving bands overran seven provinces. There was social unrest and the people were alarmed. In order to calm the people and unite them, the Government felt compelled to launch a fourth major campaign against the Communists. Then in January, 1933, just when a decisive victory was in sight, the Japanese forces launched the Battle of the Great Wall. Again, the Government had to shift forces to the north to meet the aggressor. As a result, the campaign against the Communists suffered.

In the winter of 1933, the Government began the fifth campaign against the Chinese Communists in an effort to carry out the policy of "internal pacification as a pre-requisite to resisting foreign aggression." The Communists instigated a revolt of the 19th Route Army and formed a "People's Government" in Foochow. Fortunately, the rebellion was quelled quickly. By 1934, under repeated encirclement attacks by Government troops, the Communist forces collapsed in eight guerrilla districts, and their remnants had to flee in small groups.

Chu Teh and Mao Tse-tung, facing a bleak future in Szechuan and Kwei-chow, issued on August 1, 1935, a declaration from Mao-erh-kai, proposing an "Anti-Japanese People's United Front" and demanding the formation of a so-called National People's Coalition Defense Government. Their slogan was; "The Kuomintang and the Chinese Communist Party must cooperate in order to resist Japan and to save the nation." Thus, they tried to save themselves by political means. In the winter of 1935, professors and students in a number of univer-sities and colleges in Peiping paraded the streets in protest against the Japanese-instigated "Autonomous Rule for Hopei and Chahar provinces." This protest started as a patriotic movement, but it was used by the Communists to advance their neutralism tactics. Furthermore, the Communist-directed "People's Front" was engaged in activities in various places to create ill feelings between troops under regional commanders and those under the direct command of the Gov-ernment, and to ask the local troops not to help the Government forces when the latter went after the Communists. It proceeded to sabotage the Govern-ment's policy of "effecting internal pacification before resisting external aggres-sion" under such high-sounding slogans as "Fight Japan but not the Communist"; and "Chinese must not fight Chinese."

In the spring of 1936, cornered in northern Shensi, the Chinese Commu-nists knew that they did not have the strength to undertake military venture and sought surrender from the National Government. On May 5, 1936, they issued a circular telegram calling for cessation of internal hostilities and holding of peace negotiations. Accordingly, they accepted the following 4 principles laid down by the National Government.

1.   Abide by Three People's Principles.
2.   Obey Generalissimo Chiang Kai-shek's orders.
3.   Abolish the "Red Army" and have it integrated into the National Army.
4.   Abrogate the Soviets and have them reorganized into local governments.

In the meantime, the Communists were engaged in a "peace" offensive in various provinces. They established contacts with Chang Hsueh-liang and Yang Hu-cheng, two commanders of Government troops in Shensi, leading to the De-cember 12 Incident at which Generalissimo Chiang was kidnapped. Fortunate-ly, Chang and Yang were inspired by and escorted Generalissimo Chiang to Nanking. Greatly disturbed, our people were more united than ever. Our soli-darity expedited the aggression of the Japanese militarists in implementing their continental policy. Hence, on July 7, 1937, the Japanese militarists started the Marco Polo Bridge Incident which led to full-scale war.

After the full-scale War of Resistance broke out, Generalissimo Chiang, our Supreme Commander, felt that in this war which meant life or death to our people, all the nation's soldiers and civilians, regardless of sex, should have the opportunity to serve the nation. At this time, Chinese Communist remnants, cornered in northern Shensi, made a declaration which contained the following four pledges:

1.   As the Three People's Principles can adequately meet the needs of China, the Chinese Communist Party will work for their full realization.

2.   The Chinese Communist Party will abolish its policy of armed uprising and its sovietization movement, and will abandon its program of dispossessing the landlords through violence.

3.   The Chinese Communist Party will liquidate the existing Soviet regime and hereafter practice democracy in order that the administrative authority of the nation may be unified.

4.   The Chinese Communist Party will abolish both the name and designations of the Red Army, and agree to have them reorganized into the National Revolutionary Forces and placed under the National Military Council of the National Government and to have them wait for orders to move against the Japanese.

In August, 1937, the National Military Council appointed Chu Teh and Peng Teh-huai commander and deputy commander respectively of the former Communist remnants now renamed the 18th Army Group of the National Revolutionary Forces.   This army which was composed of three divisions with Lin Piao, Ho Lung and Liu Po-cheng as divisional commanders, was assigned to the Second War Area in northern Shansi for guerrilla operations under the command of Yen Hsi-shan.

Lin Tsu-han and Chang Kuo-tao were appointed chairman and vice-chairman respectively of the Shensi-Kansu-Ninghsia Border Area Government.

Later, Communist troops under Yeh Ting and Hsiang Ying, south of the Yangtze River, were reorganized into the New Fourth Corps with Yeh as commander and Hsiang as deputy commander.   This corps, composed of four columns, was about the strength of a division and was assigned to the 3rd War Area for guerrilla operations between Nanking and Wu-hu under the command of Ku Chu-tung.

After activation, the Communist forces lacked training; their officers were of inferior caliber; their discipline was poor; and their combat effectiveness was weak.   Facing strong enemy forces, the National Military Council conserved the strength of the Communist forces.   In order to avoid heavy losses which might occur, the National Military Council did not assign regular combat on important battlefields to the Communist forces.   It was hoped that they would develop their combat effectiveness gradually.   Little did we realize that the Communist forces took advantage of this opportunity to avoid combat and conserve their strength.   They not only failed to execute the prescribed missions faithfully, but also took free actions attacking friendly forces instead of the enemy, so as to strengthen themselves.   This was the pre-determined policy of the Communists. Mao Tse-tung said in part:

"The Sino-Japanese War gives us, the Chinese Communists, an excellent opportunity for expansion. Our policy is to devote 70 per cent of our effort to this end, 20 per cent to coping with the Government, and 10 per cent to fighting the Japanese." This fully reflected what he meant.

After 1939, the Communist forces steadily grew in strength. They infiltrated into Hopei, Shantung, northern Kiangsu from northern Shansi on the one hand, and infiltrated into central Anhwei and areas north of the Yangtze River from the areas south of the river and then fled to other parts of Hupei and Anhwei. The Communists were intent on swallowing our local militia left behind enemy lines, guerrilla forces and their bases. They not only negated our war efforts but also helped the enemy strengthen his rule in the Japanese-occupied areas.

The following are the causes which enabled the Communist forces to roam at will and rendered the other forces incapable of coping with them:

1. Failures in our propaganda and education led to the lack of understanding on the part of our soldiers and civilians on Communist ruthlessness.

2. As the entire nation was solidly united with the outbreak of the War of Resistance, our people did not guard against the Communists.

3. As the Communist 18th Army Group and the New 4th Corps were given official designations of the Chinese Armed Forces, our other forces did not take necessary precautions when these two Communist forces approached them. As a result, they were incapable of coping with the enemy when they were attacked.

4. Whenever the Chinese Armed Forces fought against the Japanese, the Communists attacked the flanks of our forces. It was not possible to guard against such attacks.

5. The Communists deliberately created rumours, set traps and used any means to realize their aims. They accused certain individuals of treason or called other individuals friction specialists. Once they achieved their aims, they launched separate attacks to achieve defeat in detail.

6. With the overall situation in mind, our Supreme Command never took stern measures and frequently ordered forces being attacked to yield despite pains.

In attacking the Government and undermining the War of Resistance, the Communists initially worked their way in through the local militia and guerrilla forces. By the time they had grown in strength, they openly attacked our regular forces. Between November, 1940 and October, 1941, the official messages and cables sent by the various war areas to the Supreme Command totalled 395 engagements as a result of Communist harassments and attacks. Some of the serious and major attacks which adversely affected our forces in the War of Resistance are stated as follows:

As soon as it had crossed the Yellow River into Shansi in September, 1937, the 18th Army Group began to act without authorization. It took upon itself to organize such unlawful organizations as the Shansi-Hopei-Chahar Military District, the Shansi-Hopei-Honan Military District, the Southern Hopei Military District, the Central Hopei District, the Eastern Hopei District, the Shansi-Hopei-Chahar Border Area Government, the Northwestern Shansi Administrative Office, the Shansi-Hopei-Shantung-Honan Border Area Government and the Eastern Hopei Administrative Office to undermine our administrative system. By December, 1938, the Communists massed the forces under Ho Lung, Chao Cheng-chin and Lu Cheng-tsao, the Eastward Column, and the Youth Column to lay siege and put an end to the Hopei militia forces under Chang Yin-wu, Ting Shu-pen, Chang Hsi-chiu, Shang Chung-yeh, Yang Yu-kun and Chao Tien-ching at Po-yeh, Hsiao-tien, Pei-yi, Chi Hsien, Pei-ma-chuang, Wu-ching, An-tze, Tsan-huang, Yuan-shih, Chao Hsien, Lung-ping, Wu-an, Shang-chiao-shih and Tsan-chin-shih. As all the anti-Japanese militia organized by the Government in Hopei had been mauled, the check on the rear of the Japanese forces in North China was lessened.

After March, 1939, the attitude of the Chinese Communists worsened. They marked out a special area on the Shensi-Kansu-Ninghsia border where they subsequently set up a government of their own. They issued puppet notes without authorization, undermined national laws, and upset our finances so as to help the Japanese undermine our economic policy. Units of the Communist 18th Army Group under Hsu Hsiang-chien raced to Shantung and laid sieges against the local militia forces, such as the 1st District Peace Preservation Headquarters at Chang-ching, the 14th District Peace Preservation Headquarters at Shou-kwang and the militia at Yu-tai Hsien, Chu-yeh Hsien, Lai-wu Hsien and Mon-yin Hsien. After September, the 8th Peace Preservation Brigade at Po-hsing, the 9th Echelon in eastern Shantung, the 27th Peace Preservation Brigade at Chao-yuan and the peace preservation units at An-chiu, Lai-wu, Tung-ping and Yi Hsien and the garrison unit at Yun-cheng were wiped out by the Communists. In addition, countless people's self-defense organizations in Shantung were mopped up by the Communists. In the end, the Shantung Provincial Government was incapable of exercising its authority.

In the winter of 1939, the Communist 18th Army Group instigated and supported a revolt by about 10 newly organized Shansi regiments under the command of Po I-po, Han Chun, Shu Sheng-wu, Chang Wen-ang and others, and thus thwarted the Government winter offensive against the Japanese in the triangular area of southern Shansi.

In January, 1940, Communist forces under Hsu Hsiang-chien, Ho Lung, Lu Cheng-tsao, Yang Yung and Yang Chi-feng and the 129th and 115th Divisions were massed and launched violent attacks on Government forces in central and southern Hopei. Government forces under Sun Liang-cheng and Kao Shu-hsun were forced to retreat toward western Shantung, while those forces under Lu Chung-lin, commander-in-chief of the Hopei-Chahar War Area and concurrently governor of Hopei Province, and Chu Huai-ping were forced to retreat toward southeastern Shansi. In spite of Government orders to end the clash, the Communists moved onward in pursuit of Sun and Kao and made repeated attacks. Communist efforts aiming at the destruction of the Hopei Provincial Government rendered it incapable of exercising its authority.

Between June and July, 1940, the Communist 18th Army Group again massed on the south bank of the Yellow River. Meanwhile, Communist forces under Peng Ming-chih, Yang Yung, Yang Shang-chih, Hsiao Hua, Chen Tsai-tao, and Chao Chin-cheng and the main force of the Communist 115th Division again attacked the forces under Sun and Kao forcing them to fall back to the north of the Yellow River after bitter fighting for more than 20 days. After capture of western Shantung, the Communist 18th Army Group again extended its influence to harass eastern Honan and northern Anhwei and responded to the Communist New 4th Corps which had crossed the river to the north without authority. As it pressed against the Shantung-Kiangsu-Anhwei-Honan border area, the Japanese forces in Hopei had a respite to actively make military preparations, develop traffic communications, economic and resources. As a result, the Japanese were able to begin without hindrance the construction of Teh-Shih Railway which cut across Hopei Province. The construction of the railway was completed in November 15. In Shansi Province, Government troops under Chao Cheng-shou in northwestern Shansi and those under Wang Ching-kuo east of the Yellow River were also subjected to Communist attacks, causing great confusion in the entire province. The above was ample evidence that the Communist forces did not devote themselves to operations against the Japanese, but attacked friendly forces instead.

The withdrawal of Lu Chung-ling's and Chu Huai-ping's forces from northern China enabled the Japanese to seize control of the following communication lines there:

1. Rail lines laid—425 km.

    The Tung-Lu Line (Tung-kuan-chen—Hsin Hsien—Chang-chih)

    The Teh-Shih Line (Teh-chow—Heng-shui—Shu-lu—Shih-chia-chuang)

    The Hou-Yi Line (Hou-ma—Chu-ao—Yi-yu)

2. Highways constructed—4,409 km.

    Tsin-Pu trunk line (along the Tientsin—Pukow Railway)

    Ping-Nan trunk line (Peiping—Nankung)

    Ping-Han trunk line (along the northern sector of the Peiping—Hankow Railway)

    Tung-Pu trunk line (along the Tung-Pu Railway)

    Pai-Chin trunk line (Paikuei—Hsin Hsien—Ching-cheng)

    Tang-Sui trunk line (along the Peiping-Tientsin and Peiping-Suiyuan Railway)

    Tsin-Kao trunk line (Tientsin-Pa Hsien-Kao-pei-tien)

    Tsin-Pao trunk line (Tientsin-Jen-chiu-Paoting)

      Tsang-Shih trunk line (Tsang-chow-Hsien Hsien-Shih-chia-chuang)
      Yu-Hsing trunk line (Tsinan-Lin-cheng-Wei-pang-tai)
      Hsu-Pien trunk line (along the eastern sector of the Lung-hai Railway)
      Shih-Ching trunk line (Shih-chia-chuang-Ching-ching)
3.   Channels cleared:
      Wei River (Hsin-hsiang-Ta-ming--the Canal)
      Hsiao Ching River (Tsinan—coast of Po-hai)
      Tzu-ya River (Shih-chia-chuang-Hsien Hsien--Tientsin)
      Ta-ching River (Pao-ting—Tientsin)

The completion of the above communication lines not only facilitated Japanese transportation but also absorbed the materials from the areas along the lines to meet his military requirements. The effects achieved were beyond description.

On July 16, 1940, the Government, with a view to preventing more clashes in various parts of the country, worked out a modus vivendi with Chou En-lai and Yeh Chien-ying. Chou took it to Yenan on July 24 for implementation by Chu Teh and Peng Teh-huai. Meanwhile, all Government forces were ordered to avoid further clashes with the 18th Army Group and the New Fourth Corps. The important points in the directive were:

1. The Shensi-Kansu-Ninghsia Border Area (to comprise 18 counties by approval) was to be renamed the Northern Shensi Administrative Area, and placed temporarily under the Executive Yuan but subject to the direction of the Shensi Provincial government.

2. The areas of operations (against the Japanese) for the 18th Army Group and the New Fourth Corps were to be redelineated. The Hopei-Chahar War Area was to be abolished, and the two provinces of Hopei and Chahar, plus that part of Shantung province north of the Yellow River, were to be assigned to the Second War Area, of which Yen Hsi-shan was to remain commander and Chu Teh (a Communist) was to be appointed deputy-commander, to direct military operations in accordance with orders of the National Military Council.

3. Both the 18th Army Group and the New Fourth Corps were to be moved in their entirety to the above-designated areas within one month after receiving pertinent orders.

4. The 18th Army Group was to have three corps (of two divisions each), plus three supplementary regiments, with permission to add two more supplementary regiments later on. The New Fourth Corps was to be reorganized into two divisions.

While the Government troops consistently avoided clashes, the same could not be said of the 18th Army Group. In August, 1940, the 18th Army Group dispatched forces to southern Shantung to assist Hsu Hsiang-chien's forces of the Shantung Column in attacking Lu-tsun where the seat of Shantung Provincial Government was located. Governor Shen Hung-lieh of Shantung led his forces in the withdrawal.   After the capture of Lu-tsun, on August 14, the Communists continued to press ahead.   They never complied with the Supreme Command's stern orders to withdraw.   By the time the Japanese invaded Lu-tsun, they with-drew without a fight.   After the Japanese pulled out of Lu-tsun, they occupied it again.   They repeatedly dealt heavy blows against the Shantung Provincial Government rendering it incapable of exercising its authority.

On October, 1940, the Huang-chiao Incident broke out in northern Kiangsu. Earlier, the 18th Army Group took Lu-tsun after its occupation of western Shan-tung.   In September, the Communists moved south.   Having crossed the river to the north without authorization in July, units of the New 4th Corps under Chen Yi and Kuan Wen-wei attacked Government forces under Chen Tai-yun who was subordinated to Han Teh-chin, governor of Kiangsu and concurrently deputy commander-in-chief of the Shantung-Kiangsu War Area.   The Commu-nists took Huang-chiao east of Tai-hsing in August and Chiang-yen east of Tai-chow in September.   In early October the Communist New 4th Corps teamed up with the 18th Army Group in an enveloping attack against Han Teh-chin's forces.   In the south, there were units of the New 4th Corps under Chen Yi, Kuan Wen-wei, Wang Chien, and Li Chun.   In the north, there were units of the 18th Army Group under Peng Ming-chih, Lo Ping-hui, Huang Ke-cheng and Chang Ai-ping and one brigade of the 115th Division.   Han's forces were subjected to the enemy's surprise attacks. 5,000 troops including Li Shou-wei, commander of the 89th Corps were killed in action.   Ever since then, Han's forces found themselves surrounded by the Communists and the Japanese.   On November 29, simultaneous with the Japanese attack on Han's forces at Huai-an and Pao-ying, the Communist forces launched violent attacks on Han's forces. The fighting lasted 10 days.   Despite of the fact that both attacking forces were repelled by Han's forces, the Communists and the Japanese continued to sur-round the outskirts of Hsing-hua where the provincial government of Kiangsu was located.   They cut off the lines of communications of Han's forces and at-tempted to wipe out the Kiangsu Provincial Government rendering it incapable of exercising its authority.

Our Supreme Command realized that should such anti-guerrilla and anti-War of Resistance actions of the Communists be permitted to continue uncheck-ed in attacking our forces without authorization instead of the Japanese, our war effort would be seriously jeopardized.   However, in due consideration of the nation's solidarity and conservation of our strength, it had to accommodate itself to such Communist actions.   Gen. Ho Ying-chin, Chief of the General Staff, and Gen. Pai Chung-hsi, Vice Chief of the General Staff, dispatched a tele-gram on October 19 to the Communists reiterating the above-mentioned modus vivendi reached with Yeh Chien-ying, Chief of Staff of the Communist 18th Army Group, on July 16, and setting the end of November as the deadline for units of the New 4th Corps to arrive in the new area of operations north of the Yellow

River.   Despite receipt of this telegram, the Communist forces lacked the sincerity to accept orders.   Instead Chu Teh, Peng Teh-huai, Yeh Chien-ying and Hsiang Ying answered it glibly.   On December 8, Gen. Ho and Gen. Pai again dispatched a telegram advising the Communists to observe the modus vivendi. On December 9, an order for postponement was issued directing all units of the 18th Army Group south of the Yellow River to move to the north before December 31, and for all units of the New 4th Corps, south of the Yangtze River, to move to the north before December 31 and to cross the Yellow River northward by January 30, 1941.

By the end of 1940, units of the New 4th Corps in Chin-tan, Tantu, Chu-yung, Lang-hsi and Li-yang refused to move northward as ordered.   Instead, it made plans to control the countryside in the triangular area formed by Nanking, Shanghai and Hangchow.   On January 5, 1941, its units even attacked the Government's 40th Division with 7 regiments when the latter was being relieved.   Divided in 3 routes, the Communist launched a converging attack on San-hsi.   Hastily, the 40th Division engaged the enemy.   Whereupon, Ku-Chu-tung, commander of the 3rd War Area, took disciplinary action against the Communists between January 6 and January 14.   In one week's time, the rebel units were disarmed and disbanded.   On January 17, the National Military Council ordered the cancellation of the New 4th Corps designation.   Yeh Ting, its commander, was arrested and later court-martialed.

Subsequent to the New 4th Corps Incident, the Communists, in the name of the Chinese Communist Party Revolutionary Military Committee, appointed Chen Yi and Chang Yun-yi commander and deputy commander of the New 4th Corps and announced that the corps consisted of 7 divisions, headed by Su Yu, Chang Yun-yi etc.   While exaggerating the merits of the New 4th Corps on the one hand, they smeared Gen. Ho Ying-chin as the leader in the Pro-Japanese clique and claimed that the New 4th Corps Incident was the intrigue of the pro-Japanese clique to surrender China to Japan.   Furthermore, they staged "Anti-Ho Rally" in various places of the "Shensi-Kansu-Ninghsia Border Area" at which they launched malicious attacks.   Communist councillors Mao Tse-tung and Chen Shao-yu made 12 demands as the conditions to their attendance of the 2nd People's Political Consultative Conference so as to extort the Government. Highlights of the 12 demands are listed as follows:

1.   Rescind the "reactionary" order of January 17 and admit the errors.

2.   Take stern disciplinary actions against Ho Ying-chin, Ku Chu-tung and Shangkuan Yun-hsiang, the "ring leaders" of the Southern Anhwei Incident.

3.   Release Yeh Ting and let Yeh continue as the corps commander.

4.   Return all prisoners and weapons to the New 4th Corps.

5.   Pay gratuity to all officers and men of the New 4th Corps killed or wounded in the incident.

6.   Withdraw the anti-Communist forces from central China.

7. Arrest the leaders of the various pro-Japanese cliques and try them with our laws.

Meanwhile, the Communists stepped up their distorted propaganda activities at home and abroad to confuse peoples and cover up the rebellious activities. Their propaganda highlights are as follows:

1. Putting an end to the New 4th Corps is evidence that the KMT Government has abandoned the anti-Japanese policy, conducted military operations and surrendered to the Japanese.

2. Without the participation of the powerful Communist armies, the War of Resistance cannot be continued.

3. Use various means to instigate the overseas Chinese not to make donations to the KMT Government.

4. Contact Communists in Britain and the United States to conduct propaganda activities in their respective countries saying that civil war has broken out in China and that all assistance to China should be stopped.

As the Communists twisted the truth and made the above propaganda, the Japanese seized this opportunity to spread rumours and create dissension attempting to waver our determination to continue the sacred War of Resistance and realize his aim of aggression. At the time (March 8, 1941), Generalissimo Chiang, in making clear the Government's pains and in enabling the peoples at home and abroad to understand that the sanctions against the New 4th Corps were to straighten military discipline and strengthen our war efforts, made the following painful statement:

"The destiny of our nation and our people hinges on the unification of military orders and the successful implementation of political orders... In disposing the New 4th Corps Incident, our primary objective is to strengthen our efforts in the War of Resistance. The essentials are: (1) To deal a heavy blow against the enemy's illusion that our military discipline is shattered and our country is divided internally so as to weaken our war efforts; (2) To reiterate the importance of military discipline so that the rank and file of our armed forces are constantly aware of it and are inspired to serve the nation and strengthen the spirit of solidarity." His statement which was designed to dispel the enemy's rumours, expressed the hope that the Chinese Communists would repent to remedy what had been done wrong, so as not to be rejected by the Chinese people.

In August, 1941, parts of Chen Keng's and Po Yi-po's forces of the Communist 18th Army Group north of the Hung-Tun Highway, together with Sun Ting-kuo's force west of the Hsin River, launched a surprise attack on Chao Shao-chuan's force, one of Wang Ching-kuo's subordinate units, and captured Ma-pi. Again on August 12, they moved west to attack Lu Jui-ying's corps at Fu-shan. They captured regimental commander Kao Chiao of Lu's corps and regimental commander Li Hsi-chuan of Chao's corps and inflicted heavy losses on our forces. The combat effectiveness of our forces nearly fell apart. In late August, when the Japanese used Fu-ping (in northwestern Hopei Province) as a center to invade Shansi-Hopei border area, our Supreme Command, in an effort to conduct counter-mopping up operations, cabled our 1st and 2nd War Area forces on the north bank of the Yellow River to attack the Japanese forces in their areas in order to respond to the operations of the 18th Army Group. Subsequently, Yen Hsi-shan, commander of 2nd War Area cabled: "If the 18th Army Group releases regimental commanders Kao and Li whom it had captured in Fen-tung, our forces will then attack the Japanese in that area." On September 16, our Board of Military Operations cabled Chu Teh about their release but never received an answer.

When the Japanese converged on a Chinese corps under Wu Shih-min east of the Hsin River in Shansi in late September, 1941, the Communist 18th Army Group west of the river attacked Wu from behind rendering Wu's corps trapped between the Japanese and the 18th Army Group incapable of fighting the Japanese with its total strength. Heavy losses were sustained, and Wu committed suicide because of his defeat.

Having been subjected to the repeated attacks of the Communist 18th Army Group, our forces left behind enemy lines and our anti-Japanese organizations found themselves unable to hold on any longer. Meanwhile, the Communists continued to expand and arm themselves. With regard to the military operations against Japan, they sang out loud for "joint KMT and Communist Party leadership." Obviously, this meant that the actions of the Communist forces hereafter would not, even in name, come under the control of Supreme Command. While they established the unlawful regime on the one hand, they organized various borders, changed political set-ups, issued puppet notes and bonds, printed tax stamps and postal stamps, engaged in smuggling and opium peddling and squeezed the people constituting a divided situation on the other. Beyond the border areas, they instigated the people to oppose the draft and food taxation. Hence, ignorant people in Chien-shan in Hupei, and in Sung-tao in Szechuan-Hunan border area were fanned by the Communists into staging riots to harass the local areas.

In 1942, due to reverses in military operations, Soviet Russia found itself in a precarious situation and incapable of providing aid to foreign country. The Third International was suddenly disbanded, but Mao Tse-tung was pleased. Apart from reiterating his statement that the disbandment of Communist International had no effect on the Chinese Communists, he boasted of creative talent and independence in solving problems. Accordingly, Mao stepped up the purge and ruthlessly executed dissident cadres. As the cadres left the Communist Party in large number, the party became shaky. For a time, the Communist forces, incapable of launching large-scale operations against the Government forces, implemented the so-called "concealment policy" and shouted the slogan of "consolidation more important than development." Everywhere they went, they spread the rumours that Government forces were so weak that they could not carry on and that only the 18th Army Group and the New 4th Corps were the real strength ie fighting the Japanese. Meanwhile, they added fuel to fire by using "democracy" and "solidarity" as calls to befriend other parties, launch malicious attacks on the Government, make known their political views in an attempt to harass our rear areas and undermine our base in the War of Resistance. As prices soared and finance fluctuated, our people suffered more than ever. Through utter chaos, the Communists attempted to realize their aims of overthrowing the Government and seizing political power.

In September, 1943, the KMT 11th Plenary Meeting announced the convocation of the National Assembly one year after the termination of the War of Resistance to draft the constitution and implement constitutional rule. The second meeting of the 3rd People's Political Council decided "to solve the Communist problems through political means." Yet, the Communist reaction was that the time limit set by KMT for the implementation of constitutional rule was just empty talk to deceive people. And they continued to make active preparations for civil war. They stated that if the KMT really had in mind the implementation of democratic Government, it should accept militarily the following conditions laid down by the Communists:

1. Recognize the Communist regimes in the border areas and bases behind enemy lines and all the Communist armed forces behind enemy lines.

2. Restore the New 4th Corps and permit Communist forces to expand and be organized into 4 corps of 12 divisions.

At this time, again the Communists spread rumours and used every means to make propaganda aiming at the United States and saying that our expeditionary forces in western Yunnan, instead of fighting the Japanese with the weapons and ammunication provided by the United States, secretly stored them in the rear areas for subsequent use in the civil war. They attempted to drive a wedge between the United States and China in military cooperation. Their activities led to serious protest by Gen. Joseph W. Stilwell and indignation of American public opinion. Later, our Supreme Command and the U.S. authorities dispatched personnel who flew to western Yunnan to check the units and logistic commands. The results of the check dispelled the rumours. Nevertheless, the Communists continued to fabricate such rumours.

By the spring of 1944, Japanese forces had reached the end of their wits in the military situation. However, they made a final struggle before the arrival of the end. Fanatically, they launched offensives in the Central Plains, Hunan and Kwangsi. The situation was indeed critical. Military, the Communists ganged up with the Japanese by signing secret treaties and adopting the so-called "parallel movement" to launch converging attacks on our Government forces. Politically, they made extortions by advancing demands on the Government. Some of the major demands are listed below:

1.   That the Government give the Communist forces designations for at least 5 corps of 16 divisions.

2.   That the Government recognize the so-called "popularly elected anti-Japanese local administrations" in the Shensi-Kansu-Ninghsia Border Area, in North China, Central China and South China as well as the installations therein.

3.   That a coalition government be established.

In addition, at a time when the situation was most serious, the Communist demanded the reorganization of the Supreme Command attempting to create chaos in our command center and place our military forces in a precarious position.

On the eve of the Allied victory over Japan in 1945, the Communists boasted of 650,000 regular troops and 2,000,000 militia.   Thus, they shifted their strategy from guerrilla warfare to regular warfare, and from rural areas to cities. They attempted to launch massive moves by seizing cities.   Accordingly, they massed major forces in Hopei, Shantung and Honan and took advantage of our counter-offensive against the Japanese to attack Government forces and enter key cities abandoned by the Japanese.   They seized the nation's lifeline.   In areas along the coast, they made scattered activities and attempted to establish strong points.   The established contact with Allied forces ahead of the Government forces to seize international status as capital in their future blackmail against the Government.

On June 25, the Communists instigated our peace preservation units in Shun-hua, northern Shensi to rebel, and further swallowed neighboring units. As the captured Shun-hua Hsien and other important hsiangs and chens, they fought bitterly against Government forces.   Fighting lasted until the end of July when the Communists could no longer sustain and retreated.   Meanwhile, conflicts erupted in eastern Chekiang, western Chekiang, southern Shantung and western Shantung, greatly impeding our full-scale counteroffensive.

On August 10, the Japanese Government announced the acceptance of the proclamation of the Potsdam Conference demanding its unconditional surrender to China, the United States, Britain and Soviet Russia.   Upon receipt of Japan's declaration of surrender, the National Military Council of the Chinese Government immediately instructed all armed forces in the country to wait for orders pertaining to the acceptance of surrender in accordance with Allied agreements. In an order to the 18th Army Group, the council specifically instructed all its units to remain where they were until further orders; and, for those committed to area commanders, under any circumstances, not to make any unauthorized move.

But the Communists flatly disobeyed the council's order and Chu Teh, in the name of the "Yen-an Headquarters," issued on August 10 "Seven Orders of the Day," directing Communist forces in various places to resort to all-out violence and effect the following military movements:

1.   "For the sake of coordinating with the Soviet Red Army's entry into

China": (a) troops under Lu Cheng-tsao were to move from Shansi and Suiyuan into Chahar and Jehol; (b) troops under Chang Hsueh-shih were to move from Hopei and Chahar into Jehol and Liaoning; (c) troops under Wan Yi were to move from Shantung and Hopei into Liaoning; (d) troops under Li Yun-chang were to move from Hopei and Jehol into Liaoning and Kirin; and (e) Korean Communist troops were also to enter the Northeast Provinces.

2. "For the sake of coordinating with the Outer Mongolian troops' entry into Inner Mongolia, Suiyuan, Chahar, and Jehol": (a) troops under Ho Lung were to move northward from Suiyuan; and (b) troops under Nieh Yung-tseng were to move northward from Chahar and Jehol.

3. All troops in Shansi were to be "placed under Ho Lung's unified command and to occupy the areas along the Tatung-Pucheng Railway and in the Fen River valley."

4. In order to seize or sever "all principal arteries of communication in the country": all Communist troops along the Peiping-Liaoning Railway, the Peiping-Suiyuan Railway, the Tatung-Pucheng Railway, the Tsang-chow-Shih-chia-chuang Railway, the Cheng-ting-Tai-yuan Railway, the Pei-ching Railway, the Tao-tsing Railway, the Tientsin-Pukow Railway, the Shanghai-Nanking Railway, the Nanking-Wuhu Railway, the Shanghai-Hangchow Railway, the Canton-Kowloon Railway, the Chao-chow-Swatow Railway; and all Communist troops on both sides of principal arteries of communication in other "liberated areas" were "to go actively into attack."

5. All Communist forces in various places could send notes to the Japanese and puppet forces setting time limit for them to lay down their arms. Should they refuse, they would be destroyed resolutely.

6. Military control would be exercised in the occupied areas. Individuals who sabotaged or resisted would be dealt with as traitors.

On August 14 Chu Teh and Peng Teh-huai cabled our Supreme Commander openly defying the orders of the Supreme Command directing them to remain and await further orders. Calling himself "commander-in-chief of the Anti-Japanese Forces in the Liberated Areas of China," Chu Teh again notified Neiji Okamura to surrender his forces to the designated Communists delegates in the following areas:

1. Neih Yung-tseng would accept the surrender of the Japanese forces in north China in Fu-Ping area.

2. Chen Yi would accept the surrender of the Japanese forces in eastern China in Tien-chang area.

3. Li Hsien-nien would accept the surrender of the Japanese forces in Hupei and Honan Provinces in Ta-pieh Shan area.

4. Tseng Shen would accept the surrender of the Japanese in Kwangtung in Tung-wan area.

On August 17, the Chinese Communists, in the name of Chu Teh, presented a set of six demands to the Government:

1. In accepting the surrender of Japanese and puppet forces and in concluding agreements or treaties for that purpose, the Government should consult first the Anti-Japanese People's Armed Forces in "liberated areas" in order to reach unanimity of views.

2. All Anti-Japanese People's Armed Forces in "liberated areas" and in occupied areas should have the right, under the terms of the Potsdam Declaration and the procedure as laid down by the Allies, to accept the surrender of Japanese and puppet troops and to take over their arms and supplies.

3. The Anti-Japanese People's Armed Forces in "liberated areas" and in occupied areas should have the right to send delegates to take part in accepting Japanese surrender and in administering local affairs after the surrender.

4. All Anti-Japanese People's Armed Forces in "liberated areas" should have the right to designate representatives to the peace conference and to United Nations meetings.

5. Generalissimo Chiang should be asked to stop the civil war by assigning troops in "liberated areas" to accept the surrender of the Japanese and puppet troops they have surrounded in their areas, and by assigning "Kuomintang troops" to accept the surrender of Japanese troops they have surrounded in their own areas.

6. A multi-party conference, including also non-partisan representatives, should be called at once to form a democratic coalition government to effect democratic political and economic reforms.

Thus, the Communist forces in various areas became most active looting the weapons of the Japanese and puppet forces, intercepting Government forces and sabotaging the nation's communication nets. Furthermore, they occupied important lines of communications, impeded the advance of Government forces and expanded their areas. In addition, they teamed up with the Russian and the Mongolian forces to carve the Northeast China, Suiyuan, Chahar and Jehol provinces, and divided China throwing the nation into utter chaos after V-J Day.

In summarizing the Communist attempts to undermine our efforts in the War of Resistance, we can see that Communist fanaticism to-day is the result of their opportunism, breach of faith and inhuman measures to realize their intrigues of betraying our nation for personal gains and of communizing the world at the expense of our national interests, during the past 14 years of war against Japan. They will become more vicious in the future. If peoples throughout the world do not heighten their vigilance and take actions against them, the holocaust of mankind and the end of the world may not be too distant.

CHAPTER EIGHT
Sino-U.S. Cooperation

Section 1. Sino-U.S. Diplomatic Relations

Traditionally, the relations between the United States and the Republic of China have always been most harmonious. In 1931, when the Japanese militarists launched the Mukden Incident which unveiled the Sino-Japanese War, China appealed to the League of Nations and the signatories to the Non-War Pact to maintain justice. Although the United States did not join the League of Nations, it expressed willingness to cooperate with the League in its measures to stop the Japanese aggression. Repeatedly, the United States invoked the Nine-Power Pact to denounce Japan. On January 2, 1932, the Japanese forces invaded Chin-chow. On January 7, 1932, Secretary of State Henry A. Stimson of the United States dispatched a memorandum to China and Japan, the well-known "Stimson's Principle of Non-Recognition." The announcement of this memorandum led to the attention of the world, and provided unbounded moral assistance to China. It also dealt a heavy moral blow against Japan. Subsequently, it was adopted by the Assembly of the League of Nations and became one of the obligations to be observed by various nations toward China. In 1933, Japan invaded North China and forced China to sign the Tangku Truce Agreement. On April 17, 1934, Japan issued the absurd Amane Statement. At that time, many nations adopted the attitude of "watching a fire from the other side of the river." Britain and France merely made interpellations. The United States was the only nation which opposed Japan in consonance with the spirit of Stimson's principle non-recognition. American public opinion clearly denounced Japan on her ambition in aggression. This fully reflected the American foreign policy toward China and Japan.

When the full-scale War of Resistance broke out on July 7, 1937, American Secretary of States Cordell Hull delivered an address on July 14 in which he advocated the maintenance of international peace and justice, the avoidance of the use of arms as a means to promote national policy, the settlement of disputes between nations through peaceful means, respect of treaty dignity, disarmament, and abolition of trade barriers as a basis in establishing understanding among nations. On October 5, President Franklin D. Roosevelt, in his quarantine speech, urged all peaceloving peoples to unite and maintain peace and to quarantine by force those nations which broke international order. This marked the beginning of the American moral support to China.

During the preliminary phase of the Sino-Japanese War when the Japanese rapidly pushed into the inland of China, American public opinion regretted the situation and predicted that China would be defeated. Little did the Americans realize that one year later the spirit of China became higher and higher. Hence, as sympathy turned into respect, the United States was willing to provide material assistance to China. In July, 1939, the United States notified Japan of the abrogation of the U.S.-Japan Trade and Navigation Treaty. In January, 1940, restrictions were placed on the shipping of gasoline, scrap iron, machinery and other military materials to Japan. In July, 1941, the United States formally froze all Japanese assets in the country. This was the U.S. economic sanction against Japan. With regard to China's finance, the United States rendered assistance to stabilize Chinese currency and established Board of Foreign Exchange Stabilization Fund to maintain the exchange rate between Chinese currency and American dollars. In addition, the U.S. Import and Export Bank provided credit loans to China on four occasions totalling U.S.$120,000,000.

In October, 1941, the United States Congress passed the abolition of the Chinese Exclusion Act and legally gave Chinese nationals the right to become naturalized American citizen. On December 7, 1941, the war in the Pacific broke out. In February, 1942, the United States in consultation with Britain, notified the Chinese Government that they wish to abolish their extra-territorial rights and other special privileges provided in the past unequal treaties in China and to negotiate mutually beneficial treaty in accordance with the principle of equality. All these friendly gestures indicated the faith of the American Government and people to uphold justice. Such spirit of righteousness coincided with the traditional Chinese spirit of "reviving the extinguished States and restore families whose line of succession had been cut off" and will never be forgotten.

Section 2.   Military Cooperation

In the spring of 1941, the United States Congress passed the Lend-Lease Act to China. In November of the same year, a military mission was sent to China to help equip and train China's new army. Due to transportation difficulties and the lack of transportation means, only a small quantity of U.S. equipment arrived. However, U.S. assistance to the Chinese Air Force was more successful. In early, 1941, the United States Government gave permission for American volunteer pilots to fly U.S. fighters. On August 1, the American Volunteer Group (AVG) was formally established under then Col. Claire L. Chennault and became a part of the Chinese Armed Forces. The AVG provided effective air defense of southwestern China.

On May 6, 1941, based on the Lend-Lease Act, the United States formally signed the Lend-Lease Agreement with China. First of all, emphasis was placed on stepping up the transportation on the Yunnan-Burma Road. The lend-lease materials included trucks, spare parts, gasoline, lubricants and materials needed to widen the road. Traffic communications experts were dispatched to survey the Yunnan-Burma Road and make improvements. By the end of November, the transportability of the road rose from 4,000 tons per month to 15,000 tons per month. As the transportability of the road was rising, the United States Government planned to make available U.S.$15,000,000 loan for the construction of a railway from Burma to China, so as to greatly increase the flow of materials from Rangoon to our rear area. Unfortunately, this plan never materialized, as Japan scored military victories in Burma.

After the outbreak of the Pacific War in December, 1941, President Roosevelt proposed to name the 26 anti-Axis nations, the "United Nations" and invited the representatives of these 26 nations to meet in Washington and sign the United Nations' announcement on January 1, 1942 to show their willingness to fight against the "Axis Nations." On January 4, the United Nations appointed Generalissimo Chiang as the Supreme Commander of the China Theater (including Vietnam and Thailand) of the United Nations and the Supreme Command of this Theater was established, to be the highest strategic command on land over Southeast Asia.

In March, 1942, at the request of China, President Roosevelt sent General Stilwell to set up in Chungking the U.S. Force Command of the China Theater. In addition to commanding all American forces and certain Chinese forces on the battlefields of China, India and Burma, General Stilwell was also appointed chief of staff to the Supreme Commander of the China Theater. In order to ensure close coordination, it was prescribed that on every Thursday General Stilwell, or his representatives would participate in a conference held by the Chinese High Military Command to review the war situation of the previous week and prepare a full-scale operational plan. Meanwhile, the Flying Tigers under Gen. Chennault was re-named the U.S. 14th Air Force and remained in China to fight the Japanese. Sino-U.S. military cooperation became closer than ever.

In March, 1942, after Japan had penetrated into Burma, our military posture became increasingly difficult, and operational materials were extremely lacking. Meanwhile, the Allies concentrated their efforts in defeating Germany first. With the European Theater receiving first priority in the supply of strategic materials, little was left to supply the China Theater. China's only line of communications between Assam in India and the Yunnan Plateaus was the air supply route over the Hump in the Himalayas. As the road was frequently subjected to the attacks of windstorms and snow-storms, it was only ably to provide the gasoline, bombs and ammunition needed by the U.S. 14th Air Force under the command of Gen. Chennault. It was not possible to provide China with the most urgently needed materials such as gasoline, automobile parts, railroad equipment, guns, tanks and other heavy equipment. This unfavorable situation continued until January, 1943 when the Allies at the Casablanca Conference, decided to restore land communications to China and to step up the airlift over the Hump. In May of the same year, when the Washington Conference was held, it was felt that should China break down in her resistance, it would lead to serious consequences for the Allied forces in Asia. Deliberate considerations resulted in the concurrence to give priority to the Military Air Transport Command so as to increase the monthly airlift over the Hump to 10,000 tons. The decision was made to launch offensives in Burma after the end of the monsoon season in the fall of 1943. The offensive plans were formulated in detail later at the Quebec Conference.

At the Quebec Conference (known as the Quadrant Conference in the United States) in August, 1943, the Allies decided to employ every possible means to open the land lines of communications to China in order to provide China with adequate assistance and to achieve maximum results in the Asian Theater. Accordingly, the Southeast Asia Allied Forces Supreme Command with Adm. Lord Louis Mountbatten as its supreme commander and Gen. Stilwell as the deputy was established. The military operations in the China Theater under Generalissimo Chiang were not included in this command. Gen. Stilwell continued as Generalissimo Chiang's chief of staff and directed the Chinese and American forces in Burma. The British and American air forces in Burma were organized into the Eastern Air Command under Gen. George Stratemeyer. On October 1, the Sino-U.S. Composite Wing was activated in Kwei-lin with Col. Morse as the commander. This wing was under the unified command of Gen. Chennault. Meanwhile, in conjunction with the U.S. Army engineers, the Chinese forces in India swiftly extended the Ledo Road. Pipelines were laid parallel to the road so that the flow of automobile fuel to China could be increased. Meanwhile, the monthly airlift over the Hump rose to 20,000 tons. Flying Fortress bases were built in Szechuan and Yunnan Provinces for use by U.S. Air Force to bomb Japan proper.

In October, 1943, in accordance the Allied established plans, the Chinese forces in India moved from the Ledo Road into the Hukawng Valley to link up with Brig. Gen. Merrill's jungle force in an attempt to drive the Japanese out of northern Burma and re-open the Yunnan-Burma Road. Despite extremely inclement weather and exceedingly difficult terrain, Sino-American forces wiped out the crack Japanese 18th Division which had taken Singapore before. In an exploitation of success, our 14th and 50th Divisions were airlifted by U.S. Air Force from Yunnan to an air base in India where they were equipped with U.S. weapons and then were flown to Burma to take part in the operations in Hukawng Valley. In August, 1944, our forces captured Myitkyina Airfield, while our Expeditionary Forces crossed the Salween River from Pao-shan, Yunnan and advanced toward northern Burma for the offensive.

A strong-willed soldier, Gen. Stilwell had a strong sense of responsibility. While in China, the contributions he made toward the defeat of the Japanese were commendable. Regrettably, he lacked a deep understanding of the Chinese Communists. On October 21, 1944, he was relieved and recalled to the United States. In, time, to facilitate subsequent operations, the China-Burma-India (CBI) Theater was divided into the India-Burma Theater and the China Theater. Gen. Deniel I. Sultan and Gen. Albert C. Wedemeyer respectively commanded the U.S. forces in India-Burma and in China. In October 31, Gen. Wedemeyer arrived in China to become Generalissimo Chiang's chief of staff. Deployed along the Irrawady River north of Kalewa, the Sino-American forces planned to move south to central Burma and head for Walawbum. Adm. Mounbatten's forces launched amphibious offensives from the south in order to capture Rangoon. When the monsoon season ended, the Sino-American forces under Gen. Sultan crossed the Irrawady River. In early November, they took Toungoo. In December, they cleared the supply route to Bhamo and captured Bhamo. On January 26, 1945, they linked up with our expeditionary forces at Mongyu and opened the China-India Road. On March 24 they linked up with British forces at Kyaume.

In the winter of 1944, the GHQ Army, China Theater was activated with Gen. Ho Ying-chin as the commander-in-chief in order to gear to the Allied operations. With the headquarters in Kun-ming, it commanded 4 front armies. Its missions were to organize and train the U.S. equipped forces for final, decisive battles against the Japanese forces on the China mainland.

In January, 1945, as the Ledo Road (later known as the Stilwell Road) reached China, land transportation increased greatly. 54,000 tons of petroleum products were moved monthly by pipelines. Similarly, the air transportability over the Hump rose 46,000 tons. In order to handle these materials, the Logistic Command, GHQ Chinese Army was activated on February 1 to maintain contact with the U.S. Supply Division (the famous SOS). Initially, the logistic command was organized jointly by the United States and China with Lt. Gen. Childs as the commander. In June of the same year. Gen. Childs was recalled to the United States and was replaced by Lt. Gen. Pai Yu-sheng. In time, 35 Chinese infantry divisions and a number of special units were equipped with U.S. weapons vastly enhancing the combat effectiveness of the Chinese forces. American officers were dispatched to Kwei-lin and Kun-ming to assist in the training of the U.S. equipped forces. The training record was most outstanding. According to the Marshall report, the materials provided to China were valued over US$500,000,000 excluding transportation. However, considering the fact the U.S. assistance to other allies totalled US$20,000,000,000, what China received was small indeed. China was justified in receiving the assistance, since she had fought for so long and contributed so much to the war in Asia.

As the Sino-American forces applied increasing pressure, the Japanese forces were shaken. Subsequently, the U.S. War Department directed the 5th Army and the 9th Army which had recently defeated in Axis in Germany and

Italy, to join the battle of order in the China Theater. Under the direct and close cooperation between the GHQ Chinese Army and the U.S. Operations Command in China (under Maj. Gen. Robert B. McClure), most of the U.S. equipped Chinese units completed their training. These units coordinated with Sino-U.S. Air Force Composite Wing in dealing a heavy blow against the Japanese during the Battle of Western Hunan. Later, they recaptured Kwei-lin and Liu-chow. As the Chinese and American forces were poised for general counter-offensive, Japan accepted the terms of the Postdam Declaration and announced her unconditional surrender.

During this time, most of our forces were located in southwestern China. To seek early acceptance of the Japanese surrender and the restoration of order, our forces pushed forward on land, at sea, by air and on foot. The United States also rendered assistance in shipping and flying our forces as well as completing the repatriation of the Japanese nationals and prisoners of war, Koreans and our Taiwanese compatriots on the scheduled dates from the designated ports.

All in all, the United States moved from sympathy to assistance and co-operation with China in World War II. Such assistance which can never be forgotten has left a glorious page in the annals of the twentieth century.

CHAPTER NINE
Surrender and Demobilization

Section 1. Surrender

1. Surrender Arrangement

In the summer of 1945, sandwiched between the Chinese and American forces, the Japanese forces were about to collapse. On July 26, 1945, Japan was given the last warning, in the form of a joint proclamation by Generalissimo Chiang Kai-shek, President Truman and Prime Minister Churchill, to choose either "conditional surrender" or "prompt and utter destruction."

The following is the full text of the Proclamation by the United States, the United Kingdom and the Republic of China calling upon Japan to surrender unconditionally or suffer prompt and utter destruction:

"a. We, the President of the United States, the President of the National Government of the Republic of China and the Prime Minister of Great Britain, representing the hundreds of millions of our countrymen, have conferred and agreed that Japan shall be given an opportunity to end this war.

"b. The prodigious land, sea and air forces of the United States, the British Empire and of China are many times reinforced. Their armies and air fleets from the west are poised to strike the final blows upon Japan. Their military power is sustained and inspired by the determination of all the Allied Nations to prosecute the war against Japan until she ceases to resist.

"c. The result of the futile and senseless German resistance to the might of the aroused free people of the world stands forth in awful clarity as an example to the people of Japan. The might that now converges on Japan is immeasurably greater than that which, when applied to the resisting Nazis, necessarily laid waste the lands, the industry and the method of life of the whole German people. The full application of our military power, backed by our resolve, will win the inevitable and complete destruction of the Japanese armed forces and just as inevitably the utter destruction of the Japanese homeland.

"d. The time has come for Japan to decide whether she will continue to be controlled by those self-willed militaristic advisers whose unintelligent calculations have brought the Empire of Japan to the threshold of annihilation, or whether she will follow the path of reason.

"e. Following are our terms. We will not deviate from them. There are no alternatives. We shall brook no delay.

"f.   There must be eliminated for all time the authority and influence of those who have deceived and misled the people of Japan into embarking on world conquest, for we insist that a new order of peace, security and justice will be impossible until responsible militarism is driven from the world.

"g.   Until such a new order is established and until there is convincing proof that Japan's war-making power is destroyed, Japanese territory to be designated by the Allies shall be occupied to secure the achievement of the basic objectives we are here setting forth.

"h.   The terms of the Cairo Declaration shall be carried out and Japanese sovereignty shall be limited to the Islands of Honshu, Hokkaido, Kyushu, Shikoku and such minor islands as we determine.

"i.   The Japanese military forces, after being completely disarmed, shall be permitted to return to their homes with the opportunity to lead peaceful and productive lives.

"j.   We do not intend that the Japanese shall be enslaved as a race or destroyed as a nation, but stern justice shall be meted out to all war criminals, including those who have visited cruelties upon our prisoners.   The Japanese Government shall remove all obstacles to the revival and strengthening of democratic tendencies among the Japanese people.   Freedom of speech, of religion, and of thought, as well as respect for the human rights shall be established.

"k.   Japan shall be permitted to maintain such industries as will sustain her economy and permit the exaction of just reparations in kind, but not those which would enable her to rearm for war.   To this end, access to, as distinguished from control of, raw materials shall be permitted.   Eventual Japanese participation in world trade relations shall be permitted.

"l.   The occupying forces of the Allies shall be withdrawn from Japan as soon as the objectives have been accomplished and there has been established in accordance with the freely expressed will of the Japanese people a peacefully inclined and responsible government.

"m.   We call upon the Government of Japan to proclaim now the unconditional surrender of all Japanese armed forces, and to provide proper and adequate assurance of their good faith in such action.   The alternative for Japan is prompt and utter destruction."

The Ministry of Foreign Affairs of Japan, after receiving this ultimatum from China, the United States, and Britain called an emergency cabinet meeting and for a time refused to surrender and announced that "The Government of Japan is determined to fight to the bitter and sad end."   Subsequently, on August 5 and 7, the United States Air Force dropped atomic bombs over Hiroshima and Nagasaki in consonance with the large-scale counteroffensive that the Chinese forces were about to launch in South China.   Soviet Russia seized this opportunity to declare war on Japan.   Knowing that the fate of its ultimate defeat was beyond repair, Japan appealed to the United Nations for more lenient peace terms before it would end the war. Immediately afterwards, the Allies issued a statement giving Japan a flat refusal. However, they reiterated their explanation that the so-called "unconditional surrender does not imply the destruction of the Japanese race nor the enslavement of the Japanese people."

At 1950 hours, August 10, the Japanese Government requested Switzerland and Sweden to forward its surrender text to the Allies in which it indicated its willingness to accept the provisions of the Potsdam Declaration and to make unconditional surrender to the United Nations. However, it requested that the Emperor be retained as the titular head. On August 11, on behalf of China, the United States, Britain and Soviet Russia, U.S. Secretary of States Byrnes, in a reply to Japan, accepted its surrender request. At first, Japan made no indication. The American and British fleets which were poised for action were about to attack in force, should Japan refuse to surrender. On August 15, the Ministry of Foreign Affairs, Executive Yuan of the National Government formally received Japan's surrender message to China, the United States, Britain and Soviet Russia. On the same day, Generalissimo Chiang, our Supreme Commander, sent a telegram to Neiji Okamura, supreme commander of the Japanese forces in China, in which he directed six principles for the surrender[1] and appointed Gen. Ho Ying-chin, Commander-in-Chief of the Chinese Army, to accept the Japanese surrender in the name of the Supreme Commander, China Theater. Meanwhile, in his broadcast to the nation's people and servicemen and to the peoples in the world, Generalissimo Chiang hoped that "all men on earth—wherever they lived, in the East or West and whatever the color of their skin may be—will someday be linked together in close fellowship like members of one family and develop international understanding and mutual trust so that this world war may be the last world war. As to Japan, we will "remember not evil against others" and will not revenge. Stupendous and difficult tasks will demand greater strength and sacrifice than the years of war. We must march forward on the great road of democracy and unity and give our collective support to the ideals of lasting peace."

---

[1] Six principles:

   a. The Japanese Government has announced its unconditional surrender.

   b. The Japanese commander should direct the Japanese forces under his command to cease all military actions and dispatch representatives to Yu-shan to receive orders from General Ho Ying-chin, Commander-in-Chief of the Chinese Army.

   b. After cessation of military actions, the Japanese forces may retain their arms and equipment for the time being, maintain the status quo and order and traffic communications in their present stations while awaiting orders from General Ho Ying-chin, Commander-in-Chief of the Chinese Army.

   d. All Japanese airhraft and ships will remain in their present stations; however, Japanese ships in the Yangtze River will assefble in I-chang and Sha-shih.

   e. The Japanese forces should not destroy any facilities or material.

   f. The Japanese commander and his subordinate officers should be held personally responsible for the execution of the above orders and should reply swiftly.

The following is the text of a radio message by Generalissimo Chiang Kai-shek to the peace-loving nations of the world and the soldiers and civilians of China.

"Right will triumph over might—this great truth which we never once doubted has been finally vindicated. Our faith in justice through black and hopeless days and eight long years of struggle has today been rewarded. The historical mission of our National Revolution has at last been fulfilled.

"For the peace that lies before us we pay grateful tribute, first to the millions of our soldiers and civilians who so bravely sacrificed their lives; to our Allies who fought by our side for freedom and right; and to the Father of our Republic, Dr. Sun Yat-sen, who labored all his life-time to guide our National Revolution to success. But for him we would not be enjoying this day of victory. Above all, we the Christians all over the world, join in thanksgiving to our righteous and merciful God.

"The people of China suffered and sacrificed more each year as our long war of defense went on. But the confidence that we would emerge victorious also grew from day to day. Our fellow countrymen in the enemy-occupied areas had to endure a long night of devastation and disgrace. Today they are liberated and can see again the White Sun in the Blue Sky (China's Flag). The cheers and rejoicings of our armies and people have their deepest meaning in this new freedom of our long oppressed compatriots.

"We have won the victory. But it is not yet the final victory. The universal power of righteousness has not simply achieved one more triumph. We and the peoples of all the world fervently hope that this war may be the last war in which civilized nations engage.

"If this is really to be the last war in human history, then our people will not feel that the indescribable cruelties and humiliations they have endured are too big a price to have paid or that peace for them has been too long delayed.

"Even in periods of deepest gloom and despair our people, with a fine inherited loyalty, fortitude, magnanimity and goodwill, held to the conviction that sacrifices made for justice and humanity would surely be followed by rightful compensations.

"The greatest compensation has been the mutual trust and confidence between peace-loving peoples of the world born out of our common struggle. With the flesh and blood of their armed youth the United Nations built a long continuous dyke against the tide of aggression. All who took part in the great conflict are now allies, united not simply for temporary advantage, but rather because of a great common faith—noble and enduring—that binds us together. No intrigues can wreck this great union.

"It is my sincere belief that all men on earth—wherever they live, in the East or the West, and whatever the color of their skin may be—will someday be linked together in close fellowship like members of one family. World war is indivisible, and world peace, too, is indivisible. It has encouraged international under-standing and mutual trust, which will serve as a powerful barrier against future wars.

"I am deeply moved when I think of the teachings of Jesus Christ that we should do unto others as we would have them do unto us and love our enemies. My fellow countrymen know that "Remember not evil against others" and "Do good to all men" have been highest virtues taught by our own sages. We have always said that the violent militarism of Japan is our enemy, not the people of Japan. Although the armed forces of the enemy have been defeated and must be made to observe strictly all the terms of surrender, yet we should not for a moment think of revenge or heap abuses upon the innocent people of Japan. We can only pity them because they have been so sadly deceived and misled, and hope that they will break away from the wrong doings and crimes of their na-tion. Let all our fellow citizens—soldiers and civilians—remember this.

"The enemy's imperialistic designs on China have been thoroughly crushed. But relaxation and pride are not rewards of victory that we seek. Peace, when fighting has entirely ceased, will confront us with stupendous and difficult tasks, demanding greater strength and sacrifice than the years of war. At times we may feel that the problems of peace that descend upon us are more trying even than those we met during the war.

"I think first of one very serious problem—how to make the peoples mis-guided by Fascist rulers admit their mistakes and defeat, and recognize that our struggle for national independence, democracy and the welfare of all the people, is more in harmony with truth and human rights than their struggle for land and power by means of violence and terrorism. Permanent world peace can be established only upon the basis of democratic freedom and equality and the brotherly cooperation of all nations and races. We must march forward on the great road of democracy and unity and give our collective support to the ideals of lasting peace.

"I urge all of our friends of the Allied nations and all my own countrymen to face the fact that the peace we have gained by arms is not necessarily the be-ginning of permanent peace. Only if our enemies are conquered on the battle-ground of reason, only if they repent thoroughly of their folly and become lovers of world peace like ourselves, can we hope to satisfy the yearning of mankind for peace and achieve the final goal of the great war that has just ended."

On 18 August, Generalissimo Chiang authorized General Ho Ying-chin, C-in-C of Chinese Army, the following functions:

a. By order of the Generalissimo; to handle the surrender of all Japanese forces in the China Theater.

b. To order the war zones and front armies to handle the surrender of Japanese forces in those areas under their jurisdiction.

c.   By order of the Generalissimo, to issue orders to the Supreme Commander of the enemy forces in China Theater.

d.   By order of the Generalissimo, to work closely with U.S. military personnel in the China Theater on the surrender of enemy forces in the U.S. occupied areas and the joint occupation areas.

e.   To handle the relief of refugees and the restoration of communications and transportation in the recovered areas.

f.   To direct the war zones and front armies to reorganize the troops of the puppet regime and to punish the disobedient troops of the puppet regime in the respective areas under their jurisdiction.

g.   To be responsible for the prompt handling of the puppet regime in Nanking and for the restoration of order in Nanking and its surrounding areas, awaiting the National Government's return to the Capital.

h.   By order of the Generalissimo, to dispatch troops, during the acceptance of the surrender of the enemy forces, to those cities and seaports of military, political, economic or communications value in order to establish an advantageous situation for the handling of enemy forces and the restoration of order.

i.   May suggest to the Generalissimo for punishment those unauthorized units which accepted surrender without approval and with the intention of jeopardizing the plan for the acceptance of surrender.

j.   The enemy forces must surrender to those units authorized by the Generalissimo, and the C-in-C of the Chinese Army may punish with arms to those enemy units which surrender or hand over their defensive areas to unauthorized units, or disobey our orders and may directly punish the disobedient commanding officers or the supreme commander of the enemy forces.

k.   To direct, supervise and handle with full authority the Party and administrative matters in the recovered areas.

l.   To be in command of those units of various war zones on their way to the recovered areas and those units already in the recovered areas.   Those units of various war zones left in the rear will remain under the command of their respective war zone by direction of the National Military Council.

On 21 August, Tekeo Imai, representative of Neiji Okamura, Supreme Commander of Japanese Forces in China, and a party of seven arrived at Chichiang by air and were called before Hsiao I-su, Chief of Staff of the Chinese Army General Headquarters, who, on behalf of General Ho Ying-chin, C-in-C of Chinese Army, handed them First Memorandum back to Neiji Okamura in Nanking on 23 August by the same aircraft.   The Memorandum reads as follows:

"a.   By order of Generalissimo Chiang Kai-shek, Supreme commander of the China Theater, I, C-in-C of the Army of the China Theater, accept the surrender of Japanese high commanders, all Army, Navy, Air Force and auxiliary units in China (excluding the three Provinces of Liaoning, Kirin and Heilungchiang), Taiwan and the areas north of 16 degrees latitude in Indochina.

"b. General Neiji Okamura, Supreme Commander of Japanese forces in China, should immediately execute all the instructions of the C-in-C, Chinese Army, upon receipt of the Memorandum, as well as all Japanese forces in Taiwan and in the areas north of 16 degrees latitude in Indochina, which shall surrender under the command of General Neiji Okamura.

"c. After receipt of the Memorandum, General Neiji Okamura should immediately issue the following orders:

"(1) All Japanese Army, Navy and Air Force units and their auxiliary units in the areas under jurisdiction of the C-in-C of the Chinese Army (areas as mentioned in paragraph a.) should stop hostile action of any kind.

"(2) All Japanese Army, Navy and Air Force units and their auxiliary units should stay where they are, or have been appointed, to await further orders and should not surrender, negotiate with or hand over any supplies to military commanders not authorized by Generalissimo Chiang, or the C-in-C of the Chinese Army.

"(3) All Japanese Army, Navy and Air Force units and their auxiliary units in the areas under the jurisdiction of the C-in-C, Chinese Army, should keep their weapons, ammunition, aviation materiel, naval vessels, merchant vessels, vehicles, all transportation and communications equipment, airfields, harbors, piers, workshops, warehouses, supplies, all buildings and military installations, documents, files and intelligence materials in good shape. General Neiji Okamura is responsible for these items, until handed over to personnel authorized by the C-in-C, Chinese Army.

"(4) All Japanese Army, Navy and Air Force units and their auxiliary units in the areas under the jurisdiction of the C-in-C, Chinese Army, should maintain order in their respective areas until those units and commanding officers, authorized by Generalissimo Chiang or C-in-C, Chinese Army arrive. During this period, they should not hand over the administrative organs to any units or representatives not authorized by Generalissimo Chiang or the C-in-C, Chinese Army.

"(5) All POW's, captured civilians and officials of the Allied Nations in the areas under the jurisdiction of the C-in-C, Chinese Army, should be freed immediately, furnished with adequate clothing, food, quarters and medical care, and made ready to send to those places appointed by the C-in-C, Chinese Army.

"d. In order to supervise the execution of the orders of the C-in-C, Chinese Army, by Japanese forces, Lt. General Leng Hsin, Deputy Chief of Staff of the Chinese Army, shall come to Nanking first to set up the Advanced Post of the C-in-C, Chinese Army. All requests made by Lt. General Leng Hsin should be executed immediately.

"e. The time and place for General Neiji Okamura to personally receive the formal procedures for the surrender from the C-in-C, Chinese Army and the order of Generalissimo Chiang will be notified later after the acceptance of surrender by General MacArthur, Supreme Commander of Allied Forces."

On 27 August, Lt. General Leng Hsin, Deputy Chief of Staff of Chinese Army, flew from Chih-chiang to Nanking to set up the Advanced Post in preparation for accepting the surrender.

2. Signing of surrender

On 3 September, Japanese representatives Ohi Shigemetsu and Sajiro Umetsu signed the formal surrender treaty on board the U.S.S. Missouri, in the presence of our representative, General Hsu Yung-chang. In the meantime the signing of the surrender of Japanese forces in the China Theater was scheduled to be held on September 9 in Nanking and the GHQ Chinese Army staff and those representatives sent by the various Yuan and Ministries of the Central Government were flown from Chih-chiang to Nanking before September 8.

At 0900 hours on September 9, General Ho Ying-chin, as representative of the Supreme Commander, China Theater of the Chinese Armed Forces presided over the 20 minutes signing ceremony of the unconditional surrender of Japan in the China Theater. The document of surrender reads as follows:

a. The Imperial Government and Imperial Supreme Commander of the Japanese Empire has surrendered unconditionally to the Supreme Commander of the United Nations' Forces.

b. The First Order of the Supreme Commander of the United Nations' Forces reads: "All Japanese Army, Navy and Air Force units and their auxiliary units in the Republic of China (excluding the three Northeastern Provinces), Taiwan and in those areas north of 16 degrees latitude in Indo-China shall surrender to Generalissimo Chiang.

c. All we commanding officers of Japanese Army, Navy and Air Force units and auxiliary units in subject areas are willing to surrender unconditionally to Generalissimo Chiang.

d. I, Commander of Japanese Forces in China, have ordered all commanding officers of Japanese Army, Navy, and Air Force units, and their attached units in those areas mentioned in paragraph to surrender to the representative appointed by Generalissimo Chiang, General Ho Ying-chin, C-in-C of the Chinese Army in the China Theater and to those representatives in various areas appointed by General Ho.

e. All surrendered Japanese Army, Navy and Air Force units have stopped hostile actions immediately and have remained where they were until further orders. All weapons, ammunition, equipment, materiel, supplies, intelligence materials, maps, documents files and all other properties have been kept for the time being and all aircraft and airfield installations and equipment, naval vessels, merchant vessels, vehicles, piers, workshops, warehouses and all buildings and all other military and civilian properties owned or controlled by Japanese forces in subject areas have been kept in good shape, waiting to be handed over to the commanding officers or administrative representative authorized by Generalissimo Chiang, or his representative, General Ho Ying-chin.

    f. All POW's and civilians of United Nations captured by Japanese Army, Navy and Air Force units in subject areas will be freed immediately, protected and sent to appointed places.

    g. From now on, all Japanese Army, Navy and Air Force units shall be under the jurisdiction of Generalissimo Chiang and shall take orders from Generalissimo Chiang and his representative, General Ho Ying-chin.

    h. I, Commander of Japanese Forces in China, will transmit to all officers and men of the surrendered Japanese forces the orders issued by Generalissimo Chiang and his representative, General Ho Ying-chin, and all officers and men in subject areas are bound to obey.

    i. Any personnel of the surrendered Japanese forces will be subject to punishment for failing or delaying to fulfil the terms mentioned herein or to carry out the orders of Generalissimo Chiang and his representative, General Ho Ying-chin.

By order of the Imperial Government and the Imperial Supreme Commander of the Japanese Empire.

Signed Neiji Okamura, General of Japanese Army, Commander of the Japanese Expeditionary Forces in China in Nanking, Republic of China at 0900 hours on September 9, 1945.

Representing the Republic of China, the United States of America, the Commonwealth of Great Britain, the Soviet Union and for the benefit of the member-nations of the United Nations at war with Japan, this document of surrender is accepted in Nanking, Republic of China, at 0900 hours on 9 September 1945.

Signed Ho Ying-chin, General, 1st-grade, Chinese Army, C-in-C of Chinese Army, authorized Representative of Generalissimo Chiang Kai-shek, Supreme Commander of the China Theater.

    3. Massing of the Japanese Forces for Surrender in the China Theater:

After the signing of the Japanese surrender in Nanking, General Ho Ying-chin handed to Neiji Okamura the First Order of the C-in-C of our Armed Forces, stating that all Japanese Army, Navy and Air Force units in the Republic of China (excluding the three Northeastern Provinces), Taiwan and the areas north of latitude 16 degrees in Indo-China should surrender to those commanding officers authorized for the acceptance of surrender.

The strength of the Japanese forces during the surrender is as follows:

North China Front Army	326,244
6th Front Army in Central China	290,367
6th and 13th Corps in Nanking-Shanghai Area	330,397
23rd Corps in Kwangtung	137,386
10th Front Army in Taiwan	169,031
38th Corps in area north of the N. Lat. 16°	29,815

The above areas totalled 1,283,240 troops.

The Command agencies and units are listed below:

General headquarters   1

Front army   3

Corps   10

Division (including 1 tank division and 2 air divisions)   36

Separate brigade (including 1 cav brig)   41

Separate garrison units and columns   19

Naval special base and marines   6

For areas where units were massed, see Map 46.

4.   Surrender Disposition (See Map 47)

In order to disarm the enemy rapidly and restore general order at an early date, GHQ Chinese Army, in compliance with the instructions of the Supreme Commander, designated the following 16 districts and the senior commanders therein for the acceptance of the surrender:

a.   Gen. Lu Han, commander of the 1st Front Army, was to accept the surrender of the Japanese 38th Corps (21D, 22D (a portion) and 34th BS) assembled in northern Indo-China.   The Japanese surrendering commander was Tsuchihashi and the surrender location was Hanoi.

b.   Gen. Chang Fa-kuei, commander of the 2nd Front Army, was to accept the surrender of the Japanese 23rd Corps, 129th Division, 130th Division, 23rd BS, 81st BS and 13th IBS which were assembled in Canton.   One battalion each of the 22nd and 23rd BS was assembled in Leichow Peninsula, and the Hainan Garrison Force was assembled on Hainan Island.   The Japanese surrendering commander was Kyuichi Tanaka, and the surrender location was Canton.

c.   Gen. Yu Han-mou, commander of the 7th War Area, was to accept the surrender of the Japanese 104th Division, Chaochow-Swatow Column and one artillery battalion of the 103rd Division and 2½ infantry battalions, assembled in Swatow.   The Japanese surrendering commander was Kyuichi Tanaka of the 23rd Corps and the surrender location was Swa-tow.

d.   Gen. Wang Yao-wu, commander of the 4th Front Army, was to accept the surrender of the Japanese 20th Corps, 64th Division, 81st BS, 82nd BS, 2nd KS which were assembled in Changsha, the 68th Division in Hengyang and the 116th Division and 17th BS in Yueh-yang.   The Japanese surrendering commander was Ichiro Sakanishi of the 20th Corps and the surrender location was Chang-sha.

e.   Gen. Hsueh Yueh, commander of the 9th War Area, was to accept the surrender of the Japanese 71st BS which was assembled in Nanchang and the 11th Corps, 13th Division, 58th Division, 22nd BS, 84th BS and 87th BS in Chiuchiang.   The Japanese surrendering commander was Yukio Kassawara of the 11th Corps and the surrender location was Nan-chang.

f.   Gen. Ku Chu-tung, commander of the 3rd War Area, was to accept the surrender of the Japanese 133rd Division, 62nd BS and 91st BS assembled in Hang-chow and the Japanese marines in Amoy. The Japanese surrendering commander was Kyutaro Matsui of the 13th Corps and the surrender location was Hang-chow.

g. Gen. Tang En-po, commander of the 3rd Front Army, was to accept the surrender of the Japanese 13th Corps, 27th Division, 60th Division, 61 Division, 69th Division, 89th BS and 90th BS assembled in Shanghai and the 6th Corps, 3rd Division, 34th Division, 40th Division, 161st Division and 13th FD in Nanking. The Japanese surrendering commander in Nanking was Jiro Togawa of the 6th Corps and in Shanghai was Kyutaro Matsui of the 13th Corps.

h. Gen. Sun Wei-ju, commander of the 6th War Area, was to accept the surrender of the Japanese 6th FA (132nd Division, 83rd IBS, 85th BS, 11th IBS and 51st IBS) assembled in Hankow and the 12th IBS, 86th IBS, and 88th BS in Wu-chang. The surrender location was Han-kow.

i. Gen. Li Pin-hsien, commander of the 10th War Area, was to accept the surrender of the Japanese 65th Division assembled in Hsu-chow, the 70th Division and 1st KS in Pang-pu and the 13th IBS and 6th IBS in Anking. The Japanese surrendering commander was Jiro Togawa of the 6th Corps and the surrender location was Hsu-chow.

j. 11th War Area

(1) Gen. Sun Lien-chung was to accept the surrender of the Japanese 118th Division, 9th BS and North China Special Garrison Force assembled in Peiping and Tientsin, the Mongolian Frontier Army, the 3rd TK Division, 2nd BS, 8th BS and 3rd KS in Peiping, the 7th KS in Pao-ting, 1st BS and 21st BS in Shih-chia-chuang. The Japanese surrendering commander was Hiroshi Nemoto of the North China Front Army, and the surrender location was Peiping.

(2) Gen. Li Yen-nien was to accept the Japanese surrender in Tsi-nan, Tsingtao and Teh-chow area. The Japanese surrendering forces were the 5th BS, 12th KS and marines assembled in Tsing-tao and the 43rd Corps, 47th Division, 9th KS and 11th KS in Tsi-nan. The Japanese surrendering commander was Tadayasu Hokokawa of the 43rd Corps, and the surrender location was Tsi-nan.

k. Gen. Hu Tsung-nan, commander of the 1st War Area, was to accept the surrender of the Japanese 110th Division, assembled in Lo-yang, the 6th KS and 22nd Division (bulk) in Hsin-hsiang, and the 12th Corps and 10th KS in Cheng-chow. The Japanese surrendering commander was Takashi Takamori of the 12th Corps, and the surrender location was Lo-yang.

l. Gen. Liu Chih, commander of the 5th War Area, was to accept the surrender of the Japanese 115th Division and 14th KS assembled in Yen-cheng, the 92nd BS and 13th KS in Hsu-chang, and the 4th KS in Shang-chiu. The Japanese surrendering commander was Takashi Takamori of the 12th Corps and the surrender location was Yen-cheng.

m. Gen. Yen Hsi-shan, commander of the 2nd War Area, was to accept the surrender of the Japanese 1st Corps, 114th Division, 3rd BS, 10th IBS, 14th IBS and 5th KS at an assembly area to be determined by Gen. Yen. The Japanese surrendering commander was Raishiro Sumita, and the surrender location was Tai-yuan.

n.   Gen. Fu Tso-yi, commander of the 12th War Area, was to accept the surrender of two battalions of the Japanese assembly area to be determined by Gen. Fu.   The Japanese surrendering commander was Hiroshi Nemoto of the Mongolian Frontier Army, and the surrender location was Kuei-sui.

o.   Gen. Chen Yi was to accept the surrender of the Japanese forces in Taiwan and Penghu complex. The Japanese forces were the 10th FA, 8th FD, 9th Division, 12th Division, 50th Division, 66th Division, 71st Division, 75th BS, 76th BS, 100th BS, 103rd BS, 102nd BS, 112th BS and Penghu Garrison Force which would be assembled at a location to be determined by Gen. Chen. The Japanese surrendering commander was Reikichi Ando of the 10th FA.

5.   Conduct of the Surrender

When the C-in-C of the Chinese Army received the order to accept the surrender of the enemy, most of our main force (regular units) were in the southwest provinces, but we had to take control over the 26 strategic keypoints of Canton, Chang-sha, Wu-chang, Han-kow, Nan-chang, Chiu-chiang, An-king, Nanking, Shanghai, Hang-chow, Hsu-chow, Cheng-chow, Lo-yang, Tsing-tao, Tsinan, Peiping, Tientsin, Shan-hai-kuan, Chengte, Chih-feng, To-lun, Ku-pei-kou, Kalgan, Kuei-sui, Pao-tou, Tai-yuan, Ta-tung and Shih-chia-chuang. Therefore, GHQ Chinese Army worked out the plan for acceptance of surrender which kept the military organs of the enemy intact for the time being to act as liaison, and put the Japanese Army in Taiwan and North Indo-China and the Japanese Navy in China under the unified command of Neiji Okamura, so as to insure a smooth acceptance.   Then, all war zone and regional army commands were ordered to send their troops to the key-points by air, land, water or by foot; after their arrival, the Japanese forces were gradually concentrated and simultaneously disarmed.   When the Japanese arrived at the concentration points, they were ordered to lay down their arms, under the supervision of our troops, at the designated warehouses and then turn over a list of the weapons for us to check and receive accordingly.   Later, all the POW's were sent to concentration camps.

Beginning from September 11 1945 to mid-October, the acceptance of the surrender was carried out smoothly in all places except Taiwan, North China, Peiping, Tientsin, Tsing-tao and North Kiangsu, where the acceptance of surrender was not carried out according to plan due to the shortage of transportation and the Chinese Communists' planned interference and destruction of communications lines after October 1945. However, GHO Chinese Army, used every effort to overcome these difficulties and completed the disarming of Japanese forces in early February 1946, except for a small number of Japanese forces which were enveloped and disarmed by the Chinese Communists forces (such as one Japanese artillery battery at Wa-yao on the Eastern Section of the Lan-chow-Lien-yung-kang Railroad and 100 Japanese soldiers at Tai-an Railroad Station in Shangtung). All key-points, which were captured by Communists forces before us, were recaptured by our forces one after the other, except for Kalgan and Ku-pei-kou.

By mid-April 1946, the number of disarmed Japanese weapons, vehicles, aircraft and ships was as follows:

a. Infantry small arms

Rifle and carbine	685,897
Pistol	60,377
Lt and Hv machine gun	29,822

b. Gun   12,446

c. Ammunition

Rifle and machine gun bullet	180,994,000
Pistol bullet	2,035,000

d. Vehicles

Tank	383
Armored car	151
Truck (including special-purpose vehicle)	15,785

e. Horses   74,159

f. Aircraft   1,068

Serviceable	291
To be repaired	626
Unserviceable	151
Bomb	6,000 tons
Aviation gasoline	10,000+tons
	(3,101,927 gallons)

g. Ships and craft (totalling 1,400 ships and craft and 54,600+ tons (averaging 50– tons per craft)

Warship (90-1,000 tons, only 3 were in serviceable	19
Destroyer (approximately 100 tons per destroyer, 6 were serviceable)	7
PT Boat (3 15-ton type and 3 25-ton type) all 6 were serviceable	6
Small Submarine (2 5,000-ton type were serviceable)	3
Gunboat (8-25 ton each. Most of them were out of commission)	200

The remainder consisted of mostly unserviceable or damaged small craft and junks.

6. Utilization of Surrendered Japanese Equipment

The acceptance of surrendered Japanese party, administrative and puppet regime materials was handled by the Party and Administrative Acceptance Planning Committee consisting of representatives of all ministries and commissions of the Executive Yuan under the supervision of Chinese Army General Headquarters, while all those materials concerning regular armed forces was handled by the Chinese Army General Headquarters. At this time, as all properties looted or managed by the enemy in China were under direct control of the Japanese Ministry of Great East Asia, and only a small part such as water supply, power, communications and transportation facilities for military use was managed by Japanese forces, Neiji Okamura was ordered to hand them over as a whole in order to avoid confusion and loss of materials. Besides, as the puppet regime had already been disbanded, so those public utilities managed by them had no one responsible to turn them over; therefore, GHQ Chinese Army collected all those documents concerning public utilities for the commissioners sent by various ministries and commissions of the Executive Yuan to receive thru the Party and Administrative Acceptance Planning Committee.

On September 8, 1945, the Party and Administrative Acceptance Planning Committee started operations in Nanking and set forth that those properties or materials not belonging to the provincial or municipal government would be accepted by commissioners appointed by the ministries or commissions concerned, and those belonging to the provincial or municipal governments would be accepted by the local military and police authorities in coordination with the organizations-in-charge, according to the rules set forth by the Provincial and Municipal Party and Administrative Acceptance Committee as a whole and then turned over to the organizations concerned. By November, GHQ Chinese Army had wound up all remaining business concerning acceptance of surrendered men and materiel after the completion of the acceptance operations in various places in October and the establishment of the Nation-wide Enterprises Acceptance Committee for the Recovery Areas of the Executive Yuan; and the Party and Administrative Acceptance Planning Committee branches in various places were abolished with the establishment of the Enemy and Puppet Regime's Property Administration of the Executive Yuan.

In principle, the military equipment received was put to use. Work was resumed in factories and depots in which the machinery was serviceable. Those factories and depots in which the machinery was incomplete or lost were consolidated. The engineer equipment turned in was issued to various units. All training aids were turned over to the Engineer School. Most of the railway equipment was turned over to the Ministry of Communications for emergency repair. Most of the signal equipment was accepted by the General Station, Ministry of War. In order to form a communication net at an early date, the equipment was distributed to the various units. GHQ Army took over the puppet general radio station and the sub radio stations and reorganized them into GHQ Army radio stations attached to the various reorganized corps. In order to increase the combat effectiveness of the Chinese Army, a telegram was dispatched to the surrender-accepting areas giving permission for the corps and divisions accepting the surrender to make use of the guns, equipment and horses in accordance with their organizational requirements. A total of 116 artillery battalions were equipped with surrendered Japanese pack howitzers and field guns in the various corps and divisions. Similarly, carbines, light and heavy machine guns and pistols were distributed to regular forces and local militia and police. A number of weapons which were retained were distributed later after the reorganization. The Japanese military vehicles which had been turned in were issued to the transportation, engineer and signal regiments for use. Those vehicles requiring repair were turned over to the arsenals. Civilian vehicles were turned over to the Ministry of Communications to improve land transportation. Serviceable ships and aircraft received by the Chinese Navy and Chinese Air Force were put to use by the respective general headquarters. The damaged ships and aircraft were turned in to the respective factories for repair. All in all, the principle was to make timely use of the surrendered equipment and materials so as to increase our combat effectiveness.

7. Repatriation of Japanese POW's and Civilians

The total of Japanese and Korean servicemen and civilians in the China Theater reached 2,129,826 men, including 1,240,471 Japanese POW's and 779,874 civilians, 14,428 Korean POW's and 50,935 civilians and 44,118 men from Taiwan. All were concentrated on the Chinese Mainland, Taiwan, Hainan Island and North Indo-China and repatriated from the 12 ports of Tang-ku, Tsing-tao, Lien-yun-kang, Shanghai, Amoy, Swa-tow, Canton, Hai-kow, San-ya, Haiphong, Keelung, and Kaohsiung. We were responsible for their transportation from inland to the ports, while the United States was responsible for their sea transportation. The United States dispatched 85 LST's, one "Liberty" ship and some Japanese vessels to handle the repatriation. But, due to the shortage of vessels and the damage inflicted by the Chinese Communists to the railroads, only 1,464,303 men had been moved to the ports by April 20, 1946, and the shipment of the remaining 665,523 men was not completed until the end of June.

Section 2. Demobilization

1. Military Reorganization

a. Principle of Reorganization

After V-J Day the Chinese people longed for demobilization, and the nation needed reconstruction. Accordingly, the Government established peace and national reconstruction policy. Externally, the Government sought national unification, independence and world peace and security. Internally, it strove toward the general objective of establishing a modern, democratic and unified country. It began by reorganizing the nation's armed forces to turn them into armed forces of the nation. In 1944, the strength of the Chinese Army stood at 120 corps, 354 divisions, 31 brigades, 112 regiments, and 15 battalions. By the end of 1945, it was reduced to 89 corps, 2 cavalry corps and 253 infantry divisions showing a reduction of 34 corps, 110 divisions, 21 brigades, 83 regiments and 10 battalions (all remaining brigades, regiments and battalions were integrated into the infantry divisions). In 1946, when the basic program governing reorganization of the Government and Communist forces had been decided by the Military 3-Man Team, government forces underwent phased reorganization hoping to attain the objective of maintaining 20 corps of 60 divisions in time of peace. The reorganization was divided into two phases. During the first phase which lasted 12 months, all units were organized into 36 corps of 108 divisions (including 6 Communist corps of 18 divisions). During the second phase, the units were reduced to 20 corps of 60 divisions (including 10 Communist divisions). Special units were 15% of the Army total strength after reorganization. The first phase of this program was divided into two stages for implementation. The first stage which effected 1/3 reduction was divided into 3 periods of two months each. During the 1st period, units along the Lung-hai Railway and in the northwest (except Sinkiang) were reduced in strength. During the 2nd period, units along and south of the Yangtze River were reduced in strength. During the third period, units in northeast China, North China and Sinkiang were reduced in strength. In the implementation, other than the units in northeast China, North China and Sinkiang for which reorganization was held up due to their missions, 27 corps of 67 divisions were reorganized during the 1st period and 29 corps of 80 divisions during the 2nd period. According to the basic program, the Chinese Army would be reduced to 90 divisions. The organization of an Army division 1946 was worked out. The 70th Corps was reorganized under the new organization. Other units were to undergo reorganization after units of the 1st stage had completed their reorganization. Instead of observing the provisions governing the reorganization, the Communist forces ran wild and expanded without limit to intensify their full-scale rebellions. Though adequate, the reorganization program was never implemented in full.

b. Reorganization of Defense Establishment and Intensifying Unit Equipment and Training:

In view of the pressing need for military reorganization and build-up, the Government resolutely made the decision to reorganize the military establishment after V-J Day. The former National Military Council was reorganized into the Ministry of National Defense to bring unity to the army-navy-air force system. Next, army, navy and air force district were delineated, and a military administrative system was established and simplified as the basis for military build-up. A national defense reconstruction plan by areas was formulated of which a portion was implemented in 1946. After a detailed survey was made of the fortresses, ports and harbors along the rivers and coast, important portions were repaired and reconstructed in the spring of 1946. As to defense works on the ground, preparations were made gradually. With regard to unit equipment and training, an elite force system was instituted. National defense science and technical studies were enhanced, and ordnance and munitions industries were promoted to augment the equipment of troop units. Training regulations were written to intensify troop training so that the nation's forces might become crack outfits.

2. Resettlement of Retired Officers and Men

From the initiation of the reorganization to October 15, 1946, a total of 161,660 officers who had been passed over during the reorganization were assigned to the Officers' Group. 33,184 officers were retired or discharged. The officers who took unified examination and received change of occupation training included 26,040 who entered the Police Officers' Training Class, 4,996 who entered the Transportation Management Personnel Training Class and 39,194 who received training in agronomy, finance, land administration, local administration and civil education. In addition, 7,941 officers received no training and changed occupation after taking the unified examination. The total number of officers having changed occupation was 78,175. 33,103 officers who had been in troop units and organizations were retired or separated from service. Plans were also made for those officers who had not changed their occupations. With regard to the disposition of enlisted personnel, 53,125 were demobilized during the 1st and 2nd phase reorganization; 32,091 were sent to supply districts and the Supply Bureau; 4,716 were sent by various organizations to demobilization stations; and 2,787 reported to demobilization stations and then returned home. The remaining enlisted men were demobilized.

3. Gratuity

In August, 1938, the Gratuity Commission was organized under the National Military Council to handle the gratuity of wounded and disabled officers and men and survivor-dependents. A total of 13 gratuity divisions were established in Honan, Shensi, Chekiang, Kwangsi, Hunan, Kwangtung, Kweichow, Anhwei, Kiangsi, Hupei, Fukien, Szechuan and Shansi Provinces to commend officers and men who had distinguished themselves while serving the country. For officers who were to receive state or official funerals, orders would be published by the Executive Yuan. The amount and kinds of gratuity were increased through the years and the procedures were greatly simplified to insure proper care for wounded and disabled officers and men and survivor-dependents.

In 1946, the Gratuity Commission was deactivated and was replaced by the Gratuity Department of the Combined Service Forces.

CHAPTER TEN

Conclusion

In the course of our national revolution, our country had been subjected to the converging attacks of the Japanese militarists and the Russian and Chinese Communists. After 14 years of arduous struggle, our country finally succeeded in destroying a powerful enemy and achieving final victory in the War of Resistance. Our victory can be attributed to the inspirations of the Three People's Principles and our national consciousness which had enabled our people and servicemen to fight courageously and relentlessly under the inspiring leadership of Generalissimo Chiang. It was a case of "he who is on the right road is helped." In summary, our political thinking, political strategy and military strategy are as follows:

Political thinking: Since the overthrow of the Ching Dynasty and the mopping-up of the warlords, our country has employed the Three People's Principles to give political tutelage to our people, stimulate national consciousness and strengthen national concept. The Three People's Principles has been the impetus in our indomitable resistance against aggression. Furthermore, the political thinking of the Three People's Principles coincides with a government of the people, for the people, and by the people and is the basic factor in uniting the democratic camp to seek a common victory. Intoxicated with Nazism, infatuated with the omnipotence of military power and opposed to the trend of democracy, the Japanese militarists were doomed to fail. Political thinking is the core of modern total war. Indeed the Three People's Principles is the foundation in our War of Resistance for national reconstruction and the guarantee of our final victory.

Political strategy: The primary objective of our political strategy was to achieve internal unity, make foreign alliance and seek common victory of the democratic camp. In the beginning, the policy was to achieve "internal pacification as a pre-requisite to resisting foreign aggression" and to mop up the Communists. Later, our policy was to unite the various parties and factions and rally the people in fighting the War of Resistance. Relations with the democratic nations were promoted, anti-aggression alliances were made, and even non-aggression treaty was signed with Soviet Russia. In the end, we tolerated Russian subversion and sabotage to sign the Sino-Russian Amity Alliance Treaty in order to seek common victory of the democratic camp. Against fanatical Japanese attacks, we suffered hardships and shortages and stood firm without compromise to fight the scorched-earth War of Resistance.   At the Cairo Conference, Generalissimo Chiang favored repaying grievance with kindness and was of the opinion that the form of Japan's government should be determined by the Japanese people.   This prompted the Japanese motivation to surrender and contributed to the maintenance of order in post-war Japan.   Such thinking is of immeasurable value in our anti-Communist political strategy.

Military Strategy: Prior to July 7, 1937, our forces, in consonance with the political strategy of "internal pacification as a pre-requisite to resisting foreign aggression," offered only planned resistance against the Japanese aggression so as to gain time and mop up the Communists.   After July 7, 1937 and during the initial period of the War of Resistance, the main battlefield moved from North China to Shanghai forcing the enemy to change his favorable north-south axis of operations to unfavorable east-west uphill fight.   By means of a total War of Resistance and absolute war, our forces crushed the encroachment of the Japanese militarists; by means of attrition strategy and guerrilla-type war of movement, our forces defeated the enemy's plan of bringing the war to a speedy end.   Our operational guidance was to seize the initiative, avoid enemy strength and hit enemy vulnerable areas.   As a result, our forces scored countless minor victories, cut the enemy to size and uplifted our morale.   Instead of fighting for points and lines, our forces strove to control entire areas causing the enemy to be hopelessly bogged down.   By the time the Japanese forces launched the Pacific War, our forces staged full-scale attacks to tie down the enemy and reinforce Burma despite sacrifices in order to relieve the pressure on the Allied forces. Subsequently, when foreign aid was cut, materials were lacking and inflation resulted, our officers and men suffered increasing hardships.   In spite of the fact that there was a shortage of troops on the domestic battle field and that our equipment was obsolete, 7 corps were pulled in conjunction with 2 corps of Chinese forces in India to join force with Allied forces in counteroffensive in Burma.   By wiping out the Japanese 18th and 56th Divisions and portions of the 2nd, 49th, and 53rd Divisions, our forces helped make the operations of the British and Indian forces in the Battle of Imphal easier and stabilized the situation in India.   Although the enemy succeeded in opening the lines of communications on the mainland, our forces persisted in carrying out the Burma counteroffensive operation plans and opened the China-India Road.   During the Battle of Western Hunan, some of our forces received new equipment.   A destructive strike against the enemy's final offensive enabled our forces to recover Kwangsi.   As our forces were prepared to launch the general offensive, the Japanese, exhausted and lacking the will-to-fight, proclaimed the unconditional surrender on August 10.   Thus, the democratic camp achieved a common victory.

Regrettably, the Allied strategy placed more emphasis on Europe than on Asia and failed to bring an end to the War against Japan simultaneous with or before the defeat of Germany. Hence, the fruits of victory were grabbed by the Russians and Chinese Communists. Employing their favorite tactic of cold war, Russia and Communist China continued to infiltrate Asia, Africa and Central and South Americas. The nations in the democratic camp must apply the enemy's favorite strategy of "hitting where the opponent is most vulnerable" and seize initiative by destroying the Chinese Communists first and restoring the China mainland. This is the only way to save the world from its sad fate.

Reference Books of the History of the Sino-Japanese War (1937-1945)

Name	Author	Date of Publication
An Account of the 8-year War of Resistance	Ho Ying-chin	April, 1946
A Brief Account of the 8-year War of Resistance	Chen Cheng	December, 1946
History of the Greater East Asia War		July, 1956
A Record of the Operations of the Japanese Forces on the China Front	Ministry of National Dafense	August, 1954
Draft of the CAF Operations in the War of Resistance	GHQ CAF	January, 1951
A History of the Chinese Navy Operations	GHQ, CN	October, 1941
A Brief History of the War of Resistance	History Division, MND	1952
A History of the War of Resistance (Causes of the war)	History Bureau, MND	October, 1968
A History of the War of Resistance (An account of the Entire war)	History Bureau, MND	October, 1968
A History of the War of Resistance (Yu-kuan and Jehol Operations)	History Bureau, MND	May, 1966
A History of the War of Resistance (Wusung-Shanghai Operations of Jan. 28, 1932)	History Bureau, MND	October, 1968
A History of the War of Resistance (Operations in Area East of the Luan River and the Great Wall)	History Bureau, MND	October, 1966
A History of the War of Resistance (Operations in Eastern Hopei and Eastern Charhar)	History Bureau, MND	May, 1966

Name	Author	Date of Publication
A History of the War of Resistance (July 7 Incident and Operations in Peiping-Tientsin)	History Bureau, MND	June, 1962
A History of the War of Resistance (Operations along the Peiping-Sui-yuan Railway)	History Bureau, MND	October, 1967
A History of the War of Resistance (Operations along the northern sector of the Peiping-Hankow Railway)	History Bureau, MND	June, 1962
A History of the War of Resistance (Operations along the northern sector of the Tientsin-Pukow Railway)	History Bureau, MND	June, 1962
A History of the War of Resistance (Battle of Tai-yuan)	History Bureau, MND	June, 1962
A History of the War of Resistance (Battle of Wusung-Shanghai)	History Bureau, MND	June, 1962
A History of the War of Resistance (Battle of Hsuchow)	History Bureau, MND	June, 1963
A History of the War of Resistance (Operations along both banks of the Yellow River between the Canal and Yuan-chu)	History Bureau, MND	October, 1967
A History of the War of Resistance (Battle of Wuhan)	History Bureau, MND	June, 1963
A History of the War of Resistance (Operations of the Fukien-Kwangtung Border)	History Bureau, MND	October, 1967
A History of the War of Resistance (Battle Nanchang)	History Bureau, MND	June, 1963
A History of the War of Resistance (Battle of Sui-Tsao)	History Bureau, MND	June, 1963
A History of the War of Resistance (1st Battle of Changsha)	History Bureau, MND	June, 1963
A History of the War of Resistance (Battle of Southern Kwangsi)	History Bureau, MND	June, 1963
A History of the War of Resistance (Winter Offensive of 1939)	History Bureau, MND	October, 1965

Name	Author	Date of Publication
A History of the War of Resistance (Battle of Tsao-Yi)	History Bureau, MND	October, 1967
A History of the War of Resistance (Battle of Southern Honan)	History Bureau, MND	October, 1965
A History of the War of Resistance (Battle of Shang-kao)	History Bureau, MND	May, 1966
A History of the War of Resistance (Battle of Southern Shansi)	History Bureau, MND	May, 1966
A History of the War of Resistance (2nd Battle of Changsha)	History Bureau, MND	May, 1966
A History of the War of Resistance (3rd Battle of Changsha)	History Bureau, MND	May, 1966
A History of the War of Resistance (Operations along the Yunnan-Burma Highway)	History Bureau, MND	May, 1966
A History of the War of Resistance (Battle of Chekiang-Kiangsi)	History Bureau, MND	October, 1966
A History of the War of Resistance (Battle of Western Hupei)	History Bureau, MND	May, 1966
A History of the War of Resistance (Operations in Northern Burma and Western Yunnan)	History Bureau, MND	October, 1968
A History of the War of Resistance (Battle of Chang-teh)	History Bureau, MND	October, 1968
A History of the War of Resistance (Battle of Cental Honan)	History Bureau, MND	October, 1967
A History of the War of Resistance (Battle of Changsha-Hengyang)	History Bureau, MND	October, 1966
A History of the War of Resistance (Battle of Kweichow-Liuchow)	History Bureau, MND	October, 1967
A History of the War of Resistance (Operations on the Hunan-Kwangtung-Kiangsi border)	History Bureau, MND	May, 1966
A History of the War of Resistance (Battle of Western Honan and Northern Hupei)	History Buerau, MND	May, 1966

Name	Author	Date of Publication
A History of the War of Resistance (Battle of Western Hunan)	History Bureau, MND	May, 1966
A History of the War of Resistance (Pursuit in the Southern Theater)	History Bureau, MND	May, 1966
A History of the War of Resistance (Guerilla operation in Shantung and Kiangsu)	History Bureau, MND	May, 1966
A History of the War of Resistance (Guerilla operations in Hopei and Charhar)	History Bureau, MND	May, 1966
A History of the War of Resistance (Guerilla operations in Shansi and Suiyuan)	History Bureau, MND	May, 1960
A History of the War of Resistance (Guerilla operations in various areas)	History Bureau, MND	October, 1968
A History of the War of Resistance (Acceptance of the Japanese surrender)	History Bureau, MND	October, 1967
A History of the War of Resistance (Demobilization)	History Bureau, MND	October, 1967
An Account of the 8 year Japanese Aggression in China	History Bureau, MND	1948
International Situation and the War of Resistance	Army War College	1940
Selected Works of President Chiang Kai-shek	National War College	1960
A History of China's Foreign Affairs	Fu Chi-hsueh	1957
A Chronicle of the Repubic of China	Kao Yin-tsu	1957
A History of the Establishment of the Republic of China	Chiang Chun-chang	1957
An Account of the War of Resistance	The Commercial Press	November, 1947
A Pictorial of National Reconstruction in the War of Resistance	Chinese Cultural Trust Service	
Geography during China's War of Resistance	Wang Wei-ping	1940

Name	Author	Date of Publication
A History of the Sino-Japanese War	Chungking Bookstore	1945
Japan's Secret History in the Past 15 years	Cheng Hsueh-chia	1948
A Modern History of Japan in the Past 100 Years	Pao Tsang-lan	1958
A Modern History of China	Ho Chan-men	1958
Selected Works of Mr. Chiang Pai-li	Huang Ping-sun (ed.)	1940
An Outline of Modern Chinese History	Huang Ta-shou	1961
A History of the Chinese People in the War of Resistance	The Commercial Press	
An Account of the Chinese People in the War of Resistance	The Commercial Press	

Index

C

M

N

T

U

MAPS

MAP 1
MAP GIVING AN ACCOUNT OF FIRST PHASE OPERATIONS
(Early July, 1937 — Mid-Nov., 1938)

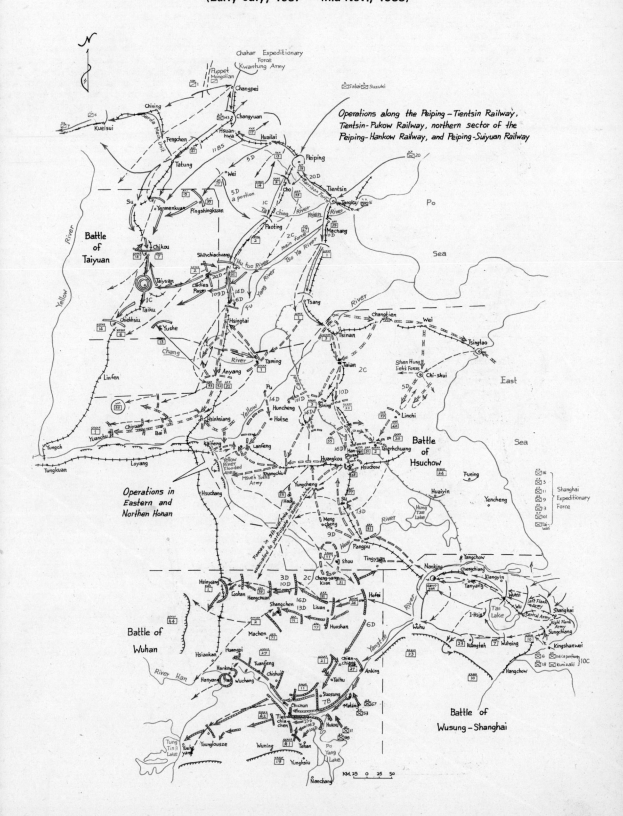

MAP 2
MAP GIVING AN ACCOUNT OF OPERATIONS IN PEIPING-TIENTSIN
(Early July — Early Aug., 1937)

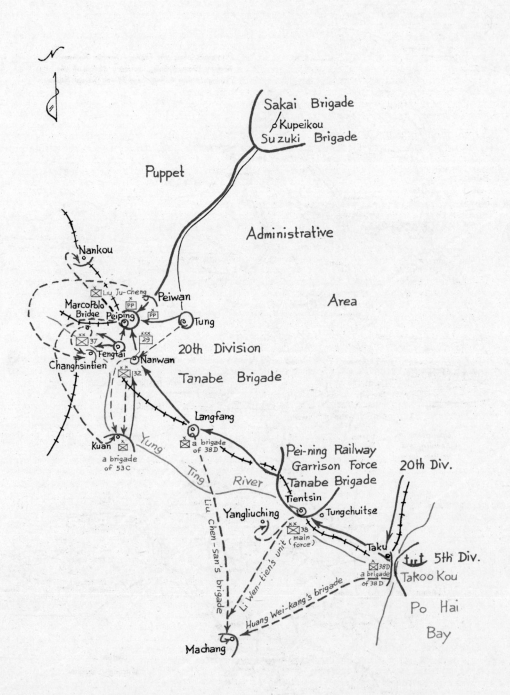

MAP 3
MAP GIVING AN ACCOUNT OF OPERATIONS ALONG
EASTERN SECTOR OF PEIPING-SUIYUAN RAILWAY
(Early Aug. – Late Aug., 1937)

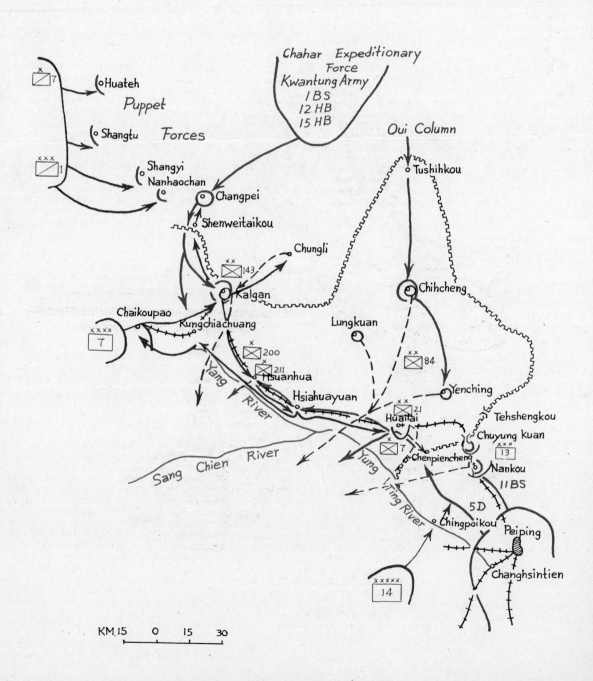

MAP 4
MAP GIVING AN ACCOUNT OF OPERATIONS ALONG NORTHERN SECTOR OF PEIPING-HANKOW RAILWAY
(Aug. 21 — Nov. 12, 1937)

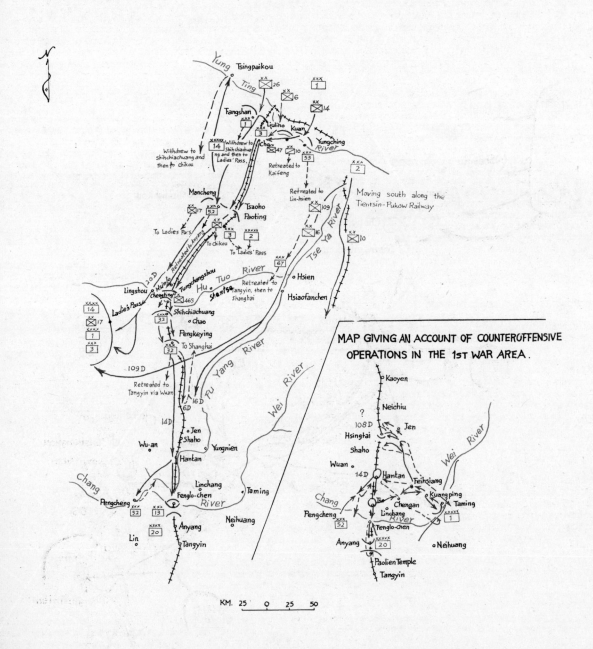

MAP GIVING AN ACCOUNT OF COUNTEROFFENSIVE OPERATIONS IN THE 1st WAR AREA.

KM. 25   0   25   50

MAP 5
MAP GIVING AN ACCOUNT OF OPERATIONS ALONG NORTHERN SECTOR OF THE TIENTSIN-PUKOW RAILWAY
(Early Sept. — Mid-Nov. 1937)

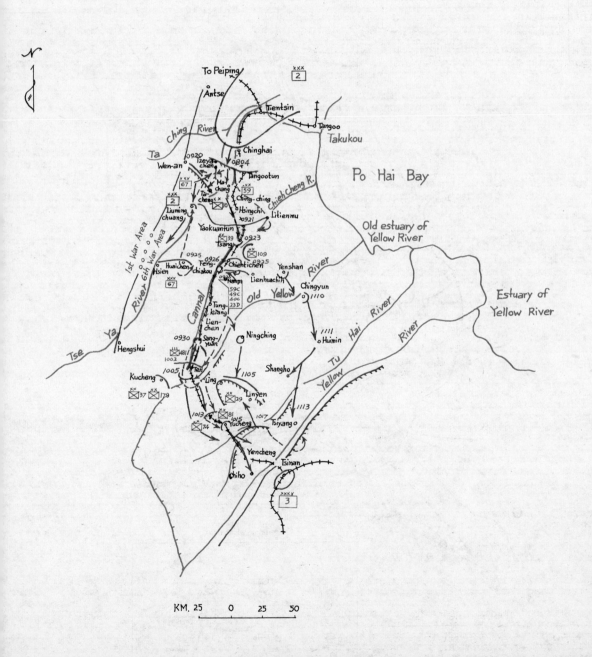

KM. 25   0   25   50

MAP 6
MAP SHOWING AN ACCOUNT OF THE BATTLE OF TAIYUAN
(Mid-Sept. — Early Nov., 1939)

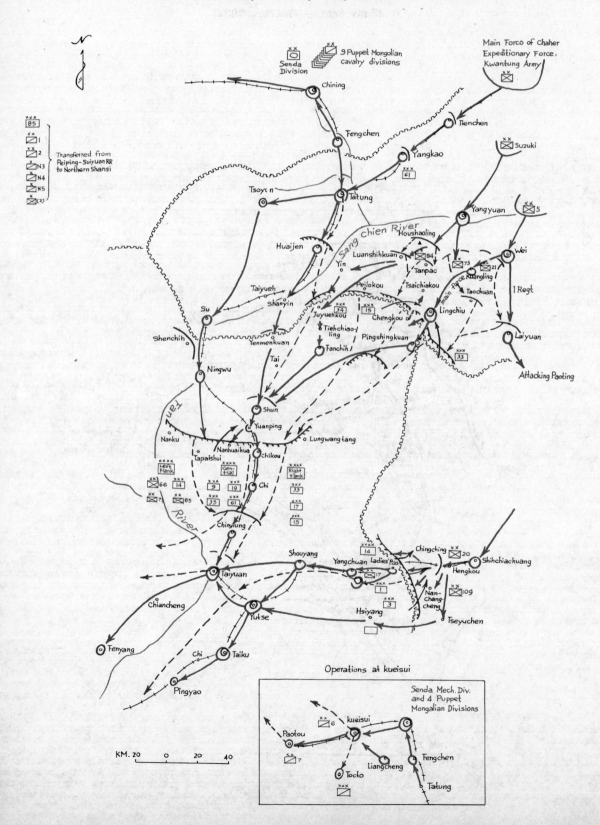

Senda Division

9 Puppet Mongolian cavalry divisions

Main Force of Chaher Expeditionary Force, Kwantung Army

Transferred from Peiping–Suiyuan RR to Northern Shansi

Chining

Fengchen

Tienchen

Yangkao

Suzuki

Tsoyin

Tatung

Yangyuan

Sang chien River

Houshaoling

Wei

Luanshihkuan

Huaijen

Tanpao

Yin

Tsaichiakou

Kuangling

Taochuan

1 Regt

Taiyueh

Shanyin

Peilokou

Su

Juyuehkou

Chengkou

Lingchiu

Laiyuan

Shenchih

Tiehchiao-ling

Pingshingkuan

Yenmenkuan

Tai

Fanchih

Attacking Paoting

Ningwu

Shun

Yuanping

Lungwangtang

Nanku

Nanhuaihua

Tapaishui

Chikou

Left Flank

Central

Right Flank

Chi

Chinjung

River

Shouyang

Yangchuan Ladies'Pas

Chingching

Shihchiachuang

Hengkou

Nan-chang-cheng

Taiyuan

Hsiyang

Tseyuchen

Chiancheng

Yutse

Fenyang

Chi

Taiku

Pingyao

Operations at kueisui

Senda Mech. Div. and 4 Puppet Mongolian Divisions

kueisui

Paotou

Liangcheng

Fengchen

Tocto

Tatung

KM. 20 0 20 40

MAP 7
MAP SHOWING AN ACCOUNT OF OPERATIONS IN THE VICINITY OF WUSUNG-SHANGHAI
(Aug. 13 — Nov. 9, 1937)

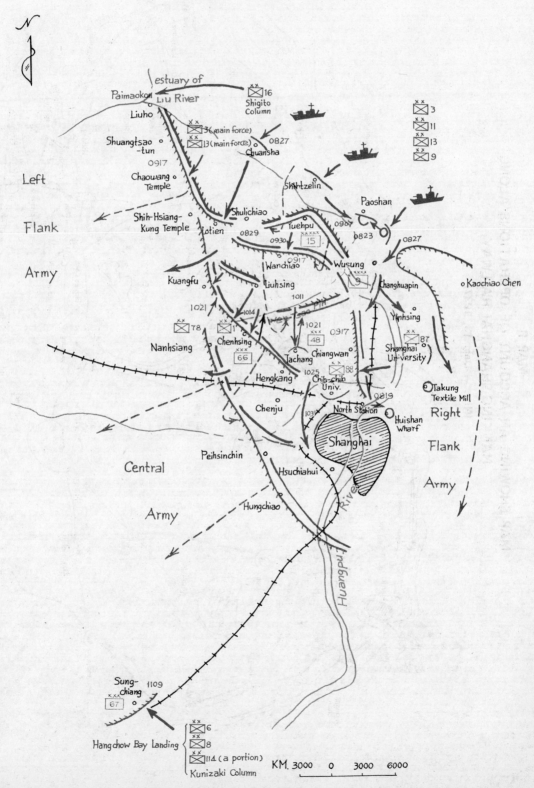

MAP 8

MAP SHOWING AN ACCOUNT OF OPERATIONS ALONG
NANKING-SHANGHAI RAILWAY

(Nov. – Dec. 13, 1937)

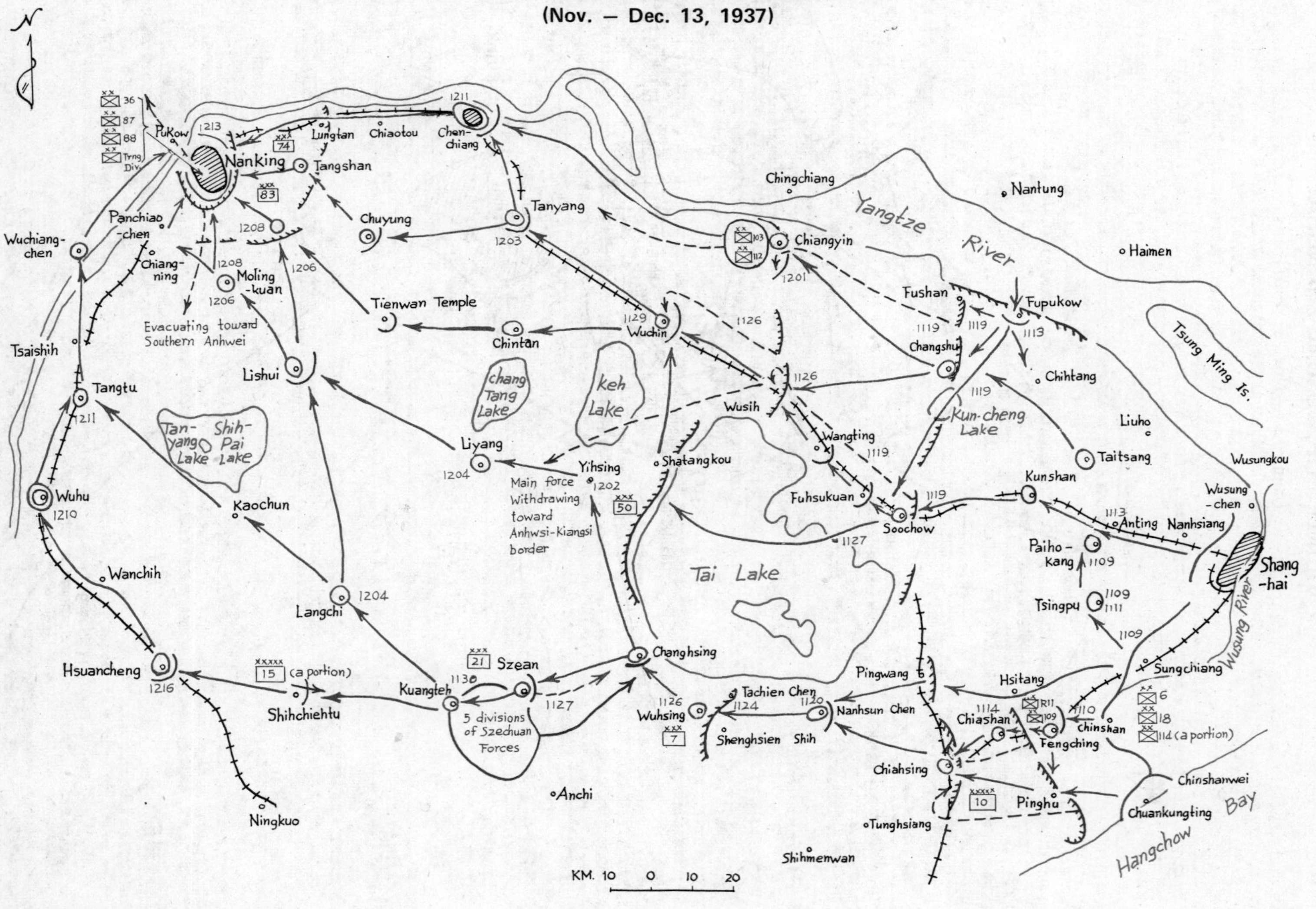

MAP 9-1
MAP SHOWING AN ACCOUNT OF THE BATTLE OF HSUCHOW
(Late Dec., 1937 – Early June, 1938)

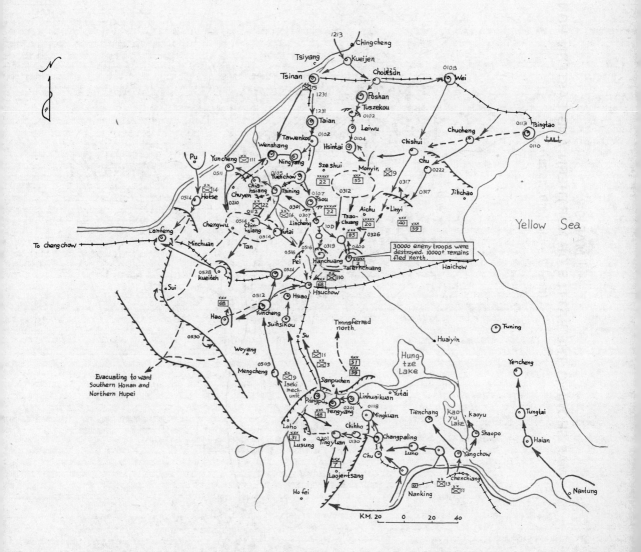

MAP 9-2

MAP SHOWING THE BATTLE OF NORTHERN AND EASTERN HONAN

(Feb. 7 – Jun. 10, 1938)

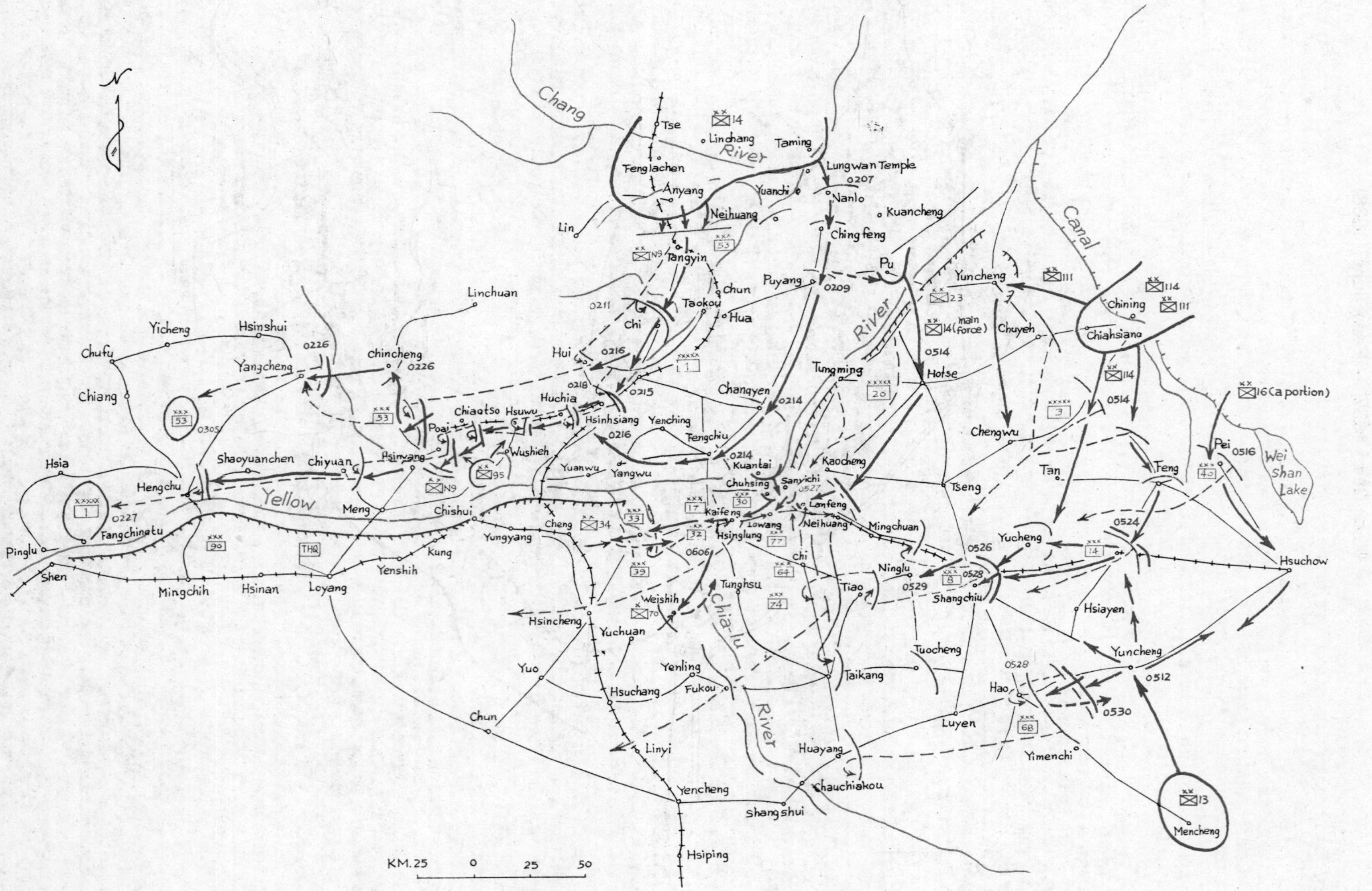

MAP 10
MAP SHOWING THE BATTLE OF WUHAN
(Mid-June — Mid-November, 1938)

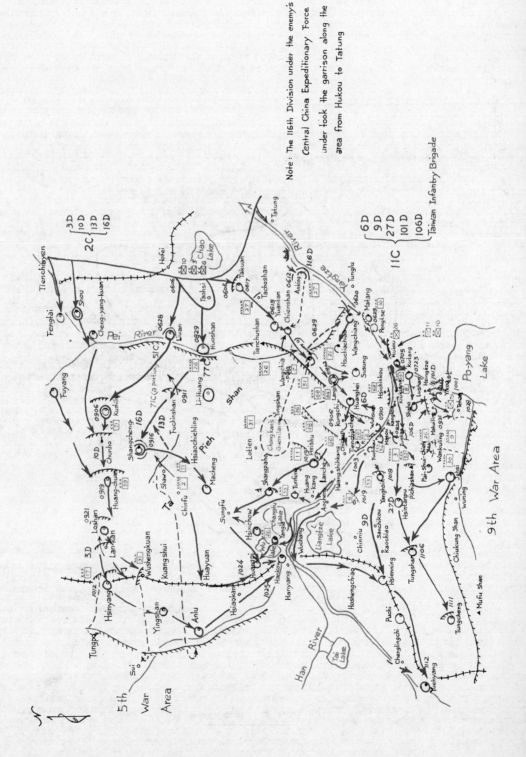

Note: The 116th Division under the enemy's Central China Expeditionary Force under took the garrison along the area from Hukou to Tatung

MAP 11
MAP SHOWING OPERATIONS IN AMOY
(Mar. 10–13, 1938)

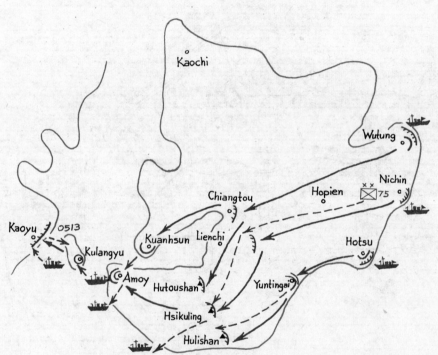

Kaochi

Wutung

Nichin

Hopien

☒ 75

Chiangtou

Kaoyu 0513

Kuanhsun Lienchi

Hotsu

Kulangyu

Amoy Hutoushan

Yuntingai

Hsikuling

Hulishan

Under the cover of more than 30 planes and powerful naval gunfire support 4 enemy groups made a forced landing

M. 1000 0 1000 2000

MAP 12
MAP SHOWING OPERATIONS DURING JAPANESE LANDING AT TAYA BAY AND THE FALL OF CANTON
(Oct. 12 — Dec. 10, 1938)

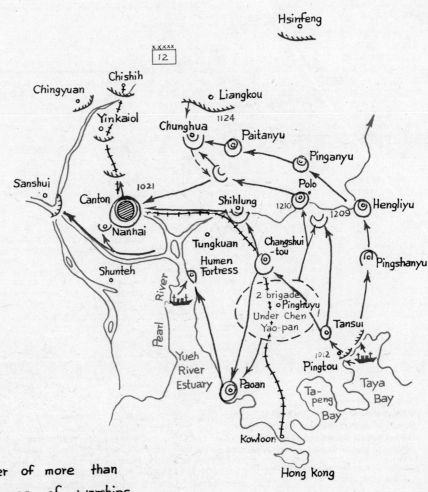

Under the cover of more than 100 planes and scores of warships, the enemy's 21st Corps (built around 3 divisons) made a surprise landing.

KM. 20   0   20   40

MAP 13
MAP GIVING AN ACCOUNT OF OPERATIONS DURING THE FIRST STAGE OF THE SECOND PHASE
(Mid-Mar., 1939 — Early Mar., 1940)

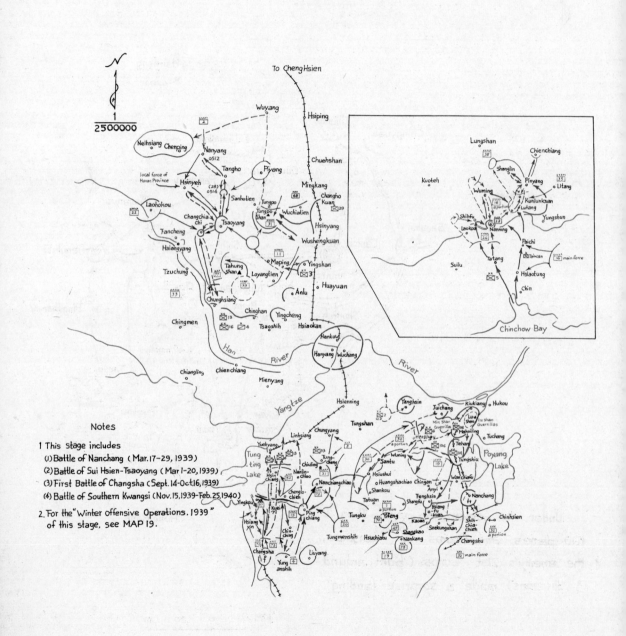

Notes

1 This stage includes
  (1) Battle of Nanchang (Mar.17-29, 1939)
  (2) Battle of Sui Hsien-Tsaoyang (Mar 1-20, 1939)
  (3) First Battle of Changsha (Sept. 14-Oct.16, 1939)
  (4) Battle of Southern Kwangsi (Nov.15, 1939-Feb.25, 1940)

2. For the "Winter offensive Operations. 1939"
   of this stage, see MAP 19.

MAP 14
MAP GIVING AN ACCOUNT OF THE BATTLE OF NANCHANG
(Mid-Feb. — Late Mar., 1939)

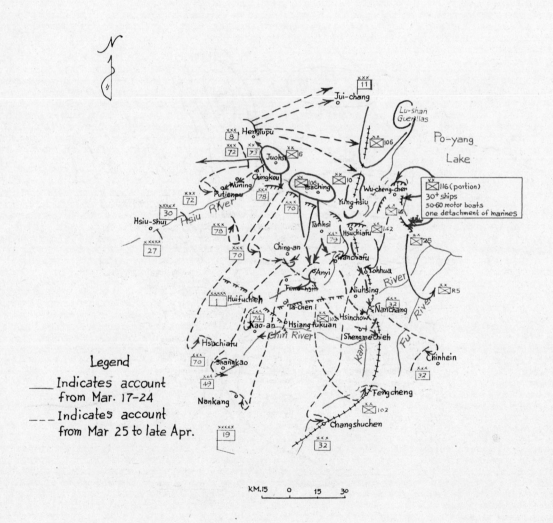

Legend

___ Indicates account from Mar. 17-24

--- Indicates account from Mar 25 to late Apr.

KM.15   0   15   30

MAP 15
MAP GIVING AN ACCOUNT OF THE
NANCHANG COUNTEROFFENSIVE OPERATIONS
(Early Apr. — Early May, 1939)

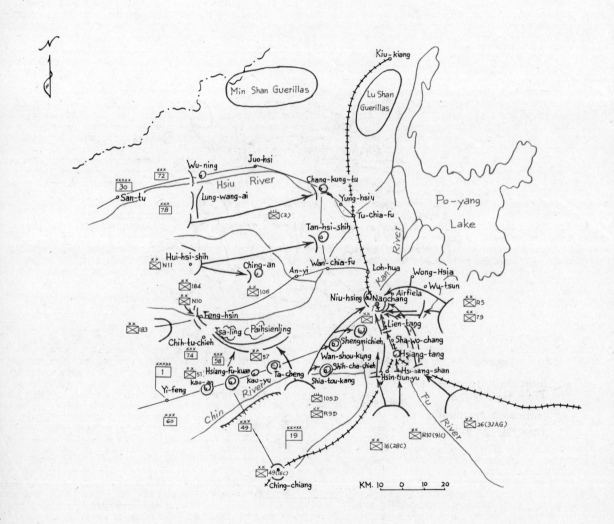

MAP 16
MAP GIVING AN ACCOUNT OF THE BATTLE OF SUI HSIEN-TSAOYANG
(Late Apr. — Mid-May, 1939)

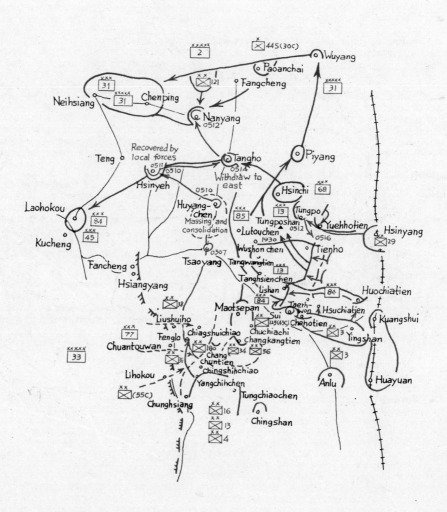

KM. 10 0 10 20

MAP 17
MAP GIVING AN ACCOUNT OF THE 1st BATTLE OF CHANGSHA
(Sept. 14 — Oct. 14, 1939)

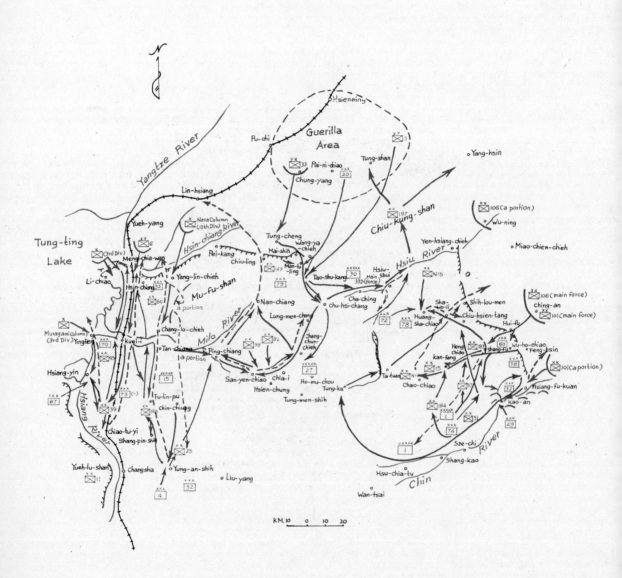

MAP 18
MAP GIVING AN ACCOUNT OF THE BATTLE OF SOUTHERN KWANGSI
(Mid-Oct., 1939 — Late Feb., 1940)

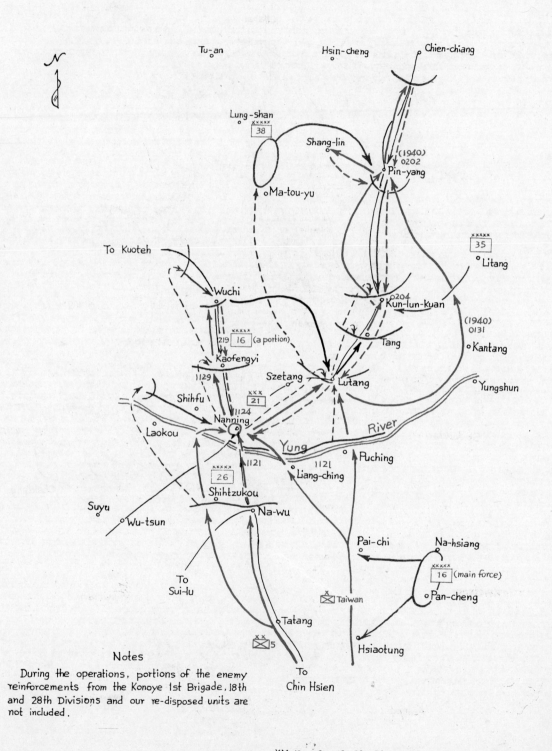

Notes

During the operations, portions of the enemy reinforcements from the Konoye 1st Brigade, 18th and 28th Divisions and our re-disposed units are not included.

KM. 10   0   10 20 30

MAP 19
MAP GIVING AN ACCOUNT OF WINTER OFFENSIVE, 1939
(Late Nov., 1939 — Mar., 1940)

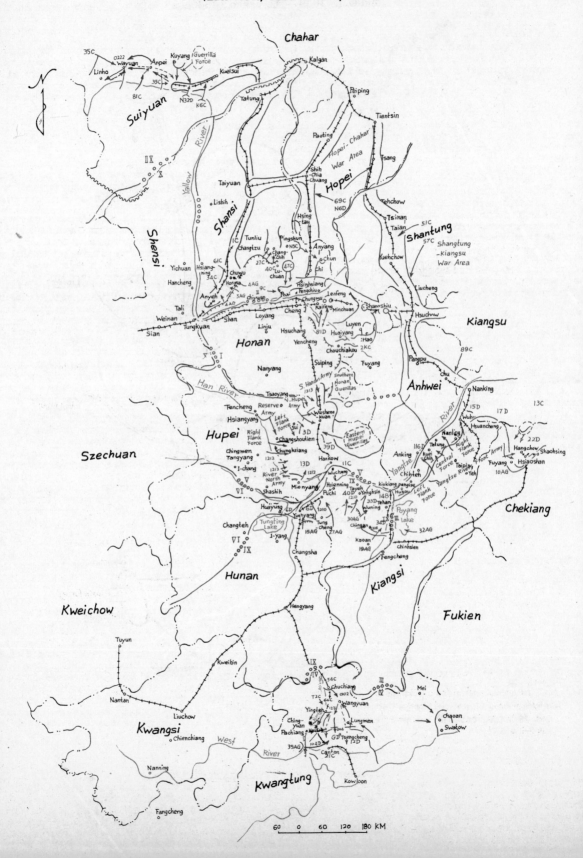

60 0 60 120 180 KM

MAP 20
MAP GIVING AN ACCOUNT OF OPERATIONS DURING THE SECOND STAGE OF THE SECOND PHASE
(Mar., 1940 — Early Dec., 1941)

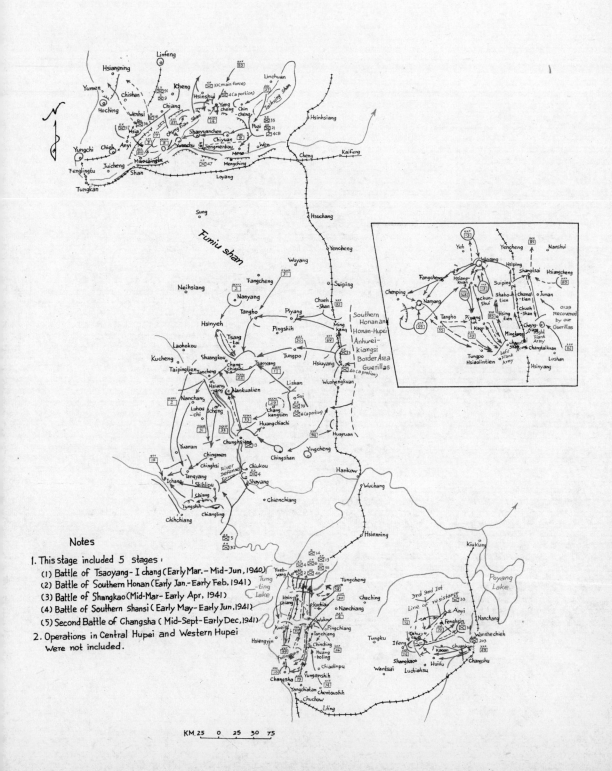

Notes

1. This stage included 5 stages :
   (1) Battle of Tsaoyang- I chang (Early Mar.– Mid-Jun , 1940)
   (2) Battle of Southern Honan (Early Jan.– Early Feb. 1941)
   (3) Battle of Shangkao (Mid-Mar– Early Apr, 1941)
   (4) Battle of Southern shansi (Early May– Early Jun, 1941)
   (5) Second Battle of Changsha (Mid-Sept– Early Dec, 1941)

2. Operations in Central Hupei and Western Hupei
   Were not included.

KM. 25 0 25 50 75

MAP 21
MAP GIVING AN ACCOUNT OF THE BATTLE OF TSAO-YANG-I-CHANG
(Early May — Mid-June., 1940)

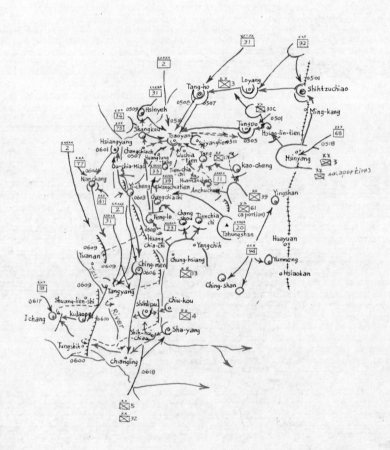

KM. 25   0   25   50

MAP 22

MAP GIVING AN ACCOUNT OF OPERATIONS IN CENTRAL HUPEI

(Late Nov. – Early Dec., 1940)

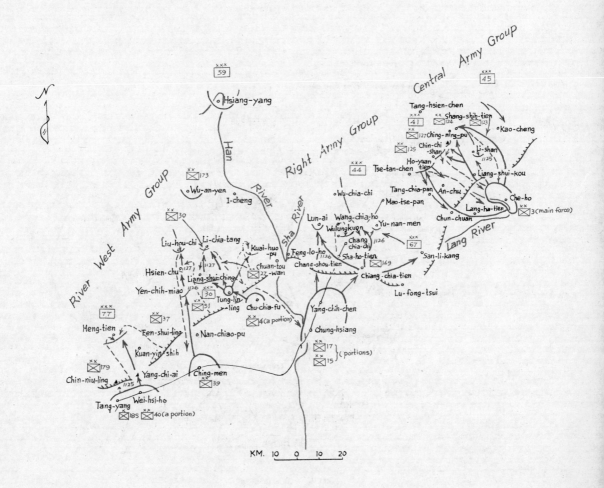

KM.   10   0   10   20

MAP 23
MAP GIVING AN ACCOUNT OF OPERATIONS IN WESTERN HUPEI
(Early March — Mid-March, 1941)

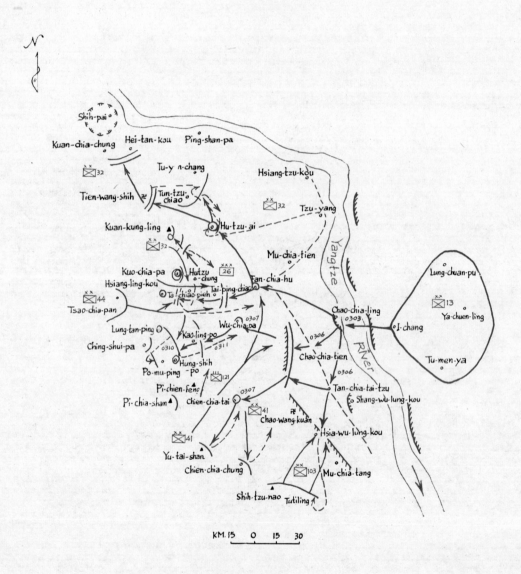

KM. 15 0 15 30

MAP 24
MAP GIVING AN ACCOUNT OF THE BATTLE OF SOUTHERN HONAN
(Late Jan. — Early Feb., 1941)

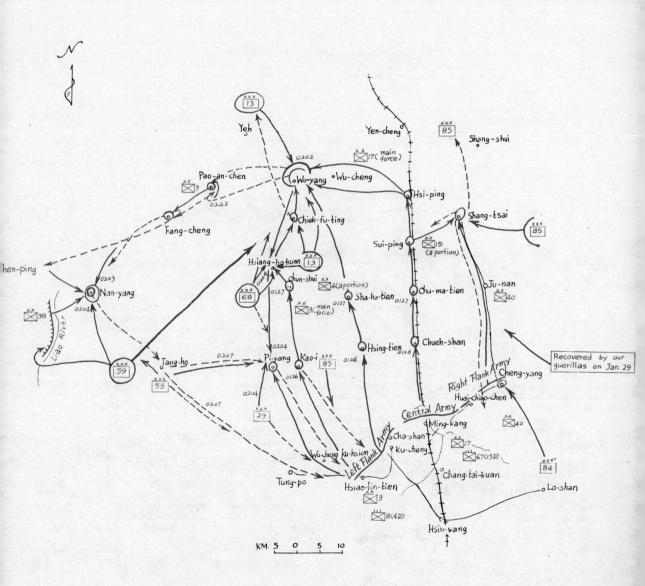

KM. 5 0 5 10

MAP 25
MAP GIVING AN ACCOUNT OF THE BATTLE OF SHANG-KAO
(Mid-Mar. — Early Apr., 1941)

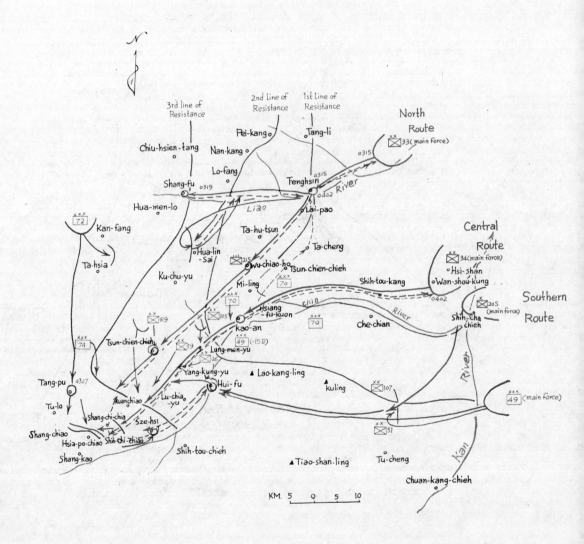

N

3rd line of Resistance

2nd Line of Resistance

1st Line of Resistance

North Route

33 (main force)

Chiu-hsien-tang

Pei-kang

Nan-kang

Tang-li

Lo-fang

o315

Shang-fu o319

Fenghsin

o315

River

o402

Hua-men-lo

Liao

Lai-pao

72

Kan-fang

Ta-hu-tsun

Ta-cheng

Central Route

34 (main force)

Hua-lin -Sai

215

Wu-chiao-ho

Tsun-chien-chieh

Hsi-shan

Ta-hsia

Ku-chu-yu

Mi-ling

70

Shih-tou-kang

Wan-shou-kung

Southern Route

o402

20S (main force)

74

Hsiang -fu-kuon

chia

River

Shih-cha chieh

105

70

kao-an

Che-chian

Tsun-chien-chieh

19

49 (-15D)

26

Lung-men-yu

Tang-pu o327

Yang-kung-yu

Lao-kang-ling

Kuling

107

River

49 (main force)

Tu-lo

Hui-fu

Kuanchiao

Lu-chia -yu

Shang-chi-chia

Sze-hsi

51

Shang-chiao

Hsia-po-chiao

Shih-chi-chiao

Shih-tou-chieh

Kan

Shang-kao

Tiao-shan-ling

Tu-cheng

Chuan-kang-chieh

KM. 5 0 5 10

MAP 26
MAP GIVING AN ACCOUNT OF THE BATTLE OF SOUTHERN SHANSI
(Early May — Early June, 1941)

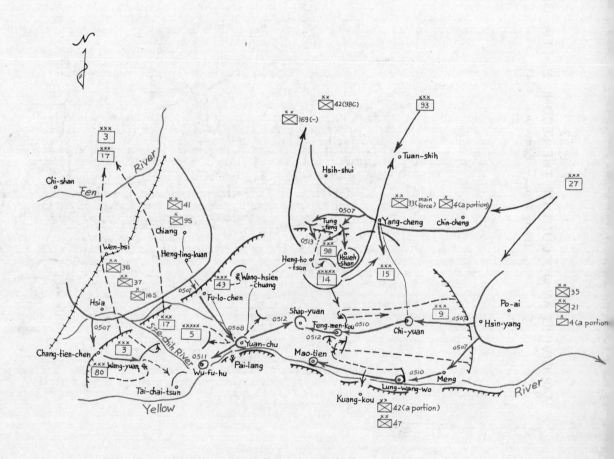

KM. 10   0   10   20

MAP 27

MAP GIVING AN ACCOUNT OF THE SECOND BATTLE OF CHANGSHA

(Early Sept. – Early Oct., 1941)

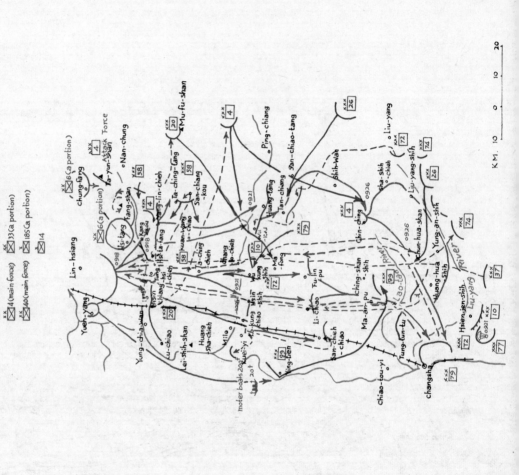

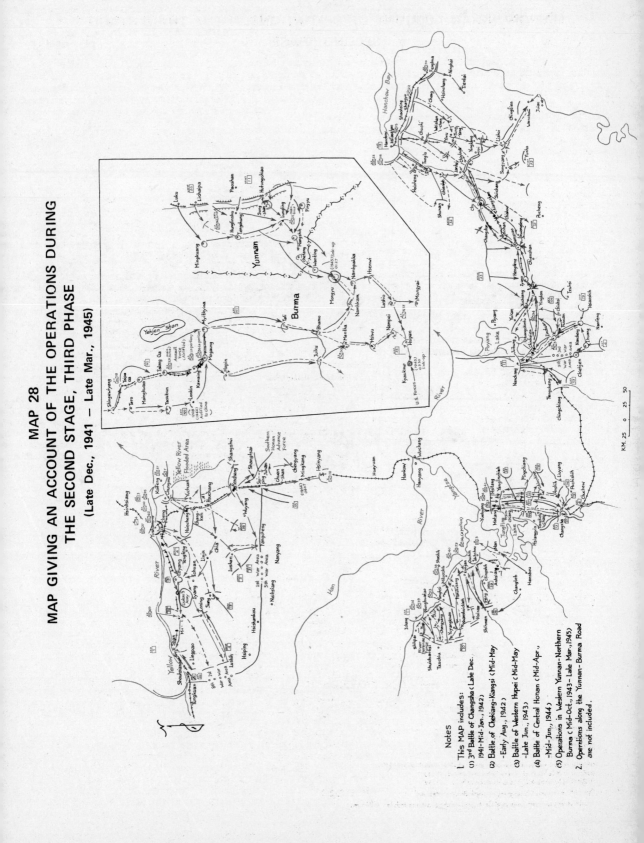

MAP 28

MAP GIVING AN ACCOUNT OF THE OPERATIONS DURING
THE SECOND STAGE, THIRD PHASE

(Late Dec., 1941 – Late Mar., 1945)

Notes

1. This MAP includes:
   (1) 3rd Battle of Changsha (Late Dec.
       1941-Mid-Jan., 1942)
   (2) Battle of Chekiang-Kiangsi (Mid-May
       -Early Aug., 1942)
   (3) Battle of Western Hupei (Mid-May
       -Late Jun., 1943)
   (4) Battle of Central Honan (Mid-Apr.,
       -Mid-Jun., 1944)
   (5) Operations in Western Yunnan-Northern
       Burma (Mid-Oct.,1943-Late Mar.,1945)

2. Operations along the Yunnan-Burma Road
   are not included.

MAP 29
MAP GIVING AN ACCOUNT OF OPERATIONS IN THE THIRD STAGE, SECOND PHASE

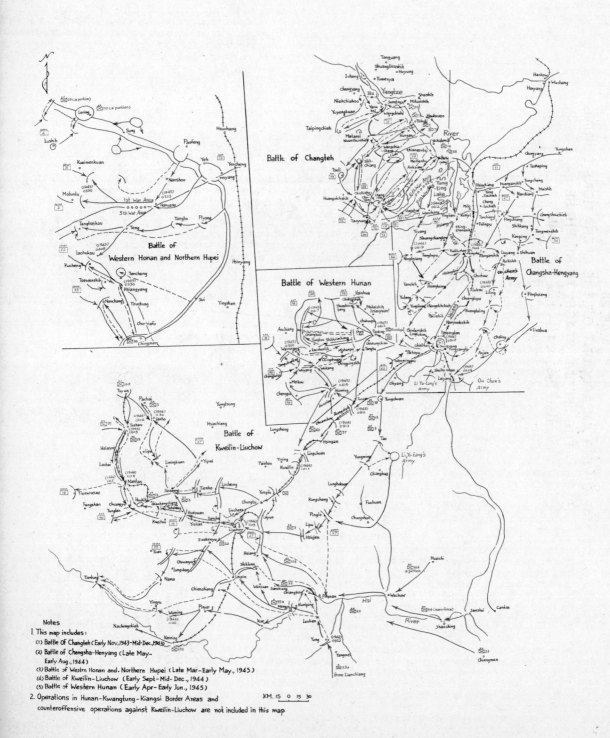

Notes

1. This map includes:

(1) Battle Of Changteh (Early Nov.,1943-Mid-Dec.,1943)

(2) Battle of Changsha-Henyang (Late May-
 Early Aug.,1944)

(3) Battle of Westrn Honan and. Northern Hupei (Late Mar-Early May., 1945)

(4) Battle of Kweilin-Liuchow (Early Sept-Mid-Dec., 1944)

(5) Battle of Western Hunan (Early Apr- Early Jun., 1945)

2. Operations in Hunan-Kwangtung-Kiangsi Border Areas and
 counteroffensive operations against Kweilin-Liuchow are not included in this map

KM. 15 0 15 30

MAP 30

MAP GIVING AN ACCOUNT OF THE THIRD BATTLE OF CHANGSHA

(Late Dec., 1941 – Mid-Jan., 1942)

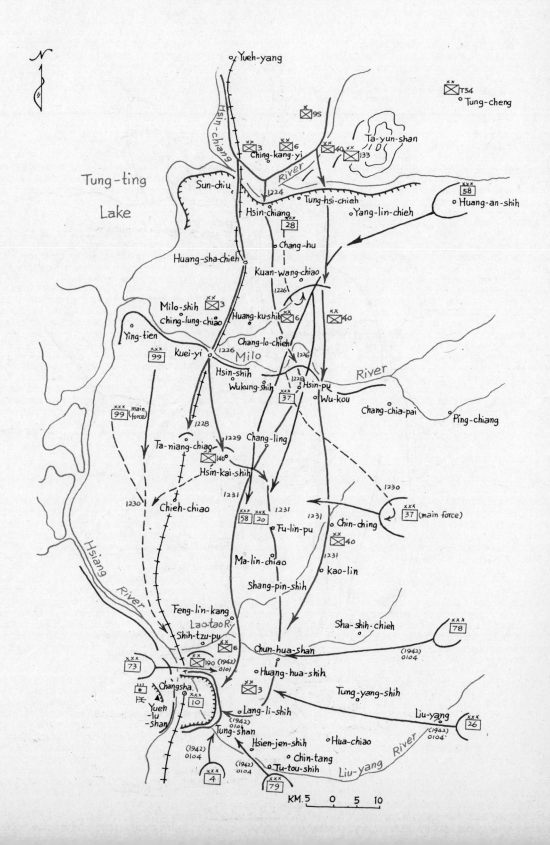

N

Yueh-yang

T54
Tung-cheng

9S

Ta-yun-shan

3
Ching-kang-yi   6   40   xx   133

Tung-ting

Lake

Sun-chiu   1224   Tung-hsi-chieh   Yang-lin-chieh   58   Huang-an-shih

Hsin-chiang
28

Chang-hu

Huang-sha-chieh   Kuan-wang-chiao
1226

Milo-shih   3
ching-lung-chiao   Huang-ku-shih   6   40

Ying-tien   Chang-lo-chieh
99   Kuei-yi   1226   Milo   1226   River

Hsin-shih   1229   Hsin-pu
Wukung-shih   37   Wu-kou

99 main force   Chang-chia-pai   Ping-chiang
1228

1229   Chang-ling
Ta-niang-chiao   140
Hsin-kai-shih   1231   37 (main force)

1230   Chieh-chiao   1231   1231
58   20   1231
Fu-lin-pu   Chin-ching
40
Ma-lin-chiao   1231   kao-lin
Shang-pin-shih

Feng-lin-kang   Sha-shih-chieh   78
Lao-tao R.
Shih-tzu-pu   6   Chun-hua-shan   (1942)
73   190 (1942)   0104
0101
Changsha   Huang-hua-shih
10   3   Tung-yang-shih   Liu-yang
Yueh   Lang-li-shih   26
-lu   (1942)
-shan   0104
Tung-shan   Hsien-jen-shih   Hua-chiao   (1942)
0104
(1942)   Chin-tang   Liu-yang River
0104   Tu-tou-shih
(1942)
4   0104
79   KM.5   0   5   10

MAP 31
MAP GIVING AN ACCOUNT OF THE THIRD BATTLE OF CHANGSHA
(Early Jan. — Mid-Jan., 1942)

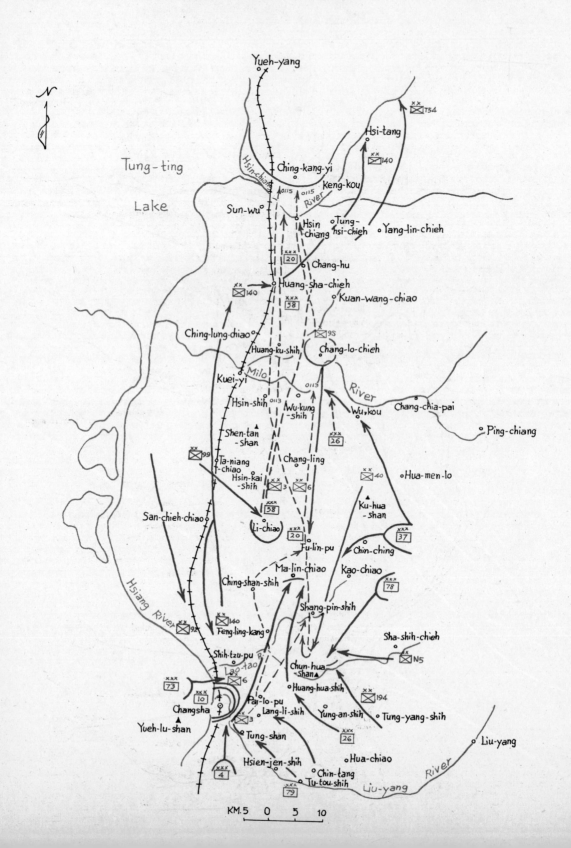

MAP 32
MAP GIVING AN ACCOUNT OF THE OPERATIONS ALONG
THE YUNNAN-BURMA ROAD
(Mid-Mar. — Early June, 1942)

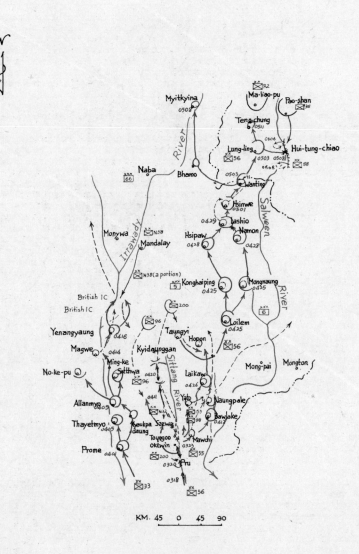

KM. 45   0   45   90

MAP 33

MAP GIVING AN ACCOUNT OF THE BATTLE OF CHEKIANG-KIANGSI

(Mid-May – Early September, 1942)

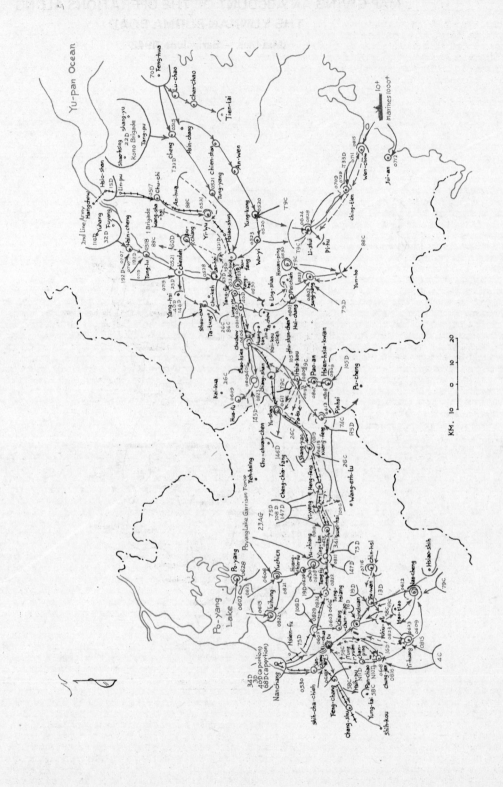

MAP 34
MAP GIVING AN ACCOUNT OF THE BATTLE OF WESTERN HUPEI
(Early May — Mid-June., 1943)

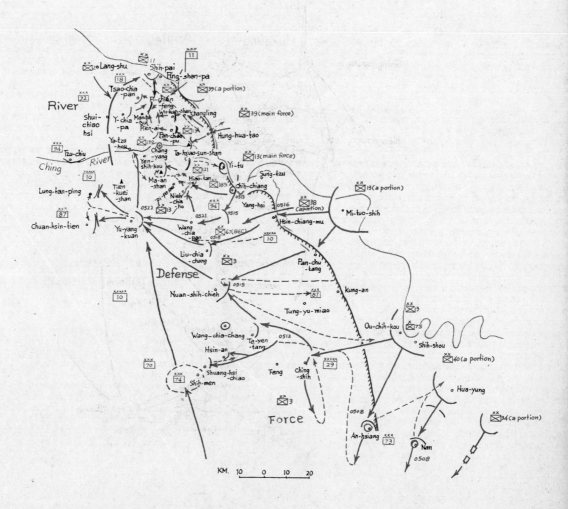

KM. 10 0 10 20

MAP 35

MAP GIVING AN ACCOUNT OF THE FIRST PHASE NORTHERN BURMA OPERATIONS OF THE CHINESE FORCES IN INDIA

(Early Nov., 1943 — Early Aug., 1944)

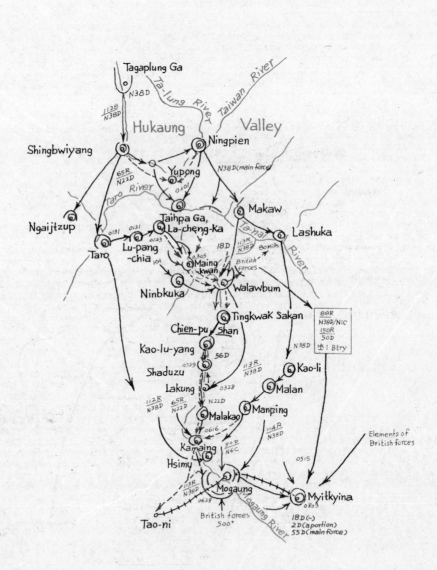

MAP 36

MAP GIVING AN ACCOUNT OF THE SECOND PHASE OPERATIONS
IN NORTHERN BURMA

(Mid-October, 1944 — Late March, 1945)

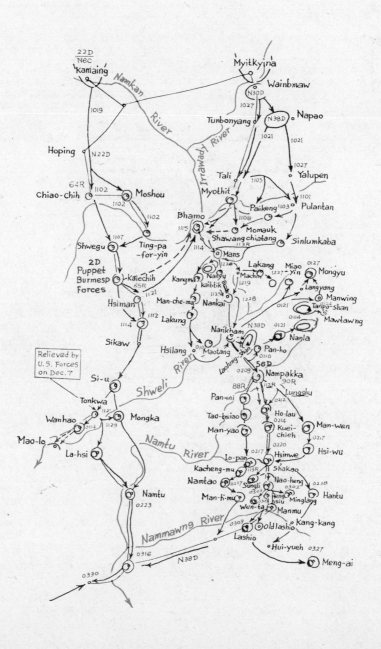

MAP 37
MAP GIVING AN ACCOUNT OF COUNTEROFFENSIVE BY CHINESE
EXPEDITIONARY FORCES IN WESTERN YUNNAN AND NORTHERN BURMA
(Mid-May, 1943 — Late Jan., 1945)

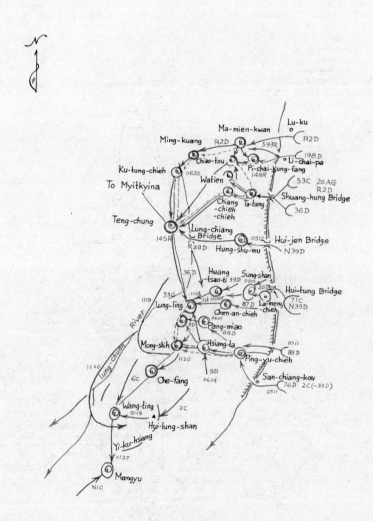

MAP 38
MAP SHOWING AN ACCOUNT OF THE BATTLE OF CHANGTEH
(Early Nov. — Late Dec., 1943)

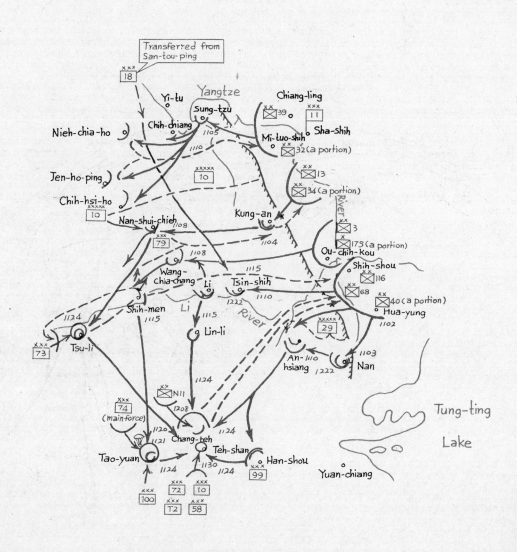

KM. 15   0   15   30

MAP 39
MAP SHOWING AN ACCOUNT OF THE BATTLE OF CENTRAL HONAN
(Mid-Apr. — Mid-June, 1944)

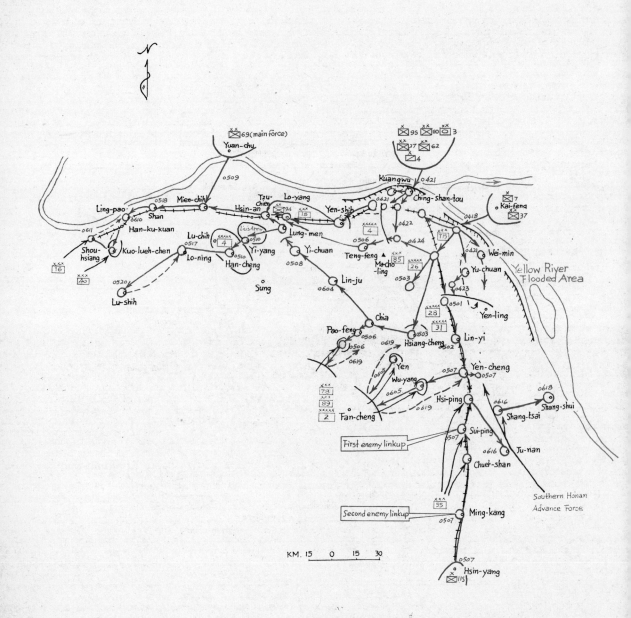

MAP 40
MAP SHOWING AN ACCOUNT OF THE BATTLE OF CHANGSHA-HENGYANG
(Late May — Early Aug., 1944)

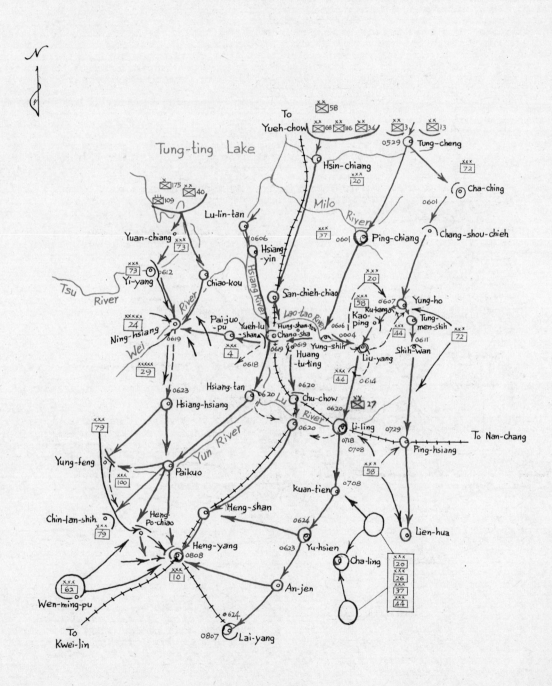

MAP 41
MAP SHOWING AN ACCOUNT OF THE BATTLE OF KWEILIN-LIUCHOW
(Early Sept. — Mid-Dec., 1944)

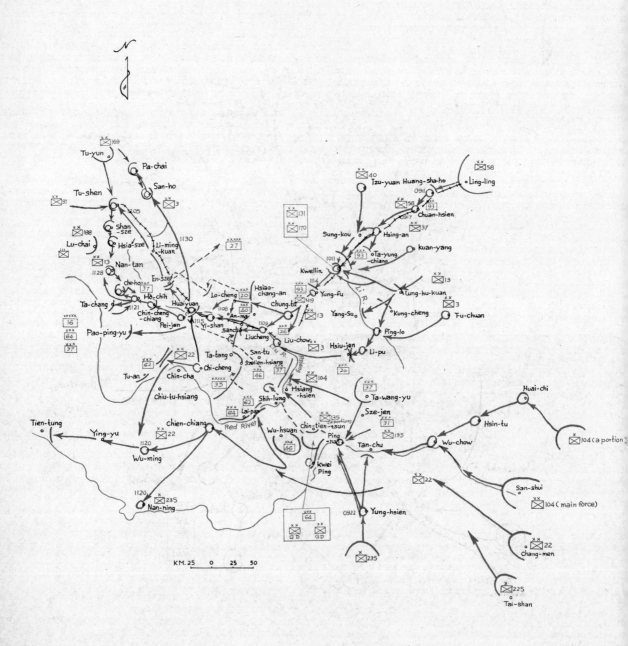

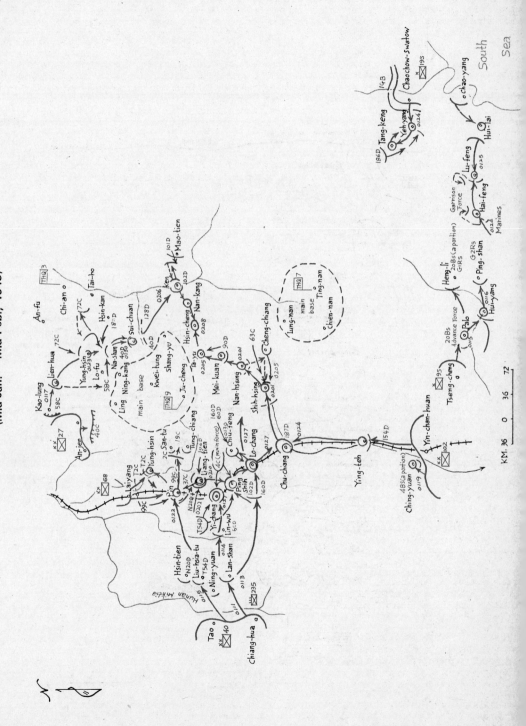

MAP 42

MAP SHOWING AN ACCOUNT OF OPERATIONS IN HUNAN-KWANGTUNG-KIANGSI BORDER AREAS

(Mid-Jan. – Mid-Feb., 1945)

MAP 43
MAP SHOWING AN ACCOUNT OF THE BATTLE OF WESTERN HONAN-NORTHERN HUPEI
(Late March — Late May, 1945)

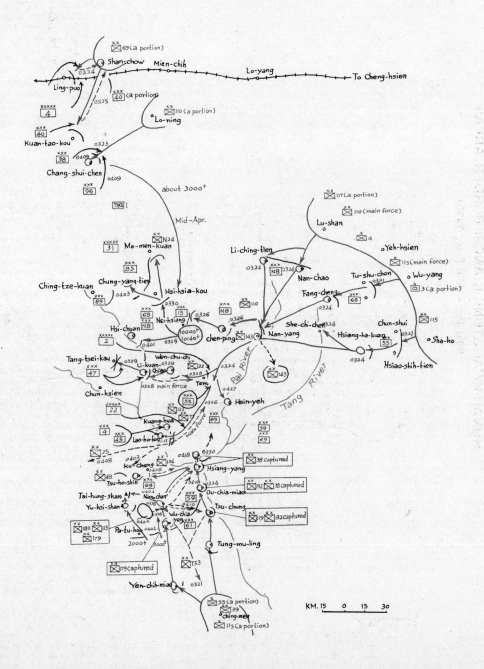

69 (a portion)

Shan-chow   Mien-chih   Lo-yang   To Cheng-hsien

0324

Ling-pao   0525   40 (a portion)

4   110 (a portion)

40   Lo-ning

Kuan-tao-kou   0323

38   0409

Chang-shui-chen   0409

96   about 3000+

THG 1   Mid-Apr.   117 (a portion)

110 (main force)

31   N24   Lu-shan

85   Mo-men-kuan   4   Yeh-hsien

Ching-tze-kuan   Chung-yang-tien   Li-ching-tien   115 (main force)

89   0403   Hsi-hsia-kou   0324   0324   Tu-shu-chen   Wu-yang

0330   N8   Nan-chao   68   3 (a portion)

68   0326   N8   Fang-cheng

Hsi-chuan   N8   Nei-hsiang   0326   110   0324   Chun-shui   115

2   10000+   She-chi-chen   324   Hsiang-ha-kuan   0321   Sha-ho

0401   0329   10140+   chen-ping   143   Nan-yang   55

Wen-chu-chi   0324   Hsiao-shih-tien

Tang-tsei-kau   0329   Li-kuan   0328   22

47   Chiao   0328   143

0328 main force   Teng   0427

Chun-hsien   55   0326   Hsin-yeh

22   122   Tang River

4   69   Kuang-hua   Main force   59

45   Lao-ho-kou   69

25   0330

0408   0402   0418

ku-cheng   124   Hsiang-yang   38 captured

48   0408

Tsu-ho-shih   69   0410   0324   132   38 captured

Tai-hung-shan   0404   Nan-chan   Ou-chia-miao

Yu-hsi-shan   0326   59   Tzu-chung

180   123   Wu-chia   0410   179   132 captured

179   Pa-tu-hoo   0402   yen   61

2000+   3000+   Tung-mu-ling

179 captured   T53

Yen-chih-miao   0321

55 (a portion)
39
ching-mey
115 (a portion)

KM. 15   0   15   30

MAP 44
MAP SHOWING AN ACCOUNT OF THE BATTLE OF WESTERN HUNAN
(Early April — Early June, 1945)

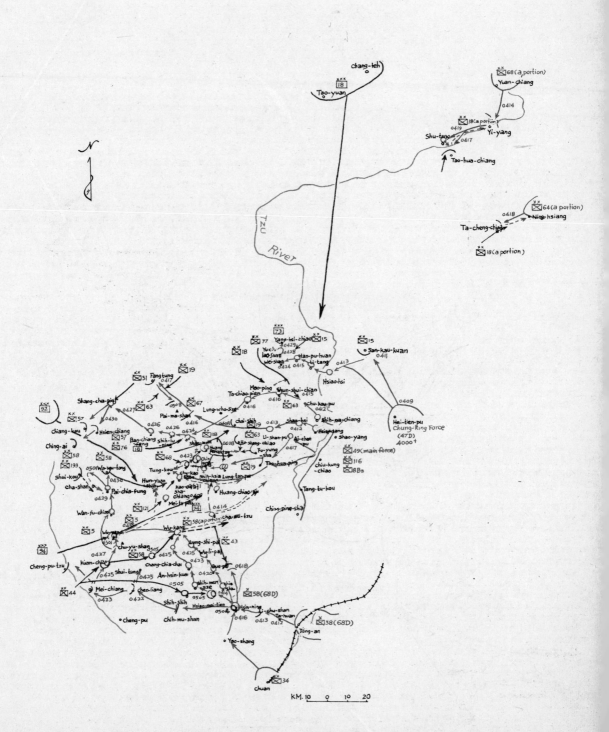

MAP 45
MAP SHOWING AN ACCOUNT OF THE KWEI-LIN-LIUCHOW
COUNTEROFFENSIVE OPERATIONS
(Late April — Late July, 1945)

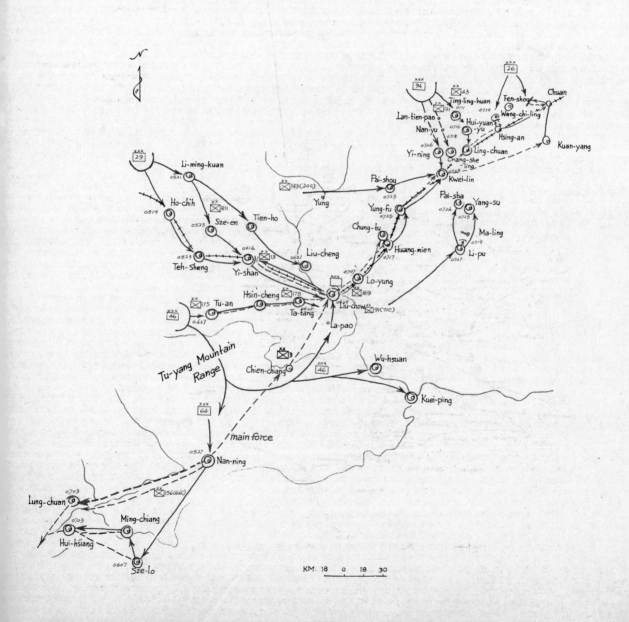

MAP 46
MAP SHOWING SURRENDER AND ASSEMBLY AREAS OF JAPANESE FORCES IN THE CHINA THEATER
(September 13, 1945)

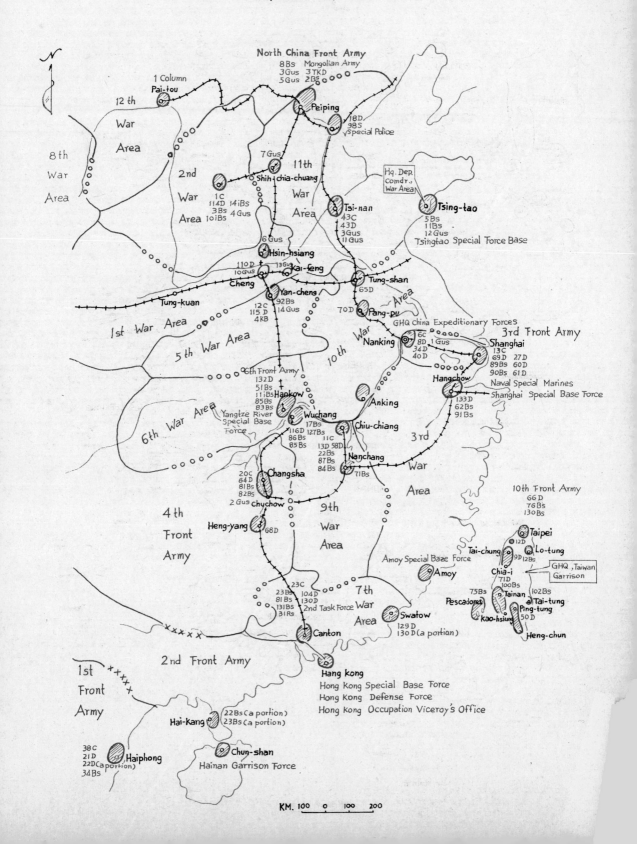

MAP 47
MAP SHOWING OVERALL SITUATION PRIOR TO THE JAPANESE SURRENDER
(September 9, 1945)

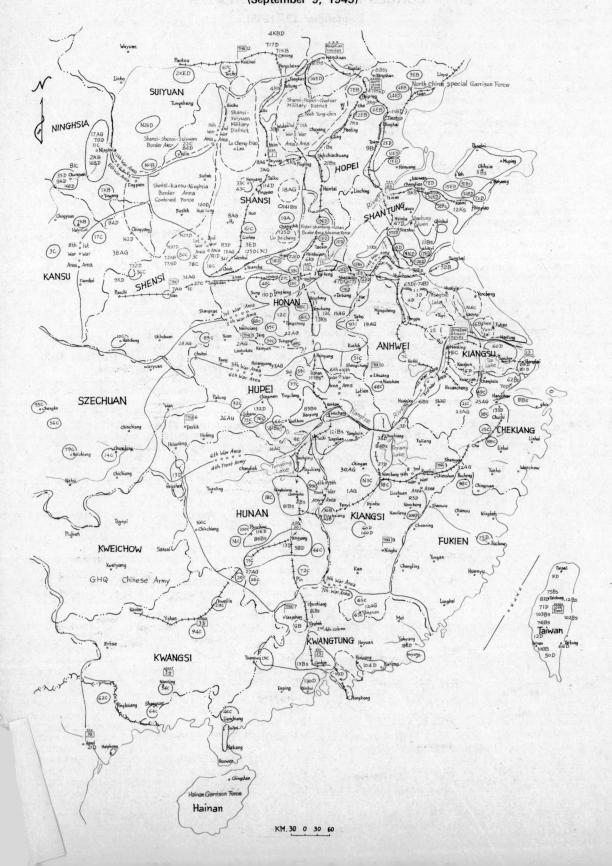

KM. 30 0 30 60